Case Studies in Finance

Managing for Corporate Value Creation

Eighth Edition

Robert F. Bruner
Kenneth M. Eades
Michael J. Schill

UNIVERSITY *of* VIRGINIA
DARDEN SCHOOL OF BUSINESS

Mc
Graw
Hill
Education

CASE STUDIES IN FINANCE: MANAGING FOR CORPORATE VALUE CREATIONS, EIGHTH EDITION

Published by McGraw-Hill Education, 2 Penn Plaza, New York, NY 10121. Copyright © 2018 by McGraw-Hill Education. All rights reserved. Printed in the United States of America. Previous editions © 2014, 2002, and 1989. No part of this publication may be reproduced or distributed in any form or by any means, or stored in a database or retrieval system, without the prior written consent of McGraw-Hill Education, including, but not limited to, in any network or other electronic storage or transmission, or broadcast for distance learning.

Some ancillaries, including electronic and print components, may not be available to customers outside the United States.

This book is printed on acid-free paper.

1 2 3 4 5 6 7 8 9 LCR 21 20 19 18 17

ISBN 978-1-259-27719-1
MHID 1-259-27719-4

Portfolio Manager: *Tim Vertovec*
Senior Product Developer: *Jennifer Upton*
Marketing Manager: *Trina Maurer*
Content Project Managers: *Melissa M. Leick, Karen Jozefowicz*
Buyer: *Susan K. Culbertson*
Content Licensing Specialist: *Beth Thole*
Compositor: *Aptara®, Inc.*

All credits appearing on page or at the end of the book are considered to be an extension of the copyright page.

Library of Congress Cataloging-in-Publication Data
Names: Bruner, Robert F., 1949-author. | Eades, Kenneth M., author. | Schill, Michael J., author.
Title: Case studies in finance: managing for corporate value creation / Robert F. Bruner, Kenneth M. Eades, Michael J. Schill.
Description: Eighth Edition. | Dubuque, IA : McGraw-Hill Education, [2018] | Series: The McGraw-Hill/Irwin series in finance, insurance, and real estate | Revised edition of the authors' Case studies in finance, [2014]
Identifiers: LCCN 2017023496| ISBN 9781259277191 (alk. paper) | ISBN 1259277194 (alk. paper)
Subjects: LCSH: Corporations—Finance—Case studies. | International business enterprises—Finance—Case studies.
Classification: LCC HG4015.5 .B78 2017 | DDC 658.15—dc23 LC record available at https://lccn.loc.gov/2017023496

The Internet addresses listed in the text were accurate at the time of publication. The inclusion of a website does not indicate an endorsement by the authors or McGraw-Hill Education, and McGraw-Hill Education does not guarantee the accuracy of the information presented at these sites.

mheducation.com/highered

The McGraw-Hill Education Series in Finance, Insurance, and Real Estate

Rose and Marquis
Financial Institutions and Markets
Eleventh Edition

Saunders and Cornett
Financial Institutions Management: A Risk Management Approach
Ninth Edition

Saunders and Cornett
Financial Markets and Institutions
Seventh Edition

INTERNATIONAL FINANCE

Eun and Resnick
International Financial Management
Eighth Edition

REAL ESTATE

Brueggeman and Fisher
Real Estate Finance and Investments
Sixteenth Edition

Ling and Archer
Real Estate Principles: A Value Approach
Fifth Edition

FINANCIAL PLANNING AND INSURANCE

Allen, Melone, Rosenbloom, and Mahoney
Retirement Plans: 401(k)s, IRAs, and Other Deferred Compensation Approaches
Tenth Edition

Altfest
Personal Financial Planning
Second Edition

Harrington and Niehaus
Risk Management and Insurance
Second Edition

Kapoor, Dlabay, Hughes, and Hart
Focus on Personal Finance: An active approach to help you achieve financial literacy
Sixth Edition

Kapoor, Dlabay, Hughes, and Hart
Personal Finance
Twelfth Edition

Walker and Walker
Personal Finance: Building Your Future
Second Edition

In dedication to
our wives

Barbara M. Bruner
Kathy N. Eades

And to the memory of
Mary Ann H. Schill

and to our children

About the Authors

Robert F. Bruner is University Professor, Distinguished Professor of Business Administration and Charles C. Abbott Professor of Business Administration and Dean Emeritus of the Darden Graduate School of Business Administration at the University of Virginia. He has taught and written in various areas, including corporate finance, mergers and acquisitions, investing in emerging markets, innovation, and technology transfer. In addition to *Case Studies in Finance*, his books include *Finance Interactive,* multimedia tutorial software in Finance (Irwin/McGraw-Hill 1997), *The Portable MBA* (Wiley 2003), *Applied Mergers and Acquisitions*, *(*Wiley, 2004), *Deals from Hell: M&A Lessons that Rise Above the Ashes* (Wiley, 2005) and *The Panic of 1907* (Wiley, 2007). He has been recognized in the United States and Europe for his teaching and case writing. *BusinessWeek* magazine cited him as one of the "masters of the MBA classroom." He is the author or co-author of over 400 case studies and notes. His research has been published in journals such as *Financial Management, Journal of Accounting and Economics, Journal of Applied Corporate Finance, Journal of Financial Economics, Journal of Financial and Quantitative Analysis,* and *Journal of Money, Credit, and Banking.* Industrial corporations, financial institutions, and government agencies have retained him for counsel and training. He has been on the faculty of the Darden School since 1982, and has been a visiting professor at Harvard, Columbia, INSEAD, and IESE. Formerly he was a loan officer and investment analyst for First Chicago Corporation. He holds the B.A. degree from Yale University and the M.B.A. and D.B.A. degrees from Harvard University. Copies of his papers and essays may be obtained from his website, http://www.darden.virginia.edu/web/Faculty-Research/Directory/Full-time/Robert-F-Bruner/ He may be reached via email at brunerr@virginia.edu.

Kenneth M. Eades is Professor of Business Administration and Area Coordinator of the Finance Department of the Darden Graduate School of Business Administration at the University of Virginia. He has taught a variety of corporate finance topics including: capital structure, dividend policy, risk management, capital investments and firm valuation. His research interests are in the area of corporate finance where he has published articles in *The Journal of Finance, Journal of Financial Economics, Journal of Financial and Quantitative Analysis,* and *Financial Management.* In addition to *Case Studies in Finance*, his books include *The Portable MBA* (Wiley 2010) *Finance Interactive*, a multimedia tutorial software in Finance (Irwin/McGraw-Hill 1997) and *Case Studies in Financial Decision Making* (Dryden Press, 1994). He has authored or co-authored over 70 case studies as well as a web-based, interactive tutorial on the pricing of financial derivatives. He has received the Wachovia Award for Excellence in Teaching Materials and the Wachovia Award for Excellence in Research. Mr. Eades is active in executive education programs at the Darden School and has served as a consultant to a number of corporations and institutions; including many commercial banks and investment banks; Fortune 500 companies and the Internal Revenue Service. Prior to joining Darden in

1988, Professor Eades was a member of the faculties at The University of Michigan and the Kellogg School of Management at Northwestern University. He has a B.S. from the University of Kentucky and Ph.D. from Purdue University. His website is http://www.darden.virginia.edu/web/Faculty-Research/Directory/Full-time/Kenneth-M-Eades/ and he may be reached via email at eades@virginia.edu.

Michael J. Schill is Professor of Business Administration of the Darden Graduate School of Business Administration at the University of Virginia where he teaches corporate finance and investments. His research spans empirical questions in corporate finance, investments, and international finance. He is the author of numerous articles that have been published in leading finance journals such as *Journal of Business, Journal of Finance, Journal of Financial Economics,* and *Review of Financial Studies*, and cited by major media outlets such as *The Wall Street Journal.* He has been on the faculty of the Darden School since 2001 and was previously with the University of California, Riverside, as well as a visiting professor at Cambridge and Melbourne. He is the current course head for Darden's core MBA finance course. He is the author or co-author of over 40 cases and technical notes, as well as a financial market simulation entitled Bond Trader. Prior to his doctoral work, he was a consultant with Marakon Associates in Stamford and London. He received a B.S. degree from Brigham Young University, an M.B.A. from INSEAD, and a Ph.D. from University of Washington. More details are available from his website, http://www.darden.virginia.edu/web/Faculty-Research/Directory/Full-time/Michael-J-Schill/ He may be reached via email at schill@virginia.edu.

Contents

Setting Some Themes

Financial Analysis and Forecasting

Estimating the Cost of Capital

Capital Budgeting and Resource Allocation

Management of the Firm's Equity: Dividends and Repurchases

Management of the Corporate Capital Structure

Analysis of Financing Tactics: Leases, Options, and Foreign Currency

Valuing the Enterprise: Acquisitions and Buyouts

Foreword

As I think about developing the next generation of leaders in business and finance, I naturally reflect on my own path. My career in business has taught some profound lessons— and so did my experience at the University of Virginia's Darden School of Business. Both life experience and school learning are critical components in the development of any leader. For that reason, I have supported wholeheartedly higher education as the path toward a promising future.

As the world keeps changing, higher education must continually adapt. Practices, processes, and business models that were once popular have faded. At the same time, the field of Finance has witnessed dramatic changes, including the advent of new valuation models, the rise of new markets and institutions, the invention of new financial instruments, the impact of new information technologies, and growing globalization. In this environment, we must think critically about the changing world, pay attention to new ideas, and adapt in sensible ways. Business schools play a critical role in the change process: theory suggests new approaches, empirical research tests them, and classroom teaching transfers knowledge. The development of new teaching materials is vital to that process.

Case studies in Finance have evolved markedly over the past 40 years. This shift reflects the revolutionary changes in markets and organization, as well as the many significant advances in theory and empirical research. Because case studies are an invaluable teaching tool, it is critical that the body of cases grows with the practice of and scholarship in Finance.

I am pleased to introduce the reader to the eighth edition of *Case Studies in Finance,* by Robert F. Bruner, Kenneth M. Eades, and Michael J. Schill. These professors exemplify the practice-oriented scholar who understands the economic foundations of Finance and the extensive varieties of its practice. They translate business phenomena into material that is accessible both to experienced practitioners and novices in Finance.

This book is a valuable contribution to the teaching materials available in the field of Finance. First, these cases link managerial decisions to capital markets and investor expectations. At the core of most is a valuation task that requires students to look to financial markets to resolve the problem. Second, these cases feature a wide range of contemporary and relevant problems, including examples in real and financial options, agency conflicts, financial innovation, investing in emerging markets, and corporate control. They also cover classic topics in Finance, including dividend policy, the mix of debt and equity financing, the estimation of future financial requirements, and the choice between mutually exclusive investments. Finally, these cases invite students to harness technology they will use in the workplace to develop key insights.

I am confident this collection will help students, scholars, and practitioners sharpen their decision-making ability, and advance the development of the next generation of leaders in Finance.

John R. Strangfeld
Chairman and Chief Executive Officer
Prudential Financial, Inc.
May 3, 2017
Newark, New Jersey

Preface

The inexplicable is all around us. So is the incomprehensible. So is the unintelligible. Interviewing Babe Ruth[1] *in 1928, I put it to him "People come and ask what's your system for hitting home runs—that so?" "Yes," said the Babe, "and all I can tell 'em is I pick a good one and sock it. I get back to the dugout and they ask me what it was I hit and I tell `em I don't know except it looked good."*

　　—Carl Sandburg[2]

Managers are not confronted with problems that are independent of each other, but with dynamic situations that consist of complex systems of changing problems that interact with each other. I call such situations <u>messes</u> *. . . Managers do not solve problems: they manage messes.*

　　—Russell Ackoff[3]

Orientation of the Book

Practitioners tell us that much in finance is inexplicable, incomprehensible, and unintelligible. Like Babe Ruth, their explanations for their actions often amount to "I pick a good one and sock it." Fortunately for a rising generation of practitioners, tools and concepts of Modern Finance provide a language and approach for excellent performance. The aim of this book is to illustrate and exercise the application of these tools and concepts in a messy world.

Focus on Value

The subtitle of this book is *Managing for Corporate Value Creation.* Economics teaches us that value creation should be an enduring focus of concern because value is the foundation of survival and prosperity of the enterprise. The focus on value also helps managers understand the impact of the firm on the world around it. These cases harness and exercise this economic view of the firm. It is the special province of finance to highlight value as a legitimate concern for managers. The cases in this book exercise valuation analysis over a wide range of assets, debt, equities, and options, and a wide range of perspectives, such as investor, creditor, and manager.

Linkage to Capital Markets

An important premise of these cases is that managers should take cues from the capital markets. The cases in this volume help the student learn to look at the capital markets in four ways. First, they illustrate important players in the capital markets such as

---

[1]George Herman "Babe" Ruth (1895–1948) was one of the most famous players in the history of American baseball, leading the league in home runs for 10 straight seasons, setting a record of 60 home runs in one season, and hitting 714 home runs in his career. Ruth was also known as the "Sultan of Swat."

[2]Carl Sandburg, "Notes for Preface," in *Harvest Poems* (New York: Harcourt Brace Jovanovich, 1960), p.11.

[3]Russell Ackoff, "The Future of Operational Research is Past," *Journal of Operational Research Society,* 30, 1 (Pergamon Press, Ltd., 1979): 93–104.

individual exemplar Warren Buffett and institutions like investment banks, commercial banks, rating agencies, hedge funds, merger arbitrageurs, private equity firms, lessors of industrial equipment, and so on. Second, they exercise the students' abilities to interpret capital market conditions across the economic cycle. Third, they explore the design of financial securities, and illuminate the use of exotic instruments in support of corporate policy. Finally, they help students understand the implications of transparency of the firm to investors, and the impact of news about the firm in an efficient market.

Respect for the Administrative Point of View

The real world is messy. Information is incomplete, arrives late, or is reported with error. The motivations of counterparties are ambiguous. Resources often fall short. These cases illustrate the immense practicality of finance theory in sorting out the issues facing managers, assessing alternatives, and illuminating the effects of any particular choice. A number of the cases in this book present practical ethical dilemmas or moral hazards facing managers—indeed, this edition features a chapter, "Ethics in Finance" right at the beginning, where ethics belongs. Most of the cases (and teaching plans in the associated instructor's manual) call for *action plans* rather than mere analyses or descriptions of a problem.

Contemporaneity and Diversity

All of the cases in this book are set in the year 2006 or after and 25 percent are set in 2015 or later. A substantial proportion (57 percent) of the cases and technical notes are new, or significantly updated. The mix of cases reflects the global business environment: 52 percent of the cases in this book are set outside the United States, or have strong cross-border elements. Finally the blend of cases continues to reflect the growing role of women in managerial ranks: 31 percent of the cases present women as key protagonists and decision-makers. Generally, these cases reflect the increasingly diverse world of business participants.

Plan of the Book

The cases may be taught in many different combinations. The sequence indicated by the table of contents corresponds to course designs used at Darden. Each cluster of cases in the Table of Contents suggests a concept module, with a particular orientation.

1. **Setting Some Themes.** These cases introduce basic concepts of value creation, assessment of performance against a capital market benchmark, and capital market efficiency that reappear throughout a case course. The numerical analysis required of the student is relatively light. The synthesis of case facts into an important framework or perspective is the main challenge. The case, "Warren E. Buffett, 2016," sets the nearly universal theme of this volume: the need to think like an investor. The updated case entitled, "The Battle for Value, 2016: FedEx Corp. vs. United Parcel Service, Inc." explores the definition of business success and its connections to themes of financial management. "Larry Puglia and the T. Rowe Price Blue Chip Growth Fund," is an updated version of cases in prior

editions that explores a basic question about performance measurement: what is the right benchmark against which to evaluate success? And finally, "Genzyme and Relational Investors: Science and Business Collide?", is a case that poses the dilemma of managing a public company when the objectives of the shareholders are not always easily aligned with the long-term objectives of the company and an activist investor is pressuring the company for change.

2. **Financial Analysis and Forecasting.** In this section, students are introduced to the crucial skills of financial-statement analysis, break-even analysis, ratio analysis, and financial statement forecasting. The section starts with a note, "Business Performance Evaluation: Approaches for Thoughtful Forecasting", that provides a helpful introduction to financial statement analysis and student guidance on generating rational financial forecasts. The case, "The Financial Detective 2016", asks students to match financial ratios of companies with their underlying business and financial strategies. "Whole Foods Market: The Deutsche Bank Report" provides students with the opportunity to reassess the financial forecast of a research analyst in light of industry dynamics. This case can also be used an opportunity for students to hone firm valuation skills with the evaluation of the analyst's "buy, hold, or sell" recommendation. "Horniman Horticulture" uses a financial model to build intuition for the relevancy of corporate cash flow and the financial effects of firm growth. The case, "Guna Fibres" asks the students to consider a variety of working capital decisions, including the impact of seasonal demand upon financing needs. Other cases address issues in the analysis of working-capital management, and credit analysis.

3. **Estimating the Cost of Capital.** This module begins with an article that is a survey of "best practices" among leading firms for estimating the cost of capital during the low interest rate regime following the 2007–08 financial crisis. The cases following the survey article expose students to the skills in estimating the cost of capital for firms and their business segments. The cases aim to exercise and solidify students' mastery of the capital asset pricing model, the dividend-growth model, and the weighted average cost of capital formula. "Roche Holdings AG: Funding the Genentech Acquisition" is a case that invites students to estimate the appropriate cost of debt for a massive debt offering. The case provides an introduction to the concept of estimating required returns. Two new cases ask the student to estimate the cost of capital for the firm. "H.J. Heinz: Estimating the Cost of Capital in Uncertain Times" gives students the opportunity to reassess the cost of capital following share price decline. "Royal Mail plc:Cost of Capital" affords students the challenge of critiquing a cost of capital estimate for recently privatized British postal service. The case "Chestnut Foods" requires students to consider arguments for and against risk-adjusted hurdle rates in a multi-divisional firm, as well as techniques for estimating divisional-specific cost of capital.

4. **Capital Budgeting and Resource Allocation.** The focus of these cases is the evaluation of individual investment opportunities as well as the assessment of corporate capital budgets. The analytical challenges range from setting the entire

capital budget for a resource-constrained firm ("Target Corporation") to basic time value of money problems ("The Investment Detective"). Key issues in this module include the estimation of Free Cash Flows, the comparison of various investment criteria (NPV, IRR, payback, and equivalent annuities), the treatment of issues in mutually exclusive investments, and capital budgeting under rationing. This module features several new cases. The first is "Centennial Pharmaceutical Corporation" provides an introduction to discounted cash flow principles by asking the student to compare values of two earnout plans. "Worldwide Paper Company" is an updated case that serves as an introduction to estimating cash flows and calculating the NPV of an investment opportunity. "Fonderia del Piemonte S.p.A." is a new addition to the book. Fonderia is an Italian company considering a capital investment in machinery that replaces existing equipment. The student must assess the incremental value to the company of investing in the new equipment. The Victoria Chemical cases give students cash flow estimates for a large capital investment opportunity ("Victoria Chemical plc (A): The Merseyside Project") as asks the student to provide a careful critique of the DCF analysis. The sequel case, ("Victoria Chemical plc (B): Merseyside and Rotterdam Projects", deepens the analysis by adding a competing and mutually exclusive investment opportunity. "The Procter and Gamble Company: Crest Whitestrips Advanced Seal" is a case that asks the student to value a new product launch but then consider the financial implications of a variety of alternative launch scenarios The case, "Jacobs Division", presents students an opportunity to consider the implications of strategic planning processes. "UVa Hospital System: The Long-term Acute Care Hospital Project", is an analysis of an investment decision within a not-for-profit environment. In addition to forecasting and valuing the project's cash flows, students must assess whether NPV and IRR are appropriate metrics for an organization that does not have stockholders. "Star River Electronics Ltd" has been updated for this edition and presents the student will a range of issues that the new CEO of the company must address, including the determination of the company's cost of capital and whether to invest in new machinery. We have used this case as an exam for the first half of the finance principles course in the MBA program.

5. **Management of the Firm's Equity: Dividends and Repurchases.** This module seeks to develop practical principles about dividend policy and share repurchases by drawing on concepts about dividend irrelevance, signaling, investor clienteles, bonding, and agency costs. The first case, "Rockboro Machine Tools Corporation", is set in 2015 and concerns a company that is changing its business strategy and considering a change in its dividend policy. The case serves as a comprehensive introduction to corporate financial policy and themes in managing the right side of the balance sheet. The second case, "EMI Group PLC", is new to this edition and features a struggling music producer in the U.K. confronted with whether it should continue to pay a dividend despite the profit pressures it is facing. And finally, "AutoZone, Inc." is a leading auto parts retailer that has been repurchasing shares over many years. The case serves as an excellent example of how share

repurchases impact the balance sheet and presents the student with the challenge of assessing the impact upon the company's stock price.

6. **Management of the Corporate Capital Structure.** The problem of setting capital structure targets is introduced in this module. Prominent issues are the use and creation of debt tax shields, the role of industry economics and technology, the influence of corporate competitive strategy, the tradeoffs between debt policy, dividend policy, and investment goals, and the avoidance of costs of distress. Following a technical note, "An Introduction to Debt Policy and Value", is a new case, "M&M Pizza", which explores the debt-equity choice within a perfect capital market environment—a capital market with full information and no costs of trading. This case provides an engaging environment for students to confront fundamental financial policy theory. "California Pizza Kitchen", is a real world analog to "M&M Pizza" as it addresses the classic dilemma entailed in optimizing the use of debt tax shields and providing financial flexibility for a national restaurant chain. The next four cases are all new to the book. "Dominion Resources: Cove Point" presents the student with the challenge of financing a large new project without creating substantial disruption to the firm's capital structure polices. The "Nokia OYJ: Financing the WP Strategic Plan" presents a similar theme as management has taken a new strategic direction and must make financing decisions that are cost effective, but also preserve financial flexibility going forward. "Kelly Solar" concerns a start-up that needs new funds for investment, but already has a significant amount of debt on the books that needs to be renegotiated before new investors will find their investment to be attractive. The case, "JC Penney Company", presents a large retail chain that is facing widespread performance challenges and needs to raise funds to offset the steadily declining cash balance that will eventually create a liquidity crisis for the company. The last case is "Horizon Lines, Inc." The case is about a company facing default on a debt covenant that will prompt the need for either Chapter 11 protection or a voluntary financial restructuring.

7. **Analysis of Financing Tactics: Leases, Options, and Foreign Currency.** While the preceding module is concerned with setting debt targets, this module addresses a range of tactics a firm might use to pursue those targets, hedge risk, and exploit market opportunities. Included are domestic and international debt offerings, leases, currency hedges, warrants, and convertibles. With these cases, students will exercise techniques in securities valuation, including the use of option-pricing theory. For example, the first case, "Baker Adhesives" explores the concept of exchange-rate risk and the management of that risk with a forward-contract hedge and a money-market hedge. "Vale SA" is new to this edition and is a Brazilian mining company that must choose between debt financing denominated in U.S. dollars, euros or British pounds. The case "J&L Railroad" presents a commodity risk problem for which students are asked to propose a specific hedging strategy using financial contracts offered on the open market or from a commercial bank. "WNG Capital, LLC" is a new case about a company that owns older aircraft that it leases to airlines as an alternative to the airline buying new aircraft. "MoGen, Inc" presents the pricing challenges associated with a

convertible bond as well as a complex hedging strategy to change the conversion price of the convertible through the purchase of options and issuance of warrants.

8. **Valuing the Enterprise: Acquisitions and Buyouts.** This module begins with an extensive introduction to firm valuation in the note "Methods of Valuation: Mergers and Acquisitions." The focus of the note includes valuation using DCF and multiples. This edition features six new cases in this module and five cases from the previous edition. The "Medfield Pharmaceuticals" introduces students to firm valuation with the reality of considering the difference between the value of firm assets in place and the value of firm growth opportunities in the context of a takeover offer for a pharmaceutical company. The case also includes important ethical considerations. "American Greetings" was in the prior edition and provides a straightforward firm valuation in the context of a repurchase decision and is designed to be an introduction to firm valuation. The new case "Ferrari: The 2015 Initial Public Offering", presents students the opportunity to value the legendary automotive company, and consider how to determine appropriate company comparables for a firm that is both an auto manufacturer and a luxury brand. The case, "Rosetta Stone: Pricing the 2009 IPO", provides an alternative IPO valuation case with additional focus on valuation with market multiples. "Sun Microsystems" is also returning from the previous edition and presents a traditional takeover valuation case with opportunities to evaluate merger synergies and cost of capital implications. The next five cases are all new to this edition. "Carter International" involves assessing the correct price to offer to acquire another hotel company. "DuPont Corporation: Sale of Performance Coatings" asks the student to assess the economics of divesting a business unit that is not meeting the strategic objectives of the firm. "Sanofi-Aventis's Tender Offer for Genzyme" is a sequel to the "Genzyme and Relational Investors: Science and Business Collide?" in which Genzyme's CEO must decide whether to accept a tender offer to acquire Genzyme. "Delphi Corporation" features a large auto parts company that has been in Chapter 11 bankruptcy for two years. The student must decide in the role of a non-secured lender whether to vote to approve the Plan of Reorganization to emerge from Chapter 11.

And finally, the module features a merger negotiation exercise ("Flinder Valves and Controls Inc.") that provides an engaging venue for investigating the distribution of value in a merger negotiation. The comprehensive nature of cases in this module makes them excellent vehicles for end-of-course classes, student term papers, and/or presentations by teams of students.

This edition offers a number of cases that give insights about investing or financing decisions in emerging markets. These include "Guna Fibres Ltd.," "Star River Electronics Ltd.," and "Baker Adhesives."

Summary of Changes for this Edition

The eighth edition represents a substantial and significant change from the seventh edition.

This edition offers 31 new or significantly updated cases and technical notes, which represents 57 percent of the book. In the interest of presenting a fresh and contemporary collection, older cases have been updated and/or replaced with new case situations such that all the cases are set in 2006 or later and 25 percent are set in 2015 or later. Several of the favorite "classic" cases from the first seven editions are available online from McGraw-Hill such that instructors who adopt this edition may copy these older cases for classroom use. These materials can be find at www.mhhe.com/bescases8e. All cases and teaching notes have been edited to sharpen the opportunities for student analysis.

Supplements

The case studies in this volume are supported by various resources that help make student engagement a success:

- A guide to the novice on case preparation, "Note to the Student: How to Study and Discuss Cases" in this volume.

- All of the cases in this book are accompanied by a full teaching note that contains suggested student study questions, a hypothetical teaching plan, and a prototypical finished case analysis. In addition, the cases also have spreadsheet files that support student and instructor preparation of the cases. These materials are available to all instructors at the book's website at www.mhhe.com/bescases8e. Also at the book's website is an instructor's resource manual that facilitates the use of these materials in a standard course by providing resources on how to design a case course and how the cases fit together.

- Two of the cases provide student counterparty roles for two negotiation exercises. The teaching materials present detailed discussions of case outcomes, one of which is designed to be used as second class period for the case. These supplemental materials can significantly extend student learning and expand the opportunities for classroom discussion.

- A companion book by Robert Bruner titled, *Socrates' Muse: Reflections on Excellence in Case Discussion Leadership* (Irwin/McGraw-Hill, 2002), is available to instructors who adopt the book for classroom use. This book offers useful tips on case method teaching. This title is available through Create, McGraw-Hill Education's on-demand and custom publishing system. Ask your learning technology representative for more details.

Acknowledgments

This book would not be possible without the contributions of many other people. Colleagues at Darden who have taught, co-authored, contributed to, or commented on these cases are Brandt Allen, Yiorgos Allayannis, Sam Bodily, Karl-Adam Bonnier, Susan Chaplinsky, John Colley, Bob Conroy, Mark Eaker, Rich Evans, Bob Fair, Paul Farris, Jim Freeland, Sherwood Frey, Bob Harris, Jared Harris, Mark Haskins, Michael Ho, Marc Lipson, Elena Loutskina, Pedro Matos, Matt McBrady, Charles Meiburg, Jud Reis, William Sihler and Robert Spekman. We are grateful for their collegiality and for the support for our casewriting efforts from the Darden School Foundation, the Mayo Center for Asset Management, the L. White Matthews Fund for Finance Casewriting, the Batten Institute, Columbia Business School, INSEAD, the University of Melbourne and the University of Virginia's McIntire School of Commerce.

Colleagues at other schools provided worthy insights and encouragement toward the development of the eight editions of *Case Studies in Finance*. We are grateful to the following persons (listed with the schools with which they were associated at the time of our correspondence or work with them):

Michael Adler, *Columbia*

Raj Aggarwal, *John Carroll*

Turki Alshimmiri, *Kuwait Univ.*

Ed Altman, *NYU*

James Ang, *Florida State*

Paul Asquith, *M.I.T.*

Bob Barnett, *North Carolina State*

Geert Bekaert, *Stanford*

Michael Berry, *James Madison*

Randy Billingsley, *VPI&SU*

Gary Blemaster, *Georgetown*

Rick Boebel, *Univ. Otago, New Zealand*

Oyvind Bohren, *BI, Norway*

John Boquist, *Indiana*

Michael Brennan, *UCLA*

Duke Bristow, *UCLA*

Ed Burmeister, *Duke*

Kirt Butler, *Michigan State*

Don Chance, *VPI&SU*

Andrew Chen, *Southern Methodist*

Barbara J. Childs, *Univ. of Texas at Austin*

C. Roland Christensen, *Harvard*

Thomas E. Copeland, *McKinsey*

Jean Dermine, *INSEAD*

Michael Dooley, *UVA Law*

Barry Doyle, *University of San Francisco*

Bernard Dumas, *INSEAD*

Craig Dunbar, *Western Ontario*

Peter Eisemann, *Georgia State*

Javier Estrada, *IESE*

Ben Esty, *Harvard*

Thomas H. Eyssell, *Missouri*

Pablo Fernandez, *IESE*

Kenneth Ferris, *Thunderbird*

John Finnerty, *Fordham*

Joseph Finnerty, *Illinois*

Steve Foerster, *Western Ontario*

Günther Franke, *Konstanz*

Bill Fulmer, *George Mason*

Louis Gagnon, *Queens*

Dan Galai, *Jerusalem*

Jim Gentry, *Illinois*

Stuart Gilson, *Harvard*

Robert Glauber, *Harvard*

Mustafa Gultekin, *North Carolina*

Benton Gup, *Alabama*

Jim Haltiner, *William & Mary*

Rob Hansen, *VPI&SU*

Philippe Haspeslagh, *INSEAD*

Gabriel Hawawini, *INSEAD*

Pekka Hietala, *INSEAD*

Rocky Higgins, *Washington*

Pierre Hillion, *INSEAD*

Laurie Simon Hodrick, *Columbia*

John Hund, *Texas*

Daniel Indro, *Kent State*

Thomas Jackson, *UVA Law*

Pradeep Jalan, *Regina*

Michael Jensen, *Harvard*

Sreeni Kamma, *Indiana*

Steven Kaplan, *Chicago*

Andrew Karolyi, *Western Ontario*

James Kehr, *Miami Univ. Ohio*

Kathryn Kelm, *Emporia State*

Carl Kester, *Harvard*

Naveen Khanna, *Michigan State*

Herwig Langohr, *INSEAD*

Dan Laughhunn, *Duke*

Ken Lehn, *Pittsburgh*

Saul Levmore, *UVA Law*

Wilbur Lewellen, *Purdue*

Scott Linn, *Oklahoma*

Dennis Logue, *Dartmouth*

Paul Mahoney, *UVA Law*

Paul Malatesta, *Washington*

Wesley Marple, *Northeastern*

Felicia Marston, *UVA (McIntire)*

John Martin, *Texas*

Ronald Masulis, *Vanderbilt*

John McConnell, *Purdue*

Richard McEnally, *North Carolina*

Catherine McDonough, *Babson*

Wayne Mikkelson, *Oregon*

Michael Moffett, *Thunderbird*

Nancy Mohan, *Dayton*

Ed Moses, *Rollins*

Charles Moyer, *Wake Forest*

David W. Mullins, Jr., *Harvard*

James T. Murphy, *Tulane*

Chris Muscarella, *Penn State*

Robert Nachtmann, *Pittsburgh*

Tom C. Nelson, *University of Colorado*

Ben Nunnally, *UNC-Charlotte*

Robert Parrino, *Texas (Austin)*

Luis Pereiro, *Universidad Torcuato di Tella*

Pamela Peterson, *Florida State*

Larry Pettit, *Virginia (McIntire)*

Tom Piper, *Harvard*

Gordon Philips, *Maryland*

John Pringle, *North Carolina*

Ahmad Rahnema, *IESE*

Al Rappaport, *Northwestern*

Allen Rappaport, *Northern Iowa*

Raghu Rau, *Purdue*

David Ravenscraft, *North Carolina*

Henry B. Reiling, *Harvard*

Lee Remmers, *INSEAD*

Jay Ritter, *Florida*

Richard Ruback, *Harvard*

Jim Schallheim, *Utah*

Art Selander, *Southern Methodist*

Israel Shaked, *Boston*

Dennis Sheehan, *Penn State*

J.B. Silvers, *Case Western*

Betty Simkins, *Oklahoma State*

Luke Sparvero, *Texas*

Richard Stapleton, *Lancaster*

Laura Starks, *Texas*

Jerry Stevens, *Richmond*

John Strong, *William & Mary*

Marti Subrahmanyam, *NYU*

Anant Sundaram, *Thunderbird*

Rick Swasey, *Northeastern*

Bob Taggart, *Boston College*

Udin Tanuddin, *Univ. Surabaya, Indonesia*

Anjan Thakor, *Indiana*

Thomas Thibodeau, *Southern Methodist*

Clifford Thies, *Shenandoah Univ.*

James G. Tompkins, *Kenesaw State*

Walter Torous, *UCLA*

Max Torres, *IESE*

Nick Travlos, *Boston College*

Lenos Trigeorgis, *Cyprus*

George Tsetsekos, *Drexel*

Peter Tufano, *Harvard*

James Van Horne, *Stanford*

Nick Varaiya, *San Diego State*

Theo Vermaelen, *INSEAD*

Michael Vetsuypens, *Southern Methodist*

Claude Viallet, *INSEAD*

Ingo Walter, *NYU*

Sam Weaver, *Lehigh*

J.F. Weston, *UCLA*

Peter Williamson, *Dartmouth*

Brent Wilson, *Brigham Young*

Kent Womack, *Dartmouth*

Karen Wruck, *Ohio State*

Fred Yeager, *St. Louis*

Betty Yobaccio, *Framingham State*

Marc Zenner, *North Carolina*

Research Assistants working under our direction have helped gather data and prepare drafts. Research assistants who contributed to various cases in this and previous editions include Darren Berry, Chris Blankenship, Justin Brenner, Anna Buchanan, Anne Campbell, Drew Chambers, Sean Carr, Jessica Chan, Jenny Craddock, Lucas Doe, Jake Dubois, Brett Durick, David Eichler, Ali Erarac, Shachar Eyal, Rick Green, Daniel Hake, Dennis Hall, Jerry Halpin, Peter Hennessy, Dot Kelly, Vladimir Kolcin, Nili Mehta, Casey Opitz, Katarina Paddack, Suprajj Papireddy, Thien Pham, Chad Rynbrandt, John Sherwood, Elizabeth Shumadine, Janelle Sirleaf, Jane Sommers-Kelly, Don Stevenson, Carla Stiassni, Sanjay Vakharia, Larry Weatherford, and Steve Wilus. We have supervised numerous others in the development of individual cases—those worthy contributors are recognized in the first footnote of each case.

A busy professor soon learns the wisdom in the adage, "Many hands make work light." we are very grateful to the staff of the Darden School for its support in this project. Excellent editorial assistance at Darden was provided by the staff of Darden Business Publishing and the Darden Case Collection. We specifically thank Leslie Mullin (Senior Editor) and Margaret Ebin, Lucinda Ewing and Debbie O'Brien (Editors). Ginny Fisher gave stalwart secretarial support. Valuable library research support was given by Karen Marsh King and Susan Norrisey. The patience, care, and dedication of these people are richly appreciated.

At McGraw-Hill, Chuck Synovec has served as Brand Manager for this book. Melissa Leick was the project manager, and Jennifer Upton served as Product Developer for this edition. Our thanks extend to those who helped us on prior editions as well, including Mike Junior, who originally recruited Bob Bruner to do this project, and Michele Janicek.

Of all the contributors, our wives, Barbara M. Bruner, Kathy N. Eades, and Mary Ann H. Schill as well as our children have endured great sacrifices as the result of our work on this book. As Milton said, "They also serve who only stand and wait." Development of this eighth edition would not have been possible without their fond patience.

All these acknowledgments notwithstanding, responsibility for these materials is ours. We welcome suggestions for their enhancement. Please let us know of your experience with these cases, either through McGraw-Hill/Irwin, or at the coordinates given below.

Robert F. Bruner
University Professor
Distinguished Professor of Business Administration
Dean Emeritus of the Darden School of Business
Darden Graduate School of Business
University of Virginia
brunerr@virginia.edu[4]

Kenneth M. Eades
Professor of Business Administration
Darden Graduate School of Business
University of Virginia
eades@virginia.edu[4]

Michael J. Schill
Professor of Business Administration
Darden Graduate School of Business
University of Virginia
schill@virginia.edu[4]

Individual copies of all the Darden cases in this and previous editions may be obtained promptly from McGraw-Hill/Irwin's Create (http://create.mcgraw-hill.com) or from Darden Business Publishing (telephone: 800-246-3367; https://store.darden.virginia.edu/). Proceeds from these case sales support case writing efforts. Please respect the copyrights on these materials.

---

[4]Students should know that we are unable to offer any comments that would assist their preparation of these cases without the prior express request of their instructors.

Note to the Student: How to Study and Discuss Cases

"Get a good idea and stay with it. Dog it and work at it until it's done, and done right."
   —Walt Disney

You enroll in a "case method" course, pick up the book of case studies or the stack of loose-leaf cases, and get ready for the first class meeting. If this is your first experience with case discussions, the odds are that you are clueless and a little anxious about how to prepare for this course. That's fairly normal but something you should try to break through quickly in order to gain the maximum from your studies. Quick breakthroughs come from a combination of good attitude, good "infrastructure," and good execution—this note offers some tips.

Good Attitude

Students learn best that which they teach themselves. Passive and mindless learning is ephemeral. Active and mindful learning simply sticks. The case method makes learning sticky by placing you in situations that require invention of tools and concepts *in your own terms.* The most successful case students share a set of characteristics that drive self-teaching:

1. **Personal initiative, self-reliance.** Case studies rarely suggest how to proceed. Professors are more like guides on a long hike: they can't carry you, but they can show you the way. You must arrive at the destination under your own power. You must figure out the case on your own. To teach yourself means that you must sort ideas out in ways that make sense to you, personally. To teach yourself is to give yourself two gifts: the idea you are trying to learn, and greater self-confidence in your own ability to master the world.

2. **Curiosity, a zest for exploration as an end in itself.** Richard P. Feynman, who won the Nobel Prize in Physics in 1965, was once asked whether his key discovery was worth it. He replied, ". . . [the Nobel Prize is] a pain in the . . . I don't like honors . . . The prize is the pleasure of finding the thing out, the kick in the discovery, the observation that other people use it [my work]—those are the real things, the honors are unreal to me."[1]

---

[1]Richard P. Feynman, *The Pleasure of Finding Things Out,* Cambridge, Perseus Publishing, 1999, page 12.

3. **A willingness to take risks.** Risk-taking is at the heart of all learning. Usually one learns more from failures than successes. The banker, Walter Wriston, once said, "Good judgment comes from experience. Experience comes from bad judgment."

4. **Patience and persistence.** Case studies are messy, a realistic reflection of the fact that managers don't manage problems, they manage messes.[2] Initially, reaching a solution will seem to be the major challenge. But once you reach *a* solution, you may discover other possible solutions, and face the choice among the best alternatives.

5. **An orientation to community and discussion.** Much of the power of the case method derives from a willingness to *talk* with others about your ideas and/or your points of confusion. This is one of the paradoxes of the case method: you must teach yourself, but not in a vacuum. The poet, T.S. Eliot, said, "there is no life not lived in community." Talking seems like such an inefficient method of sorting through the case, but if exploration is an end in itself then talking is the only way. Furthermore, talking is an excellent means of testing your own mastery of ideas, of rooting out points of confusion, and generally, of preparing you for professional life.

6. **Trust in the process.** The learnings from a case-method course are impressive. They arrive cumulatively over time. In many cases, the learnings continue well after the course has finished. Occasionally, these learnings hit you with the force of a tsunami. But generally, the learnings creep in quietly, but powerfully, like the tide. After the case course, you will look back and see that your thinking, mastery, and appreciation have changed dramatically. The key point is that you should not measure the success of your progress on the basis of any single case discussion. Trust that in the cumulative work over many cases you will gain the mastery you seek.

Good Infrastructure

"Infrastructure" consists of all the resources that the case student can call upon. Some of this is simply given to you by the professor: case studies, assignment questions, supporting references to textbooks or articles, and computer data or models. But you can go much farther to help yourself. Consider these steps:

1. **Find a quiet place to study. Spend at least 90 minutes there for each case study.** Each case has subtleties to it, which you will miss unless you can concentrate. After two or three visits, your quiet place will take on the attributes of a

---

[2]One of the iconic professors in operations research, Russell Ackoff, once wrote, "Managers are not confronted with problems that are independent of each other, but with dynamic situations that consist of complex systems of changing problems that interact with each other. I call such situations messes . . . Managers do not solve problems: they manage messes." ((Russell Ackoff, "The Future of Operational Research is Past," *Journal of Operational Research Society,* 30, 1 (Pergamon Press, Ltd., 1979): 93–104.))

habit: you will slip into a working attitude more easily. Be sure to spend enough time in the quiet place to give yourself a chance to really engage the case.

2. **Access a business dictionary.** If you are new to business and finance, some of the terms will seem foreign; if English is not your first language, *many* of the terms will seem foreign if not bizarre. Get into the habit of looking up terms that you don't know. The benefit of this becomes cumulative. You can find good definitions online.

3. **Skim the business news each day; read a substantive business magazine or blog regularly; follow the markets.** Reading a newspaper or magazine helps build a *context* for the case study you are trying to solve at the moment, and helps you make connections between the case study and current events. The terminology of business and finance that you see in the publications helps reinforce your use of the dictionary, and hastens your mastery of terms you will see in the cases. Your learning by reading business periodicals is cumulative. Some students choose to follow a good business news website on the Internet. These have the virtue of being inexpensive and efficient, but they tend to screen too much. Having the printed publication in your hands, and leafing through it, helps the process of *discovery*, which is the whole point of the exercise.

4. **Learn the basics of spreadsheet modeling on a computer.** Many case studies now have supporting data available for analysis in spreadsheet files, such as Microsoft Excel. Analyzing the data on a computer rather than by hand both speeds up your work, and extends your reach.

5. **Form a study group.** The ideas in many cases are deep; the analysis can get complex. *You will learn more, and perform better in class participation by discussing the cases together in a learning team before you come to class.* Your team should devote an average of an hour to each case. High performance teams show a number of common attributes:

   a. Members commit to the success of the team.

   b. The team plans ahead, leaving time for contingencies.

   c. The team meets regularly.

   d. Team members show up for meetings and are *prepared* to contribute.

   e. There may or may not be a formal leader, but assignments are clear. Team members meet their assigned obligations.

6. **Get to know your professor.** In the case method, students inevitably learn more from one another than from the instructor. But the teacher is part of the learning infrastructure too: a resource to be used wisely. Never troll for answers in advance of a case discussion. Do your homework; use classmates and learning teams to clear up most questions so that you can focus on the meatiest issues with the teacher. Be very organized and focused about what you would like to discuss. Remember that teachers like to learn too: if you reveal a new insight about a case or bring a clipping about a related issue in current events, the professor and student both gain from their time together. Ultimately, the best payoff to the professor is the "aha" in the student's eyes when he or she masters an idea.

Good Execution

Good attitude and infrastructure must be employed properly—and one needs good execution. The extent to which a student learns depends on how the case study is approached. What can one do to gain the maximum from the study of these cases?

1. **Reading the case**. The very first time you read any case, look for the forest not the trees. This requires that your first reading be quick. Do not begin taking notes on the first round; instead, read the case like a magazine article. The first few paragraphs of a well-constructed case usually say something about the problem—read those carefully. Then quickly read the rest of the case, seeking mainly a sense of the scope of the problems, and what information the case contains to help resolve them. Leaf through the exhibits, looking for what information they hold, rather than for any analytical insights. At the conclusion of the first pass, read any supporting articles or notes that your instructor may have recommended.

2. **Getting into the case situation. Develop your "awareness."** With the broader perspective in mind, the second and more detailed reading will be more productive. The reason is that as you now encounter details, your mind will be able to organize them in some useful fashion rather than inventorying them randomly. Making linkages among case details is necessary toward solving the case. At this point you can take the notes that will set up your analysis.

   The most successful students project themselves into the position of the decision-maker because this perspective helps them link case details as well as develop a stand on the case problem. Assignment questions may help you do this; but it is a good idea to get into the habit of doing it yourself. Here are the kinds of questions you might try to answer in preparing every case:

   a. Who are the protagonists in the case? Who must take action on the problem? What do they have at stake? What pressures are they under?

   b. In what business is the company? What is the nature of its product? What is the nature of demand for that product? What is the firm's distinctive competence? With whom does it compete?[3] What is the structure of the industry? Is the firm comparatively strong or weak? In what ways?

   c. What are the goals of the firm? What is the firm's strategy in pursuit of these goals? (The goals and strategy might be explicitly stated, or they may be implicit in the way the firm does business.) What are the firm's apparent functional policies in marketing (e.g., push- versus-pull strategy), production

---

[3]Think broadly about competitors. Mark Twain wrote in *A Connecticut Yankee in King Arthur's Court,* "The best swordsman in the world doesn't need to fear the second best swordsman in the world; no, the person for him to be afraid of is some ignorant antagonist who has never had a sword in his hand before; he doesn't do the thing he ought to do, and so the expert isn't prepared for him; he does the thing he ought not to do; and it often catches the expert out and ends him on the spot."

(e.g., labor relations, use of new technology, distributed production vs. centralized), and finance (e.g., the use of debt financing, payment of dividends)? Financial and business strategies can be inferred from analysis of financial ratios and a sources and uses of funds statement.

D. How well has the firm performed in pursuit of its goals? (The answer to this question calls for simple analysis using financial ratios, such as the DuPont system, compound growth rates, and measures of value creation.)

The larger point of this phase of your case preparation is to broaden your awareness of issues. Perhaps the most successful investor in history, Warren Buffett, said, "Any player unaware of the fool in the market, probably is the fool in the market."[4] Awareness is an important attribute of successful managers.

3. **Defining the problem.** A common trap for many executives is to assume that the issue at hand is the real problem worthiest of their time, rather than a symptom of some larger problem that *really* deserves their time. For instance, a lender is often asked to advance funds to help tide a firm over a cash shortfall. Careful study may reveal that the key problem is not a cash shortfall, but rather product obsolescence, unexpected competition, or careless cost management. Even in cases where the decision is fairly narrowly defined (such as in a capital expenditure choice), the "problem" generally turns out to be the believability of certain key assumptions. Students who are new to the case method tend to focus narrowly in defining problems and often overlook the influence which the larger setting has on the problem. In doing this the student develops narrow specialist habits, never achieving the general manager perspective. It is useful and important for you to define the problem yourself, and in the process, validate the problem as suggested by the protagonist in the case.

4. **Analysis: run the numbers and go to the heart of the matter.** Virtually all finance cases require numerical analysis. This is good because figure-work lends rigor and structure to your thinking. But some cases, reflecting reality, invite you to explore blind alleys. If you are new to finance, even these explorations will help you learn.[5] The best case students develop an instinct for where to devote their analysis. Economy of effort is desirable. If you have invested wisely in problem definition, economical analysis tends to follow. For instance, a student might assume that a particular case is meant to exercise financial forecasting skills and will spend two or more hours preparing a detailed forecast, instead of preparing a simpler forecast in one hour and conducting a sensitivity analysis based on key assumptions in the next hour. An executive rarely thinks of a situation as having to do with a forecasting method or discounting or any other technique, but rather

---

[4]Buffett was quoted by Michael Lewis in his book, *Liar's Poker.*

[5]Case analysis is often iterative: an understanding of the big issues invites an analysis of details—then the details may restructure the big issues and invite the analysis of other details. In some cases, getting to the "heart of the matter" will mean just such iteration.

thinks of it as a problem of judgment, deciding on which people or concepts or environmental conditions to bet. The best case analyses get down to the *key bets* on which the executive is wagering the prosperity of the firm, and his or her career. Get to the business issues quickly, and avoid lengthy churning through relatively unimportant calculations.

5. **Prepare to participate: take a stand.** To develop analytical insights without making recommendations is useless to executives, and drains the case study experience of some of its learning power. A stand means having a point of view about the problem, a recommendation, and an analysis to back up both of them. The lessons most worth learning all come from taking a stand. From that truth flows the educative force of the case method. In the typical case, the student is projected into the position of an executive who must do something in response to a problem. It is this choice of what to do that constitutes the executive's "stand." Over the course of a career, an executive who takes stands gains wisdom. If the stand provides an effective resolution of the problem, so much the better for all concerned. If it does not, however, the wise executive analyzes the reasons for the failure and may learn even more than from a success. As Theodore Roosevelt wrote:

   > *The credit belongs to the man[6] who is actually in the arena—whose face is marred by dust and sweat and blood . . . who knows the great enthusiasms, the great devotions— and spends himself in a worthy cause—who at best if he wins knows the thrills of high achievement—and if he fails, at least fails while daring greatly so that his place shall never be with those cold and timid souls who know neither victory nor defeat.*

6. **In class: participate actively in support of your conclusions, but be open to new insights.** Of course, one can have a stand without the world being any wiser. To take a stand in case discussions means to participate actively in the discussion and to advocate your stand until new facts or analyses emerge to warrant a change.[7] Learning by the case method is not a spectator sport. A classic error many students make is to bring into the case method classroom the habits of the lecture hall (i.e., passively absorbing what other people say). These habits fail miserably in the case method classroom because they only guarantee that one absorbs the truths and fallacies uttered by others. The purpose of case study is to develop and exercise *one's own* skills and judgment. This takes practice and participation, just as in a sport. Here are two good general suggestions: (1) defer significant note-taking until after class and (2) strive to contribute to every case discussion.

7. **Immediately after class: jot down notes, corrections and questions.** Don't overinvest in taking notes during class—that just cannibalizes "air time" in which you could be learning through discussing the case. But immediately after, collect

---

[6]Today, a statement such as this would surely recognize women as well.

[7]There is a difference between taking a stand and pigheadedness. Nothing is served by clinging to your stand to the bitter end in the face of better analysis or common sense. Good managers recognize new facts and arguments as they come to light, and adapt.

your learnings and questions in notes that will capture your thinking. Of course, ask a fellow student or your teacher questions that will help clarify issues that still puzzle you.

8. **Once a week, flip through notes. Make a list of your questions, and pursue answers.** Take an hour each weekend to review your notes from class discussions during the past week. This will help build your grasp of the flow of the course. Studying a subject by the case method is like building a large picture with small mosaic tiles. It helps to step back to see the big picture. But the main objective should be to make an inventory of anything you are unclear about: terms, concepts, and calculations. Work your way through this inventory with classmates, learning teams, and ultimately the instructor. This kind of review and follow-up builds your self-confidence and prepares you to participate more effectively in future case discussions.

Conclusion: Focus on Process, and Results Will Follow

View the case method experience as a series of opportunities to test your mastery of techniques and your business judgment. If you seek a list of axioms to be etched in stone, you are bound to disappoint yourself. As in real life, there are virtually no "right" answers to these cases in the sense that a scientific or engineering problem has an exact solution. Jeff Milman has said, "The answers worth getting are never found in the back of the book." What matters is that you obtain a way of thinking about business situations that you can carry from one job (or career) to the next. In the case method it is largely true that *how you learn is what you learn.*[8]

---

[8] In describing the work of case teachers, John H. McArthur has said, "How we teach is what we teach."

Ethics in Finance

"The first thing is character, before money or anything else."
    —J. P. Morgan (in testimony before the U.S. Congress)

"The professional concerns himself with doing the right thing rather than making money, knowing that the profit takes care of itself if the other things are attended to."
    —Edwin LeFevre, *Reminiscences of a Stock Operator*

Integrity is paramount for a successful career in finance and business, as practitioners remind us. One learns, rather than inherits, integrity. And the lessons are everywhere, even in case studies about finance. To some people, the world of finance is purely mechanical, devoid of ethical considerations. The reality is that ethical issues are pervasive in finance. Still, disbelief that ethics matter in finance can take many forms.

- "It's not my job," says one person, thinking that a concern for ethics belongs to a CEO, an ombudsperson, or a lawyer. But if you passively let someone else do your thinking, you expose yourself to complicity in unethical decisions of others. Even worse is the possibility that if everyone assumes that someone else owns the job of ethical practice, then perhaps *no one* owns it and that therefore the enterprise has no moral compass at all.

- Another person says, "When in Rome, do as the Romans do. It's a dog-eat-dog world: we have to play the game their way if we mean to do business there." Under this view, everybody is assumed to act ethically relative to their local environment so that it is inappropriate to challenge unethical behavior. This is moral relativism. The problem with this view is that it presupposes that you have no identity, that you are defined like a chameleon by the environment around you. Relativism is the enemy of personal identity and character. You *must* have a view if you are rooted in any cultural system. Prepare to take a stand.

- A third person says, "It's too complicated. Civilization has been arguing about ethics for 3,000 years. You expect me to master it in my lifetime?" The response must be that we use complicated systems dozens of times each day without full mastery of their details. Perhaps the alternative would be to live in a cave, a simpler life but much less rewarding. Moreover, as courts have been telling the business world for centuries, ignorance of the law is no defense: if you want to succeed in the field of finance, you must grasp the norms of ethical behavior.

There is no escaping the fact that ethical reasoning is vital to the practice of business and finance. Tools and concepts of ethical reasoning belong in the financial toolkit alongside other valuable instruments of financial practice.

Ethics and economics were once tightly interwoven. The patriarch of economics, Adam Smith, was actually a scholar of moral philosophy. Though the two fields may have diverged in the last century, they remain strong complements.[i] Morality concerns norms and teachings. Ethics concerns the process of making morally *good* decisions, or as Andrew Wicks wrote, "Ethics has to do with pursuing—and achieving—laudable ends."[ii] The *Oxford English Dictionary* defines "moral" as "Of knowledge, opinions, judgments, etc.; Relating to the nature and application of the distinction between right and wrong."[iii] "Ethics," on the other hand, is defined as "The science of morals."[iv] To see how decision-making processes in finance have ethical implications, consider the following case studies.

1. Fraud. For several decades, Bernard Madoff operated a money management firm that reported annual returns of about 10% in good years and bad, performance that was astonishing for its regularity.[v] Madoff claimed that he was able to earn such reliable returns from investing in the shares of mature companies, along with a "collar" (put and call options that limited the risk). He marketed his services to investors on the strength of his reported performance, his years in the investment business, and his ethnic and social affinity in prominent clubs and communities. But in the Panic of 2008, worried investors sought to withdraw their investments from the Madoff firm. On December 10, 2008, Bernard Madoff admitted to F.B.I. agents that his investment fund was "one big lie," exploiting some 13,500 individual investors and charities.[vi] Investigation and court proceedings eventually revealed that Madoff had operated a massive "Ponzi scheme," in which the investments by new investors were used to pay high returns to existing investors. The collapse of his firm cost investors some $50 billion in losses.[vii] Madoff was convicted of 11 Federal crimes and received a sentence of 150 years in jail. A number of other individuals, charities, and firms were investigated, indicted, convicted, and/or fined on related charges. Several[1] analysts over the years warned that Madoff's performance was unrealistic and probably fraudulent; but the SEC took no action. Afterward, the agency issued a 477-page report[viii] of an internal investigation that resulted in disciplinary actions against eight SEC employees, but no terminations. This was the largest Ponzi scheme in history and generated an enormous range of accusations of negligence or complicity in the fraud.

2. Negligence. In 2011, the Financial Crisis Inquiry Commission delivered a report on the Panic of 2008 that found "a systemic breakdown in accountability and ethics. The integrity of our financial markets and the public's trust in those markets are essential to the economic well-being of our nation. The soundness and the sustained prosperity of the financial system and our economy rely on the notions of fair dealing, responsibility, and transparency. In our economy, we expect businesses and individuals to pursue profits, at the same time that they produce products and services of quality and conduct themselves well. . . . Unfortunately—as

---

[1]Harry Markopoulos of Rampart Investment Management raised concerns with the SEC in May, 2000. In 2001, Michael Ocrant, editor of MARHedge published an article questioning the possibility of Madoff's performance. Also in 2001, Erin Arvedlund published an article in *Barrons* questioning the consistency of Madoff's returns.

has been the case in past speculative booms and busts—we witnessed an erosion of standards of responsibility and ethics that exacerbated the financial crisis. This was not universal, but these breaches stretched from the ground level to the corporate suites. They resulted not only in significant financial consequences but also in damage to the trust of investors, businesses, and the public in the financial system. . . . This report catalogues the corrosion of mortgage-lending standards and the securitization pipeline that transported toxic mortgages from neighborhoods across America to investors around the globe. Many mortgage lenders set the bar so low that lenders simply took eager borrowers' qualifications on faith, often with a willful disregard for a borrower's ability to pay. . . . These trends were not secret. As irresponsible lending, including predatory and fraudulent practices, became more prevalent, the Federal Reserve and other regulators and authorities heard warnings from many quarters. Yet the Federal Reserve neglected its mission "to ensure the safety and soundness of the nation's banking and financial system and to protect the credit rights of consumers." It failed to build the retaining wall before it was too late. And the Office of the Comptroller of the Currency and the Office of Thrift Supervision, caught up in turf wars, preempted state regulators from reining in abuses. . . . In our inquiry, we found dramatic breakdowns of corporate governance, profound lapses in regulatory oversight, and near fatal flaws in our financial system."[ix]

3. <u>Incentives that distort values.</u> From August, 2015 to May, 2016, the share prices of Valeant Pharmaceutical fell about 90%.[x] This destruction of share value reflected the accumulated doubts about the adequacy of the firm's disclosure of accounting results and material information pertaining to its strategy and risks. The company had grown rapidly by acquisition and by sharply raising the prices of product lines that it had purchased. Congress began an investigation into the firm's practices and complained that Valeant was withholding information. Short-sellers alleged that Valeant used a related firm, Phillidor, to book fake sales—Valeant denied this, but then ceased its ties to Phillidor and shut down its operations. The board of directors sacked its CEO. And a prominent backer of Valeant, activist investor, Bill Ackman, "deeply and profoundly apologize[d]" to investors for his support of Valeant's management. Analysts cited liberal option-based executive compensation as one stimulus for Valeant's aggressive behavior.

Laws and regulations often provide a "bright red line" to constrain bad behavior. But ethics demand an even higher standard. Bernard Madoff broke the law against fraudulent behavior. His family, friends, and associates seem to have looked the other way over the years, rather than urging him not to proceed. Leading up to the Panic of 2008, many watchdogs grew lax and neglected their duties to the wider public. And in the case of Valeant, managers and directors of the company fueled a toxic culture of growth at any cost to others.

Why One Should Care about Ethics in Finance

Managing in ethical ways is not merely about avoiding bad outcomes. There are at least five positive arguments for bringing ethics to bear on financial decision-making.

Sustainability. Unethical practices are not a foundation for enduring, sustainable, enterprise. This first consideration focuses on the *legacy* one creates through one's financial transactions. What legacy do you want to leave? To incorporate ethics into our finance mindset is to think about the kind of world that we would like to live in, and that our children will inherit.

One might object that in a totally anarchic world, unethical behavior might be the only path to life. But this only begs the point: we don't live in such a world. Instead, our world of norms and laws ensures a corrective process against unethical behavior.

Ethical behavior builds trust. Trust rewards. The branding of products seeks to create a bond between producer and consumer: a signal of purity, performance, or other attributes of quality. This bond is built by trustworthy behavior. As markets reveal, successfully branded products command a premium price. Bonds of trust tend to pay. If the field of finance were purely a world of one-off transactions, it would seem ripe for opportunistic behavior. But in the case of repeated entry into financial markets and transactions, for instance by active buyers, intermediaries, and advisors, reputation can count for a great deal in shaping the expectations of counterparties. This implicit bond, trust, or reputation can translate into more effective and economically attractive financial transactions and policies.

Surely, ethical behavior should be an end in itself. If you are behaving ethically only to get rich, then you are hardly committed to that behavior. Some might even see this as an imperfect means by which justice expresses itself.

Ethical behavior builds teams and leadership which underpin process excellence. Standards of global best practice emphasize that good business processes drive good outcomes. Stronger teams and leaders result in more agile and creative responses to problems. Ethical behavior contributes to the strength of teams and leadership by aligning employees around shared values, and building confidence and loyalty.

An objection to this argument is that in some settings promoting ethical behavior is no guarantee of team-building. Indeed, teams might blow apart over disagreement about what is ethical or what action is appropriate to take. But typically, this is not the fault of ethics, rather of team processes for handling disagreements.

Ethics sets a higher standard than laws and regulations. To a large extent, the law is a crude instrument: it tends to trail rather than anticipate behavior; it contains gaps that become recreational exploitation for the aggressive business person; Justice may neither be swift nor proportional to the crime; and as Andrew Wicks said, it "puts you in an adversarial posture with respect to others which may be counterproductive to other objectives in facing a crisis."[xi] To use only the law as a basis for ethical thinking is to settle for the lowest common denominator of social norms. As former Chairman of the Securities and Exchange Commission, Richard Breeden, said, "It is not an adequate ethical standard to want to get through the day without being indicted."[xii]

Some might object to this line of thinking by claiming that in a pluralistic society, the law is the only baseline of norms on which society can agree. Therefore, isn't the law a "good enough" guide to ethical behavior? Lynn Paine argued that this leads to a "compliance" mentality and that ethics takes one farther. She wrote, "Attention to law, as an important source of managers' rights and responsibilities, is integral to, but not a substitute for, the ethical point of view—a point of view that is attentive to rights, responsibilities, relationships, opportunities to improve and enhance human well-being, and virtue and moral excellence."[xiii]

Reputation and conscience. Motivating ethical behavior only by appealing to benefits and avoiding costs is inappropriate. By some estimates, the average annual income for a lifetime of crime (even counting years spent in prison) is large—it seems that crime *does* pay. If income were all that mattered, most of us would switch into this lucrative field. The business world features enough cheats and scoundrels to offer any professional the opportunity to break promises, or worse, for money. Ethical professionals decline these opportunities for reasons having to do with the kind of people they want to be. Amar Bhide and Howard Stevenson wrote, "The businesspeople we interviewed set great store on the regard of their family, friends, and the community at large. They valued their reputations, not for some nebulous financial gain but because they took pride in their good names. Even more important, since outsiders cannot easily judge trustworthiness, businesspeople seem guided by their inner voices, by their consciences. . . . We keep promises because it is right to do so, not because it is good business."[xiv]

For Whose Interests Are You Working?

Generally the financial executive or deal designer is an agent acting on behalf of others. For whom are you the agent? Two classic schools of thought emerge.

- **Stockholders.** Some national legal frameworks require directors and managers to operate a company in the interests of its shareholders. The shareholder focus lends a clear objective: do what creates shareholders' wealth. This would seem to limit charitable giving, "living wage" programs, voluntary reduction of pollution, and enlargement of pension benefits for retirees—all of these loosely gather under the umbrella of "social responsibility" movement in business. Milton Friedman (1962), perhaps the most prominent exponent of the stockholder school of thought, argued that the objective of business is to return value to its owners and that to divert the objective to other ends is to expropriate shareholder value and threaten the survival of the enterprise. Also, the stockholder view would argue that if all companies deviated, the price system would cease to function well as a carrier of information about the allocation of resources in the economy. The stockholder view is perhaps dominant in the U.S., U.K, and other countries in the Anglo-Saxon sphere.

- **Stakeholders.** The alternative view admits that stockholders are an important constituency of the firm, but that other groups such as employees, customers, suppliers, and the community also have a stake in the activities and success of the firm. Edward Freeman (1984) argued that the firm should be managed in the interest of the broader spectrum of constituents. The manager would necessarily be obligated to account for the interests and concerns of the various constituent groups in arriving at business decisions—the aim would be to satisfy them all, or at least the most concerned stakeholders on each issue. The complexity of this kind of decision-making can be daunting and slow. In addition, it is not always clear which stakeholder interests are relevant in making specific decisions. Such a definition seems to depend highly on the specific context, which would seem to challenge the ability to achieve equitable treatment of different stakeholder groups and across time. But the important contribution of this view is to suggest a relational view of the firm and to stimulate the manager to consider the diversity of those relationships.

Adding complexity to the question of whose interests one serves is the fact that often one has many allegiances—not only to the firm or client, but also to one's community, family, etc. Obligations that one has as an employee or professional are only a subset of obligations one has on the whole.

What is "good"? Consequences, Duties, Virtues.

One confronts ethical issues when one must choose among alternatives on the basis of right versus wrong. The ethical choices may be stark where one alternative is truly right and the other truly wrong. But in professional life the alternatives typically differ more subtly as in choosing which alternative is *more* right or *less* wrong. Ernest Hemingway said that what is moral is what one feels good after and what is immoral is what one feels bad after. Since feelings about an action could vary tremendously from one person to the next, this simplistic test would seem to admit moral relativism as the only course, an ethical "I'm OK, You're OK" approach. Fortunately 3,000 years of moral reasoning lend frameworks for greater definition of what is "right" and "wrong."

"Right" and "wrong" defined by *consequences*. An easy point of departure is to focus on outcomes. An action might be weighed in terms of its utility[xv] for society. Who is hurt or helped must be taken into consideration. Utility can be assessed in terms of the pleasure or pain for people. People choose to maximize utility. Therefore, right action is that which produces the greatest good for the greatest number of people.

"Utilitarianism" has proved to be controversial. Some critics feared that this approach might endorse gross violations of norms that society holds dear including the right to privacy, the sanctity of contracts, and property rights, when weighed in the balance of consequences for all. And the calculation of utility might be subject to special circumstances or open to interpretation, making the assessment rather more situation-specific than some philosophers could accept.

Utilitarianism was the foundation for modern neoclassical economics. Utility has proved to be difficult to measure rigorously and remains a largely theoretical idea. Yet utility-based theories are at the core of welfare economics and underpin analyses of phenomena varying as widely as government policies, consumer preferences, and investor behavior.

"Right" and "wrong" defined by *duty or intentions*. Immoral actions are ultimately self-defeating. A practice of writing bad checks, for instance, if practiced universally, would result in a world without check-writing and probably very little credit. Therefore you should act on rules which you would require to be applied universally[xvi]. You should treat a person as an end, never as a means. It is vital to ask whether an action would show respect for other persons and whether that action was something a rational person would do—"If everyone behaved this way, what kind of world would we have?"

Critics of this perspective argue that its universal view is too demanding, indeed, impossible for a businessperson to observe. For instance, the profit motive focuses on the manager's duty to just one company. But Norman Bowie responds, "Perhaps focusing on issues other than profits . . . will actually enhance the bottom line . . . .Perhaps we should view profits as a consequence of good business practices rather than as the goal of business."[xvii]

"Right" and "wrong" defined by *virtues*. Finally, a third tradition[xviii] in philosophy argues that the debate over "values" is misplaced: the focus should be on *virtues* and the qualities of the practitioner. The attention to consequences or duty is fundamentally a focus on *compliance*. Instead, one should consider whether an action is consistent with being a virtuous person. This view argues that personal happiness flowed from being virtuous, and not merely from comfort (utility) or observance (duty). It acknowledges that vices are corrupting. And it focuses on personal pride: "If I take this action would I be proud of what I see in the mirror? If it were reported tomorrow in the newspaper, would I be proud of myself?" Warren Buffett, CEO of Berkshire Hathaway, and one of the most successful investors in modern history issues a letter to each of his operating managers each year emphasizing the importance of personal integrity: He said that Berkshire can afford financial losses, but not losses in reputation. He wrote, "Make sure everything you do can be reported on the front page of your local newspaper written by an unfriendly, but intelligent reporter."[xix]

Critics of virtue-based ethics raise two objections. First, a virtue to one person may be a vice to another. Solomon (1999) points out that Confucius and Nietzsche, two other virtue ethicists, held radically different visions of virtue: Confucius extolled virtues such as respect and piety. In contrast, Nietzsche extolled risk-taking, war-making, and ingenuity. Thus, virtue ethics may be context-specific. Second, virtues can change over time. What may have been regarded as "gentlemanly" behavior (i.e., formal politeness) in the 19th Century, might have been seen by feminists in the late 20th Century as insincere and manipulative.

Discrete definition of "right" and "wrong" remains a subject of ongoing discourse. But the practical person can abstract from these and other perspectives useful guidelines toward ethical work:

- How will my action affect others? What are the consequences?
- What are my motives and my duty here? How does this decision affect them?
- Does this action serve the best that I can be?

What Can *You* Do to Promote Ethical Behavior in Your Firm?

An important contributor to unethical business practices is the existence of a work environment that promotes such behavior. Leaders in corporate work places need to be proactive in shaping a high performance culture that sets high ethical expectations. The leader can take a number of steps to shape an ethical culture.

Adopt a code of ethics. One dimension of ethical behavior is to acknowledge some code by which one intends to live. Corporations, too, can adopt codes of conduct that shape ethical expectations. Firms recognize the "problem of the commons" inherent in unethical behavior by one or a few employees. In 1909, the Supreme Court decided that a corporation could be held liable for the actions of its employees.[xx] Since then, companies have sought to set expectations for employee behavior, including codes of ethics.[xxi] **Exhibits 1 and 2** give excerpts of codes from J.P. Morgan Chase and General Electric Company—they are clear statements that define right behavior. Corporate codes are viewed by some critics as cynical efforts that seem merely to respond to executive liability that might arise from white collar and other economic crimes. Companies and their executives may be held liable for employee behavior, even if the employee acted contrary to instructions. Mere observance of guidelines in order to reduce liability is a legalistic approach to ethical behavior. Instead, Lynn Paine (1994) urged firms to adopt an "integrity strategy" that uses ethics as the driving force within a corporation. Deeply-held values would become the foundation for decision making across the firm and would yield a frame of reference that would integrate functions and businesses. By this view, ethics defines what a firm stands for.

In addition, an industry or professional group can organize a code of ethics. One example relevant for finance professionals is the Code of Ethics of the CFA Institute, the group that confers the Chartered Financial Analyst (CFA) designation on professional securities analysts and portfolio managers. An excerpt of the CFA Institute Code of Ethics is given in **Exhibit 3**.

Talk about ethics within your team and firm. Many firms seek to reinforce a culture of integrity with a program of seminars and training in ethical reasoning. A leader can stimulate reflection through informal discussion of ethical developments (e.g., indictments, convictions, civil lawsuits) in the industry or profession or of ethical issues that the team may be facing. This kind of discussion (without preaching) signals that it is on the leader's mind and is a legitimate focus of discussion. One executive regularly raises issues such as these informally over lunch and morning coffee. Leaders believe ethical matters are important enough to be the focus of team discussions.

Find and reflect on your dilemmas. The challenge for many finance practitioners is that ethical dilemmas are not readily given to structured analysis, in the same way one values a firm or balances the books. Nevertheless, one can harness the questions raised in the field of ethics to lend some rigor to one's reflections. Laura Nash (1981) abstracted a list of twelve questions on which the thoughtful practitioner might reflect in grappling with an ethical dilemma:

1. Have I defined the problem correctly and accurately?
2. If I stood on the other side of the problem, how would I define it?
3. What are the origins of this dilemma?
4. To whom and what am I loyal, as a person and as a member of a firm?
5. What is my intention in making this decision?

6. How do the likely results compare with my intention?

7. Can my decision injure anyone? How?

8. Can I engage the affected parties in my decision before I decide or take action?

9. Am I confident that my decision will be valid over a long period of time as it may seem at this moment?

10. If my boss, the CEO, the directors, my family, or community learned about this decision, would I have misgivings?

11. What signals (or symbols) might my decision convey, if my decision were understood correctly? If misunderstood?

12. Are there exceptions to my position, "special circumstances" under which I might make an alternative decision?

Act on your reflections. This may be the toughest step of all. The field of ethics can lend structure to one's thinking but has less to say about the action to be taken. Confronting a problem of ethics within a team or organization, one can consider a hierarchy of responses, from questioning and coaching to "whistle blowing" (either to an internal ombudsperson or if necessary to an outside source), and possibly, to exit from the organization.

Conclusion

Analysis of ethical issues in finance is vital. The cases of Bernard Madoff and other major business scandals show that ethical issues pervade the financial environment. Ethics is one of the pillars on which stands success in finance—it builds sustainable enterprise, trust, organizational strength, and personal satisfaction. Therefore, the financial decision maker must learn to identify, analyze, and act on ethical issues that may arise. Consequences, duties, and virtues stand out as three important benchmarks for ethical analysis. Nevertheless, the results of such analysis are rarely clear-cut. But real business leaders will take the time to sort through the ambiguities and do "the right thing" in the words of Edwin LeFevre. These and other ethical themes will appear throughout finance case studies and one's career.

References and Recommended Readings

Achampong, F., and Zemedkun, W. 1995. "An empirical and ethical analysis of factors motivating managers' merger decisions," *Journal of Business Ethics*. 14: 855–865.

Bhide, A., and H. H. Stevenson, 1990. "Why be honest if honesty doesn't pay," *Harvard Business Review* September-October, pages 121–129.

Bloomenthal, Harold S., 2002. *Sarbanes-Oxley Act in Perspective* St. Paul, MN: West Group.

Boatright, J.R., 1999. *Ethics in Finance*, Oxford: Blackwell Publishers.

Bowie, N.E., "A Kantian approach to business ethics," in R. E. Frederick, ed., *A Companion to Business Ethics*, Malden, MA: Blackwell pages 3–16.

Carroll, A. B. 1999. "Ethics in management," in R. E. Frederick, ed., *A Companion to Business Ethics*, Malden, MA: Blackwell pages 141–152.

CFA Institute 2014. "Code of Ethics and Standard of Professional Conduct" (Charlottesville, Virginia) http://www.cfapubs.org/doi/pdf/10.2469/ccb.v2014.n6.1

Frederick, R.E., *A Companion to Business Ethics*, Oxford: Blackwell Publishers.

Freeman, R.E., 1984. *Strategic Management: A Stakeholder Approach* Boston: Pittman.

Friedman, M., 1962. *Capitalism and Freedom*, Chicago: University of Chicago Press.

General Electric Company 2005. "Integrity: The Spirit and Letter of Our Commitment" (June 2005). Downloaded from https://www.sec.gov/Archives/edgar/data/1262449/000119312508061906/dex142.htm.

Jensen, M., 2005. "The agency costs of overvalued equity," *Financial Management* (Spring): 5–19.

Kidder, R., 1997. "Ethics and the bottom line: Ten reasons for businesses to do right," *Insights on Global Ethics*, Spring, pages 7–9.

Murphy, P.E. 1997. "80 Exemplary Ethics statements," cited in L.H. Newton, "A passport for the corporate code: from Borg Warner to the Caux Principles," in Robert E. Frederick, *A Companion to Business Ethics*, Malden, MA: Blackwell, 1999, pages 374–385.

Nash, L.L. 1981. "Ethics without the sermon," *Harvard Business Review,* November-December, pages 79–90.

Paine, L.S. 1994. "Managing for organizational integrity," *Harvard Business Review*, March-April, 106–117.

Paine, L.S., 1999. "Law, ethics, and managerial judgment," in R. E. Frederick, ed., *A Companion to Business Ethics*, Malden, MA: Blackwell pages 194–206.

Paine, L.S. 2003. *Value Shift: Why Companies Must Merger Social and Financial Imperatives to Achieve Superior Performance* New York: McGraw-Hill.

Pulliam S., 2003. A staffer ordered to commit fraud balked, and then caved. *The Wall Street Journal* June 23, 2003. Page A1.

Sen, A. 1987. *On Ethics and Economics* Oxford: Blackwell Publishers.

Shafer, W. 2002. "Effects of materiality, risk, and ethical perceptions on fraudulent reporting by financial executives," *Journal of Business Ethics.* 38(3): 243–263.

Solomon, R., 1999. "Business ethics and virtue." in R. E. Frederick, ed., *A Companion to Business Ethics*, Malden, MA: Blackwell pages 30–37.

Solomon, D., 2003. WorldCom moved expenses to the balance sheet of MCI. *The Wall Street Journal* March 31, 2003. Downloaded from http://online.wsj.com/article_print/0,,SB104907054486790100,00.html.

Werhane, P. 1988. "Two ethical issues in Mergers and Acquisitions," *Journal of Business Ethics* 7, 41–45.

Werhane, P. 1990. "Mergers, acquisitions, and the market for corporate control," *Public Affairs Quarterly* 4(1): 81–96.

Werhane, P. 1997. "A note on moral imagination." Charlottesville VA: Darden Case Collection, catalogue number UVA-E-0114.

Werhane, P. 1999. "Business ethics and the origins of contemporary capitalism: economics and ethics in the work of Adam Smith and Herbert Spencer" in R. E. Frederick, ed., *A Companion to Business Ethics*, Malden, MA: Blackwell pages 325–341.

Wicks, A., 2003. "A note on ethical decision making." Charlottesville VA: Darden Case Collection catalogue number UVA-E-0242.

EXHIBIT 1 | J.P. Morgan Chase & Co. Excerpts from Code of Conduct and Code of Ethics for Finance Professionals[xxii]

JPMC Finance Officers and Finance Professionals must act honestly, promote ethical conduct and comply with the law . . . They are specifically required to:

• Carry out their responsibilities honestly, in good faith and with integrity, due care and diligence . . .

• Comply with applicable government laws, rules and regulations . . .

• Never . . . coerce, manipulate, mislead or fraudulently influence the firm's independent auditors . . .

• Protect the confidentiality of non-public information relating to JPMC and its clients . . .

• Address actual or apparent conflicts of interest . . .

• Promptly report . . . any known or suspected violation . . .

. . .

JPMC strictly prohibits intimidation or retaliation against anyone who makes a good faith report about a known or suspected violation of this Policy, or of any law or regulation.

EXHIBIT 2 | Excerpts from "The Spirit and the Letter:" General Electric's "Code of Conduct"

Statement of integrity

We have been ranked first for integrity and governance. But none of that matters if each of us does not make the right decisions and take the right actions. . . . Do not allow anything—not "making the numbers," competitive instincts or even a direct order from a superior—to compromise your commitment to integrity. . . . Leaders must address employees' concerns about appropriate conduct promptly and with care and respect.

There is no conflict between excellent financial performance and high standards of governance and compliance—in fact, the two are mutually reinforcing.

. . .

- Obey the applicable laws and regulations . . .
- Be honest, fair and trustworthy . . .
- Avoid all conflicts of interest . . .
- Foster an atmosphere [of] fair employment practices . . .
- Strive to create a safe workplace and to protect the environment.
- . . . Sustain a culture where ethical conduct is recognized, valued and exemplified by all employees.

Source: "Integrity: The Spirit and Letter of Our Commitment" General Electric Company, June 2005, page 3. A longer version of this resource is also available at https://www.sec.gov/Archives/edgar/data/1262449/000119312508061906/dex142.htm.

EXHIBIT 3 | CFA Institute Code of Ethics, 2014

High ethical standards are critical to maintaining the public's trust in financial markets and in the investment profession. . . .
- Act with integrity, competence, diligence, respect . . .
- Place . . . the interests of clients above their own personal interests.
- Use reasonable care and exercise independent professional judgment . . .
- Practice and encourage others. . . .
- Promote the integrity of . . . capital markets.
- Maintain and improve their professional competence . . .

Source: CFA Institute 2014. "Code of Ethics and Standard of Professional Conduct" (Charlottesville, Virginia) http://www.cfapubs.org/doi/pdf/10.2469/ccb.v2014.n6.1

Endnotes

[i]Sen (1987) and Werhane (1999) have argued that Smith's masterpiece, *Wealth of Nations*, is incorrectly construed as a justification for self-interest, and that it speaks more broadly about virtues such as prudence, fairness, and cooperation.

[ii]Wicks (2003) page 5.

[iii]*Oxford English Dictionary* 1989. Vol. IX, page 1068.

[iv]*Ibid.* Vol. V, page 421.

[v]"The Con of the Century," *The Economist,* December 18, 2008 at http://www.economist.com/node/12818310.

[vi]Mark Seal, "Madoff's World," *Vanity Fair,* April, 2009 at http://www.vanityfair.com/news/2009/04/bernard-madoff-friends-family-profile.

[vii]Henriques, Diana and Zachery Kouwe, "Prominent Trader Accused of Defrauding Clients," *New York Times,* December 11, 2008.

[viii]"Investigation of Failure of the SEC to Uncover Bernard Madoff's Ponzi Scheme," U.S. Securities and Exchange Commission, Office of Investigations, August 31, 2009.

[ix]*The Financial Crisis Inquiry Report,"* 2011, Philip Angelides, Chair, pages xxii, xxiii, and xxvii–xxviii.

[x]For further information on the Valeant case study, see Stephen Gandel, "What Caused Valeant's Epic 90% plunge," *Fortune,* March 20, 2016, at http://fortune.com/2016/03/20/valeant-timeline-scandal/. And see Miles Johnson, "What went wrong with Ackman and Valeant—the alternative edition" *Financial Times,* March 30, 2017 at https://ftalphaville.ft.com/2017/03/30/2186644/what-went-wrong-with-ackman-and-valeant-the-alternative-edition/.

[xi]Wicks (2003) page 11.

[xii]Quoted in K.V. Salwen, 1991 "SEC Chief's criticism of ex-managers of Salomon suggests civil action is likely," *Wall Street Journal* Nov. 20, A10.

[xiii]Paine (1999), pages 194–195.

[xiv]Bhide and Stevenson, 1990, pages 127–128.

[xv]The Utilitarian philosophers, Jeremy Bentham (1748–1832), James Mill (1773–1836), and John Stuart Mill (1806–1873), argued that the utility (or usefulness) of ideas, actions, and institutions could be measured in terms of their consequences.

[xvi]The philosopher, Immanuel Kant (1724–1804) sought a foundation for ethics in the purity of one's motives.

[xvii]Bowie (1999) page 13.

[xviii]This view originates in ancient Greek philosophy, starting from Socrates, Plato, and Aristotle.

[xix]Russ Banham, "The Warren Buffett School," *Chief Executive,* December 2002, downloaded from http://www.robertpmiles.com/BuffettSchool.htm, May 19, 2003.

[xx]See *New York Central v. United States*, 212 US 481.

[xxi]Murphy (1997) compiles 80 exemplary ethics statements.

[xxii]Source: J.P. Morgan Chase & Company, website: https://www.jpmorganchase.com/corporate/About-JPMC/ab-code-of-ethics.htm downloaded May 18, 2017.

## PART 1

Setting Some Themes

Warren E. Buffett, 2015

On August 10, 2015, Warren E. Buffett, chair and CEO of Berkshire Hathaway Inc., announced that Berkshire Hathaway would acquire the aerospace-parts supplier Precision Castparts Corporation (PCP). In Buffett's largest deal ever, Berkshire would purchase all of PCP's outstanding shares for $235 per share in cash, a 21% premium over the trading price a day earlier. The bid valued PCP's equity at $32.3 billion.[1] The total transaction value would be $37.2 billion, including assuming PCP's outstanding debt—this was what analysts called the "enterprise value." "I've admired PCP's operation for a long time. For good reasons, it is the supplier of choice for the world's aerospace industry, one of the largest sources of American exports,"[2] Buffett said. After the announcement, Berkshire Hathaway's Class A[3] shares moved down 1.1% at market open, a loss in market value of $4.05 billion.[4] PCP's share price jumped 19.2% at the news[5]; the S&P 500 Composite Index opened up 0.2%. **Exhibit 1.1** illustrates the recent share-price performance for Berkshire Hathaway, PCP, and the S&P 500 Index. **Exhibit 1.2** presents recent consolidated financial statements for the firm.

---

[1]The difference between enterprise value and equity value is the amount of debt outstanding. On August 10, 2015, PCP's debt amounted to about $4.9 billion—this differs from the debt indicated in **Exhibit 1.9**, which was dated March 31, 2015.

[2]Tomi Kilgore, "Warren Buffett's $3.72 Billion Buy of Precision Castparts is His Biggest Buyout Ever," Marketwatch, August 10, 2015 http://www.marketwatch.com/story/warren-buffetts-372-billion-buy-of-precision-castparts-is-his-biggest-buyout-deal-ever-2015-08-10 (accessed Dec. 12, 2016).

[3]Each Class A common share is entitled to one vote per share. Class B common stock possesses dividend and distribution rights equal to one-fifteen-hundredth (1/1,500) of such rights of Class A common stock. Each Class B common share possesses voting rights equivalent to one-ten-thousandth (1/10,000) of the voting rights of a Class A share.

[4]The per-share change in Berkshire Hathaway's Class A share price at the date of the announcement was $1,895. The company had 811,755 Class A shares outstanding and 1,247,366,163 Class B shares outstanding. Class B common shares are equivalent to 1/1500th of Class A common shares.

[5]The per-share change in PCP share price after the announcement was $37.28. The stock closed at $193.88 on August 7, 2015, and opened on August 10, 2015, at $231.16.

The acquisition of PCP, Berkshire Hathaway's largest deal ever, renewed public interest in its sponsor, Buffett. In many ways, he was an anomaly. One of the richest individuals in the world (with an estimated net worth of about $66.5 billion according to *Forbes*), he was also respected and even beloved. Though he had accumulated perhaps the best investment record in history (a compound annual increase in wealth for Berkshire Hathaway of 21.6% from 1965 to 2014),[6] Berkshire Hathaway paid him only $100,000 per year to serve as its CEO. While Buffett and other insiders controlled 39.5% of Berkshire Hathaway, he ran the company in the interests of all shareholders. "We will not take cash compensation, restricted stock, or option grants that would make our results superior to [those of Berkshire's investors]," Buffett said. "I will keep well over 99% of my net worth in Berkshire. My wife and I have never sold a share nor do we intend to."[7]

Buffett was the subject of numerous laudatory articles and at least eight biographies, yet he remained an intensely private individual. Although acclaimed by many as an intellectual genius, he shunned the company of intellectuals and preferred to affect the manner of a down-home Nebraskan (he lived in Omaha) and a tough-minded investor. In contrast to the investment world's other "stars," Buffett acknowledged his investment failures both quickly and publicly. Although he held an MBA from Columbia University and credited his mentor, Benjamin Graham, with developing the philosophy of value-based investing that had guided Buffett to his success, he chided business schools for the irrelevance of their finance and investing theories.

Numerous writers sought to distill the essence of Buffett's success. What were the key principles that guided Buffett? Could those principles be applied broadly in the 21st century, or were they unique to Buffett and his time? By understanding those principles, analysts hoped to illuminate the acquisition of PCP. What were Buffett's probable motives in the acquisition? What did Buffett's offer say about his valuation of PCP, and how would it compare with valuations for other comparable firms? Would Berkshire's acquisition of PCP prove to be a success? How would Buffett define success?

Berkshire Hathaway Inc.

Berkshire Hathaway was incorporated in 1889 as Berkshire Cotton Manufacturing and eventually grew to become one of New England's biggest textile producers, accounting for 25% of U.S. cotton-textile production. In 1955, Berkshire Cotton Manufacturing merged with Hathaway Manufacturing and began a secular decline due to inflation, technological change, and intensifying competition from foreign rivals. In 1965, Buffett and some partners acquired control of Berkshire Hathaway, believing that its financial decline could be reversed.

Over the next 20 years, it became apparent that large capital investments would be required for the company to remain competitive, and that even then the financial returns

---

[6]In comparison, the annual average total return on all large stocks from 1965 to the end of 2014 was 9.9%. (See Warren Buffett, annual letter to shareholders, 2014.)

[7]Warren Buffett, annual letter to shareholders, 2001. Warren Buffett has since pledged to donate 99% of his net worth to philanthropic foundations. See http://givingpledge.org.

would be mediocre. Fortunately, the textile group generated enough cash in the early years to permit the firm to purchase two insurance companies headquartered in Omaha: National Indemnity Company and National Fire & Marine Insurance Company. Acquisitions of other businesses followed in the 1970s and 1980s; Berkshire Hathaway exited the textile business in 1985.

The investment performance of a share in Berkshire Hathaway had astonished most observers. As shown in **Exhibit 1.3**, a $100 investment in Berkshire Hathaway stock on September 30, 1976, would compound to a value of $305,714 as of July 31, 2015, approximately 39 years later. The investment would result in a 305,614% cumulative return, 22.8% when annualized. Over the same period, a $100 investment in the S&P 500 would compound to a value of $1,999 for a cumulative return of 1,899.1% or 8.0% annualized.[8]

In 2014, Berkshire Hathaway's annual report described the firm as "a holding company owning subsidiaries engaged in a number of diverse business activities."[9] Berkshire Hathaway's portfolio of businesses included:

- *Insurance:* Insurance and reinsurance[10] of property and casualty risks worldwide and with reinsurance of life, accident, and health risks worldwide in addition (e.g., GEICO, General Re).

- *Railroad:* A long-lived asset with heavy regulation and high capital intensity, the company operated one of the largest railroad systems in North America (i.e., BNSF).

- *Utilities and Energy:* Generate, transmit, store, distribute, and supply energy through the subsidiary Berkshire Hathaway Energy company.

- *Manufacturing:* Numerous and diverse manufacturing businesses were grouped into three categories: (1) industrial products, (2) building products, and (3) consumer products (e.g., Lubrizol, PCP).

- *Service and Retailing:* Providers of numerous services, including fractional aircraft-ownership programs, aviation pilot training, electronic-components distribution, and various retailing businesses, including automotive dealerships (e.g., NetJets, Nebraska Furniture Mart).

- *Finance and Financial Products:* Manufactured housing and related consumer financing; transportation equipment, manufacturing, and leasing; and furniture leasing (e.g., Clayton Homes, ULTX, XTRA).

Exhibit 1.4 gives a summary of revenues, operating profits, capital expenditures, depreciation, and assets for Berkshire Hathaway's various business segments. The company's investment portfolio also included equity interests in numerous publicly traded companies, summarized in **Exhibit 1.5**.

---

[8]The annualized return calculation assumes a 39-year period (actual time period is 38 years 10 months).

[9]Berkshire Hathaway Inc. annual report, 2004.

[10]Reinsurance was insurance for insurance companies, a way of transferring or "ceding" some of the financial risk insurance companies assumed in insuring cars, homes, and businesses to another insurance company, the reinsurer. Insurance Information Institute, "Reinsurance," November 2014, http://www.iii.org/issue-update/reinsurance (accessed Dec. 9, 2016).

Buffett's Investment Philosophy

Warren Buffett was first exposed to formal training in investing at Columbia University, where he studied under Benjamin Graham. A coauthor of the classic text, *Security Analysis*, Graham developed a method of identifying undervalued stocks (that is, stocks whose prices were less than their intrinsic value). This became the cornerstone of modern value investing. Graham's approach was to focus on the value of assets, such as cash, net working capital, and physical assets. Eventually, Buffett modified that approach to focus also on valuable franchises that were unrecognized by the market.

Over the years, Buffett had expounded his philosophy of investing in his chair's letter to shareholders in Berkshire Hathaway's annual report. By 2005, those lengthy letters had acquired a broad following because of their wisdom and their humorous, self-deprecating tone. The letters emphasized the following elements:

1. **Economic reality, not accounting reality.** Financial statements prepared by accountants conformed to rules that might not adequately represent the *economic* reality of a business. Buffett wrote:

   Because of the limitations of conventional accounting, consolidated reported earnings may reveal relatively little about our true economic performance. Charlie [Munger, Buffett's business partner] and I, both as owners and managers, virtually ignore such consolidated numbers . . . Accounting consequences do not influence our operating or capital-allocation process.[11]

   Accounting reality was conservative, backward looking, and governed by generally accepted accounting principles (GAAP), even though investment decisions should be based on the economic reality of a business. In economic reality, intangible assets such as patents, trademarks, special managerial expertise, and reputation might be very valuable, yet, under GAAP, they would be carried at little or no value. GAAP measured results in terms of net profit, while in economic reality the results of a business were its *flows of cash.*

   A key feature of Buffett's approach defined economic reality at the level of the business itself, not the market, the economy, or the security—he was a *fundamental analyst* of the business. His analysis sought to judge the simplicity of the business, the consistency of its operating history, the attractiveness of its long-term prospects, the quality of management, and the firm's capacity to create value.

2. **The cost of the lost opportunity.** Buffett compared an investment opportunity against the next-best alternative, the lost opportunity. In his business decisions, he demonstrated a tendency to frame his choices as either/or decisions rather than yes/no decisions. Thus an important standard of comparison in testing the attractiveness of an acquisition was the potential rate of return from investing in the common stocks of other companies. Buffett held that there was no fundamental difference between buying a business outright and buying a few shares of that business in the equity market. Thus for him, the comparison of an investment against other returns available in the market was an important benchmark of performance.

---

[11]Berkshire Hathaway Inc. annual report, 2004.

3. **Embrace the time value of money.** Buffett assessed intrinsic value as the present value of future expected performance:

> [All other methods fall short in determining whether] an investor is indeed buying something for what it is worth and is therefore truly operating on the principle of obtaining value for his investments . . . Irrespective of whether a business grows or doesn't, displays volatility or smoothness in earnings, or carries a high price or low in relation to its current earnings and book value, the investment shown by the discounted-flows-of-cash calculation to be the cheapest is the one that the investor should purchase.[12]

Enlarging on his discussion of intrinsic value, Buffett used an educational example:

> We define intrinsic value as the discounted value of the cash that can be taken out of a business during its remaining life. Anyone calculating intrinsic value necessarily comes up with a highly subjective figure that will change both as estimates of future cash flows are revised and as interest rates move. Despite its fuzziness, however, intrinsic value is all important and is the only logical way to evaluate the relative attractiveness of investments and businesses.
>
> To see how historical input (book value) and future output (intrinsic value) can diverge, let us look at another form of investment, a college education. Think of the education's cost as its "book value." If it is to be accurate, the cost should include the earnings that were foregone by the student because he chose college rather than a job. For this exercise, we will ignore the important non economic benefits of an education and focus strictly on its economic value. First, we must estimate the earnings that the graduate will receive over his lifetime and subtract from that figure an estimate of what he would have earned had he lacked his education. That gives us an excess earnings figure, which must then be discounted, at an appropriate interest rate, back to graduation day. The dollar result equals the intrinsic economic value of the education. Some graduates will find that the book value of their education exceeds its intrinsic value, which means that whoever paid for the education didn't get his money's worth. In other cases, the intrinsic value of an education will far exceed its book value, a result that proves capital was wisely deployed. In all cases, what is clear is that book value is meaningless as an indicator of intrinsic value.[13]

To illustrate the mechanics of this example, consider the hypothetical case presented in **Exhibit 1.6**. Suppose an individual has the opportunity to invest $50 million in a business—this is its cost or book value. This business will throw off cash at the rate of 20% of its investment base each year. Suppose that instead of receiving any dividends, the owner decides to reinvest all cash flow back into the business—at this rate, the book value of the business will grow at 20% per year. Suppose that the investor plans to sell the business for its book value at the end of the fifth year. Does this investment create value for the individual? One determines this by discounting the future cash flows to the present at a cost of equity of 15%. Suppose that this is the investor's opportunity cost, the required return that could have been earned elsewhere at comparable risk. Dividing the present value of future cash flows (i.e., Buffett's intrinsic value) by the cost of the

---

[12]Berkshire Hathaway Inc. annual report, 1992.

[13]Berkshire Hathaway Inc. annual report, 1992.

investment (i.e., Buffett's book value) indicates that every dollar invested buys securities worth $1.23. Value is created.

Consider an opposing case, summarized in **Exhibit 1.7**. The example is similar in all respects, except for one key difference: the annual return on the investment is 10%. The result is that every dollar invested buys securities worth $0.80. Value is destroyed.

Comparing the two cases in **Exhibits 1.6** and **1.7**, the difference in value creation and destruction is driven entirely by the relationship between the expected returns and the discount rate: in the first case, the spread is positive; in the second case, it is negative. Only in the instance where expected returns equal the discount rate will book value equal intrinsic value. In short, book value or the investment outlay may not reflect the economic reality. One needs to focus on the prospective rates of return, and how they compare to the required rate of return.

4. **Measure performance by gain in intrinsic value, not accounting profit.** Buffett wrote:

> Our long-term economic goal . . . is to maximize Berkshire's average annual rate of gain in intrinsic business value on a per-share basis. We do not measure the economic significance or performance of Berkshire by its size; we measure by per-share progress. We are certain that the rate of per-share progress will diminish in the future—a greatly enlarged capital base will see to that. But we will be disappointed if our rate does not exceed that of the average large American corporation.[14]

The gain in intrinsic value could be modeled as the value added by a business above and beyond the charge for the use of capital in that business. The gain in intrinsic value was analogous to the economic-profit and market-value-added measures used by analysts in leading corporations to assess financial performance. Those measures focus on the ability to earn returns in excess of the cost of capital.

5. **Set a required return consistent with the risk you bear.** Conventional academic and practitioner thinking held that the more risk one took, the more one should get paid. Thus discount rates used in determining intrinsic values should be determined by the risk of the cash flows being valued. The conventional model for estimating the cost of equity capital was the capital asset pricing model (CAPM), which added a risk premium to the long-term risk-free rate of return, such as the U.S. Treasury bond yield. In August 2015, a weighted average of Berkshire Hathaway's cost of equity and debt capital was about 0.8%.[15]

Buffett departed from conventional thinking by using the rate of return on the long-term (e.g., 30-year) U.S. Treasury bond to discount cash flows—in August 2015, the yield on the 30-year U.S. Treasury bond was 2.89%. Defending this practice, Buffett argued that he avoided risk, and therefore should use a risk-free

---

[14]Berkshire Hathaway Inc. annual report, 2004.

[15]Berkshire Hathaway's cost of equity was 9.2%, which reflected a beta of 0.90, an expected market return of 9.90%, and a risk-free rate of 2.89%. The yield on corporate bonds rated AA was 3.95%—and after a 39% expected marginal tax rate, the cost of debt would be 2.3%. Weights of capital were 16.9% for debt and 83.1% for equity. In contrast, the beta for PCP was 0.38. Analysts expected that PCP's cash flows would grow indefinitely at about the long-term expected real growth rate of the U.S. economy, 2.5%.

discount rate. His firm used little debt financing. He focused on companies with predictable and stable earnings. He or his vice chair, Charlie Munger, sat on the boards of directors, where they obtained a candid inside view of the company and could intervene in management decisions if necessary. Buffett once said, "I put a heavy weight on certainty. If you do that, the whole idea of a risk factor doesn't make sense to me. Risk comes from not knowing what you're doing."[16] He also wrote:

> We define risk, using dictionary terms, as "the possibility of loss or injury." Academics, however, like to define "risk" differently, averring that it is the relative volatility of a stock or a portfolio of stocks—that is, the volatility as compared to that of a large universe of stocks. Employing databases and statistical skills, these academics compute with precision the "beta" of a stock—its relative volatility in the past—and then build arcane investment and capital allocation theories around this calculation. In their hunger for a single statistic to measure risk, however, they forget a fundamental principle: it is better to be approximately right than precisely wrong.[17]

6. **Diversify reasonably.** Berkshire Hathaway represented a diverse portfolio of business interests. But Buffett disagreed with conventional wisdom that investors should hold a broad portfolio of stocks in order to shed company-specific risk. In his view, investors typically purchased far too many stocks rather than waiting for one exceptional company. Buffett said:

> Figure businesses out that you understand and concentrate. Diversification is protection against ignorance, but if you don't feel ignorant, the need for it goes down drastically.[18]

7. **Invest based on information, analysis, and self-discipline, not on emotion or hunch.** Buffett repeatedly emphasized awareness and information as the foundation for investing. He said, "Anyone not aware of the fool in the market probably is the fool in the market."[19] Buffett was fond of repeating a parable told to him by Graham:

> There was a small private business and one of the owners was a man named Market. Every day, Mr. Market had a new opinion of what the business was worth, and at that price stood ready to buy your interest or sell you his. As excitable as he was opinionated, Mr. Market presented a constant distraction to his fellow owners. "What does he know?" they would wonder, as he bid them an extraordinarily high price or a depressingly low one. Actually, the gentleman knew little or nothing. You may be happy to sell out to him when he quotes you a ridiculously high price, and equally happy to buy from him when his price is low. But the rest of the time, you will be wiser to form your own ideas of the value of your holdings, based on full reports from the company about its operation and financial position.[20]

---

[16]Jim Rasmussen, "Buffett Talks Strategy with Students," *Omaha World-Herald*, January 2, 1994, 26.

[17]Berkshire Hathaway Inc. annual report, 1993; Andrew Kilpatrick, *Of Permanent Value: The Story of Warren Buffett* (Birmingham, AL: AKPE, 1994): 574.

[18]*Forbes*, October 19, 1993; Kilpatrick, 574.

[19]Quoted in Michael Lewis's *Liar's Poker* (New York: Norton, 1989): 35.

[20]Berkshire Hathaway Inc. annual report, 1987. This quotation was paraphrased from James Grant's *Minding Mr. Market* (New York: Times Books, 1993): xxi.

Buffett used this allegory to illustrate the irrationality of stock prices as compared to true intrinsic value. Graham believed that an investor's worst enemy was not the stock market, but oneself. Superior training could not compensate for the absence of the requisite temperament for investing. Over the long term, stock prices should have a strong relationship with the economic progress of the business. But daily market quotations were heavily influenced by momentary greed or fear and were an unreliable measure of intrinsic value. Buffett said:

> As far as I am concerned, the stock market doesn't exist. It is there only as a reference to see if anybody is offering to do anything foolish. When we invest in stocks, we invest in businesses. You simply have to behave according to what is rational rather than according to what is fashionable.[21]

Accordingly, Buffett did not try to "time the market" (i.e., trade stocks based on expectations of changes in the market cycle)—his was a strategy of patient, long-term investing. As if in contrast to Mr. Market, Buffett expressed more contrarian goals: "We simply attempt to be fearful when others are greedy and to be greedy only when others are fearful."[22] Buffett also said, "Lethargy bordering on sloth remains the cornerstone of our investment style,"[23] and "The market, like the Lord, helps those who help themselves. But unlike the Lord, the market does not forgive those who know not what they do."[24]

8. **Look for market inefficiencies.** Buffett scorned the academic theory of capital-market efficiency. The efficient-markets hypothesis (EMH) held that publicly known information was rapidly impounded into share prices, and that as a result, stock prices were fair in reflecting what was known about the company. Under EMH, there were no bargains to be had, and trying to outperform the market would be futile. "It has been helpful to me to have tens of thousands turned out of business schools that taught that it didn't do any good to think," Buffett said.[25]

> I think it's fascinating how the ruling orthodoxy can cause a lot of people to think the earth is flat. Investing in a market where people believe in efficiency is like playing bridge with someone who's been told it doesn't do any good to look at the cards.[26]

9. **Align the interests of agents and owners.** Explaining his significant ownership interest in Berkshire Hathaway, Buffett said, "I am a better businessman because I am an investor. And I am a better investor because I am a businessman."[27]
   As if to illustrate this sentiment, he said:

> A managerial "wish list" will not be filled at shareholder expense. We will not diversify by purchasing entire businesses at control prices that ignore long-term economic consequences

---

[21]Peter Lynch, *One Up on Wall Street* (New York: Penguin Books, 1990): 78.

[22]Berkshire Hathaway Inc. annual report, 1986.

[23]Berkshire Hathaway Inc. annual report, 1990.

[24]Berkshire Hathaway Inc. letters to shareholders, 1977–83.

[25]Kilpatrick, 353.

[26]L. J. Davis, "Buffett Takes Stock," *New York Times*, April 1, 1990.

[27]*Forbes*, October 19, 1993; Kilpatrick, 574.

to our shareholders. We will only do with your money what we would do with our own, weighing fully the values you can obtain by diversifying your own portfolios through direct purchases in the stock market.[28]

For four out of six Berkshire directors, more than 50% of the family net worth was represented by shares in Berkshire Hathaway. The senior managers of Berkshire Hathaway subsidiaries either held shares in the company or were compensated under incentive plans that imitated the potential returns from an equity interest in their business unit, or both.[29]

Precision Castparts

"In the short run, the market is a voting machine but in the long run, it is a weighing machine."
—Benjamin Graham[30]

The vote was in and the market's reaction to Berkshire Hathaway's acquisition of PCP indicated disapproval. The market ascribed $4.05 billion less value to Berkshire Hathaway after the announced acquisition than before it. At the same time, the value of PCP jumped more than $5 billion, close to 20% of the market value of the firm. The market seemed to be saying that Buffett and Berkshire had overpaid for the business.

Buffett didn't seem to think so. And despite his age, he didn't appear to be slowing down. PCP was the largest acquisition in a string of large purchases over the past several years, including Duracell, Kraft, Heinz, and Burlington Northern Santa Fe, totaling more than $70 billion in deal value in all. These acquisitions, along with many more over the years, followed a similar blueprint (**Exhibit 1.8**). The gist of the acquisition criteria seemed to be relatively straightforward—Berkshire Hathaway looked for well-run businesses producing consistent results offered at a fair price. As Berkshire Hathaway stated in its press release following the PCP acquisition:

> PCP fits perfectly into the Berkshire model and will substantially increase our normalized per-share earning power. Under CEO Mark Donegan, PCP has become the world's premier supplier of aerospace components (most of them destined to be original equipment, though spares are important to the company as well). Mark's accomplishments remind me of the magic regularly performed by Jacob Harpaz at IMC, our remarkable Israeli manufacturer of cutting tools. The two men transform very ordinary raw materials into extraordinary products that are used by major manufacturers worldwide. Each is the da Vinci of his craft. PCP's products, often delivered under multi year contracts, are key components in most large aircraft.[31]

---

[28]"Owner-Related Business Principles," Berkshire Hathaway annual report, 2004.

[29]In April 2005, the U.S. Securities and Exchange Commission interviewed Buffett in connection with an investigation into the insurance giant AIG and its dealings with Berkshire Hathaway's General Reinsurance unit. Buffett reported that he had questioned General Re's CEO about the transactions with AIG, but that he never learned any details.

[30]as quoted in Berkshire Hathaway Inc. letter to shareholders, 1993.

[31]PCP press release, August 10, 2015.

PCP manufactured complex metal components and products for very specific applications, mainly in the critical aerospace and power applications. The components were used in products with highly complex engineering processes, such as large jet-aircraft engines. Its customer base was concentrated and sophisticated, including General Electric, Pratt & Whitney, and Rolls-Royce, for whom they had been supplying castings for multiple decades.[32]

Exhibit 1.9 presents PCP's income statement and balance sheet ending March 31, 2015. **Exhibit 1.10** provides financials on comparable firms. **Exhibit 1.11** provides valuation multiples for comparable firms. The beta of PCP, measured after the acquisition announcement, was 0.38.

Conclusion

The announcement of Berkshire Hathaway's acquisition of PCP prompted some critical commentary. The Economist magazine wrote,

> But [Buffett] is far from a model for how capitalism should be transformed. He is a careful, largely ethical accumulator of capital invested in traditional businesses, preferably with oligopolistic qualities, whereas what America needs right now is more risk-taking, lower prices, higher investment and much more competition. You won't find much at all about these ideas in Mr. Buffett's shareholder letters.[33]

Conventional thinking held that it would be difficult for Warren Buffett to maintain his record of 21.6% annual growth[34] in shareholder wealth. Buffett acknowledged that "a fat wallet is the enemy of superior investment results."[35] He stated that it was the firm's goal to meet a 15% annual growth rate in intrinsic value. Would the PCP acquisition serve Berkshire Hathaway's long-term goals? Was the bid price appropriate? How did Berkshire Hathaway's offer measure up against the company's valuation implied by the multiples for comparable firms? Did Berkshire Hathaway overpay for PCP? Was the market's reaction rational?

Or did Buffett pay a fair price for a great business? If so, what determines a fair price? What makes a great business? And why would Berkshire Hathaway be interested in buying PCP? Why would PCP be interested in selling itself to Berkshire Hathaway? What value did Berkshire Hathaway bring to the equation?

[32]PCP annual report, 2014.

[33]"The Other Side of Warren Buffett," *Economist*, August 13, 2016.

[34]Berkshire Hathaway Inc. letter to shareholders, 2014.

[35]Garth Alexander, "Buffett Spends $2bn on Return to His Roots," *Times* (London), August 17, 1995.

EXHIBIT 1.1 | Relative Share Price Performance of Berkshire Hathaway Class A Share, PCP, and the S&P 500 January 1, 2015, to August 13, 2015

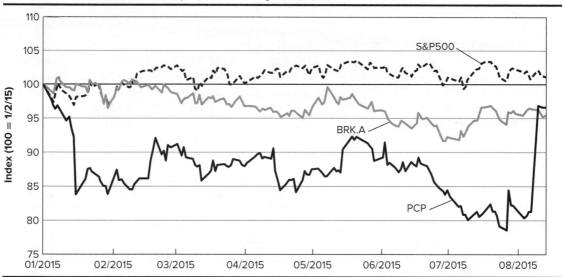

Note: PCP = Precision Castparts; BRK.A = Berkshire Hathaway Class A shares; S&P500 = Standard & Poor's 500 Index.

Data source: Google Finance.

EXHIBIT 1.2 I Berkshire Hathaway Condensed Consolidated Financial Statements

	2011	2012	2013	2014
Income Statement				
(In millions, except per share data, unless otherwise specified)				
Revenue	$143,700	$162,500	$182,200	$194,700
Operating expenses	123,080	134,810	147,770	163,340
Income from operations	20,620	27,690	34,430	31,360
Net interest expense	5,310	5,450	5,630	3,250
Income before income tax expense	15,310	22,240	28,800	28,110
Income tax expense	4,570	6,920	8,950	7,940
Consolidated net income	$ 10,075	$ 15,310	$ 19,850	$ 20,170

	2011	2012	2013	2014
Balance Sheet				
(In millions, except per share data, unless otherwise specified)				
Assets:				
Current assets	$ 79,220	$ 91,200	$ 91,500	$107,900
Net property, plant and equipment	100,400	106,900	122,200	137,200
Deferred tax assets	10,540	9,780	8,430	8,430
Other assets	213,040	229,320	271,270	281,070
Total assets	$403,200	$437,200	$493,400	$534,600
Liabilities & Shareholder Equity:				
Current liabilities	$ 34,200	$ 47,290	$ 44,470	$ 48,510
Deferred tax liabilities	47,650	53,670	65,870	70,370
Long-term debt	58,890	50,810	65,590	71,930
Other long-term liabilities	93,460	93,830	92,970	100,790
Total liabilities	234,200	245,600	268,900	291,600
Shareholders' equity	169,000	191,600	224,500	243,000
Total liabilities and stockholders' equity	$403,200	$437,200	$493,400	$534,600

Data source: Factset.

EXHIBIT 1.3 | Berkshire Hathaway Class A Shares versus S&P 500 Index over 39 Years

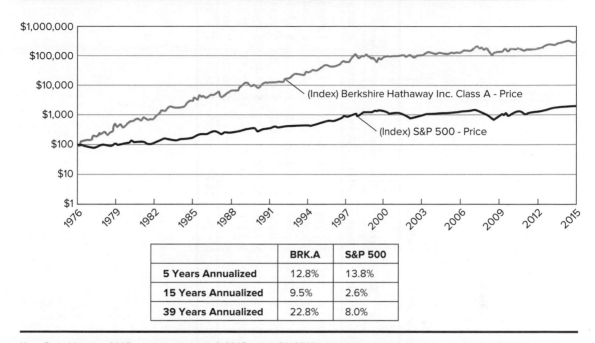

	BRK.A	S&P 500
5 Years Annualized	12.8%	13.8%
15 Years Annualized	9.5%	2.6%
39 Years Annualized	22.8%	8.0%

Note: Period listed as 2015 represents January 1, 2015 to July 31, 2015.

Data source: Yahoo! Finance.

EXHIBIT 1.4 | Business-Segment Information for Berkshire Hathaway Inc. (dollars in millions)

Segment	Revenues		EBIT		Capital Expenditures		Depreciation		Total Assets	
	2014	2015	2014	2015	2014	2015	2014	2015	2014	2015
Insurance Group	$ 45,623	$ 45,856	$ 7,025	$ 6,387	$ 94	$ 115	$ 69	$ 77	$225,432	$219,451
Manufacturing	$ 36,773	$ 36,136	$ 4,811	$ 4,893	$ 1,324	$ 1,292	$ 943	$ 938	$ 34,509	$ 34,141
Service & Retailing	$ 60,916	$ 71,689	$ 1,981	$ 2,222	$ 832	$ 912	$ 620	$ 665	$ 16,722	$ 22,170
Railroad	$ 23,239	$ 21,967	$ 6,169	$ 6,775	$ 5,243	$ 5,651	$ 1,804	$ 1,932	$ 62,916	$ 66,613
Utility and Energy	$ 17,614	$ 18,231	$ 2,711	$ 2,851	$ 6,555	$ 5,876	$ 2,177	$ 2,451	$ 71,482	$ 74,221
Finance & Financial Products	$ 6,526	$ 6,964	$ 1,839	$ 2,086	$ 1,137	$ 2,236	$ 602	$ 610	$ 32,164	$ 37,621
Other	$ 3,982	$ 9,978	$ 3,569	$ -	$ -	$ -	$ -	$ -	$ 60,714	$ 98,040
Total	$194,673	$210,821	$28,105	$25,214	$15,185	$16,082	$6,215	$6,673	$503,939	$552,257

Source: SEC documents.

EXHIBIT 1.5 | Major Investees of Berkshire Hathaway (dollars in millions)

Shares**	Company	Percentage of Company Owned	Cost*	Market
			(in millions)	
151,610,700	American Express Company	14.8	$ 1,287	$14,106
400,000,000	The Coca-Cola Company	9.2	1,299	16,888
18,513,482	DaVita HealthCare Partners Inc.	8.6	843	1,402
15,430,586	Deere & Company	4.5	1,253	1,365
24,617,939	DIRECTV	4.9	1,454	2,134
13,062,594	The Goldman Sachs Group, Inc.	3.0	750	2,532
76,971,817	International Business Machines Corp.	7.8	13,157	12,349
24,669,778	Moody's Corporation	12.1	248	2,364
20,060,390	Munich Re	11.8	2,990	4,023
52,477,678	The Procter & Gamble Company	1.9	336	4,683***
22,169,930	Sanofi	1.7	1,721	2,032
96,890,665	U.S. Bancorp	5.4	3,033	4,355
43,387,980	USG Corporation	30.0	836	1,214
67,707,544	Wal-Mart Stores, Inc.	2.1	3,798	5,815
483,470,853	Wells Fargo & Company	9.4	11,871	26,504
	Others		10,180	15,704
	Total Common Stocks Carried at Market		$55,056	$117,470

*Actual purchase price and tax basis; GAAP "cost" differs in a few cases because of write-ups or write-downs that have been required under GAAP rules.

**Excludes shares held by pension funds of Berkshire subsidiaries.

***Held under contract of sale for this amount.

Source: Berkshire Hathaway Inc. letter to shareholders, 2014.

EXHIBIT 1.6 | Hypothetical Example of Value Creation

Assume:
- Five-year investment horizon, when you liquidate at "book" or accumulated investment value
- Initial investment is $50 million
- No dividends are paid, all cash flows are reinvested
- Return on equity = 20%
- Cost of equity = 15%

Year	0	1	2	3	4	5
Investment or **book** equity value	50	60	72	86	104	124

Market value (or intrinsic value) = Present value @ 15% of 124 = $61.65

Market/book = $61.65/50.00   = $1.23

Value created: $1.00 invested becomes $1.23 in market value.

Source: Author analysis.

EXHIBIT 1.7 | Hypothetical Example of Value Destruction

Assume:
- Five-year investment horizon, when you liquidate at "book" or accumulated investment value
- Initial investment of $50 million
- No dividends are paid, all cash flows are reinvested
- Return on equity = 10%
- Cost of equity = 15%

Year	0	1	2	3	4	5
Investment or **book** equity value	50	55	60	67	73	81

Market value (or intrinsic value) = Present value @ 15% of $81 = $40.30

Market/book = $40.30/50.00   = $0.80

Value destroyed: $1.00 invested becomes $0.80 in market value.

Source: Author analysis.

EXHIBIT 1.8 | Berkshire Hathaway Acquisition Criteria

We are eager to hear *from principals or their representatives* about businesses that meet all of the following criteria:

1. Large purchases (at least $75 million of pretax earnings unless the business will fit into one of our existing units)
2. Consistent earning power demonstrated (Future projections are of no interest to us, nor are turnaround situations.)
3. Businesses earning good returns on equity while employing little or no debt
4. Management in place (We can't supply it.)
5. Simple businesses (If there's lots of technology, we won't understand it.)
6. Offering price (We don't want to waste our time or that of the seller by talking, even preliminarily, about a transaction when price is unknown.)

The larger the company, the greater will be our interest: We would like to make an acquisition in the $5 billion to $20 billion range. *We are not interested, however, in receiving suggestions about purchases we might make in the general stock market.*

We will not engage in unfriendly takeovers. We can promise complete confidentiality and a very fast answer—customarily within five minutes—as to whether we're interested. We prefer to buy for cash, but will consider issuing stock when we receive as much in intrinsic business value as we give. *We don't participate in auctions.*

Charlie and I frequently get approached about acquisitions that don't come close to meeting our tests: We've found that if you advertise an interest in buying collies, a lot of people will call hoping to sell you their cocker spaniels. A line from a country song expresses our feeling about new ventures, turnarounds, or auction-like sales: "When the phone don't ring, you'll know it's me."

Source: Berkshire Hathaway Inc. annual report, 2014.

EXHIBIT 1.9 | PCP Consolidated Financial Statements

	12 Months Ending March 31		
	2013	2014	2015*
Income Statement			
(In millions, except per share data, unless otherwise specified)			
Revenue	$8,347	$ 9,533	$10,005
Operating expenses[1]	6,188	6,874	7,393
Income from operations	2,159	2,659	2,612
Net interest expense	31	71	65
Income before income tax expense	2,128	2,588	2,547
Income tax expense	695	830	816
Consolidated net income from continuing operations[2]	$1,433	$ 1,758	$ 1,731

	2011	2012	2013	2014
Balance Sheet				
(In millions, except per share data, unless otherwise specified)				
Assets:				
Current assets			$ 5,507	$ 5,972
Net property, plant, and equipment			2,300	2,474
Other assets			10,779	10,982
Total assets			$18,586	$19,428
Liabilities & Shareholder Equity:				
Current liabilities			$ 1,608	$ 2,827
Long-term debt			3,569	3,493
Pension obligation			442	678
Other long-term liabilities			1,554	1,473
Total liabilities			7,173	8,471
Shareholders' equity[3]			11,413	10,957
Total liabilities and stockholders' equity			$18,586	$19,428

*Note - Fiscal year ends March 31. Period listed as 2015 represents March 31, 2014 to March 31, 2015

Note: The market value of PCP's equity shortly before the announcement of the acquisition by Berkshire Hathaway was $31,208 million.

Data source: Edgar.

[1]Excludes restructuring charges.

[2]Excludes equity in unconsolidated investments.

[3]Excludes noncontrolling interests.

EXHIBIT 1.10 | Comparable Firms

(dollars in millions)

| Company | Shares O/S | Price Per Share | | Div. Per Share | Total Assets | Total Liabilities | Cash and Equiv | ST Debt | LT Debt | Net Debt | Rev | EBITDA | EBIT | Net Income |
		Low	High											
Alcoa	1,216.7	$ 15.77	$ 16.03	$0.12	$37,399	$22,605	$1,877	$ 83	$8,769	$6,975	$23,906	$3,556	$2,185	$2,043
LISI	54.0	$ 21.30	$ 21.50	$0.37	$ 1,387	$ 677	$ 111	$ 46	$ 246	$ 181	$ 1,307	$ 193	$ 131	$ 81
ThyssenKrupp	565.9	$ 20.64	$ 20.85	$0.11	$41,547	$38,348	$4,122	$1,071	$6,651	$3,600	$41,304	$2,290	$1,314	$ 210
Allegheny Technologies	108.7	$ 34.59	$ 35.41	$0.72	$ 6,583	$ 3,861	$ 270	$ 18	$1,509	$1,257	$ 4,223	$ 283	$ 106	($3)
Carpenter Technology	53.1	$ 61.75	$ 63.35	$0.72	$ 3,058	$ 1,553	$ 120	$ 0	$ 604	$ 484	$ 2,173	$ 382	$ 212	$ 133
Precision Castparts	141.8	$209.61	$211.36	$0.12	$19,428	$ 8,471	$ 474	$1,093	$3,493	$4,112	$10,005	$2,927	$2,602	$1,530

Note: Dollar values are in millions except for share prices and dividends per share, which are in dollar units. Shares outstanding (O/S) are stated in millions.

ALCOA, INC., engages in lightweight metals engineering and manufacturing. Its products are used worldwide in aircraft, automobiles, commercial transportation, packaging, oil and gas, defense, and industrial applications.

LISI SA engages in the manufacturing of multifunctional fasteners and assembly components for three business sectors: Aerospace, Automotive, and Medical.

THYSSENKRUPP AG engages in the production of steel. The Components Technology business area offers components for the automotive, construction, and engineering sectors.

ALLEGHENY TECHNOLOGIES, INC., engages in the manufacture of specialty materials and components for different industries, which include aerospace and defense, oil and gas, and chemical processing, as well as electrical energy.

CARPENTER TECHNOLOGY CORP. engages in developing, manufacturing, and distributing cast/wrought and powder-metal stainless steels. It operates through Specialty Alloys Operations and Performance Engineered Products segments.

Data sources: Company reports; Factset.

EXHIBIT 1.11 I Valuation of PCP Based on Multiples for Comparable Firms

Line	Company Name	MV Equity	Enterprise Value	Book Value	CY'14				Enterprise Value as Multiple of:			MV of Equity as Multiple of:	
					Rev	EBITDA	EBIT	Net Income	Revenue	EBITDA	EBIT	Net Income	Book Value
1	Alcoa	$13,637	$23,164	$10,599	$23,906	$3,556	$2,185	$2,043	0.97x	6.51x	10.60x	6.68x	1.29x
2	LISI	$ 1,332	$ 1,517	$ 709	$ 1,307	$ 193	$ 131	$ 81	1.16x	7.86x	11.56x	16.36x	1.88x
3	ThyssenKrupp	$ 9,460	$12,924	$ 3,182	$41,304	$2,290	$1,314	$ 210	0.31x	5.64x	9.84x	45.05x	2.97x
4	Allegheny Technologies	$ 1,804	$ 3,193	$ 2,598	$ 4,223	$ 283	$ 106	($3)	0.76x	11.28x	30.09x	NM	0.69x
5	Carpenter Technology	$ 1,627	$ 2,220	$ 1,326	$ 2,173	$ 382	$ 212	$ 133	1.02x	5.81x	10.47x	12.25x	1.23x
6	Median	$ 1,804	$ 3,193	$ 2,598	$ 4,223	$ 382	$ 212	$ 133	0.97x	6.51x	10.60x	14.31x	1.29x
7	Mean	$ 5,572	$ 8,603	$ 3,683	$14,583	$1,341	$ 790	$ 493	0.84x	7.42x	14.51x	20.08x	1.61x
	Precision Castparts			$10,929	$10,005	$2,927	$2,602	$1,530					
8	Implied Value - Median[1]								$9,705	$19,055	$27,581	$21,894	$14,098
9	Implied Value - Mean[1]								$8,404	$21,718	$37,755	$30,722	$17,596

Data Source: Factset.

[1]The calculation of the implied values for PCP based on the median of the peer firms' multiples takes the product of the median value of the multiples of comparable firms (line 8) and multiples it times the relevant base (revenue, EBITDA, EBIT, net income, or book value) for PCP. The same method is used for the calculation of the implied value based on the average or mean of the peer firms' multiples (line 9). For instance, the implied value based on the median multiple of EBIT ($37,755 million) is derived by multiplying 14.51 (the mean EBIT multiple for the comparable firms) times $2,602 million (the EBIT of PCP).

The Battle for Value, 2016: FedEx Corp. versus United Parcel Service, Inc.

2015 was a transformative year for FedEx with outstanding financial results, more powerful customer solutions, and actions to generate increased long-term value for shareowners. We believe FedEx is on a dynamic trajectory that will make 2016 very successful. Our company has never been better positioned to build shareowner value.
  —**FedEx CEO Frederick W. Smith,** *Annual Report 2015*

Our 2015 results demonstrate that UPS can thrive in [today's] challenging environment, as shown by our continued ability to meet the expectations of customers and investors alike. The continued execution of our proven strategies will enable UPS to maintain positive momentum in the coming year and beyond.
  —**UPS CEO David Abney,** *Annual Report 2015*

On April 29, 2016, FedEx Corp., the American courier delivery company, received final government approval on its bid to acquire TNT Express (TNT), a Dutch logistics and delivery firm with road and air delivery services all over the world, for $4.8 billion. Ever since FedEx made the public bid to acquire TNT, many industry insiders expected TNT's strong European road network to bolster FedEx's presence in a region and market in which it had failed to compete with its long-standing rival, United Parcel Service, Inc. (UPS), for a bigger share of the world's ever-increasing e-commerce shipments.

The approval came as a bitter blow to American package-delivery rival UPS, which had tried to buy TNT in 2013, only to be blocked by European Union regulators who viewed the potential merger as obstructing healthy competition. Still, UPS had plenty to celebrate. The company had just announced record first-quarter sales of $14.4 billion, up 3.2% over the same quarter the previous year, driven by growth in both its domestic and international small-package segments. The company was starting to see its recent investments in technology and productivity improvements pay off, with its cost per package falling 1.9% for the same period. This was impressive for a company whose return on equity the previous year was a whopping 210%.

Against this backdrop, industry observers wondered how the titanic struggle between FedEx and UPS would develop, particularly for investors in the two firms. Was the performance of the companies in recent years predictive of the future? International reach and extensive logistics services were widely seen as the litmus test for corporate survival of delivery companies in the new millennium. Which company was better positioned to attract the capital necessary to win this competitive battle?

United Parcel Service, Inc.

Founded in 1907, UPS was the largest package-delivery company in the world. Consolidated parcel delivery, both on the ground and through the air, was the primary business of the company, although increasingly the company offered more-specialized transportation and logistics services.

Known in the industry as "Big Brown," UPS had its roots in Seattle, Washington, where 19-year-old Jim Casey started a bicycle-messenger service called American Messenger Company. After merging with a rival firm, Motorcycle Delivery Company, the company focused on department-store deliveries, and that remained true until the 1940s. Renamed United Parcel Service of America, UPS started an air-delivery service in 1929 by putting packages on commercial passenger planes. The company entered its strongest period of growth during the post–World War II economic boom and, by 1975, UPS had reached a milestone when it promised package delivery to every address in the continental United States. That same year the company expanded outside the country with its first delivery to Ontario, Canada. The following year, UPS began service in West Germany with 120 of its trademark-brown delivery vans.

The key to the success of UPS, later headquartered in Atlanta, Georgia, was efficiency. According to *BusinessWeek*, "Every route is timed down to the traffic light. Each vehicle was engineered to exacting specifications. And the drivers . . . endure a daily routine calibrated down to the minute."[1] But this demand for machinelike precision met with resistance by UPS's heavily unionized labor force.

For most of the company's history, UPS stock was owned solely by UPS's managers, their families, former employees, or charitable foundations owned by UPS. The company acted as the market maker with its own shares, buying or selling shares at a fair

---

[1]Todd Vogel and Chuck Hawkins, "Can UPS Deliver the Goods in a New World?" *BusinessWeek*, June 4, 1990.

market value determined by the board of directors each quarter.[2] By the end of the millennium, company executives determined that UPS needed the added flexibility of publicly traded stock in order to pursue a more aggressive acquisition strategy.

In November 1999, UPS became a public company through a public equity offering and corporate reorganization. Before this reorganization, the financially and operationally conservative company had been perceived as slow and plodding. Although much larger than FedEx, UPS had been unable to effectively compete directly in the overnight-delivery market, largely because of the enormous cost of building an air fleet. But after going public, UPS initiated an aggressive series of acquisitions, beginning with a Miami-based freight carrier operating in Latin America and a franchise-based chain of stores providing packing, shipping, and mail services called Mail Boxes Etc. (later renamed The UPS Store) with more than 4,300 domestic and international locations.

More assertive than ever before, the UPS of the new millennium was the product of extensive reengineering efforts and a revitalized business focus. Whereas the company had traditionally been the industry's low-cost provider, UPS now began investing heavily in a full range of highly specialized business services. As a sign of this shift, the company revamped its logo for the first time since 1961, emphasizing its activities in the wider supply-chain industry. The expansive "What can brown do for you?" campaign was also launched around this time to promote UPS's business-facing logistics and supply-chain services.

Another example was UPS's extensive push into more complex industries like health care. Health care logistic services (which were bucketed into the company's supply-chain and freight segments) allowed pharmaceutical and medical-device companies to outsource their logistics to UPS pharmacists, who were able to fulfill, pack, and ship customers' orders from UPS's worldwide health care warehouses, even when medications included temperature specifications or required cross-border transport. By 2015, this segment had experienced huge growth and saw no signs of slowing in the face of the world's aging population that increasingly wanted home delivery of health care products.

Alongside its health care offerings, UPS also looked to emerging markets for growth. In 2014, CEO David Abney claimed that "growing internationally and diversifying our customer base"[3] across regions was a top priority for UPS. By 2015, international package operations accounted for 21% of revenues. **Exhibit 2.1** presents segment (ground and express) and geographic (international and U.S. domestic) revenue data for both FedEx and UPS. The company also invested in information technology to improve

---

[2]In setting its share price, the board considered a variety of factors, including past and current earnings, earnings estimates, the ratio of UPS's common stock to its debt, the business and outlook of UPS, and the general economic climate. The opinions of outside advisers were sometimes considered. The stock price had never decreased in value. The employee stock purchases were often financed with stock hypothecation loans from commercial banks. As the shares provided the collateral for those loans, the assessment made by the outside lenders provided some external validation for the share price.

[3]Reuters, "UPS Names Operating Chief David Abney as Its New CEO," CNBC, June 6, 2014, http://www.cnbc.com/2014/06/06/ups-names-operating-chief-david-abney-as-its-new-ceo.html (accessed Nov. 28, 2016).

its profitability. In 2013, for example, UPS launched cutting-edge route-optimization software for its drivers that was intended to set the stage for even more personalized service offerings and efficient deliveries when its rollout was complete in 2017.

By 2015, UPS offered package-delivery services in more than 220 countries and territories (with every address in the United States and Europe covered) and was moving more than 18 million packages and documents through its network every day. Its immense volumes in the higher-margin ground segment and aligned assets that served both ground and express shipments gave it a margin advantage compared to FedEx. UPS employed 440,000 people and had 104,926 vehicles and 650 jet aircraft.[4] UPS reported revenues of $58 billion and net profit of nearly $5 billion. **Exhibit 2.2** provides recent operating results for UPS.

FedEx Corporation

FedEx first took form as Fred Smith's undergraduate term paper for a Yale University economics class. Smith's strategy dictated that FedEx would purchase the planes that it required to transport packages, whereas all other competitors used the cargo space available on passenger airlines. In addition to using his own planes, Smith's key innovation was a hub-and-spoke distribution pattern, which permitted cheaper and faster service to more locations than his competitors could offer. In 1971, Smith invested his $4 million inheritance and raised $91 million in venture capital to launch the firm—the largest venture-capital start-up at the time.

In 1973, on the first night of continuous operation, 389 FedEx employees delivered 186 packages overnight to 25 U.S. cities. In those early years, FedEx, then known as Federal Express Corporation, experienced severe losses, and Smith was nearly ousted from his chair position. By 1976, FedEx finally saw a modest profit of $3.6 million on an average daily volume of 19,000 packages. Through the rest of the 1970s, FedEx continued to grow by expanding services, acquiring more trucks and aircraft, and raising capital. The formula was successful. In 1981, FedEx generated more revenue than any other U.S. air-delivery company.

By 1981, competition in the industry had started to rise. Emery Air Freight began to imitate FedEx's hub system and to acquire airplanes, and UPS began to move into the overnight air market. The United States Postal Service (USPS) positioned its overnight letter at half the price of FedEx's, but quality problems and FedEx's "absolutely positively overnight" ad campaign quelled that potential threat. In 1983, FedEx reached $1 billion in revenues and seemed poised to own the market for express delivery.

During the 1990s, FedEx proved itself as an operational leader, even receiving the prestigious Malcolm Baldrige National Quality Award from the president of the United States. FedEx was the first company ever to win in the service category. Part of this success could be attributed to deregulation and to operational strategy, but credit could also be given to FedEx's philosophy of "People-Service-Profit," which reflected its emphasis on customer focus, total quality management, and employee participation. Extensive attitude surveying, a promote-from-within policy, effective grievance procedures that sometimes resulted in a chat with Fred Smith himself, and an emphasis on

---

[4]UPS Form 10-K.

personal responsibility and initiative not only earned FedEx a reputation as a great place to work, but also helped to keep the firm largely free of unions.

FedEx's growth occurred within the context of fundamental change in the business environment. Deregulation of the domestic airline industry after 1977 permitted larger planes to replace smaller ones, thereby permitting FedEx to purchase several Boeing 727s starting in 1978, which helped reduce its unit costs. Deregulation of the trucking industry also permitted FedEx to establish an integrated regional trucking system that lowered its unit costs on short-haul trips, enabling the company to compete more effectively with UPS. Rising inflation and global competitiveness compelled manufacturers to manage inventories more closely and to emulate the just-in-time supply programs of the Japanese, creating a heightened demand for FedEx's rapid and carefully monitored movement of packages. And, finally, technological innovations enabled FedEx to achieve important advances in customer ordering, package tracking, and process monitoring.

Despite making its name as the pioneer of the overnight-delivery market, FedEx continued to expand beyond its lower-margin express offerings throughout the first decade of the 2000s. In addition to purchasing Kinko's 1,200 retail stores and eventually rebranding them as FedEx Office (a full-service print-and-ship retail chain), in 2012, FedEx started to move its capex focus from its crown-jewel express segment (where capital expenditures from 2013 to 2015 were mainly used to modernize its outdated fleet) to higher-margin ground services in order to increase capacity in its U.S. ground network.[5] By 2015, these efforts had paid off: FedEx Ground's revenues had grown significantly over the past five years, and the company was providing faster deliveries to more U.S locations than its competition, in large part due to its industry-leading automation-optimized efficiency. The ground segment's independent operation of drivers and trucks as separate from its parallel express-network assets, however, gave rival UPS and its integrated asset system the margin advantage.[6]

By the end of 2015, FedEx had net income of over $1 billion on revenues of about $48 billion. **Exhibit 2.3** provides recent operating results for FedEx. FedEx Express's aircraft fleet consisted of 647 aircraft, FedEx Ground had about 95,000 ground vehicles and trailers, and FedEx Freight operated approximately 65,000 vehicles and trailers. The company operated with more than 325,000 team members and handled more than 11 million packages daily across its ground and express services.[7]

The U.S. Delivery Market–Changing Shape

Barclays estimated the 2015 U.S. package delivery market to be $90 billion.[8] The market was commonly segmented along three dimensions: weight, mode of transit, and timeliness of service. The weight categories consisted of letters (weighing 0–2.0 pounds),

---

[5]Allison Landry, Daniel Schuster, and Kenneth Ryan, "FedEx Corporation—Ground is the New Black," Credit Suisse, February 27, 2015.

[6]Keith Schoonmaker, "UPS, Inc.," Morningstar, No. 27249776 from Investext Current Reports database.

[7]FedEx Corporation annual report, 2015.

[8]Brandon Oglenski, Eric Morgan, and Van Kegel, "North American Transportation and Shipping Equity Research," Barclays, May 2, 2016.

packages (2.0–150 pounds), and freight (over 151 pounds). The mode of transit categories were air (i.e., express) and ground. Time categories were overnight, deferred delivery (second-day delivery), three-day delivery, and, lastly, regular delivery, which occurred four or more days after pickup.

The rise of e-commerce had created a colossal shift in package-delivery density, as low-density residential deliveries from e-commerce sales had overtaken higher-density business-to-business package deliveries that had once driven sales at the large shipping companies. As online retailers outpaced their brick-and-mortar peers, e-commerce sales skyrocketed; in 2015 alone, e-commerce sales grew 14.6%, according to the U.S. Department of Commerce."[9] Many believed that FedEx's package volume was poised to benefit most from this growth due to the numerous online retailers that employed FedEx for timely deliveries, but recently it was UPS that had the upper hand, with market share of 54% for U.S. e-commerce shipments in 2014, leaving FedEx with 30%, and USPS the remaining 16%.[10]

As the booming e-commerce market grew, many high-volume e-tailers, such as Amazon, commanded bigger discounts from their shipping partners. In 2012, Amazon had launched Amazon Logistics, with its own delivery-van network. A growing number of retailers, such as Wal-Mart and Amazon, were even starting to explore unmanned aerial vehicles as a potential alternative means of delivery. By 2014, Amazon was upstaging its private shipping vendors by offering Sunday delivery and same-day delivery service in various cities through the USPS. As retailers looked for downstream solutions to managing deliveries, an expectation arose that the delivery market, already polarized between high-value, next-day-guaranteed services and economy options, could see the economy segment suffer at the expense of retailers' own initiatives.[11] Others expected shippers to experience a potential shift in demand away from pricier express deliveries as consumers favored free shipping on their online orders through ground service.

Competition

Amid these mixed expectations for future demand, a closer look at the industry's 2015 revenues in the United States revealed that the air-express segment's revenues were fairly evenly split across FedEx and UPS, whereas in the ground segment, UPS reaped the majority of sales. See **Figure 2.1**.

Although higher-margin ground operations were attractive to shippers, complications in the segment arose from the lower density of residential deliveries common among ground orders. To continue to grow their ground operations without focusing on those low-density last-mile trips, both UPS and FedEx contracted USPS's Parcel Select Ground service, which helped businesses move shipments at the back end of their deliveries. Through the service, the private companies delivered packages to the local post

---

[9]Stefany Zaroban, "U.S. E-commerce Grows 14.6% in 2015," Internet Retailer, February 17, 2016, https://www.internetretailer.com/mobile/2016/02/17/us-e-commerce-grows-146-2015 (accessed Jan. 23, 2017).

[10]Robert Lazich, ed., *Market Share Reporter*, 26th ed., vol. II (Farmington Hills, MI: Gale, 2016): 719.

[11]Gill Plimmer, "E-commerce Groups Rush to Deliver the Goods," *Financial Times*, December 19, 2014, https://www.ft.com/content/a061a558-876f-11e4-bc7c-00144feabdc0 (accessed Dec. 10, 2016).

FIGURE 2.1 I   U.S. package market revenue share (%), by segment—2015.

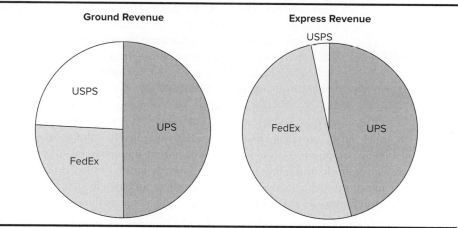

Data source: Brandon Oglenski, Eric Morgan, and Van Kegel, "North American Transportation and Shipping Equity Research," Barclays, May 2, 2016: 31.

office, after which USPS handled the last-mile drop-off. FedEx referred to this partnership with USPS, which launched in 2009, as SmartPost, while UPS's version, launched in 2011, was offered as SurePost, and the service allowed the shipping companies to offer customers even cheaper pricing without wasting van and driver resources.

This similarity of execution on these partnered ground operations reflected the long-standing competition between FedEx and UPS and their frequently parallel strategies. **Exhibit 2.4** provides a detailed summary of the major events marking the competitive rivalry between FedEx and UPS. Significant dimensions of this rivalry included the following:

- **Customer focus**. Both companies emphasized their focus on the customer. This meant listening carefully to the customer's needs, providing customized solutions rather than standardized products, and committing to service relationships.

- **Pricing**. The shipping rivals always moved in lockstep on parcel-pricing fees. In the face of e-commerce retailers adopting the frequent use of large packages for lightweight products, however, the shippers who priced parcels by weight alone started to take a margin hit when those poorly priced packages took up valuable space in delivery trucks. In order to maximize the profitability of e-commerce deliveries, in May 2014, FedEx announced that it would start using dimensional weight to calculate the billable price for all ground packages, effective at the start of 2015. UPS quickly followed with the same announcement the following month.

- **Operational reengineering**. Given the intense price competition, the reduction of unit costs became a priority. Cost reduction was achieved through the exploitation of economies of scale, investment in technology, and business-process reengineering, which sought to squeeze unnecessary steps and costs out of the service process.

- **Information technology**. Information management became central to the operations of both UPS and FedEx. Every package handled by FedEx, for instance, was logged into COSMOS (Customer, Operations, Service, Master Online System), which transmitted data from package movements, customer pickups, invoices, and deliveries to a central database at the Memphis, Tennessee, headquarters. UPS relied on DIADs (Delivery Information Acquisition Devices), which were handheld units that drivers used to scan package barcodes and record customer signatures.

- **Service expansion**. FedEx and UPS increasingly pecked at each other's service offerings. In 2011, for example, UPS launched MyChoice, which allowed customers to control the time of their deliveries online. FedEx quickly followed suit in 2013, launching Delivery Manager, which allowed customers to schedule dates, times, and locations of deliveries from their phones. FedEx even launched a repair shop for devices like iPhones and Nooks in 2012, capitalizing on its retail space and existing shipping capabilities.

- **Logistics services**. The largest shipping innovations entailed offering integrated logistics services to large corporate clients. These services were aimed at providing total inventory control to customers, including purchase orders, receipt of goods, order entry and warehousing, inventory accounting, shipping, and accounts receivable. While this service line was initially developed as a model wherein the shippers stored, tracked, and shipped across client's brick-and-mortar stores, these services eventually expanded to include shipping directly to consumers, as in the health care segment.

The impact of the fierce one-upmanship between FedEx and UPS was clearly reflected in their respective investment expenditures. From 2010 to 2015, capital expenditures for FedEx and UPS increased by 54% and 71%, respectively. During this period, FedEx's aggressive growth strategy, evident in its acquisitions and its investment in the relatively outdated Express aircraft fleet, nearly doubled those of "Big Brown," which benefited from its more modern fleet.

International Package-Delivery Market

In 2015, the global parcel-shipping market was dominated by UPS, FedEx, and DHL, with international services representing 22% and 28% of revenues for UPS and FedEx that year, respectively. FedEx made significant investments in developing European delivery capabilities in the 1980s before eventually relinquishing its European hub in 1992, causing it to rely on local partners to deliver to Europe for the ensuing decade. In 1995, FedEx expanded its routes in Latin America and the Caribbean, and later introduced FedEx AsiaOne, a next-business-day service between Asian countries and the United States via a hub in Subic Bay, Philippines.

UPS broke into the European market in earnest in 1988, with the acquisition of 10 European courier services. To enhance its international delivery systems, UPS created a system that coded and tracked packages and automatically billed customers for customs duties and taxes. In 2012, UPS expanded its European offerings by purchasing Kiala, a European company that gave customers delivery options at nearby shops and gas stations close to their homes, before replicating the service for UK customers the following year. By 2015, the company planned to double its investment in Europe to nearly $2 billion over five years.[12]

Much like the U.S. domestic market, the international package-delivery market of the first decade of the 2000s was given its greatest boost by the explosion of e-commerce. Compared to same-country online shopping, cross-border shipping was only a fraction of global e-commerce spending in 2015, but it was the piece that was growing most quickly, at an annual rate of over 25%.[13] Websites like Amazon Marketplace and Etsy allowed shoppers to purchase goods from sellers all over the world, while expecting an ease of shipping similar to that provided by domestic retailers. As a result of this growing segment of online sales, FedEx, UPS, and others were quickly adapting their service offerings to make cross-border shopping as smooth as possible. FedEx, for example, purchased Bongo in 2014, later rebranded as FedEx Cross Border, which aimed to help retailers face cross-border selling issues, including regulatory compliance and credit-card-fraud protection, while connecting them to global consumers.

Performance Assessment

Virtually all interested observers—customers, suppliers, investors, and employees—watched the competitive struggle between UPS and FedEx for hints about the next stage of the drama. The conventional wisdom was that if a firm were operationally excellent, strong financial performance would follow. Indeed, FedEx had set a goal of producing "superior financial returns,"[14] while UPS targeted "a long-term competitive return."[15] Had the two firms achieved their goals? Moreover, did the trends in financial performance suggest whether strong performance could be achieved in the future? In pursuit of answers to those questions, the following exhibits afford several possible avenues of analysis.

Financial Success

The success of the two companies could be evaluated based on a number of financial and market performance measures. **Exhibit 2.5** presents the share prices, earnings per share (EPS), and price–earnings ratios for the two firms. Also included are the annual total return from holding each share (percentage gain in share price plus dividend yield) and the economic value add, reflecting the value created or destroyed each year by deducting a charge for capital from the firm's net operating profit after taxes. **Exhibits 2.2** and **2.3** present a variety of analytical ratios computed from the financial statements of each firm.

---

[12]Laura Stevens, "Borders Matter Less and Less in E-Commerce," *Wall Street Journal*, June 23, 2015, http://www.wsj.com/articles/SB11295793630700694761804581015971594095608 (accessed Nov. 9 2016).

[13]http://www.wsj.com/articles/SB11295793630700694761804581015971594095608.

[14]FedEx website, http://investors.fedex.com/investor-home/default.aspx (accessed Jan. 20, 2017).

[15]UPS website, https://pressroom.ups.com/pressroom/ContentDetailsViewer.page?ConceptType=FactSheets&id=1426321650156-161 (accessed Jan. 20, 2017).

The thinking of the several securities analysts who followed FedEx and UPS in 2015 and 2016 reflected the uncertainty surrounding the future performance for the two arch-rival shipping companies. **Exhibits 2.6** and **2.7** contain excerpts from various equity research reports that indicate the analysts' outlook held for UPS and FedEx.

Operational Success

Beyond their financial performance, the rival companies' strengths and successes could also be examined using various measures of operational excellence:

- Marketing: In 2015, brand consultancy Interbrand's annual ranking of top global brands ranked UPS at number 29 and FedEx at 86,[16] representing little change from UPS's rank of 27 and FedEx's distant 92 for 2014. This favoring of UPS reflected the payoffs of its full-service-promoting campaigns of the early years of the 2000s.

- Employee satisfaction: *Fortune* magazine's annual ranking of the world's most-admired companies was based on nine factors related to financial performance and corporate reputation, with four of those factors specifically relating to HR attributes (quality of management, ability to attract and retain talented people, innovation, and product and service quality). In 2015, *Fortune* awarded FedEx with the number 12 spot overall, with UPS coming in at number 24. FedEx's apparent excellence with regard to talent management was also reflected by the Great Place to Work Institute, naming FedEx Express as one of the top global companies to work for for the fourth year in a row.[17] The more unionized UPS, where strikes were not uncommon, seemed to lag behind its rival in its commitment to its employees.

- Holiday performance: High-volume holiday-delivery performance was always seen as a strong test of a shipping company's effectiveness, and FedEx and UPS traditionally adopted different strategies approaching the peak season. Despite the holidays of 2013 and 2014 favoring FedEx's automation at its hubs, its independent-contractor model (paying ground drivers by package rather than by hour) and practice of turning down peak volumes based on quantities customers shipped during nonpeak months, by 2015, the tide had turned. That year, UPS finally managed to prove its peak execution capabilities; its strategy of increasing capacity to handle higher volumes allowed it to achieve an on-time-delivery rate nearing 98% the week before Christmas. For the same period, FedEx struggled to handle a late surge of e-commerce shipments that were delivered after the holiday (though the company wouldn't provide numbers).[18]

---

[16] Best Global Brands 2015 report, http://interbrand.com/wp-content/uploads/2016/02/Best-Global-Brands-2015-report.pdf (accessed Jan. 4, 2017).

[17] FedEx Form 10-K, 2015.

[18] Nick Carey, "Third Time's a Charm for UPS at Christmas, but FedEx Stumbles," December 29, 2015, http://www.reuters.com/article/us-ups-fedex-peak-idUSKBN0UC1KP20151229 (accessed Jan. 4, 2017).

- Customer satisfaction: The American Customer Satisfaction Index (ACSI), the only national, cross-industry measure of companies' perceptions among consumers, ranked shipping companies each year based on nearly 10,000 customers' responses concerning ease of tracking, package condition on arrival, helpfulness of in-store staff, and other factors related to recent delivery experiences. Until 2009, FedEx was ranked number one, but the two shippers leveled out in recent years, and by 2014 and 2015, both UPS and FedEx remained neck and neck, having identical ACSI scores of 82, well above USPS's scores of 73 and 75 for the same years.[19]

Outlook for FedEx and UPS

Observers of the air-express package-delivery industry pondered the recent performance of the two leading firms and their prospects. What had been the impact of the intense competition between the two firms? Which firm was doing better? The companies faced a watershed moment with the growth of e-commerce and FedEx's aggressive push into Europe. Might their past performance contain clues about the prospects for future competition?

---

[19]ACSI Utilities, Consumer Shipping, and Health Care Report 2015, May 12, 2015, http://marketing.theacsi. org/acton/attachment/5132/f-0037/1/-/-/-/-/ACSI%20Utilities%20Consumer%20Shipping%20and%20 Health%20Care%20Report%202015.pdf (accessed Jan. 5, 2016).

EXHIBIT 2.1 | Revenues for FedEx and UPS by Business and Geography Segment (Millions)

FedEx	2010	2011	2012	2013	2014	2015
Geography						
U.S. Domestic Revenue	24,852	27,461	29,837	30,948	32,259	34,216
International Revenue	9,882	11,843	12,843	13,339	13,308	13,237
Business						
FedEx Express	21,555	24,581	26,515	27,171	27,121	27,239
FedEx Ground	7,439	8,485	9,573	10,578	11,617	12,984
FedEx Freight	4,321	4,911	5,282	5,401	5,757	6,191
FedEx Services*	1,419	1,327	1,310	1,137	1,072	1,039
UPS	**2010**	**2011**	**2012**	**2013**	**2014**	**2015**
Geography						
U.S. Domestic Revenue	36,795	39,347	40,428	41,772	43,840	45,309
International Revenue	12,750	13,758	13,699	13,666	14,392	13,054
Business						
U.S. Domestic Package						
Next-Day Air	5,835	6,229	6,412	6,443	6,581	6,570
Deferred	2,975	3,299	3,392	3,437	3,672	3,903
Ground	20,932	22,189	23,052	24,194	25,598	26,274
International Package	11,133	12,249	12,124	12,429	12,988	12,149
Supply-Chain & Freight	8,670	9,139	9,147	8,935	9,393	9,467

*FedEx Services provides back-office support to FedEx's three transportation segments and printing and retail support to customers through FedEx Office.

Data source: Company SEC filings.

EXHIBIT 2.2 | Operating Results for UPS Inc. (period ending Dec. 31, in millions)

	2010	2011	2012	2013	2014	2015
Revenue	49,545	53,105	54,127	55,438	58,232	58,363
Operating Income (EBIT)	5,641	6,080	1,343	7,034	4,968	7,668
Interest Expense	354	348	393	380	353	341
Net Income	3,338	3,804	807	4,372	3,032	4,844
Capital Expenditures	1,389	2,005	2,153	2,065	2,328	2,379
Cash and Marketable Securities	4,081	4,275	7,924	5,245	3,283	4,726
Accounts Receivable	6,117	6,246	6,111	6,502	6,661	7,134
Total Current Assets	11,569	12,284	15,591	13,387	11,218	13,208
Net Prop., Plant, and Equip.	17,387	17,621	17,894	17,961	18,281	18,352
Total Asssets	33,597	34,077	38,818	35,553	35,440	38,311
Current Liabilities	5,902	6,514	8,390	7,131	8,621	10,696
Total Debt	10,846	11,128	12,870	10,872	10,779	14,334
Total Stockholders' Equity	8,047	7,108	4,733	6,488	2,158	2,491

	2010	2011	2012	2013	2014	2015	
Growth							**CAGR ('10–'15)**
Revenue Growth		7.2%	1.9%	2.4%	5.0%	0.2%	17.8%
Total Asset Growth		1.4%	13.9%	−8.4%	−0.3%	8.1%	14.0%
Operating Income Growth		7.8%	−77.9%	423.8%	−29.4%	54.3%	35.9%
Net Income Growth		14.0%	−78.8%	441.8%	−30.6%	59.8%	45.1%
Asset Efficiency Ratios							
Working Capital Turnover	8.7	9.2	7.5	8.9	22.4	23.2	Revenue/(C. Assets – C. Liab.)
PPE Turnover	2.8	3.0	3.0	3.1	3.2	3.2	Revenue/PPE
Capital Expenditure %	2.8%	3.8%	4.0%	3.7%	4.0%	4.1%	Capital Exp./Revenue
Total Asset Turnover	1.5	1.6	1.4	1.6	1.6	1.5	Revenue/Total Assets
Liquidity and Leverage Ratios							
Current Ratio	2.0	1.9	1.9	1.9	1.3	1.2	C. Assets/C. Liab.
Cash Ratio	0.7	0.7	0.9	0.7	0.4	0.4	Cash & Mkt. Sec./Curr. Liab.
Total Debt/Equity Ratio	1.3	1.6	2.7	1.7	5.0	5.8	Total Debt/Total St. Eq.
Times Interest Earned	15.9	17.5	3.4	18.5	14.1	22.5	Op. Income/Interest Exp.
Profitability Ratios							
Operating Margin	11%	11%	2%	13%	9%	13%	EBIT/Revenue
Net Profit Margin	7%	7%	1%	8%	5%	8%	Net Income/Revenue
Return on Assets	11%	12%	3%	13%	10%	14%	(N. Inc. + Int. Exp.)/T. Assets
Return on Equity	41%	54%	17%	67%	141%	194%	Net Income/Tot. St. Eq.
Economic Profit (millions)*	$1,873	$2,189	−$602	$2,832	$1,946	$3,255	

*Economic Profit (EVA) is calculated as EBIT *(1 − t) − CofC × (T. Debt + T. St. Eq), where t = 40% and CofC = 8%.

Data source: Capital IQ, Morningstar, company annual reports.

EXHIBIT 2.3 | Operating Results for FedEx Corp. (period ending May 31, in millions)

	2010	2011	2012	2013	2014	2015
Revenue	34,734	39,304	42,680	44,287	45,567	47,453
Operating Income (EBIT)	1,998	2,378	3,186	4,434	3,815	1,867
Interest Expense	79	86	52	82	160	235
Net Income	1,184	1,452	2,032	2,716	2,324	1,050
Capital Expenditures	2,816	3,434	4,007	3,375	3,533	4,347
Cash and Marketable Securities	1,952	2,328	2,843	4,917	2,908	3,763
Accounts Receivable	4,163	4,581	4,704	5,044	5,460	5,719
Total Current Assets	7,284	8,285	9,056	11,274	9,683	10,941
Net Prop., Plant, and Equip.	14,385	15,543	17,248	18,484	19,550	20,875
Total Asssets	24,902	27,385	29,903	33,567	33,070	37,069
Current Liabilities	4,645	4,882	5,374	5,750	5,312	5,957
Total Debt	1,930	1,685	1,667	2,990	4,737	7,268
Total Stockholders' Equity	13,811	15,220	14,727	17,398	15,277	14,993

	2010	2011	2012	2013	2014	2015	
Growth							**CAGR ('10–'15)**
Revenue Growth		13.16%	8.59%	3.77%	2.89%	4.14%	36.62%
Total Assets Growth		9.97%	9.19%	12.25%	−1.48%	12.09%	48.86%
Operating Income Growth		19.02%	33.98%	39.17%	−13.96%	−51.06%	−6.56%
Net Income Growth		22.64%	39.94%	33.66%	−14.43%	−54.82%	−11.32%
Asset Efficiency Ratios							
Working Capital Turnover	13.16	11.55	11.59	8.02	10.42	9.52	Revenue/(C. Assets − C. Liab.)
PPE Turnover	2.41	2.53	2.47	2.40	2.33	2.27	Revenue/PPE
Capital Expenditure %	8.1%	8.7%	9.4%	7.6%	7.8%	9.2%	Capital Exp./Revenue
Asset Turnover	1.39	1.44	1.43	1.32	1.38	1.28	Revenue/Total Assets
Liquidity and Leverage Ratios							
Current Ratio	1.57	1.70	1.69	1.96	1.82	1.84	C. Assets/C. Liab.
Cash Ratio	0.42	0.48	0.53	0.86	0.55	0.63	Cash & Mkt. Sec./Curr. Liab.
Total Debt/Equity Ratio	0.1	0.1	0.1	0.2	0.3	0.5	Total Debt/Total St. Eq.
Times Interest Earned	25.3	27.7	61.3	54.1	23.8	7.9	Op. Income/Interest Exp.
Profitability Analysis							
Operating Margin	5.75%	6.05%	7.46%	10.01%	8.37%	3.93%	EBIT/Revenue
Net Profit Margin	3.41%	3.69%	4.76%	6.13%	5.10%	2.21%	Net Income/Revenue
Return on Assets	5.07%	5.62%	6.97%	8.34%	7.51%	3.47%	(N. Inc. + Int. Exp.)/T. Assets
Return on Equity	8.57%	9.54%	13.80%	15.61%	15.21%	7.00%	Net Income/Tot. St. Eq.
Economic Profit (millions)*	−$60	$74	$600	$1,029	$688	−$661	

*Economic Profit (EVA) is calculated as EBIT * (1 − t) − CofC x (T. Debt + T. St. Eq), where t = 40% and CofC = 8%.

Data source: Capital IQ, Morningstar, company annual reports.

EXHIBIT 2.4 | Timeline of Selective Competitive Developments

FedEx Corp.		United Parcel Service, Inc.
• Offers 10:30 a.m. delivery	**1982**	• Establishes next-day air service
• Acquires Gelco Express and launches operations in Asia-Pacific	**1984**	
• Establishes European hub in Brussels	**1985**	• Begins intercontinental air service between United States and Europe
• Introduces handheld barcode scanner to capture detailed package information	**1986**	
• Offers warehouse services for IBM, National Semiconductor, Laura Ashley	**1987**	
	1988	• Establishes UPS's first air fleet
		• Offers automated customs service
• Acquires Tiger International to expand its international presence	**1989**	• Expands international air service to 180 countries
• Wins Malcolm Baldrige National Quality Award	**1990**	• Introduces 10:30 a.m. guarantee for next-day air
	1991	• Begins Saturday delivery
		• Offers electronic-signature tracking
• Offers two-day delivery	**1992**	• Expands delivery to over 200 countries
	1993	• Provides supply-chain solutions through UPS Logistics Group
• Launches website for package tracking	**1994**	• Launches website for package tracking
• Acquires air routes serving China	**1995**	• Offers guaranteed 8 a.m. overnight delivery
• Establishes Latin American division		
• Creates new hub at Roissy–Charles de Gaulle Airport in France	**1999**	• Makes UPS stock available through a public offering
• Launches business-to-consumer home-delivery service	**2000**	• Acquires all-cargo air service in Latin America
• Carries U.S. Postal Service packages	**2001**	• Acquires Mail Boxes Etc. retail franchise
• Acquires American Freightways Corp.		• Begins direct flights to China
• Expands home delivery to cover 100% of the U.S. population	**2002**	• Offers guaranteed next-day home delivery
• Acquires Kinko's retail franchise	**2003**	
• Establishes Chinese headquarters	**2004**	
• Acquires Parcel Direct, leading parcel consolidator		• Reduces domestic ground-delivery time
	2005	• Purchases Menlo Worldwide Forwarding, adding heavy-air-freight shipment capability
• Launches around-the-world flights		
• Develops new Asia-Pacific hub in Ghangzhou, China		
• Acquires UK domestic express company ANC and Flying-Cargo Hungary	**2006**	• Acquires Overnite, expanding ground-freight services in North America
• Acquires Prakash Air Freight in India		• Launches first nonstop delivery service between the U.S. and Guangzhou, China

(continued)

EXHIBIT 2.4 | Timeline of Selective Competitive Developments (*continued*)

FedEx Corp.		United Parcel Service, Inc.
		• Launches HealthCare Services
	2007	
• Launches FedEx Freight AM, a flat-rate service with a money-back guarantee delivery by 10:30 am	**2008**	
	2009	
	2010	
• Launches HealthCare Solutions, offering shipping and supply-chain management for health companies	**2011**	
		• Launches new brand platform to promote expanded logistics and supply-chain management abilities
• Launches TechConnect, repair shop for consumer electronics		• Launches UPS MyChoice, allowing consumers to control package deliveries online
• Launches FedEx Delivery Manager, giving U.S. customers flexible options to schedule delivery	**2012**	
• Acquires GENCO, third-party logistics providers in North America, expanding ground service	**2013**	• Acquires Kiala, a European company allowing retailers to deliver goods to shoppers' chosen retail location
• Acquires Bongo International, a cross- border enablement technology	**2014**	• Launches ORION, proprietary route-optimization software for drivers, and UPS Access Point, a convenient local-store alternative to home delivery
	2016	• Acquires i-parcel, allowing foreign shoppers to easily purchase goods on a retailer's site
		• Acquires trucker broker, Coyote Logistics, expanding freight logistics

Data source: Compiled by author from company documents and news outlets.

EXHIBIT 2.5 | Financial and Market Performance

FedEx	2012	2013	2014	2015
Stock Price, Dec. 31 Close	91.72	143.77	173.66	148.99
Dividends Declared in $ Per Share	0.52	0.56	0.6	0.8
Basic EPS (period ending May 31)	6.44	8.61	7.56	3.7
Common Shares Outstanding (Mill)	317.0	318.0	287.0	282.4
Price/Earnings	14.7	27.8	22.0	37.9
Annual Return		57.4%	21.2%	−13.7%
Cumul. Annual Return		57.4%	78.6%	64.8%

UPS	2012	2013	2014	2015
Stock Price, Dec. 31 Close	73.73	105.08	111.17	96.23
Dividends Declared in $ Per Share	2.28	2.48	2.68	2.92
Basic EPS	0.84	4.65	3.31	5.38
Common Shares Outstanding (Mill)	953.0	924.0	905.0	886.0
Price/Earnings	88.5	67.1	27.6	22.0
Annual Return		45.9%	8.3%	−10.8%
Cumul. Annual Return		45.9%	54.2%	43.4%

Standard & Poor's 500 Index	2012	2013	2014	2015
Index Level, Dec. 31 Close	1,426.19	1,848.36	2,058.90	2,043.94
Annual Return		29.6%	11.4%	−0.7%
Cumul. Annual Return		29.6%	41.0%	40.3%

Data source: Google Finance, Morningstar, Value Line, and Capital IQ.

EXHIBIT 2.6 | Recent Equity Analysts' Outlook for UPS

Morgan Stanley	"The USPS is a real competitor in the B2C market, and has lower unit delivery costs than either UPS or FedEx. While USPS service may not be as good, the government operated network can still affect the parcel market pricing. . . . The most important strategic question facing UPS is: What is more important to UPS–to maintain margins even in the face of market share losses or to maintain market share dominance even if that means lower margins over time? We suspect UPS will aim to minimize market share losses while maintaining a high ROIC. Over the long run, it may not be possible to achieve both, which is why we think UPS should go after market share aggressively."[1]
Macquarie	"It's tough to be negative on UPS given its impressive return and cash flow metrics, but from a relative basis, we see much more upside potential from FDX. We think FDX's recent underperformance vs. UPS, transports, and the broader market reflects overblown concerns about its China exposure & Express skepticism."[2]
Morningstar	"Despite its extensive unionization and asset intensity, UPS produces returns on invested capital about double its cost of capital and margins well above its competitors'; we credit the firm's leading package density and outstanding operational efficiency, enhanced by years of consistent and extensive technology investment. UPS has turned to health care markets and developing nations for growth, and we think the company has ample runway left to build speed. Even existing operations have revenue expansion potential via pricing power because UPS operates within a somewhat rational oligopoly in its largest market, U.S. high-service parcel delivery."[3]

[1]William Greene, Alexander Vecchio, and Diane Huang, "Greene/United Parcel Service—The Most Important Strategic Question," Morgan Stanley, No. 25356723 from Investext Current Reports database (accessed Feb. 3, 2017).

[2]Kelly Dougherty, Matt Frankel, and Cleo Zagrean, "UPS—It's All about the Peak," Macquarie Group, No. 27249020 from Investext Current Reports database (accessed Feb. 3, 2017).

[3]Keith Schoonmaker, "UPS, Inc.," Morningstar, No. 27249776 from Investext Current Reports database (accessed Feb. 3, 2017).

Source: Analyst reports from specified sources.

EXHIBIT 2.7 | Recent Equity Analysts' Outlook for FedEx

Morningstar	"We expect FedEx to increase revenue 4.5% per year on average through fiscal 2020. Our revenue projections assume ground sales grow at nearly 10% annually, based on organic growth (including from e-commerce shipments) plus clients downshifting from express and continued expansion of SmartPost, a low-priced product that uses a partnership with the postal service for final-mile delivery. Ground margins are likely to remain the highest of any sector . . . [Our] estimates produce consolidated operating margins of about 11.5% . . . due largely to our projection that FedEx will expand the portion of its revenue earned from higher-margin ground operations."[1]
Barclays	"Global trade and urgent Express shipments remain subdued, likely a function of soft Industrial demand. However, ground volume growth of 9% this quarter lends credibility to a stronger consumer this holiday season, especially driven by e-commerce purchases . . . With e-commerce becoming a greater driver of revenue and FedEx clearly delivering cost and capacity constraint, we are becoming incrementally positive on the package networks relative to more industrial exposed large cap transports. Our estimates move slightly higher on stronger Ground growth."[2]
Macquarie	"Ground & Express do face ongoing FY2016 headwinds, but favorable pricing and volume should help drive improvement in FY2017 and beyond, especially as FedEx continues to gain share. We've long viewed FedEx as [a] burgeoning cash-flow story that's been meaningfully de-risked thanks to solid Express execution. The TNT acquisition carries its own acquisition risk but should also meaningfully boost LT growth prospects as FDX finds its global footprint and materially improves its EU cost positon, especially in the all-important e-commerce growth segment. . . . FedEx is in the midst of a meaningful improvement in profitability and cash generation, both of which underlie our continued positive stance on the company."[3]

[1]Keith Schoonmaker, "FedEx Corp.," Morningstar, No. 27901878 from Investext Current Reports database (accessed Feb. 3, 2017).

[2]Brandon Oglenski, Eric Morgan, and Van Kegel, "FedEx Corp–Some Holiday Cheer," Barclay's, No. 27771203 from Investext Current Reports database (accessed Feb. 3, 2017).

[3]Kelly Dougherty, Matt Frankel, and Cleo Zagrean, "FedEx–Still the One," Macquarie Group, No. 27761106 from Investext Current Reports database (accessed Feb. 3, 2017).

Source: Analyst reports from specified sources.

Larry Puglia and the T. Rowe Price Blue Chip Growth Fund

By late 2016, Larry J. Puglia had been managing the $33 billion T. Rowe Price Blue Chip Growth Fund (Blue Chip Growth Fund) for more than 23 years. One of the fund's original managers, Puglia had been the sole manager of the open-ended mutual fund since 1997 and had generated superior returns on average for his investors over the life of the fund.[1]

Since inception in mid-1993 through September 30, 2016, the fund had returned an average annual total return of 10.12%, outperforming the 9.12% return of the fund's benchmark, the Standard & Poor's 500 Index (S&P 500).[2] For most fund managers, beating the S&P 500 in any single year was an accomplishment, yet Puglia had served his investors well by performing better than competitor funds both in bull markets, such as that of the late 1990s, as well as the bear markets, such as that of the first decade of the 2000s. **Exhibit 3.1** presents a summary of the Blue Chip Growth Fund. **Exhibits 3.2** and **3.3** show the fund's performance and annual return versus its benchmark and other funds in the large-cap growth category.

---

[1]An open-end mutual fund was an investment vehicle that pooled the funds of individual investors to buy a portfolio of securities, stocks, bonds, and/or money-market instruments; investors owned a pro rata share of the overall investment portfolio. Investors purchased and redeemed shares of open-end funds directly from the fund issuer. Shares did not trade on the secondary market such as the New York Stock Exchange (NYSE). In contrast, closed-end mutual funds issued a fixed number of shares which then traded on secondary markets such as the NYSE. This case study focuses on open-end mutual funds.

[2]The S&P 500 was a market-capitalization-weighted index of shares of the 500 largest companies traded on both the New York and American Stock Exchanges.

This public-sourced case was prepared by Dorothy C. Kelly, CFA (MBA '92), under the supervision of Kenneth M. Eades, Professor of Business Administration. The financial support of the Darden Foundation and the Mayo Center for Asset Management are gratefully acknowledged. It is based on "The Fidelity Magellan Fund, 1995," UVA-F-1126 (Charlottesville, VA: Darden Business Publishing, 1995) by Robert F. Bruner, University Professor, Distinguished Professor of Business Administration, and Dean Emeritus. It was written using publicly available information as a basis for class discussion rather than to illustrate effective or ineffective handling of an administrative situation. Copyright © 2016 by the University of Virginia Darden School Foundation, Charlottesville, VA. All rights reserved. *To order copies, send an e-mail to sales@dardenpublishing.com. No part of this publication may be reproduced, stored in a retrieval system, used in a spreadsheet, or transmitted in any form or by any means—electronic, mechanical, photocopying, recording, or otherwise—without the permission of the Darden School Foundation.*

While Puglia, working out of T. Rowe Price's Baltimore, Maryland, headquarters, rarely had the best overall performance in any given year, and other managers had beaten his results over short-term periods, his overall long-term performance relative to the index was truly impressive. He ranked 20th out of 558 U.S. stock mutual funds with a single portfolio manager, and Morningstar had awarded the Blue Chip Growth Fund its coveted five-star rating for the fund's five-year performance, placing it in the top 10% of 1,285 mutual funds investing in large-capitalization growth stocks.[3] Puglia had also been nominated by Morningstar as one of five finalists for Domestic Fund Manager of the Year in 2013. The fund had been recognized as an IBD Best Mutual Funds 2016 Awards winner by *Investor's Business Daily* (IBD).[4] In addition, *Money Magazine* consistently named the fund to its annual selection of best funds, and *Kiplinger's Personal Finance* magazine included the fund on its list of 25 favorite funds.

Puglia's results seemed to contradict conventional academic theories, which suggested that, in markets characterized by high competition, easy entry, and informational efficiency, it would be extremely difficult to beat the market on a sustained basis. Observers wondered what might explain such consistent outperformance by a fund manager and how it could be sustained.

The Mutual-Fund Market[5]

The global mutual-fund market represented $37.2 trillion in worldwide assets at the end of 2015. Investment companies in the United States accounted for almost half the global market, with $18.1 trillion in assets; U.S. investment company assets first topped $1 trillion in 1990, growing to $5.8 trillion in 1998 and $18.1 trillion in 2015. Ninety-three million individuals and 44% of U.S. households owned mutual funds in 2015. In 2015, individual investors owned about 86% of the assets held by U.S. investment companies.

Mutual funds provided several benefits for individual retail investors. First, they gave investors the ability to diversify their portfolios—that is, invest in many different securities simultaneously, thereby reducing the risks associated with owning any single stock. By purchasing shares in a mutual fund, investors without significant amounts of capital could efficiently diversify their portfolios, investing as if they had the sizable amount of capital usually necessary to achieve such efficiency. Mutual funds also offered scale economies in trading and transaction costs, economies unavailable to the typical individual investor. Second, mutual funds provided retail investors with professional management and expertise devoted to analysis of securities, which in theory could lead to higher-than-average returns. A

---

[3]Morningstar, T. Rowe Price Blue Chip Growth Fund TRBCX, release date June 7, 2016: 13.

[4]Paul Katzeff, "12 Blue-Chip Beauties That This Top Money Manager Likes Now," *Investor's Business Daily*, May 6, 2016, http://www.investors.com/etfs-and-funds/mutual-funds/amazon-ross-facebook-driving-a-t-rowe-price-marquee-manager/ (accessed Dec. 16, 2016).

[5]Investment Company Institute, Worldwide Regulated Open-End Fund Assets and Flows, Second Quarter 2016, https://www.ici.org/research/stats/worldwide/ww_q2_16 (accessed Dec. 16, 2016).

third view was that the mutual-fund industry provided, according to one observer, "an insulating layer between the individual investor and the painful vicissitudes of the marketplace"[6]:

> This service, after all, allows individuals to go about their daily lives without spending too much time on the aggravating subject of what to buy and sell and when, and it spares them the even greater aggravation of kicking themselves for making the wrong decision. . . . Thus, the money management industry is really selling "more peace of mind" and "less worry," though it rarely bothers to say so.[7]

Between 1970 and 2015, the number of mutual funds offered in the United States grew from 361 to 9,520. This total included many different types of funds; each pursued a specific investment focus and could be classified in one of several categories, such as aggressive-growth, growth, growth-and-income, international, option, balanced, or a variety of bond or fixed-income funds.[8] Funds could be further segmented by company size based on the market capitalization (market cap), calculated by multiplying the number of shares outstanding by share price. Investors could, for example, opt to invest in large-cap, mid-cap, or small-cap growth funds. Funds whose principal focus of investing was common stocks or equities represented the largest segment of the industry.[9]

The growth in the number and types of mutual funds reflected a major shift in retirement plans for U.S. workers. Prior to the 1980s, most workers were covered by traditional defined-benefit (DB) pension plans, which were funded by employers and managed by institutional money managers hired by the employers. Changes to the U.S. tax code in the 1970s set the stage for a major shift, which would have broad implications for the mutual-fund industry. First, the Employee Retirement Income Security Act of 1974 established the self-directed Individual Retirement Account (IRA) through which workers could save and invest individually for their retirement on a tax-deferred basis. Second, large U.S. companies began to replace their DB pension plans with defined-contribution (DC) plans such as 401(k) and 403(b) plans. The new plans, named for the relevant sections of the U.S. tax code, shifted the burden and responsibility of saving and managing retirement assets from corporate employers to individual employees. **Exhibit 3.4** shows the growth in retirement-plan assets over the period from 1975 to 2015. By 2015, $7.1 trillion of IRA and DC plan assets were invested through mutual funds.[10]

---

[6]Bruner.

[7]Contrarious, "Good News and Bad News," *Personal Investing*, August 26, 1987, 128.

[8]Aggressive-growth funds sought to maximize capital gains by investing in companies with the potential to grow rapidly. Growth funds invested in more mature companies that were expected to continue growing faster than the general economy. Growth-and-income funds invested in companies with longer track records that were expected to increase in value and provide a steady income stream. International funds invested in foreign companies. Option funds sought to maximize current returns by investing in dividend-paying stocks on which call options were traded. Balanced funds attempted to conserve the purchasing power of principal by investing in bonds for current income and stocks for capital appreciation.

[9]Bruner.

[10]Investment Company Institute, "Investment Company Factbook 2015."

The shift into DC plans created a broader customer base for the mutual-fund industry, as well as a deeper penetration of the total market for financial services. With DC plans, each worker had an individual investment account that could hold multiple mutual funds, whereas a company's DB plan held the assets of tens of thousands of workers in a single investment account. Funds owned in an employee's name after a vesting period remained in the employee's name even if they switched employers. By 2015, 44.1% or 54.9 million U.S. households owned mutual funds, up from 5.7% or 4.6 million U.S. households in 1980.[11]

The breadth of mutual-fund alternatives tended to encourage fund switching, especially from one type of fund to another within a family of funds. The switching behavior reflected the increased participation of growing numbers of relatively inexperienced and unskilled retail investors; their interest in market-timing-oriented investment strategies; and the greater range of mutual funds from which to choose, all of which increased volatility in the market. In short, as the mutual-fund industry grew and segmented, mutual-fund money became "hotter" (tended to turn over faster).[12]

As a result of the growth in the industry, the institutional investors who managed mutual funds, pension funds, and hedge funds[13] on behalf of individual investors grew in power and influence. By 2015, mutual funds owned 31% of the outstanding stock of U.S. companies.[14] The power and influence of institutional asset managers was apparent in their trading muscle—their ability, coupled with their willingness, to move huge sums of money in and out of securities.[15] The rising role of institutional investors investing on behalf of millions of individual account holders resulted in increases in trading volume, average-trade size, and block trading (a single trade of more than 10,000 shares).[16]

---

[11]Investment Company Institute, "Investment Company Factbook 2009" and "Investment Company Factbook 2015."

[12]Bruner.

[13]Hedge funds, like mutual funds, were investment vehicles that pooled investors' money and invested the aggregated funds in financial instruments to generate a positive return. Unlike mutual funds, hedge funds were lightly regulated and were thus restricted to accredited investors meeting net-worth and/or income requirements set by the U.S. Securities and Exchange Commission. Hedge funds were often structured as limited partnerships in which the fund managers acted as general partners, charging management fees of 1% to 2% of the fund's assets plus performance fees up to 20% of profits. Investors were required to "lock up" their invested capital for a year or more. Most hedge funds were structured such that the portfolio could hold not only "long" investment positions like their mutual fund counterparts, but also "short" positions designed to profit from expected declines in asset prices. Like their mutual-fund counterparts, hedge funds could be categorized into a variety of segments. Among the most common were long-short equity funds, market-neutral funds, event-driven funds which sought to profit from events such as mergers and acquisitions, and global macro funds, which sought to profit from global economic trends. Worldwide growth in hedge funds had exploded since the 1990s, rising from approximately $38 billion in assets in 1990, to more than $3 trillion in assets under management in 2015. Traditionally, hedge funds had been little known and unregulated, but their growth as an investment vehicle had attracted increasing regulatory scrutiny in the United States.

[14]Investment Company Institute, "Investment Company Factbook 2016."

[15]Bruner.

[16]Bruner.

Mutual-Fund Basics[17]

When individuals invested in an open-ended mutual fund, their ownership was proportional to the number of shares purchased. The value of each share was called the fund's net asset value (NAV). The NAV, computed after market close each day, was the fund's total assets less liabilities divided by the number of mutual-fund shares outstanding, or:

$$\text{Net asset value (NAV)} = \frac{\text{Market value of fund assets} - \text{Liabilities}}{\text{Fund shares outstanding}}$$

The investment performance of a mutual fund was measured as the increase or decrease in NAV plus the fund's income distributions during the period (i.e., dividends and capital gains), expressed as a percentage of the fund's NAV at the beginning of the investment period, or:

$$\text{Annual total return} = \frac{\text{Change in NAV} + \text{Dividends} + \text{Capital-gain distributions}}{\text{NAV(at the beginning of the period)}}$$

Investors in mutual funds generally paid two types of fees for their investments: one-time transaction fees and ongoing management fees. A fund's transaction fee, or sales load, covered sales commissions paid to brokers for selling the fund. The sales load could be a front-end or back-end load. A front-end sales load shaved off as much as 6% of an individual's initial investment. A back-end load, in contrast, enabled investors to invest all of their money and defer paying the sales load until they redeemed the shares. Some companies eschewed the use of brokers and pursued a no-load strategy, selling funds directly to investors.

In addition to any sales load imposed, investors paid fees for the ongoing management and operation of the mutual fund. Expenses included management fees for managing the investments, administrative costs, advertising and promotion expenses, and distribution and service fees. Expenses were calculated as a percentage of the fund's total assets (the expense ratio), and were charged to all shareholders proportionally. Expense ratios ranged from as low as 0.2% to as high as 2.0%. As seen in **Exhibit 3.5**, expense ratios were lower for index funds (funds designed to replicate the performance of a specific market index) than they were for actively managed funds which sought to outperform a market index. Because the expense ratio was regularly deducted from the portfolio, it reduced the fund's NAV, thereby lowering the fund's gross returns. Depending on the magnitude of the fund's expense ratio, the net effect of loads and expense ratios on shareholder returns could be substantial.[18]

Another drag on shareholders' returns was the tendency to keep some portion of fund assets in cash either to invest in attractive investment opportunities or to meet shareholder redemptions. As economist and industry observer Henry Kaufman warned

---

[17]Bruner.

[18]For instance, suppose you had invested $10,000 in a fund that appreciated 10% annually, which you then sold out after three years. Also, suppose the fund carried an expense ratio of 2% and a front-end load of 4%. The fees would cut your pretax profit by 35%—from $3,310 to $2,162.

in 1994, a sudden economy-wide shock from interest rates or commodity prices could spook investors into panic-style redemptions from mutual funds, which could force the funds themselves to liquidate investments, sending security prices into a tailspin.[19] Unlike the banking industry, which enjoyed the liquidity afforded by the U.S. Federal Reserve to respond to the effects of panic by depositors, the mutual-fund industry enjoyed no such government-backed reserve, and thus fund managers often carried a certain amount of cash to meet redemptions.[20]

A final drag on shareholders' returns was taxes. Mutual funds collected taxable dividends for the shares they held and generated taxable capital gains whenever they sold securities at a profit. Dividends received and capital gains and losses were reflected in the daily NAV. The funds could avoid paying corporate taxes on dividends earned and capital gains realized during the year if they distributed the investment income to shareholders prior to year-end. The distribution shifted the tax liability from the investment company to individual shareholders.

Mutual funds generally distributed the year's realized capital gains and dividend income to shareholders in December. Dividends and capital gains had, of course, been collected and realized throughout the year, and were reflected in the daily NAV as they occurred. On the day of the distribution, the NAV was reduced by the amount of the distribution. As an example, imagine a mutual fund with an NAV of $10 per share that had realized capital gains of $1.12 per share during the year. In December, the mutual fund would distribute $1.12 per share to its investors and the new NAV would be $8.88. Thus an investor with 100 shares who chose to receive the distribution in cash would have $112 in cash plus 100 shares worth $888 for a total investment value of $1,000. An investor who held 100 shares with an NAV of $10 prior to a distribution that he chose to reinvest would hold the original 100 shares with a new NAV of $8.88 plus 12.612 new shares ($1.12 × 100 shares/8.88 per share), for a total of 112.612 shares worth $1,000 ($8.88 × 12.612 shares). When funds were held in taxable rather than tax-deferred accounts, capital gains distributions triggered both unexpected and unwanted tax liabilities for investors, and reduced the net returns to investors.

Most mutual-fund managers relied on some variation of the two classic schools of securities analysis for choosing investments[21]:

Technical analysis: This approach involved the identification of profitable investment opportunities based on trends in stock prices, volume, market sentiment, and the like.

Fundamental analysis: This approach relied on insights afforded by an analysis of the economic fundamentals of a company and its industry: supply and demand, costs, growth prospects, and the like.

While variations on those approaches produced above-average returns in certain years, there was no guarantee that they would produce such returns consistently over time.[22]

---

[19] Henry Kaufman, "Structural Changes in the Financial Markets: Economic and Policy Significance," Federal Reserve Bank of Kansas, 1994.

[20] Bruner.

[21] Bruner.

[22] Bruner.

Performance of the Mutual-Fund Industry

The two most frequently used measures of mutual-fund performance were (1) the annual growth rate of NAV assuming reinvestment of all dividend and capital-gain distributions (the total return on investment) and (2) the absolute dollar value today of an investment made at some time in the past. Those measures were then compared with the performance of a benchmark portfolio such as the Russell 2000 Index or the S&P 500 Composite Index. **Exhibit 3.6** provides performance data on a range of mutual-fund categories. The Russell, S&P 500, Dow Jones, and Value Line indices offered benchmarks for the investment performance of hypothetical stock portfolios.[23]

Academicians criticized those performance measures for failing to adjust for the relative risk of the mutual fund. Over long periods, as **Exhibit 3.7** shows, different types of securities yielded different levels of total return, and each type of security was associated with differing degrees of risk (measured as the standard deviation of returns). Thus the relationship between risk and return was reliable both on average and over time. For instance, it would be expected that a conservatively managed mutual fund would yield a lower return—precisely because it took fewer risks.[24]

After adjusting for the risk of the fund, academic research indicated that mutual funds had the ability to perform up to the market on a gross-return basis, but when all expenses were factored in, the funds underperformed the market benchmarks. In a paper first published in 1968, Michael Jensen reported that gross risk-adjusted returns were −0.4% and that net risk-adjusted returns (i.e., net of expenses) were −1.1%. Later studies found that, in a sample of 70 mutual funds, net risk-adjusted returns were essentially zero, and some analysts attributed this general result to the average 1.3% expense ratio of mutual funds and their tendency to hold cash.[25]

In his best-selling book, *A Random Walk Down Wall Street*, a classic investment tome first published in 1973, Burton Malkiel, an academic researcher, concluded that a passive buy-and-hold strategy (of a large, diversified portfolio) would do as well for the investor as the average mutual fund.[26] Malkiel wrote:

> Even a dart-throwing chimpanzee can select a portfolio that performs as well as one carefully selected by the experts. This, in essence, is the practical application of the theory of efficient markets. . . . The theory holds that the market appears to adjust so quickly to information about individual stocks and the economy as a whole, that no technique of selecting a portfolio—neither technical nor fundamental analysis—can consistently outperform a strategy of simply buying and holding a diversified group of securities such as those that

---

[23]The Dow Jones indices of industrial companies, transportation companies, and utilities reflected the stocks of a small number (e.g., 30) of large blue-chip companies, all traded on the NYSE and the NASDAQ. The Value Line Index was an equal-weighted stock index containing 1,700 companies from the NYSE, American Stock Exchange, NASDAQ, and over-the-counter market; it was also known as the Value Line Investment Survey. The Russell 2000 measured the performance of 2,000 of the smallest companies in the Russell 3000 index of the biggest U.S. stocks. As any index sample became larger, it reflected a greater weighting of smaller, high-growth companies.

[24]Bruner.

[25]Bruner.

[26]Bruner.

make up the popular market averages. . . . [o]ne has to be impressed with the substantial volume of evidence suggesting that stock prices display a remarkable degree of efficiency. . . . If some degree of mispricing exists, it does not persist for long. "True value will always out" in the stock market.[27]

Many scholars accepted and espoused Malkiel's view that the stock market followed a "random walk," where the price movements of the future were uncorrelated with the price movements of the past or present. This view denied the possibility that there could be momentum in the movements of common stock prices. According to this view, technical analysis was the modern-day equivalent of alchemy.[28] Academics also dismissed the value and effectiveness of fundamental analysis. They argued that capital markets' information was efficient–that the data, information, and analytical conclusions available to any one market participant were bound to be reflected quickly in share prices.[29]

The belief that capital markets incorporated all the relevant information into existing securities' prices was known as the *efficient market hypothesis* (EMH), and was widely, though not universally, accepted by financial economists. If EMH were correct and all current prices reflected the true value of the underlying securities, then arguably it would be impossible to beat the market with superior skill or intellect.[30]

Economists defined three levels of market efficiency, which were distinguished by the degree of information believed to be reflected in current securities' prices. The *weak form* of efficiency maintained that all past prices for a stock were incorporated into today's price; prices today simply followed a random walk with no correlation with past patterns. *Semistrong* efficiency held that today's prices reflected not only all past prices, but also all publicly available information. Finally, the *strong* form of market efficiency held that today's stock price reflected *all* the information that could be acquired through a close analysis of the company and the economy.[31] "In such a market," as one economist said, "we would observe lucky and unlucky investors, but we wouldn't find any superior investment managers who can consistently beat the market."[32]

Proponents of EMH were both skeptical and highly critical of the services provided by active mutual-fund managers. Paul Samuelson, the Nobel Prize–winning economist, said:

> [E]xisting stock prices already have discounted in them an allowance for their future prospects. Hence . . . one stock [is] about as good or bad a buy as another. To [the] passive investor, chance alone would be as good a method of selection as anything else.[33]

---

[27]Burton G. Malkiel, *A Random Walk Down Wall Street* (New York: Norton, 1990), 186, 211.

[28]Bruner.

[29]Bruner.

[30]Sean D. Carr, "Bill Miller and Value Trust," UVA-F-1481 (Charlottesville, VA: Darden Business Publishing, 2005).

[31]Carr.

[32]Richard A. Brealey, Stewart C. Myers, and Franklin Allen, *Principles of Corporate Finance*, 8th ed. (New York: McGraw–Hill Irwin, 2006): 337.

[33]Malkiel, 182.

Tests supported Samuelson's view. For example, in June 1967, *Forbes* magazine established an equally weighted portfolio of 28 stocks selected by throwing darts at a dartboard. By 1984, when the magazine retired the feature article, the initial $28,000 portfolio with $1,000 invested in each stock was worth $131,698, a 9.5% compound rate of return. This beat the broad market averages and almost all mutual funds. *Forbes* concluded, "It would seem that a combination of luck and sloth beats brains."[34]

Despite the teachings of EMH and the results of such tests, some money managers—such as Larry Puglia—had significantly outperformed the market over long periods. In reply, Malkiel suggested that beating the market was much like participating in a coin-tossing contest where those who consistently flip heads are the winners.[35] In a coin-tossing game with 1,000 contestants, half will be eliminated on the first flip. On the second flip, half of those surviving contestants are eliminated. And so on, until, on the seventh flip, only eight contestants remain. To the naïve observer, the ability to flip heads consistently looks like extraordinary skill. By analogy, Malkiel suggested that the success of a few superstar portfolio managers could be explained as luck.[36]

Not surprisingly, the community of professional asset managers viewed those scholarly theories with disdain. Dissension also grew in the ranks of academicians as research exposed anomalies inconsistent with the EMH. For example, evidence suggested that stocks with low price-to-earnings (P/E) multiples tended to outperform those with high P/E multiples. Other evidence indicated positive serial correlation (i.e., momentum) in stock returns from week to week or from month to month. The evidence of these anomalies was inconsistent with a random walk of prices and returns.[37]

The most vocal academic criticism came from the burgeoning field of "behavioral finance," which suggested that greed, fear, and panic could be much more significant factors in determining stock prices than mainstream theories would suggest. Critics of EMH argued that events such as the stock-market crash of October 1987 were inconsistent with the view of markets as fundamentally rational and efficient. Lawrence Summers, economist and past president of Harvard University, argued that the 1987 crash was a "clear gap with the theory. If anyone did seriously believe that price movements are determined by changes in information about economic fundamentals, they've got to be disabused of that notion by [the] 500-point drop" which erased more than 22% of market value in a single day.[38] Following the 1987 crash, Yale University economist Robert Shiller concluded: "The efficient market hypothesis is the most remarkable error in the history of economic theory. This is just another nail in its coffin."[39]

Market events such as the Internet bubble of the late 1990s and the global financial crisis of 2007–2009 further added to the belief that market participants were not always

---

[34]Malkiel, 164.

[35]Malkiel, 175–176.

[36]Bruner.

[37]Bruner.

[38]B. Donnelly, "Efficient-Market Theorists Are Puzzled by Recent Gyrations in Stock Market," *Wall Street Journal*, October 23, 1987, 7.

[39]Donnelly.

rational and the EMH was flawed. Yet, despite the mounting evidence of its shortcomings, the EMH remained the dominant model in the academic community.[40]

The Rise of Passive Investing

More than 20 years after graduating from Princeton University in 1951, where he wrote his senior thesis on "The Economic Role of the Investment Company," John C. Bogle founded the Vanguard Group and established a fund whose investment goal was to match—not beat—the performance of a market index. Bogle's First Index Investment Trust launched on December 31, 1975, and was quickly dismissed as folly by many. Investors, critics proclaimed, would not be satisfied with receiving average returns.

Over time, Bogle's fund, which tracked the S&P 500, and was eventually renamed the Vanguard 500 Index Fund, proved critics wrong. Without expensive portfolio managers or research analysts to compensate, the fund charged a low expense ratio of 0.16%. Without portfolio managers trading in and out of securities, the fund's turnover rate was 3%, meaning that year-end capital-gains distributions were negligible, making the fund extremely tax efficient for taxable investors.

At least some investors decided that the benefits of being average outweighed the costs of trying to be above average. From approximately $11 million in assets in 1975, the fund grew to $262.80 billion in assets on September 30, 2016.[41] Vanguard also grew. By December 2015, the company employed 14,000 individuals and offered more than 300 U.S. and non-U.S. funds, serving more than 20 million investors from approximately 170 countries.[42]

Vanguard's success was noticed. In particular, other investment companies developed and offered index funds, and by 2015, $2.2 trillion was invested in index-based mutual funds.[43] **Exhibit 3.8** shows the growing percentage of assets invested in equity index funds from 2000 to 2015, and **Exhibit 3.9** shows how outflows from actively managed funds matched the inflows to passively managed investment funds from 2009 to 2015.[44]

Larry Puglia and the T. Rowe Price Blue Chip Growth Fund

At a time when many investors were eschewing actively managed funds such as Puglia's in favor of passive investments designed to track stock-market indices, Puglia's investment performance stood out. Morningstar, the well-known statistical service for

---

[40]Carr.

[41]The Vanguard Group website, https://institutional.vanguard.com/iippdf/pdfs/FS40R.pdf (accessed Dec. 16, 2016).

[42]www.Vanguard.com (accessed Dec. 15, 2016).

[43]2015 Investment Company Factbook, p. 218.

[44]Similar to an index mutual fund were index exchange-traded funds (ETFs). An ETF was designed to track an index, but unlike an index fund, shares of an ETF traded on a stock exchange, like shares of common stock. Investors bought and sold ETFs within the same day and paid a commission for each transaction. ETFs were more tax efficient than owning a mutual fund and they allowed investors to trade intraday, rather than only trading at the end-of-day NAV as was done for a mutual fund.

the investment community, gave the Blue Chip Growth Fund its second-highest rating, four stars for overall performance, placing it in the top 32.5% of 1,482 funds in its category. Morningstar rated funds with at least a three-year history based on risk-adjusted return (including the effects of transaction fees such as sales loads and redemption fees) with emphasis on downward variations and consistent performance. According to Morningstar, a high rating could reflect above-average returns, below-average risk, or both.[45]

Puglia graduated *summa cum laude* from the University of Notre Dame and went one to earn an MBA from the Darden School of Business, where he graduated with highest honors. A Certified Public Accountant (CPA), Puglia also held the Chartered Financial Analyst (CFA) designation. Puglia learned his first lessons about investing from his father, a traditional buy-and-hold investor. "He would buy good companies and literally hold them for 15 or 20 years."[46]

Puglia, 56, joined T. Rowe Price in 1990 as an analyst following the financial services and pharmaceutical industries. He worked closely with portfolio manager Tom Broadus (co-manager of the Blue Chip Growth Fund from mid-1993 until leaving the fund on May 1, 1997), who provided additional lessons about investing. Broadus warned the young analyst that his investment style would sometimes be out of sync with the market. Part of the portfolio manager's job, he told Puglia, was to recognize that and lose as little as possible.[47]

When the Blue Chip Growth Fund launched in 1993, its managers engaged in considerable debate over "what constituted a 'blue-chip growth company.' Some people felt we should own the old Dow Jones smokestack companies; others said we needed to own the Ciscos and the Microsofts. After giving it a lot of thought, we decided that it was durable, sustainable earnings-per-share growth that confers blue-chip status on a company. That's what allows it to garner an above-average price-earnings ratio, and that's what allows you to really hold such an investment for the long term and allows your wealth to compound. So that's basically what we're trying to do—we're trying to find companies with durable, sustainable earnings-per-share growth, and we want to hold those companies for the long term."[48]

---

[45]The Morningstar Rating for funds reflected a mutual fund's historical risk-adjusted performance as of a specific date. Funds were rated for up to three time periods (3, 5, and 10 years). These separate ratings were then weighted and averaged to produce an overall rating. Morningstar computed risk-adjusted return by subtracting a risk penalty (as determined by the amount of variation in the fund's monthly returns) from the fund's load-adjusted excess return. Funds were then ranked within their respective Morningstar categories and assigned stars. The top 10% of funds in each category received five stars, the next 22.5% received four stars, the next 35% received three stars, the next 22.5% received two stars, and the bottom 10% received one star.

[46]William Long, "Investing It: Investing with Larry Puglia; T. Rowe Price Blue Chip Growth Fund," July 12, 1998, http://www.nytimes.com/1998/07/12/business/investing-it-investing-with-larry-puglia-t-rowe-price-blue-chip-growth-fund.html (accessed Dec. 16, 2016).

[47]Katzeff.

[48]Maria Crawford Scott, "A Search for the Blue Chips: Durable, Sustainable Earnings Growth," *AAII Journal* (November 2000).

The fund's objective was long-term capital growth, with income only a secondary consideration. Consequently, Puglia invested in well-established large and medium-sized companies that he believed had potential for above-average earnings growth. More specifically, Puglia looked for companies with leading market positions, seasoned management that allocated capital effectively, and strong returns on invested capital.[49] To be included in his portfolio, a company needed several things[50]:

1. Growing market share and market size. In Puglia's view, a leading market position conferred both cost advantages and pricing advantages. A company with superior market share generally made its products more cheaply, and also enjoyed more pricing flexibility. As important as growing market share was growing market size. Superior market share in a declining marketplace was not a good indicator, so Puglia also evaluated the market for a company's products and how large the total addressable market could grow over time.

2. Competitive advantage(s): Puglia used Harvard Business School professor Michael Porter's competitive analysis to identify companies with sustainable competitive advantage, what legendary value investor Warren Buffett referred to as "economic castles protected by unbreachable moats."[51]

3. Strong fundamentals including above-average earnings growth, stable-to-improving margins, strong free cash flow, and return on equity.

4. Seasoned management with a demonstrated track record: Puglia looked for evidence of management's ability to allocate capital to the highest-return businesses and pare away low-returning businesses; and to manage expenses aggressively. He compared a company that generates superior return and has strong free-cash flow but lacks strong management to a fast ship without a rudder. Sooner or later, it will run aground.

Puglia was assisted in this process by a very highly regarded global research team that included more than 250 industry analysts, as well as portfolio managers responsible for other funds. Together, members of the research team covered more than 2,300 public companies around the globe, almost two-thirds of global markets by market capitalization.[52] The firm's recruiting and internal mentoring programs allowed it to attract and develop talented investment analysts, who formed a pool of well-trained and experienced candidates for portfolio manager positions.

T. Rowe Price's culture and structure encouraged and facilitated close and frequent collaboration between managers and analysts and equity and fixed-income professionals.

---

[49]Grace L. Williams, "14 Blue Chip Stocks for the Slow-Growth Era," *Barron's*, September 2, 2014.

[50]"Apple, Michael Kors, Visa, eBay: Larry Puglia's Bets" *Investor's Business Daily*, December 4, 2012, http://www.nasdaq.com/article/apple-michael-kors-visa-ebay-larry-puglias-bets-cm195628#ixzz4O6gSqIlE (accessed Dec. 16, 2016).

[51]Berkshire Hathaway Inc. annual letter to shareholders, 1995, http://www.berkshirehathaway.com/letters/1995.html (accessed Jan. 3, 2017).

[52]T. Rowe Price website, https://www3.troweprice.com/usis/corporate/en/about/investment-philosophy.html (accessed Dec. 16, 2016).

Its performance evaluation and compensation practices rewarded collaboration and focused on long-term, rather than short-term, results.[53] Management regularly promoted the strength and contributions of the research team to clients, directly or through its website, and shared research supporting its approach to active management.

Puglia, like most of the firm's portfolio managers, had initially served as an analyst, and considered analyst recommendations and insights from the research team to be instrumental to the stock-selection process. With assistance from the research team and robust firm resources, he focused on identifying companies with durable free-cash-flow growth.

Although most investment candidates were identified through analyst recommendations, Puglia also employed other identification methods, including screening databases for various characteristics, such as steady earnings growth and return on equity over one, three, and five years. Puglia explained, "We'll look under every stone," searching news reports, economic data, and even rivals' portfolios for investment ideas. "There are plenty of other managers out there with excellent track records," he said, "and we're willing to learn from others where possible."[54]

Identifying a potential investment through screening was only one quantitative aspect of the investment research and decision-making process. For each company of interest, Puglia calculated the company's "self-sustaining growth rate," multiplying return on equity by 1 minus the payout ratio (percentage of earnings paid out in dividends). A company with a 25% return on equity paying out 10% of earnings in dividends, would, for example, have a self-sustaining growth rate of 22.5%.[55] Recognizing the limitations of return on equity or other measures based upon GAAP or book accounting, Puglia and the research team also used free cash flow extensively in quantitative analysis and stock selection. If a company met Puglia's quantitative criteria, he and the research team would do further qualitative research, including meeting with corporate management and corroborating their assertions and other data with customers, suppliers, and competitors.

According to Morningstar, $10,000 invested in the Blue Chip Growth Fund at its inception in mid-1993 would have grown to $94,021 in assets on September 30, 2016. Puglia's fund significantly outperformed the average growth for the large-cap-growth category of $56,185 and growth from investing in the S&P 500, which returned $76,100. As news of Puglia's performance record spread, more and more investors moved their money to the Blue Chip Growth Fund, such that over the life of the fund, more than $15 billion of new money was added to the fund's assets under management. Even so, Puglia remained modest; he knew his investing style would not always be in sync with the markets and that the fund's returns could vary quite a bit at times from the S&P 500. During those times, Puglia would recall the advice of his former co-manager to recognize the shift and lose as little as possible.

---

[53]https://www3.troweprice.com/usis/personal-investing/planning-and-research/t-rowe-price-insights/investments/equities/long-term-benefits-of-the-t--rowe-price-approach-to-active-manag.html?van=complete-active-study (accessed Dec. 16, 2016).

[54]Long.

[55]Derived from an example in Long.

Conclusion

Judged from an historical perspective, Puglia's investment success seemed exceptional. His long-run, market-beating performance defied conventional academic theories. Investors, scholars, and market observers wondered about the sources of such superior performance and about its sustainability. At of the end of 2016, was it rational for an equity investor to buy shares in the Blue Chip Growth Fund, or for that matter any actively managed fund? Investors and other observers wondered whether and for how long Puglia could continue to outperform the market. In particular, they wondered whether he would be able to sustain his performance under the weight of having $30 billion in assets to invest.

EXHIBIT 3.1 | Morningstar, Inc., Report on T. Rowe Price Blue Chip Growth Fund: Summary[1]

T. Rowe Price Blue Chip Growth Fund TRBCX

Morningstar Analyst Rating
NAV

NAV $	NAV Day Change %	Yield TTM %	Total Assets $ Bil	Status	Min. Inv.	Load	Expenses	Morningstar Rating™	Category	Investment Style
70.53	+0.37I0.53	0.00	30.7	Open	$2,500	None	0.71%	★★★★★	Large Growth	▦ Large Growth

Growth of 10,000 06-06-2006 - 06-06-2016

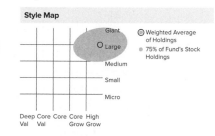

— T. Rowe Price Blue Chip Growth Fund $24,101.23
— Large Growth $19,527.63
— S&P 500 TR USD $20,644.16

2007   2008   2009   2010   2011   2012   2013   2014   2015   2016

3 Year Average Morningstar Risk Measures

Risk vs. Category (1467)	+Avg
Return vs. Category (1467)	+Avg

Low   Avg   High

Investment Strategy

The investment seeks long-term capital growth; income is a secondary objective. The fund will normally invest at least 80% of its net assets (including any borrowings for investment purposes) in the common stocks of large- and medium-sized blue chip growth companies. It focuses on companies with leading market positions, seasoned management, and strong financial fundamentals. The fund may sell securities for a variety of reasons, such as to secure gains, limit losses, or redeploy assets into more promising opportunities.

Pillars

Process	Positive
Performance	Positive
People	Positive
Parent	Positive
Price	Positive
Rating	

Style Map

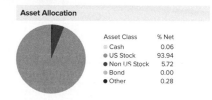

Giant
Large   ◉ Weighted Average of Holdings
Medium   ● 75% of Fund's Stock Holdings
Small
Micro

Deep Core Core Core High
Val   Val   Grow Grow

Performance 06-06-2016

	YTD	1 Mo	1 Yr	3 Yr Ann	5 Yr Ann	10 Yr Ann
Growth of 10,000	9,744	10,357	10,088	14,930	19,639	24,154
Fund	−2.56	3.57	0.88	14.29	14.45	9.22
+/- S&P 500 TR USD	−6.77	0.79	−2.14	2.84	1.64	1.69
+/- Category	−2.65	0.17	2.26	3.17	3.34	1.70
% Rank in Cat	86	41	26	7	3	13
# of Funds in Cat	1,648	1,659	1,580	1,444	1,270	915

*Currency is displayed in BASE

Top Holdings 03-31-2016

	Weight %	Last Price	Day Chg %	52 Week Range
T Amazon.com Inc	6.89	726.73 BASE	0.16]	419.14 − 731.50
T Alphabet Inc C	4.42	716.55 BASE	−0.80 [	515.18 − 789.87
T Facebook Inc A	4.37	118.79 BASE	0.27]	72.00 − 135.60
T The Priceline Group Inc	3.61	— BASE	3.64]	954.02 − 1,476.52
T Microsoft Corp	3.13	52.13 BASE	0.66]	39.72 − 56.85

% Assets in Top 5 Holdings   22.42

TIncrease   YDecrease   RNew to Portfolio

Asset Allocation

Asset Class	% Net
● Cash	0.06
● US Stock	93.94
● Non US Stock	5.72
● Bond	0.00
● Other	0.28

Management

Start Date
06-30-1993

Larry J. Puglia

Top Sectors 03-31-2016

	Fund	3 Yr High	3 Yr Low	Cat Avg	Fund ▼Cat Avg	
t Consumer Cyclical	25.67	26.02	24.12	18.15		
d Healthcare	23.07	26.25	23.07	17.76		
a Technology	22.51	22.51	14.96	26.71		
p Industrials	11.92	14.72	10.94	10.17		
y Financial Services	10.34	11.09	10.10	10.05		

0   10   20   30   40

Dividend and Capital Gains Distributions

Distribution Date	Distribution NAV	Long-Term Capital Gain	Short-Term Capital Gain	Return of Capital	Dividend Income	Distribution Total
12-14-2015	71.50	2.3600	0.0000	0.0000	0.0000	2.3600
12-12-2014	66.04	3.2600	0.0000	0.0000	0.0000	3.2600
12-14-2012	44.89	0.0000	0.0000	0.0000	0.1400	0.1400
12-30-2011	38.65	0.0000	0.0000	0.0000	0.0100	0.0100
12-14-2011	37.37	0.0000	0.0000	0.0000	0.0400	0.0400

T. Rowe Price Blue Chip Growth Fund TRBCX

Performance

Growth of 10,000 05-31-2016

Legend: ■ TRBCX ■ Category LG ■ Index S&P 500 TR USD

2006	2007	2008	2009	2010	2011	2012	2013	2014	2015	YTD	History
9.73	13.02	−42.62	42.57	16.42	1.50	18.41	41.57	9.28	11.15	−3.18	TRBCX
15.79	5.49	−37.00	26.46	15.06	2.11	16.00	32.39	13.69	1.38	3.57	S&P 500 TR USD
7.05	13.35	−40.67	35.68	15.53	−2.46	15.34	33.92	10.00	3.60	−0.51	Category (LG)
−6.07	7.53	−5.63	16.10	1.35	−0.61	2.41	9.19	−4.41	9.76	−6.75	+/− S&P 500 TR USD
2.67	−0.33	−1.96	6.89	0.89	3.96	3.07	7.65	−0.72	7.55	−2.67	+/− Category (LG)
—	—	—	—	—	—	—	—	—	—	—	Income USD
—	—	—	—	—	—	—	—	—	—	—	Capital Gains USD
—	—	—	—	—	—	—	—	—	—	—	Net Assets USD Mil
25	48	69	20	39	17	18	8	60	3	86	% Rank in Category
LG	LG	LG	LG	LG	LG	LG	LG	LG	LG	LG	Fund Category

Trailing Total Returns 06-06-2016

Legend: ► TRBCX ◄ Category: LG ◄ Index: S&P 500 TR USD

Large Growth
■ Top Quartile
■ 2nd Quartile
■ 3rd Quartile
■ Bottom Quartile

1 Day	1 Wk	1 Mo	3 Mo	YTD	1 Yr	3 Yr	5 Yr	10 Yr	15 Yr	Total Return %
0.53	0.66	3.57	5.84	−2.56	0.88	14.29	14.45	9.22	6.27	TRBCX
0.49	0.53	2.78	6.05	4.22	3.02	11.46	12.81	7.53	5.53	S&P 500 TR USD
0.45	0.62	3.40	5.70	0.10	−1.38	11.13	11.11	7.52	4.80	Category (LG)
0.04	0.12	0.79	−0.21	−6.77	−2.14	2.84	1.64	1.69	0.74	+/− S&P 500 TR USD
0.07	0.04	0.17	0.14	−2.65	2.26	3.17	3.34	1.70	1.47	+/− Category (LG)
36	39	41	47	86	26	7	3	13	12	Rank in Category

Tax Analysis 05-31-2016

	1 Mo	3 Mo	6 Mo	YTD	1 Yr	3 Yr	5 Yr	10 Yr	15 Yr	Since Incpt.
Pretax Return	2.61	7.98	−3.68	−3.18	0.30	13.49	13.26	9.07	6.32	10.05
Tax-adjusted Return	2.61	7.98	−4.41	−3.18	−0.47	12.78	12.80	8.80	6.12	9.73
% Rank in Category	22	43	49	71	12	3	1	6	7	—
Tax Cost Ratio	—	—	—	—	0.76	0.63	0.41	0.25	0.18	—

Potential Cap Gains Exposure %   38.59

EXHIBIT 3.3 | Morningstar Performance Comparison of T. Rowe Price Blue Chip Growth Fund, the Large-Cap Growth Category, and the Broad Market Index (Average Total Returns %–Sept. 30, 2016)

	1-Month	3-Month	6-Month	YTD	1-Year	3-Year	5-Year	10-Year
TRP Blue Chip Growth Fund	1.48	7.52	7.24	1.35	11.34	11.56	17.86	9.11
S&P 500 Index	0.02	3.85	6.4	7.84	15.43	11.16	16.37	7.24
Large-Cap Growth Category	0.64	5.59	6.12	3.45	10.46	9.23	14.98	7.52
+/− S&P 500 Index	1.46	3.67	0.83	−6.48	−4.09	0.4	1.49	1.87
+/− Large-Cap Growth Category	0.84	1.93	1.11	−2.09	0.88	2.33	2.88	1.6
Rank in Category	15	18	25	79	40	14	5	14

Data source: Morningstar, T. Rowe Price Blue Chip Growth Fund TRBCX, at http://performance.morningstar.com/fund/performance-return.action?t=TRBCX&region=usa&culture=en-US (accessed Nov. 21, 2016).

Note: Average total return includes changes in principal value, reinvested dividends, and capital gain distributions. For periods of one year or longer, the returns are annualized. For periods less than one year, the return figures are not annualized and represent total return for the period.

EXHIBIT 3.4 | Retirement Plan Assets by Categories 1975 and 2015 (billions of dollars, end-of-period)

	1975		2015		1975–2015
	Retirement Assets ($B)	Percent	Retirement Assets ($B)	Percent	CAGR
IRAs	3	1%	7,329*	31%	22%
DC plans	91	19%	6,734	28%	11%
Private-sector DB plans	174	37%	2,791	12%	7%
State and local government DB plans	104	22%	3,664	15%	9%
Federal DB plans	42	9%	1,512	6%	9%
Annuities	55	12%	1,948	8%	9%
TOTAL	469	100%	23,978	100%	10%

CAGR = compound annual growth rate.

Data source: Created by author based on data from Investment Company Institute, https://www.ici.org/research/stats/retirement (accessed Dec. 16, 2016).

*Data are estimated.

EXHIBIT 3.5 | Expense Ratios of Actively Managed and Index Funds in Basis Points 1996–2015

Note: Expense ratios are measured as asset-weighted averages. Data exclude mutual funds available as investment choices in variable annuities and mutual funds that invest primarily in other mutual funds.

Data source: Created by author based on data from Investment Company Institute and Lipper, https://www.ici.org/pressroom/news/16_news_trends_expenses (accessed Dec. 16, 2016).

EXHIBIT 3.6 | Morningstar Performance Comparison of U.S. Mutual-Fund Categories

Name	1 Month(%)	YTD(%)	3 Month(%)	1 Year(%)	3 Year(%)	5 Year(%)
Small Value	5.03	16.37	5.30	11.31	5.89	12.11
Small Blend	4.20	12.92	4.04	8.72	5.34	11.83
Mid-Cap Value	2.62	11.48	1.77	7.91	6.20	12.21
Large Value	2.72	9.49	1.33	7.06	6.46	11.81
Mid-Cap Blend	2.08	8.45	0.75	5.43	5.42	11.57
Small Growth	2.04	7.74	1.84	4.71	4.35	11.31
Large Blend	1.63	6.29	−0.33	4.54	7.04	12.17
Mid-Cap Growth	0.43	3.41	−1.72	1.44	4.92	10.62
Large Growth	−1.78	1.57	−1.57	0.04	7.21	12.40

Note: Data through November 11, 2016. Returns are simple averages. For periods of one year or longer, the returns are annualized. For periods of less than one year, the return figures are not annualized and represent total return for the period.

Data source: Morningstar.

EXHIBIT 3.7 | Mean and Standard Deviation of Annual Returns by Major U.S. Asset Category

Series (1926–2014)	Geometric Mean	Arithmetic Mean	Standard Deviation
Large company stocks	10.1%	12.1%	20.1%
Small company stocks	12.2	16.7	32.1
Long-term corporate bonds	6.1	6.4	8.4
Long-term government	5.7	6.1	10.0
Intermediate-term government	5.3	5.4	5.6
U.S. Treasury bills	3.5	3.5	3.1
Inflation	2.0%	3.0%	4.1%

Data source: *Stocks, Bonds, Bills, and Inflation 2014 Yearbook* (Chicago: Ibbotson Associates, 2015): 34.

EXHIBIT 3.8 | Percentage of Equity Mutual Funds' Total Net Assets Invested in Index Funds 2000–2015

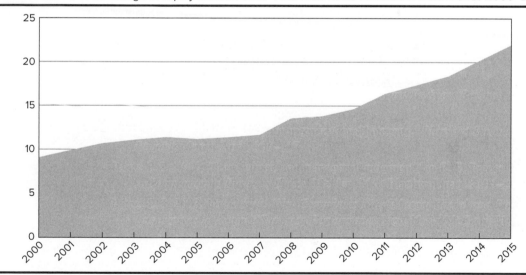

Data source: Created by author based on data from Investment Company Institute, http://www.icifactbook.org/ch2/16_fb_ch2 (accessed Dec. 16, 2016).

EXHIBIT 3.9 | Monthly Cumulative Flows to and Net-Share Issuance of U.S. Equity Mutual Funds and Index Exchange-Traded Funds (ETFs) January 2007–December 2015 (in billions of dollars)

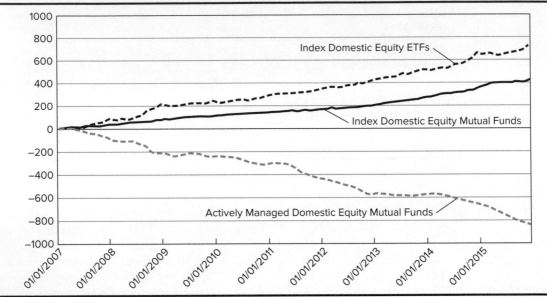

Note: Equity mutual fund flows include net new cash flow and reinvested dividends. Data exclude mutual funds that invest primarily in other mutual funds.

Data source: Created by author based on data from Investment Company Institute, http://www.icifactbook.org/ch2/16_fb_ch2 (accessed Dec. 16, 2016).

Genzyme and Relational Investors: Science and Business Collide?

For Marblehead Neck, Massachusetts, it was an unusually warm morning in April 2009, so Henri Termeer decided to take a leisurely walk on the beach. Termeer had some serious issues to consider and often found that the fresh sea air and solitude did wonders for his thought process. For more than 20 years, Termeer had been the chairman and CEO of Genzyme Corporation, based in Cambridge, Massachusetts. Under his watch, Genzyme had grown from an entrepreneurial venture to one the country's top-five biotechnology firms (**Exhibit 4.1** shows Genzyme's financial statements).

There were bumps along the way accompanying Termeer's achievements, and a recent event was one of them. The week before, Termeer had sat in a presentation by Ralph Whitworth, cofounder and principal of a large activist investment fund, Relational Investors (RI). Whitworth's company now had a 2.6% stake[1] in Genzyme (**Exhibit 4.2** shows Genzyme's top 10 shareholders). Whitworth had a history of engagements with the board of directors of numerous companies, and in several instances, the CEO had been forced to resign. In January, when RI had announced its initial 1% investment in Termeer's company, the two men had met for a meeting at the JP Morgan Healthcare Conference, and the discussion had been amicable. Whitworth and his team then traveled in April to Genzyme's headquarters and talked about Genzyme's core business, value creation, and the lack of transparency in some of the company's communications.

Termeer was proud of his company's accomplishments, shown by the number of people with rare diseases who had been successfully treated with Genzyme's products. He was also pleased with the long-term growth in the price of Genzyme's stock, which had easily outperformed the market over the last several years. In fact, the company had just

---

[1]Relational Investors Form 13F, March 31, 2009.

posted record revenues of \$4.6 billion for 2008. Although the 2007–08 financial crisis had affected the stock market overall, Genzyme, along with the biotechnology industry, was faring better than most (see **Exhibit 4.3** for charts on Genzyme's stock performance).

But a bigger blow came about a month after Termeer's first introduction to Whitworth. An operational problem surfaced in the company's plant in Allston, Massachusetts, followed by an official warning letter from the U.S. Food and Drug Administration (FDA) on February 27, 2009. The company responded to the FDA by publicly disclosing its manufacturing issues. Genzyme began conducting a quality assessment of its system, and Whitworth had expressed his confidence in the company's actions to address the issues. Recent news on the impending health care reform bill also hit companies in the health care sector hard. Genzyme's stock price, which had declined by 21% over five trading days, had yet to recover.

On top of handling Whitworth's demands, Termeer had to prepare for the shareholders' annual meeting scheduled for May 21. As Termeer mulled over the sequence of past events, the name of Whitworth's RI fund suggested to him that relationship building was its modus operandi and that perhaps Whitworth genuinely wanted to help Genzyme increase its performance. Up to this time, Termeer had not considered RI to be a threat, but if there were other corporate activists or hedge funds monitoring his company and looking to set its corporate policy, then maybe he should take note that Genzyme now had an "activist" investor. What should he do?

Biotechnology

Cheeses, beer, and wine had at least one thing in common: the application of biological science in the form of bacteria processing. The use of living organisms to stimulate chemical reactions had been taking place for thousands of years. But since the mid-20th century, when revolutionary research in genetics led to the description of the structure of DNA, molecular biology had been transformed into a thriving industry. Products among the 1,200 plus biotechnology companies in 2008 included innovations in the treatment of multiple sclerosis, rheumatoid arthritis, cancer, autoimmune disorders, and diabetes.

Biotechnology drugs were normally far more complex to produce than the chemical-based blockbuster drugs developed by Big Pharma companies. The U.S. Supreme Court recognized patent rights on genetically altered life forms in the early 1980s, and the U.S. Congress passed the Orphan Drug Act in 1983. Intended to attract investment for research and development (R&D) in the treatment of rare diseases (those affecting less than 200,000 people), the act gave companies that brought successful drugs to market a seven-year monopoly on sales.[2]

This exclusive sales incentive was not a free lunch, however; its purpose was to offset the numerous uncertainties in biotechnology development. Many of these uncertainties pertained to the U.S. drug approval process itself, one of the most rigorous in the world. In addition to the extremely high cost of R&D, a lengthy process was required to get new products to market. After a particular disease was targeted, its treatment went

---

[2]Steven Silver, "Biotechnology," *Standard and Poor's Industry Surveys* (August 19, 2010): 9.

through a series of chemical tests to determine therapeutic effectiveness and to uncover potential side effects. Preclinical studies were then done by testing animals over a period of years. Only then could the company submit an investigational new drug application to the FDA to begin clinical testing on humans.

Clinical trials on humans consisted of three phases: (1) testing the drug's safety by giving small doses to relatively healthy people; (2) administering the drug to patients suffering from the targeted disease or condition; and (3) employing random double-blind tests to eliminate bias in the process. Typically, one group of patients was given the potential drug, and the other group was given an inert substance or placebo. Due to the rigorous nature of the clinical trials, only about 5% to 10% of drugs that reached the testing stage ultimately received approval for marketing.[3] Not surprisingly, the biotechnology industry's R&D spending as a percentage of revenues was among the highest of any U.S. industry group.

The level of R&D expenditures made it crucial to get new drugs to market quickly. The FDA's Center for Drug Evaluation and Research was responsible for reviewing therapeutic biological products and chemical-based drugs. Unfortunately, inadequate funding and staffing of the FDA resulted in missed deadlines and a low level of final approvals. In 2008, the regulator approved 24 new drugs, out of which only 6 were biologic.[4] By 2009, it was estimated that, on average, new products took more than eight years to get through the clinical development and regulatory process.

The industry weathered the financial storms in 2007–08 relatively well, as demand for biotechnology products depended more on the population's health than the economy (see **Exhibit 4.4** for financial metrics for Genzyme and its major competitors). This was particularly true for large-cap companies with strong cash flows that did not need to access capital markets. Of more importance to some industry observers was that strong biotechnology companies might come under increased merger and acquisition (M&A) pressure from Big Pharma because these companies faced patent expirations on key blockbuster drugs in the coming years.[5]

Genzyme Corporation

Henry Blair, a Tufts University scientist, and Sheridan Snyder founded Genzyme in 1981 to develop products based on enzyme technologies.[6] Using venture capital funding, they purchased a small company, Whatman Biochemicals Ltd., which was absorbed into Genzyme. In 1983 (the same year that the Orphan Drug Act was passed), they recruited Henri Termeer to be president, joining the other 10 employees. Termeer had spent the previous 10 years with Baxter Travenol (later Baxter International), including several years running its German subsidiary. He left his lucrative position at Baxter to join the start-up. Shortly after Termeer became CEO, Genzyme raised $28.5 million in its 1986 IPO and began trading on the NASDAQ (ticker: GENZ).

---

[3]Silver, 6.

[4]Silver, 5.

[5]Silver, 9.

[6]An enzyme is basically one of a number of proteins produced by the body that functions as a catalyst for a biochemical process.

An accidental meeting between Termeer and a former Baxter colleague turned into a masterful acquisition for Genzyme. On a return flight from Chicago to Boston in 1989, Termeer and Robert Carpenter, chairman and CEO of Integrated Genetics (IG), based in Framingham, Massachusetts, discussed the businesses and finances of the two companies. Several months later, Genzyme purchased IG with its own stock for the equivalent of $31.5 million or less than $3 per share. Overnight Genzyme's expertise received a considerable boost in several areas of biotechnology: molecular biology, protein and nuclear acid chemistry, and enzymology.[7] Carpenter served as executive vice president of Genzyme for the next two years and was elected to the board of directors in 1994 (**Exhibit 4.5** lists Genzyme board members).

Avoiding the glamorous blockbuster drug industry, Termeer established Genzyme's footprint in the treatment of genetic disorders. His goal was to create targeted drugs to completely cure these diseases, despite the statistically small populations that were afflicted. In the company's formative years, Termeer focused R&D on lysosomal storage disorders (LSDs). Commonalities among LSD patients were inherited life-threatening enzyme deficiencies that allowed the buildup of harmful substances. Cures were aimed at creating the genetic material to generate the deficient enzymes naturally in these patients.

Genzyme's most rewarding product was the first effective long-term enzyme replacement therapy for patients with a confirmed diagnosis of Type I Gaucher's disease. This inherited disease was caused by deficiency of an enzyme necessary for the body to metabolize certain fatty substances. The deficiency produced several crippling conditions such as bone disease, enlarged liver or spleen, anemia, or thrombocytopenia (low blood platelet count).

Initially, the product was known as Ceredase and received a great deal of attention for its life-saving treatment. It was approved by the FDA in 1991 and protected by the Orphan Drug Act, but its success was not without controversy. The price for Ceredase was $150,000 per patient, per year, making it one of the most expensive drugs sold at the time. Genzyme argued that the price reflected the extraordinary expense of production; a year's supply for a single patient required enzyme extraction from approximately 20,000 protein-rich placentas drawn from a multitude of hospitals around the world.[8] By 1994, however, Genzyme's laboratories had developed Cerezyme, a genetically engineered replacement for Ceredase that was administered via intravenous infusion. Cerezyme was approved by the FDA in 1995 and also qualified for protection under the Orphan Drug Act.

Further successes against LSDs included Fabrazyme (to treat Fabry disease) and Myozyme (to treat Pompe disease). Fabry disease was caused by GL-3, a substance in cells lining the blood vessels of the kidney. Pompe disease shrank a patient's muscles, eventually affecting the lungs and heart. These two drugs, along with Cerezyme, formed the core business of the company and were developed and sold by its genetic disease segment (GD).

---

[7]Bruce P. Montgomery, updated by Steven Meyer and Jeffrey L. Covell, "Genzyme Corporation," *International Directory of Company Histories*, ed. Jay P. Pederson, 77 (Detroit: St. James Press), 165.

[8]Montgomery, 166.

Termeer was particularly proud of Genzyme's scientific team for developing Myozyme. Pompe disease was a debilitating illness that affected both infants and adults. The symptoms for adults included a gradual loss of muscle strength and ability to breathe. Depending on the individual, the rate of decline varied, but patients eventually needed a wheelchair and ultimately died prematurely most often because of respiratory failure. The symptoms were similar for infants, but progressed at a faster rate, so death from cardiac or respiratory failure occurred within the first year of life. The first human trials for Myozyme were conducted on a small sample of newborns and resulted in 100% of the infants surviving their first year. This success was so dramatic that the European regulators approved the drug for infants and for adults.

Concurrent with the company's focus on genetic disorders, it also invested in the development of hyaluronic acid-based drugs to reduce the formation of postoperative adhesions. Initially, it raised funds in 1989 through a secondary stock offering and an R&D limited partnership. The research the company conducted was significantly advanced by the acquisition of Biomatrix, Inc., in 2000, forming the biosurgery segment (BI).

Termeer also searched for nascent biotechnology research companies that had good products but limited capital or marketing capabilities. As a result, he created numerous alliances and joint ventures, providing funding in exchange for a share of future revenue streams. As one example, Genzyme formed a joint venture in 1997 with GelTex Pharmaceuticals, which specialized in the treatment of conditions in the gastrointestinal tract. GelTex's first drug, RenaGel, bound dietary phosphates in patients with chronic kidney dysfunction.

After 1997, Termeer completed a host of acquisitions. To some extent, the opportunity for these acquisitions resulted from the economic woes of other biotechnology firms whose clinical failures affected their funding abilities, resulting in research cuts and layoffs. Smaller start-up firms were vulnerable to economic stress if their flagship drug failed to succeed in time. These conditions suited Termeer, who had begun a broad strategy to diversify. But his strategy was not without risks because even drugs acquired in late-stage development had not yet been approved by the FDA.

Many of Genzyme's acquisitions were new drugs in various stages of development (**Exhibit 4.6** shows Genzyme's major acquisitions). They were generally considered to be incomplete biotechnologies that required additional research, development, and testing before reaching technological feasibility. Given the risk that eventual regulatory approval might not be obtained, the technology may not have been considered to have any alternative future use. In those cases, Genzyme calculated the fair value of the technology and expensed it on the acquisition date as in-process research and development (IPR&D).

Over time, Genzyme reorganized or added business segments based on its own R&D results and the addition of acquired firms. By December 2008, the company was organized into four major segments: GD, cardiometabolic and renal (CR), BI, and hematologic oncology (HO). (**Exhibit 4.7** displays segment product offerings and the fraction of 2008 revenues generated by each product).

In its presentation, RI had analyzed the performance of Genzyme's business segments using a metric called *cash flow return on investment* or CFROI. The idea was to quantify the profit generated with respect to the capital that was invested in each business line (**Exhibit 4.8** shows the CFROI estimates by RI for 2008). Termeer asked Genzyme's CFO to review the analysis. He believed the performance of the GD division was correct, but he was not sure about the low performance of the other segments.

The goal of Termeer's diversification strategy was to create solutions for curing more common diseases and to broaden the groups of patients who benefited.[9] Termeer was also a member of the board of directors of Project HOPE, an international nonprofit health education and humanitarian assistance organization. Through a partnership with Project HOPE, Genzyme provided life-saving treatment at no cost to patients in developing countries, particularly those with inadequate health care services or medical plans.

Like most biotechnology firms, Genzyme did not pay dividends to its shareholders. As it stated, "We have never paid a cash dividend on our shares of stock. We currently intend to retain our earnings to finance future growth and do not anticipate paying any cash dividends on our stock in the foreseeable future."[10] The company had repurchased shares of its common stock amounting to $231.5 million in 2006 and $143 million in 2007, but these were offset by issuances of shares to honor option exercises. There was no open market share repurchase program.

In terms of operations, the $200 million manufacturing facility Genzyme had built in Allston produced the company's primary genetic drugs, Cerezyme, Fabrazyme, and Myozyme. A new facility was being constructed in Framingham, and major international facilities were located in England, Ireland, and Belgium. Administrative activities, sales, and marketing were all centered in Cambridge and Framingham. All was well until the first quarter of 2009, when Termeer received the FDA warning letter in February outlining deficiencies in the Allston plant. The "significant objectionable conditions" fell into four categories: maintenance of equipment, computerized systems, production controls, and failure to follow procedures regarding the prevention of microbiological contamination.[11] The problems in the Allston plant could be traced back to Termeer's decision to stretch the production capacity of the plant to meet an unanticipated demand for Myozyme. Production had increased, but the strain placed on the complex processes eventually led to the problems cited by the FDA. Anything that disrupted the production of the plant concerned Termeer because it produced Genzyme's best-selling products, and those medications were critical to the well-being of the patients who used them.

Relational Investors

If only one word were used to describe 52-year-old Ralph Whitworth, cofounder of Relational Investors, it would be "performance." While attending high school in Nevada, he raced his red 1965 Pontiac GTO against friends on the desert roads near his home town of Winnemucca, outperforming them all. After obtaining a JD from

---

[9]Geoffrey Gagnon, "So This Is What a Biotech Tycoon Looks Like," *Boston Magazine*, June 2008.

[10]Genzyme Corporation, 10-K filing, 2009.

[11]David Armstrong, "FDA Warns Genzyme on Plant Conditions—Agency's Critique of Production Could Further Delay Biotech Company's Pompe Drug," *Wall Street Journal,* March 11, 2009.

Georgetown University Law Center, Whitworth accepted a job with T. Boone Pickens, the famous "corporate raider" of the 1980s, and gained what he called "a PhD in capitalism" in the process.[12] He left Pickens in 1996 to found RI with David Batchelder whom he had met while working for Pickens. The largest initial investment was the $200 million that came from the California Public Employees' Retirement System (CalPERS). In recognition of RI's performance, CalPERS had invested a total of $1.3 billion in RI by 2008. (**Exhibit 4.9** illustrates RI's annual performance.)

RI was commonly classified by observers as an "activist" investment fund. The typical target firm was a company whose discounted cash flow analysis provided a higher valuation than the company's market price. Whitworth trained his executives to view the gap between a company's intrinsic value and its market price as the result of an entrenched management taking care of itself at the expense of its shareholders.[13] Specifically, Whitworth felt the value gap came primarily from two sources: (1) money not being spent efficiently enough to earn adequate returns, and/or (2) the company suffered from major corporate governance issues.[14] Common causes of underperformance were firm diversification strategies that were not providing an adequate return to shareholders, poor integration results with a merger partner or acquisition, or the misalignment of management incentives.

Once a firm was targeted, RI typically took a 1% to 10% stake in it and then engaged management with questions backed up by a RI detailed analysis. Depending upon the particular responses from executives and directors, Whitworth would follow one of several paths. For example, he might request certain changes or consider making criticisms public. Resistance might result in isolated pressure on one or more executives or board members. In other instances, Whitworth might request a seat on the board, suggest a change in executive management or board composition, or initiate a proxy fight.[15] Management and board compensation was a favorite target of RI criticism—one that was never well received by the target firm. Similar to most people's view of an athlete, Whitworth had no objections regarding high compensation for executives, so long as they performed. (**Exhibit 4.10** illustrates some of RI's major corporate governance engagements in the past.)

As one example, in late 2006, Whitworth and Batchelder contacted the board of Home Depot requesting changes in the company's strategy. By then, RI had purchased $1 billion of Home Depot stock. Specifically, they criticized CEO Robert Nardelli's decision to shift the company's focus to a lower-margin commercial supply business, which Nardelli considered a growth opportunity. This proved to be commercially unsuccessful. As a result, Nardelli had increased revenues, which was in keeping with his board-approved incentive contract, but earnings suffered. After the engagement of RI, Batchelder joined the board, and Nardelli was ousted.

---

[12]Francesco Guerrera and James Politi, "The Lone Ranger of Boardroom Battles," *Financial Times,* February 25, 2008.

[13]Jonathan R. Laing, "Insiders, Look Out!," *Barron's,* February 19, 2007.

[14]Aaron Bernstein and Jeffery M. Cunningham, "The Alchemist," *Directorship*, June/July 2007.

[15]Laing, "Insiders, Look Out!"

In another instance, this time with Sovereign Bancorp, corporate governance was the key issue. One director was found to have executed private transactions in branch offices. Another had an undisclosed ownership in a landscaping company that the bank hired. Instead of the more normal compensation of $80,000 paid to board members of similarly sized banks, Sovereign Bancorp's board members received $320,000 a year.[16] After uncovering these events and fighting with the board, Whitworth succeeded in being elected to it, and the CEO Jay Sidhu was ousted.

At its peak, RI's engagements comprised a total portfolio of $8.4 billion at the end of third quarter 2007. Given the drop in share prices following the financial crisis and the impact of several redemptions from investors, RI's portfolio value had been reduced to $4.3 billion by the end of March 2009. (**Exhibit 4.11** lists the amount of RI's engagements as of September 30 for each year since 2001 as well as the active engagements that RI had as of March 31, 2009).

Which Path to Follow?

When Termeer finished his walk on the beach, he returned to the office, where he reviewed Whitworth's presentation slides. The main slide illustrated RI's calculation of the present value of each of Genzyme's divisions plus its R&D pipeline. The sum of these, representing RI's valuation of Genzyme, is compared to the company's current stock price (**Exhibit 4.12** shows RI's valuation analysis of Genzyme). It showed that Genzyme's share price was trading at $34 below its fundamental value—a significant discount. RI then offered recommendations as to how Genzyme could address this:

1. Improve capital allocation decision making to ensure that spending would be focused on the investment with the highest expected return.
2. Implement a share-buyback or dividend program.
3. Improve board composition by adding more members with financial expertise.
4. Focus executive compensation on the achievement of performance metrics.

Termeer reflected on the first two items on the RI list. During his presentation, Whitworth stated how impressed he was with Genzyme's growth and complemented Termeer on how well he had been able to create significant shareholder value. But Whitworth anticipated that the years of successful growth were about to lead to high positive cash flow for several years. (**Exhibit 4.13** shows how RI expected Genzyme to generate significant cash flow in the coming years.) That positive cash flow would create new challenges for Termeer. Whitworth explained that CEOs often failed to realize that value-adding investment opportunities were not available at the level of the cash flows being produced. As the CEOs continued to invest the large cash flows into lower-return investments, the market would eventually react negatively to the overinvestment problem and cause the share price to decline. Whitworth argued that it was better for

---

[16]Bernstein and Cunningham, 13.

management to distribute the newly found cash flow as part of a share repurchase program. Moreover, he thought Genzyme could leverage its share repurchases by obtaining external funding because Genzyme's balance sheet could support a significant increase in debt.

Termeer realized it would be difficult for him to change his conservative views about leverage, particularly in light of the fact that he had been so successful in building the company without relying on debt.[17] The thought of using debt to enhance a share repurchase program was doubly difficult for him to accept. But even more important was his opinion that one had to take a long-term view to succeed in biotechnology. Whitworth seemed to see investments as simply a use of cash, whereas Termeer saw investments as being critical to the business model and survival of Genzyme. In fact, the higher cash flow level would make it easier to fund the investments because it would reduce or eliminate the need to access capital markets. Termeer had always envisioned a future where diagnostics and therapeutics would be closer together, and now he recognized that this future would require Genzyme to pursue a variety of technologies on an on-going basis.

Then Termeer's eyes caught the third item on the list about adding board members with financial expertise. This brought to mind the earlier demands by another activist investor, Carl Icahn, who had purchased 1.5 million shares of Genzyme during third quarter 2007.[18] Termeer had strongly protested Icahn's involvement, and with the support of the board made a public plea to shareholders that ultimately led Icahn to sell his Genzyme shares and turn his attention to Biogen Idec, another major biotechnology company.[19]

In Termeer's mind, Icahn was more than just an activist investor. During his long career, Icahn had earned the title of "corporate raider" by taking large stakes in companies that often culminated in a takeover or, at a minimum, in a contentious proxy fight. Earlier in the year, Icahn had taken a large position in MedImmune, Inc., and helped arrange the sale of the company to AstraZeneca PLC. Were the current circumstances such that Icahn would see another opportunity to target Genzyme again? Where would Whitworth stand on this? "After all, at the end of the day, both Icahn and Whitworth are just after the cash flow," said Termeer.

Other recent events were on Termeer's mind as well. Genentech, the second-largest U.S. biotechnology firm and one of Genzyme's competitors, had just lost a bitterly contested hostile takeover from Roche Holding AG at the start of 2009. This takeover reminded Termeer of the possibility that some Big Pharma companies were looking to expand their operations into biotechnology.

As Termeer reflected on the last 26 years spent creating and building Genzyme, he realized that Whitworth's RI fund had been a shareholder for less than a year and held only 2.6% of the shares. It was no surprise these two men held such different viewpoints of what Genzyme had to offer to its owners and to society. Termeer, aware that he

---

[17]Geoffrey Gagnon, "So This Is What a Biotech Tycoon Looks Like."

[18]Capital IQ, "Genzyme Corporation," Public Ownership, Detailed, History—Carl Icahn LLC.

[19]Gagnon, "Biotech Tycoon."

needed a strategy for dealing with Whitworth, had identified three different approaches he could take:

1. Fight Whitworth as he had fought Icahn. To do this, he would need to enlist the board to join him in what would be a public relations battle for shareholder support.

2. Welcome Whitworth onto the board to reap the benefits of his experience in how to create shareholder value. In this regard, he could think of Whitworth as a free consultant.

3. Manage Whitworth by giving him some items on his list of demands but nothing that would compromise the core mission of Genzyme.

He had arranged for a phone call with Whitworth in the following week. Regardless of his approach, Termeer expected that Whitworth would probably request a hearing at the board meeting, which was scheduled two days before the annual shareholders' meeting on May 21. The prospect of such a meeting with the board only served to emphasize the importance of Termeer's having a strategy for the upcoming call with Whitworth and making decisions that would be in the best interest of his company.

EXHIBIT 4.1 | Income Statements

Amounts in $ thousands	2006	2007	2008
Revenue			
Net product sales	$2,887,409	$3,457,778	$4,196,907
Net service sales	282,118	326,326	366,091
Research & development revenue	17,486	29,415	42,041
Total revenues	3,187,013	3,813,519	4,605,039
Operating Costs			
Cost of products and services sold	735,671	927,330	1,148,562
Selling and administrative expenses	1,010,400	1,187,184	1,338,190
Research & development	649,951	737,685	1,308,330
Amortization of goodwill	209,355	201,105	226,442
Purchase of in-process R&D	552,900	106,350	0
Charges for impaired assets	219,245	0	2,036
Other operating expenses	3,377,522	3,159,654	4,023,560
Operating income (loss)	(190,509)	653,865	581,479
Investment income	56,001	70,196	51,260
Interest expense	(15,478)	(12,147)	(4,418)
Equity method investments	88,935	20,465	(3,139)
All other income (expense)	8,373	3,295	356
Total other income (expenses)	137,831	81,809	44,059
Income before income taxes	(52,678)	735,674	625,538
Provision for income taxes	35,881	(255,481)	(204,457)
Net income (loss)	($16,797)	$480,193	$421,081
Earnings per share			
Basic	($0.06)	$1.82	$1.57
Diluted	($0.06)	$1.74	$1.50

Data source: Genzyme Corporation, 10-K filing, 2008.

EXHIBIT 4.1 | Balance Sheets (*continued*)

Amounts in $ thousands	2006	2007	2008
Assets			
Cash and equivalents	$492,170	$867,012	$572,106
Short-term investments	119,894	80,445	57,507
Accounts receivable	746,746	904,101	1,036,940
Inventory	374,644	439,115	453,437
Other current assets	256,047	331,158	396,145
Total current assets	1,989,501	2,621,831	2,516,135
Property, plant & equipment—net	1,610,593	1,968,402	2,306,567
Investments—long term	740,103	602,118	427,403
Goodwill	1,298,781	1,403,828	1,401,074
Other intangibles	1,492,038	1,555,652	1,654,698
Other long-term assets	60,172	162,544	365,399
Total Assets	$7,191,188	$8,314,375	$8,671,276
Liabilities			
Accounts payable	$98,063	$128,380	$127,869
Accrued expenses payable	532,295	645,645	765,386
Current portion—long-term debt	6,226	696,625	7,566
Other short-term liabilities	14,855	13,277	13,462
Current Liabilities	651,439	1,483,927	914,283
Long-term debt	809,803	113,748	124,341
Other liabilities	69,235	103,763	326,659
Total Liabilities	1,530,477	1,701,438	1,365,283
Shareholders' Equity (a)			
Common stock and paid-in capital	5,108,904	5,387,814	5,783,460
Retained earnings	551,807	1,225,123	1,522,533
Total Equity	5,660,711	6,612,937	7,305,993
Total Liabilities and Shareholders' Equity	$7,191,188	$8,314,375	$8,671,276
Shares outstanding at December 31 (000)	263,026	266,008	270,704

Data source: Genzyme Corporation, 10-K filings, 2007 and 2008.

EXHIBIT 4.1 I   Statement of Cash Flows   (*continued*)

Amounts in $ thousands	2006	2007	2008
Cash from operations			
Net income	($16,797)	$480,193	$421,081
Depreciation & amortization	331,389	338,196	374,664
Stock-based compensation	208,614	190,070	187,596
Change in operating assets	(73,311)	(117,862)	(90,615)
Purchase of in-process R&D	552,900	106,350	0
Charge for impaired assets	219,243	0	2,036
Deferred income tax benefit	(279,795)	(106,140)	(195,200)
Other operating cash flows	(53,674)	27,865	59,613
Cash from operations	888,569	918,672	759,175
Cash from investing			
Capital expenditure	(333,675)	(412,872)	(597,562)
Acquisitions, net of acquired cash	(568,953)	(342,456)	(16,561)
Net sale (purchase) of investments	13,168	205,614	188,127
Net sale (purchase) of equity securities	132,588	(1,282)	(80,062)
Other investing activities	(79,540)	(40,060)	(75,482)
Cash from investing	(836,412)	(591,056)	(581,540)
Cash from financing			
Net long-term debt issued/repaid	(4,501)	(5,909)	(693,961)
Issuance of common stock	158,305	285,762	318,753
Repurchase of common stock	0	(231,576)	(143,012)
Other financing activities	(5,751)	(1,051)	45,679
Cash from financing	148,053	47,226	(472,541)
Net change in cash & equivalents	$200,210	$374,842	($294,906)

Data source: Genzyme Corporation, 10-K filing, 2008.

EXHIBIT 4.2 | Top 10 Shareholders, March 31, 2009

	Shares Held	%
Clearbridge Advisors, LLC	15,103,597	5.7%
Barclays Global Investors, UK, Ltd.	11,974,523	4.5%
Wellington Management Co., LLP	10,790,760	4.0%
State Street Global Advisors, Inc.	9,326,639	3.5%
The Vanguard Group, Inc.	9,066,174	3.4%
Sands Capital Management, LLC	8,372,483	3.1%
UBS Global Asset Management	7,722,011	2.9%
Fidelity Investments	6,995,691	2.6%
Relational Investors LLC	6,942,506	2.6%
PRIMECAP Management Company	6,330,985	2.4%
SG Gestion	5,804,357	2.2%
Massachusetts Financial Services Company	5,522,034	2.1%
Total shares outstanding:	267,019,462	

Data source: Forms 13F filed by investors.

EXHIBIT 4.3 | Genzyme (GENZ) vs. S&P 500 (S&P) and NASDAQ Biotechnology Index (NBI), Weekly Close—Base = 1/1/2003

— GENZ ✱ NBI --- S&P

Genzyme Daily Closing Price (GENZ)

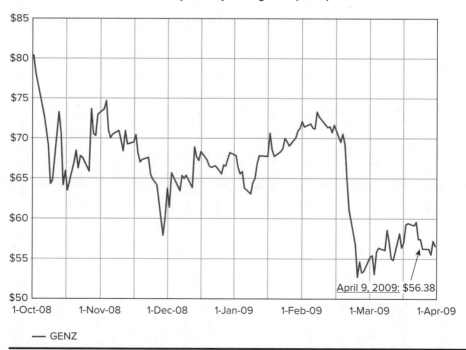

— GENZ

Data source: Bloomberg.

EXHIBIT 4.4 | Biotechnology Financial Metrics as of December 2008

Amounts in $ millions	Genzyme * GENZ	Amgen AMGN	Biogen Idec BIIB	Celgene CELG	Cephalon CEPH	Genentech DNA	Gilead Sci. GILD
Beta	0.70	0.65	0.75	0.80	0.70	n/a	0.65
Price as of 12/31/2008	$66.37	$57.75	$47.63	$55.28	$77.04	$82.91	$51.14
Market capitalization	$17,967	$60,464	$13,720	$25,381	$5,295	$87,304	$46,528
Revenues	$4,605	$15,003	$4,098	$2,255	$1,975	$10,531	$5,336
Return on Assets (ROA)	5.0	11.8	9.1	n/a	6.7	n/a	31.3
Return on Equity (ROE)	6.1	21.9	13.8	n/a	15.9	n/a	52.8
Net income	$421	$4,196	$783	($1,534)	$223	$3,427	$2,011
Net profit margin	9.1%	28.0%	19.1%	−68.0%	11.3%	32.5%	37.7%
EPS (weighted avg.)	$1.57	$3.92	$2.68	($3.47)	$3.28	$3.21	$2.18
P/E (trailing)	42.3	14.7	17.8	n/a	23.5	25.8	23.4
Dividends	$0	$0	$0	$0	$0	$0	$0
Share buybacks (a)	($143)	($2,268)	($739)	$0	($43)	($780)	($1,970)
Research & development	$1,308	$3,030	$1,072	$931	$362	$2,800	$722
R&D as % of revenues	28.4%	20.2%	26.2%	41.3%	18.3%	26.6%	13.5%
Cash flow—operations	$759	$5,988	$1,564	$182	($2)	$3,955	$2,204
Cash flow—investing	(582)	(3,165)	(366)	(522)	(108)	(1,667)	(178)
Cash flow—financing	(472)	(3,073)	(1,236)	214	(184)	(269)	(1,535)
Inc (Dec) in Cash Flow	($295)	($250)	($38)	($126)	($294)	$2,019	$491
Cash Flow/share	($1.10)	($0.23)	($0.13)	($0.28)	($4.32)	$1.89	$0.53
Book value	$7,306	$20,386	$5,806	$3,490	$1,503	$15,671	$4,152
Book value/share	$26.99	$19.47	$20.16	$7.60	$21.87	$14.88	$4.56
Price/book	2.5	3.0	2.4	7.3	3.5	5.6	11.2
Debt/Equity	1.8%	49.9%	19.2%	0.0%	68.8%	14.9%	31.4%
Debt/Debt & Equity	1.8%	33.3%	16.1%	0.0%	40.8%	12.9%	23.9%
Interest coverage ratio	144.1	17.6	22.7	n/a	7.3	67.2	228.8

Notes: (a) Share buybacks for Genzyme and Cephalon represent purchases to satisfy option exercises.

Data Sources: Company 10-K filings, 2008; Silver, "Biotechnology" exhibits.

EXHIBIT 4.5 | Board of Directors, March 31, 2009

Director	Committee	Experience
Henri A. Termeer (1983)		Chairman of Genzyme since 1988; deputy chairman of the Federal Reserve Bank of Boston; worked for Baxter laboratories for 10 years.
Charles L. Cooney (1983)	Compensation (Chairman); Corporate Governance	Distinguished professor of chemical and biochemical engineering at MIT (joined in 1970). Principal of BioInformation Associates, Inc., a consulting firm.
Douglas A. Berthiaume (1988)	Audit (Chairman); Compensation	Chairman, president, and CEO of Waters Corporation since 1994 (manufacturer of high-performance liquid chromatography instrumentation).
Robert J. Carpenter (1994)	Compensation	President of Boston Medical Investors, Inc. (invests in health care companies); chairman of Hydra Biosciences (ion-channel-based drugs); chairman of Peptimmune Inc. from 2002–07 (treatment of autoimmune diseases); cofounder of GelTex in 1991; CEO of Integrated Genetics until purchased by Genzyme in 1989.
Victor J. Dzau, MD (2000)	Corporate Governance; Compensation	Chancellor for Health Affairs and president and CEO of Duke University Health System.
Senator Connie Mack III (2001)	Corporate Governance (Chairman), Audit	Served as senior policy advisor at two law firms (King & Spalding LLP and Shaw Pittman); U.S. senator from Florida from 1989 to 2001.
Gail K. Boudreaux (2004)	Audit	EVP, United Healthcare Group (since May 2008). Former president of Blue Cross and Blue Shield of Illinois; held various positions over 20 years at Aetna Group Insurance.
Richard F. Syron (2006)	Corporate Governance; Audit	Chairman and CEO of FHLMC (Freddie Mac) from 2003 to 2008; held executive positions at Thermo Electron from 1999 to 2003 (developed technology instruments).

Note: Date in parentheses is the first year elected to the board.

Data source: Genzyme Corporation, 14A filing, April 13, 2009.

EXHIBIT 4.6 | Acquisitions: 1997–2007 (in millions of dollars)

Date	Value	In-process R&D	Company Acquired	Drug or Business Acquired	Segment
1997	$112	$0	PharmaGenics, Inc.	Created Genzyme molecular oncology	HO
2000	1,284	118	GelTex	Obtained RenaGel (formerly a joint venture)	CR
2000	875	82	Biomatrix, Inc.	Became Genzyme Biosurgery division	BI
2001	17	17	Focal	Surgical biomaterials	BI
2003	596	158	SangStat Medical Corp.	Immune system treatment—Thymoglobulin	Other
2004	1,030	254	Ilex Oncology, Inc.	Cancer drugs—Campath and Clolar	HO
2005	659	12	Bone Care Int'l	Treatment of kidney disease—Hectorol	CR
2005	50	9	Verigen	Cartilage repair—MACI (launch in 2012)	BI
2005	12	7	Avigen	AV201—Parkinson's disease (launch in 2016)	GD
2006	589	553	AnorMED	Mozobil—stem cell transplant (approved 12/2008)	HO
2007	$350	$106	Bioenvision	Evoltra (launch 2010–13)	HO

Data Sources: LexisNexis, "Genzyme Corporation" Mergers and Acquisitions; Genzyme Corporation 10-K filings, 2000–07; Montgomery, 165.

EXHIBIT 4.7 | Main Products by Segment

Segment	Product	% of 2008 Total Revenues
Genetic Diseases (GD): The core business of the company focused on products to treat patients with genetic and other chronic debilitating diseases.	**Cerezyme**: Enzyme replacement therapy for Type 1 Gaucher's Disease; launched in 1995	29.5%
	Fabrazyme: intended to replace the missing enzyme alpha-Galactosidase in patients with the inherited Fabry disease; launched in 2001.	11.8%
	Myozyme: Lysosomal glycogen-specific enzyme for use in patients with infantile-onset of Pompe disease; launched in 2006.	7.1%
	Aldurazyme: for treatment of Mucopolysaccharidosis I (MPS I), a deficiency of a lysosomal enzyme, alpha-L-iduronidase; launched in 2003.	3.6%
	Other genetic diseases	1.1%
Cardiometabolic and Renal (CR): Treatment of renal, endocrine, and cardiovascular diseases.	**Renagel/Renvela**: Used by patients with chronic kidney disease on dialysis for the control of serum phosphorus.	16.1%
	Hectorol: Treatment of secondary hyperparathyroidism in patients with stage 3 or 4 chronic kidney disease and on dialysis. Acquired via purchase of Bone Care in 2005.	3.1%
	Thyrogen: Treatment for thyroid cancer to allow patients to avoid traditional hypothyroidism treatment.	3.5%
	Other cardiometabolic and renal	0.0%
Biosurgery (BI): Orthopaedic products; formed via purchase of Biomatrix, Inc., in 2000.	**Synvisc**: a local therapy to reduce osteoporosis knee pain, facilitating increased mobility.	6.3%
	Sepra: a family of products used by to prevent adhesions after abdominal and pelvic open surgery, including a C-section, hysterectomy, myomectomy, colectomy, or hernia repair.	3.2%
	Other biosurgery	1.2%
Hematologic Oncology (HO): cancer treatment products		2.4%
Other product revenue (Other)		11.1%

Data source: Genzyme Corporation, 10-K filings, 2008 and 2009.

EXHIBIT 4.8 | Genzyme—Estimates of CFROI by Segment (2008)

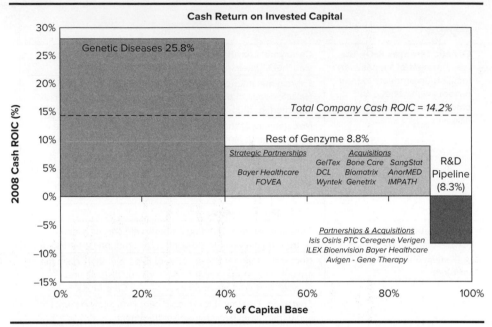

Note: Cash ROIC = Adjusted Cash Profits/Average Invested Capital.

Source: Relational Investors.

EXHIBIT 4.9 | Relational Investors—Calendar Year Performance (%)

	2002	2003	2004	2005	2006	2007	2008
Relational Investors	0.55%	40.77	16.49	9.89	9.29	−10.01	−40.01%
S&P	−22.12%	28.69	10.87	4.89	15.81	5.54	−37.01%
Alpha	22.67%	12.08	5.62	5.00	−6.52	−15.55	−4.00%

Note: RI was not required to disclose publicly its performance results. CalPERS disclosed its investment returns in RI's Corporate Governance Fund, and this serves as a good proxy for RI's performance.

Data source: "Performance Analysis for the California Public Employers' Retirement System," Wilshire Consulting (Santa Monica, CA), September 30, 2010.

EXHIBIT 4.10 | Relational Investors—High-Profile Corporate Governance Engagements

Company	Engagement Period (a)	Max. % of company	MV (b) $ millions	Corporate Governance Issues	Actions/Results
Baxter	Q1 /2004 to Q1/2009	5.1% in Q4/2007	$1,882	Ineffective board dynamics—emphasized growth at any cost. Poor capital allocation objectives.	Board hired new CEO in 2004, with 25 years experience at Abbott Labs. Revamped executive compensation.
Home Depot	Q4/2006 to Q1/2009	2.2% in Q2/2008	$ 858	CEO moved from core franchise to invest in commercial building supply business. His incentive contract emphasized revenues and earnings, not returns on equity.	Batchelder placed on board in May 2007; resulted in CEO being ousted. Forced company to abandon commercial building supply business.
National Semiconductor	Q3/2001 to Q1/2009	15.3% in Q1/2008	$ 715	Analog chip maker investing in digital chips to compete with Intel—margins @ 45% compared with competitors' 60%.	RI provided choice to stay with digital chips requiring 16% growth or stop spending and achieve 10.5%. Board chose the latter.
Sprint Nextel	Q1/2007 to Q4/2008	1.9% in Q4/2007	$ 697	Wanted to reverse the merger with Nextel and reduce focus on new subscribers.	Balance sheet was not stress-tested adequately, and reversal was abandoned.
Sovereign Bancorp	Q2/2004 to Q1/2009	8.9% in Q2/2008	$ 434	Related party transactions & other conflicts. Board members compensation of $320,000/year.	Whitworth joined board & ousted CEO, who sold part of bank without shareholder approval.
Waste Management	Q1/1998 to Q4/2004	1.3% in Q2/2004	$ 224	Questionable accounting practices; insider sales ahead of bad news.	Whitworth served on board from 1998 to 2004. He served as chairman from August to November 1999.

NOTES: (a) Represents end-of-quarter periods until the time of the case (3/2009);

(b) Represents the MV when RI held its maximum % in the company. RI's position in $ may have been higher at another time.

Sources: Relational Investors, 13F filings to March 31, 2009.

Jonathan R. Laing, "Insider's Look Out," *Barron's*, February 19, 2007.

Aaron Bernstein and Jeffrey M. Cunningham, "Whitworth: The Alchemist in the Boardroom," *Directorship*, June/July 2007.

EXHIBIT 4.11 | Relational Investors—Portfolio Investments

Total market value of equity positions held by RI (as of Sept. 30 each year)

	Total Invested ($ millions)
2001	$ 554
2002	$1,062
2003	$1,878
2004	$3,199
2005	$6,910
2006	$5,974
2007	$8,063
2008	$4,974
2009*	$4,282

*March 31, 2009.

Data source: Relational Investors, Form 13F.

List of RI's active engagements (as of 3/31/2009)

Company	Value ($000) 3/31/2009	% of RI's Total	% Owned by RI
The Home Depot, Inc.	$856,826	22.1%	2.1%
Baxter International Inc.	568,012	14.6%	1.8%
Genzyme Corporation	412,315	10.6%	2.6%
Unum Group	398,879	10.3%	9.6%
Occidental Petroleum Corp.	292,752	7.5%	0.6%
Yahoo! Inc.	269,789	7.0%	1.5%
National Semiconductor Corp.	231,011	6.0%	9.8%
Burlington Northern	211,631	5.5%	1.0%
SPDR Trust Series 1	204,733	5.3%	0.3%
Freeport-McMoran	100,610	2.6%	0.6%
Others (under $100 million each)	334,000	8.6%	n/a
Total Investments	$3,880,558	100.0%	

Data source: Relational Investors, Form 13F.

EXHIBIT 4.12 | Relational Investors' Fundamental Valuation of Genzyme

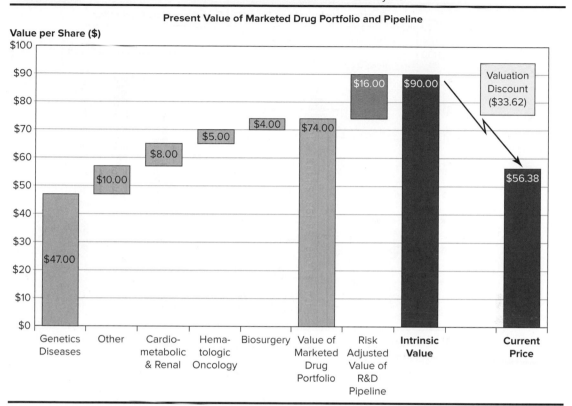

Source: Relational Investors.

EXHIBIT 4.13 | Relational Investors' Estimates of Genzyme's Free Cash Flow

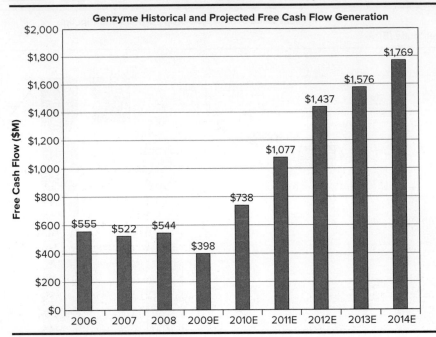

Genzyme Historical and Projected Free Cash Flow Generation

Source: Relational Investors.

## PART 2

Financial Analysis and Forecasting

Business Performance Evaluation: Approaches for Thoughtful Forecasting

Every day, fortunes are won and lost on the backs of business performance assessments and forecasts. Because of the uncertainty surrounding business performance, the manager should appreciate that forecasting is not the same as fortune-telling; unanticipated events have a way of making certain that specific forecasts are never exactly correct. This note purports, however, that thoughtful forecasts greatly aid managers in understanding the implications of various outcomes (including the most probable outcome) and identify the key bets associated with a forecast. Such forecasts provide the manager with an appreciation of the odds of business success.

This note examines principles in the art and science of thoughtful financial forecasting for the business manager. In particular, it reviews the importance of (1) understanding the financial relationships of a business enterprise, (2) grounding business forecasts in the reality of the industry and macroenvironment, (3) modeling a forecast that embeds the implications of business strategy, and (4) recognizing the potential for cognitive bias in the forecasting process. The note closes with a detailed example of financial forecasting based on the example of the Swiss food and nutrition company Nestle.

Understanding the Financial Relationships of the Business Enterprise

Financial statements provide information on the financial activities of an enterprise. Much like the performance statistics from an athletic contest, financial statements provide an array of identifying data on various historical strengths and weaknesses

This technical note was prepared by Professor Michael J. Schill. Special thanks go to Vladimir Kolcin for data-collection assistance and to Lee Ann Long-Tyler and Ray Nedzel for technical assistance. Copyright © 2015 by the University of Virginia Darden School Foundation, Charlottesville, VA. All rights reserved. *To order copies, send an e-mail to* sales@dardenbusinesspublishing.com. *No part of this publication may be reproduced, stored in a retrieval system, used in a spreadsheet, or transmitted in any form or by any means—electronic, mechanical, photocopying, recording, or otherwise—without the permission of the Darden School Foundation.*

across a broad spectrum of business activities. The income statement (also known as the profit-and-loss statement) measures *flows* of costs, revenue, and profits over a defined period of time, such as a year. The balance sheet provides a *snapshot* of business investment and financing at a particular point in time, such as the end of a year. Both statements combine to provide a rich picture of a business's financial performance. The analysis of financial statements is one important way of understanding the mechanics of the systems that make up business operations.

Interpreting Financial Ratios

Financial ratios provide a useful way to identify and compare relationships across financial statement line items.[1] Trends in the relationships captured by financial ratios are particularly helpful in modeling a financial forecast. The comparison of ratios across time or with similar firms provides diagnostic tools for assessing the health of the various systems in the enterprise. These tools and the assessments obtained with them provide the foundation for financial forecasting.

We review common financial ratios for examining business operating performance. It is worth noting that there is wide variation in the definition of financial ratios. A measure such as return on assets is computed many different ways in the business world. Although the precise definitions may vary, there is greater consensus on the interpretation and implication of each ratio. This note presents one such definition and reviews the interpretation.

Growth rates: Growth rates capture the year-on-year percentage change in a particular line item. For example, if total revenue for a business increases from $1.8 million to $2.0 million, the total revenue growth for the business is said to be 11.1% [(2.0 − 1.8)/1.8]. Total revenue growth can be further decomposed into two other growth measures: unit growth (the growth in revenue due to an increase in units sold) and price growth (the growth in revenue due to an increase in the price of each unit). In the above example, if unit growth for the business is 5.0%, the remaining 6.1% of total growth can be attributed to increases in prices or price growth.

Margins: Margin ratios capture the percentage of revenue that flows into profit or, alternatively, the percentage of revenue not consumed by business costs. Business profits can be defined in many ways. Gross profit reports the gains to revenue after subtracting the direct expenses. Operating profit reports the gains to revenue after subtracting all associated operating expenses. Operating profit is also commonly referred to as earnings before interest and taxes (EBIT). Net profit reports the gains to revenue after subtracting all associated expenses, including financing expenses and taxes. Each of these measures of profits have an associated margin. For example, if operating profit is $0.2 million and total revenue is $2.0 million, the operating

---

[1]The analogy of athletic performance statistics is again useful in understanding how ratios provide additional meaningful information. In measuring the effectiveness of a batter in baseball, the batting average (number of hits ÷ number of at bats) may be more useful than simply knowing the number of hits. In measuring the success of a running back in football, the ratio of rushing yards gained per carry may be more useful than simply knowing the total rushing yards gained.

margin is 10% (0.2/2.0). Thus, for each revenue dollar, an operating profit of $0.10 is generated and $0.90 is consumed by operating expenses. The margin provides the analyst with a sense of the cost structure of the business. Common definitions of margin include the following:

$$\text{Gross margin} = \text{Gross profit/Total revenue}$$

where gross profit equals total revenue less the cost of goods sold.

$$\text{Operating margin} = \text{Operating profit/Total revenue}$$

where operating profit equals total revenue less all operating expenses (EBIT).

$$\text{NOPAT margin} = \text{Net operating profit after tax (NOPAT)/Total revenue}$$

where NOPAT equals EBIT multiplied by $(1 - t)$, where t is the prevailing marginal income tax rate. NOPAT measures the operating profits on an after-tax basis without accounting for tax effects associated with business financing.

$$\text{Net profit margin} = \text{Net income/Total revenue}$$

where net income or net profit equals total revenue less all expenses for the period. A business that has a high gross margin and low operating margin has a cost structure that maintains high indirect operating expenses such as the costs associated advertising or with property, plant, or equipment (PPE).

Turnover: Turnover ratios measure the productivity, or efficiency, of business assets. The turnover ratio is constructed by dividing a measure of volume from the income statement (i.e., total revenue) by a related measure of investment from the balance sheet (i.e., total assets). Turnover provides a measure of how much business flow is generated per unit of investment. Productive or efficient assets produce high levels of asset turnover. For example, if total revenue is $2.0 million and total assets are $2.5 million, the asset-turnover measure is 0.8 times (2.0/2.5). Thus, each dollar of total asset investment is producing $0.80 in revenue or, alternatively, total assets are turning over 0.8 times a year through the operations of the business. Common measures of turnover include the following:

$$\text{Accounts receivable turnover} = \text{Total revenue/Accounts receivable}$$

Accounts receivable turnover measures how quickly sales on credit are collected. Businesses that take a long time to collect their bills have low receivable turnover because of their large receivable levels.

$$\text{Inventory turnover} = \text{Cost of goods sold/Inventory}$$

Inventory turnover measures how inventory is working in the business, and whether the business is generating its revenue on large levels or small levels of inventory. For inventory turnover (as well as payable turnover) it is customary to use cost of sales as the volume measure because inventory and purchases are on the books at cost rather than at the expected selling price.

$$\text{PPE turnover} = \text{Total revenue/Net PPE}$$

PPE turnover measures the operating efficiency of the fixed assets of the business. Businesses with high PPE turnover are able to generate large amounts of revenue on relatively small amounts of PPE, suggesting high productivity or asset efficiency.

$$\text{Asset turnover} = \text{Total revenue/Total assets}$$

$$\text{Total capital turnover} = \text{Total revenue/Total capital}$$

Total capital is the amount of capital that investors have put into the business and is defined as total debt plus total equity. Since investors require a return on the total capital they have invested, total capital turnover provides a good measure of the productivity of that investment.

$$\text{Accounts payable turnover} = \text{Cost of goods sold/Accounts payable}$$

Accounts payable turnover measures how quickly purchases on credit are paid. Businesses that are able to take a long time to pay their bills have low payable turnover because of their large payables levels.

An alternative and equally informative measure of asset productivity is a "days" measure, which is computed as the investment amount divided by the volume amount multiplied by 365 days. This measure captures the average number of days in a year that an investment item is held by the business. For example, if total revenue is $2.0 million and accounts receivable is $0.22 million, the accounts receivable days measure is calculated as 40.2 days (0.22/2.0 × 365). The days measure can be interpreted as that the average receivable is held by the business for 40.2 days before being collected. The lower the days measure, the more efficient is the investment item. If the accounts receivable balance equals the total revenue for the year, the accounts receivable days measure is equal to 365 days as the business has 365 days of receivables on their books. This means it takes the business 365 days, on average, to collect their accounts receivable. While the days measure does not actually provide any information that is not already contained in the respective turnover ratio (as it is simply the inverse of the turnover measure multiplied by 365 days), many managers find the days measure to be more intuitive than the turnover measure. Common days measures include the following:

$$\text{Accounts receivable days} = \text{Accounts receivable/Total revenue} \times 365 \text{ days}$$

$$\text{Inventory days} = \text{Inventory/Cost of goods sold} \times 365 \text{ days}$$

$$\text{Accounts payable days} = \text{Accounts payable/Cost of goods sold} \times 365 \text{ days}$$

Return on investment: Return on investment captures the profit generated per dollar of investment. For example, if operating profit is $0.2 million and total assets are $2.5 million, pretax return on assets is calculated as operating profit divided by total assets (0.2/2.5), or 8%. Thus, the total dollars invested in business assets are generating pretax operating-profit returns of 8%. Common measures of return on investment include the following:

$$\text{Return on equity (ROE)} = \text{Net income/Shareholders' equity}$$

where shareholders' equity is the amount of money that shareholders have put into the business. Since net income is the money that is available to be distributed back to equity investors, ROE provides a measure of the return the business is generating for the equity investors.

$$\text{Return on assets (ROA)} = \text{NOPAT/Total assets}$$

where NOPAT equals EBIT $\times$ $(1 - t)$, EBIT is the earnings before interest and taxes, and t is the prevailing marginal income tax rate. Like many of these ratios, there are many other common definitions. One common alternative definition of ROA is the following:

$$\text{Return on assets (ROA)} = \text{Net income/Total assets}$$

and, lastly,

$$\text{Return on capital (ROC)} = \text{NOPAT/Total capital}$$

Since NOPAT is the money that can be distributed back to both debt and equity investors and total capital measures the amount of capital invested by both debt and equity investors, ROC provides a measure of the return the business is generating for all investors (both debt and equity). It is important to observe that return on investment can be decomposed into a margin effect and a turnover effect. That relationship means that the same level of business profitability can be attained by a business with high margins and low turnover, such as Nordstrom, as by a business with low margins and high turnover, such as Wal-Mart. This decomposition can be shown algebraically for the ROC:

$$\text{ROC} = \text{NOPAT margin} \times \text{Total capital turnover}$$

$$\frac{\text{NOPAT}}{\text{Total capital}} = \frac{\text{NOPAT}}{\text{Total revenue}} \times \frac{\text{Total revenue}}{\text{Total capital}}$$

Notice that the equality holds because the quantity for total revenue cancels out across the two right-hand ratios. ROE can be decomposed into three components:

$$\text{ROC} = \text{Net profit margin} \times \text{Total capital turnover} \times \text{Total capital leverage}$$

$$\frac{\text{Net income}}{\text{Shareholders' equity}} = \frac{\text{Net income}}{\text{Total revenue}} \times \frac{\text{Total revenue}}{\text{Total capital}} \times \frac{\text{Total capital}}{\text{Shareholders' equity}}$$

This decomposition shows that changes in ROE can be achieved in three ways: changes in net profit margin, changes in total capital productivity, and changes in total capital leverage. This last measure is not an operating mechanism but rather a financing mechanism. Businesses financed with less equity and more debt generate higher ROE but also have higher financial risk.

Using Financial Ratios in Financial Models

Financial ratios provide the foundation for forecasting financial statements because financial ratios capture relationships across financial statement line items that tend to be preserved over time. For example, one could forecast the dollar amount of gross profit for next year through an explicit independent forecast. However, a better approach is to forecast two ratios: a revenue growth rate and a gross margin. Using these two ratios in combination one can apply the growth rate to the current year's revenue, and then use the gross margin rate to yield an implicit dollar forecast for gross profit. As an example, if we estimate revenue growth at 5% and operating margin at 24%, we can apply those ratios to last year's total revenue of $2.0 million to derive an implicit gross profit forecast of $0.5 million [$2.0 \times (1 + 0.05) \times 0.24$]. Given some familiarity with the financial ratios of a business, the ratios are generally easier to forecast with accuracy than are the expected dollar values. The approach to forecasting is thus to model future financial statements based on assumptions about future financial ratios.

Financial models based on financial ratios can be helpful in identifying the impact of particular assumptions on the forecast. For example, models can easily allow one to see the financial impact on dollar profits of a difference of one percentage point in operating margin. To facilitate such a scenario analysis, financial models are commonly built in electronic spreadsheet packages such as Microsoft Excel. Good financial forecast models make the forecast assumptions highly transparent. To achieve transparency, assumption cells for the forecast should be prominently displayed in the spreadsheet (e.g., total revenue growth rate assumption cell, operating margin assumption cell), and then those cells should be referenced in the generation of the forecast. In this way, it becomes easy not only to vary the assumptions for different forecast scenarios, but also to scrutinize the forecast assumptions.

Grounding Business Forecasts in the Reality of the Industry and Macroenvironment

Good financial forecasts recognize the impact of the business environment on the performance of the business. Financial forecasting should be grounded in an appreciation for industry- and economy-wide pressures. Because business performance tends to be correlated across the economy, information regarding macroeconomic business trends should be incorporated into a business's financial forecast. If, for example, price increases for a business are highly correlated with economy-wide inflation trends, the financial forecast should incorporate price growth assumptions that capture the available information on expected inflation. If the economy is in a recession, then the forecast should be consistent with that economic reality.

Thoughtful forecasts should also recognize the industry reality. Business prospects are dependent on the structure of the industry in which the business operates. Some industries tend to be more profitable than others. Microeconomic theory provides some explanations for the variation in industry profitability. Profitability within an industry is likely to be greater if (1) barriers to entry discourage industry entrants, (2) ease of industry exit facilitates redeployment of assets for unprofitable players, (3) industry participants exert bargaining power over buyers and suppliers, or (4) industry consolidation reduces price competition.[2] **Table 5.1** shows the five most and the five least profitable industries in the United States based on median pretax ROAs for all public firms from

---

[2]Michael E. Porter, "How Competitive Forces Shape Strategy," *Harvard Business Review* 57, no. 2 (March–April 1979): 137–45.

TABLE 5.1 | Most profitable and least profitable U.S. industries: 2005–2014.

Most Profitable Industries	Median Firm ROA	Least Profitable Industries	Median Firm ROA
Tobacco Products	18%	Chemicals and Allied Products	−25%
Building Materials, Retail	16%	Metal Mining	−14%
Leather and Leather Products	13%	Mining and Quarrying	−4%
Apparel and Accessory Stores	11%	Building Construction	−2%
Apparel	10%	Oil and Gas Extraction	−1%

2005 to 2014. Based on the evidence, firms operating in the apparel and accessory retail industry should have systematically generated more profitable financial forecasts over that period than did firms in the metal-mining industry. One explanation for the differences in industry profitability is the ease of industry exit. In the retail industry, unprofitable businesses are able to sell their assets easily for redeployment elsewhere. In the mining industries, where asset redeployment is much more costly, industry capacity may have dragged down industry profitability.

Being within a profitable industry, however, does not ensure superior business performance. Business performance also depends on the competitive position of the firm within the industry. **Table 5.2** shows the variation of profitability for firms within the U.S. apparel and accessory stores industry from 2005 to 2014. Despite being one of the most profitable industries as shown in **Table 5.1**, there is large variation in profitability within the industry. All five firms at the bottom of the profitability list generated median ROAs that were actually negative (Delia's, Frederick's, Bakers Footwear, Pacific Sunwear, and Coldwater Creek). Good forecasting considers the ability of a business to sustain performance given the structure of its industry and its competitive position within that industry.

Abnormal profitability is difficult to sustain over time. Competitive pressure tends to bring abnormal performance toward the mean. To show that effect, we can sort all U.S. public companies for each year from 2005 to 2015 into five groups (group 1 with low profits through group 5 with high profits) based on their annual ROAs and sales growth. We then follow what happened to the composition of those groups over the next

TABLE 5.2 | Most and least profitable firms within the apparel and accessory stores retail industry: 2005–2014. Rankings in Tables 5.1 and 5.2 are based on all firms from Compustat organized into industries by 2-digit SIC codes.

Most Profitable Firms	Median Firm ROA	Least Profitable Firms	Median Firm ROA
Francesca's	53%	Delia's	−29%
Buckle	38%	Frederick's	−17%
TJX	27%	Bakers Footwear	−10%
Ross Stores	26%	Pacific Sunwear	−6%
J. Crew	26%	Coldwater Creek	−5%

FIGURE 5.1 | Firm-ranking annual transitions by profitability and sales growth. Firms are sorted for each year into five groups by either annual pretax ROA or sales growth. For example, in the ROA panel, group 1 comprises the firms with the lowest 20% of ROA for the year; group 5 comprises the firms with the highest 20% of ROA for the year. The figure plots the mean ranking number for all U.S. public firms in the Compustat database from 2005 to 2015.

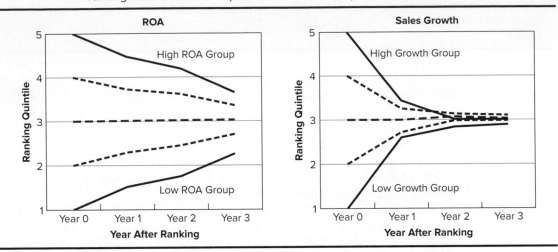

three years. The results of this exercise are captured in **Figure 5.1**. The ROA graph shows the mean group rankings for firms in subsequent years. For example, firms that ranked in group 5 with the top ROA at year 0 tend to have a mean group ranking of 4.5 in year 1, 4.3 in year 2, and 3.7 in year 3. Firms that ranked in group 1 with the lowest ROA at year 0 tend to have a mean group ranking of 1.5 in year 1, 1.7 in year 2, and 2.2 in year 3. There is a systematic drift toward average performance (3.0) over time. The effect is even stronger vis-à-vis sales growth. **Figure 5.1** provides the transition matrix for average groups sorted by sales growth. Here we see that, by year 2, the average sales growth ranking for the high-growth group is virtually indistinguishable from that of the low-growth group.

Figure 5.1 illustrates that business is fiercely competitive. It is naïve to assume that superior business profitability or growth can continue unabated for an extended period. Abnormally high profits attract competitive responses that eventually return profits to their normal levels.

Modeling a Base-Case Forecast that Incorporates Expectations for Business Strategy

With a solid understanding of the business's historical financial mechanics and of the environment in which the business operates, the forecaster can incorporate the firm's operating strategy into the forecast in a meaningful way. All initiatives to improve revenue growth, profit margin, and asset efficiency should be explicitly reflected in the financial forecast. The forecast should recognize, however, that business strategy does not play out in isolation. Competitors do not stand still. A good forecast recognizes that business strategy also begets competitive response. All modeling of the effects of business strategy should be tempered with an appreciation for the effects of aggressive competition.

One helpful way of tempering the modeling of business strategy's effects is to complement the traditional bottom-up approach to financial forecasting with a top-down approach. The top-down approach starts with a forecast of industry sales and then works back to the particular business of interest. The forecaster models firm sales by modeling market share within the industry. Such a forecast makes more explicit the challenge that sales growth must come from either overall industry growth or market share gain. A forecast that explicitly demands a market share gain of, say, 20% to 24%, is easier to scrutinize from a competitive perspective than a forecast that simply projects sales growth without any context (e.g., at an 8% rate).

Another helpful forecasting technique is to articulate business perspectives into a coherent qualitative view on business performance. This performance view encourages the forecaster to ground the forecast in a qualitative vision of how the future will play out. In blending qualitative and quantitative analyses into a coherent story, the forecaster develops a richer understanding of the relationships between the financial forecast and the qualitative trends and developments in the enterprise and its industry.

Forecasters can better understand their models by identifying the forecast's value drivers, which are those assumptions that strongly affect the overall outcome. For example, in some businesses the operating margin assumption may have a dramatic impact on overall business profitability, whereas the assumption for inventory turnover may make little difference. For other businesses, the inventory turnover may have a tremendous impact and thus becomes a value driver. In varying the assumptions, the forecaster can better appreciate which assumptions matter and thus channel resources to improve the forecast's precision by shoring up a particular assumption or altering the business strategy to improve the performance of a particular line item.

Lastly, good forecasters understand that it is more useful to think of forecasts as ranges of possible outcomes rather than as precise predictions. A common term in forecasting is the "base-case forecast." A base-case forecast represents the best guess outcome or the expected value of the forecast's line items. In generating forecasts, it is also important to have an unbiased appreciation for the range of possible outcomes, which is commonly done by estimating a high-side and a low-side scenario. In this way, the forecaster can bound the forecast with a relevant range of outcomes and can best appreciate the key bets of the financial forecast.

Recognizing the Potential for Cognitive Bias in the Forecasting Process

A substantial amount of research suggests that human decision making can be systematically biased. Bias in financial forecasts creates systematic problems in managing and investing in the business. Two elements of cognitive bias that play a role in financial forecasting are *optimism bias* and *overconfidence bias*. This note defines optimism bias

FIGURE 5.2 | Optimism and overconfidence biases in forecasting the sales growth rate.

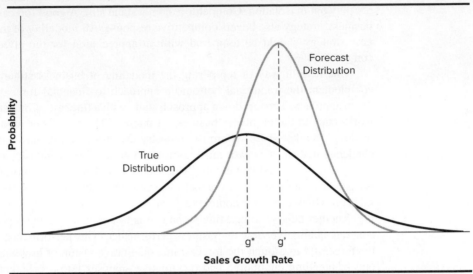

as a systematic positive error in the *expected value* of an unknown quantity, and defines the overconfidence bias as a systematic negative error in the *expected variance* of an unknown quantity. The definitions of those two terms are shown graphically in **Figure 5.2**. The dark curve shows the true distribution of the sales growth rate. The realization of the growth rate is uncertain, with a higher probability of its being in the central part of the distribution. The expected value for the sales growth rate is g*; thus, the proper base-case forecast for the sales growth rate is precisely g*. The light curve shows the distribution expected by the average forecaster. This distribution is biased for two reasons. First, the expected value is too high. The forecaster expects the base-case sales growth rate to be g', rather than g*. Such positive bias for expected value is termed optimistic. Second, the dispersion of the distribution is too tight. This dispersion is captured by the variance (or standard deviation) statistic. Because the forecast dispersion is tighter than the true dispersion, the forecaster exhibits negative variance bias, or overconfidence—the forecaster believes that the forecast is more precise than it really is.

A description and the implications of an experiment on forecasting bias among MBA students is provided in an Appendix to this note.

Nestle: An Example

In 2013, Nestle was one of the world's largest food and health companies. Headquartered in Switzerland, the company was truly a multinational organization with factories in 86 countries around the world. Suppose that in early 2014, we needed to forecast the financial performance of Nestle for the end of 2014. We suspected that one sensible place to start was to look at the company's performance over the past few years. **Exhibit 5.1** provides Nestle's income statement and balance sheet for 2012 and 2103.

One approach to forecasting the financial statements for 2014 is to forecast each line item from the income statement and balance sheet independently. Such an approach, however, ignores the important relationships among the different line items (e.g., costs and revenues tend to grow together). To gain an appreciation for those relationships, we calculate a variety of ratios (**Exhibit 5.1**). In calculating the ratios, we notice some interesting patterns. First, sales growth declined sharply in 2013, from 7.4% to 2.7%. The sales decline was also accompanied by much smaller decline in profitability margins; operating margin declined from 14.9% to 14.1%. Meanwhile, the asset ratios showed modest improvement; total asset turnover improved only slightly, from 0.7× to 0.8×. Asset efficiency improved across the various classes of assets (e.g., accounts receivable days improved in 2013, from 53.0 days to 48.2 days; PPE turnover also improved, from 2.8× to 3.0×). Overall in 2013 Nestle's declines in sales growth and margins were counteracted with improvements in asset efficiency such that return on assets improved from 6.9% to 7.1%. Because return on assets comprises both a margin effect and an asset-productivity effect, we can attribute the 2013 improvement in return on assets to a denominator effect—Nestle's asset efficiency improvement. The historical ratio analysis gives us some sense of the trends in business performance.

A common way to begin a financial forecast is to extrapolate current ratios into the future. For example, a simple starting point would be to assume that the 2013 financial ratios hold in 2014. If we make that simplifying assumption, we generate the financial forecast presented in **Exhibit 5.2**. We recognize this forecast as naïve, but it provides a straw-man forecast through which the relationships captured in the financial ratios can be scrutinized. In generating the forecast, all the line-item figures are built on the ratios used in the forecast. The financial line-item forecasts are computed as referenced to the right of each figure based on the ratios below. Such a forecast is known as a financial model. The design of the model is thoughtful. By linking the dollar figures with the financial ratios, the model preserves the existing relationships across line items and can be easily adjusted to accommodate different ratio assumptions.

Based on the naïve model, we can now augment the model with qualitative and quantitative research on the company, its industry, and the overall economy. In early 2014, Nestle was engaged in important efforts to expand the company product line in foods with all-natural ingredients as well the company presence in the Pacific Asian region. These initiatives required investment in new facilities. It was hoped that the initiatives would make up for ongoing declines in some of Nestle's important product offerings, particularly prepared dishes. Nestle was made up of seven major business units: powdered and liquid beverages (22% of total sales), water (8%), milk products and ice cream (18%), nutrition and health science (14%), prepared dishes and cooking aids (15%), confectionary (11%), and pet care (12%). The food processing industry had recently seen a substantial decline in demand for its products in the developing world. Important macroeconomic factors had led to sizable declines in demand from this part of the world. The softening of growth had led to increased competitive pressures within the industry that included such food giants as Mondelez, Tyson, and Unilever.

Based on this simple business and industry assessment, we take the view that Nestle will maintain its position in a deteriorating industry. We can adjust the naïve 2014 forecast based on that assessment (**Exhibit 5.3**). We suspect that the softening of demand in developing markets and the prepared dishes line will lead to zero sales growth for Nestle in 2014. We also expect the increased competition within the industry will increase amount spent on operating expenses to an operating expense-to-sales ratio of 35%. Those assumptions give us an operating margin estimate of 12.9%. We expect the increased competition to reduce Nestle's ability to work its inventory such that inventory turnover returns to the average between 2012 and 2013 of 5.53. We project PPE turnover to decline to 2.8× with the increased investment in new facilities that are not yet operational. Those assumptions lead to an implied financial forecast. The resulting projected after-tax ROA is 6.3%. The forecast is thoughtful. It captures a coherent view of Nestle based on the company's historical financial relationships, a grounding in the macroeconomic and industry reality, and the incorporation of Nestle's specific business strategy.

We recognize that we cannot anticipate all the events of 2014. Our forecast will inevitably be wrong. Nevertheless, we suspect that, by being thoughtful in our analysis, our forecast will provide a reasonable, unbiased expectation of future performance. **Exhibit 5.4** gives the actual 2014 results for Nestle. The big surprise was that the effect of competition was worse than anticipated. Nestle's realized sales growth was actually negative, and its operating margin dropped from 14.9% and 14.1% in 2012 and 2013, respectively, to 11.9% in 2014. Our asset assumptions were fairly close to the outcome, although the inventory turnover and PPE turnover were a little worse than we had expected. Overall, the ROA for Nestle dropped from 7.1% in 2013 to 5.3% in 2014. Although we did not complete a high-side and a low-side scenario in this simple example, we can hope that, had we done so, we could have appropriately assessed the sources and level of uncertainty of our forecast.

Appendix

To test for forecasting bias among business school forecasters, an experiment was performed in 2005 with the 300 first-year MBA students at the Darden School of Business at the University of Virginia. Each student was randomly assigned to both a U.S. public company and a year between 1980 and 2000.[3] Some students were assigned the same company, but no students were assigned the same company *and* the same year. The students were asked to forecast sales growth and operating margin for their assigned company for the subsequent three years. The students based their forecasts on the

---

[3]More precisely, the population of sample firms was all U.S. firms followed by Compustat and the Value Line Investment Survey. To ensure meaningful industry forecast data, we required that each firm belong to a meaningful industry, which is to say that multiform, industrial services, and diversified industries were not considered). We also required that Value Line report operating profit for each firm. To maintain consistency in the representation of firms over time, the sample began with a random identification of 25 firms per year. The forecast data were based on Value Line forecasts during the summer of the first year of the forecast. All historical financial data were from Compustat.

following information: industry name, firm sales growth and operating margin for the previous three years, historical and three-year prospective industry average growth and margins, and certain macroeconomic historical and three-year forecast data (real gross national product [GNP] growth, inflation rates, and the prevailing Treasury bill yield). To avoid biasing the forecasts based on subsequent known outcomes, students were given the name of their firm's industry but not the firm's name. For the same reason, the students were not given the identity of the current year. The responses were submitted electronically and anonymously. Forecast data from students who agreed to allow their responses to be used for research purposes were aggregated and analyzed. Summary statistics from the responses are presented in **Figure 5.3**.

The median values for the base-case forecast of expected sales growth and operating margin are plotted in **Figure 5.3**. The sales growth panel suggests that students tended to expect growth to continue to improve over the forecast horizon (years 1 through 3). The operating margin panel suggests that students expected near-term performance to be constant, followed by later-term improvement. To benchmark the forecast, we can compare the students' forecasts with the actual growth rates and operating margins realized by the companies. We expect that if students were unbiased in their forecasting, the distribution of the forecasts should be similar to the distribution of the actual results. **Figure 5.3** also plots the median value for the actual realizations. We observe that sales growth for these randomly selected firms did not improve but stayed fairly constant, whereas operating margins tended to decline over the extended term. The gap between the two lines represents the systematic bias in the students' forecasts. Because the bias in both cases is positive, the results are consistent with systematic optimism in the students' forecasts. By the third year, the optimism bias is a large 4 percentage points for the sales growth forecast and almost 2 percentage points for the margin forecast.

FIGURE 5.3 | Median expected and actual financial forecast values for a random sample of U.S. companies. This figure plots the median forecast and actual company realization for sales growth and operating margin over the three-year historical period and the three-year forecast period based on the responses from MBA students in an experiment.

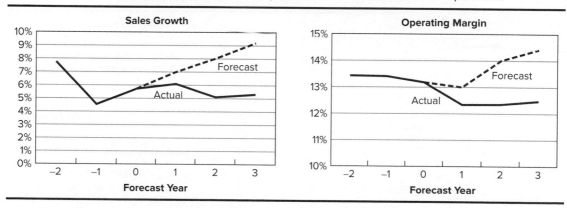

Although the average student tended to exhibit an optimistic bias, there was variation in the bias across different groups of students. The forecast bias was further examined across two characteristics: gender and professional training. For both sales growth and operating margin, the test results revealed that males and those whose professional backgrounds were outside finance exhibited the most optimistic bias. For example, the bias in the third-year margin forecast was 0.7% for those with professional finance backgrounds and 1.9% for those outside finance; and 2.6% for the male students and just 0.8% for the female students.

In generating forecasts, it is also important to have an unbiased appreciation for the precision of the forecast, which is commonly done by estimating a high-side and a low-side scenario. To determine whether students were unbiased in appreciating the risk in forecast outcomes, they were asked to provide a high-side and a low-side scenario. The high-side scenario was defined explicitly as the 80th percentile level. The low-side scenario was defined as the 20th percentile level. **Figure 5.4** plots the median high-side and low-side scenarios, as well as the expected base-case forecast presented in **Figure 5.3**. For the three-year horizon, the median high-side forecast was 4 percentage points above the base case and the low-side forecast was 4 percentage points below the base case. The actual 80th percentile performance was 8 percentage points above the base case and the actual 20th percentile was 12 percentage points below the base case. The results suggest that the true variance in sales growth is substantially greater than that estimated by the students. The same is also true of the operating margin. The estimates provided by the students are consistent with strong overconfidence (negative variance bias) in the forecast.

FIGURE 5.4 | Median base-case, high-side, and low-side forecasts versus the actual 20th and 80th performance percentiles for sales growth and operating margin. This figure plots the median base-case, high-side, and low-side forecasts for sales growth and operating margin over the three-year forecast period based on the responses from MBA students in an experiment. The low-side and high-side performance levels were defined as the students' estimate of the 20th and 80th percentile levels. The actual company 20th and 80th performance percentiles for sales growth and operating margin are also plotted.

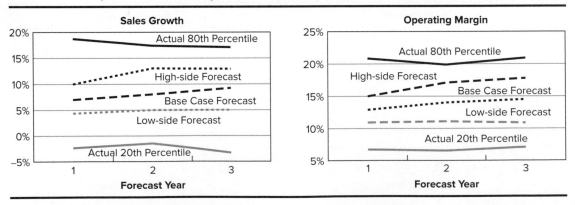

EXHIBIT 5.1 | Financial Statements for Nestle SA (in billions of Swiss francs)

	2012	2013
(1) Sales	89.9	92.4
(2) Cost of sales	47.5	48.1
(3) Gross profit	42.4	44.3
(4) Operating expenses	29.0	31.2
(5) Operating profit	13.4	13.1
(6) Net interest expense	0.7	0.6
(7) Profit before taxes	12.7	12.4
(8) Taxes	3.3	3.3
(9) Profit after taxes	9.4	9.2
(10) Accounts receivable	13.1	12.2
(11) Inventory	8.9	8.4
(12) Other current assets	12.0	9.5
(13) Net property, plant, and equipment	32.7	31.0
(14) Other non current assets	59.2	59.3
(15) Total assets	125.9	120.5
(16) Accounts payable	14.6	16.1
(17) Short-term debt	18.4	11.4
(18) Other current liabilities	5.6	5.5
(19) Current liabilities	38.6	32.9
(20) Long-term debt	9.0	10.4
(21) Non current liabilities	15.6	13.0
(22) Book equity	62.7	64.1
(23) Total liabilities and equity	125.9	120.5
Sales growth	7.4%	2.7%
Gross margin (3/1)	47.2%	47.9%
Operating exp/Sales (4/1)	32.3%	33.8%
Operating margin (5/1)	14.9%	14.1%
Interest expense/Debt (6/(17+20))	2.6%	2.9%
Tax rate (8/7)	25.7%	26.2%
Receivable turnover (1/10)	6.9	7.6
Accounts receivable days (10/1*365 days)	53.0	48.2
Inventory turnover (2/11)	5.3	5.7
Inventory days (11/2*365 days)	68.7	63.6
Other current assets/Sales (12/1)	13.4%	10.3%
PPE turnover (1/13)	2.8	3.0
Other noncurrent asset turnover (1/14)	1.5	1.6
Total asset turnover (1/15)	0.7	0.8
Return on assets (5*(1−.35)/15)	6.9%	7.1%
Accounts payable days (16/2*365 days)	112.4	121.9
Other curr liab/Sales (18/1)	6.2%	5.9%
Non curr liab/Sales (21/1)	17.4%	14.1%

Note: Although including both turnover and days ratios is redundant, doing so illustrates the two perspectives.

EXHIBIT 5.2 | Naïve Financial Forecast for Nestle SA (in billions of Swiss francs)

	2012	2013	2014E	
(1) Sales	89.9	92.4	94.9	Sales13 * (1 + Sales growth)
(2) Cost of sales	47.5	48.1	49.4	Sales14 − Gross profit
(3) Gross profit	42.4	44.3	45.5	Sales14 * Gross margin
(4) Operating expenses	29.0	31.2	32.0	Sales14 * [Operating exp/Sales]
(5) Operating profit	13.4	13.1	13.4	Gross profit − Operating expenses
(6) Net interest expense	0.7	0.6	0.8	[Int. Expense/Debt] * (STD + LTD)
(7) Profit before taxes	12.7	12.4	12.6	Op profit − Net interest exp
(8) Taxes	3.3	3.3	3.3	Tax rate * Profit before tax
(9) Profit after taxes	9.4	9.2	9.3	Profit before taxes − Taxes
(10) Accounts receivable	13.1	12.2	12.5	Sales14 * AR days/365
(11) Inventory	8.9	8.4	8.6	Cost of sales/Inv turnover
(12) Other current assets	12.0	9.5	9.7	Sales14 * [Other curr assets/Sales]
(13) Net property, plant, and equipment	32.7	31.0	31.9	Sales14/PPE turnover
(14) Other non current assets	59.2	59.3	61.0	Sales14/Other NC asset turnover
(15) Total assets	125.9	120.5	123.7	
(16) Accounts payable	14.6	16.1	16.5	Cost of Sales14 * AP days/365
(17) Short-term debt	18.4	11.4	17.2	Plug = TA-AP-OCA-LTD-NCL-BE
(18) Other current liabilities	5.6	5.5	5.6	Sales14 * [Other curr liab/Sales]
(19) Current liabilities	38.6	32.9	39.3	
(20) Long-term debt	9.0	10.4	10.4	Maintain '13
(21) Non current liabilities	15.6	13.0	5.6	Sales14 * [Non curr liab/Sales]
(22) Book equity	62.7	64.1	68.5	BE13 + PAT-5DIV
(23) Total liabilities and equity	125.9	120.5	123.7	
Sales growth	7.4%	2.7%	2.7%	Maintain '13
Gross margin (3/1)	47.2%	47.9%	47.9%	Maintain '13
Operating exp/Sales (4/1)	32.3%	33.8%	33.8%	Maintain '13
Operating margin (5/1)	14.9%	14.1%	14.1%	
Interest expense/Debt (6/(17+20))	2.6%	2.9%	2.9%	Maintain '13
Tax rate (8/7)	25.7%	26.2%	26.2%	Maintain '13
Receivable turnover (1/10)	6.9	7.6	7.6	
Accounts receivable days (10/1*365 days)	53.0	48.2	48.2	Maintain '13
Inventory turnover (2/11)	5.3	5.7	5.7	Maintain '13
Inventory days (11/2*365 days)	68.7	63.6	63.6	
Other current assets/Sales (12/1)	13.4%	10.3%	10.3%	Maintain '13
PPE turnover (1/13)	2.8	3.0	3.0	Maintain '13
Other noncurrent asset turnover (1/14)	1.5	1.6	1.6	Maintain '13
Total asset turnover (1/15)	0.7	0.8	0.8	Maintain '13
Return on assets (5*(1−.35)/15)	6.9%	7.1%	7.1%	
Accounts payable days (16/2*365 days)	112.4	121.9	121.9	Maintain '13
Other curr liab/Sales (18/1)	6.2%	5.9%	5.9%	Maintain '13
Non curr liab/Sales (21/1)	17.4%	14.1%	14.1%	Maintain '13

EXHIBIT 5.3 | Revised Financial Forecast for Nestle SA (in billions of Swiss francs)

	2012	2013	2014E	
(1) Sales	89.9	92.4	92.4	Sales13 * (1 + Sales growth)
(2) Cost of sales	47.5	48.1	48.1	Sales14 − Gross profit
(3) Gross profit	42.4	44.3	44.3	Sales14 * Gross margin
(4) Operating expenses	29.0	31.2	32.3	Sales14 * [Operating exp/Sales]
(5) Operating profit	13.4	13.1	11.9	Gross profit − Operating expenses
(6) Net interest expense	0.7	0.6	0.8	[Int. Expense/Debt] * (STD + LTD)
(7) Profit before taxes	12.7	12.4	11.1	Op profit − Net interest exp
(8) Taxes	3.3	3.3	2.9	Tax rate * Profit before tax
(9) Profit after taxes	9.4	9.2	8.2	Profit before taxes − Taxes
(10) Accounts receivable	13.1	12.2	12.2	Sales14 * AR days/365
(11) Inventory	8.9	8.4	8.7	Cost of sales/Inv turnover
(12) Other current assets	12.0	9.5	9.5	Sales14 * [Other curr assets/Sales]
(13) Net property, plant, and equipment	32.7	31.0	33.6	Sales14/PPE turnover
(14) Other non current assets	59.2	59.3	59.3	Sales14/Other NC asset turnover
(15) Total assets	125.9	120.5	123.3	
(16) Accounts payable	14.6	16.1	16.1	Cost of Sales14 * AP days/365
(17) Short-term debt	18.4	11.4	18.6	Plug = TA-AP-OCA-LTD-NCL-BE
(18) Other current liabilities	5.6	5.5	5.5	Sales14 * [Other curr liab/Sales]
(19) Current liabilities	38.6	32.9	40.2	
(20) Long-term debt	9.0	10.4	10.4	Maintain '13
(21) Non current liabilities	15.6	13.0	5.5	Sales14 * [Non curr liab/Sales]
(22) Book equity	62.7	64.1	67.3	BE13 + PAT-5DIV
(23) Total liabilities and equity	125.9	120.5	123.3	
Sales growth	7.4%	2.7%	**0.0%**	**No growth in '14**
Gross margin (3/1)	47.2%	47.9%	47.9%	Maintain '13
Operating exp/Sales (4/1)	32.3%	33.8%	**35.0%**	**Increased competition**
Operating margin (5/1)	14.9%	14.1%	12.9%	
Interest expense/Debt (6/(17+20))	2.6%	2.9%	2.9%	Maintain '13
Tax rate (8/7)	25.7%	26.2%	26.2%	Maintain '13
Receivable turnover (1/10)	6.9	7.6	7.6	
Accounts receivable days (10/1*365 days)	53.0	48.2	48.2	Maintain '13
Inventory turnover (2/11)	5.3	5.7	**5.53**	**Average turnover more appropriate**
Inventory days (11/2*365 days)	68.7	63.6	66.0	
Other current assets/Sales (12/1)	13.4%	10.3%	10.3%	Maintain '13
PPE turnover (1/13)	2.8	3.0	**2.8**	**Average turnover more appropriate**
Other noncurrent asset turnover (1/14)	1.5	1.6	1.6	Maintain '13
Total asset turnover (1/15)	0.7	0.8	0.7	Maintain '13
Return on assets (5*(1−.35)/15)	6.9%	7.1%	6.3%	
Accounts payable days (16/2*365 days)	112.4	121.9	121.9	Maintain '13
Other curr liab/Sales (18/1)	6.2%	5.9%	5.9%	Maintain '13
Non curr liab/Sales (21/1)	17.4%	14.1%	14.1%	Maintain '13

EXHIBIT 5.4 | Actual Financial Performance for Nestle SA (in billions of Swiss francs)

	2012	2013	2014A
(1) Sales	89.9	92.4	91.9
(2) Cost of sales	47.5	48.1	47.6
(3) Gross profit	42.4	44.3	44.3
(4) Operating expenses	29.0	31.2	33.4
(5) Operating profit	13.4	13.1	10.9
(6) Net interest expense	0.7	0.6	0.6
(7) Profit before taxes	12.7	12.4	10.3
(8) Taxes	3.3	3.3	3.4
(9) Profit after taxes	9.4	9.2	6.9
(10) Accounts receivable	13.1	12.2	13.5
(11) Inventory	8.9	8.4	9.2
(12) Other current assets	12.0	9.5	11.3
(13) Net property, plant, and equipment	32.7	31.0	34.6
(14) Other non current assets	59.2	59.3	64.9
(15) Total assets	125.9	120.5	133.5
(16) Accounts payable	14.6	16.1	17.4
(17) Short-term debt	18.4	11.4	8.8
(18) Other current liabilities	5.6	5.5	6.7
(19) Current liabilities	38.6	32.9	32.9
(20) Long-term debt	9.0	10.4	12.4
(21) Non current liabilities	15.6	13.0	16.3
(22) Book equity	62.7	64.1	71.9
(23) Total liabilities and equity	125.9	120.5	133.5
Sales growth	7.4%	2.7%	−0.6%
Gross margin (3/1)	47.2%	47.9%	48.2%
Operating exp/Sales (4/1)	32.3%	33.8%	36.4%
Operating margin (5/1)	14.9%	14.1%	11.9%
Interest expense/Debt (6/(17 + 20))	2.6%	2.9%	3.0%
Tax rate (8/7)	25.7%	26.2%	32.8%
Receivable turnover (1/10)	6.9	7.6	6.8
Accounts receivable days (10/1*365 days)	53.0	48.2	53.5
Inventory turnover (2/11)	5.3	5.7	5.2
Inventory days (11/2*365 days)	68.7	63.6	70.4
Other current assets/Sales (12/1)	13.4%	10.3%	12.3%
PPE turnover (1/13)	2.8	3.0	2.7
Other noncurrent asset turnover (1/14)	1.5	1.6	1.4
Total asset turnover (1/15)	0.7	0.8	0.7
Return on assets (5*(1−.35)/15)	6.9%	7.1%	5.3%
Accounts payable days (16/2*365 days)	112.4	121.9	133.9
Other curr liab/Sales (18/1)	6.2%	5.9%	7.2%
Non curr liab/Sales (21/1)	17.4%	14.1%	17.7%

The Financial Detective, 2016

Financial characteristics of companies vary for many reasons. The two most prominent drivers are industry economics and firm strategy.

Each industry has a financial norm around which companies within the industry tend to operate. An airline, for example, would naturally be expected to have a high proportion of fixed assets (airplanes), while a consulting firm would not. A steel manufacturer would be expected to have a lower gross margin than a pharmaceutical manufacturer because commodities such as steel are subject to strong price competition, while highly differentiated products like patented drugs enjoy much more pricing freedom. Because of each industry's unique economic features, average financial statements will vary from one industry to the next.

Similarly, companies *within* industries have different financial characteristics, in part because of the diverse strategies that can be employed. Executives choose strategies that will position their company favorably in the competitive jockeying within an industry. Strategies typically entail making important choices in how a product is made (e.g., capital intensive versus labor intensive), how it is marketed (e.g., direct sales versus the use of distributors), and how the company is financed (e.g., the use of debt or equity). Strategies among companies in the same industry can differ dramatically. Different strategies can produce striking differences in financial results for firms in the same industry.

The following paragraphs describe pairs of participants in a number of different industries. Their strategies and market niches provide clues as to the financial condition and performance that one would expect of them. The companies' common-sized financial statements and operating data, as of early 2016, are presented in a standardized format in **Exhibit 6.1**. It is up to you to match the financial data with the company descriptions. Also, try to explain the differences in financial results *across* industries.

This case was prepared by Jenelle Sirleaf (MBA '17) under the direction of Kenneth M. Eades, Professor of Business Administration, and was derived from earlier versions prepared under the direction of Robert F. Bruner, University Professor, Distinguished Professor of Business Administration, and Dean Emeritus. It was written as a basis for class discussion rather than to illustrate effective or ineffective handling of an administrative situation. Copyright © 2016 by the University of Virginia Darden School Foundation, Charlottesville, VA. All rights reserved. *To order copies, send an e-mail to* sales@dardenbusinesspublishing. com. *No part of this publication may be reproduced, stored in a retrieval system, used in a spreadsheet, or transmitted in any form or by any means—electronic, mechanical, photocopying, recording, or otherwise— without the permission of the Darden School Foundation.*

Airlines

Companies A and B are airline companies. One firm is a major airline that flies both domestically and internationally and offers additional services including travel packages and airplane repair. The company owns a refinery to supply its own jet fuel as a hedge to fuel-price volatility. In 2008, this company merged with one of the largest airline carriers in the United States.

The other company operates primarily in the United States, with some routes to the Caribbean and Latin America. It is the leading low-cost carrier in the United States. One source of operating efficiency is the fact that the company carries only three different aircraft in its fleet, making maintenance much simpler than for legacy airlines that might need to service 20 or 30 different aircraft models. This company's growth has been mostly organic—it expands its routes by purchasing new aircraft and the rights to fly into new airports.

Beer

Of the beer companies, C and D, one is a national brewer of mass-market consumer beers sold under a variety of brand names. This company operates an extensive network of breweries and distribution systems. The firm also owns a number of beer-related businesses—such as snack-food and aluminum-container manufacturing companies—and several major theme parks. Over the past 12 years, it has acquired several large brewers from around the globe.

The other company is the largest craft brewer in the United States. Like most craft brewers, this company produces higher-quality beers than the mass-market brands, but production is at a lower volume and the beers carry premium prices. The firm is financially conservative.

Computers

Companies E and F sell computers and related equipment. One company sells high-performance computing systems ("supercomputers") to government agencies, universities, and commercial businesses. It has experienced considerable growth due to an increasing customer base. The company is financially conservative.

The other company sells personal computers as well as handheld devices and software. The firm has been able to differentiate itself by using its own operating system for its computers and by creating new and innovative designs for all its products. These products carry premium prices domestically and globally. The company follows a vertical integration strategy starting with owning chip manufacturers and ending with owning its own retail stores.

Hospitality

Companies G and H are both in the hospitality business. One company operates hotels and residential complexes. Rather than owning the hotels, this firm chooses to manage or franchise its hotels. The company receives its revenues each month based on long-term contracts with the hotel owners, who pay a percentage of the hotel revenues as a management fee or franchise fee. Much of this company's growth is inorganic—the company buys the rights to manage existing hotel chains and also the rights to use the hotel's brand name. This company has also pursued a strategy of repurchasing a significant percentage of the shares of its own common stock.

The other company owns and operates several chains of upscale, full-service hotels and resorts. The firm's strategy is to maintain market presence by owning all of its properties, which contributes to the high recognition of its industry-leading brands.

Newspapers

Companies I and J are newspaper companies. One company owns and operates two newspapers in the southwestern United States. Due to the transition of customer preference from print to digital, the company has begun offering marketing and digital-advertising services and acquiring firms in more profitable industries. The company has introduced cost controls to address cost-structure issues such as personnel expenses.

Founded in 1851, the other company is renowned for its highly circulated newspaper offered both in print and online formats. This paper is sold and distributed domestically as well as around the world. Because the company is focused largely on one product, it has strong central controls that have allowed it to remain profitable despite the fierce competition for subscribers and advertising revenues.

Pharmaceuticals

Companies K and L manufacture and market pharmaceuticals. One firm is a diversified company that sells both human pharmaceuticals as well as health products for animals. This company's strategy is to stay ahead of the competition by investing in the discovery and development of new and innovative drugs.

The other company focuses on generic pharmaceuticals and medical devices. Most of this company's growth has been inorganic—the growth strategy has been to engage in highly leveraged acquisitions, and it has participated in more than 100 during the past eight years. The goal of acquiring new businesses is to enhance the value of the proven drugs in the company's portfolio rather than gamble on discoveries of new drugs for the future.

Power

Companies M and N are in the power-generation industry. One company focuses on solar power. This includes the manufacturing and selling of power systems as well as maintenance services for those systems.

The other company owns large, mostly coal-powered electric-power-generation plants in countries around the world. Most of its revenues result from power-purchase agreements with a country's government that buy the power generated. Some of its U.S. assets include regulated public utilities.

Retail

Companies O and P are retailers. One is a leading e-commerce company that sells a broad range of products, including media (books, music, and videos) and electronics, which together account for 92% of revenues. One-third of revenues are international and 20% of sales come from third-party sellers (i.e., sellers who transact through the company's website to sell their own products rather than those owned by the company). A growing portion of operating profit comes from the company's cloud-computing business. With its desire to focus on customer satisfaction, this company has invested considerably in improving its online technologies.

The other company is a leading retailer in apparel and fashion accessories for men, women, and children. The company sells mostly through its upscale brick-and-mortar department stores.

EXHIBIT 6.1 | Common-Sized Financial Data and Ratios

	Airlines		Beer		Computers		Hospitality		Newspaper		Pharmaceuticals		Power		Retail	
Assets %	A	B	C	D	E	F	G	H	I	J	K	L	M	N	O	P
Cash & ST Investments	6	10	5	15	14	41	7	2	25	35	1	13	5	25	30	8
Receivables	4	2	3	9	10	18	4	18	9	14	5	11	7	8	10	3
Inventory	1	1	2	9	1	16	0	0	0	2	3	10	2	7	16	25
Current Assets—Other	5	4	3	3	5	9	4	3	2	4	2	2	5	6	0	4
Current Assets—Total	**17**	**16**	**14**	**35**	**31**	**84**	**15**	**23**	**36**	**56**	**11**	**35**	**19**	**46**	**56**	**39**
Net Property, Plant, & Equipment	42	75	14	64	8	4	53	17	25	23	3	23	62	19	33	49
Long-Term Marketable Securities	0	1	0	1	56	0	0	0	13	0	0	10	0	0	0	0
Goodwill & Intangibles	28	0	70	0	3	2	9	39	5	19	85	26	8	3	7	6
Assets—Other	13	8	2	1	2	9	23	21	21	2	1	6	12	33	4	7
Assets—Total	**100**	**100**	**100**	**100**	**100**	**100**	**100**	**100**	**100**	**100**	**100**	**100**	**100**	**100**	**100**	**100**
Liabilities & Equity %																
Accounts Payable	5	2	6	7	12	4	2	10	4	6	1	4	5	5	31	17
Debt in Current Liabilities	3	5	4	0	4	0	4	5	8	0	2	0	7	1	5	0
Current Liabilities—Other	24	19	8	11	12	20	8	38	12	12	8	19	7	8	15	20
Current Liabilities—Total	**33**	**26**	**21**	**17**	**28**	**24**	**15**	**53**	**23**	**18**	**11**	**23**	**19**	**13**	**52**	**38**
Long-Term Debt	13	16	32	0	18	0	14	63	10	0	62	22	50	4	13	36
Deferred Taxes	0	14	9	5	8	0	1	0	0	0	12	0	3	0	2	0
Liabilities—Other	34	6	4	3	4	5	18	43	32	28	3	13	12	7	14	15
Liabilities—Total	**80**	**63**	**66**	**29**	**59**	**29**	**47**	**159**	**66**	**46**	**88**	**59**	**83**	**24**	**80**	**89**
Stockholders' Equity	20	37	34	71	41	71	53	(59)	34	54	12	41	17	76	20	11
Total Liabilities & Equity	**100**	**100**	**100**	**100**	**100**	**100**	**100**	**100**	**100**	**100**	**100**	**100**	**100**	**100**	**100**	**100**
Income/Expenses %																
Revenue	100	100	100	100	100	100	100	100	100	100	100	100	100	100	100	100
Cost of Goods Sold	(70)	(60)	(39)	(48)	(60)	(69)	(63)	(26)	(39)	(101)	(23)	(24)	(81)	(74)	(67)	(63)
Finance Div. Operating Exp.	0	0	0	0	0	0	0	0	0	0	0	0	0	0	0	(1)
Interent Expense—Finance Division	0	0	0	0	0	0	0	0	0	0	0	0	0	0	0	(0)
Gross Profit	**30**	**40**	**61**	**52**	**40**	**31**	**37**	**74**	**61**	**(1)**	**77**	**76**	**19**	**26**	**33**	**36**
SG&A Expense	(4)	(4)	(32)	(36)	(6)	(12)	(12)	(23)	(45)	0	(26)	(33)	(1)	(7)	(19)	(28)
R & D Exp.	0	0	0	0	(3)	(13)	0	0	0	0	(3)	(24)	0	0	0	0
Depreciation & Amort.	(5)	(5)	0	0	0	0	(13)	(4)	(4)	5	0	0	0	(4)	0	0
Other Operating Expense	(5)	(12)	3	0	0	0	0	0	0	0	(23)	0	0	0	(0)	0
Earnings before Interest and Taxes	**16**	**19**	**32**	**16**	**30**	**6**	**13**	**47**	**12**	**(5)**	**25**	**19**	**18**	**14**	**2**	**8**
Net Interest Expense	(1)	(2)	(4)	0	(0)	0	(2)	(5)	(2)	(2)	(15)	(0)	(6)	0	(0)	(1)
Other	3	0	1	(0)	1	0	(3)	2	(4)	0	(12)	(4)	(4)	1	(0)	(0)
Pretax Income	**18**	**17**	**29**	**16**	**31**	**6**	**8**	**44**	**6**	**(7)**	**(1)**	**14**	**8**	**15**	**1**	**7**
Income Tax Expense	(7)	(6)	(6)	(6)	(8)	(2)	(3)	(14)	(2)	0	(2)	(2)	(3)	0	(0)	(3)
Earnings of Discontinued Ops.	0	0	0	0	0	0	0	0	0	0	0	0	0	0	0	0
Extraord. Item & Account Change	0	0	0	0	0	0	0	0	0	0	0	0	0	0	0	0
Minority Int. in Earnings	0	0	(4)	0	0	0	0	0	0	0	0	0	(3)	0	0	0
Net Income	**11**	**11**	**19**	**10**	**23**	**4**	**5**	**30**	**4**	**(7)**	**(3)**	**12**	**2**	**15**	**1**	**4**

111

EXHIBIT 6.1 | Common-Sized Financial Data and Ratios *(continued)*

	Airlines		Beer		Computers		Hospitality		Newspaper		Pharmaceuticals		Power		Retail	
	A	B	C	D	E	F	G	H	I	J	K	L	M	N	O	P
Market Data																
Beta	1.20	1.10	0.95	0.95	0.95	1.20	1.15	1.15	1.15	0.95	1.15	0.75	1.15	1.50	1.05	1.00
Price/Earnings	10.0	10.9	24.2	34.0	12.8	22.0	59.8	24.0	34.9	nmf	18.3	22.9	27.2	9.7	nmf	19.2
Price to Book	3.9	2.4	4.2	3.9	5.0	2.8	0.3	nmf	2.7	0.8	5.5	6.1	1.8	1.2	25.5	6.4
Dividend Payout (%)	7.9	0.0	88.2	0.0	21.8	0.0	0.0	29.5	41.8	(39.4)	0.0	88.7	91.5	0.0	0.0	197.5
Liquidity																
Current Ratio	0.52	0.60	0.64	2.01	1.11	3.50	1.02	0.43	1.53	3.17	1.04	1.53	0.99	3.48	1.08	1.04
Quick Ratio	0.31	0.44	0.41	1.35	0.90	2.45	0.72	0.37	1.45	2.82	0.62	1.03	0.63	2.49	0.77	0.30
Asset Management																
Inventory Turnover	37.0	85.4	5.9	8.5	62.8	3.9	109.7	nmf	nmf	61.2	2.3	1.6	17.6	4.6	7.7	4.9
Receivables Turnover	16.5	43.3	13.0	25.3	13.6	5.3	8.8	13.1	7.1	8.3	4.3	5.9	5.8	9.3	17.8	11.7
Fixed Assets Turnover	1.9	1.0	2.2	2.4	10.8	22.0	0.6	14.1	2.4	4.8	7.6	2.5	0.6	2.5	5.5	4.1
Debt Management																
Total Debt/Total Assets (%)	79.6	62.9	66.0	28.5	58.9	29.1	47.4	159.0	65.7	45.7	87.7	59.0	83.0	24.2	79.5	88.7
LT Debt/Shareholders' Equity (%)	62.4	43.5	95.2	0.1	44.8	0.0	26.2	nmf	29.3	0.0	501.9	54.6	292.5	5.2	61.5	320.9
Interest Coverage	13.6	10.0	6.5	nmf	97.2	nmf	4.8	8.1	4.2	nmf	1.7	23.2	1.9	74.1	4.9	10.2
DuPont Analysis																
Net Profit Margin (%)	11.1	10.6	19.0	10.3	22.8	3.8	4.9	30.1	4.0	(6.6)	(2.8)	12.1	2.0	15.3	0.6	4.2
Asset Turnover	0.8	0.8	0.3	1.5	0.9	1.1	0.3	2.4	0.6	1.0	0.3	0.6	0.4	0.5	1.8	1.7
Return on Equity (%)	46.0	23.6	19.7	21.9	46.2	5.8	2.9	nmf	8.1	(14.8)	(5.0)	16.1	11.2	10.4	4.9	36.2

nmf = not a meaningful figure

Data sources: S&P Research Insight, Capital IQ, and Value Line Investment Survey.

Whole Foods Market: The Deutsche Bank Report

The latest numbers coming out of Whole Foods Market, Inc. (Whole Foods) in May 2014 took Deutsche Bank research analyst Karen Short and her team by surprise. On May 6, Whole Foods reported just $0.38 per share in its quarterly earnings report, missing Wall Street's consensus of $0.41 and cutting earnings guidance for the remainder of the year. The company's share price fell 19% to $38.93 the next day as Whole Foods' management acknowledged that it faced an increasingly competitive environment that could compress margins and slow expansion. The only upbeat news was the 20% increase in the company's quarterly dividend, up from $0.10 to $0.12 per share. Short and her team knew this was not the first time the market believed Whole Foods had gone stale. In 2006, Whole Foods' stock had also declined 20% over fears of slowing growth and increasing competition, but had since bounced back and outperformed both its competition and the broader market (see **Exhibit 7.1** for stock price performance). Nevertheless, it was time for Short and her team to discuss how the news altered their outlook for the company in a revised analyst report. The main point of discussion would certainly be whether Whole Foods still had a recipe for success.

The Grocery Industry

The U.S. grocery industry as a whole had historically been a low-growth industry, and, as a result of fierce competition, had typically maintained low margins. In 2012, the industry recorded over $600 billion in sales, a 3% increase from the previous year.[1] Real demand growth was strongly tied to population growth, and consensus estimates for nominal long-term growth rate were between 2% and 3%.[2] Key segments included

---

[1]Whole Foods Market annual report, 2013.

[2]Hoover's Inc., *Grocery Stores & Supermarkets Industry Report*, 2015.

conventional grocers such as Kroger, Publix, Safeway, and Albertsons; supercenters such as Wal-Mart and Target; natural grocers such as Whole Foods, Sprouts Farmers Market (Sprouts), and The Fresh Market (Fresh Market); and wholesalers such as Costco and Sam's Club. Conventional grocers remained the primary destination for shoppers, but competition from Wal-Mart, wholesalers, and other low-price vendors had driven down conventional grocers' share of food dollars for over a decade; for example, Wal-Mart was the largest food retailer in the United States in 2014, with 25% market share.[3] **Exhibit 7.2** provides market share information for the U.S. grocery market. The narrow margins and limited growth opportunities favored large competitors that could leverage efficiencies in purchasing and distribution to pass savings on to the consumer. As a result, many small competitors had been acquired or forced to close. Consumers were extremely price conscious and came to expect promotions (which were largely funded by manufacturers), and most shoppers did not have strong attachments to particular retail outlets.

Given this environment, companies relentlessly searched for opportunities to achieve growth and improve margins. Many grocers had implemented loyalty programs to reward repeat shoppers, and most were trying to improve the in-store customer experience, for instance by using self-checkout lines and other operational adjustments to reduce checkout times, a source of frequent complaints. Given the high percentage of perishable goods in the industry, supply chain management was essential, and companies were using improved technology to more efficiently plan their inventories. Grocers also began promoting prepared foods, which could command higher margins and reach consumers who did not regularly cook their own meals. Finally, most major grocers offered private-label products, which allowed them to offer low prices while still capturing sufficient margins.

Despite operating in a competitive and low-growth industry, natural grocers had grown rapidly over the past two decades. Increasingly health-conscious consumers were concerned about the source and content of their food, which fueled natural grocers' sustained growth (over 20% per year since 1990) despite their comparatively higher prices.[4] In 2012, natural and organic products accounted for $81 billion in total sales in the United States, a 10% increase from the previous year.[5] Organic products, which were more narrowly defined than natural products, accounted for about $28 billion of these sales and were expected to top $35 billion by the end of 2014.[6] **Exhibit 7.3** provides growth forecast and share data on the natural and organic segments. As of 2014, 45% of Americans explicitly sought to include organic food in their meals, and more than half of the country's 18–29-year-old population sought it out.[7] By specializing in such products, natural grocers were able to carve out a profitable niche: the three leading natural grocers (Whole Foods, Sprouts, and Fresh Market) had EBITDA margins of

---

[3]Hoover's Inc.

[4]USDA, Organic Market Overview, 2014.

[5]Whole Foods Market annual report, 2013.

[6]USDA.

[7]Rebecca Riffkin, "Forty-Five Percent of Americans Seek Out Organic Food," Gallup, August 7, 2014.

9.5%, 7.7%, and 9.1% respectively, whereas Kroger, the leading conventional supermarket, had an EBITDA margin of only 4.5%.[8] **Exhibits 7.4** and **7.5** contain operating and financial information for selected companies in the U.S. grocery industry.

As expected, the segment's attractiveness sparked increasing competition from both new entrants and established players from the other competing segments. Wal-Mart, Kroger, and others launched organic offerings targeted at health-conscious consumers, often at a much lower price point than similar products at natural grocers. While Whole Foods, other natural grocers, independent retailers, and food cooperatives were the primary source of organic products in the 1990s, by 2006, half of the country's organic food was sold through conventional supermarkets.[9] By 2014, organic products were available in over 20,000 natural food stores and nearly three out of four conventional grocers.[10]

Even in the face of this competition, Whole Foods maintained a position as the market leader for the natural and organic industry. As many grocers joined the natural and organic bandwagon, Whole Foods defended against misrepresentative claims. Whole Foods had recently introduced a system to rate fresh produce on a number of criteria, including sustainability and other characteristics important to natural and organic customers.[11] The company's website listed over 75 substances that were prohibited in all of its products and published additional measures for meat, seafood, and produce selection to ensure consumers had insight into the quality of their food. Whole Foods was the only U.S. retailer that labeled genetically modified foods, an area of some concern to health-conscious consumers.

Despite its remarkable growth, the natural and organic industry was not without its critics. Several academic and government studies had concluded that organic products were not significantly more nutritious than nonorganic goods and claimed that the inefficiency of organic production could harm the environment. Moreover, the continuing lack of official legal definitions of terms such as "natural" arguably made them effectively meaningless: one botanist argued the segment was "99% marketing and public perception."[12]

Whole Foods Market

Whole Foods traced its roots to 1978, when John Mackey and Renee Lawson opened a small organic grocer called SaferWay in Austin, Texas. Two years later, it partnered with Craig Weller and Mark Skiles of Clarksville Natural Grocery to launch the first Whole Foods Market, one of the country's first natural and organic supermarkets. In 1984, the company began expanding within Texas and in 1988 made its first move across state lines by acquiring the Louisiana-based Whole Foods Company; the next year

---

[8]Author calculations using companies' 10-Ks.

[9]Carolyn Dimitri and Lydia Oberholtzer, "Expanding Demand for Organic Foods Brings Changes in Marketing," Amber Waves, March 1, 2010.

[10]USDA.

[11]Whole Foods Market annual report, 2013.

[12]"Victim of Success," *The Economist*, August 2, 2014.

it launched its first store in California. The company went public in 1992 and grew rapidly during the 1990s through both new store openings and acquisitions. Whole Foods launched its first international store in Canada in 2002 and acquired a natural supermarket chain in the United Kingdom in 2004.[13] The company had consistently maintained high growth throughout the new century by increasing same-store sales and expanding its store count; same-store sales grew more than 5% in every year except 2008 and 2009, when the global financial crisis brought America into a severe recession. By 2013, the company's growth strategy had moved away from acquisitions, and management saw improving same-store sales and continued new openings as its primary growth opportunities.[14] Same-store sales—the most important growth criteria Wall Street used to evaluate retailers—had grown by at least 7% every year since 2010, far above other established grocers' growth rates even after it began expanding its natural and organic offerings. The company had done all of this with no debt financing. Looking forward, Whole Foods management planned to eventually operate over 1,000 stores, up from the 362 it operated as of the end of fiscal year 2013.[15] **Exhibit 7.6** contains store count and same-store sales growth history for Whole Foods and other industry players.

Whole Foods positioned itself as "the leading retailer of natural and organic foods" and defined its mission as promoting "the vitality and well-being of all individuals by supplying the highest quality, most wholesome foods available."[16] The company's sole operating segment was its natural and organic markets and nearly 97% of its revenues came from the United States. By 2013, the average Whole Foods store carried 21,000 SKUs and approximately 30% of sales outside the bakery and prepared-food segments were organic. Whole Foods reported $551 million in net income on $12.9 billion in sales in 2013, making it the clear leader of natural and organic grocers even though its numbers were still rather small compared to Kroger's net income of $1.5 billion on more than $98 billion in sales.[17]

Facing increased competition in the segment, many analysts believed that Whole Foods' biggest challenge was its reputation for high prices. For instance, Whole Foods charged $2.99 for a pound of organic apples, compared to $1.99 at Sprouts and even less at Costco.[18] Indeed, many consumers derisively described the store as "Whole Paycheck," and the company had historically opened its stores in high-income areas. In response to this image, the company had already begun marketing private labels (365 and 365 Everyday Value), begun competitive price matching and promotional sales, and launched a printed value guide (*The Whole Deal*) that featured coupons, low-budget recipes, and other tips for price-conscious consumers.[19] Additionally, many Whole Foods supporters often pointed out that they were willing to pay a premium price for a premium product.

---

[13]Company website.

[14]Whole Foods Market annual report, 2013.

[15]Tom Ryan, "Whole Foods Market Aims for 1,000 Stores in the U.S.," *Forbes*, July 5, 2011.

[16]Whole Foods Market annual report, 2013.

[17]Whole Foods Market annual report, 2013.

[18]"Victim of Success."

[19]Whole Foods Market annual report, 2013.

The Research Report

The recent collapse of Whole Foods' stock price had caught Short and her team flat-footed. After all, heated competition in the grocery space was nothing new, even for Whole Foods, but the company had nonetheless maintained both its favorable margins and high growth rate for years. Short, along with many other analysts across Wall Street, had been strongly in the bull camp prior to the recent earnings report. Short's report from the past month recommended to investors that Whole Foods stock was a "buy" and worth $60 per share. This argument was based on ongoing gains to expected revenue growth and EBITDA margins in the coming year (the report built in expectations of revenue growth of 11% and 14%, respectively, in 2014 and 2015; and EBITDA margins of 9.4% and 9.8%, respectively, in 2014 and 2015). The main question now facing the team was whether to adjust its financial forecast for Whole Foods in light of recent news. **Exhibit 7.7** contains a version of the forecast model with the assumptions used for Short's previous report. As an additional benchmark, **Exhibit 7.8** reports prevailing capital market information. As Short reconsidered her position, her team fleshed out the case for both a bearish and bullish view on Whole Foods.

From the bears' perspective, the natural and organic market was becoming saturated as more companies offered organic products at lower cost. This competition would soon compress Whole Foods' margins, while at the same time stealing market share and causing same-store sales to slow or even decline.[20] Several analysts had downgraded Whole Foods after the company issued its disappointing quarterly results.[21] A report put out the previous week by another bank noted that 85% of Whole Foods' stores were within three miles of a Trader Joe's—a privately owned natural grocer—up from 44% in 2005; similar overlap with Sprouts had grown from 3% to 16% and with Fresh Market from 1% to 14%. Moreover, Whole Foods was running out of dense, highly educated, high-income neighborhoods to open new stores in, which could either force the company to rely more on low-price offerings or slow its rapid expansion.[22] Such a shift in strategy could take the company into uncharted territory and risk its reputation as a premium brand. Finally, the bears were concerned that the new competitive reality would cause the market to fundamentally revalue Whole Foods. The company had long traded at a substantial premium, at times exceeding Kroger's market value, despite the latter company's substantial size advantage (compared to Whole Foods, Kroger had 7.3 times as many stores that generated 7.6 times as many sales and 3.6 times as much EBITDA). Such a premium could only be justified if Whole Foods could continue growing, both at its existing stores and in terms of its overall footprint. The team noted that even if it cut the price target from

[20]Karen Short and Shane Higgins, "The Bear vs. Bull Thesis; We Remain in the Bull Camp," Deutsche Bank, 2014.

[21]Annie Gasparro, "Slow to Cut Prices, Whole Foods is Punished," *Wall Street Journal*, May 7, 2014.

[22]Edward Kelly, Judah Frommer, and Lauren Wood, "Analysis of Emerging Headwinds Suggests Pullback May Not be a Buying Opportunity," Credit Suisse, 2014.

$60 to $40, Whole Foods would still trade at a premium to its competitors in the conventional grocers' segment.

The bulls believed the combination of Whole Foods' leadership in natural and organic offerings, shifting consumer preferences, and organic food's small but rapidly growing market provided ample runway for sustained growth at high margins.[23] As the clear leader in the segment, Whole Foods was well positioned to benefit from consumers' increasingly health-conscious decision making. Moreover, Whole Foods was not just another retailer that offered natural products; it was the standard bearer and thought leader for the industry, making it top of mind for anyone interested in the type of healthy products Whole Foods brought into the mainstream. Its competitors were merely imitating what Whole Foods pioneered and continued to lead, giving the company a sustainable advantage.[24] While competition could put downward pressure on some of Whole Foods' prices, the company had the stature to maintain its margin targets even with competitive price cuts by driving sales toward higher-margin categories like prepared foods, where the grocer could more readily differentiate its products. Moreover, the company's high prices gave it more room to adjust prices on goods where it directly competed with lower-cost retailers; past work by Short's team had shown that Whole Foods could match Kroger on 10,000 SKUs–equivalent to all the non private-label nonperishable products the company offered—and still maintain nearly a 35% gross margin, which was within Whole Foods' target range.[25] Similar analyses against other competitors also suggested ample room to selectively compete on prices while maintaining its overall margin targets. Additionally, Whole Foods had opportunities to reduce operating expenses, which the bulls thought would offset decline in revenue from pricing pressure over the next few years. While some analysts were concerned that Whole Foods' expansion would take it into lower-income areas that were distinct from the company's historical target market, the bulls believed that Whole Foods private-label products offered a chance to provide similar, high-quality products at a more accessible price point while protecting margins and providing a promising new avenue for growth.[26] While the bulls acknowledged that Whole Foods traded at a premium, they thought the company's higher growth rates, attractive margins, and position as a market leader provided ample justification for its higher valuation.

Whole Foods' CEO John Mackey was firmly in the bull camp. While he acknowledged that Whole Foods' best-in-the-industry sales per square foot and margins would attract competition, he claimed: "We are and will be able to compete successfully" and that the pricing gap between Whole Foods and the competition would not disappear.[27] More importantly, he claimed that no competitor offered the quality of products that Whole Foods could, regardless of how these competitors chose to market their products. Alluding to the lack of a clear legal definition for natural foods, he alleged that

---

[23]Short and Higgins.

[24]Short and Higgins.

[25]Short and Higgins.

[26]Scott Davis, "Whole Foods Holistic Growth Plan," *Forbes*, April 30, 2014.

[27]Author interview with John Mackey, March 22, 2016.

many competitors marketed standard commercial meat and other perishable goods under misleading labels, and said that Whole Foods could more aggressively advertise its superior quality to maintain its differentiation from the competition. Similarly, the company was making investments to improve the customer experience, already seen by many as one of its stronger points, by shortening wait times and offering higher-quality self-service food. Behind the scenes, it was reallocating support personnel on a regional rather than store-by-store basis in an effort to cut costs. After hinting at several projects in the pipeline that would help Whole Foods thrive in the new reality of stronger competition, he said that Whole Foods "is not sitting still. We are still very innovative!"

EXHIBIT 7.1 | Share Price Performance of Whole Foods Market Indexed to S&P 500 Index (January 2005 to April 2014)

Data source: Yahoo! Finance, author analysis.

EXHIBIT 7.2 | Select Market Share Data

Grocery Sales by Channel	Actual 2011	2016
Traditional Supermarkets	40.1%	37.4%
Supercenters	17.2%	18.5%
Convenience Stores	15.1%	15.6%
Wholesale Clubs	8.5%	9.0%
Drug Stores	5.5%	5.9%
Mass Merchandisers	4.4%	2.8%
Limited Assortment Grocery Stores	2.7%	3.7%
Dollar Stores	2.2%	2.3%
Other	4.3%	4.9%

Top Grocery Retailers in North America	2012 Revenue ($ billions)
Wal-Mart	145.0
Kroger	96.3
Costco	87.3
Target	73.1
Safeway	44.5
Loblaw Cos.	31.8
Publix	27.5
Ahold USA Retail	27.3
7-Eleven	22.0
C&S Wholesale Grocers	21.4
Delhaize America	19.5
H-E-B Grocery Co.	19.4
Sobeys	17.7
Dollar General Corp.	16.1
Meijer, Inc.	14.6
Wakefern Food Corp.	13.6
Metro Inc.	12.0
Whole Foods Market	11.7

Source: *Market Share Reporter* (Farmington Hills, MI: Gale, 2014) and author analysis.

EXHIBIT 7.3 | U.S. Store Count Forecast—Natural and Organic Share versus Total Industry

	2013	2014	2015	2016	2017	2018
Conventional Supermarkets	36,092	36,092	36,092	36,092	36,092	36,092
Natural and Organic Subtotal	1,367	1,572	1,808	2,079	2,391	2,750
Assumed Growth Rate		15%	15%	15%	15%	15%
N&O Share of Industry	3.6%	4.2%	4.8%	5.4%	6.2%	7.1%

Data source: Deutsche Bank Research; Food Marketing Institute.

EXHIBIT 7.4 | Selected Operating Data for Comparable Companies

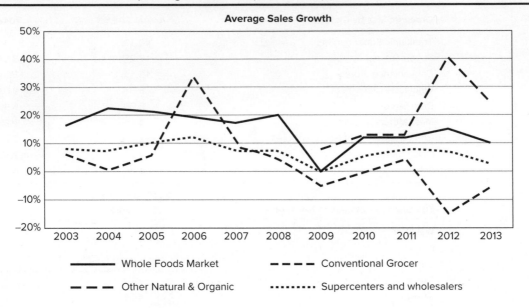

Average Sales Growth

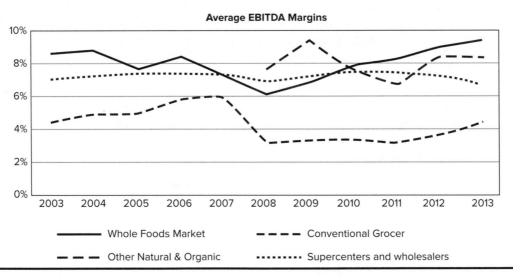

Average EBITDA Margins

Note: "Other natural & organic" is composed of Sprouts and Fresh Market. "Conventional grocer" is composed of Kroger, Safeway, and SuperValu. "Supercenters and wholesalers" is composed of Wal-Mart and Costco.

Source: Company SEC filings, 2003–2013.

EXHIBIT 7.5 | Selected Financial Data for Comparable Companies (in millions of USD, except percentages, ratios, and per share data; financial statement data as of fiscal year 2013)

Company	Sales	EBITDA	Market Cap of Equity	Total Debt	Beta	Bond Credit Rating
Natural & Organic						
Whole Foods Market	12,917	1,222	14,481	0	0.70	N.A.
Sprouts Farmers Market	2,438	187	4,102	304	0.75	BB−
The Fresh Market	1,512	138	1,554	25	0.80	N.A.
Conventional Grocers						
Kroger	98,375	4,428	23,679	11,311	0.70	BBB
Safeway	36,139	1,579	7,899	4,451	0.75	BBB
Supervalu	17,155	720	1,876	2,531	1.00	B−
Supercenters and Wholesalers						
Wal-Mart	476,294	35,742	251,747	55,245	0.60	AA
Target	72,596	6,452	36,806	14,089	0.75	A
Costco	105,156	3,999	49,257	4,985	0.75	A+

Data sources: Value Line, Mergent Online, YCharts, Yahoo! Finance, Standard and Poor's, company SEC filings, and author estimates.

EXHIBIT 7.6 | Store Growth Statistics for Whole Foods and Other Industry Comparables

	2008	2009	2010	2011	2012	2013
Total Stores						
Trader Joe's						400
Whole Foods Market	275	284	299	311	335	362
Sprouts	36	40	43	103	148	167
Fresh Market	86	92	100	113	129	151
Natural Grocers						72
Fairway						14
Other Natural and Organic Retailers						200
Kroger	2,481	2,469	2,460	2,435	2,424	2,640
Safeway	1,739	1,725	1,694	1,678	1,641	1,335
SuperValu	2,474	2,421	2,349	2,394	2,434	2,396
Wal-Mart (including Sam's Club, U.S. only)	4,258	4,360	4,413	4,479	4,625	4,835
Costco (U.S., Canada, & Mexico)	512	527	540	592	606	634

	2008	2009	2010	2011	2012	2013
Same-Store Sales Growth						
Whole Foods Market	4.0%	−4.0%	7.0%	8.0%	8.0%	7.0%
Sprouts	9.0%	2.6%	2.3%	5.1%	9.7%	10.7%
Fresh Market	−1.5%	−1.1%	5.0%	5.4%	5.7%	3.2%
Kroger (excluding fuel)	5.3%	3.1%	2.5%	4.9%	3.5%	3.6%
Safeway (excluding fuel)	1.5%	−4.9%	−0.5%	4.9%	1.6%	0.2%
SuperValu (including fuel)	0.5%	−1.2%	−5.1%	−6.0%	−2.8%	−2.4%
Wal-Mart (U.S. only)	3.5%	−0.8%	−0.6%	1.6%	2.4%	−0.5%
Costco (including fuel)	8.0%	−4.0%	7.0%	10.0%	7.0%	6.0%

Data source: Company SEC filings; Deutsche Bank Research; Food Marketing Institute.

EXHIBIT 7.7 | Deutsche Bank Model (in millions of USD, except per share figures)

At Fiscal Year End	Actual 2011	Actual 2012	Actual 2013	Forecast 2014	Forecast 2015
Store Growth	4.0%	7.7%	8.1%	10.5%	12.6%
Sales Growth	12.2%	15.7%	10.4%	11.1%	14.0%
EBITDA Margin	8.5%	9.0%	9.5%	9.4%	9.8%
Tax Rate	38.1%	38.4%	38.8%	39.0%	39.0%
Current Asset Turnover	7.0	5.6	6.5	7.0	7.1
Current Liabilities Turnover	10.5	10.9	10.7	10.5	10.5
Net PP&E/Store	6.4	6.5	6.7	6.7	6.7
Annual Dep. & Amort./Store	1.00	0.93	0.94	0.94	0.94
Stores	311	335	362	400	450
Sales	10,108	11,699	12,917	14,351	16,360
EBITDA	859	1,055	1,222	1,352	1,600
Dep. & Amort.	311	311	339	376	423
EBIT	548	744	883	976	1,176
Taxes	209	286	343	381	459
Net Income	339	458	540	596	717
Shares Outstanding	350	364	372	372	372
Earnings per Share	0.97	1.26	1.45	1.60	1.93
Current Assets	1,453	2,103	1,980	2,050	2,304
Current Liabilities	880	977	1,088	1,238	1,406
Net Working Capital	573	1,126	892	812	898
Net PP&E	1,997	2,193	2,428	2,680	3,018
Return on Capital	13.2%	13.8%	16.3%	17.1%	18.3%

Data source: Company financial reports, Deutsche Bank research, and author estimates.

EXHIBIT 7.8 I   Demographic and Capital Markets Data

U.S. Population Growth Rates

2014–2015	0.82%
2015–2060 (Compound Annual Growth Rate)	0.70%

Yield on U.S. Treasuries

6 Months	0.05%
1 Year	0.10%
3 Years	0.90%
5 Years	1.65%
30 Years	3.40%

Average Yields on U.S. Corporate Bonds

	5-Year Maturity	30-Year Maturity
AA	1.90%	4.29%
A	2.09%	4.39%
BBB	2.49%	4.80%
BB	4.00%	6.83%
B	4.90%	n/a

Data sources: Bloomberg and U.S. Census Bureau.

Horniman Horticulture

Bob Brown hummed along to a seasonal carol on the van radio as he made his way over the dark and icy roads of Amherst County, Virginia. He and his crew had just finished securing their nursery against some unexpected chilly weather. It was Christmas Eve 2015, and Bob, the father of four boys ranging in age from 5 to 10, was anxious to be home. Despite the late hour, he fully anticipated the hoopla that would greet him on his return and knew that it would be some time before even the youngest would be asleep. He regretted that the boys' holiday gifts would not be substantial; money was again tight this year. Nonetheless, Bob was delighted with what his company had accomplished. Business was booming. Revenue for 2015 was 15% ahead of 2014, and operating profits were up even more.

Bob had been brought up to value a strong work ethic. His father had worked his way up through the ranks to become foreman of a lumber mill in Southwest Virginia. At a young age, Bob began working for his father at the mill. After earning a degree in agricultural economics at Virginia Tech, he married Maggie Horniman in 2003. Upon his return to the mill, Bob was made a supervisor. He excelled at his job and was highly respected by everyone at the mill. In 2010, facing the financial needs of an expanding family, he and Maggie began exploring employment alternatives. In late 2012, Maggie's father offered to sell the couple his wholesalenursery business, Horniman Horticulture, near Lynchburg, Virginia. The business and the opportunity to be near Maggie's family appealed to both Maggie and Bob. Pooling their savings, the proceeds from the sale of their house, a minority-business-development grant, and a sizable personal loan from Maggie's father, the Browns purchased the business for $999,000. It was agreed that Bob would run the nursery's operations and Maggie would oversee its finances.

Bob thoroughly enjoyed running his own business and was proud of its growth over the previous three years. The nursery's operations filled 52 greenhouses and 40 acres of productive fields and employed 12 full-time and 15 seasonal employees.

Sales were primarily to retail nurseries throughout the mid-Atlantic region. The company specialized in such woody shrubs as azaleas, camellias, hydrangeas, and rhododendrons, but also grew and sold a wide variety of annuals, perennials, and trees.[1] Over the previous two years, Bob had increased the number of plant species grown at the nursery by more than 40%.

Bob was a "people person." His warm personality had endeared him to customers and employees alike. With Maggie's help, he had kept a tight rein on costs. The effect on the business's profits was obvious, as its profit margin had increased from 3.1% in 2013 to an expected 5.8% in 2015. Bob was confident that the nursery's overall prospects were robust.

With Bob running the business full time, Maggie primarily focused on attending to the needs of her active family. With the help of two clerks, she oversaw the company's books. Bob knew that Maggie was concerned about the recent decline in the firm's cash balance to below $10,000. Such a cash level was well under her operating target of 8% of annual revenue. But Maggie had shown determination to maintain financial responsibility by avoiding bank borrowing and by paying suppliers early enough to obtain any trade discounts.[2] Her aversion to debt financing stemmed from her concern about inventory risk. She believed that interest payments might be impossible to meet if adverse weather wiped out their inventory.

Maggie was happy with the steady margin improvements the business had experienced. Some of the gains were due to Bob's response to a growing demand for more-mature plants. Nurseries were willing to pay premium prices for plants that delivered "instant landscape," and Bob was increasingly shifting the product mix to that line. Maggie had recently prepared what she expected to be the end-of-year financial summary (**Exhibit 8.1**).[3] To benchmark the company's performance, Maggie used available data for the few publicly traded horticultural producers (**Exhibit 8.2**).

Across almost any dimension of profitability and growth, Bob and Maggie agreed that the business appeared to be strong. They also knew that expectations could change quickly. Increases in interest rates, for example, could substantially slow market demand. The company's margins relied heavily on the hourly wage rate of $10.32, currently required for H2A-certified nonimmigrant foreign agricultural workers. There was some debate within the U.S. Congress about the merits of raising this rate.

Bob was optimistic about the coming year. Given the ongoing strength of the local economy, he expected to have plenty of demand to continue to grow the business.

---

[1]Over the past year, Horniman Horticulture had experienced a noticeable increase in business from small nurseries. Because the cost of carrying inventory was particularly burdensome for those customers, slight improvements in the credit terms had been accompanied by substantial increases in sales.

[2]Most of Horniman's suppliers provided 30-day payment terms, with a 2% discount for payments received within 10 days.

[3]As compensation for the Browns' services to the business, they had drawn an annual salary of $50,000 (itemized as an SG&A expense) for each of the past three years. This amount was effectively the family's entire income.

Because much of the inventory took two to five years to mature sufficiently to sell, his top-line expansion efforts had been in the works for some time. Bob was sure that 2016 would be a banner year, with expected revenue hitting a record 30% growth rate. In addition, he looked forward to ensuring long-term-growth opportunities with the expected closing next month on a neighboring 12-acre parcel of farmland.[4] But for now, it was Christmas Eve, and Bob was looking forward to taking off work for the entire week. He would enjoy spending time with Maggie and the boys. They had much to celebrate for 2015 and much to look forward to in 2016.

---

[4]With the acquisition of the additional property, Maggie expected 2016 capital expenditures to be $75,000. Although she was not planning to finance the purchase, prevailing mortgage rates were running at 6.5%. The expected depreciation expense for 2016 was $46,000.

EXHIBIT 8.1 I Projected Financial Summary for Horniman Horticulture (in thousands of dollars)

	2012	2013	2014	2015
Profit and loss statement				
Revenue	788.5	807.6	908.2	1048.8
Cost of goods sold	402.9	428.8	437.7	503.4
Gross profit	385.6	378.8	470.5	545.4
SG&A expense	301.2	302.0	356.0	404.5
Depreciation	34.2	38.4	36.3	40.9
Operating profit	50.2	38.4	78.2	100.0
Taxes	17.6	13.1	26.2	39.2
Net profit	32.6	25.3	52.0	60.8
Balance sheet				
Cash	120.1	105.2	66.8	9.4
Accounts receivable	90.6	99.5	119.5	146.4
Inventory[1]	468.3	507.6	523.4	656.9
Other current assets[2]	20.9	19.3	22.6	20.9
Current assets	699.9	731.6	732.3	833.6
Net fixed assets (NFAs)[3]	332.1	332.5	384.3	347.9
Total assets	1,032.0	1,064.1	1,116.6	1,181.5
Accounts payable	6.0	5.3	4.5	5.0
Wages payable	19.7	22.0	22.1	24.4
Other payables	10.2	15.4	16.6	17.9
Current liabilities	35.9	42.7	43.2	47.3
Net worth	996.1	1,021.4	1,073.4	1,134.2
Capital expenditure	22.0	38.8	88.1	4.5
Purchases[4]	140.8	145.2	161.2	185.1

[1]Inventory investment was valued at the lower of cost or market. The cost of inventory was determined by accumulating the costs associated with preparing the plants for sale. Costs that were typically capitalized as inventory included direct labor, materials (soil, water, containers, stakes, labels, chemicals), scrap, and overhead.

[2]Other current assets included consigned inventory, prepaid expenses, and assets held for sale.

[3]NFAs included land, buildings and improvements, equipment, and software.

[4]Purchases represented the annual amount paid to suppliers.

EXHIBIT 8.2 | Financial Ratio Analysis and Benchmarking

	2012	2013	2014	2015	Benchmark[1]
Revenue growth	2.9%	2.4%	12.5%	15.5%	(1.8)%
Gross margin (gross profit/revenue)	48.9%	46.9%	51.8%	52.0%	48.9%
Operating margin (op. profit/revenue)	6.4%	4.8%	8.6%	9.5%	7.6%
Net profit margin (net profit/revenue)	4.1%	3.1%	5.7%	5.8%	2.8%
Return on assets (net profit/total assets)	3.2%	2.4%	4.7%	5.1%	2.9%
Return on capital (net profit/total capital)	3.3%	2.5%	4.8%	5.4%	4.0%
Receivable days (AR/revenue × 365)	41.9	45.0	48.0	50.9	21.8
Inventory days (inventory/COGS × 365)	424.2	432.1	436.5	476.3	386.3
Payable days (AP/purchases × 365)	15.6	13.3	10.2	9.9	26.9
NFA turnover (revenue/NFA)	2.4	2.4	2.4	3.0	2.7

[1]Benchmark figures were based on 2014 financial ratios of publicly traded horticultural producers.

Guna Fibres, Ltd.

Surabhi Kumar, managing director and principal owner of Guna Fibres, Ltd. (Guna), discovered the problem when she arrived at the parking lot of the company's plant one morning in early January 2012. Customers for whom rolls of fiber yarn were intended had been badgering Kumar to fill their orders in a timely manner, yet trucks that had been loaded just the night before were being unloaded because the government tax inspector, stationed at the company's warehouse, would not clear the trucks for departure. The excise tax had not been paid; the inspector required a cash payment, but in seeking to draw funds that morning, Vikram Malik, the bookkeeper, discovered that the company had overdrawn its bank account—the third time in as many weeks. The truck drivers, independent contractors, cursed loudly as they unloaded the trucks, refusing to wait while the company and government settled their accounts.

This shipment would not leave for at least another two days, and angry customers would no doubt require an explanation. Before granting a loan with which to pay the excise tax, the branch manager of the All-India Bank & Trust Company had requested a meeting with Kumar for the next day to discuss Guna's financial condition and its plans for restoring the firm's liquidity.

Kumar told Malik, "This cash problem is most vexing. I don't understand it. We're a very profitable enterprise, yet we seem to have to depend increasingly on the bank. Why do we need more loans just as our heavy selling season begins? We can't repeat this blunder."

Company Background

Guna was founded in 1972 to produce nylon fiber at its only plant in Guna, India, about 500 km south of New Delhi. By using new technology and domestic raw materials, the firm had developed a steady franchise among dozens of small, local textile weavers. It supplied synthetic fiber yarns used to weave colorful cloths for making

This case was written by Thien T. Pham (MBA '90), Robert F. Bruner, and Michael J. Schill as a basis for class discussion. The names and institutions in this case are fictitious. The financial support of the Batten Institute is gratefully acknowledged. Copyright © 2013 by the University of Virginia Darden School Foundation, Charlottesville, VA. All rights reserved. *To order copies, send an e-mail to sales@dardenbusinesspublishing.com. No part of this publication may be reproduced, stored in a retrieval system, used in a spreadsheet, or transmitted in any form or by any means—electronic, mechanical, photocopying, recording, or otherwise—without the permission of the Darden School Foundation.*

saris, the traditional women's dress of India. On average, each sari required eight yards of cloth. An Indian woman typically would buy three saris a year. With India's female population at around 600 million, the demand for saris accounted for more than 14 billion yards of fabric. This demand was currently being supplied entirely from domestic textile mills that, in turn, filled their yarn requirements from suppliers such as Guna.

Synthetic Textile Market

The demand for synthetic textiles was stable, with year-to-year growth and predictable seasonal fluctuations. Unit demand increased with both population and national income. In addition, India's population celebrated hundreds of festivals each year, in deference to a host of deities, at which saris were traditionally worn. The most important festival, the Diwali celebration in midautumn, caused a seasonal peak in the demand for new saris, which in turn caused a seasonal peak in demand for nylon textiles in late summer and early fall. Thus the seasonal demand for nylon yarn would peak in midsummer. Unit growth in the industry was expected to be 15% per year.

Consumers purchased saris and textiles from cloth merchants located in villages throughout the country. A cloth merchant usually was an important local figure who was well known to area residents and who generally granted credit to support consumer purchases. Merchants maintained relatively low levels of inventory and built stocks of goods only shortly before and during the peak selling season.

Competition was keen among those merchants' suppliers (the many small textile-weaving mills) and was affected by price, service, and the credit they could grant to the merchants. The mills essentially produced to order, building their inventories of woven cloth shortly in advance of the peak selling season and keeping only maintenance stocks at other times of the year.

The yarn manufacturers competed for the business of the mills through responsive service and credit. The suppliers to the yarn manufacturers provided little or no trade credit. Being near the origin of the textile chain in India, the yarn manufacturers essentially banked the downstream activities of the industry.

Production and Distribution System

Thin profit margins had prompted Kumar to adopt policies against overproduction and overstocking, which required Guna to carry inventories through the slack selling season. She had adopted a plan of seasonal production, which meant that the yarn plant would operate at peak capacity for two months of the year and at modest levels the rest of the year. That policy imposed an annual ritual of hirings and layoffs.

To help ensure prompt service, Guna maintained two distribution warehouses, but getting the finished yarn quickly from the factory in Guna to the customers was a challenge. The roads were narrow and mostly in poor repair. A truck was often delayed negotiating the trip between Kolkata and Guna, a distance of about 730 km. Journeys were slow and dangerous, and accidents were frequent.

Company Performance

Guna had experienced consistent growth and profitability (see **Exhibit 9.1** for firm's recent financial statements). In 2011, sales had grown at an impressive rate of 18%. Recent profits were INR25 million, down from INR36 million in 2010.[1] Kumar expected Guna's growth to continue with gross sales reaching more than INR900 million in 2012 (**Exhibit 9.2**).[2]

Reassessment

After the episode in the parking lot, Kumar and her bookkeeper went to her office to analyze the situation. She pushed aside two items on her desk to which she had intended to devote her morning: a message from the transportation manager regarding a possible change in the inventory policy (**Exhibit 9.3**) and a proposal from the operations manager for a scheme of level annual production (**Exhibit 9.4**).

To prepare a forecast on a business-as-usual basis, Kumar and Malik agreed on various parameters. Cost of goods sold would run at 73.7% of gross sales—a figure that was up from recent years because of increasing price competition. Annual operating expenses would be about 6% of gross annual sales. Operating expenses were up from recent years to include the addition of a quality-control department, two new sales agents, and four young nephews in whom Kumar hoped to build allegiance to the family business. Kumar had long felt pressure to hire family members to company management. The four new fellows would join 10 other family members on her team. Although the company's income tax rate of 30% accrued monthly, positive balances were paid quarterly in March, June, September, and December. The excise tax (at 15% of sales) was different from the income tax and was collected at the factory gate as trucks left to make deliveries to customers and the regional warehouses. Kumar expected to pay dividends of INR5.0 million per quarter to the 11 members of her extended family who owned the entirety of the firm's equity. For years, Guna had paid substantial dividends. The Kumar family believed that excess funds left in the firm were at greater risk than if the funds were returned to shareholders.

Accounts receivable collections in any given month had been running steadily at the rate of 48 days, comprised of 40% of the previous month's gross sales plus 60% of the gross sales from the month before that. The cost of the raw materials for Guna's yarn production ran about 55% of the gross sale price. To ensure sufficient raw material on hand, it was Guna's practice each month to purchase the amount of raw materials expected to be sold in two months. The suppliers Guna used had little ability to provide credit such that accounts payable were generally paid within two weeks. Monthly direct labor and other direct costs associated with yarn manufacturing were equivalent to about 34% of purchases in the previous month.[3] Accounts payable ran at about half of the month's purchases. As a matter of policy, Kumar wanted to see a cash balance of at

---

[1] INR = Indian rupees.

[2] At the time, the rupee exchange rate for U.S. dollars was roughly at the rate of INR50 per dollar.

[3] The 73.7% COGS rate assumption was determined based on these purchases and direct cost figures:
$73.7\% = 55\% + 55\% \times 34\%$.

least INR7.5 million. To sustain company expansion, capital expenditures were anticipated to run at INR3.5 million per quarter.

Guna had a line of credit at the All-India Bank & Trust Company, where it also
maintained its cash balances. All-India's short-term interest rate was currently 14.5%,
but Kumar was worried that inflation and interest rates might rise in the coming year. By
terms of the bank, the seasonal line of credit had to be reduced to a zero balance for at
least 30 days each year. The usual cleanup month had been October,[4] but last year Guna
had failed to make a full repayment at that time. Only after strong assurances by Kumar
that she would clean up the loan in November or December had the lending officer re-
luctantly agreed to waive the cleanup requirement in October. Unfortunately, the credit
needs of Guna did not abate as rapidly as expected in November and December, and
although his protests increased each month, the lending officer had agreed to meet
Guna's cash requirements with loans. Now he was refusing to extend any more seasonal
credit until Kumar presented a reasonable financial plan for the company that demonstrated its ability to clean up the loan by the end of 2012.

Financial Forecast

With some experience in financial modeling, Malik used the agreed-upon assumptions
to build out a monthly forecast of Guna's financial statements (**Exhibit 9.5**). To summarize the seasonal pattern of the model, Malik handed Kumar a graph showing the
projected monthly sales and key balance sheet accounts (**Exhibit 9.6**). After studying
the forecasts for a few moments, Kumar expostulated:

> The loan officer will never accept this forecast as a basis for more credit. We need a new
> plan, and fast. Maintaining this loan is critical for us to scale up for the most important
> part of our business season. Please go over these assumptions in detail and look for any
> opportunities to improve our debt position.

Then looking toward the two proposals she had pushed aside earlier, she muttered, "Perhaps
these proposals will help."

---

[4]The selection of October as the loan-cleanup month was imposed by the bank on the grounds of tradition.
Seasonal loans of any type made by the bank were to be cleaned up in October. Kumar had seen no reason
previously to challenge the bank's tradition.

EXHIBIT 9.1 | Guna's Annual Income Statements
(in millions of Indian rupees)

	2010	2011
Gross Sales	644.8	758.7
Excise Tax	96.7	113.8
Net Sales	548.1	644.9
Cost of Goods	445.0	538.6
Gross Profits	103.1	106.3
Operating Expenses	35.0	48.3
Depreciation	7.7	9.1
Interest Expense	9.1	12.4
Profit Before Tax	51.4	36.5
Income Tax	15.5	10.9
Net Profit	35.9	25.6
Cash	9.0	7.6
Accounts Receivable	23.9	26.7
Inventory	29.7	34.5
Total Current Assets	62.6	68.8
Gross Plant, Property, and Equipment (PPE)	88.7	100.9
Accumulated Depreciation	11.7	14.8
Net PPE	77.0	86.1
Total Assets	139.6	154.9
Accounts Payable	6.0	8.2
Notes to Bank	0.0	8.0
Accrued Taxes	−0.6	−0.9
Total Current Liabilities	5.4	15.3
Owners' Equity	134.2	139.6
Total Liabilities and Equity	139.6	154.9

Source: All exhibits created by case writer.

EXHIBIT 9.2 | Guna's Monthly Sales, 2011 Actual and 2012 Forecast (in millions of Indian rupees)

	2011 (Actual)	2012 (Forecast)
January	20.1	26.2
February	23.1	28.9
March	34.2	44.5
April	70.4	88.0
May	120.7	138.9
June	152.9	175.9
July	141.9	163.2
August	71.4	85.8
September	40.2	50.3
October	34.2	44.5
November	27.2	35.3
December	22.1	27.7
Year	758.7	909.0

EXHIBIT 9.3 | Message from Transportation Manager

January 2, 2012

To: S. Kumar
From: R. Sikh

As you asked me to, I have been tracking our supply shipments over the past year. I have observed a substantial improvement in the reliability of the shipments. As a result, I would propose that we reduce our raw-material inventory requirement from 60 days to 30 days. This would reduce the amount of inventory we are carrying by one month, and should free up a lot of space in the warehouse. I am not sure if that will affect any other department since we will be buying the same amount of material, but it would make inventory tracking a lot easier for me. Please let me know so we can implement this in January such that I don't purchase any additional raw material this month.

EXHIBIT 9.4 | Message from Operations Manager

January 7, 2012

To: S. Kumar
From: L. Gupta

You asked me to estimate the production efficiencies arising from a scheme of level annual production where our production rate is level over the year rather than highly seasonal as it currently is. To provide for the estimated production needs in 2012 and 2013 with level production, I recommend that purchases shift to INR50 million per month.

There are significant operating advantages to be gained withthis operating scenario:

- Seasonal hirings and layoffs would no longer be necessary, permitting us to cultivate a stronger work force and, perhaps, to suppress labor unrest. You will recall that the unions have indicated that reducing seasonal layoffs will be one of their major negotiating objectives this year.
- Level production entails lower manufacturing risk. With the load spread throughout the year, we would suffer less from equipment breakdowns and could better match the routine maintenance with the demand on the plant and equipment.

With level production my team believes that direct labor and other direct manufacturing costs could be reduced from a forecasted 34% of purchases down to 29% of purchases.

EXHIBIT 9.5 | Monthly Financial Statement Forecast (in millions of Indian rupees)

Assumptions

Excise Tax Rate	15%
Annual Operating Expenses/Annual Gr Sales	6.0%
Depreciation/Gross PPE	10%
Interest Rate on Borrowings (and Deposits)	14.5%
Income Tax Rate	30%
Dividends Paid (in March, June, Sep, Dec)	5.0
Implied Operating Margin	26.3%

Minimum Cash Balance	7.5
Accounts Receivable Collection	
In One Month	40%
In Two Months	60%
Purchases/Gr Sales in Two Months	55%
Direct Labor/Purchases Last Month	34%
Capital Expenditures (every third month)	3.50
Accounts Payable/Purchases	50%

	Nov-11	Dec-11	Jan-12	Feb-12	Mar-12	Apr-12	May-12	Jun-12	Jul-12	Aug-12	Sep-12	Oct-12	Nov-12	Dec-12	2012	Jan-13	Feb-13
Gross Sales[1]	27.2	22.1	26.2	28.9	44.5	88.0	138.9	175.9	163.2	85.8	50.3	44.5	35.3	27.7	909.0	34.0	36.2
Excise Taxes[2]			3.9	4.3	6.7	13.2	20.8	26.4	24.5	12.9	7.5	6.7	5.3	4.2	136.3		
Net Sales			22.2	24.6	37.8	74.8	118.0	149.5	138.7	72.9	42.8	37.8	30.0	23.5	772.6		
Cost of Goods Sold			19.3	21.3	32.8	64.9	102.3	129.6	120.2	63.2	37.1	32.8	26.0	20.4	669.9		
Gross Profit			3.0	3.3	5.0	9.9	15.7	19.9	18.4	9.7	5.7	5.0	4.0	3.1	102.7		
Operating Expenses[3]			4.5	4.5	4.5	4.5	4.5	4.5	4.5	4.5	4.5	4.5	4.5	4.5	54.5		
Depreciation[4]			0.8	0.8	0.9	0.9	0.9	0.9	0.9	0.9	0.9	0.9	0.9	1.0	10.7		
Interest Expense[5]			0.1	0.2	0.6	1.4	2.6	3.7	4.2	3.4	2.0	1.0	0.6	0.4	20.3		
Profit Before Taxes			-2.5	-2.3	-1.0	3.1	7.7	10.7	8.8	0.9	-1.8	-1.5	-2.1	-2.8	17.2		
Income Taxes			-0.8	-0.7	-0.3	0.9	2.3	3.2	2.6	0.3	-0.5	-0.4	-0.6	-0.8	5.2		
Net Profit			-1.8	-1.6	-0.7	2.2	5.4	7.5	6.2	0.6	-1.2	-1.0	-1.5	-2.0	12.0		
Dividend					5.0			5.0			5.0			5.0			

[1] Gross Sales × Exercise Tax Rate

[2] Gross Sales × (Raw Material Cost % + Direct Labor Cost %)

[3] Annual Operating Expenses ÷ 12

[4] Gross PPE × Depreciation Rate ÷ 12

[5] Notes Payable $(t - 1)$ × Interest Rate ÷ 12

EXHIBIT 9.5 | Monthly Financial Statement Forecast (in millions of Indian rupees) *(continued)*

	Dec-11	Jan-12	Feb-12	Mar-12	Apr-12	May-12	Jun-12	Jul-12	Aug-12	Sep-12	Oct-12	Nov-12	Dec-12
Cash	7.6	7.5	7.5	7.5	7.5	7.5	7.5	7.5	7.5	7.5	7.5	7.5	7.5
Accounts Receivable[6]	26.7	27.7	32.9	50.1	103.0	179.9	247.5	256.9	171.9	90.0	62.9	50.3	37.1
Inventory	34.5	45.1	80.5	140.6	198.4	218.7	166.7	90.2	60.9	51.5	40.6	38.4	44.3
Total Current Assets	68.8	80.3	120.9	198.2	308.9	406.1	421.7	354.6	240.3	149.0	111.0	96.2	88.9
Gross PPE[7]	100.9	100.9	100.9	104.4	104.4	104.4	107.9	107.9	107.9	111.4	111.4	111.4	114.9
Accumulated Depreciation	14.8	15.6	16.5	17.4	18.2	19.1	20.0	20.9	21.8	22.7	23.6	24.6	25.5
Net PPE	86.1	85.3	84.4	87.0	86.2	85.3	87.9	87.0	86.1	88.7	87.8	86.8	89.4
Total Assets	154.9	165.6	205.3	285.2	395.0	491.4	509.6	441.6	326.4	237.7	198.7	183.0	178.3
Accounts Payable[8]	8.2	12.2	24.2	33.2	48.4	44.9	23.6	13.8	12.2	9.7	7.6	9.4	9.9
Note Payable[9]	8.0	17.1	47.2	119.1	215.7	307.9	345.4	278.4	163.9	86.9	51.5	36.1	38.6
Accrued Taxes[10]	-0.9	-1.7	-2.4	-2.6	-1.7	0.6	0.0	2.6	2.9	0.0	-0.4	-1.1	-1.9
Total Current Liabilities	15.3	27.7	69.1	154.6	262.3	353.3	369.0	294.9	179.0	96.6	58.6	44.4	46.6
Shareholders' Equity[11]	139.6	137.9	136.2	130.6	132.7	138.1	140.6	146.8	147.4	141.1	140.1	138.6	131.6
Total Liabilities & Equity	154.9	165.6	205.3	285.2	395.0	491.4	509.6	441.6	326.4	237.7	198.7	183.0	178.3

Inventory Detail	Nov-11	Dec-11	Jan-12	Feb-12	Mar-12	Apr-12	May-12	Jun-12	Jul-12	Aug-12	Sep-12	Oct-12	Nov-12	Dec-12	2012
Purchases[12]	14.4	15.9	24.5	48.4	76.4	96.7	89.7	47.2	27.7	24.5	19.4	15.2	18.7	19.9	508.2
Direct Labor and Other Mftg Costs[13]		4.9	5.4	8.3	16.5	26.0	32.9	30.5	16.0	9.4	8.3	6.6	5.2	6.4	171.4
Cost of Goods Sold			19.3	21.3	32.8	64.9	102.3	129.6	120.2	63.2	37.1	32.8	26.0	20.4	
Inventory[14]		34.5	45.1	80.5	140.6	198.4	218.7	166.7	90.2	60.9	51.5	40.6	38.4	44.3	

[6] AR(t − 1) + GSales(t) − 40% × GSales(t − 1) − 60% × GSales(t − 2)

[7] Gross PPE(t − 1) + Capex(t)

[8] 50% × Purchases(t)

[9] Total Assets − AP − AccTax − ShrEquity

[10] AccTax(t − 1) + IncTax(t) or 0 if positive balance and month of quarterly payment

[11] ShrEquity(t − 1) + NetProfit(t) − Dividend(t)

[12] 55% × GSales(t + 2)

[13] 35% × Purchases(t − 1)

[14] Inventory(t − 1) + Purchases(t) + Direct Labor(t) − COGS(t)

EXHIBIT 9.6 | Forecast of Accounts by Month

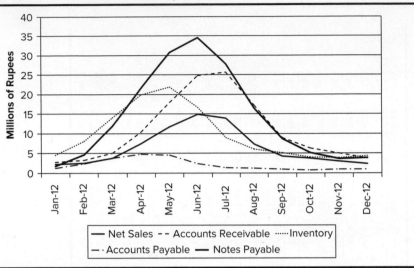

## PART 3

Estimating the Cost of Capital

"Best Practices" in Estimating the Cost of Capital: An Update

—W. Todd Brotherson, Kenneth M. Eades, Robert S. Harris, and Robert C. Higgins

"Cost of capital is so critical to things we do, and CAPM has so many holes in it—and the books don't tell you which numbers to use . . . so at the end of the day, you wonder a bit if you've got a solid number. Am I fooling myself with this well-disciplined, quantifiable number?"
—*A Corporate Survey Participant*

Theories on cost of capital have been around for decades. Unfortunately for practice, the academic discussions typically stop at a high level of generality, leaving important questions for application unanswered. Recent upheavals in financial markets have only made the practitioner's task more difficult. This paper updates our earlier work on the state of the art in cost of capital estimation to identify current best practices that emerge. Unlike many broadly distributed multiple choice or fill-in-the-blank surveys, our findings are based on conversations with practitioners at highly regarded corporations and leading financial advisors. We also report on advice from best-selling textbooks and trade books. We find close alignment among all these groups on use of common theoretical frameworks to estimate the cost of capital and on many aspects of estimation. We find large variation, however, for the joint choices of the risk-free rate of return, beta and the equity market risk premium, as well as for the adjustment of capital costs for specific investment risk. When compared to our 1998 publication, we find that practice has changed some since the late 1990s but there is still no consensus on important practical issues. The paper ends with a synthesis of messages from best practice companies and financial advisors and our conclusions.

"Best Practices in Estimating the Cost of Capital: An Update" by W. Todd Brotherson, Kenneth M. Eades, Robert S. Harris, and Robert C. Higgins from *Journal of Applied Finance,* Vol. 23, No. 1, 2013. Used by permission of Financial Management Association, Tampa, FL.

The authors thank Bob Bruner for collaboration on prior research. His duties as a dean, however, prevent his joining this effort. We thank MSCI for sharing Barra data. The research would not have been possible without the cooperation of the companies and financial advisors surveyed. These contributions notwithstanding, any errors remain the authors'.

W. Todd Brotherson is Assistant professor at Southern Virginia University in Buena Vista, VA. Kenneth M. Eades is a Professor at the Darden Graduate School of Business Administration at the University of Virginia in Charlottesville, VA. Robert S. Harris is a Professor at the Darden Graduate School of Business Administration at the University of Virginia in Charlottesville, VA. Robert C. Higgins is Professor Emeritus at the Foster School of Business at the University of Washington in Seattle, WA.

Over the years, theoretical developments in finance converged into compelling recommendations about the cost of capital to a corporation. By the early 1990s, a consensus had emerged prompting descriptions such as "traditional . . . textbook . . . appropriate," "theoretically correct," "a useful rule of thumb" and a "good vehicle." In prior work with Bob Bruner, we reached out to highly regarded firms and financial advisors to see how they dealt with the many issues of implementation.[1] Fifteen years have passed since our first study. We revisit the issues and see what now constitutes best practice and what has changed in both academic recommendations and in practice.

We present evidence on how some of the most financially sophisticated companies and financial advisors estimate capital costs. This evidence is valuable in several respects. First, it identifies the most important ambiguities in the application of cost of capital theory, setting the stage for productive debate and research on their resolution. Second, it helps interested companies to benchmark their cost of capital estimation practices against best-practice peers. Third, the evidence sheds light on the accuracy with which capital costs can be reasonably estimated, enabling executives to use the estimates more wisely in their decision-making. Fourth, it enables teachers to answer the inevitable question, "But how do companies really estimate their cost of capital?"

The paper is part of a lengthy tradition of surveys of industry practice. For instance, Burns and Walker (2009) examine a large set of surveys conducted over the last quarter century into how U.S. companies make capital budgeting decisions. They find that estimating the weighted average cost of capital is the primary approach to selecting hurdle rates. More recently, Jacobs and Shivdasani (2012) report on a large-scale survey of how financial practitioners implement cost of capital estimation. Our approach differs from most papers in several important respects. Typically studies are based on written, closed-end surveys sent electronically to a large sample of firms, often covering a wide array of topics, and commonly using multiple choice or fill-in-the-blank questions. Such an approach typically yields low response rates and provides limited opportunity to explore subtleties of the topic. For instance, Jacobs and Shivdasani (2012) provide useful insights based on the Association for Finance Professionals (AFP) cost of capital survey. While the survey had 309 respondents, AFP (2011, page 18) reports this was a response rate of about 7% based on its membership companies. In contrast, we report the result of personal telephone interviews with practitioners from a carefully chosen group of leading corporations and financial advisors. Another important difference is that many existing papers focus on how well accepted modern financial techniques are among practitioners, while we are interested in those areas of cost of capital estimation where finance theory is silent or ambiguous and practitioners are left to their own devices.

The following section gives a brief overview of the weighted-average cost of capital. The research approach and sample selection are discussed in Section II. Section III reports the general survey results. Key points of disparity are reviewed in Section IV.

---

[1]To provide a self-contained article we draw directly on portions of our earlier work, Bruner, Eades, Harris, and Higgins (1998), which also discusses surveys from earlier years.

Section V discusses further survey results on risk adjustment to a baseline cost of capital, and Section VI highlights some institutional and market forces affecting cost of capital estimation. Section VII offers conclusions and implications for the financial practitioner.

I. The Weighted-Average Cost of Capital

A key insight from finance theory is that any use of capital imposes an opportunity cost on investors; namely, funds are diverted from earning a return on the next best equal-risk investment. Since investors have access to a host of financial market opportunities, corporate uses of capital must be benchmarked against these capital market alternatives. The cost of capital provides this benchmark. Unless a firm can earn in excess of its cost of capital on an average-risk investment, it will not create economic profit or value for investors.

A standard means of expressing a company's cost of capital is the weighted-average of the cost of individual sources of capital employed. In symbols, a company's weighted-average cost of capital (or WACC) is:

$$WACC = (W_{debt}(1 - t)K_{debt}) + (W_{equity}K_{equity}), \tag{1}$$

where:

K = *component cost of capital.*

W = *weight of each component as percent of total capital.*

t = *marginal corporate tax rate.*

For simplicity, this formula includes only two sources of capital; it can be easily expanded to include other sources as well.

Finance theory offers several important observations when estimating a company's WACC. First, the capital costs appearing in the equation should be current costs reflecting current financial market conditions, not historical, sunk costs. In essence, the costs should equal the investors' anticipated internal rate of return on future cash flows associated with each form of capital. Second, the weights appearing in the equation should be market weights, not historical weights based on often arbitrary, out-of-date book values. Third, the cost of debt should be after corporate tax, reflecting the benefits of the tax deductibility of interest.

Despite the guidance provided by finance theory, use of the weighted-average expression to estimate a company's cost of capital still confronts the practitioner with a number of difficult choices.[2] As our survey results demonstrate, the most nettlesome component of WACC estimation is the cost of equity capital; for unlike readily avail-

---

[2]Even at the theoretical level, the use of standard net present value (NPV) decision rules (with, for instance, WACC as a discount rate) does not capture the option value of being able to delay an irreversible investment expenditure. As a result, a firm may find it better to delay an investment even if the current NPV is positive. Our survey does not explore the ways firms deal with this issue; rather we focus on measuring capital costs.

able yields in bond markets, no observable counterpart exists for equities. This forces practitioners to rely on more abstract and indirect methods to estimate the cost of equity capital.

II. Sample Selection

This paper describes the results of conversations with leading practitioners. Believing that the complexity of the subject does not lend itself to a written questionnaire, we wanted to solicit an explanation of each firm's approach told in the practitioner's own words. Though our telephone interviews were guided by a series of questions, the conversations were sufficiently open-ended to reveal many subtle differences in practice.

Since our focus is on the gaps between theory and application rather than on average or typical practice, we aimed to sample practitioners who were leaders in the field. We began by searching for a sample of corporations (rather than investors or financial advisors) in the belief that they had ample motivation to compute WACC carefully and to resolve many of the estimation issues themselves. Several publications offer lists of firms that are well-regarded in finance; of these, we chose Fortune's 2012 listing of Most Admired Companies.[3] Working with the Hay Group, Fortune creates what it terms "the definitive report card on corporate reputations." Hay provided us with a listing of companies ranked by the criterion "wise use of assets" within industry. To create our sample we only used companies ranked first or second in their industry. We could not obtain raw scores that would allow comparisons across industries.

The 2012 Fortune rankings are based on a survey of 698 companies, each of which is among the largest in its industry. For each of 58 industry lists, Hay asks executives, directors, and analysts to rate companies in their own industry on a set of criteria. Starting with the top two ranked firms in each industry, we eliminated companies headquartered outside North America (eight excluded).[4] We also eliminated the one firm classified as a regulated utility (on the grounds that regulatory mandates create unique issues for capital budgeting and cost of capital estimation) and the seven firms in financial services (inclusive of insurance, banking, securities and real estate). Forty-seven companies satisfied our screens. Of these, 19 firms agreed to be interviewed and are included in the sample given in Table I. Despite multiple concerted attempts we made to contact appropriate personnel at each company, our response rate is lower than Bruner, Eades, Harris, and Higgins (1998) but still much higher than typical cost of capital surveys. We suspect that increases in the number of surveys and in the demands on executives' time influence response rates now versus the late 1990s.

---

[3]For instance, Institutional Investor publishes lists of firms with the best Chief Financial Officers (CFOs), or with special competencies in certain areas. We elected not to use such lists because special competencies might not indicate a generally excellent finance department, nor might a stellar CFO. The source used by Bruner et al. (1998) is no longer published. Our approach, however, mirrors that earlier work.

[4]This screen was also used in Bruner et al. (1998). Our reasons for excluding these firms were the increased difficulty of obtaining interviews, and possible difficulties in obtaining capital market information (such as betas and equity market premiums).

TABLE I. Three Survey Samples

Full titles of textbooks and trade books are listed in the references at the end of this paper.

Company Sample	Advisor Sample	Textbook/Trade Book Sample
AmerisourceBergen	Bank of America Merrill	Textbooks
Caterpillar	Lynch	Brigham and Ehrhardt (2013)
Chevron	Barclays Capital	Ross, Westerfield and Jaffe (2013)
Coca Cola	Credit Suisse	Brealey, Myers, and Allen (2011)
Costco Wholesale	Deutsche Bank AG	Higgins (2012)
IBM	Evercore Partners	
International Paper	Goldman Sachs & Co.	Trade books
Intuit	Greenhill & Co, LLC	Koller, Goedhart, and Wessels (2005)
Johnson Controls	JP Morgan	Ibbotson (2012)
PepsiCo	Lazard	
Qualcomm	Morgan Stanley	
Sysco	UBS	
Target		
Texas Instruments		
Union Pacific		
United Technologies		
UPS		
W.W. Grainger		
Walt Disney		

We approached corporate officers first with an email explaining our research. Our request was to interview the individual in charge of estimating the firm's WACC. We then arranged phone conversations. We promised our interviewees that, in preparing a report on our findings, we would not identify the practices of any particular company by name—we have respected this promise in the presentation that follows.

In the interest of assessing the practices of the broader community of finance practitioners, we surveyed two other samples:

- Financial advisors. Using a "league table" of merger and acquisition advisors from Thomson's Securities Data Commission (SDC) Mergers and Acquisitions database, we drew a sample of the most active advisors based on aggregate deal volume in M&A in the United States for 2011. Of the top twelve advisors, one firm chose not to participate in the survey, giving us a sample of eleven.

  We applied approximately the same set of questions to representatives of these firms' M&A departments.[5] Financial advisors face a variety of different

---

[5]Specific questions differ, reflecting the facts that financial advisors infrequently deal with capital budgeting matters and that corporate financial officers infrequently value companies.

pressures regarding cost of capital. When an advisor is representing the sell side of an M&A deal, the client wants a high valuation but the reverse may be true when an advisor is acting on the buy side. In addition, banks may be engaged by either side of the deal to provide a Fairness Opinion about the transaction. We wondered whether the pressures of these various roles might result in financial advisors using assumptions and methodologies that result in different cost of capital estimates than those made by operating companies. This proved not to be the case.

- Textbooks and Trade books. In parallel with our prior study, we focus on a handful of widely-used books. From a leading textbook publisher we obtained names of the four best-selling, graduate-level textbooks in corporate finance in 2011. In addition, we consulted two popular trade books that discuss estimation of the cost of capital in detail.

III. Survey Findings

Table II summarizes responses to our questions and shows that the estimation approaches are broadly similar across the three samples in several dimensions:

- Discounted Cash Flow (DCF) is the dominant investment evaluation technique.
- WACC is the dominant discount rate used in DCF analyses.
- Weights are based on *market* not book value mixes of debt and equity.[6]
- The after-tax cost of debt is predominantly based on *marginal* pretax costs, and *marginal* tax rates.[7]
- The Capital Asset Pricing Model (CAPM) is the dominant model for estimating the cost of equity. Despite shortcomings of the CAPM, our companies and financial advisors adopt this approach. In fact, across both companies and financial advisors, only one respondent did not use the CAPM.[8]

These practices parallel many of the findings from our earlier survey. First, the "best practice" firms show considerable alignment on many elements of practice. Second, they base their practice on financial economic models rather than on rules of thumb or arbitrary decision rules. Third, the financial frameworks offered by leading texts and trade books are fundamentally unchanged from our earlier survey.

---

[6]The choice between target and actual proportions is not a simple one. Because debt and equity costs depend on the proportions of each employed, it might appear that the actual proportions must be used. However, if the firm's target weights are publicly known and if investors expect the firm to move to these weights, then observed costs of debt and equity may anticipate the target capital structure.

[7]In practice, complexities of tax laws such as tax-loss carry forwards and carry backs, investment tax credits, state taxes, and international tax treatments complicate the situation. Graham and Mills (2008) estimate effective marginal tax rates. While most companies in their sample hit the statutory marginal rate, the average effective marginal tax rate turned out to be about 5% lower.

[8]See, for instance, Brealey, Myers, and Allen (2011) pgs. 196-199 for a high-level review of some of the empirical evidence and the textbook authors' rationale for continued use of the CAPM.

TABLE II. General Survey Results

Questions	Corporations	Financial Advisors	Textbooks/Trade Books
1. Do you use DCF techniques to evaluate investment opportunities?	95% Yes, as primary tool; some also consider transactions and trading multiples, real options, IRR and payback analysis, and ROI within a specified time period 4% No	100% Yes	100% Yes
2. Do you use any form of a cost of capital as your discount rate in your DCF analysis?	84% Yes 11% No 5% Decline to answer	100% Yes	100% Yes
3. For your cost of capital, do you form any combination of capital cost to determine a WACC?	95% Yes 5% No (not for valuation, but does use WACC for strategic comparisons)	100% Yes	100% Yes
4. What weighting factors do you use? A) Target weights vs. current debt/equity? B) Market vs. book weights?	A) 37% Target; 37% Current; 26% Not Reported B) 74% MV equity and debt; 21% MV equity with BV debt; 5% BV both	A) 73% Target/Optimal; 27% Current B) 100% MV equity and debt	A) 50% Market; 50% Target B) 100% MV equity and debt
5. How do you estimate your before tax cost of debt?	26% U.S. Treasury yield + spread 21% Marginal/YTM outstanding debt 21% Weighted avg outstanding issues 5% Banker's estimate 5% Current yield 5% Current rate, bank debt 11% Other 5% N/A	55% Current yield to maturity 45% New debt yield to maturity	83% Yield to maturity 17% Marginal cost of new debt
6. What tax rate do you use?	95% Effective marginal or statutory 5% Other	100% Effective marginal or statutory	67% Marginal income tax rate 33% Statutory corporate tax rate

(continued)

TABLE II. General Survey Results *(continued)*

Questions	Corporations	Financial Advisors	Textbooks/Trade Books
7. How do you estimate your cost of equity? (If you do not use CAPM, skip to question 12.)	90% CAPM 5% CAPM with dividend discount model and bond/stock relationship as a check 5% Modified required return model using beta	100% CAPM	100% CAPM Also mention dividend discount/ growth, arbitrage pricing, and Fama-French models
8. As usually written, the CAPM version of the cost of equity has three terms: a risk free rate, a volatility or beta factor, and a market risk premium. Is this consistent with your company's approach?	95% Yes 5% No	100% Yes	100% Yes
9. What do you use for the risk-free rate (both maturity and measurement)?	52% 10-year Treasuries 21% 20-year Treasuries 21% 30-year Treasuries 5% N/A 21% use something other than the spot yield to maturity (e.g., some form of historical averaging)	73% 10-year Treasuries 18% 20-year Treasuries 9% 30-year Treasuries 36% use some historical average rather than the spot yield to maturity	50% Long-term Treasuries 33% Long-term Treasuries less historical "term premium" 17% Match tenor of Treasury to that of investment
10. What do you use as your volatility or beta factor?	53% Explicitly reference Bloomberg betas 26% Use a published source (other than Bloomberg) or a third party advisors; three of these mention Barra 37% Mention self-calculated betas but some may use Bloomberg for this 26% Mention comparisons across sources (32% of respondents mentioned (unsolicited) unlevering/relevering beta)	73% Fundamental beta from Barra 44% Beta from Bloomberg 18% Self-calculated historical beta or other published source (27% of respondents mentioned (unsolicited) unlevering/relevering beta)	100% Mention published sources (One recommends levering industry beta to company target capital structure)

(continued)

TABLE II. General Survey Results *(continued)*

Questions	Corporations	Financial Advisors	Textbooks/Trade Books

11. What do you use as your market risk premium?	43% Cite historical data only
	  • 32% cite Ibbotson
	  • 11% mention another source
	16% Judgment using various cited sources
	16% Bloomberg
	16% Forward-looking calculation (other than Bloomberg)
	5% Ask bank
	5% No specific methodology reported
	Of 9 who reported a specific number, range was 4.87-9.02%, and mean was 6.49%
		73% Cite historical data—Ibbotson
		18% Forward-looking DDM
		9% Use a "range": No specific methodology reported
		
		Of 10 who reported a specific number, range was 4.0-8.5%, and mean was 6.6%
			100% Mention historical excess returns
			50% Recommend arithmetic averages; 17% geometric in some instances; 33% are silent
			87% Mention various other approaches

12. Do you use data from comparable companies in estimating the cost of capital? If so, how (e.g., averages for a subset of firms you feel are comparable)?	26% Yes, in order to get betas to relever or to select appropriate risk class 32% No 42% Indirectly as a check or reference	82% Use comps normally as benchmark 18% Use comps only if firm's WACC looks unreliable	67% Recommend estimating an industry asset beta and relevering to the target's capital structure
13. Having estimated your company's cost of capital, do you make any further adjustments to reflect the risk of individual investment opportunities?	53% Yes 37% No 5% Unsure 5% Decline to answer Slightly less than half of "Noes" make adjustments when deemed necessary but say this is infrequent.	91% Yes/As appropriate 9% No	33% Discuss further adjustments for small cap and industry 33% Adjust for project risk and division 33% Ignore the issue
14. How frequently do you re-estimate your company's cost of capital?	5% Monthly 21% Quarterly 16% Semi-annually 53% Annually 5% Occasionally Generally, many said that in addition to scheduled reviews, they re-estimate as needed for significant events such as acquisitions and high-impact economic events.	Not asked	Not mentioned

(continued)

TABLE II. General Survey Results *(continued)*

Questions	Corporations	Financial Advisors	Textbooks/Trade Books
15. Have financial market conditions of the last few years caused you to change the way you estimate and use the cost of capital?	26% Yes 63% No 5% Unsure 5% Not internally, but advising IBs have made adjustments	27% Yes 64% No 9% No response	One notes recent volatility as one reason practitioners use "target" weights rather than raw "market" weights when measuring capital structure
16. Is the cost of capital used for purposes other than project analysis in your company? (For example, to evaluate divisional performance?)	42% Yes 47% No 5% Indirectly 5% Decline to answer	Not asked	67% Discuss in context of performance measurement and EVA 33% Are silent
17. Do you distinguish between strategic and operational investments? Is cost of capital used differently in these two categories?	68% Yes 32% No If do distinguish, is cost of capital used differently (N=13): 23% Yes; 39% No; 30% Maybe; 5% N/A	Not asked	Not mentioned
18. What methods do you use to estimate terminal value? Do you use the same discount rate for the terminal value as for the interim cash flows?	Not asked	100% Both multiples and perpetual growth DCF model 55% Have no preference between models 27% Prefer perpetuity model 18% Prefer multiples approach 91% Use same WACC for TV 9% Did not specify	All recommend DCF equations. 50% recommend also using multiples and triangulating on value. There is no discussion of differing discount rates for terminal value and interim cash flows.
19. In valuing a multidivisional company, do you aggregate the values of the individual divisions, or just value the firm as a whole? If you value each division separately, do you use a different cost of capital for each one?	Not asked	100% "Usually"/"Typically" value the enterprise 100% Value the parts if size, risk, or other factors merit the consideration 91% Use separate WACCs 9% Did not specify	All recommend varying the discount rate to reflect the risk of the cash flows. Only one (17%) discusses valuation by parts.

(continued)

TABLE II. General Survey Results *(continued)*

Questions	Corporations	Financial Advisors	Textbooks/Trade Books
20. In your valuations do you use any different methods to value synergies or strategic opportunities (e.g., higher or lower discount rates, options valuation)?	Not asked	82% Value cash flows differently when warranted 73% Use a different discount rate for the risk 9% Use a different growth rate 27% cited NOLs as an example 45% cited synergies or strategic opportunities as examples	Not mentioned
21. How long have you been with the company? What is your job title?	Years with firm: Range: 2–32; Mean: 15.2 Years in finance: Range: 4–32; Mean: 18.5 All senior, except two	Mean: 11.0 years (current bank) Mean: 13.5 years (banking career) 1 Principal, 1 COO, 8 MD/D/EDs, 1 VP	N/A

On the other hand, disagreements exist within and among groups on matters of application, especially when it comes to using the CAPM to estimate the cost of equity. The CAPM states that the required return (K) on any asset can be expressed as:

$$K = R_f + \beta(R_m - R_f), \tag{2}$$

where:

R_f = *interest rate available on a risk-free asset.*

R_m = *return required to attract investors to hold the broad market portfolio of risky assets.*

β = *the relative risk of the particular asset.*

According to CAPM then, the cost of equity, K_{equity}, for a company depends on three components: returns on riskfree assets (R_f), the stock's equity "beta" which measures risk of the company's stock relative to other risky assets ($\beta = 1.0$ is average risk), and the market risk premium ($R_m - R_f$) necessary to entice investors to hold risky assets generally versus risk-free instruments. In theory, each of these components must be a forward-looking estimate. Our survey results show substantial disagreements, especially in terms of estimating the market risk premium.

A. The Risk-Free Rate of Return

As originally derived, the CAPM is a single period model, so the question of which interest rate best represents the risk-free rate never arises. In a multi period world typically characterized by upward-sloping yield curves, the practitioner must choose. The difference between realized returns on short-term U.S. Treasury-bills and long-term T-bonds has averaged about 150 basis points over the longrun; so choice of a risk-free rate can have a material effect on the cost of equity and WACC.[9]

Treasury bill yields are more consistent with the CAPM as originally derived and reflect risk-free returns in the sense that T-bill investors avoid material loss in value from interest rate movements. However, long-term bond yields more closely reflect the default-free holding period returns available on long-lived investments and thus more closely mirror the types of investments made by companies.

Our survey results reveal a strong preference on the part of practitioners for long-term bond yields. As shown in Table II (Question 9), all the corporations and financial advisors use Treasury bond yields for maturities of 10 years or greater, with the 10-year rate being the most popular choice. Many corporations said they matched the term of the risk-free rate to the tenor of the investment. In contrast, a third of the sample books suggested subtracting a term premium from long-term rates to approximate a shorter term yield. Half of the books recommended long-term rates but were not precise on the choice of maturity.

---

[9]This was estimated as the difference in arithmetic mean returns on longterm government bonds and U.S. Treasury bills over the years 1900–2008, using data from E. Dimson and P. Marsh as cited in Brealey, Myers, and Allen (2011) in Table 7.1 at page 158.

Because the yield curve is ordinarily relatively flat beyond ten years, the choice of which particular long-term yield to use often is not a critical one. However, at the time of our survey, Treasury markets did not display these "normal" conditions in the wake of the financial crisis and expansionary monetary policy. In the year we conducted our survey (2012), the spread between 10- and 30-year Treasury yields averaged 112 basis points.[10] While the text and trade books do not directly address the question of how to deal with such markets, it is clear that some practitioners are looking for ways to "normalize" what they see as unusual circumstances in the government bond markets. For instance, 21% of the corporations and 36% of the financial advisors resort to some historical average of interest rates rather than the spot rate in the markets. Such an averaging practice is at odds with finance theory in which investors see the current market rate as the relevant opportunity. We return to this issue later in the paper.

B. Beta Estimates

Finance theory calls for a forward-looking beta, one reflecting investors' uncertainty about the future cash flows to equity. Because forward-looking betas are unobservable, practitioners are forced to rely on proxies of various kinds. Often this involves using beta estimates derived from historical data.

The usual methodology is to estimate beta as the slope coefficient of the market model of returns:

$$R_{it} = \alpha_i + \beta_i(R_{mt}),\tag{3}$$

where:

R_{it} = *return on stock I in time period (e.g., day, week, month) t.*

R_{mt} = *return on the market portfolio in period t.*

α_i = *regression constant for stock i.*

β_i = *beta for stock i.*

In addition to relying on historical data, use of this equation to estimate beta requires a number of practical compromises, each of which can materially affect the results. For instance, increasing the number of time periods used in the estimation may improve the statistical reliability of the estimate but risks including stale, irrelevant information. Similarly, shortening the observation period from monthly to weekly, or even daily, increases the size of the sample but may yield observations that are not normally distributed and may introduce unwanted random noise. A third compromise involves choice of the market index. Theory dictates that R_m is the return on the "market portfolio," an unobservable portfolio consisting of *all* risky assets, including human

---

[10]Over the period 1977-2012 the difference between the yields on 10- and 30-year Treasury bonds averaged 29 basis points. However, for the period after the financial crisis this spread has been much higher in the midst of expansive Federal Reserve policy. For the period 2008–2012, the difference averaged 103 basis points. During 2012 when we conducted our survey it averaged 112 basis points. As we write in mid-January 2013, the yields on 10-, 20-, and 30-year Treasury bonds are 1.89%, 2.66%, and 3.06% respectively. Calculations use Federal Reserve H-15 interest rate data.

TABLE III.   **Compromises Underlying Beta Estimates and Their Effect on Estimated Betas of Sample Companies**

	Bloomberg*	Value Line*	Barra
Number of observations	102	260	statistical models using
Time interval	weekly over 2 yrs.	weekly over 5 yrs.	company characteristics
Market index proxy	S&P 500	NYSE composite	
Sample mean beta	0.96	0.93	0.91
Sample median beta	0.98	0.90	0.96

*With the Bloomberg service it is possible to estimate a beta over many differing time periods, market indices, and smoothed or unadjusted. The figures presented here represent the baseline or default-estimation approach used if one does not specify other approaches. Value Line states that "the Beta coefficient is derived from a regression analysis of the relationship between weekly percentage changes in the price of a stock and weekly percentage changes in the NYSE Index over a period of five years. In the case of shorter price histories, a smaller time period is used, but two years is the minimum. The betas are adjusted for their long-term tendency to converge toward 1.00."

capital and other non traded assets, in proportion to their importance in world wealth. Beta providers use a variety of stock market indices as proxies for the market portfolio on the argument that stock markets trade claims on a sufficiently wide array of assets to be adequate surrogates for the unobservable market portfolio.

Another approach is to "predict" beta based on underlying characteristics of a company. According to Barra, the "predicted beta, the beta Barra derives from its risk model, is a forecast of a stock's sensitivity to the market. It is also known as fundamental beta because it is derived from fundamental risk factors . . . such as size, yield, and volatility—plus industry exposure. Because we re-estimate these risk factors daily, the predicted beta reflects changes in the company's underlying risk structure in a timely manner."[11] Table III shows the compromises underlying the beta estimates of three prominent providers (Bloomberg, Value Line and Barra) and their combined effect on the beta estimates of our sample companies. The mean beta of our sample companies is similar from all providers, 0.96 from Bloomberg, 0.93 according to Value Line, and 0.91 from Barra. On the other hand, the averages mask differences for individual companies. Table IV provides a complete list of sample betas by provider.

Over half of the corporations in our sample (Table II, Question 10) cite Bloomberg as the source for their beta estimates, and some of the 37% that say they calculate their own may use Bloomberg data and programs. 26% of the companies cite some other published source and 26% explicitly compare a number of beta sources before making a final choice. Among financial advisors, there is strong reliance on fundamental betas with 89% of the advisors using Barra as a source. Many advisors (44%) also

---

[11] Barra (2007) on page 18. The actual quote from 2007 mentions monthly updating. In obtaining Barra data, we learned that updates are now daily so have substituted that in the quotes since we did not find an updated reference.

TABLE IV.   Betas for Corporate Survey Respondents

	Bloomberg Betas						
	2-year raw	5-year raw	2-year adjusted	5-year adjusted	Value Line Beta	Barra Beta	Range Max-Min
AmerisourceBergen	0.60	0.61	0.74	0.74	0.70	0.64	0.14
Caterpillar	1.48	1.45	1.32	1.30	1.35	1.47	0.18
Chevron	1.11	1.01	1.07	1.01	0.95	0.99	0.16
Coca-Cola	0.58	0.55	0.72	0.70	0.60	0.53	0.19
Costco Wholesale	0.64	0.73	0.76	0.82	0.75	0.64	0.18
IBM	0.85	0.83	0.90	0.89	0.85	0.73	0.17
International Paper	1.37	1.57	1.25	1.38	1.40	1.37	0.32
Intuit	0.92	0.71	0.95	0.80	0.90	0.77	0.24
Johnson Controls	1.56	1.41	1.38	1.28	1.30	1.40	0.29
PepsiCo	0.34	0.46	0.56	0.64	0.60	0.54	0.30
Qualcomm	1.10	0.85	1.07	0.90	0.85	1.10	0.26
Sysco	0.62	0.79	0.75	0.86	0.70	0.60	0.26
Target	0.54	1.07	0.69	1.04	0.90	0.82	0.53
Texas Instruments	1.13	0.92	1.09	0.95	0.90	0.97	0.23
Union Pacific	1.14	1.08	1.09	1.05	1.15	0.96	0.19
United Technologies	1.17	0.99	1.12	0.99	1.00	0.96	0.21
UPS	0.85	0.92	0.90	0.95	0.85	0.84	0.11
W.W. Grainger	0.98	0.91	0.98	0.94	0.95	1.05	0.14
Walt Disney	1.20	1.10	1.13	1.06	1.00	0.96	0.24
Mean	**0.96**	**0.94**	**0.97**	**0.96**	**0.93**	**0.91**	**0.23**
Median	**0.98**	**0.92**	**0.98**	**0.95**	**0.90**	**0.96**	**0.21**
Standard Deviation	**0.34**	**0.30**	**0.23**	**0.20**	**0.23**	**0.28**	**0.09**

Value Line betas are as of January 11, 2013.

Bloomberg betas are as of Jan 22, 2013. The adjusted beta is calculated as 2/3 times the raw beta plus 1/3 times 1.0.

Barra betas are from January 2013. Source: Barra. The Barra data contained herein are the property of Barra, Inc. Barra, its affiliates and information providers make no warranties with respect to any such data. The Barra data contained herein is used under license and may not be further used, distributed or disseminated without the express written consent of Barra.

use Bloomberg. About a third of both companies and financial advisors mentioned levering and unlevering betas even though we did not ask them for this information. And in response to a question about using data from other firms (Table II, Question 12), the majority of companies and all advisors take advantage of data on comparable companies to inform their estimates of beta and capital costs.[12]

Within these broad categories, the comments in Table V indicate that a number of survey participants use more pragmatic approaches which combine published beta estimates or adjust published estimates in various heuristic ways.

---

[12] Conroy and Harris (2011) compare the impacts of various approaches to using comparable company data to estimate the cost of capital for firms in the S&P 500.

TABLE V.   Choice of Beta

We asked our sample companies and advisors "what do you use as your beta estimate?" A sampling of responses shows the choice is not always a simple one.

"We use Bloomberg's default calculation. We take special care to support beta chosen if doing an acquisition or major investment."

"We use Bloomberg (both historical and historical adjusted) plus Barra and calibrate based on comparing the results."

"We use our beta and check against those of competitors. We unlever the peers and then relever to our capital structure. The results come pretty close to our own beta, so that's confirming."

"We use the median beta of comparable companies, based on analysis of size and business. We have a third party identify comparable companies and betas."

We use Barra and Bloomberg and triangulate based on those numbers. The problem comes up for getting a pure play for a division or a company that hasn't been public for a long time. We then have to pick comparable companies."

"Each line of business has its own peer group of companies and cost of capital. Using five-year betas from Bloomberg, we find an average unlevered beta for the peer group and then relever to our corporate-wide capital structure."

C. Equity Market Risk Premium

This topic prompted the greatest variety of responses among survey participants. Finance theory says the equity market risk premium should equal the excess return expected by investors on the market portfolio relative to riskless assets. How one measures expected future returns on the market portfolio and on riskless assets is a problem left to practitioners. Because expected future returns are unobservable, past surveys of practice have routinely revealed a wide array of choices for the market risk premium. For instance, Fernandez, Aguirreamalloa, and Corres (2011) survey professors, analysts and companies on what they use as a U.S. market risk premium. Of those who reported a reference to justify their choice, the single most mentioned source was Ibbotson/Morningstar, but even among those citing this reference, there was a wide dispersion of market risk premium estimates used. Carleton and Lakonishok (1985) demonstrate empirically some of the problems with such historical premiums when they are disaggregated for different time periods or groups of firms. Dimson, Marsh, and Staunton (2011a, 2011b) discuss evidence from an array of markets around the globe.

How do our best practice companies cope? Among financial advisors, 73% extrapolate historical returns into the future on the presumption that past experience heavily conditions future expectations. Among companies, 43% cite historical data and another 16% use various sources inclusive of historical data. Unlike the results of our earlier study (1998) in which historical returns were used by all companies and advisors, we found a number of respondents (18% of financial advisors and 32% of companies) using forward-looking estimates of the market risk premium. The advisors cited versions of the dividend discount model. The companies used a variety of methods including Bloomberg's version of the dividend discount model.[13]

---

[13]In our conversations, company respondents sometimes noted they used the Bloomberg estimate of the market risk premium but did not have detailed knowledge of the calculation. As described by Bloomberg, their estimates of country risk premiums are based on projections of future dividends in a multistage dividend discount model. At the time of our survey, the U.S. country risk premium from Bloomberg was in the range of 8-9%, well above averages from historical returns. See Harris and Marston (2001, 2013) for discussion of changing risk premiums over time.

TABLE VI.   Historical Averages to Estimate the Equity Market Risk Premium, $(R_m - R_f)$

Figures are the annual average risk premium calculated over the period 1926-2011 based on data drawn from Table II-I, Ibbotson (2012), where the Rm was drawn from the "Large Company Stocks" series, and Rf drawn from the "Long-Term Government Bonds" and "U.S. Treasury Bills" series.

	Relative to T-Bill Returns	Relative to T-Bond Returns
Arithmetic Mean	8.2%	5.7%
Geometric Mean	6.0%	3.9%

Even when historical returns are used to estimate the market risk premium, a host of differences emerge including what data to use and what method to use for averaging. For instance, a leading textbook cites U.S. historical data back to 1900 from Dimson and Staunton (as cited by Brealey, Myers, and Allen (2011), p.158) while 73% of our financial advisors cite Ibbotson data which traces U.S. history back to 1926. Among companies, only 32% explicitly cite Ibbotson as their main reference for data and 11% cite other historical sources.[14]

Even using the same data, another chief difference was in their use of *arithmetic* versus *geometric* averages. The arithmetic mean return is the simple average of past returns. Assuming the distribution of returns is stable over time and that periodic returns are independent of one another, the arithmetic return is the best estimator of expected return. The geometric mean return is the internal rate of return between a single outlay and one or more future receipts. It measures the compound rate of return investors earned over past periods. It accurately portrays historical investment experience. Unless returns are the same each time period, the geometric average will always be less than the arithmetic average and the gap widens as returns become more volatile.[15]

Based on Ibbotson data (2012) from 1926 to 2011, Table VI illustrates the possible range of equity market risk premiums depending on use of the geometric as opposed to the arithmetic mean equity return and on use of realized returns on T-bills as opposed to T-bonds. Even wider variations in market risk premiums can arise when one changes the historical period for averaging or decides to use data from outside the United States. For instance, Dimson, Marsh, and Staunton (2011a) provide estimates of historical equity risk premiums for a number of different countries since 1900.

Since our respondents all used longer-term Treasuries as their risk-free rate, the right-most column of Table VI most closely fits that choice. Even when respondents explicitly referenced the arithmetic or geometric mean of historical returns, many rounded the figure or used other data to adjust their final choice. The net result is a wide array of choices for the market risk premium. For respondents who provided a numerical

---

[14]With only minor exceptions, our respondents used U.S. data rather than rely on global indices for both their estimates of beta and the market risk premium. Dimson, Marsh, and Staunton (2011a) discuss historical estimates of the market risk premium using data from many countries.

[15]See Brealey, Myers, and Allen (2011), pages 158–159 for the argument to support use of an arithmetic mean. For large samples of returns, the geometric average can be approximated as the arithmetic average minus one half the variance of realized returns.

TABLE VII.   Choice of the Market Risk Premium

"What do you use as your market risk premium?" A sampling of responses from our best practice companies shows the choice can be a complicated one.

"We take an average of arithmetic mean and geometric mean for equity risk premium."

"5.5%–6.5%. Reflects a judgmental synthesis of various academic views and financial market perspectives."

"Estimate a forward-looking risk premium. Use a methodology that incorporates S&P P/E ratio. It is a more volatile metric than using a historical risk premium. Use historicals as a sanity check."

"6.5%–7%. We ask several banks how we compare to comparable companies, including comparable size and industry."
"Use the long-term (1926–2011) Ibbotson's S&P 500 premium over the risk-free rate."

Comments from financial advisors also were revealing. While some simply responded that they use a published historical average, others presented a more complex picture.

"We used to apply the geometric mean, and then we switched to arithmetic. Now we use 4.6-6.6%, so we'll show for both ends of that distribution. Based mainly on Ibbotson, but may add to that for emerging market companies."

"Forward-looking estimate using dividend discount model . . . bank's proprietary model, which is forward-looking and uses S&P price level, plus projections and payout to get an implied cost of equity"

figure (Table II, Question 11), the average for companies was 6.49%, very close to the average of 6.6% from financial advisors. These averages mask considerable variation in both groups. We had responses as low as 4% and as high as 9%. The 4% value is in line with the Ibbotson (2012) historical figures using the geometric mean spread between stocks and long-term government bonds. The upper end of 9% comes from forward-looking estimates done in 2012 when U.S. financial markets reflected a very low interest rate environment.[16] We add a word of caution in how to interpret some of the differences we found in the market risk premium since the ultimate cost of capital calculation depends on the joint choice of a risk premium, the risk-free rate and beta. We return to this issue when we illustrate potential differences in the cost of capital.

As shown in Table VII, comments in our interviews exemplify the diversity among survey participants. This variety of practice displays the challenge of application since theory calls for a forward-looking risk premium, one that reflects current market sentiment and may change with market conditions. What is clear is that there is substantial variation as practitioners try to operationalize the theoretical call for a market risk premium. And, as is clear in some of the respondent comments, volatility in markets has made the challenge even harder. Compared to our earlier study (1998) in which respondents almost always applied historical averages, current practice shows a wider variation in approach and considerable judgment. This situation points the way for valuable future research on the market risk premium.

IV. The Impact of Various Assumptions for Using CAPM

To illustrate the effect of these various practices on estimated capital costs, we mechanically selected the two sample companies with the largest and smallest range of beta estimates in Table IV. We estimated the hypothetical cost of equity and WACC

---

[16]Harris and Marston (2001, 2013) discuss evidence that the market risk premium is inversely related to interest rates.

for Target Corporation, which has the widest range in estimated betas, and for UPS which has the smallest range. Our estimates are "hypothetical" in that we do not adopt any information supplied to us by the companies and financial advisors but rather apply a range of approaches based on publicly available information as of early 2013. Table VIII gives Target's estimated costs of equity and WACCs under various combinations of riskfree rate, beta, and market risk premiums. Three clusters of possible practice are illustrated, each in turn using betas as provided by Bloomberg, Value Line, and Barra. The first approach, adopted by a number of our respondents, uses a 10-year T-bond yield and a risk premium of 6.5% (roughly the average response from both companies and financial advisors). The second approach also uses a 6.5% risk premium but moves to a 30-year rate to proxy the long-term interest rate. The third method uses the ten-year Treasury rate but a risk premium of 9%, consistent with what some adopters of a forward-looking risk premium applied. We repeated these general procedures for UPS

The resulting ranges of estimated WACCs for the two firms are as follows:

	Maximum WACC	Minimum WACC	Difference in Basis Points
Target	8.58%	4.58%	400
UPS	9.17%	6.62%	255

The range from minimum to maximum is considerable for both firms, and the economic impact potentially stunning. To illustrate this, the present value of a level perpetual annual stream of $10 million would range between $117 million and $218 million for Target, and between $109 million and $151 million for UPS.

Given the positive yield curve in early 2013, the variations in our illustration are explained by choices for all three elements in applying the CAPM: the risk-free rate, beta, and the equity market premium assumption. Moreover, we note that use of a 10-year Treasury rate in these circumstances leads to quite low cost of capital estimates if one sticks to traditional risk premium estimates often found in textbooks which are in the range of 6%. From talking to our respondents, we sense that many are struggling with how to deal with current market conditions that do not fit typical historical norms, a topic we discuss in more detail in Section VI.

V. Risk Adjustments to WACC

Finance theory is clear that the discount rate should rise and fall in concert with an investment's risk and that a firm's WACC is an appropriate discount rate only for average-risk investments by the firm. High-risk, new ventures should face higher discount rates, while replacement and repair investments should face lower ones. Attracting capital requires that prospective return increase with risk. Most practitioners accept this reasoning but face two problems when applying it. First, it is often not clear precisely how much a given investment's risk differs from average, and second, even when this amount is known, it is still not obvious how large an increment should be added to, or subtracted from, the firm's WACC to determine the appropriate discount rate.

TABLE VIII.   Variations in Cost of Capital (WACC) Estimates for Target Corporation Using Different Methods of Implementing the Capital Asset Pricing Model

Data are as of January 22, 2013. The CAPM is used to estimate the cost of equity. Interest rates are from Bloomberg and the Federal Reserve. The cost of debt is assumed to be 4.21% (average of Aaa and Baa yields). We approximated the capital structure and tax rate using the market value of equity and the most recent financial statements, yielding debt as 32% of capital and a 34% tax rate.

1. Ten-year Treasury rate plus risk premium of 6.5%

(Most common choice of proxy for risk-free rate and average risk premium used by respondents)

$R_f = 1.92\%$, yield to maturity on 10-year U.S. Treasury bond

$R_m - R_f = 6.50\%$, average value for respondents

Beta Service	Cost of Equity K_e	Cost of Capital WACC
Bloomberg (default), $\beta = .54$	5.42%	4.58%
Bloomberg (5-year, adj.), $\beta = 1.04$	8.67%	6.81%
Value Line, $\beta = .90$	7.76%	6.18%
Barra, $\beta = .82$	7.24%	5.83%

2. Thirty-year Treasury rate plus risk premium of 6.5%

(Longer-term maturity choice favored by some analysts)

$R_f = 3.03\%$, yield to maturity on 30-year U.S. Treasury bond

$R_m - R_f = 6.5\%\%$, average value for respondents

Beta Service	Cost of Equity K_e	Cost of Capital WACC
Bloomberg (default), $\beta = .54$	6.54%	5.34%
Bloomberg (five year, adj.), $\beta = 1.04$	9.79%	7.57%
Value Line, $\beta = .90$	8.88%	6.94%
Barra, $\beta = .82$	8.36%	6.59%

3. Ten-year Treasury rate plus risk premium of 9.0%

(Consistent with some applications of a forward-looking risk premium estimate)

$R_f = 1.92\%$, yield to maturity on 10-year U.S. Treasury bond

$R_m - R_f = 9.0\%$, upper-end of risk premium estimates

Beta Service	Cost of Equity K_e	Cost of Capital WACC
Bloomberg (default), $\beta = .54$	6.71%	5.51%
Bloomberg (five year, adj.), $\beta = 1.04$	11.27%	8.58%
Value Line, $\beta = .90$	10.01%	7.72%
Barra, $\beta = .82$	9.29%	7.23%

We probed the extent to which respondents alter discount rates to reflect risk differences in questions about variations in project risk, strategic investments, terminal values, multidivisional companies, and synergies (Table II, Questions 13 and 17–20). Responses indicate that the great preponderance of financial advisors and text authors strongly favor varying the discount rate to capture differences in risk (Table II, Questions 13, 19, and 20). Corporations, on the other hand, are more evenly split, with a sizeable minority electing not to adjust discount rates for risk differences among individual projects (Table II, Questions 13 and 17). Comparing these results with our earlier study, it is worth noting that while only about half of corporate respondents adjust discount rates for risk, this figure is more than double the percentage reported in 1998. Despite continuing hesitance, companies are apparently becoming more comfortable with explicit risk adjustments to discount rates.

A closer look at specific responses suggests that respondents' enthusiasm for risk-adjusting discount rates depends on the quality of the data available. Text authors live in a largely data-free world and thus have no qualms recommending risk adjustments whenever appropriate. Financial advisors are a bit more constrained. They regularly confront real-world data, but their mission is often to value companies or divisions where extensive market information is available about rates and prices. Correspondingly, virtually all advisors questioned value multi division businesses by parts when the divisions differed materially in size and risk, and over 90% are prepared to use separate division WACCs to reflect risk differences. Similarly, 82% of advisors value merger synergies and strategic opportunities separately from operating cash flows, and 73% are prepared to use different discount rates when necessary on the various cash flows.

There is a long history of empirical research on how shareholder returns vary across firm size, leading some academics to suggest that a small cap premium should be added to the calculated cost of capital for such firms.[17] Our study focuses on large public companies, so it is not surprising that firm responses do not reveal any such small cap adjustments. In contrast, financial advisors work with a wide spectrum of companies and are thus more likely to be sensitive to the issue—as indeed they are. Among financial advisors interviewed, 91% said they would at times increase the discount rate when evaluating small companies. Of those who did make size adjustments, half mentioned using Ibbotson (2012) data which show differences in past returns among firms of different size. The adjustment process varied among advisors, as the following illustrative quotes suggest. "Adjustments are discretionary, but we tend to adjust for extreme size." "We have used a small cap premium, but we don't have a set policy to make adjustments. It is fairly subjective." "We apply a small cap premium only for microcap companies." "We use a small cap premium for $300 million and below."

In important ways corporate executives face a more complex task than financial advisors or academics. They must routinely evaluate investments in internal opportunities, and new products and technologies, for which objective, third party information is

---

[17]Banz (1981) and Renganum (1981) first identified that firms with smaller market capitalization had earned higher average returns than stocks generally and higher than those predicted even if one adjusts for risk using the CAPM. Fama and French (1992) identify size as a critical factor in explaining differences in returns. Pratt and Grabowski (2010) discuss size adjustments and the use of Ibbotson data on size groupings.

TABLE IX.   Adjusting Discount Rates for Risk

When asked whether they adjusted discount rates for project risk, companies provided a wide range of responses.

"Yes, but [the process] is fairly ad hoc. There's not a formal number."

"We don't risk adjust, [but] we make sure we're on target by using sensitivity analysis and checking key assumptions."

"For new deals, we add 20% to the cost of capital."

"Yes, we make adjustments for different countries."

"We make subjective adjustments [to our discount rate] for new technologies or products or customers, all of which carry more uncertainty."

"We use a hurdle rate that is intentionally higher than our WACC. Recent WACC has been 9.64% and the hurdle rate is 15%, and then we add qualitative considerations for the final decision."

"Generally no further adjustments are made unless specifics are identified at the project level that would be very different risk. For instance, a contractual cash flow might be treated as a debt equivalent cash flow and given a lower discount rate."

nonexistent. Moreover, they work in an administrative setting where decision rights are widely dispersed, with headquarters defining procedures and estimating discount rates, and various operating people throughout the company analyzing different aspects of a given project. As Table IX reveals, these complexities lead to a variety of creative approaches to dealing with risk. A number of respondents describe making discount rate adjustments to distinguish among divisional capital costs, international as opposed to domestic investments, and leased versus purchased assets. In other instances, however, respondents indicated they hold the discount rate constant and deal with risk in more qualitative ways, sometimes by altering the project cash flows being discounted.

Why do corporations risk-adjust discount rates in some settings and use different, often more *ad hoc,* approaches in others? Our interpretation is that risk-adjusted discount rates are more likely to be used when the analyst can establish relatively objective financial market benchmarks for what the risk adjustment should be. At the division level, data on comparable companies inform division cost of capital estimates. Debt markets provide surrogates for the risks in leasing cash flows, and international financial markets shed light on cross-country risk differences. When no such benchmarks exist, practitioners look to other more informal methods for dealing with risk. In our view, then, practical use of risk-adjusted discount rates occurs when the analyst can find reliable market data indicating how comparablerisk cash flows are being valued by others.

The same pragmatic perspective was evident when we asked companies how frequently they re-estimated their capital costs (Table II, Question 14). Even among firms that re-estimate costs frequently, there was reluctance to alter the underlying methodology employed or to revise the way they use the number in decision making. Firms also appear sensitive to administrative costs, evidencing reluctance to make small adjustments but prepared to revisit the numbers at any time in anticipation of major decisions or in response to financial market upheavals. Benchmark companies recognize a certain ambiguity in any cost number and are willing to live with approximations. While the bond market reacts to minute basis point changes in interest rates,

TABLE X.   **Re-estimating the Cost of Capital**

"How frequently do you re-estimate your company's cost of capital? Here are responses from best practice companies.

"[We re-estimate] annually unless a fundamental event that is a game changer occurs, such as the banking crisis in 2008."

"[We re-estimate] once a year around May since this is right before impairment testing."

"We re-estimate twice a year and for special events such as a major acquisition."

"We calculate the hurdle rate each year. We try to avoid any changes less than plus or minus 25 basis points."

"Formally, we re-estimate our cost of capital every quarter, but generally we have used 10% for a long time, which seems to have been successful so far."

TABLE XI.   **Judgments Related to Financial Market Conditions**

Some of our best practice companies and advisors noted that their choice of a risk-free rate attempted to remove any unusual conditions they saw in current market yields. We asked "What do you use for a risk-free rate?" and heard the following:

"20-year U.S. government bonds. If it seems to be unusually high or low, we may use a trailing average or other modified number."

"Use a five-year rolling average in order to smooth out volatility associated with current/recent market trends."

"Historically had used the spot rate yield to maturity on 10-year government bonds, but more recently have changed to thinking about factors driving government interest rates, so we have moved away from the spot rate and toward the average yield over last 10 years."

investments in real assets involve much less precision, due largely to greater uncertainty, decentralized decision-making, and time consuming decision processes. As noted in Table X, one respondent evidences an extreme tolerance for rough estimates in saying that the firm re-estimates capital costs every quarter, but has used 10% for a long time because it "seems to have been successful so far." Our interpretation is that the mixed responses to questions about risk adjusting and re-estimating discount rates reflect an often sophisticated set of practical considerations. Chief among them are the size of the risk differences among investments, the volume and quality of information available from financial markets, and the realities of administrative costs and processes. When conditions warrant, practitioners routinely employ risk adjustments in project appraisal. Acquisitions, valuing divisions and cross-border investments, and leasing decisions were frequently cited examples. In contrast, when conditions are not favorable, practitioners are more likely to rely on cruder capital cost estimates and cope with risk differences by other means.

VI. Recent Institutional and Market Developments

As discussed in the prior section, our interviews reveal that the practice of cost of capital estimation is shaped by forces that go beyond considerations found in usual academic treatments of the topic. A feature that was more pronounced than in our prior study is the influence of a wide array of stakeholders. For instance, a number of companies voiced that any change in estimation methods would raise red flags with auditors looking for process consistency in key items such as impairment estimates. Some advisors mentioned similar concerns, citing their work in venues where consistency and precedent were major considerations (e.g., fairness opinions, legal settings). Moreover, some companies noted that they "outsourced" substantial parts of their estimation to advisors or data providers. These items serve as a reminder that the art of cost of capital estimation and its use are part of a larger process of management—not simply an application of finance theory.

The financial upheaval in 2008–2009 provided a natural test of respondents' commitment to existing cost of capital estimation methodologies and applications. When confronted with a major external shock, did companies make wholesale changes or did they keep to existing practices? When we asked companies and advisors if financial market conditions in 2008–2009 caused them to change the way they estimate and use the cost of capital (Table II, Question 15), over three-fifths replied "No." In the main, then, there was not a wholesale change in methods. That said, a number of respondents noted discomfort with cost of capital estimation in recent years. Some singled out high volatility in markets. Others pointed to the low interest rate environment resulting from Federal Reserve policies to stimulate the U.S. economy. Combining low interest rates and typical historical risk premiums created capital cost estimates that some practitioners viewed as "too low." One company was so distrustful of market signals that it placed an arbitrary eight percent floor under any cost of capital estimate, noting that "since 2008, as rates have decreased so drastically, we don't feel that [the estimate] represents a long-term cost of capital. Now we don't report anything below 8% as a minimum [cost of capital]."

Among the minority who did revise their estimation procedures to cope with these market forces, one change was to put more reliance on historical numbers when estimating interest rates as indicated in Table XI. This is in sharp contrast to both finance theory and what we found in our prior study. Such rejection of spot rates in favor of historical averages or arbitrary numbers is inconsistent with the academic view that historical data do not accurately reflect current attitudes in competitive markets. The academic challenge today is to better articulate the extent to which the superiority of spot rates still applies when markets are highly volatile and when governments are aggressively attempting to lower rates through such initiatives as quantitative easing.

Another change in estimation methods since our earlier study is reflected in the fact that more companies are using forward-looking risk premiums as we reported earlier and illustrated in Table VII. Since the forward-looking premiums cited by our respondents were higher than historical risk premiums, they mitigated or offset to some degree the impact of low interest rates on estimated capital costs.[18]

---

[18]Pratt and Grabowski (2010) provide a discussion of estimating forward looking risk premiums. Harris and Marston (2001, 2013) discuss evidence that the market risk premium is inversely related to interest rates.

VII. Conclusions

Our research sought to identify the "best practice" in cost of capital estimation through interviews with leading corporations and financial advisors. Given the huge annual expenditure on capital projects and corporate acquisitions each year, the wise selection of discount rates is of material importance to senior corporate managers.

Consistent with our 1998 study of the same topic, this survey reveals broad acceptance of the WACC as the basis for setting discount rates. In addition, the survey reveals general alignment between the advice of popular textbooks and the practices of leading companies and corporate advisors in many aspects of the estimation of WACC. The main continuing area of notable disagreement is in the details of implementing the CAPM to estimate the cost of equity. This paper outlines the varieties of practice in CAPM use, the arguments in favor of different approaches, and the practical implications of differing choices.

In summary, we believe that the following elements represent "best current practice" in the estimation of WACC:

- Weights should be based on *market-value* mixes of debt and equity.

- The after-tax cost of debt should be estimated from *marginal* pretax costs, combined with *marginal* tax rates.

- CAPM is currently the preferred model for estimating the cost of equity.

- Betas are drawn substantially from published sources. Where a number of statistical publishers disagree, best practice often involves judgment to estimate a beta. Moreover, practitioners often look to data on comparable companies to help benchmark an appropriate beta.

- Risk-free rate should match the tenor of the cash flows being valued. For most capital projects and corporate acquisitions, the yield on the U.S. government Treasury bond of ten or more years in maturity would be appropriate.

- Choice of an equity market risk premium is the subject of considerable controversy both as to its value and method of estimation. While the market risk premium averages about 6.5% across both our "best practice" companies and financial advisors, the range of values starts from a low of around 4% and ends with a high of 9%.

- Monitoring for changes in WACC should be keyed to major investment opportunities or significant changes in financial market rates, but should be done at least annually. Actually flowing a change through a corporate system of project appraisal and compensation targets must be done gingerly and only when there are material changes.

- WACC should be risk-adjusted to reflect substantive differences among different businesses in a corporation. For instance, financial advisors generally find the corporate WACC to be inappropriate for valuing different parts of a corporation. Given publicly traded companies in different businesses, such risk adjustment involves only modest revision in the WACC and CAPM approaches already used. Corporations also cite the need to adjust capital costs across national boundaries. In situations where market proxies for a particular type of risk class are not available, best practice involves finding other means to account for risk differences.

Best practice is largely consistent with finance theory. Despite broad agreement at the theoretical level, however, several problems in application can lead to wide divergence in estimated capital costs. Based on our results, we believe that two areas of practice cry out for further applied research. First, practitioners need additional tools for sharpening their assessment of relative project and market risk. The variation in company specific beta estimates from different published sources can create substantial differences in capital cost estimates. Moreover, the use of risk-adjusted discount rates appears limited by lack of good market proxies for different risk profiles. We believe that appropriate use of comparablerisk, cross-industry or other risk categories deserves further exploration. Second, practitioners could benefit from further research on estimating the equity market risk premium. Current practice still relies primarily on averaging past data over often lengthy periods and yields a wide range of estimates. Use of forward-looking valuation models to estimate the implied market risk premium could be particularly helpful to practitioners dealing with volatile markets. As the next generation of theories sharpens our insights, we feel that research attention to the implementation of existing theory can make for real improvements in practice.

In fundamental ways, our conclusions echo those of our study fifteen years ago. Our conversations with practitioners serve as a reminder that cost of capital estimation is part of the larger art of management—not simply an application of finance theory. There is an old saying that too often in business we measure with a micrometer, mark with a pencil, and cut with an ax. Despite the many advances in finance theory, the particular "ax" available for estimating company capital costs remains a blunt one. Best practice companies can expect to estimate their weighted average cost of capital with an accuracy of no more than plus or minus 100 to 150 basis points. This has important implications for how managers use the cost of capital in decision making. First, do not mistake capital budgeting for bond pricing. Despite the tools available, effective capital appraisal continues to require thorough knowledge of the business and wise business judgment. Second, be careful not to throw out the baby with the bath water. Do not reject the cost of capital and attendant advances in financial management because your finance people cannot provide a precise number. When in need, even a blunt ax is better than nothing. ■

References

Association for Finance Professionals, 2011, "Current Trends in Estimating and Applying the Cost of Capital: Report of Survey Results," www.AFPonline.org, accessed March 2011.

Banz, R., 1981, "The Relationship between Return and Market Value of Common Stock," *Journal of Financial Economics* 9 (No. 1), 3–18.

Barra, 2007, *Barra Risk Model Handbook*, MSCI Barra, www.Barra.com/support/library.

Brealey, R., S. Myers, and F. Allen, 2011, *Principles of Corporate Finance*, 10th ed., New York, NY, McGraw-Hill.

Brigham, E. and M. Ehrhardt, 2013, *Financial Management: Theory and Practice*, 14th ed., Mason, OH, South-Western Publishing.

Bruner, R., K. Eades, R. Harris, and R. Higgins, 1998, "Best Practices in Estimating the Cost of Capital: Survey and Synthesis," *Financial Practice and Education* 8 (No. 1), 13–28.

Burns, R. and J. Walker, 2009, "Capital Budgeting Surveys: The Future is Now," *Journal of Applied Finance* 19 (No. 1–2), 78–90.

Carleton, W.T. and J. Lakonishok, 1985, "Risk and Return on Equity: The Use and Misuse of Historical Estimates," *Financial Analysts Journal* 41 (No. 1), 38–48.

Conroy, R. and R. Harris, 2011, "Estimating Capital Costs: Practical Implementation of Theory's Insights" *Capital Structure and Financing Decisions: Theory and Practice* (K. Baker and J. Martin, eds.), New York, NY, John Wiley & Sons.

Dimson, E., P. Marsh, and M. Staunton, 2011a, "Equity Premia Around the World," London Business School Working Paper.

Dimson, E., P. Marsh, and M. Staunton, 2011b, *The Dimson-Marsh-Staunton Global Investment Returns Database* (the "DMS Database"), New York, NY, Morningstar Inc.

Fama, E.F. and K.R. French, 1992, "The Cross-section of Expected Returns," *Journal of Finance* 47 (No. 2), 27–465.

Fernandez, P., J. Aguirreamalloa, and L. Corres, 2011, "US Market Risk Premium used in 2011 by Professors, Analysts and Companies: A Survey with 5,731 Answers," IESE Business School Working Paper.

Graham, J. and L. Mills, 2008, "Using Tax Return Data to Simulate Corporate Marginal Tax Rates," *Journal of Accounting and Economics* 46 (No. 2–3), 366–380.

Harris, R. and F. Marston, 2001, "The Market Risk Premium: Expectational Estimates Using Analysts' Forecasts," *Journal of Applied Finance* 11 (No. 1), 6–16.

Harris, R. and F. Marston, 2013, "Changes in the Market Risk Premium and the Cost of Capital: Implications for Practice," *Journal of Applied Finance* 23 (No. 1), 34–47.

Higgins, R.C., 2012, *Analysis for Financial Management*, 10th Ed., New York, NY, McGraw-Hill.

Ibbotson, SBBI, 2012, *Classic Yearbook, Market Results for Stocks, Bonds, Bills and Inflation 1926–2011,"* Morningstar.

Jacobs, M.T. and A. Shivdasani, 2012, "Do You Know Your Cost of Capital?" *Harvard Business Review* (July).

Koller, T., M. Goedhart, and D. Wessels, 2005, *Valuation: Measuring and Managing the Value of Companies*, 5th Ed., Hoboken, NJ, John Wiley & Sons, Inc.

Pratt, S. and R. Grabowski, 2010, *Cost of Capital: Applications and Examples* 4th Ed., Hoboken, NJ, John Wiley and Sons.

Reinganum, M.R. 1981, "Misspecification of Capital Asset Pricing: Empirical Anomalies Based on Earnings' Yields and Market Values," *Journal of Financial Economics* 9 (No. 1), 19–46.

Ross, S., R. Westerfield, and J. Jaffe, 2013, *Corporate Finance*, 10th Ed., New York, NY, McGraw-Hill.

Roche Holding AG: Funding the Genentech Acquisition

We are confident that we will have the financing available when the money is needed . . . The plan is to use as financing partly our own funds and then obviously bonds and then commercial paper and traditional bank financing. We will start by going to the bond market first.[1]

—Roche Chairman Franz Hume

In July 2008, Swiss pharmaceutical company Roche Holding AG (Roche) made an offer to acquire all remaining outstanding shares of U.S. biotechnology leader Genentech for (U.S. dollars) USD89.00 per share in cash. Six months later, with equity markets down 35%, Roche announced its recommitment to the deal with a discounted offer of USD86.50 in cash per share of Genentech stock.

To pay for the deal, Roche needed a massive USD42 billion in cash. To meet the need, management planned to sell USD32 billion in bonds at various maturities from 1 year to 30 years and in three different currencies (U.S. dollar, euro, and British pound). The sale would begin with the dollar-denominated offering and followed up soon after with rounds of offerings in the other currencies.

In mid-February 2009, Roche was ready to move forward with what was anticipated to be the largest bond offering in history. With considerable ongoing turmoil in world financial markets and substantial uncertainty surrounding the willingness of Genentech minority shareholders to sell their shares for the reduced offer of USD86.50, Roche's financing strategy was certainly bold.

---

[1] Sam Cage, "Roche Goes Hostile, Cuts Genentech Bid to $42 Billion," *Reuters*, January 30, 2009.

This case, based on publicly available data, was prepared by Brett Durick (MBA '11), Drew Chambers (MBA '11), and Michael J. Schill, Robert F. Vandell Research Associate Professor of Business Administration. This case is dedicated to Courtney Turner Chambers, in recognition of the sacrifice and contribution of all Darden partners. Copyright © 2011 by the University of Virginia Darden School Foundation, Charlottesville, VA. All rights reserved. *To order copies, send an e-mail to* sales@dardenbusinesspublishing.com. *No part of this publication may be reproduced, stored in a retrieval system, used in a spreadsheet, or transmitted in any form or by any means—electronic, mechanical, photocopying, recording, or otherwise—without the permission of the Darden School Foundation.*

Roche

In 1894, Swiss banker Fritz Hoffmann-La Roche, 26, joined Max Carl Traub to take over a small factory on Basel's Grenzacherstrasse from druggists Bohny, Hollinger & Co. Following a difficult first two years, Hoffmann-La Roche bought out his partner and entered F. Hoffmann-La Roche & Co. in the commercial register.

In the early years, the company's primary products included sleeping agents, antiseptics, and vitamins; by the late 1930s, the company had already expanded to 35 countries, an expansion that continued in the decades following the Second World War. In 1990, the company, by then known as Roche, acquired a majority stake in Genentech, a South San Francisco biotechnology company, for USD2.1 billion. Genentech's research focused primarily on developing products based on gene splicing or recombinant DNA to treat diseases such as cancer and AIDS. The acquisition gave Roche a strong foothold in the emerging biologics market as well as stronger presence in the U.S. market.

Since the 1990s, Roche had maintained focus on its two primary business units, pharmaceuticals and medical diagnostics; in 2004, Roche sold its over-the-counter consumer health business to Bayer AG for nearly USD3 billion. In 2008, Roche expanded its diagnostics business with the acquisition of Ventana Medical Systems for USD3.4 billion.

By the end of 2008, Roche's total revenue was just shy of (Swiss francs) CHF50 billion. The pharmaceutical division contributed 70% of the total Roche revenue and over 90% of the operating profit. Roche was clearly one of the leading pharmaceuticals in the world. **Exhibit 11.1** provides a revenue breakdown of Roche's 2008 revenue by geography and therapeutic area, as well as a detailed overview of Roche's top selling pharmaceutical products. Roche and Genentech's financial statements are detailed in **Exhibit 11.2** and **11.3**, respectively, and the stock performance of the two companies is shown in **Exhibit 11.4**.

Market Conditions

The past 18 months had been historic for global financial markets, with dramatic declines in equity and credit markets. Since October 2007, world equity market prices had declined over 45%. Large numbers of commercial and investment banks had failed. The global labor market was shedding jobs, resulting in sharp increases in unemployment rates. Broad economic activity was also affected, with large declines in overall economic activity.

In response to what some feared would become the next Great Depression, world governments made massive investments in financial and industrial institutions. In an effort to stimulate liquidity, central banks had lowered interest rates. The market uncertainty was accompanied by a massive "flight to quality" as global investors moved capital to government securities (particularly U.S. Treasuries), thereby driving government yields to historic lows. **Exhibit 11.5** shows the prevailing yield curve in U.S. dollars, euros, and British pounds. With benchmark yields declining but overall borrowing rates rising, the credit spreads (the difference between corporate yields and benchmark yields) were expanding to historic levels. **Exhibit 11.6** contains the prevailing credit spreads over benchmark yields for U.S. industrial corporate bonds based on bond ratings from bond-rating agency Standard and Poor's. **Exhibit 11.7** plots historical trends in yields of bonds by various credit ratings over the past two years. **Exhibit 11.8** provides a definitional overview of Standard and Poor's credit ratings. Roche's current credit rating with Standard and Poor's was AA−, and with Moody's was Aa1. **Exhibit 11.9** details median values for various financial ratios for companies rated within a particular category for 2007 and 2008.

Despite the uncertainty in the credit markets, corporate transactions were reawakening in the pharmaceutical industry. Pfizer had recently agreed to acquire Wyeth for USD68 billion. In the deal, five banks had agreed to lend Pfizer USD22.5 billion to pay for the deal, and Pfizer was funding the remaining USD45.5 billion through issuance of a combination of cash and stock.

The Bond Offering Process

The issuance of publicly traded bonds, in addition to the pricing and marketing of the deal, required the satisfaction of certain legal requirements. Because of the complexity and importance of these two processes, corporations typically hired investment bankers to provide assistance. Given the size of the deal, Roche hired three banks as joint lead managers for the U.S. dollar deal (Banc of America Securities, Citigroup Global Markets, and JPMorgan) and four bankers for the euro and pound sterling deals (Barclays Capital, BNP Paribas, Deutsche Bank, and Banco Santander).

Because Roche's bonds would be publicly traded, it had to file with the appropriate regulatory agencies in the countries where the bonds would be issued. Simultaneous with the drafting of the documentation by legal teams, the underwriting banks' debt capital markets and syndication desks began the marketing process. The initial phase of this process was the "road show." During the road show, management teams for Roche and the banks held initial meetings with investors from all over the world. The Roche management team expected to meet with investors in many of the major investment centers in the United States and Europe.

Given the global nature of Roche's business, the banks determined that a mix of bonds at different maturities and in different currencies was the best option. By matching differing maturities and currencies to the company's operating cash flows in those currencies, Roche was able to reduce exchange rate risk. **Exhibit 11.10** provides an overview of the different currency and maturity tranches planned in the offering. The final amounts raised from each offering, along with the coupon rate, were not yet determined because pricing was expected to be highly influenced by investor demand. To ensure that the bond offering raised the targeted proceeds, the coupon rate was set to approximate the anticipated yield, such that the bond traded at par. Following market conventions, the U.S. dollar bonds would pay interest semiannually, and the euro and sterling issues would pay interest annually.

The coupon payments of the shorter durations were to be floating, and the interest to be paid was equivalent to the short-term interbank interest rate (LIBOR) plus a credit spread. The longer durations were to have fixed coupon payments for the duration of the bond. Investors typically referenced the "price" of bonds as the spread over the applicable risk-free rate. The risk-free rate was commonly established as the respective government borrowing rate and was referred to as the *benchmark*, *sovereign*, or *Treasury rate*. The logic of the credit spread was that bonds were riskier than the benchmark bonds, so to entice investors, the issuer had to offer a price over the risk-free rate.

During the road show, banks received feedback from investors on the demand for each tranche. Determining the final size and pricing of each issue was an iterative process between the investors, banks, and issuer. In the case of Roche, if investors showed strong demand for the four-year euro tranche, Roche could decide to either issue more at that price (thus reducing the amount of another tranche) or lower the coupon and pay a lower interest rate on the four-year euro issue. The banks' process of determining demand and receiving orders for each issue was known as *book-building*. Bond prices were set based on prevailing yields of bond issues by similar companies. **Exhibit 11.11** and **11.12** provide a sample of prevailing prices and terms of company bonds traded in the market, in addition to various equity market and accounting data.

The Genentech Deal

On July 21, 2008, Roche publicly announced an offer to acquire the 44.1% of Genentech's outstanding shares that it did not already own. The offer price of USD89.00 represented a 19% premium over the previous one-month share prices for Genentech. Roche management believed that economies justified the premium with an estimate that, following the transaction, the combined entity could realize USD750 million to USD850 million in operational efficiencies. Following the offer, Genentech's stock price shot up beyond the USD89.00 offer price with the anticipation that Roche would increase its offer.

On August 13, 2008, a special committee of Genentech's board of directors (those without direct ties to Roche) responded to Roche's offer. The committee stated that the offer "substantially undervalues the company." Without the support of Genentech's board of directors, Roche needed either to negotiate with the board or take the offer directly to shareholders with what was known as a *tender offer*. In that case, shareholders would receive a take-it-or-leave-it offer. If sufficient shareholders "tendered" their shares, the deal would go through regardless of the support of the board.

Over the next six months, capital markets fell into disarray. As credit markets deteriorated, Genentech shareholders realized that Roche might not be able to finance an increased bid for the company, and the share price continued to decline through the end of the year. Contemporaneously with the deal, Genentech awaited the announcement of the clinical trial results for several of its next generation of potential drugs, including its promising cancer drug Avastin.

On January 30, 2009, Roche announced its intention to launch a tender offer for the remaining shares at a reduced price of USD86.50. The revised offer was contingent on Roche's ability to obtain sufficient financing to purchase the shares. The announcement was accompanied by a 4% price drop of Genentech's share price to USD80.82. Bill Tanner, analyst at Leerink Swann, warned Genentech shareholders that the stock was overvalued and that if upcoming Genentech drug trials showed mediocre results then the stock would fall into the USD60 range. He encouraged shareholders to take the sure

USD86.50 offer claiming that "DNA's [the stock ticker symbol for Genentech] best days may be over."[2]

Jason Napadano, analyst at Zach's Investment Research, claimed that Roche was trying "to pull the wool over the eyes of Genentech shareholders." He continued, "Roche is trying to get this deal done before the adjuvant colon cancer data comes out and Genentech shareholders are well aware of that. I don't know why they would tender their shares for [USD]86.50, which is only 10% above today's price, when they can get closer to $95 to $100 a share if they wait."[3]

The Financing Proposal

Unlike Pfizer in its acquisition of Wyeth, Roche could not issue equity to Genentech shareholders. Roche was controlled by the remnants of its founder in the Oeri, Hoffman, and Sacher families. The company maintained two classes of shares, *bearer* and *Genussscheine* (profit-participation) shares. Both share classes had equal economic rights (i.e., same dividends, etc.) and traded on the Swiss Stock Exchange, but the bearer shares were the only shares with voting rights, and the founding family controlled just over 50% of the bearer shares. This dual-share structure existed before modern shareholder rights legislation in Switzerland and was grandfathered in. In the event Roche were to issue equity to Genentech shareholders, this dual-class share structure would have to be revisited, and the family might lose control. Given this ownership structure, Roche was forced to finance the deal entirely of debt and current cash on hand.

When Roche originally announced the transaction, the company had intended to finance the acquisition with a combination of bonds and loans from a variety of commercial banks. The collapse of the financial markets caused many of the commercial banks to demand a much higher interest rate on the loans than originally anticipated by Roche. As a result of the change in market conditions, Roche was limited to the bond market for the majority of its financing. Despite the magnitude of the debt-financing need, the investment banks assisting in the deal expected that Roche's cash flow was stable enough to manage the additional level of debt.

To ensure that Roche raised the necessary capital, it was important to correctly anticipate the required yield on each bond and set the coupon rate at the rate that would price the bond at par. This was done by simply setting the coupon rate equal to the anticipated yield. With such a substantial amount of money riding on the deal, it was critical that Roche correctly set the price, despite the immense uncertainty in capital markets.

---

[2]Bob O'Brien, "Analysts Debate Strategy Behind Sourer Offer," *Barron's*, January 30, 2009.
[3]O'Brien.

EXHIBIT 11.1 | 2008 Revenue Breakdown (sales in millions of Swiss francs)

By Geography	Share	Product (Indication)	Sales
North America	41%	MabThera/Rituxin (lymphoma, leukemia, rheumatoid arthritis)	5,923
Western Europe	29%	Avastin (colorectal, breast, lung, and kidney cancer)	5,207
CEMAI[1]	9%	Herceptin (breast cancer)	5,092
Japan	9%	CellCept (transplantation)	2,099
Latin America	6%	NeoRecormon/Epogin (anemia)	1,774
Asia-Pacific	5%	Peasys (hepatitis)	1,635
Others	1%	Tarceva (lung cancer, pancreatic cancer)	1,215
		Lucentis (macular degeneration)	960
By Therapeutic Category	**Share**	Tamiflu (influenza)	609
Oncology	55%	Xolair (asthma)	560
Inflammation and autoimmune diseases, transplantation	9%	Valcyte/Cymevene (herpes)	553
		Xenical (weight loss and control)	502
Central nervous system	3%	Pulmozyme (cystic fibrosis)	496
Respiratory	3%	Nutropin (growth hormone deficiency)	413
Metabolic diseases, bone diseases	8%	Neutrogin (neutropenia associated with chemotherapy)	404
Infectious diseases	1%	Rocephin (bacterial infections)	344
Cardiovascular diseases	3%	Activase, TNKase (heart attack)	342
Virology	9%	Madopar (Parkinson's disease)	311
Renal anemia	4%		
Ophthalmology	3%		
Others	2%		

Data source: Roche 2008 annual report.

[1]CEMAI: Central and Eastern Europe, the Middle East, Africa, Central Asia, and the Indian Subcontinent. This acronym appears to be unique to Roche.

EXHIBIT 11.2 | Roche Financial Statements, Financial Years Ended December 31 (in millions of Swiss francs)

Income statement	2004	2005	2006	2007	2008
Revenue	31,092	36,958	43,432	48,376	47,904
COGS	7,718	9,270	13,096	13,738	13,605
Gross margin	23,374	27,688	30,336	34,638	34,299
Operating expense					
Sales and marketing	10,423	11,816	11,588	11,576	11,317
Research and development	5,154	5,672	7,286	8,327	8,720
Other operating	1,572	1,011	0	0	0
Operating income	6,225	9,189	11,462	14,735	14,262
Net interest expense (income)	311	(742)	(443)	(791)	(488)
Other non operating expenses (income)	(677)	769	(682)	222	589
Income tax	1,865	2,284	3,436	3,867	3,317
Minority interest	−457	−943	−1,291	−1,676	−1,875
Net income	6,606	5,923	7,880	9,761	8,969
Balance sheet					
Total cash and ST investments	12,999	20,885	24,996	24,802	21,438
Total other current assets	16,680	14,741	15,899	18,032	17,166
Net PP&E	12,408	15,097	16,417	17,832	18,190
Other noncurrent assets	16,359	18,472	17,102	17,699	19,295
Total assets	58,446	69,195	74,414	78,365	76,089
Total current liabilities	10,134	9,492	12,692	14,454	12,104
Long-term debt	7,077	9,322	6,191	3,831	2,971
Unearned revenue	0	183	163	243	174
Other noncurrent liabilities	13,237	16,864	15,924	14,354	16,361
Total liabilities	30,448	35,861	34,970	32,882	31,610
Common stock	160	160	160	160	160
Retained earnings	35,960	38,624	44,251	50,922	52,081
Treasury stock	−4,326	−3,485	−2,102	−1,017	−
Comprehensive inc. and other	−3,796	−1,965	−2,865	−4,582	−7,762
Total shareholder equity	27,998	33,334	39,444	45,483	44,479
Total liabilities and SE	58,446	69,195	74,414	78,365	76,089

Data source: Capital IQ.

EXHIBIT 11.3 | Genentech Financial Statements (in millions of U.S. dollars)

Income statement	2004	2005	2006	2007	2008
Revenue	4,621	6,633	9,284	11,724	13,418
COGS	805	1,155	1,366	1,767	1,971
Gross margin	3,816	5,478	7,918	9,957	11,447
Operating expense					
Sales and marketing	1,088	1,435	2,014	2,256	2,405
Research and development	816	1,118	1,588	2,250	2,573
Other operating	739	946	1,110	1,212	1,400
Operating income	1,173	1,979	3,206	4,239	5,069
Net interest expense (income)	(83)	(93)	(156)	(224)	(75)
Other non operating expenses (income)	36	59	(35)	38	(286)
Income tax	435	734	1,290	1,657	2,004
Minority interest	0	0	0	0	0
Net income	785	1,279	2,107	2,768	3,426
Balance sheet					
Total cash and ST investments	1,665	2,365	2,493	3,975	6,198
Total other current assets	1,760	2,021	3,211	4,778	3,875
Net PP&E	2,091	3,349	4,173	4,986	5,404
Other noncurrent assets	3,887	4,412	4,965	5,201	6,310
Total assets	9,403	12,147	14,842	18,940	21,787
Total current liabilities	1,238	1,660	2,010	3,918	3,095
Long-term debt	412	2,083	2,204	2,402	2,329
Unearned revenue	268	220	199	418	444
Other noncurrent liabilities	703	714	951	297	248
Total liabilities	2,621	4,677	5,364	7,035	6,116
Common stock	21	21	21	21	21
Additional paid in capital	8,003	9,263	10,091	10,695	12,044
Retained earnings	(1,533)	(2,067)	(838)	992	3,482
Comprehensive inc. and other	291	253	204	197	124
Total shareholder equity	6,782	7,470	9,478	11,905	15,671
Total liabilities and SE	9,403	12,147	14,842	18,940	21,787

Data source: Capital IQ.

EXHIBIT 11.4 | Stock Price Performance of Roche and Genentech, February 2007 to February 2009 (in Swiss francs and U.S. dollars, respectively)[1]

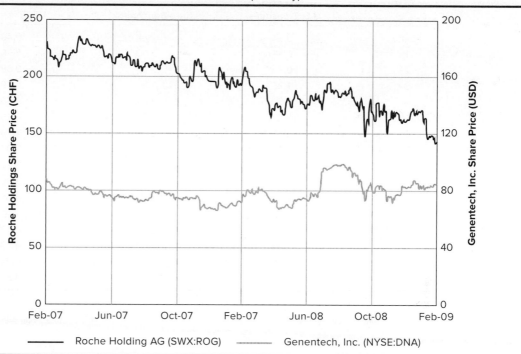

Data source: Capital IQ.

[1]Correspondence of values between axes is approximate, based on exchange rates on February 28, 2007. The average rate for the period was USD1.13/CHF1.00.

EXHIBIT 11.5 | Annual Yield Rate to Maturity (U.S. Dollar, Euro, British Pound), February 2009 (in percent)

	U.S. Treasuries	Euro Benchmark[1]	UK Sovereign
6-mo	0.34	n/a	0.48
1	0.48	2.09	0.56
2	0.93	2.26	0.88
3	1.35	2.55	1.39
4	1.50	2.81	1.85
5	1.87	3.01	2.29
6	n/a	3.19	2.79
7	2.18	3.35	3.06
8	2.67	3.48	3.25
9	2.80	3.60	3.50
10	2.85	3.70	3.66
12	n/a	3.87	n/a
15	3.45	3.99	4.13
20	3.91	3.99	4.29
25	3.90	3.83	4.34
30	3.59	3.69	4.35

Data source: Bloomberg.

[1]The euro benchmark is obtained from the midrate of the euro versus the EURIBOR mid-interest rate swap.

EXHIBIT 11.6 | U.S. Yield Spreads of U.S. Industrial Corporate Bonds over Comparable Maturity of U.S. Treasuries for S&P's Bond-Rating Categories, February 2009 (in basis points)

Rating	Years to maturity						
	1	2	3	5	7	10	30
AAA	90	82	77	90	136	114	170
AA	210	201	198	202	224	204	242
A+	211	201	217	226	243	226	242
A	279	261	278	277	290	275	263
A−	289	271	287	286	303	284	273
BBB+	406	387	409	406	412	406	394
BBB	417	398	422	424	435	418	411
BBB−	493	497	510	520	527	509	506

Data source: Bloomberg.

EXHIBIT 11.7 | History of U.S. Bond Yields for 30-Year Maturities, February 2006 to February 2009 (in percent)

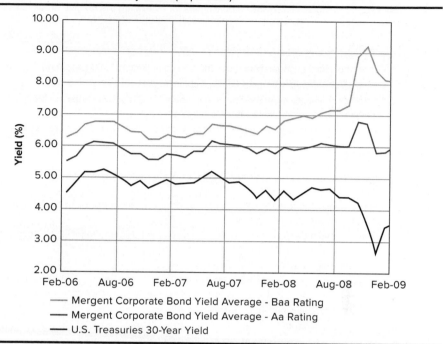

Data source: Datastream, Mergent Bond Record.

EXHIBIT 11.8 | S&P Credit Ratings Overview

S&P's global bond-rating scale provides a benchmark for evaluating the relative credit risk of issuers and issues worldwide.

Investment grade

AAA	Extremely strong capacity to meet financial commitments. Highest rating
AA	Very strong capacity to meet financial commitments
A	Strong capacity to meet financial commitments, but somewhat susceptible to adverse economic conditions and changes in circumstances
BBB	Adequate capacity to meet financial commitments, but more subject to adverse economic conditions

Speculative grade

BB	Less vulnerable in the near-term but faces major ongoing uncertainties to adverse business, financial, and economic conditions
B	More vulnerable to adverse business, financial, and economic conditions but currently has the capacity to meet financial commitments
CCC	Currently vulnerable and dependent on favorable business, financial, and economic conditions to meet financial commitments
CC	Currently highly vulnerable
C	A bankruptcy petition has been filed or similar action taken, but payments of financial commitments are continued
D	Payment default on financial commitments

Ratings from "AA" to "CCC" may be modified by the addition of a plus (+) or minus (−) sign to show relative standing within the major rating categories. The Moody's bond-rating service had a similar rating scale but denoted an S&P "BBB" rating, for example, as "Baa."

Data source: *Guide to Credit Rating Essentials,* Standard and Poor's, http://www2.standardandpoors.com/spf/pdf/fixedincome/SP_CreditRatingsGuide.pdf (accessed February 16, 2011).

EXHIBIT 11.9 | Median Financial Ratio Values for all U.S. Rated Industrial Companies, 2007 and 2008

	Number of Companies	Debt/ (Debt + BookEq)	EBITDA/ Int. Expense	EBIT/ Int. Expense	Debt/ EBITDA
2007					
AAA	26	0.51	95.47	74.06	2.26
AA	189	0.30	35.92	31.05	0.85
A	539	0.41	12.45	9.86	1.63
BBB	924	0.50	8.20	6.11	2.66
BB	470	0.52	6.59	4.63	2.82
B	335	0.71	3.71	2.30	4.66
2008					
AAA	18	0.51	113.97	81.62	3.25
AA	182	0.26	43.97	31.21	0.81
A	559	0.43	12.78	9.89	1.81
BBB	924	0.50	8.23	6.42	2.47
BB	417	0.52	6.40	4.51	2.82
B	321	0.75	3.41	2.10	4.92

Data source: Case writer analysis of Compustat data.

EXHIBIT 11.10 | Plan for Currency and Maturity of Roche Bond Offering Tranches[1]

U.S. Dollar-Denominated		
Maturity	**Amount (in billions of U.S. dollars)**	**Coupon**
1 year	3.00	Floating rate
2 years	1.25	Floating rate
3 years	2.50	Fixed rate
5 years	2.75	Fixed rate
10 years	4.50	Fixed rate
30 years	2.50	Fixed rate

Euro-denominated		
Maturity	**Amount (in billions of euros)**	**Coupon**
1 year	1.50	Floating rate
4 years	5.25	Fixed rate
7 years	2.75	Fixed rate
12 years	1.75	Fixed rate

Sterling-denominated		
Maturity	**Amount (in billions of British pounds)**	**Coupon**
6 years	1.25	Fixed rate

Data source: Company documents.

[1]Prevailing exchange rates at the time were CHF1.67/GBP1.00, CHF1.18/USD1.00, and CHF1.48/EUR1.00.

EXHIBIT 11.11 | Prevailing Prices of Sample of Recently Rated Corporate Bonds (Mid-February 2009)

Company	Issue Date	Maturity	Years Remaining to Maturity	S&P Rating	Amount Issued (millions)	Coupon	Price
U.S. dollar-denominated							
Altria	2/3/2009	2/6/2014	5	BBB	525	7.75	105.835
Altria	2/3/2009	2/6/2019	10	BBB	2,200	9.25	104.612
Altria	2/3/2009	2/6/2039	30	BBB	1,500	10.2	105.079
AT&T	1/29/2009	2/15/2014	5	A	1,000	4.85	99.790
AT&T	1/29/2009	2/15/2019	10	A	2,250	5.8	98.877
AT&T	1/29/2009	2/15/2039	30	A	2,250	6.55	96.626
Johnson & Johnson	6/23/2008	7/15/2038	29	AAA	700	5.85	111.000
McKesson	2/9/2009	2/15/2014	5	BBB+	350	6.5	103.372
McKesson	2/9/2009	2/15/2019	10	BBB+	350	7.5	106.156
Novartis	2/10/2009	2/10/2014	5	AA−	2,000	4.125	101.778
Novartis	2/10/2009	2/10/2019	10	AA−	3,000	5.125	100.746
Pfizer	2/3/2004	2/15/2014	5	AA	750	4.5	105.660
Schering-Plough	11/26/2003	12/1/2013	5	AA−	1,250	5.3	103.820
Schering-Plough	9/17/2007	9/15/2037	29	AA−	1,000	6.55	101.332
Verizon	11/4/2008	11/1/2018	10	A	2,000	8.75	118.582
Verizon	11/4/2008	3/31/2039	30	A	1,250	8.95	124.467
Warner Chilcott	2/1/2006	2/1/2015	6	BB−	600	8.75	95.000
Euro-denominated							
Anheuser-Busch InBev	2/9/2009	2/27/2014	5	BBB+	750	6.57	100.558
Imperial Tobacco	2/10/2009	2/17/2016	7	BBB	1,500	8.375	101.048
John Deere	1/19/2009	1/24/2014	5	A	600	7.5	105.801
Schering-Plough	10/1/2007	10/1/2014	6	AA−	1,500	5.375	99.710
Volkswagen	1/30/2009	2/9/2012	3	A−	2,500	5.625	100.332
Volkswagen	1/30/2009	2/9/2016	7	A−	1,000	7	100.238
Pound sterling-denominated							
Bayer AG	5/23/2006	5/23/2018	9	A−	350	5.625	100.817
Imperial Tobacco	2/10/2009	2/17/2022	13	BBB	1,000	9	107.062
Tesco	2/17/2009	2/24/2014	5	A−	600	5	100.284

Data source: Case writer analysis using Bloomberg data.

EXHIBIT 11.12 | Selected Comparable Companies' Data for 2008 (in millions of U.S. dollars)[1]

	Shareholder Equity	Total Debt	Cash and Equivalents	EBITDA	Interest Expense	Current Rating
Bayer AG	21,381	21,779	2,740	8,183	1,626	A−
Schering-Plough	10,529	8,176	3,373	2,917	536	AA−
Johnson & Johnson	46,100	11,852	10,768	19,001	435	AAA
Pfizer	57,556	17,290	2,122	20,929	516	AA
Wyeth	19,174	11,739	10,016	7,954	492	A+
GlaxoSmithKline	15,900	25,211	8,758	15,388	1,291	A+
Merck & Co	21,080	6,240	4,368	7,854	251	AA−
AstraZeneca	15,912	11,848	4,286	12,553	714	AA
Warner Chilcott	1,350	963	36	508	94	BB−
Roche Holding	41,569	4,051	4,870	16,751	213	AA−
Roche + Genentech (pro forma)	41,569	46,051	4,870	16,751	2,303	

Data source: Capital IQ and case writer analysis.

[1]Because the Genentech financial figures were already consolidated in the Roche financial statements, only the debt and interest expense was expected to vary. The pro-forma interest expense was based on an arbitrary 5% interest rate.

H. J. Heinz: Estimating the Cost of Capital in Uncertain Times

To do a common thing uncommonly well brings success.
  —**H. J. Heinz Founder Henry John Heinz**

As a financial analyst at the H. J. Heinz Company (Heinz) in its North American Consumer Products division, Solomon Sheppard, together with his co-workers, reviewed investment proposals involving a wide range of food products. Most discussions in his office focused on the potential performance of new products and reasonableness of cash flow projections. But as the company finished its 2010 fiscal year at the end of April—with financial markets still in turmoil from the onset of the recession that started at the end of 2007—the central topic of discussion was the company's weighted average cost of capital (WACC).

At the time, there were three reasons the cost of capital was a subject of controversy. First, Heinz's stock price had just finished a two-year roller coaster ride: Its fiscal year-end stock price dropped from $47 in 2008 to $34 in 2009, then rose back to $47 in 2010, and a vigorous debate ensued as to whether the weights in a cost of capital calculation should be updated to reflect these changes as they occurred. Second, interest rates remained quite low—unusually so for longer-term bond rates; there was concern that updating the cost of capital to reflect these new rates would lower the cost of capital and therefore bias in favor of accepting projects. Third, there was a strong sense that, as a result of the recent financial meltdown, the appetite for risk in the market had changed, but there was no consensus as to whether this should affect the cost of capital of the company and, if so, how.

When Sheppard arrived at work on the first of May, he found himself at the very center of that debate. Moments after his arrival, Sheppard's immediate supervisor asked him to provide a recommendation for a WACC to be used by the North American Consumer Products division. Recognizing its importance to capital budgeting decisions in the firm, he vowed to do an "uncommonly good" job with this analysis, gathered the most recent data readily available, and began to grind the numbers.

Heinz and the Food Industry

In 1869, Henry John Heinz launched a food company by making horseradish from his mother's recipe. As the story goes, Heinz was traveling on a train when he saw a sign advertising 21 styles of shoes, which he thought was clever. Since 57 was his lucky number, the entrepreneur began using the slogan "57 Varieties" in his advertising. By 2010, the company he eventually founded had become a food giant, with $10 billion in revenues and 29,600 employees around the globe.

Heinz manufactured products in three categories: Ketchup and Sauces, Meals and Snacks, and Infant Nutrition. Heinz's strategy was to be a leader in each product segment and develop a portfolio of iconic brands. The firm estimated that 150 of the company's brands held either the number one or number two position in their respective target markets.[1] The famous Heinz Ketchup, with sales of $1.5 billion a year or 650 million bottles sold, was still the undisputed world leader. Other well-known brands included Weight Watchers (a leader in dietary products), Heinz Beans (in 2010, the brand sold over 1.5 million cans a day in Britain, the "biggest bean-eating nation in the world"), and Plasmon (the gold standard of infant food in the Italian market).[2] Well-known brands remained the core of the business with the top 15 brands accounting for about 70% of revenues, and each generating over $100 million in sales.

Heinz was a global powerhouse. It operated in more than 200 countries. The company was organized into business segments based primarily on region: North American Consumer Products, U.S. Foodservice, Europe, Asia Pacific, and Rest of World. About 60% of revenues were from outside the United States and the North American Consumer Products and Europe segments were of comparable size. Increasingly, the company was focusing on emerging markets, which had generated 30% of recent growth and comprised 15% of total sales.

The most prominent global food companies based in the United States included Kraft Foods, the largest U.S.-based food and beverage company; Campbell Soup Company, the iconic canned food maker; and Del Monte Foods, one of largest producers and distributers of premium-quality branded food and pet products focused on the U.S. market (and a former Heinz subsidiary). Heinz also competed with a number of other global players such as Nestlé, the world leader in sales, and Unilever, the British-Dutch consumer goods conglomerate.

Recent Performance

With the continued uncertainty regarding any economic recovery and deep concerns about job growth over the previous two years, consumers had begun to focus on value in their purchases and to eat more frequently at home. This proved a benefit for those companies providing food products and motivated many top food producers and distributors to focus on core brands. As a result, Heinz had done well in both 2009 and 2010, with positive sales growth and profits above the 2008 level both years, although

---

[1] "H. J. Heinz Corporate Profile," http://www.heinz.com/our-company/press-room.aspx (accessed Sep. 27, 2010).

[2] http://www.heinz.com/our-company/press-room.aspx.

FIGURE 12.1 | Heinz stock price and normalized S&P 500 Index.

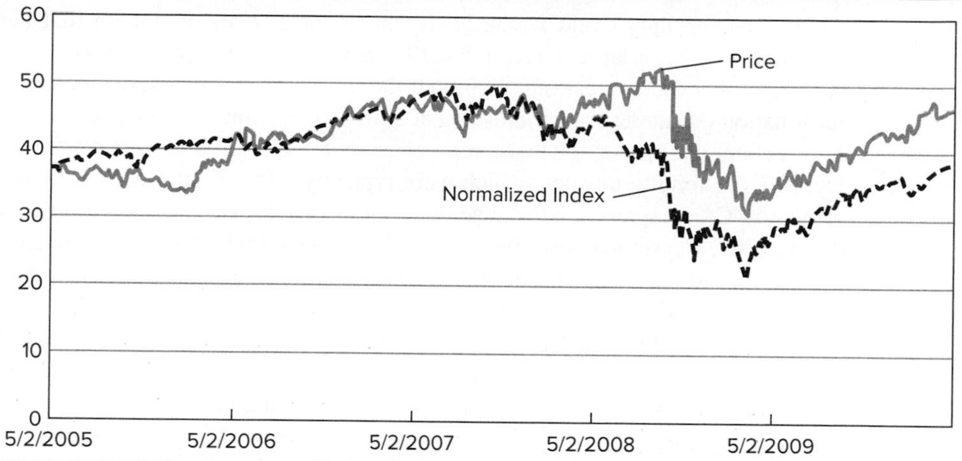

Data sources: S&P 500 and Yahoo! Finance.

2010 profits were lower than those in 2009. These results were particularly striking since a surge in the price of corn syrup and an increase in the cost of packaging had necessitated price increases for most of its products. Overseas sales growth, particularly in Asia, had also positively affected the company's operations. **Exhibit 12.1** and **Exhibit 12.2** present financial results for the years 2008, 2009, and 2010.

The relation between food company stock prices and the economy was compli-cated. In general, the performance of a food products company was not extremely sensi-tive to market conditions and might even benefit from market uncertainty. This was clear to Heinz CFO Art Winkelblack, who in early 2009 had remarked, "I'm sure glad we're selling food and not washing machines or cars. People are coming home to Heinz."[3] Still an exceptionally prolonged struggle or another extreme market decline could drive more consumers to the private-label brands that represented a step down from the Heinz brands. While a double-dip recession seemed less likely in mid-2010, it was clear the economy continued to struggle, and this put pressure on margins.

While the stock price for Heinz had been initially unaffected by adverse changes in the economy and did not decline with the market, starting in the third quarter of 2008, Heinz's stock price began tracking the market's movement quite closely. **Figure 12.1** plots the Heinz stock price against the S&P Index (normalized to match Heinz's stock price at the start of the 2005 fiscal year). The low stock price at the start of 2009 had been characterized by some as an over-reaction and, even with the subsequent recovery, it was considered undervalued by some.[4]

---

[3]Andrew Bary, "The Return of the Ketchup Kid," *Barron's,* January 26, 2009.

[4]Bary; the same article noted that Heinz had "an above-average portfolio of brands, led by its commanding global ketchup franchise" and, even at January 2009 prices, could be a takeover target.

Cost of Capital Considerations

Recessions certainly could wreak havoc on financial markets. Given that the recent downturn had been largely precipitated by turmoil in the capital markets, it was not surprising that the interest rate picture at the time was unusual. **Exhibit 12.3** presents information on interest rate yields. As of April 2010, short-term government rates and even commercial paper for those companies that could issue it were at strikingly low levels. Even long-term rates, which were typically less volatile, were low by historic standards. Credit spreads, which had drifted upwards during 2008 and jumped upwards during 2009, had settled down but were still somewhat high by historic standards. Interestingly, the low level of long-term rates had more than offset the rise in credit spreads, and borrowers with access to debt markets had low borrowing costs.

Sheppard gathered some market data related to Heinz (also shown in **Exhibit 12.3**). He easily obtained historic stock price data. Most sources he accessed estimated the company's beta using the previous five years of data at about 0.65.[5] Sheppard obtained prices for two bonds he considered representative of the company's outstanding borrowings: a note due in 2032 and a note due in 2012. Heinz had regularly accessed the commercial paper market in the past, but that market had recently dried up. Fortunately, the company had other sources for short-term borrowing and Sheppard estimated these funds cost about 1.20%.

What most surprised Sheppard was the diversity of opinions he obtained regarding the market risk premium. Integral to calculating the required return on a company's equity using the capital asset pricing model, this rate reflected the incremental return an investor required for investing in a broad market index of stocks rather than a riskless bond. When measured over long periods of time, the average premium had been about 7.5%.[6] But when measured over shorter time periods, the premium varied greatly; recently the premium had been closer to 6.0% and by some measures even lower. Most striking were the results of a survey of CFOs indicating that expectations were for an even lower premium in the near future—close to 5.0%. On the other hand, some asserted that market conditions in 2010 only made sense if a much higher premium—something close to 8%—were assumed.

As Sheppard prepared for his cost of capital analysis and recommendation, he obtained recent representative data for Heinz's three major U.S. competitors (**Exhibit 12.4**). This information would allow Sheppard to generate cost-of-capital estimates for these competitors as well as for Heinz. Arguably, if market conditions for Heinz were unusual at the time, the results for competitors could be more representative for other companies in the industry. At the very least, Sheppard knew he would be more comfortable with his recommendation if it were aligned with what he believed was appropriate for the company's major competitors.

---

[5]Sheppard was sufficiently curious as to whether this number was still relevant that he calculated his own estimated of beta from the last year of daily returns. His estimate was 0.54, close to the five-year estimate from Value Line, but still notably lower.

[6]After some research, Sheppard was confident that the appropriate rate was the arithmetic mean (simple average) of past annual returns rather than the geometric mean in this context. The reason was that the arithmetic mean appropriately calculates the present value of a distribution of future cash flows.

EXHIBIT 12.1 | Income Statement (numbers in thousands except per-share amounts; fiscal year ends in April)

	2008	2009	2010
Revenue	9,885,556	10,011,331	10,494,983
Costs of goods sold	6,233,420	6,442,075	6,700,677
Gross profit	3,652,136	3,569,256	3,794,306
SG&A expense	2,081,801	2,066,810	2,235,078
Operating income	1,570,335	1,502,446	1,559,228
Interest expense	323,289	275,485	250,574
Other income (expense)	(16,283)	92,922	(18,200)
Income before taxes	1,230,763	1,319,883	1,290,454
Income taxes	372,587	375,483	358,514
Net income after taxes	858,176	944,400	931,940
Adjustments to net income	(13,251)	(21,328)	(67,048)
Net income	844,925	923,072	864,892
Diluted EPS	2.61	2.89	2.71
Dividends per share	1.52	1.66	1.68

Data source: H. J. Heinz SEC filings, 2008–10.

EXHIBIT 12.2 | Balance Sheet (numbers in thousands except per-share amounts; fiscal year ends in April)

	2008	2009	2010
Cash	617,687	373,145	483,253
Net receivables	1,161,481	1,171,797	1,045,338
Inventories	1,378,216	1,237,613	1,249,127
Other current assets	168,182	162,466	273,407
Total current assets	3,325,566	2,945,021	3,051,125
Net fixed assets	2,104,713	1,978,302	2,091,796
Other noncurrent assets	5,134,764	4,740,861	4,932,790
Total assets	10,565,043	9,664,184	10,075,711
Accounts payable	1,247,479	1,113,307	1,129,514
Short-term debt	124,290	61,297	43,853
Current portion of long-term debt	328,418	4,341	15,167
Other current liabilities	969,873	883,901	986,825
Total current liabilities	2,670,060	2,062,846	2,175,359
Long-term debt	4,730,946	5,076,186	4,559,152
Other noncurrent liabilities	1,276,217	1,246,047	1,392,704
	6,007,163	6,322,233	5,951,856
Equity	1,887,820	1,279,105	1,948,496
Total liabilities and equity	10,565,043	9,664,184	10,075,711
Shares outstanding (in millions of dollars)	311.45	314.86	317.69

Data source: H. J. Heinz SEC filings, 2008–10.

EXHIBIT 12.3 | Capital Market Data (yields and prices as of the last trading day in April of the year indicated)

Average Historic Yields	2003	2004	2005	2006	2007	2008	2009	2010
1-year	1.22%	1.55%	3.33%	4.98%	4.89%	1.85%	0.49%	0.41%
5-year	2.85%	3.63%	3.90%	4.92%	4.51%	3.03%	2.02%	2.43%
10-year	3.89%	4.53%	4.21%	5.07%	4.63%	3.77%	3.16%	3.69%
30-year[1]	4.79%	5.31%	4.61%	5.17%	4.89%	4.49%	4.05%	4.53%
Moody's Aaa	5.53%	5.87%	5.21%	5.95%	5.40%	5.51%	5.45%	5.13%
Moody's Baa	6.65%	6.58%	5.97%	6.74%	6.31%	6.87%	8.24%	6.07%
3-month commercial paper	1.21%	1.08%	2.97%	4.90%	5.22%	1.91%	0.22%	0.24%

Heinz Capital Market Prices of Typical Issues	2009	2010
Heinz stock price	$34.42	$46.87
Bond price: 6.750% coupon, semiannual bond due 3/15/32 (Baa rated)	91.4	116.9
Bond price: 6.625% coupon, semiannual bond due 10/15/12 (Baa rated)	116.5	113.7

Note that bond data were slightly modified for teaching purposes.

Data sources: Federal Reserve, Value Line, Morningstar, and case writer estimates.

[1]The 20-year yield is used for 2003–05, when the 30-year was not issued.

EXHIBIT 12.4 | Comparable Firm Data

	Kraft	Campbell Soup	Del Monte
Financial Summary			
Revenues (in millions of dollars)	40,386	7,589	3,739
Book value of equity (in millions of dollars)	25,972	728	1,827
Book value of debt (in millions of dollars)	18,990	2,624	1,290
Market Data			
Beta	0.65	0.55	0.70
Shares outstanding (in millions of dollars)	1,735	363	182
Share price (dollars as of close April 30, 2010)	29.90	35.64	15.11
Typical Standard & Poor's bond rating	BBB—	A	BB
Representative yield on long-term debt	5.12%	4.36%	6.19%

Data sources: Value Line; H. J. Heinz SEC filings, 2008–10; case writer estimates; Morningstar.

Royal Mail plc: Cost of Capital

As Hillary Hart, senior financial analyst at the British postal service company Royal Mail plc (Royal Mail), approached company headquarters near Blackfriars Bridge in London, she reflected on the momentous nature of the seven years she had spent in that building. During that time, the company had faced important changes in broad demand for letters and parcels, significant restructuring of government regulation, competitive entry into its long-standing monopoly position, deep workforce cuts, wide-scale labor negotiations and strikes, and, lastly, the transition from 500 years as a government-owned enterprise to a massive for-profit company traded on the London Stock Exchange.

Now on July 21, 2015, Hart had an upcoming meeting with several senior managers of the company. Central to the meeting was an evaluation of the cost of capital for Royal Mail. The cost of capital had become a point of discussion for two reasons. First, since privatization, Royal Mail was increasingly looking to shed its government-based decision-making policies of the past for a more market-based orientation. The adoption of an investor-oriented cost-of-capital benchmark provided an important step in moving forward the governance of company investment policy. That said, it was by no means easy to shift company objectives toward rewarding investors and away from a focus on facilitating national employment and communication needs. Second, the company was under an important review by the British regulatory authority, the Office of Communications (Ofcom). Deregulation of private postal services was still very much an experiment in Britain. Due to recent competitive events in the country, Ofcom was reevaluating existing regulatory policies. The cost of capital provided an appropriate benchmark by which to properly assess the profitability of Royal Mail's operations and the viability of Royal Mail's operations under the existing regulatory policies.

Royal Mail plc

Royal Mail originated in 1516 when King Henry VIII established Sir Brian Tuke as "Master of the Posts" with the charge to organize a postal service to carry mail between British cities. Throughout its long history, Royal Mail proved to be the world's foremost pioneer in postal services. The company introduced many features that became ubiquitous to postal services worldwide. In 1661, the Royal Mail postmaster introduced the first postmark with the declaration [in his own spelling], "A stamp is invented that is putt upon every letter shewing the day of the moneth that every letter comes to the office, so that no Letter Carrier may dare detayne a letter from post to post; which before was usual."[1] In the late 1700s, Royal Mail was the first postal service to operate a fleet of independent mail coaches and outfit postal carriers in uniforms. In 1840, Royal Mail was the first mail service to offer letter delivery services throughout the entire country for a single rate. To certify postage prepayment in such a system, Royal Mail invented the postage stamp. The original postage stamp, the Penny Black, was a one-penny stamp bearing the face of Queen Victoria (see **Exhibit 13.1**), and provided prepaid postage for letters of up to half an ounce to be delivered anywhere in Great Britain and Ireland. In recognition of Royal Mail's role in developing the first postage stamp, British stamps remained throughout the world as the only postage stamps that did not specify the country of issuance on the stamp. In the mid-19th century, Royal Mail introduced letter boxes where senders could simply deposit letters to be sent with the affixed paid postage.

Now, due to the dramatic changes in postal services demand at the beginning of the 21st century, it was once again a time for innovation at Royal Mail. In 2006, the British government had removed Royal Mail's monopoly status, allowing private companies to compete in collecting and sorting mail in the United Kingdom. With the change, government regulation was reduced, and Royal Mail was freed to set its own postage rates. Over the next six years, Royal Mail responded by increasing the price of First-Class postage from 32 pence to 60 pence.

In 2011, Parliament passed the important Postal Services Act. In this Act, the Postal Services Commission was disbanded and the regulatory purview of postal services in the United Kingdom shifted to the Ofcom. The intent was to dramatically alter the regulation of Royal Mail. Despite the increased liberties, however, the Act designated that Royal Mail was required to maintain six-days-a-week, one-price-goes-anywhere universal service for letters regardless of the ownership structure of the company.

A decision to privatize the British mail service followed a government conclusion that Royal Mail was less efficient and disciplined than many other post offices elsewhere in Europe, and that it "urgently needed commercial confidence, capital, and corporate experience to modernize quickly and effectively."[2] This need followed a sustained worldwide decline in letter volume in the first decade of the twenty-first century as a result of the substitution of electronic communication. Vince Cable, the UK's Business Secretary, had argued his position before the House of Commons: "The government's decision on the sale is practical, it is logical, it is a commercial decision designed to put Royal Mail's future in a long-term sustainable business."[3] Over the years since deregulation, the financial performance of Royal Mail improved and its operating margin was

---

[1] John G. Hendy, *The History of the Early Postmarks of the British Isles from Their Introduction Down to 1840,* (London: L. Upcott Gill, 1905), 204.

[2] "The Privatisation of Royal Mail," National Audit Office, March 27, 2014, 5.

[3] Jennifer Rankin, "Royal Mail Privatization Will Not Affect Postal Delivery," *The Guardian,* July 10, 2013.

up fourfold. Cash flow for the company had grown from negative GBP504 million in fiscal year 2009 to positive GBP282 million in fiscal year 2013.

The privatization of Royal Mail came in October 2013, when the British government sold 60% of its 1 billion shares of Royal Mail to the public for 330 pence each. The transaction generated proceeds of GBP2 billion. Of the shares sold, 73% were sold to institutional investors and 23% were sold to 690,000 individual investors.[4]

On Royal Mail's first day of trading on the London Stock Exchange, its share price rose 38% to 455 pence. Despite high-profile strikes by postal workers who were strongly opposed to the privatization, the share price for Royal Mail rose in the months following the sale. By January 2014, the share price was trading at over 600 pence, a more than 80% increase over the sale price. Although the share price suffered a substantial price reversal in mid-2014, over the first six months of 2015 Royal Mail shares had recovered and closed on July 20th at 511 pence. **Exhibit 13.2** provides a history of returns to Royal Mail equity investors relative to returns in the broad FTSE 100 Index since October 2013. Despite the strong and growing profits and assets, there was still substantial uncertainty about the value of the shares.

Two sources of uncertainty were competition and regulation. In April 2012, the Dutch postal service company TNT had entered the UK door-to-door postal services market with a subsidiary business that would eventually become known as Whistl. Over the ensuing years, the financial viability of the venture had proved challenging. Just last month, Whistl management had announced that the company would be suspending its door-to-door business to focus on its bulk mail processing service in Britain. It would rely on Royal Mail's infrastructure for the "final mile" of delivery service. Two thousand Whistl employees were laid off. The British government responded by calling into question Ofcom's regulatory policies. In response, Ofcom began a high-profile review of the postal services market in an effort to stimulate competition. One concern was that Royal Mail maintained pricing power in the market such that it could engage in anticompetitive pricing. Such allegations raised the question of what was the appropriate level of profitability for a firm such as Royal Mail.

Moya Greene, CEO of Royal Mail, expressed the company's willingness to fully comply with the review. She also indicated that Royal Mail was facing difficulties of its own but was determined to continue to get better. She specifically stated:

> This has been a challenging year. Through a continued focus on efficiency and tight cost control, we have offset the impact of lower than anticipated UK parcel revenue this year, so that operating profit before transformation costs is in line with our expectations. It has also been a year of innovation, with a range of new initiatives delivered at pace. We have introduced around 30 new projects, including services, products and promotions, to improve our customer offering.[5]

One example was the recent announcement that the company was pursuing an efficiency objective by purchasing 76,000 hand-held scanner devices from Zebra

---

[4]National Audit Office, 43.

[5] Royal Mail plc Full Year Results 2014–15, Royal Mail plc, May 21, 2015.

Technologies. Other initiatives included upstream investment opportunities such as the acquisition of online shopping platforms such as Mallzee and StoreFeeder.

Just that morning, Greene had issued an update on the company performance for the most recent quarter and emphasized substantial success and concerns. She reported that strong performance from the parcels business was offsetting declines in letter delivery revenue, and that the company was committed to investing in innovation and efficiency.[6] She cautioned that the rest of year's performance would depend on the critically important Christmas period. **Exhibit 13.3** shows historical data on Royal Mail unit volume. **Exhibits 13.4** and **13.5** provide historical financial statements for Royal Mail.

The Cost of Capital

The cost of capital was theoretically defined as the prevailing return that investors could earn on alternative investments of similar risk. As such, it was inherently a figure determined by market forces rather than by the company. One attractive feature of the cost of capital was that it provided an opportunity cost benchmark for evaluating investment returns. Business returns that were expected to exceed the cost of capital were considered value creating to investors since the expected returns exceeded what investors could generate on their own with investments of similar risk. Business returns that were expected to be less than the cost of capital were considered value destroying to investors. Moreover, the cost of capital provided an estimate of the fair return for investors in competitive businesses. It was expected that businesses in competitive markets would, on average, earn their cost of capital.

In estimating the cost of capital it was common to consider all capital used in the business. To estimate the opportunity cost of total business capital, it was common to use a weighted average of the prevailing required return values for the various types of investors in the business, such as debt holders and equity holders. This approach was called the weighted average cost of capital (WACC).

In response to the burgeoning interest in a cost of capital estimate for Royal Mail, Hart had asked a colleague, Kyle Brooks, to provide an estimate. Given the unique nature of Royal Mail's business and its limited life in public capital markets, Hart recognized that this was not an easy task. Still, Brooks had quickly generated an estimate of 3.828% and provided a stack of documentation. **Exhibit 13.6** provides his analysis and summary. **Exhibits 13.7** through **13.9** provide his supporting documents.

---

[6]Royal Mail plc press release, July 21, 2015.

EXHIBIT 13.1 | The Penny Black, the World's First Postage Stamp (Issued in 1840)

Source: "Penny black," posted to public domain by the General Post Office of the United Kingdom of Great Britain and Ireland, August 28, 2007, https://commons.wikimedia.org/wiki/File:Penny_black.jpg (accessed Jan. 3, 2017).

EXHIBIT 13.2 | Cumulative Weekly Total Stock Returns—Royal Mail and FTSE 100 Index

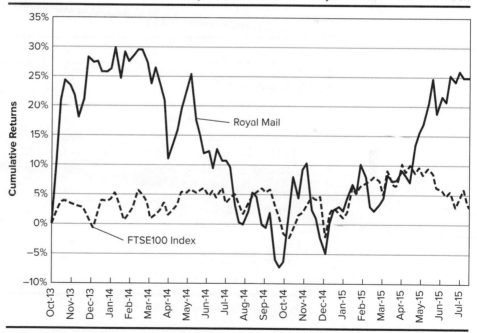

Source: Created by author using data from Investing.com.

EXHIBIT 13.3 | Royal Mail Unit Volume History (Millions of Units, Period Ending March 31)

	2012	2013	2014	2015
Letters				
Addressed letters	15,147	13,869	13,342	13,009
Unaddressed letters	3,077	3,258	3,143	3,157
Total	18,224	17,127	16,485	16,166
Growth rate		−6.0%	−3.7%	−1.9%
Parcels				
Royal Mail core network	950	994	991	1,015
Parcelforce worldwide	66	70	77	86
Total	1,016	1,064	1,068	1,101
Growth rate		4.7%	0.4%	3.1%

Source: Company annual reports.

EXHIBIT 13.4 | Royal Mail Consolidated Income Statement (Reported as of the End of March in Millions of GBP)

	2014	2015
Revenue	9,357	9,328
People costs	5,209	5,230
Distribution and conveyance costs	1,796	1,764
Infrastructure costs	1,047	1,019
Other operating costs	578	575
Transformation costs	241	145
Earnings before interest and tax	486	595
Finance costs	71	30
Finance income	4	4
Profit before tax	419	569
Tax	110	138
Profit for the period	309	431
Earnings per share	30.6 pence	42.8 pence

Source: Royal Mail annual report, 2015.

EXHIBIT 13.5 | Royal Mail Consolidated Balance Sheet (Reported as of the End of March in Millions of GBP)

	2014	2015
Noncurrent assets		
Property, plant, and equipment	1,989	1,933
Goodwill and intangible assets	392	482
Retirement benefit asset	1,723	3,179
Other noncurrent assets	55	80
	4,159	5,674
Current assets		
Inventories	22	20
Trade and other receivables	926	949
Cash and current financial assets	369	348
	1,317	1,317
Total assets	5,476	6,991
Current liabilities		
Trade and other payables	1,652	1,668
Financial loans and borrowing	286	290
	1,938	1,958
Noncurrent liabilities		
Financial loans and borrowings	860	559
Deferred tax liabilities	151	474
Other liabilities	126	154
	1,137	1,187
Total equity		
Share capital	10	10
Retained earnings	2,332	3,843
Other equity	59	−7
	2,401	3,846

Source: Royal Mail annual report, 2015.

EXHIBIT 13.6 | Kyle Brooks's Cost-of-Capital Analysis

TO:	Hillary Hart
FROM:	Kyle Brooks
DATE:	July 17, 2015
SUBJECT:	RM's cost of capital

Based on the following assumptions, my estimate of Royal Mail's cost of capital is 3.828%.

Capital Structure

Since Royal Mail is funded with both debt and equity, I used the weighted average cost of capital (WACC) method. Based on the March 2015 balance sheet, current debt as a proportion of total capital makes up 6%, noncurrent debt as a proportion of total capital makes up 12%, and equity accounts for 82%:

Capital Sources	Book Values (in millions of GBP)	
Current debt	290	6 % of total capital
Noncurrent debt	559	12% of total capital
Equity	3,846	82% of total capital

Cost of Debt

My estimate of Royal Mail's cost of debt was 3.188%, which is the weighted average between the 0.9% rate Royal Mail is paying on its current debt and the 4.375% rate it is paying on its noncurrent debt. For the noncurrent debt rate I used the coupon rate from a recent bond. On July 29, 2014, Royal Mail issued a 10-year bond with an annual coupon of 4.375%. The bond was rated by S&P at BBB. S&P recently reaffirmed that rating, and the bond is currently trading at a price of 106.

I used a tax rate of 20%, which is the marginal tax rate for similar corporations in the United Kingdom, to estimate the after-tax cost of debt.

Cost of Equity

I estimated the cost of equity at 4.11% based on the prevailing dividend yield for Royal Mail. This was calculated by dividing last year's dividend of 21 pence by the current share price of 511 pence. The dividend yield is a good estimate of the cost of equity because it indicates exactly what equity holders received over the past year on their investment.

I also looked at an estimate based on the capital-asset-pricing model (CAPM). My CAPM estimate of Royal Mail's cost of equity was 5.321%. To get this number, I used a risk-free rate of 1.551%, the average yield on the 5-year government bond over the past 18 months. Because of the short period since Royal Mail has been privatized, there were few estimates of beta. But recently the equity research firm Chambers and Thompson published a beta estimate for Royal Mail of 0.65, so I used that. For my market risk premium I used 5.8%. This estimate comes from a rigorous academic survey of British investors that was published a few months ago. However, for my estimate of the cost of equity I selected the dividend yield estimate over the CAPM estimate because I felt it more prudent to be conservative.

Weighted Average

Based on these assumptions, my estimate of Royal Mail's cost of capital was 3.828%.

$$\text{WACC} = K_d(1 - t) \times D/(D + E) + K_e \times E/(D + E)$$
$$= 3.188\% \times (1 - 20\%) \times 18\% + 4.11\% \times 82\%$$

(continued)

EXHIBIT 13.6 | Kyle Brooks's Cost-of-Capital Analysis   (*continued*)

Comparables Estimates

To confirm my estimate I calculated the weighted average cost of capital for five comparable publicly traded companies. My estimates were:

National Grid:	3.853%
Severn Trent:	3.136%
Tesco:	5.475%
United Utilities:	3.281%
Vodafone:	5.660%

Since the comparable estimates are in the same general range as my 3.828% estimate for Royal Mail, I felt like my estimate was a reasonable representation of the true cost of capital for Royal Mail.

Source: Created by author.

EXHIBIT 13.7 | One-Month Interbank Lending Rate and Government Bond Yields (%)

	1-Month Bond	5-Year Bond	10-Year Bond
Jan-14	0.47	1.78	2.71
Feb-14	0.47	1.80	2.72
Mar-14	0.47	1.87	2.74
Apr-14	0.47	1.86	2.67
May-14	0.48	1.80	2.57
Jun-14	0.48	1.99	2.67
Jul-14	0.47	1.98	0.62
Aug-14	0.47	1.70	2.37
Sep-14	0.47	1.78	2.43
Oct-14	0.47	1.56	2.25
Nov-14	0.47	1.30	1.93
Dec-14	0.47	1.20	1.76
Jan-15	0.48	0.91	1.34
Feb-15	0.48	1.28	1.79
Mar-15	0.48	1.09	1.58
Apr-15	0.48	1.30	1.84
May-15	0.48	1.26	1.80
Jun-15	0.51	1.46	2.03

Data source: Bank of England Statistical Interactive Database, http://www.bankofengland.co.uk/boeapps/iadb/Index.asp?first=yes&SectionRequired=I&HideNums=-1&ExtraInfo=true&Travel=Nix.

EXHIBIT 13.8 | UK Corporate Benchmark Bond Yields for 10-Year Maturity in GBP (July 14, 2015)

Credit Rating	Yield
AAA	2.503
AA	2.839
A	3.356
BBB	3.776
BB	4.773
B	5.883

Sources: Thomson Reuters and author estimates.

EXHIBIT 13.9 | Financial Data for Comparables (Market Data as of July 14, 2015, Other Data is Most Recent Available)

Company	Industry
National Grid	Electricity and gas utility
Severn Trent	Water utility
Tesco	Food retailer
United Utilities	Water utility
Vodafone	Telecommunications

	National Grid	Severn Trent	Tesco	United Utilities	Vodafone
Price per share (pence)	855	2,190	200	900	230
Dividend per share (pence)	42	80	15	36	16
Shares outstanding (millions)	3,730	239	8,096	682	26,440
Market capitalization (millions)	31,892	5,234	16,192	6,138	60,812
Book equity (millions)	11,911	1,078	14,715	2,216	70,802
Book debt (millions)	25,950	4,622	11,213	6,042	25,362
Beta	0.60	0.79	0.87	0.67	0.86
Credit rating	BBB−	BBB+	BB+	BBB+	BBB+

Data source: *Financial Times,* https://markets.ft.com/data/equities.

Chestnut Foods

In early 2014, stock performance at Minneapolis-based Chestnut Foods (Chestnut) had failed to meet expectations for several years running, and senior management was hard-pressed to talk about much else. CFO Brenda Pedersen, eager to reverse the trend, had begun advocating two strategic initiatives: a $1 billion investment in company growth and the adoption of a more progressive corporate identity. At a restaurant overlooking the Mississippi River, Pedersen hosted an informal meeting of company VPs to build support; exchanges had been highly spirited, but no consensus had materialized. Then, on her drive home from the restaurant, she received a call from Claire Meyer, VP of Food Products, who had attended the dinner. Given the tone of the meeting, Pedersen wasn't surprised to get a call so soon, but what Meyer shared floored the CFO. "It just came up on Twitter. My admin saw it and texted me. I'm not going to say I told you so."

Meyer read her the tweet. "Van Muur buys 10% of Chestnut, seeks seats on board and a new management direction." Meyer filled in the details: based on filings earlier in the day with the U.S. Securities and Exchange Commission, Rollo van Muur, a high-profile activist investor, had quietly and unexpectedly purchased 10% of the company and was asserting the right to two seats on the board. In addition, Van Muur was recommending that the Instruments division be sold off "to keep the focus where it belongs."

Pedersen drove in shocked silence and processed the information while Meyer waited patiently on the line, not sure what to expect. When Pedersen finally responded, she fell back on humor: "Well, that's one way to move the discussion along, but he could have just come to dinner with us." By the end of the night, she had spoken with CEO Moss Thornton and organized a team of lawyers and finance staff to assess the company's options.

The Company

Chestnut Foods began in north Minneapolis in 1887, when 22-year-old Otto Chestnut (born Otto Kestenbaum in Bavaria) opened a bakery that made lye rolls and pretzels, then stumbled into success as a supplier of sandwiches to the St. Paul, Minneapolis,

This case was prepared by Michael J. Schill, Professor of Business Administration, and Donald Stevenson, Gist Learning LLC. The individuals and entities in this case are fictitious. The case draws on an antecedent case "Teletech Corporation, 2005" (UVA-F-1485) by Robert F. Bruner and Sean D. Carr. Copyright © 2015 by the University of Virginia Darden School Foundation, Charlottesville, VA. All rights reserved. *To order copies, send an e-mail to* sales@dardenbusinesspublishing.com. *No part of this publication may be reproduced, stored in a retrieval system, used in a spreadsheet, or transmitted in any form or by any means—electronic, mechanical, photocopying, recording, or otherwise—without the permission of the Darden School Foundation.*

& Manitoba Railway. Six years later, on a trip to Chicago, Illinois, to visit the Columbian Exposition, Chestnut happened to come upon the Maxwell Street Market, a vibrant melting-pot community of merchants of eastern European descent. At the market, he had a chance meeting with Lem Vigoda and George Maszk, founders of V&M Classic Foods, which provided a range of meat and fish products as well as preserves and condiments. Through them he witnessed a nascent ad hoc distribution system to neighborhood groceries in the rapidly growing city. A vision of wholesale food production and distribution struck him, and he returned to Minneapolis determined to realize it.

By 1920, as regional grocery chains had begun to materialize, Chestnut, since joined by his sons Thomas and Andrew, had purchased V&M among other food businesses. Their plan was for the expanded Chestnut to stock the regional grocery chains across the upper Midwest, while also continuing to supply railroad dining cars and, beginning in 1921, a Chestnut chain of automats in Chicago and Detroit. Otto Chestnut died in 1927 at age 62, but the company was well positioned to weather the Great Depression; in 1935, the Chestnut brothers sold the automat division to Horn & Hardart, then used the proceeds to purchase farmland in Florida and central California. In the postwar period, as the supermarket model emerged, Chestnut grew with it, both organically and through acquisition, going public in 1979. By 2013, the company was valued at $1.8 billion, with annual profits of more than $130 million.

Chestnut sought to "provide hearty sustenance that gets you where you're going." The firm had two main business segments: Food Products, which produced a broad range of fresh, prepackaged, and processed foods for retail and food services, and Instruments, which delivered systems and specialized equipment used in the processing and packaging of food products. Instruments provided a variety of quality control and automation services used within the company. The company took increasing pride in the high quality of its manufacturing process and believed it to be an important differentiator among both investors and consumers.

In recent years, Chestnut's shares had failed to keep pace with either the overall stock market or industry indexes for foods or machinery (see **Exhibit 14.1**). The company's credit rating with Standard & Poor's had recently declined one notch to A−. Securities analysts had remarked on the firm's lackluster earnings growth, pointing to increasing competition in the food industry due to shifting demands. One prominent Wall Street analyst noted on his blog, "Chestnut has become as vulnerable to a hostile takeover as a vacant umbrella on a hot beach."

Food Products Division

The Food Products division provided a range of prepackaged and frozen products related to the bread and sandwich market for both institutional food services and retail grocery distribution throughout North America, and some limited distribution in parts of Central and South America. Revenues for the segment had long been stable; the company achieved an average annual growth rate of 2% during 2010 through 2013. In 2013, segment net operating profit after tax (NOPAT) and net assets were $88 million and $1.4 billion, respectively. Looking to the foreseeable future, operating margins were expected to be tight such that return on capital for the division was expected to be 6.3%.

From its long association with the sandwich market prior to the advent of fast food, through its expansion in the 1950s and 1960s, Chestnut had consistently retained portions of the market for institutional ready-to-bake frozen bread dough, bread and rolls, and ready-to-bake soft pretzels. Premium-quality versions of these were packaged and sold in supermarkets under both the Chestnut brand and store brands.

Despite repeated efforts over the years to expand into other markets, the specialty bread and pretzel market remained Chestnut's primary driver of growth, reliant on scale, multiple outlets and packaging formats, and product innovation, most recently with Chestnut Classic Rapid-Rise Soft Pretzels, a newly formulated ready-to-bake product that produced oven-fresh pretzels in 10 minutes, including preheating. Particularly since the 1980s, after Chestnut had gone public and as demand for fresh produce, diverse ethnic cuisines, and health-conscious snacks had begun to increase, the firm made a series of moves designed to broaden its range of offerings, but the industry remained highly competitive and the returns on those alternative products modest. Nevertheless, customer surveys reflected consistently high ratings for product quality, freshness, and flavor. Chestnut was frequently referred to in popular culture, particularly in the northern states. Its well-known catchphrase "You'll make it with Chestnut," was synonymous with warm, hearty bread for people on the move.

Instruments Division

Since its earliest days amid the bustling flour mills and rail lines of Minneapolis, Minnesota, Chestnut's management had maintained a shared value that technology, properly harnessed, could improve quality and efficiency across production processes, and over the years, the company had developed a strong expertise in food process instruments. The success of companies such as Toledo Scale, founded in Toledo in 1901 before merging to become Columbus, Ohio-based, Swiss-owned Mettler-Toledo in 1989, was not lost on Otto Chestnut himself, although thoughts of such diversification were repeatedly deferred. Yet as a more cyclical and diverse industry (with products providing advanced capabilities to utilities, military and aerospace programs, and industrial and residential applications in addition to food production), precision instruments seemed to complement the food industry and to present opportunities for growth overseas. In 1991, Chestnut capitalized on an opportunity to purchase Consolidated Automation Systems, a medium-sized food-processing-instrument equipment company based in Thunder Bay, Ontario, and the Instruments division was born. This proved very successful and was followed by the purchase in 1997 of Redhawk Laboratories, a small manufacturer of computer-controlled precision equipment based in Troy, New York.

Although 20% of the division's revenue was derived internally from the Chestnut' Products division, the Instruments division produced equipment and automation support for a wide range of food producers in North America. Demand, much of it from overseas, was strong, but required substantial investments in R&D and fixed assets.

Instruments division sales had increased by nearly 20% in 2013. Segment NOPAT was $46 million, and net assets were $600 million. The expected return on capital for the division over the foreseeable future was 7.7%.

Recent Developments

Concerned above all else with the poor stock-price performance, and mindful of the importance of scale to profitability in the precision instrument industry, Pederson hoped to sustain corporate growth opportunities by raising $1 billion to invest in the expansion of the Instruments division. She had been delighted with the market's strong interest for the high-value-added offerings the division maintained and believed that funneling investment in its direction was the way forward for Chestnut. She believed that the 7.7% expected returns for this division could be maintained with additional company investment. She also believed that the tradition-laden company name failed to capture the firm's strategic direction and that the name "CF International" better reflected the growth and modern dynamism envisioned by leadership.

At the dinner meeting, as over the past few weeks, her initiative had generated partisan reactions from the company's two divisions. Curiously, much of the discussion at dinner focused on the rather pedestrian topic of the company hurdle rate. Meyer had strongly contended from her perspective in Food Products that the two segments of the business were different enough that they warranted separate hurdle rates; Rob Suchecki, VP of Instruments, was ardent in his opposition.

SUCHECKI: Look, Claire, to investors, the firm is just a big black box. They hire us to take care of what's inside the box and judge us by the dividends coming out of the box. Our job as managers should be to put their money where the returns are best. Consistent with this reality, our company has a long-standing policy of using a single common hurdle rate. If that hurdle rate takes from an underperforming division and gives to a more profitable division, isn't that how it's supposed to work? We're all well aware that investors consider past profits unacceptable.[1]

MEYER: Rob, the question is how you define profitability. High-return investments are not necessarily the best investments, and to be fair, our investors are way more savvy than you are giving them credit for; they have a wide range of information sources and analytic tools at their disposal and have a firm grasp on what is going on inside the company. They appreciate the risk and return of the different business units, and they adjust performance expectations accordingly. So to this type of investor, different hurdle rates for the different levels of risk reflects how things really are.

---

[1]Recently, the company's return on capital had been 6.7%. Company management applied a corporate hurdle rate of 7.0% to all capital projects and to the evaluation of business unit performance. See **Exhibit 2** for the company weighted average cost of capital (WACC) calculation, **Exhibit 3** for the prevailing capital market rates, and **Exhibit 4** for comparable firm information.

SUCHECKI: But Claire, multiple hurdle rates create all sorts of inequities that are bound to create discord among the ranks. If you set the hurdle rate for Food Products lower than the firm-wide hurdle rate, you're just moving your division's goalposts closer to the ball. You haven't improved performance, you've only made it easier to score!

MEYER: You've got to realize, Rob, that we are playing in different leagues. Each part of the business has to draw on capital differently, because the rules for each unit are different. If Food Products was on its own, investors would be happy with a lower return because Food Products' risk is so much lower. Stability has its perks. And likewise, if Food Products could raise capital on its own, we'd surely get that capital at a cheaper rate.

SUCHECKI: Different leagues? The fact is that we *don't* raise capital separately; we raise it as a firm, based on our overall record. Our debt is Chestnut debt and our equity is Chestnut equity. It's a simple fact that investors expect returns that beat our corporate cost of capital of 7.0%. It is only by growing cash flow *company-wide* that investors are rewarded for their risk capital. In fact, being diversified as a company most likely helps reduce our borrowing costs, letting us borrow more as a unit than we could separately.

MEYER: Rob, you know very well the kind of problems that thinking creates. If 7.0% is always the hurdle, the company will end up overinvesting in high-risk projects. Why? Because sensible, low-risk projects won't tend to clear the hurdle. Before long, the company will be packed with high-risk projects, and 7.0% will no longer be enough to compensate investors for the higher risk. By not accommodating multiple hurdle rates, we are setting ourselves up for all sorts of perverse investment incentives. The Food Products division is getting starved for capital, penalized for being a safer bet, while the Instruments division is getting overfed, benefitting from a false sense of security.

SUCHECKI: Hold on, I object! The reason Food Products is not getting capital is because there's no growth in your division. Instruments is coming on like gangbusters. Why would investors want us to put additional capital into a business that is barely keeping up with inflation?

At this point, pens and paper napkins were procured for Meyer, who presented the group with a diagram illustrating her argument (**Figure 14.1**) before continuing.

MEYER: With a plot of risk versus return, the dashed line is our current corporate hurdle rate based on the average risk of the company. The solid line is a theoretical hurdle rate that adjusts for the risk of businesses within the company. Food Products is marked with an "F." It is expected to earn 6.3% on capital, which doesn't clear the corporate hurdle rate, but if you adjust for risk, it *does* clear it, and it *is* profitable! Instruments is the opposite. It's marked on the graph with an "I." It can expect 7.7% returns, which clears the corporate hurdle. But since it is inherently riskier, the risk-adjusted hurdle rate exceeds 7.7%. Unless we are careful to adjust for that risk, it remains a hidden cost, and we are fooling ourselves.

FIGURE 14.1. | Meyer's diagram of constant versus risk-adjusted hurdle rates.

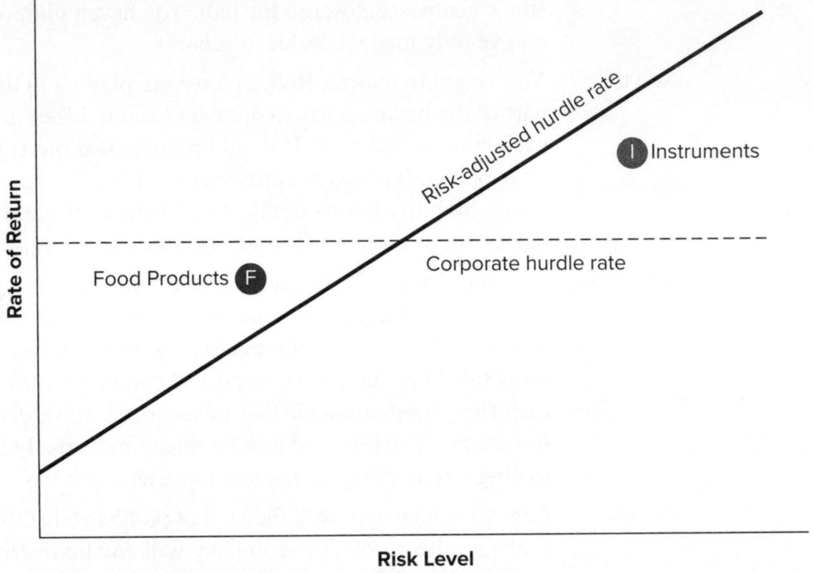

Source: Created by case writer.

SUCHECKI: Claire, I believe it is pure speculation to claim that the risk adjustment line you've sketched out is anywhere close to that steep. Second, even if you are theoretically correct, I believe there is practical wisdom in maintaining a single, simple, consistent, and understandable performance criterion. A single measure of the cost of money makes NPV results consistent, at least in economic terms. If Chestnut adopts multiple rates for discounting cash flows, the NPV and economic-profit calculations are going to lose their meaning, and business segments won't be able to make comparisons.

At this point, Pederson had finally managed to rein in the heated debate and redirect the conversation to matters that were less controversial.

The Future of Chestnut

It had been quite a night. Pedersen realized that she didn't have the time to resolve all the issues before her to influence Rollo van Muur's attack on management, but any proposal she made needed to be clear on its merits. Her thoughts returned to the discussion between the VPs. Was the historical Chestnut way of doing business as defensible as Suchecki made it sound? Was Instruments underperforming, as Van Muur and Meyer asserted? She knew that Van Muur's purchases had been prompted by Chestnut' depressed share price. In light of this development, weren't her investment and identity proposals all the more relevant?

EXHIBIT 14.1 | Value of $1.00 Invested from January 2010 to December 2013 (weekly adjusted close)

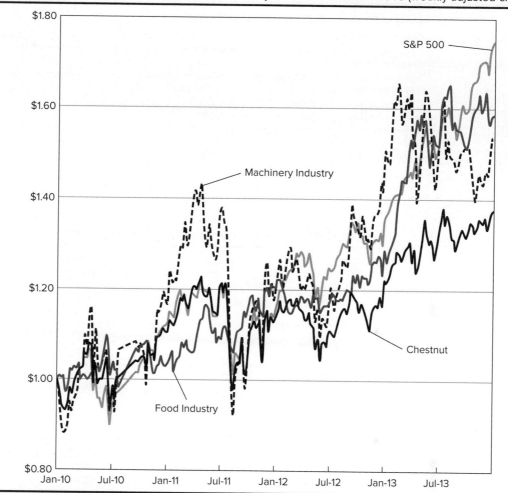

Data source: Yahoo! Finance and case writer data.

EXHIBIT 14.2 | Estimation of WACC for Chestnut Foods (year-end 2013)

Chestnut Foods Hurdle Rate as of December 2013: 7.0%

Chestnut uses a hurdle rate that reflects prevailing rates of return in financial markets using a weighted average of both debt and equity securities. The current mix of debt and equity in Chestnut's capital structure on a market-value basis is 20% debt and 80% equity. The prevailing yield on debt of similar credit risk is estimated at 3.5%. Based on a marginal corporate tax rate of 37%, the after-tax cost of debt is 2.2%. The cost of equity for Chestnut is estimated at 8.2% based on the CAPM with a beta of 0.9, a market risk premium of 6.0%, and a risk-free rate of 2.8%.[*] Based on these estimates, the WACC is 7.0%.

[*]An alternative model that uses a market risk premium of 9% and a risk-free rate of 0.1% gives a similar cost-of-equity estimate.

EXHIBIT 14.3 | Capital Market Data, December 2013

	Yield
30-Day Treasury Bill	0.1%
10-Year Treasury Bond	2.8%
10-Year Corporate Bonds of Industrial Companies	
AAA	2.8%
AA	2.9%
A+	3.2%
A	3.3%
A−	3.5%
BBB+	3.8%
BBB	4.1%
BBB-	4.6%
BB+	5.8%
BB	6.5%
BB−	6.5%
B+	6.8%
B	8.4%
B−	9.0%
Historical Market Risk Premium (Equity Market Index Less Government Debt)	6.0%

Data source: Bloomberg, case writer estimates.

EXHIBIT 14.4 | Financial Data for Industry Comparables, December 2013 (dollar figures in millions)

	Equity Beta	S&P Bond Rating	Total Debt	Total Equity (Book Value)	Total Equity (Market Value)
Chestnut Foods	0.90	A−	461	1,544	1,840
Food Processing					
Boulder Brands	0.55	B+	298	355	958
Campbell Soup	0.60	BBB+	4,832	1,349	13,223
ConAgra Foods	0.70	BBB−	9,590	5,472	13,805
Diamond Foods	0.75	B−	593	167	578
Flowers Foods	0.50	BBB−	923	1,076	4,429
General Mills	0.55	BBB+	8,645	6,633	31,245
Hormel Foods	0.65	A	250	3,311	11,759
Kellogg	0.60	BBB+	7,358	3,545	21,841
J. M. Smucker	0.70	BBB+	2,241	5,168	10,904
Tyson Foods	0.80	BBB	1,942	6,285	11,469
Instruments					
Badger Meter	1.06	BBB−*	89	197	723
Dresser-Rand	1.40	BB	1,287	1,297	4,549
Flowserve	1.30	BBB−	1,200	1,870	10,767
Honeywell	1.25	A	8,829	17,467	74,330
Idex	1.15	BBB	774	1,573	5,933
Measurement Specialties	1.35	BBB*	129	331	944
Mettler-Toledo	1.10	A*	413	935	7,154
Wendell Instruments	0.52	NA	0	98	230

*Identifies bond ratings that are estimated by case writer.

(continued)

EXHIBIT 14.4 | Financial Data for Industry Comparables, December 2013 (dollar figures in millions) *(continued)*

Food Processing	Company Description
Boulder Brands	Food products focusing on health and wellness, including gluten-free, diabetic-friendly, and low-fat offerings such as soy milk, buttery spreads, snack bars, and entrée alternatives; based in Boulder, CO.
Campbell Soup	Condensed and ready-to-serve convenience food products; based in Camden, NJ.
ConAgra Foods	Consumer and commercial food products across frozen, refrigerated, and shelf-stable temperature classes; based in Omaha, NE.
Diamond Foods	Packaged nuts and snack products for consumer and commercial channels; based in San Francisco, CA.
Flowers Foods	Baked goods for warehouse and direct-to-store delivery; based in Thomasville, GA.
General Mills	Branded and unbranded food products for consumer and commercial distribution; based in Minneapolis, MN.
Hormel Foods	Fresh and refrigerated meat, snack, and specialty food products for retail and food service distribution; based in Austin, MN.
Kellogg	Ready-to-eat cereals and convenience food products; based in Battle Creek, MI.
J. M. Smucker	Coffee, fruit spread, beverage, and specialty food products for retail and wholesale distribution; based in Orrville, OH.
Tyson Foods	Fresh beef, pork, and chicken, and related prepared food products for retail and wholesale distribution; based in Springdale, AR.
Instruments	
Badger Meter	Water meters for municipal water utilities; pipeline flow measurement for food and beverage, pharmaceutical, utility, and HVAC industries; based in Milwaukee, WI.
Dresser-Rand	Rotating equipment for oil, gas, and petrochemical industries; based in Houston, TX.
Flowserve	Pumps, valves, seals, and boiler systems for petroleum, chemical, water, mining, pharmaceutical, and other industries; based in Irving, TX.
Honeywell	Electric controls, surveillance, monitoring, and associated software for defense, air traffic control, utilities, and industry; based in Minneapolis, MN.
Idex	Pumps, flow measurement for food, chemical, industrial, and energy industries; pumps, air compressors, and optical components for health, scientific, defense, and aerospace applications; based in Lake Forest, IL.
Measurement Specialties	Equipment sensors for vehicle, medical, home appliance, aerospace, and industrial applications; based in Hampton, VA.
Mettler-Toledo	Weighing, chemical, and assorted laboratory instruments for food retail, industrial, and scientific research applications; based in Columbus, OH.
Wendell Instruments	Control and monitoring instrumentation for fast-food restaurants; young company based in Tucson, AZ.

Data source: Bloomberg, Yahoo! Finance, Value Line, and case writer estimates.

## PART 4

Capital Budgeting and Resource Allocation

Target Corporation

On November 14, 2006, Doug Scovanner, CFO of Target Corporation, was preparing for the November meeting of the Capital Expenditure Committee (CEC). Scovanner was one of five executive officers who were members of the CEC (**Exhibit 15.1**). On tap for the 8:00 a.m. meeting the next morning were 10 projects representing nearly $300 million in capital-expenditure requests. With the fiscal year's end approaching in January, there was a need to determine which projects best fit Target's future store growth and capital-expenditure plans, with the knowledge that those plans would be shared early in 2007, with both the board and investment community. In reviewing the 10 projects coming before the committee, it was clear to Scovanner that five of the projects, representing about $200 million in requested capital, would demand the greater part of the committee's attention and discussion time during the meeting.

The CEC was keenly aware that Target had been a strong performing company in part because of its successful investment decisions and continued growth. Moreover, Target management was committed to continuing the company's growth strategy of opening approximately 100 new stores a year. Each investment decision would have long-term implications for Target: an underperforming store would be a drag on earnings and difficult to turn around without significant investments of time and money, whereas a top-performing store would add value both financially and strategically for years to come.

Retail Industry

The retail industry included a myriad of different companies offering similar product lines (**Exhibit 15.2**). For example, Sears and JCPenney had extensive networks of stores that offered a broad line of products, many of which were similar to Target's product lines. Because each retailer had a different strategy and a different customer base, truly comparable stores were difficult to identify. Many investment analysts, however, focused on Wal-Mart and Costco as important competitors for Target, although for different reasons. Wal-Mart operated store formats similar to Target, and most Target stores

This case was prepared by David Ding (MBA '08) and Saul Yeaton (MBA '08) under the supervision of Kenneth Eades, Professor of Business Administration. It was written as a basis for class discussion rather than to illustrate effective or ineffective handling of an administrative situation. Copyright © 2008 by the University of Virginia Darden School Foundation, Charlottesville, VA. All rights reserved. *To order copies, send an e-mail* sales@dardenbusinesspublishing.com. *No part of this publication may be reproduced, stored in a retrieval system, used in a spreadsheet, or transmitted in any form or by any means—electronic, mechanical, photocopying, recording, or otherwise—without the permission of the Darden School Foundation.*

operated in trade areas where one or more Wal-Mart stores were located. Wal-Mart and Target also carried merchandising assortments, which overlapped on many of the same items in such areas as food, commodities, electronics, toys, and sporting goods.

Costco, on the other hand, attracted a customer base that overlapped closely with Target's core customers, but there was less often overlap between Costco and Target with respect to trade area and merchandising assortment. Costco also differed from Target in that it used a membership-fee format.[1] Most of the sales of these companies were in the broad categories of general merchandise and food. General merchandise included electronics, entertainment, sporting goods, toys, apparel, accessories, home furnishing, and décor, and food items included consumables ranging from apples to zucchini.

Wal-Mart had become the dominant player in the industry with operations located in the United States, Argentina, Brazil, Canada, Puerto Rico, the United Kingdom, Central America, Japan, and Mexico. Much of Wal-Mart's success was attributed to its "everyday low price" pricing strategy that was greeted with delight by consumers but created severe challenges for local independent retailers who needed to remain competitive. Wal-Mart sales had reached $309 billion for 2005 for 6,141 stores and a market capitalization of $200 billion, compared with sales of $178 billion and 4,189 stores in 2000. In addition to growing its top line, Wal-Mart had been successful in creating efficiency within the company and branching into product lines that offered higher margins than many of its commodity type of products.

Costco provided discount pricing for its members in exchange for membership fees. For fiscal 2005, these fees comprised 2.0% of total revenue and 72.8% of operating income. Membership fees were such an important factor to Costco that an equity analyst had coined a new price-to-membership-fee-income ratio metric for valuing the company.[2] By 2005, Costco's sales had grown to $52.9 billion across its 433 warehouses, and its market capitalization had reached $21.8 billion. Over the previous five years, sales excluding membership fees had experienced compound growth of 10.4%, while membership fees had grown 14.6% making the fees a significant growth source and highly significant to operating income in a low-profit-margin business.

In order to attract shoppers, retailers tailored their product offerings, pricing, and branding to specific customer segments. Segmentation of the customer population had led to a variety of different strategies, ranging from price competition in Wal-Mart stores to Target's strategy of appealing to style-conscious consumers by offering unique assortments of home and apparel items, while also pricing competitively with Wal-Mart on items common to both stores. The intensity of competition among retailers had resulted in razor-thin margins making every line item on the income statement an important consideration for all retailers.

The effects of tight margins were felt throughout the supply chain as retailers constantly pressured their suppliers to accept lower prices. In addition, retailers used offshore sources as low-cost substitutes for their products and implemented methods such as just-in-time inventory management, low-cost distribution networks, and high sales

---

[1]Sam's Club, which was owned by Wal-Mart, also employed a membership-fee format and represented 13% of Wal-Mart revenues.

[2]"Costco Wholesale Corp. Initiation Report," Wachovia Capital Markets, September 18, 2006.

per square foot to achieve operational efficiency. Retailers had found that profit margins could also be enhanced by selling their own brands, or products with exclusive labels that could be marketed to attract the more affluent customers in search of a unique shopping experience.

Sales growth for retail companies stemmed from two main sources: creation of new stores and organic growth through existing stores. New stores were expensive to build, but were needed to access new markets and tap into a new pool of consumers that could potentially represent high profit potential depending upon the competitive landscape. Increasing the sales of existing stores was also an important source of growth and value. If an existing store was operating profitably, it could be considered for renovation or upgrading in order to increase sales volume. Or, if a store was not profitable, management would consider it a candidate for closure.

Target Corporation

The Dayton Company opened the doors of the first Target store in 1962, in Roseville, Minnesota. The Target name had intentionally been chosen to differentiate the new discount retailer from the Dayton Company's more upscale stores. The Target concept flourished. In 1995, the first SuperTarget store opened in Omaha, Nebraska, and in 1999, the Target.com website was launched. By 2000, the parent company, Dayton Hudson, officially changed its name to Target Corporation.[3]

By 2005, Target had become a major retailing powerhouse with $52.6 billion in revenues from 1,397 stores in 47 states (**Exhibit 15.3** and **Exhibit 15.4**). With sales of $30 billion in 2000, the company had realized a 12.1% sales growth over the past five years and had announced plans to continue its growth by opening approximately 100 stores per year in the United States in the foreseeable future. While Target Corporation had never committed to expanding internationally, analysts had been speculating that domestic growth alone would not be enough to sustain its historic success. If Target continued its domestic growth strategy, most analysts expected capital expenditures would continue at a level of 6% to 7% of revenues, which equated to about $3.5 billion for fiscal year 2006.

In contrast with Wal-Mart's focus on low prices, Target's strategy was to consider the customer's shopping experience as a whole. Target referred to its customers as guests and consistently strived to support the slogan, "Expect more. Pay less." Target focused on creating a shopping experience that appealed to the profile of its "core guest": a college-educated woman with children at home who was more affluent than the typical Wal-Mart customer. This shopping experience was created by emphasizing a store décor that gave just the right shopping ambience. The company had been highly successful at promoting its brand awareness with large advertising campaigns; its advertising expenses for fiscal 2005 were $1.0 billion or about 2.0% of sales and 26.6% of operating profit. In comparison, Wal-Mart's advertising dollars amounted to 0.5% of

---

[3]The Dayton Company merged with J. L. Hudson Company in 1969. After changing its name to Target, the company renamed the Dayton-Hudson stores as Marshall Field's. In 2004, Marshall Field's was sold to May Department Stores, which was acquired by Federated Department Stores in 2006; all May stores were given the Macy's name that same year.

sales and 9.2% of operating income. Consistent advertising spending resulted in the Target bull's-eye logo's (**Exhibit 15.5**) being ranked among the most recognized corporate logos in the United States, ahead of the Nike "swoosh."

As an additional enhancement to the customer shopping experience, Target offered credit to qualified customers through its REDcards: Target Visa Credit Card and Target Credit Card. The credit-card business accounted for 14.9% of Target's operating earnings and was designed to be integrated with the company's overall strategy by focusing only on customers who visited Target stores.

Capital-Expenditure Approval Process

The Capital Expenditure Committee was composed of a team of top executives that met monthly to review all capital project requests (CPRs) in excess of $100,000. CPRs were either approved by the CEC, or in the case of projects larger than $50 million, required approval from the board of directors. Project proposals varied widely and included remodeling, relocating, rebuilding, and closing an existing store to building a new store.[4] A typical CEC meeting involved the review of 10 to 15 CPRs. All of the proposals were considered economically attractive, as any CPRs with questionable economics were normally rejected at the lower levels of review. In the rare instance when a project with a negative net present value (NPV) reached the CEC, the committee was asked to consider the project in light of its strategic importance to the company.

CEC meetings lasted several hours as each of the projects received careful scrutiny by the committee members. The process purposefully was designed to be rigorous because the CEC recognized that capital investment could have significant impact on the short-term and long-term profitability of the company. In addition to the large amount of capital at stake, approvals and denials also had the potential to set precedents that would affect future decisions. For example, the committee might choose to reject a remodeling proposal for a store with a positive NPV, if the investment amount requested was much higher than normal and therefore might create a troublesome precedent for all subsequent remodel requests for similar stores. Despite how much the projects differed, the committee was normally able to reach a consensus decision for the vast majority of them. Occasionally however, a project led to such a high degree of disagreement within the committee that the CEO made the final call.

Projects typically required 12 to 24 months of development prior to being forwarded to the CEC for consideration. In the case of new store proposals, which represented the majority of the CPRs, a real-estate manager assigned to that geographic region was responsible for the proposal from inception to completion and also for reviewing and presenting the proposal details. The pre-CPR work required a certain amount of expenditures that were not recoverable if the project were ultimately rejected by CEC. More important than these expenditures, however, were the "emotional sunk costs" for the real-estate managers who believed strongly in the merits of their proposals and felt significant disappointment if any project was not approved.

---

[4]Target expected to allocate 65% of capital expenditures to new stores, 12% to remodels and expansions, and 23% to information technology, distribution, etc.

The committee considered several factors in determining whether to accept or reject a project. An overarching objective was to meet the corporate goal of adding about 100 stores a year while maintaining a positive brand image. Projects also needed to meet a variety of financial objectives, starting with providing a suitable financial return as measured by discounted cash-flow metrics: NPV and IRR (internal rate of return). Other financial considerations included projected profit and earnings per share impacts, total investment size, impact on sales of other nearby Target stores, and sensitivity of NPV and IRR to sales variations. Projected sales were determined based on economic trends and demographic shifts but also considered the risks involved with the entrance of new competitors and competition from online retailers. And lastly, the committee attempted to keep the project approvals within the capital budget for the year. If projects were approved in excess of the budgeted amount, Target would likely need to borrow money to fund the shortfall. Adding debt unexpectedly to the balance sheet could raise questions from equity analysts as to the increased risk to the shareholders as well as to the ability of management to accurately project the company's funding needs.

Other considerations included tax and real-estate incentives provided by local communities as well as area demographics. Target typically purchased the properties where it built stores, although leasing was considered on occasion. Population growth and affluent communities were attractive to Target, but these factors also invited competition from other retailers. In some cases, new Target stores were strategically located to block other retailers despite marginal short-term returns.

When deciding whether to open a new store, the CEC was often asked to consider alternative store formats. For example, the most widely used format was the 2004 version of a Target store prototype called P04, which occupied 125,000 square feet, whereas a SuperTarget format occupied an additional 50,000 square feet to accommodate a full grocery assortment. The desirability of one format over another often centered on whether a store was expected to eventually be upgraded. Smaller stores often offered a higher NPV; but the NPV estimate did not consider the effect of future upgrades or expansions that would be required if the surrounding communities grew, nor the advantage of opening a larger store in an area where it could serve the purpose of blocking competitors from opening stores nearby.

The committee members were provided with a capital-project request "dashboard" for each project that summarized the critical inputs and assumptions used for the NPV and IRR calculations. The template represented the summary sheet for an elaborate discounted cash flow model. For example, the analysis of a new store included incremental cash flow projections for 60 years over which time the model included a remodeling of the store every 10 years. **Exhibit 15.6** provides an example of a dashboard with a detailed explanation of the "Store Sensitivities" section. The example dashboard shows that incremental sales estimates, which were computed as the total sales expected for the new store less the sales cannibalized from Target stores already located in the general vicinity. Sales estimates were made by the Research and Planning group. The R&P group used demographic and other data to make site-specific forecasts. Incremental sales were computed as total sales less those cannibalized from other Target stores. The resulting NPV and IRR metrics were divided between value created by store sales and credit-card activity. NPV calculations used a 9.0% discount rate for cash flows related to the store cash flows and a 4.0% discount rate for credit-card cash flows. The different discount rates were chosen to represent the different costs of capital for funding store operations versus funding credit-card receivables.

The dashboards also presented a variety of demographic information, investment-cost details and sensitivity analyses. An important sensitivity feature was the comparison of the project's NPV and IRR to the prototype. For example, the P04 store had an NPV of about $10 million and an IRR of 13%.[5] The sensitivity calculations answered the question of how much a certain cost or revenue item needed to change in order for the project to achieve the same NPV or IRR that would be experienced for the typical P04 or SuperTarget store.

The November Meeting

Of the 10 projects under consideration for the November CEC meeting, Doug Scovanner recognized that five would be easily accepted, but that the remaining five CPRs were likely to be difficult choices for the committee. These projects included four new store openings (Gopher Place, Whalen Court, The Barn, and Goldie's Square) and one remodeling of an existing store into a SuperTarget format (Stadium Remodel). **Exhibit 15.7** contains a summary of the five projects, and **Exhibit 15.8** contains the CPR dashboards for the individual projects.

As was normally the case, all five of the CPRs had positive NPVs, but Scovanner wondered if the projected NPVs were high enough to justify the required investment. Further, with stiff competition from other large retailers looking to get footholds in major growth areas, how much consideration should be given to short-term versus long-term sales opportunities? For example, Whalen Court represented a massive investment with relatively uncertain sales returns. Should Scovanner take the stance that the CEC should worry less about Whalen Court's uncertain sales and focus more on the project as a means to increase Target's brand awareness in an area with dense foot traffic and high-fashion appeal? Goldie's Square represented a more typical investment level of $24 million for a SuperTarget. The NPV, however, was small at $317,000, well below the expected NPV of a SuperTarget prototype, and would be negative without the value contribution of credit-card sales.

As CFO, Scovanner was also aware that Target shareholders had experienced a lackluster year in 2006, given that Target's stock price had remained essentially flat (**Exhibit 15.9**). Stock analysts were generally pleased with Target's stated growth policy and were looking for decisions from management regarding investments that were consistent with the company maintaining its growth trajectory. In that regard, Scovanner recognized that each of the projects represented a growth opportunity for Target. The question, however, was whether capital was better spent on one project or another to create the most value and the most growth for Target shareholders. Thus Scovanner believed that he needed to rank the five projects in order to be able to recommend which ones to keep and which ones to reject during the CEC meeting the next day.

---

[5]These NPV and IRR figures exclude the impact of the credit card.

EXHIBIT 15.1 | Executive Officers and Capital Expenditure Committee Members

Timothy R. Baer	Executive Vice President, General Counsel, and Corporate Secretary	
Michael R. Francis	Executive Vice President, Marketing	
John D. Griffith	Executive Vice President, Property Development	CEC
Jodeen A. Kozlak	Executive Vice President, Human Resources	
Troy H. Risch	Executive Vice President, Stores	CEC
Janet M. Schalk	Executive Vice President, Technology Services and Chief Information Officer	
Douglas A. Scovanner	Executive Vice President and Chief Financial Officer	CEC
Terrence J. Scully	President, Target Financial Services	
Gregg W. Steinhafel	President	CEC
Robert J. Ulrich	Chairman and Chief Executive Officer	CEC

Chairman and CEO **Bob Ulrich,** 62. Ulrich began his career at Dayton-Hudson as a merchandising trainee in 1967. He advanced to the position of CEO of Target Stores in 1987 and to the position of Dayton-Hudson's CEO in 1994.

EVP and CFO **Doug Scovanner,** 49. Scovanner was named Target CFO in February 2000 after previously serving as CFO of Dayton-Hudson.

President of Target Stores **Gregg Steinhafel,** 50. Steinhafel began his career at Target as a merchandising trainee in 1979. He was named president in 1999.

EVP of Stores **Troy Risch,** 37. Risch was promoted to EVP in September 2006.

EVP of Property Development **John Griffith,** 44. Griffith was promoted to EVP in February 2005 from the position of senior vice president of Property Development he had held since February 2000.

Source: Target Corporation, used with permission.

EXHIBIT 15.2 | Retail Company Financial Information

	Revenue ($ billions)	Basic EPS	Debt ($ billions)	Debt Rating (S&P)	Beta	Fiscal Year Ended	Market Capitalization as of Oct. 31, 2006 ($ billions)
Bed Bath & Beyond Inc.	$5.8	$1.95	$0.0	BBB	1.05	Feb-06	$11.4
Best Buy Co., Inc.	$30.8	$2.33	$0.6	BBB	1.25	Feb-06	$26.2
Costco Wholesale Corp.	$52.9	$2.24	$0.8	A	0.85	Aug-05	$24.1
Dick's Sporting Goods, Inc.	$2.6	$1.47	$0.2	Not Rated	1.15	Jan-06	$1.3
JCPenney Company, Inc.	$18.8	$4.30	$3.5	BB+	1.05	Jan-06	$16.6
Kohl's Corporation	$13.4	$2.45	$1.2	BBB	0.90	Jan-06	$23.1
Sears Holdings Corporation	$49.1	$5.63	$4.0	BB+	NMF	Jan-06	$26.9
Wal-Mart Stores, Inc.	$315.7	$2.68	$38.8	AA	0.80	Jan-06	$199.9
Target Corporation	**$52.6**	**$2.73**	**$9.9**	**A+**	**1.05**	**Jan-06**	**$50.1**

Data Source: Yahoo! Finance and Value Line Investment Survey.

EXHIBIT 15.3 | Target Income Statements ($ millions)

Fiscal Year Ending	28 Jan 2006	29 Jan 2005
Net revenues	52,620	46,839
Cost of goods sold	34,927	31,445
Depreciation, depletion, and amortization	1,409	1,259
Gross income	16,284	14,135
Selling, general, and admin expenses	11,961	10,534
Earnings before interest and taxes (EBIT)	4,323	3,601
Net interest expense	463	570
Pretax income	3,860	3,031
Income taxes	1,452	1,146
Net income before extra items	2,408	1,885
Gain (loss) sale of assets		1,313
Net income after extra items	2,408	3,198
Capital expenditures (net of disposals)	3,330	3,012
Capital expenditures/sales	6.3%	6.4%

Data source: Target Corporation annual reports.

EXHIBIT 15.4 | Balance Sheet Statements ($ millions)

Fiscal Year Ending	28 Jan 2006	29 Jan 2005	31 Jan 2004
Assets			
Cash and cash equivalents	1,648	2,245	708
Accounts receivable (net)	5,666	5,069	4,621
Inventory	5,838	5,384	4,531
Other current assets	1,253	1,224	3,092
Total current assets	14,405	13,922	12,952
Property, plant, and equipment, net	19,038	16,860	15,153
Other assets	1,552	1,511	3,311
Total assets	**34,995**	**32,293**	**31,416**
Liabilities			
Accounts payable	6,268	5,779	4,956
Current portion of LT debt and notes payable	753	504	863
Income taxes payable	374	304	382
Other current liabilities	2,193	1,633	2,113
Total current liabilities	9,588	8,220	8,314
Long-term debt	9,119	9,034	10,155
Other liabilities	2,083	2,010	1,815
Total liabilities	**20,790**	**19,264**	**20,284**
Shareholders' equity			
Common equity	2,192	1,881	1,609
Retained earnings	12,013	11,148	9,523
Total liabilities and shareholders' equity	**34,995**	**32,293**	**31,416**

Data source: Target Corporation annual reports.

EXHIBIT 15.5 | Target Logo

Source: Target Corporation, used with permission.

EXHIBIT 15.6 | Example of a Capital Project Request Dashboard

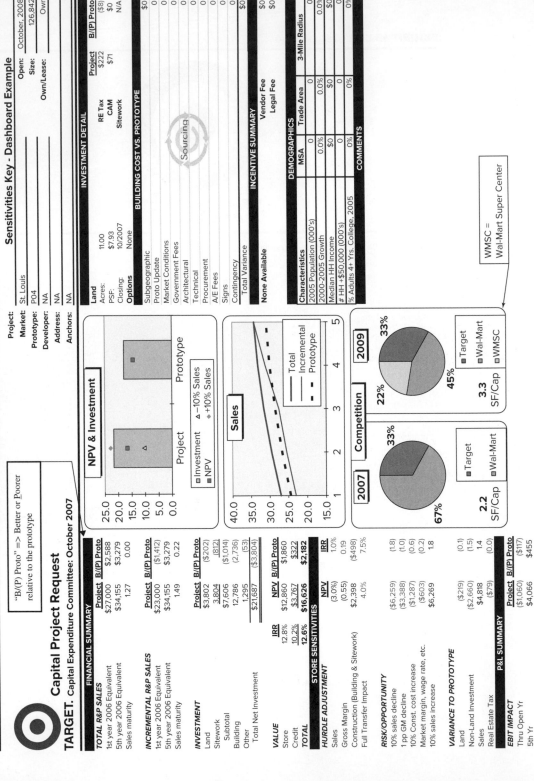

EXHIBIT 15.6 | Example of a Capital Project Request Dashboard *(continued)*

Dashboard Sensitivities Key (use with "Sensitivities Key-Dashboard Example")
Dashboard Example: P04; Store NPV: $12,860; Store IRR: 12.8%

HURDLE ADJUSTMENT (CPR Dashboard)

Sales
NPV	(3.0%)	Sales could decrease (3.0%) and still achieve Prototype Store NPV
IRR	1.0%	Sales would have to increase 1.0% to achieve Prototype Store IRR

Gross Margin
NPV	(0.55)	Gross Margin could decrease (0.55) pp and still achieve Prototype Store NPV
IRR	0.19	Gross Margin would have to increase 0.19 pp to achieve Prototype Store IRR

Construction (Building & Sitework)
NPV	$2,398	Construction costs could increase $2,398 and still achieve Prototype Store NPV
IRR	($498)	Construction costs would have to decrease ($498) to achieve Prototype Store IRR

Full Transfer Impact
Prototype Assumption: A nearby store transferring sales to a new store, fully recovers these sales by the 5th yr.
Sensitivity Assumption: If transfer sales are NOT fully recovered by the transferring store in year 5:
NPV	4.0%	Sales would have to increase 4.0% to achieve Prototype Store NPV
IRR	7.5%	Sales would have to increase 7.5% to achieve Prototype Store IRR

RISK/OPPORTUNITY

10% Sales Decline
NPV	($6,259)	If sales decline by 10%, Store NPV would decline by ($6,259)
IRR	(1.8)	If sales decline by 10%, Store IRR would decline by (1.8) pp

1pp GM Decline
NPV	($3,388)	If margin decreased by 1 pp, Store NPV would decline by ($3,388)
IRR	(1.0)	If margin decreased by 1 pp, Store IRR would decline by (1.0) pp

10% Construction Cost Increase
NPV	($1,287)	If construction costs increased by 10%, Store NPV would decline by ($1,287)
IRR	(0.6)	If construction costs increased by 10%, Store IRR would decline by (0.6) pp

Market Margin, Wage Rate, etc.
NPV	($603)	If we applied market specific assumptions, Store NPV would decrease by ($603)
IRR	(0.2)	If we applied market specific assumptions, Store IRR would decrease by (0.2) pp

10% Sales Increase
NPV	$6,269	If sales increased by 10%, Store NPV would increase by $6,269
IRR	1.8	If sales increased by 10%, Store IRR would increase by 1.8 pp

VARIANCE TO PROTOTYPE

The example dashboard with a Store NPV of $12,850 is $1,860K above Prototypical Store NPV. The following items contributed to the variance:

Land
NPV	($219)	Land cost contributed a negative ($219) to the variance from Prototype
IRR	(0.1)	Land cost contributed a negative (0.1) pp to the variance from Prototype

Non-Land Investment
NPV	($2,660)	Building/Sitework costs contributed a negative ($2,660) to the variance from Prototype
IRR	(1.5)	Building/Sitework costs contributed a negative (1.5) pp to the variance from Prototype

Sales
NPV	$4,818	Sales contributed a positive $4,818 to the variance from Prototype
IRR	1.4	Sales contributed a positive 1.4 pp to the variance from Prototype

Real Estate Taxes
NPV	($79)	Real Estate Taxes contributed a negative ($79) to the variance from Prototype
IRR	(0.0)	Real Estate Taxes contributed a negative (0.0) pp to the variance from Prototype

APPROX $ IMPACT ON STORE NPV

	Cost	NPV	%
Land:	$100K	($110K)	110%
Sitework:	$100K	($70K)	70%
Building:	$100K	($85K)	85%
On-going Exp:	$100K	($1M)	x10

On-going Expense: eg. Real Estate Taxes, Operating Expense
Assumes Store Opening occurs 1 year after closing.

Source: Target Corporation, used with permission.

EXHIBIT 15.7 | Economic Analysis Summary of Project Proposals

		Net Present Value*			Trade Area**			
	Investment ($000)	Base Case NPV ($000)	10% Sales Decline ($000)	IRR	Population	Population Increase 2000–2005	Median Income	% Adults 4+ yrs. college
Gopher Place	$23,000	$16,800	($4,722)	12.3%	70,000	27%	$56,400	12%
Whalen Court	$119,300	$25,900	($16,611)	9.8%	632,000	3%	$48,500	45%
The Barn	$13,000	$20,500	($4,066)	16.4%	151,000	3%	$38,200	17%
Goldie's Square	$23,900	$300	($4,073)	8.1%	222,000	16%	$56,000	24%
Stadium Remodel	$17,000	$15,700	($7,854)	10.8%	N/A	N/A	$65,931	42%

*NPV is computed using 9.0% as discount rate for store cash flows and 4.0% for credit-card cash flows.

**Trade area is the geographical area from which 70% of store sales will be realized.

Gopher Place was a request for $23.0 million to build a P04 store scheduled to open in October 2007. The prototype NPV would be achieved with sales of 5.3% below the R&P forecast level. This market was considered an important one, with five existing stores already in the area. Wal-Mart was expected to add two new supercenters in response to favorable population growth in the trade area, which was considered to have a very favorable median household income and growth rate. Because of the high density of Target stores, nearly 19% of sales included in the forecasts were expected to come from existing Target stores.

EXHIBIT 15.7 I Economic Analysis Summary of Project Proposals *(continued)*

Whalen Court was a request for $119.3 million to build a unique single-level store scheduled to open in October 2008. The prototype NPV could be achieved with sales of 1.9% above the R&P forecast level. Although Target currently operated 45 stores in this market, the Whalen Court market represented a rare opportunity for Target to enter the urban center of a major metropolitan area. Unlike other areas, this opportunity provided Target with major brand visibility and essentially free advertising for all passersby. Considering Target's larger advertising budget, the request for more than $100 million of capital investment could be balanced against the brand awareness benefits it would bring. Further, this opportunity was only available for a limited time. Unlike the majority of Target stores, this store would have to be leased. Thus if it was not approved at the November meeting, the property would surely be leased by another retailer.

The Barn was a request for $13.0 million to build a P04 store scheduled to open in March 2007. The prototype NPV was achievable with sales of 18.1% below the R&P forecast level. This project was being resubmitted after initial development efforts failed because of a disagreement with the developer. This small rural area was an extreme contrast to Whalen Court. The small initial investment allowed for a large return on investment even if sales growth turned out to be less than expected. This investment represented a new market for Target as the two nearest Target stores were 80 and 90 miles away.

Goldie's Square was a request for $23.9 million to build a SuperTarget store scheduled to open in October 2007. The prototype NPV required sales 45.1% above the R&P forecast level. This area was considered a key strategic anchor for many retailers. The Goldie's Square center included Bed Bath & Beyond, JCPenney, Circuit City, and Borders. Target currently operated 12 stores in the area and was expected to have 24 eventually. Despite the relatively weak NPV figures, this was a hotly contested area with an affluent and fast-growing population, which could afford good brand awareness should the growth materialize.

Stadium Remodel was a request for $17.0 million to remodel a SuperTarget store opening March 2007. As a remodel, there was no prototype NPV for comparison. The recent sales decline and deteriorating facilities at this location could lead to tarnishing the brand image. This trade area had supported Target stores since 1972 and had already been remodeled twice previously. The $17 million investment would certainly give a lift to the lagging sales.

Source: Target Corporation, used with permission.

231

EXHIBIT 15.8 | Individual Capital Project Request "Dashboards"

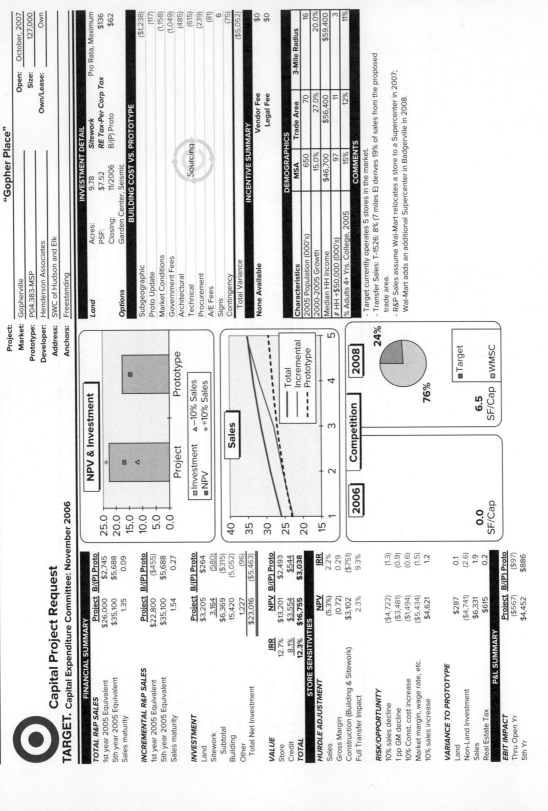

EXHIBIT 15.8 | Individual Capital Project Request "Dashboards" (continued)

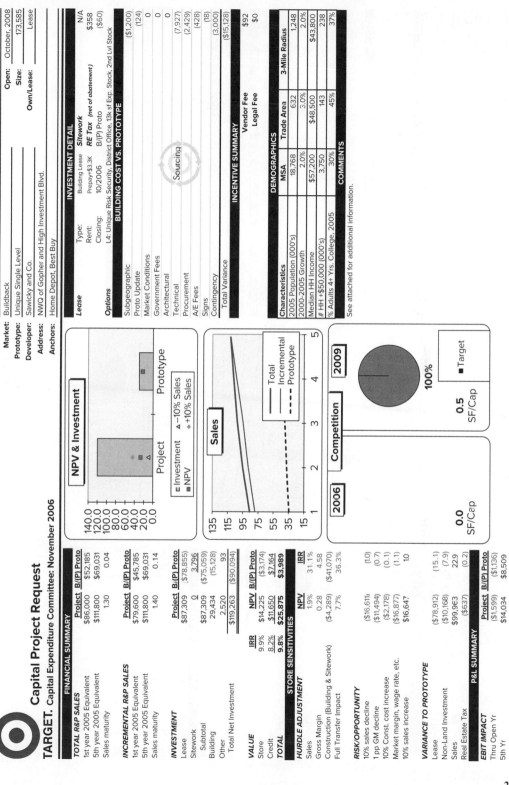

EXHIBIT 15.8 | Individual Capital Project Request "Dashboards" (continued)

Capital Project Request

TARGET. Capital Expenditure Committee: November 2006

Project:		"The Barn"		
Market:	Moose Land		Open:	March, 2007
Prototype:	P04.383-MSP		Size:	126,842
Developer:	Hulbert Ventures		Own/Lease:	Own
Address:	NWQ of Badger and Wolverine			
Anchors:	Lowe's			

INVESTMENT DETAIL

Land	Acres:	11.48	Sitework		Fixed Cost	$136
	PSF:	$0.02	RE Tax-Per Corp. Tax			$62
	Closing:	4/2006	B/(P) Proto			
	L3: Enhanced Risk Security					

BUILDING COST VS. PROTOTYPE

Options		
Subgeographic		$523
Proto Update		(22)
Market Conditions		(410)
Government Fees		0
Architectural		(95)
Technical		(122)
Procurement		(91)
A/E Fees		(76)
Signs		(9)
Contingency		(75)
Total Variance		($378)

INCENTIVE SUMMARY

None Available	Vendor Fee	$0
	Legal Fee	$0

DEMOGRAPHICS

Characteristics	MSA	Trade Area	3-Mile Radius
2005 Population (000's)	135	151	19
2000–2005 Growth	3.0%	3.0%	7.0%
Median HH Income	$36,600	$38,200	$47,300
# HH +$50,000 (000's)	20	22	4
% Adults 4+ Yrs. College, 2005	16%	17%	34%

COMMENTS

- Target is entering a new small market. The nearest Target stores are 80 miles NE, 80 miles S, 90 miles NW.
- R&P Sales assume Target is part of a major retail development of 600K sf.
- See attached Resubmission Summary.

FINANCIAL SUMMARY

TOTAL R&P SALES

	Project	B/(P) Proto	
1st year 2005 Equivalent	$24,000	$2,043	
5th year 2005 Equivalent	$30,500	$2,729	
Sales maturity	1.27	0.01	

INVESTMENT

	Project	B/(P) Proto	NPV	B/(P) Proto
Land	$10	$3,390	$17,406	$7,326
Sitework	2,303	290		
Subtotal	$2,313	$3,680	$3,121	$279
Building	9,705	(378)		
Other	998	121		
Total Net Investment	$13,017	$3,423	$20,527	$7,605

VALUE

	IRR		NPV	
Store	17.5%			
Credit	8.2%			
TOTAL	16.4%			

STORE SENSITIVITIES

HURDLE ADJUSTMENT

	NPV	IRR
Sales	(18.1%)	(23.2%)
Gross Margin	(2.35)	(3.04)
Construction (Building & Sitework)	$8,908	$6,973

RISK/OPPORTUNITY

10% sales decline	($4,066)	(1.9)
1 pp GM decline	($3,111)	(1.5)
10% Const. cost increase	($988)	(1.0)
Market margin, wage rate, etc.	($2,999)	(1.4)
10% sales increase	$4,096	1.9

VARIANCE TO PROTOTYPE

Land	$3,675	3.2
Non-Land Investment	($570)	(0.3)
Sales	$3,603	1.4
Real Estate Tax	$617	0.2

NPV & Investment

Legend: Investment, NPV — Project, Prototype; ▲ −10% Sales, ◆ +10% Sales

Sales

Legend: Total, Incremental, Prototype

Competition

2006

23%, 10%, 67%
Legend: WMSC, Sam's Club, Kmart
5.7 SF/Cap

2008

13%, 20%, 9%, 58%
Legend: Target, WMSC, Sam's Club, Kmart
6.4 SF/Cap

Sourcing

EXHIBIT 15.8 | Individual Capital Project Request "Dashboards" (*continued*)

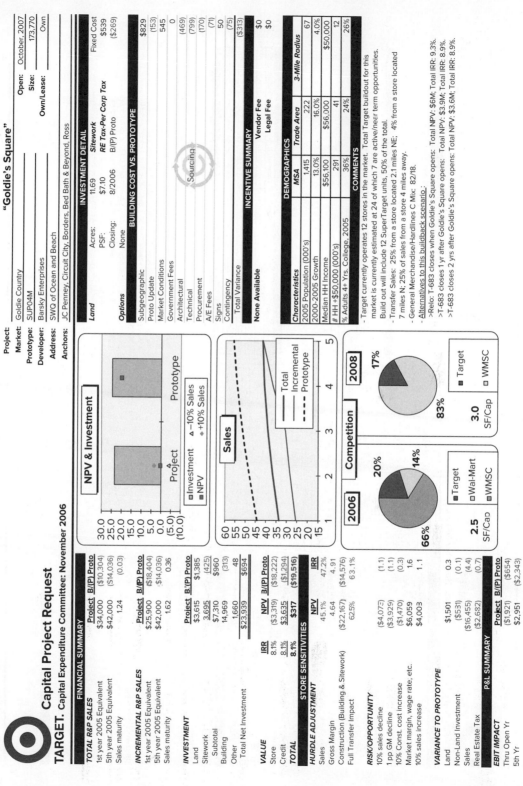

Capital Project Request

TARGET. Capital Expenditure Committee: November 2006

	Project:			"Goldie's Square"
Market:	Goldie Country		Open:	October, 2007
Prototype:	SUP04M		Size:	173,770
Developer:	Barsky Enterprises		Own/Lease:	Own
Address:	SWQ of Ocean and Beach			
Anchors:	JC Penney, Circuit City, Borders, Bed Bath & Beyond, Ross			

FINANCIAL SUMMARY

TOTAL R&P SALES

	Project	B/(P) Proto
1st year 2005 Equivalent	$34,000	($10,304)
5th year 2005 Equivalent	$42,000	($14,036)
Sales maturity	1.24	(0.03)

INCREMENTAL R&P SALES

	Project	B/(P) Proto
1st year 2005 Equivalent	$25,900	($18,404)
5th year 2005 Equivalent	$42,000	($14,036)
Sales maturity	1.62	0.36

INVESTMENT

	Project	B/(P) Proto
Land	$3,615	$1,385
Sitework	3,635	(425)
Subtotal	$7,310	$960
Building	14,969	(313)
Other	1,660	48
Total Net Investment	$23,939	$694

VALUE	IRR	NPV	B/(P) Proto
Store	8.1%	($3,319)	($18,222)
Credit	8.1%	$3,635	($1,294)
TOTAL	**8.1%**	**$317**	**($19,516)**

STORE SENSITIVITIES

HURDLE ADJUSTMENT

	NPV	IRR
Sales	45.1%	47.2%
Gross Margin	4.64	4.91
Construction (Building & Sitework)	($22,167)	($14,576)
Full Transfer Impact	62.5%	63.1%

RISK/OPPORTUNITY

10% sales decline	($4,073)	(1.1)
1 pp GM decline	($3,929)	(1.1)
10% Const. cost increase	($1,470)	(0.3)
Market margin, wage rate, etc.	$6,059	1.6
10% sales increase	$4,003	1.1

VARIANCE TO PROTOTYPE

Land	$1,501	0.3
Non-Land Investment	($531)	(0.1)
Sales	($16,455)	(4.4)
Real Estate Tax	($2,682)	(0.7)

P&L SUMMARY

EBIT IMPACT

	Project	B/(P) Proto
Thru Open Yr	($1,921)	($654)
5th Yr	$2,951	($2,343)

INVESTMENT DETAIL

Land			Sitework	
	Acres:	11.69	RE Tax-Per Corp Tax	
	PSF:	$7.10	B/(P) Proto	
	Closing:	8/2006		
	None			

Options	Fixed Cost
	BUILDING COST VS. PROTOTYPE
Subgeographic	$829
Proto Update	(153)
Market Conditions	545
Government Fees	0
Architectural	(469)
Technical	(799)
Procurement	(170)
A/E Fees	(71)
Signs	50
Contingency	(75)
Total Variance	($313)

Sourcing

INCENTIVE SUMMARY

	Vendor Fee	$0
None Available	Legal Fee	$0

DEMOGRAPHICS

Characteristics	MSA	Trade Area	3-Mile Radius
2005 Population (000's)	1,415	222	67
2000-2005 Growth	13.0%	16.0%	4.0%
Median HH Income	$56,100	$56,000	$50,000
# HH +$50,000 (000's)	291	41	12
% Adults 4+ Yrs. College, 2005	36%	24%	26%

COMMENTS

- Target currently operates 12 stores in the market. Total Target buildout for this
  market is currently estimated at 24 of which 7 are active/near term opportunities.
  Build out will include 12 SuperTarget units, 50% of the total.
- Transfer Sales: 25% from a store located 2.1 miles NE; 4% from a store located
  7 miles N; 25% of sales from a store 4 miles away.
- General Merchandise/Hardlines C Mix: 82/18.
- % Adults 4+ Yrs. College, 2005
- Alternatives to this buildback scenario :
  - >Relo: T-683 closes when Goldie's Square opens: Total NPV: $6M; Total IRR: 9.3%.
  - >T-683 closes 1 yr after Goldie's Square opens: Total NPV: $3.9M; Total IRR: 8.9%.
  - >T-683 closes 2 yrs after Goldie's Square opens: Total NPV: $3.6M; Total IRR: 8.9%.

NPV & Investment

30.0, 25.0, 20.0, 15.0, 10.0, 5.0, 0.0, (5.0), (10.0) — Project / Prototype

■ Investment ■ NPV ▲ −10% Sales ◆ +10% Sales

Sales — Total, Incremental, Prototype — 60, 55, 50, 45, 40, 35, 30, 25, 20, 15 — 1 2 3 4 5

Competition

2006	2008
66%, 20%, 14%	83%, 17%
2.5 SF/Cap	3.0 SF/Cap
■ Target ■ Wal-Mart ■ WMSC	■ Target ■ WMSC

235

EXHIBIT 15.8 | Individual Capital Project Request "Dashboards" *(continued)*

TARGET. Capital Project Request
Capital Expenditure Committee: November 2006

Project:	"Stadium Remodel"	
Market:	Boardwalk	
Scope:	Interior Remodel	
Prototype Before & After:	SUP1.1 / S04	
Expansion Availability:	Not Site Constrained	
Offsite Whse/Dist Office:	N/A	

Remodel Cycle:	Cycle 3 2007
Last Remodel:	NA
Own/Lease:	Own
Sides Before & After:	484 / 455
POG Length:	24'/28'

FINANCIAL SUMMARY

TOTAL R&P SALES	Project	B/(P) Proto
1st year 2005 Equivalent	$64,000	$19,677
5th year 2005 Equivalent	$64,000	$7,940
Sales maturity	1.00	(0.26)

INCREMENTAL R&P SALES	Project
1st year 2005 Equivalent	$9,300
5th year 2005 Equivalent	$9,300
Sales maturity	1.00

INVESTMENT	Project	B/(P) Proto
Land	$0	$5,000
Sitework	1,173	2,097
Subtotal	$1,173	$7,097
Building	12,411	2,245
Other	3,271	(1,618)
Total Net Investment	$16,855	$7,724

VALUE	IRR	NPV
Store	12.5%	$14,911
Credit	4.6%	$828
TOTAL	10.8%	$15,739

STORE SENSITIVITIES

HURDLE ADJUSTMENT	NPV	IRR
Sales		Remodel
Gross Margin		
Construction (Building & Sitework)		

RISK/OPPORTUNITY	Project	B/(P) Proto
10% sales decline	($7,854)	(1.8)
1 pp GM decline	($6,457)	(1.5)
10% Const. cost increase	($910)	(0.3)
Market margin, wage rate, etc.	($11,317)	(2.7)
10% sales increase	$6,216	15

P&L SUMMARY

EBIT IMPACT	Project	B/(P) Proto
Thru Open Yr	($6,103)	($4,812)
5th Yr	$1,272	($4,025)

PROJECT DETAIL

Write Off	$1061 ($657 Bldg, $43 Roof, $361 Other)
RE Tax-Per Corp Tax	$332
B/(P) Proto	($62)

SQUARE FOOTAGE

	Total	Sales	Stock	Support
Original Sq Ft	203,300	153,019	35,245	15,036
Additional Sq Ft		(10,544)	12,870	(2,326)
Total Sq Ft After Remodel	203,300	142,475	48,115	12,710
SUP04 Prototype	177,376	136,616	27,500	13,260
B/(P) Prototype	25,924	5,859	20,615	20,615
B/(P) Guide 1st FY			20,615	(550)

DEMOGRAPHICS

Characteristics	MSA	Trade Area	3-Mile Radius
2005 Population (000's)	806	113	84
2000-2005 Growth	5.0%	16.0%	15.0%
Median HH Income	$50,774	$65,931	$64,597
# HH +$50,000 (000's)	158	29	21
% Adults 4+ Yrs. College, 2005	28%	42%	44%

COMMENTS

- Entered market in 1972. Currently operate 8 stores in this market.
- A successful store at a strong long-term location serving an affluent family-oriented trade area.
- 2006 YTD Sales Trend: –0.9%.
- Post-remodel sales assume a 17% sales lift over R&P base case sales. Base case sales assume a (10)% impact from buildback (3.3 miles, October 2007); the store is also in the process of being impacted by Park Place South.
- Current Value of T-0530: $18.8M; R&P base case sales; Prototypical Interior Remodel in 2007; Tax benefit of depreciable property write-off: $0.4M; Rank: 783 of 1395.
- General Merchandise/Hardlines C Mix: 68/32; based on T-0530 historical trend.
- Options: New Entrance System, Relocate Pharmacy, Relocate Electrical Room.
- Scope: Refrigeration Replacement, 4 Phases of Grocery Staging, Flooring Replacement, Roof Replacement, Temp Pharmacy, New Food Avenue, New Starbucks, New Optical, New Portrait Studio, New Signage.

NPV & Investment

Sales

Source: Target Corporation, used with permission.

EXHIBIT 15.9 | Stock Price Performance 2002–06

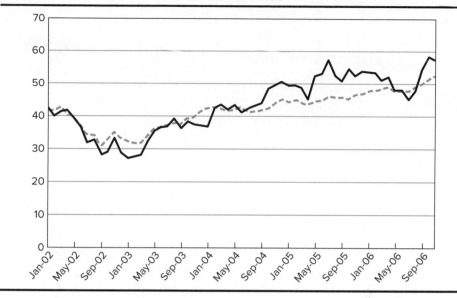

Data source: Yahoo! Finance.

The Investment Detective

The essence of capital budgeting and resource allocation is a search for good investments in which to place the firm's capital. The process can be simple when viewed in purely mechanical terms, but a number of subtle issues can obscure the best investment choices. The capital-budgeting analyst, therefore, is necessarily a detective who must winnow bad evidence from good. Much of the challenge is in knowing what quantitative analysis to generate in the first place.

Suppose you are a new capital-budgeting analyst for a company considering investments in the eight projects listed in **Exhibit 16.1**. The CFO of your company has asked you to rank the projects and recommend the "four best" that the company should accept.

In this assignment, only the quantitative considerations are relevant. No other project characteristics are deciding factors in the selection, except that management has determined that projects 7 and 8 are mutually exclusive.

All the projects require the same initial investment, $2 million. Moreover, all are believed to be of the same risk class. The firm's weighted average cost of capital has never been estimated. In the past, analysts have simply assumed that 10% was an appropriate discount rate (although certain officers of the company have recently asserted that the discount rate should be much higher).

To stimulate your analysis, consider the following questions:

1. Can you rank the projects simply by inspecting the cash flows?

2. What criteria might you use to rank the projects? Which quantitative ranking methods are better? Why?

3. What is the ranking you found by using quantitative methods? Does this ranking differ from the ranking obtained by simple inspection of the cash flows?

4. What kinds of real investment projects have cash flows similar to those in **Exhibit 16.1**?

EXHIBIT 16.1 | Projects' Free Cash Flows (dollars in thousands)

Project number: Initial investment		1 $(2,000)	2 $(2,000)	3 $(2,000)	4 $(2,000)	5 $(2,000)	6 $(2,000)	7 $(2,000)	8 $(2,000)
Year	1	$ 330	$1,666		$ 160	$ 280	$ 2,200*	$ 1,200	$ (350)
	2	330	334*		200	280		900*	(60)
	3	330	165		350	280		300	60
	4	330			395	280		90	350
	5	330			432	280		70	700
	6	330			440*	280			1,200
	7	330*			442	280			$2,250*
	8	$1,000			444	280*			
	9				446	280			
	10				448	280			
	11				450	280			
	12				451	280			
	13				451	280			
	14				452	280			
	15			$10,000*	$(2,000)	$ 280			
Sum of cash flow benefits		$3,310	$2,165	$10,000	$ 3,561	$4,200	$ 2,200	$ 2,560	$4,150
Excess of cash flow over initial investment		$ 1,310	$ 165	$ 8,000	$ 1,561	$2,200	$ 200	$ 560	$ 2,150

*Indicates year in which payback was accomplished.

Centennial Pharmaceutical Corporation

In early 2014, the board of directors of Centennial Pharmaceutical Corporation (CPC) was debating its next move regarding an earnout plan (EP) that was currently in effect for managing one of its business units. The EP had originally been structured for CloneTech management as part of the consideration for the company when CPC bought CloneTech in 2013. The EP served as a performance incentive to CloneTech's management by stipulating bonus payments to them based on the level of CloneTech's earnings during its first four years as a CPC business unit. CPC's board of directors understood the effectiveness of an earnout when acquiring a closely held company. The bonus payments motivated the newly acquired managers to work as efficiently as possible with CPC management and therefore create the most value for themselves and CPC shareholders.

But the EP had recently become infeasible due to CPC's acquisition of Pharma-New. PharmaNew had several lines of business, one of which was Strategic Research Projects (SRP), which performed the same cloning research as CloneTech. Part of the synergies that CPC hoped to realize from PharmaNew would occur by combining the CloneTech and SRP operations. Once that combination was completed, however, it would no longer be possible to directly measure the performance of CloneTech as a separate entity. If the earnings could not be directly attributable to CloneTech, the original EP could not continue to be in force. Therefore, CPC's board had constructed a revised EP based on the joint performance of CloneTech and SRP and had presented it to CloneTech management for their consideration. Unfortunately, the proposed revision had not been well received by CloneTech management, who felt that their economic position had been materially compromised by the uncertainty of SRP's future performance.

The Pharmaceutical Industry

The key challenge for a pharmaceutical was to maintain a pipeline of new drugs to bring to the market. A large part of a pharma company's profits was due to the profits of new drugs, which were protected from being copied for 20 years by U.S. patent law. Once a drug lost patent protection and became generic, many of the company's competitors rushed to produce the drug under their own brand names. Such competition usually drove the price down close to the cost of production, leaving the original producer and founder of the drug with a dramatically lower volume and margin. Thus, it was either feast or famine for a pharmaceutical through large profits when it first created a new drug or little to no profits when the drug lost its patent protection. Patents, therefore, served as incentives for pharmas to invest in research that produced lucrative new drugs. Consumers were rewarded with new treatments for ailments, but they had to pay "monopoly rents" to the founder of the drug as long as it enjoyed patent protection. In the long term, however, the low cost of production for a drug eventually rewarded the consumer with the choice of many brands at low prices once the patent protection was lifted.

The challenge for the U.S. drug industry was complicated further by the need to receive approval from the Federal Drug Administration (FDA) for any drug before it could be taken to the market. The approval process often took years to complete and sometimes became an insurmountable hurdle that prevented the drug from being marketed in the United States. Thus, the drug business was fraught with chances: the chance of discovering a viable drug, the chance of getting FDA approval, and the chance that a competitor might be first to make the same discovery. To combat the odds of not finding the next blockbuster drug, such as Viagra or Celebrex,[1] companies were forced to maintain a constant research effort with a wide spectrum of potential drug breakthroughs. Only a small percentage of research dollars were directly responsible for a successful new drug. With so few drugs reaching the market, it was all the more important for the company to have a large portfolio of potential new drugs in the pipeline at all times. Accordingly, stock analysts looked carefully at R&D budgets and announcements of possible new breakthroughs by pharmaceuticals in order to judge their market value.

CPC

In 2012, CPC was a USD20 billion U.S.-based company with 55% of its revenues coming from North America, 25% from Europe, 15% from Asia, and the remaining 5% from 20 countries around the world.[2] The company was growing in North America, but most of its growth was coming from its international markets. For the past several years, CPC had enjoyed strong growth in sales and profits, which had resulted in an A debt rating from Moody's. In the 1990s, however, CPC had run into financial problems resulting from class-action lawsuits in the United States related to the side effects of several of its drugs. In an effort to cut costs and survive the cash-flow

---

[1]Viagra was a highly successful treatment for erectile dysfunction. Celebrex was a nonsteroid and anti-inflammatory medication often used to treat the pain and inflammation associated with arthritis.

[2]USD = U.S. dollars.

losses, management decided to reduce R&D for several years, gambling that they could pick the right areas on which to focus their research efforts and, therefore, not overly compromise the firm's future. Although CPC returned to profitability and settled all the lawsuits for considerably less than expected, the reduction of its R&D budget proved to be a flawed strategy.

In 2002, in an attempt to buy the research that CPC had not been producing internally, management began a strategy of acquiring specialized biochemical research companies, including CloneTech, which was a small privately owned company in Belgium. Like CloneTech, most of the companies acquired by CPC had five to ten principal owners who were scientists in charge of the company's research. All the firms were purchased using a combination of CPC shares and an earnout contract. CPC's board preferred to use an earnout structure for acquisitions that involved a promising, but as yet unproven product. By providing for specific payments to the owner/managers as a function of profit targets, an earnout served to keep the senior managers/scientists actively involved in the company aware of its full value potential.[3] In this case, as the profits of the newly formed CPC subsidiary met the various profit targets, the CloneTech management team would receive a percentage of the performance pool.

The Earnout Plan

Exhibit 17.1 presents the original earnout plan (EP) utilized in the CloneTech acquisition. The EP stipulated an annual bonus schedule (ABS), which defined bonuses to management based on the earnings levels achieved for each of CloneTech's first four years as part of CPC. For the first year (2013), management could receive 100% of the 2013 bonus (EUR2 million) by meeting or exceeding target earnings of EUR10 million.[4] Lower bonuses would be realized for earnings less than EUR10 million: a bonus of EUR1.5 million (75% of EUR2 million) was payable for earnings between EUR9 million and EUR10 million, and EUR1.0 million (50% of EUR2 million) would be distributed for earnings between EUR8 million and EUR9 million. Failure to reach an earnings level of EUR8 million in the first year would mean no bonuses for management in 2013.

In addition to the ABS, the EP recognized the risky nature of biotech research with the inclusion of a multiyear bonus schedule (MBS). The MBS was a cumulative-earnings feature that allowed CloneTech management to receive bonus payments, in years 2, 3, and 4, which had not been fully distributed in one or more of the prior years. For example, CloneTech management could receive a full bonus of EUR2 million in 2013 and 2014 by earning EUR11 million in 2013 and EUR13 million in 2014. The full 100% bonuses would be distributed each year because earnings exceeded each year's respective target amounts in the ABS. The same bonus dollars, however, could also be realized if CloneTech earned EUR7 million in 2013 and EUR15 million in

---

[3]Earnouts sometimes used sales targets in combination with profit targets. In addition, the contracts usually contained precise definitions of costs to avoid disputes about how corporate overhead, for example, was allocated to the business unit.

[4]EUR = euros.

2014. Under this scenario, management would receive no ABS bonus for 2013 but would earn an ABS bonus of EUR2 million for 2014 plus a "cumulative bonus" of an additional EUR2 million, based on the MBS, for the EUR22 million of cumulative earnings for 2013 and 2014.

The flexibility of the EP was such that CloneTech management could potentially earn the entire EUR8 million bonus pool by reporting zero earnings for the first three years and EUR53.7 million in the last year. This facet was important because CloneTech had earned only EUR7 million in 2013, which was below the minimum threshold for bonus distributions. Despite having "underperformed" in 2013, CloneTech managers were optimistic that the entire bonus pool remained within reach once the full impact of their research was reflected in future profits. Moreover, their optimism was buoyed by the fact that half of the profits in 2013 had been earned in the fourth quarter alone, which suggested the possibility of a turnaround in the company's performance for the following years. Like most biotechs, CloneTech's historical profits varied substantially, so predicting future earnings was highly problematic.

As CloneTech was finishing its first year as an acquired company, CPC purchased another pharmaceutical company, PharmaNew. PharmaNew was a German-based company with a business unit called Strategic Research Projects (SRP), which was doing the exact same cloning research as CloneTech. CPC believed that much of the value in buying PharmaNew would come from moving CloneTech to the SRP facilities in Hamburg to allow the two groups of scientists to work together. The newly combined business unit would create significant cost savings and allow the combined labs to achieve faster and more productive results. Once the two entities were combined, however, it would no longer be possible to measure CloneTech's performance as a separate entity for purposes of the earnout agreement. According to the original EP, in the event that CloneTech was consolidated with another business unit, CPC was required to make a good-faith adjustment to the earnout schedule in order to avoid compromising the bonus incentives of CloneTech management.

Exhibit 17.2 presents CPC's revised EP that had been proposed to CloneTech management. The revised EP retained many of the basic features of the original EP. For example, bonus levels were paid according to gradations of target earnings each year, no bonuses were paid below the minimum-earnings level, and a cumulative-earnings feature remained in place.[5] The proposal, however, also had a number of important differences from the original EP. In particular, all the earnings targets had been adjusted by adding SRP's expected earnings to CloneTech's earnings targets for the remaining three years. The earnings numbers added to CloneTech's targets were exactly the numbers CPC had used to determine the value of SRP as part of the PharmaNew acquisition. Likewise, the target-earnings figures used in the original EP were exactly the earnings numbers used by CPC to determine the fair price to pay for CloneTech the previous year. Because of the similarities of their research, CPC's investment bankers predicted that both entities would experience 20% earnings growth.

---

[5]The cumulative feature was only operative in the last year of the revised EP. Therefore, managers could not use multiyear earnings to their benefit until the fourth year, at which time any bonus funds remaining could potentially be realized based on the sum of the earnings for years two, three, and four.

Perhaps the most important difference of the revised EP was CPC's proposal to convert EUR4 million of the bonus pool into a series of guaranteed payments over the remaining three years: EUR1 million in year 2, EUR1 million in year 3, and EUR2 million in year 4. Therefore, regardless of CloneTech or SRP's performance, CloneTech management was guaranteed to receive EUR4 million over the life of the revised EP. But in order to realize the full EUR8 million, the combined earnings of CloneTech and SRP together would have to reach the newly defined earnings targets.

The negative reaction of CloneTech management toward the revised EP surprised CPC's board of directors. The board thought they had made a good faith effort to preserve, if not improve, the economic value of its original agreement with CloneTech management; however, the board had not done a formal valuation of the original and revised EPs. To do so required a discounted-cash-flow analysis for both contracts (using the current interest-rate data in **Exhibit 17.3**).

EXHIBIT 17.1 | CloneTech's Original Earnout Program (in millions of euros)[1]

Annual Bonus Schedule

	Year 1		Year 2		Year 3		Year 4	
	CloneTech Earnings Level	Annual Bonus Payment	CloneTech Earnings Level	Annual Bonus Payment	CloneTech Earnings Level	Annual Bonus Payment	CloneTech Earnings Level	Annual Bonus Payment
100% Bonus Level Earnings	10.00	2.00	12.00	2.00	14.40	2.00	17.28	2.00
75% Bonus Level Earnings	9.00	1.50	10.80	1.50	12.96	1.50	15.55	1.50
50% Bonus Level Earnings	8.00	1.00	9.60	1.00	11.52	1.00	13.82	1.00

Multiyear Bonus Schedule

	Year 2		Year 3		Year 4	
	Cumulative Earnings Level	Cumulative Bonus Potential	Cumulative Earnings Level	Cumulative Bonus Potential	Cumulative Earnings Level	Cumulative Bonus Potential
100% Bonus Level Earnings	22.00	4.00	36.40	6.00	53.68	8.00
75% Bonus Level Earnings	19.80	3.00	32.76	4.50	48.31	6.00
50% Bonus Level Earnings	17.60	2.00	29.12	3.00	42.94	4.00

Source: Created by author.

[1]Bonus payments were made each year based on the Annual Bonus Schedule and, if appropriate, the Multiyear Bonus Schedule. MBS payments were distributed when the sum of all annual payments to date were less than the Cumulative Bonus Potential for that year.

EXHIBIT 17.2 | CloneTech's Revised Earnout Program (in millions of euros)[1]

	Annual Bonus Schedule—Year 2				Annual Bonus Schedule—Year 3			
	CloneTech Earnings Level	SRP's Earnings Level	Combined Earnings Level	Annual Bonus Payment	CloneTech Earnings Level	SRP's Earnings Level	Combined Earnings Level	Annual Bonus Payment
100% Bonus Level Earnings	12.00	50.00	62.00	1.33	14.40	60.00	74.40	1.33
75% Bonus Level Earnings	10.80	50.00	60.80	1.00	12.96	60.00	72.96	1.00
50% Bonus Level Earnings	9.60	50.00	59.60	0.67	11.52	60.00	71.52	0.67

	Annual Bonus Schedule—Year 4				Multiyear Bonus Schedule			
	CloneTech Earnings Level	SRP's Earnings Level	Combined Earnings Level	Annual Bonus Payment	CloneTech Cumulative Earnings	SRP's Cumulative Earnings	Combined Cumulative Earnings	Cumulative Bonus Potential
100% Bonus Level Earnings	17.28	72.00	89.28	1.33	43.68	182.00	225.68	4.00
75% Bonus Level Earnings	15.55	72.00	87.55	1.00	39.31	182.00	221.31	3.00
50% Bonus Level Earnings	13.82	72.00	85.82	0.67	34.94	182.00	216.94	2.00

Source: Created by author.

[1]Bonus payments were made each year based on the Annual Bonus Schedule and, if appropriate, the Multiyear Bonus Schedule. MBS payments were distributed when the sum of all annual payments to date were less than the Cumulative Bonus Potential for year 4. In addition to bonus payments, guaranteed payments of EUR1 million, EUR1 million, and EUR2 million were paid at the end of years 2, 3, and 4, respectively.

EXHIBIT 17.3 | Capital-Market Conditions as of January 6, 2014

Eurozone Aaa Government Yields	
3-year	0.47%
5-year	1.03%
10-year	2.20%
20-year	2.92%

Corporate Yields (3–5 year)	
Aaa	1.02%
Aa	1.32%
A	1.58%
Baa	2.33%

Data sources: Datastream and "Statistics," European Central Bank, January 14, 2016, http://www.ecb.europa.eu/stats/html/index.en.html (accessed May 31, 2016).

Worldwide Paper Company

In January 2016, Bob Prescott, the controller for the Blue Ridge Mill, was considering the addition of a new on-site longwood woodyard. The addition would have two primary benefits: to eliminate the need to purchase shortwood from an outside supplier and create the opportunity to sell shortwood on the open market as a new market for Worldwide Paper Company (WPC). Now the new woodyard would allow the Blue Ridge Mill not only to reduce its operating costs but also to increase its revenues. The proposed woodyard utilized new technology that allowed tree-length logs, called longwood, to be processed directly, whereas the current process required shortwood, which had to be purchased from the Shenandoah Mill. This nearby mill, owned by a competitor, had excess capacity that allowed it to produce more shortwood than it needed for its own pulp production. The excess was sold to several different mills, including the Blue Ridge Mill. Thus adding the new longwood equipment would mean that Prescott would no longer need to use the Shenandoah Mill as a shortwood supplier and that the Blue Ridge Mill would instead compete with the Shenandoah Mill by selling on the shortwood market. The question for Prescott was whether these expected benefits were enough to justify the $18 million capital outlay plus the incremental investment in working capital over the six-year life of the investment.

Construction would start within a few months, and the investment outlay would be spent over two calendar years: $16 million in 2016 and the remaining $2 million in 2017. When the new woodyard began operating in 2017, it would significantly reduce the operating costs of the mill. These operating savings would come mostly from the difference in the cost of producing shortwood on-site versus buying it on the open market and were estimated to be $2.0 million for 2017 and $3.5 million per year thereafter.

Prescott also planned on taking advantage of the excess production capacity afforded by the new facility by selling shortwood on the open market as soon as possible. For 2017, he expected to show revenues of approximately $4 million, as the facility came on-line and began to break into the new market. He expected shortwood sales to reach $10 million in 2018 and continue at the $10 million level through 2022. Prescott

This case was prepared by Professor Kenneth M. Eades. It was written as a basis for class discussion rather than to illustrate effective or ineffective handling of an administrative situation. Copyright © 2002 by the University of Virginia Darden School Foundation, Charlottesville, VA. All rights reserved. *To order copies, send an email to* sales@dardenbusinesspublishing.com. *No part of this publication may be reproduced, stored in a retrieval system, used in a spreadsheet, or transmitted in any form or by any means—electronic, mechanical, photocopying, recording, or otherwise—without the permission of the Darden School Foundation.*

estimated that the cost of goods sold (before including depreciation expenses) would be 75% of revenues, and SG&A would be 5% of revenues.

In addition to the capital outlay of $18 million, the increased revenues would necessitate higher levels of inventories and accounts receivable. The total working capital would average 10% of annual revenues. Therefore the amount of working capital investment each year would equal 10% of incremental sales for the year. At the end of the life of the equipment, in 2022, all the net working capital on the books would be recoverable at cost, whereas only 10% or $1.8 million (before taxes) of the capital investment would be recoverable.

Taxes would be paid at a 40% rate, and depreciation was calculated on a straight-line basis over the six-year life, with zero salvage. WPC accountants had told Prescott that depreciation charges could not begin until 2017, when all the $18 million had been spent, and the machinery was in service.

Prescott was conflicted about how to treat inflation in his analysis. He was reasonably confident that his estimates of revenues and costs for 2016 and 2017 reflected the dollar amounts that WPC would most likely experience during those years. The capital outlays were mostly contracted costs and therefore were highly reliable estimates. The expected shortwood revenue figure of $4.0 million had been based on a careful analysis of the shortwood market that included a conservative estimate of the Blue Ridge Mill's share of the market plus the expected market price of shortwood, taking into account the impact of Blue Ridge Mill as a new competitor in the market. Because he was unsure of how the operating costs and the price of shortwood would be impacted by inflation after 2017, Prescott decided not to include it in his analysis. Therefore the dollar estimates for 2018 and beyond were based on the same costs and prices per ton used in 2017. Prescott did not consider the omission critical to the final decision because he expected the increase in operating costs caused by inflation would be mostly offset by the increase in revenues associated with the rise in the price of shortwood.

WPC had a company policy to use 10% as the hurdle rate for such investment opportunities. The hurdle rate was based on a study of the company's cost of capital conducted 10 years ago. Prescott was uneasy using an outdated figure for a discount rate, particularly because it was computed when 30-year Treasury bonds were yielding 4.7%, whereas currently they were yielding less than 3% (**Exhibit 18.1**).

EXHIBIT 18.1 | Cost-of-Capital Information

Interest Rates: January 15, 2016			
Bank loan rates (LIBOR)		**Market risk premium**	
1-year	1.15%	Historical average	6.0%
Government bonds		**Corporate bonds (10-year maturities)**	
1-year	0.49%	Aaa	2.45%
5-year	1.46%	Aa	3.38%
10-year	2.04%	A	3.85%
30-year	2.82%	Baa	5.05%

Worldwide Paper Financial Data
Balance-sheet accounts (in millions of dollars)

Bank loan payable (LIBOR + 1%)	500
Long-term debt	2,500
Common equity	500
Retained earnings	2,000

Per-share data

Shares outstanding (millions)	500
Book value per share	$ 5.00
Recent market value per share	$24.00

Other

Bond rating	A
Beta	1.10

Source: Datastream

Fonderia del Piemonte S.p.A.

In November 2015, Martina Bellucci, managing director of Fonderia del Piemonte S.p.A., was considering the purchase of a Thor MM-9 automated molding machine. This machine would prepare the sand molds into which molten iron was poured to obtain iron castings. The Thor MM-9 would replace an older machine and would offer improvements in quality and some additional capacity for expansion. Similar molding-machine proposals had been rejected by the board of directors for economic reasons on three previous occasions, most recently in 2014. This time, given the size of the proposed expenditure of nearly EUR2 million,[1] Bellucci was seeking a careful estimate of the project's costs and benefits and, ultimately, a recommendation of whether to proceed with the investment.

The Company

Fonderia del Piemonte specialized in the production of precision metal castings for use in automotive, aerospace, and construction equipment. The company had acquired a reputation for quality products, particularly for safety parts (i.e., parts whose failure would result in loss of control for the operator). Its products included crankshafts, transmissions, brake calipers, axles, wheels, and various steering-assembly parts. Customers were original-equipment manufacturers (OEMs), mainly in Europe. OEMs were becoming increasingly insistent about product quality, and Fonderia del Piemonte's response had reduced the rejection rate of its castings by the OEMs to 70 parts per million.

This record had won the company coveted quality awards from BMW, Ferrari, and Peugeot, and had resulted in strategic alliances with those firms: Fonderia del Piemonte and the OEMs exchanged technical personnel and design tasks; in addition, the OEMs shared confidential market-demand information with Fonderia del Piemonte, which increased the precision of the latter's production scheduling. In certain instances, the

---

[1]EUR = euros; USD = U.S. dollars.

This case was prepared by Professors Robert F. Bruner and Michael J. Schill from field research and public information and draws its structure and some data from an antecedent case written by Brandt Allen. Fonderia del Piemonte is a fictional company representing the issues that faced actual firms. The author gratefully acknowledges the financial support of the Batten Institute. Copyright © 2016 by the University of Virginia Darden School Foundation, Charlottesville, VA. All rights reserved. *To order copies, send an e-mail* sales@dardenbusinesspublishing.com. *No part of this publication may be reproduced, stored in a retrieval system, used in a spreadsheet, or transmitted in any form or by any means—electronic, mechanical, photocopying, recording, or otherwise—without the permission of the Darden School Foundation.*

OEMs had provided cheap loans to Fonderia del Piemonte to support capital expansion. Finally, the company received relatively long-term supply contracts from the OEMs and had a preferential position for bidding on new contracts.

Fonderia del Piemonte, located in Turin, Italy, had been founded in 1912 by Bellucci's great-great-grandfather, Benito Bellucci, a naval engineer, to produce castings for the armaments industry. In the 1920s and 1930s, the company expanded its customer base into the automotive industry. Although the company barely avoided financial collapse in the late 1940s, Benito Bellucci predicted a postwar demand for precision metal casting and positioned the company to meet it. From that time, Fonderia del Piemonte grew slowly but steadily; its sales for calendar-year 2015 were expected to be EUR1.3 billion. It was listed for trading on the Milan stock exchange in 1991, but the Bellucci family owned 55% of the common shares of stock outstanding. The company's beta was estimated at 1.25.[2]

The company's traditional hurdle rate of return on capital deployed was 7%, although this rate had not been reviewed since 2012. In addition, company policy sought payback of an entire investment within five years. At the time of the case, the market value of the company's capital was 33% debt and 67% equity. The prevailing borrowing rate Fonderia del Piemonte faced on its loans was 2.6%. The company's effective tax rate was about 43%, which reflected the combination of national and local corporate income-tax rates.

Bellucci, age 57, had assumed executive responsibility for the company 15 years earlier, upon the death of her father. She held a doctorate in metallurgy and was the matriarch of an extended family. Only a son and a niece worked at Fonderia del Piemonte, however. Over the years, the Bellucci family had sought to earn a rate of return on its equity investment of 12%—this goal had been established by Benito Bellucci and had never once been questioned by management.

The Thor MM-9 Machine

Sand molds used to make castings were currently prepared in a semiautomated process at Fonderia del Piemonte. Workers stamped impressions in a mixture of sand and adhesive under heat and high pressure. The process was relatively labor intensive, required training and retraining to obtain consistency in mold quality, and demanded some heavy lifting from workers. Indeed, medical claims for back injuries in the molding shop had doubled since 2012 as the mix of Fonderia del Piemonte's casting products shifted toward heavy items. Items averaged 25 kg in 2015.

The new molding machine would replace six semiautomated stamping machines that together had originally cost EUR423,000. Cumulative depreciation of EUR169,200 had already been charged against the original cost and six years of depreciation charges remained over the total useful life of 10 years. Fonderia del Piemonte's management believed that those semiautomated machines would need to be replaced after six years. Bellucci had recently received an offer of EUR130,000 for the six machines.

---

[2]The current yield on euro-denominated bonds issued by the Italian governments was 1.7%. Bellucci assumed that the equity risk premium would be 5%. Also, she believed that current bond yields in Europe effectively impounded an expectation of no inflation over the next 10 years.

The current six machines required 12 workers per shift[3] (24 in total) at EUR14.66 per worker per hour, plus the equivalent of two maintenance workers, each of whom was paid EUR15.70 an hour, plus maintenance supplies of EUR6,000 a year. Bellucci assumed that the semiautomated machines, if kept, would continue to consume electrical power at the rate of EUR15,300 a year.

The Thor MM-9 molding machine was produced by an American company in Allentown, Pennsylvania. Fonderia del Piemonte had received a firm offering price of USD1.9 million from the American firm. Since the prevailing exchange rate between the euro and the U.S. dollar was 1.06 USD per euro, the price in euros was EUR1.8 million. The estimate for modifications to the plant, including wiring for the machine's power supply, was EUR100,000. Allowing for EUR50,000 for shipping, installation, and testing, the total cost of the Thor MM-9 machine was expected to be EUR1.95 million, all of which would be capitalized and depreciated for tax purposes over eight years. Bellucci assumed that, at a high and steady rate of machine utilization, the Thor MM-9 would be worthless after the eighth year and need to be replaced.

The new machine would require two skilled operators (one per shift), each receiving EUR22.72 an hour (including benefits), and contract maintenance of EUR120,000 a year, and would incur power costs of EUR40,000 yearly. In addition, the automatic machine was expected to save at least EUR30,000 yearly through improved labor efficiency in other areas of the foundry.

With the current machines, more than 30% of the foundry's floor space was needed for the wide galleries the machines required; raw materials and in-process inventories had to be staged near each machine in order to smooth the workflow. With the automated machine, almost half of that space would be freed for other purposes—although at present there was no need for new space.

Certain aspects of the Thor MM-9 purchase decision were difficult to quantify. First, Bellucci was unsure whether the tough collective-bargaining agreement her company had with the employees' union would allow her to lay off the 24 operators of the semiautomated machines. Reassigning the workers to other jobs might be easier, but the only positions needing to be filled were unskilled jobs, which paid EUR9.13 an hour. The extent of any labor savings would depend on negotiations with the union. Second, Bellucci believed that the Thor MM-9 would result in even higher levels of product quality and lower scrap rates than the company was now boasting. In light of the ever-increasing competition, this outcome might prove to be of enormous, but currently unquantifiable, competitive importance. Finally, the Thor MM-9 had a theoretical maximum capacity that was 30% higher than that of the six semiautomated machines; but those machines were operating at only 90% of capacity, and Bellucci was unsure when added capacity would be needed. There was plenty of uncertainty about the economic outlook in Europe, and the latest economic news suggested that the economies of Europe might be headed for a slowdown.

---

[3]The foundry operated two shifts a day. It did not operate on weekends or holidays. At maximum, the foundry would produce for 210 days a year.

Victoria Chemicals plc (A): The Merseyside Project[1]

Late one afternoon in January 2008, Frank Greystock told Lucy Morris, "No one seems satisfied with the analysis so far, but the suggested changes could kill the project. If solid projects like this can't swim past the corporate piranhas, the company will never modernize."

Morris was plant manager of Victoria Chemicals' Merseyside Works in Liverpool, England. Her controller, Frank Greystock, was discussing a capital project that Morris wanted to propose to senior management. The project consisted of a GBP12 million[2] expenditure to renovate and rationalize the polypropylene production line at the Merseyside plant in order to make up for deferred maintenance and to exploit opportunities to achieve increased production efficiency.

Victoria Chemicals was under pressure from investors to improve its financial performance because of the accumulation of the firm's common shares by a well-known corporate raider, Sir David Benjamin. Earnings had fallen to 180 pence per share at the end of 2007 from around 250 pence per share at the end of 2006. Morris thus believed that the time was ripe to obtain funding from corporate headquarters for a modernization program for the Merseyside Works—at least she had believed this until Greystock presented her with several questions that had only recently surfaced.

Victoria Chemicals and Polypropylene

Victoria Chemicals, a major competitor in the worldwide chemicals industry, was a leading producer of polypropylene, a polymer used in an extremely wide variety of products (ranging from medical products to packaging film, carpet fibers, and

[1]The author wishes to acknowledge the helpful comments of Dr. Frank H. McTigue, the literary color of Anthony Trollope, and the financial support of the Citicorp Global Scholars Program.

[2]GBP = British pounds.

automobile components) and known for its strength and malleability. Polypropylene was essentially priced as a commodity.

The production of polypropylene pellets at Merseyside Works began with propylene, a refined gas received in tank cars. Propylene was purchased from four refineries in England that produced it in the course of refining crude oil into gasoline. In the first stage of the production process, polymerization, the propylene gas was combined with a diluent (or solvent) in a large pressure vessel. In a catalytic reaction, the polypropylene precipitated to the bottom of the tank and was then concentrated in a centrifuge.

The second stage of the production process compounded the basic polypropylene with stabilizers, modifiers, fillers, and pigments to achieve the desired attributes for a particular customer. The finished plastic was extruded into pellets for shipment to the customer.

The Merseyside Works production process was old, semicontinuous at best, and, therefore, higher in labor content than its competitors' newer plants. The Merseyside Works plant was constructed in 1967.

Victoria Chemicals produced polypropylene at Merseyside Works and in Rotterdam, Holland. The two plants were of identical scale, age, and design. The managers of both plants reported to James Fawn, executive vice president and manager of the Intermediate Chemicals Group (ICG) of Victoria Chemicals. The company positioned itself as a supplier to customers in Europe and the Middle East. The strategic-analysis staff estimated that, in addition to numerous small producers, seven major competitors manufactured polypropylene in Victoria Chemicals' market region. Their plants operated at various cost levels. **Exhibit 20.1** presents a comparison of plant sizes and indexed costs.

The Proposed Capital Program

Morris had assumed responsibility for the Merseyside Works only 12 months previously, following a rapid rise from the entry position of shift engineer nine years before. When she assumed responsibility, she undertook a detailed review of the operations and discovered significant opportunities for improvement in polypropylene production. Some of those opportunities stemmed from the deferral of maintenance over the preceding five years. In an effort to enhance the operating results of Merseyside Works, the previous manager had limited capital expenditures to only the most essential. Now what previously had been routine and deferrable was becoming essential. Other opportunities stemmed from correcting the antiquated plant design in ways that would save energy and improve the process flow: (1) relocating and modernizing tank-car unloading areas, which would enable the process flow to be streamlined; (2) refurbishing the polymerization tank to achieve higher pressures and thus greater throughput; and (3) renovating the compounding plant to increase extrusion throughput and obtain energy savings.

Morris proposed an expenditure of GBP12 million on this program. The entire polymerization line would need to be shut down for 45 days, however, and because the Rotterdam plant was operating near capacity, Merseyside Works' customers would buy from competitors. Greystock believed the loss of customers would not be permanent.

The benefits would be a lower energy requirement[3] as well as a 7% greater manufacturing throughput. In addition, the project was expected to improve gross margin (before depreciation and energy savings) from 11.5% to 12.5%. The engineering group at Merseyside Works was highly confident that the efficiencies would be realized.

Merseyside Works currently produced 250,000 metric tons of polypropylene pellets a year. Currently, the price of polypropylene averaged GBP675 per ton for Victoria Chemicals' product mix. The tax rate required in capital-expenditure analyses was 30%. Greystock discovered that any plant facilities to be replaced had been completely depreciated. New assets could be depreciated on an accelerated basis[4] over 15 years, the expected life of the assets. The increased throughput would necessitate an increase of work-in-process inventory equal in value to 3.0% of cost of goods. Greystock included in the first year of his forecast preliminary engineering costs of GBP500,000 spent over the preceding nine months on efficiency and design studies of the renovation. Finally, the corporate manual stipulated that overhead costs be reflected in project analyses at the rate of 3.5% times the book value of assets acquired in the project per year.[5]

Greystock had produced the discounted-cash-flow (DCF) summary given in **Exhibit 20.2**. It suggested that the capital program would easily hurdle Victoria Chemicals' required return of 10% for engineering projects.

Concerns of the Transport Division

Victoria Chemicals owned the tank cars with which Merseyside Works received propylene gas from four petroleum refineries in England. The Transport Division, a cost center, oversaw the movement of all raw, intermediate, and finished materials throughout

---

[3]Greystock characterized the energy savings as a percentage of sales and assumed that the savings would be equal to 1.25% of sales in the first 5 years and 0.75% in years 6 through 10. Thereafter, without added aggressive green spending, the energy efficiency of the plant would revert to its old level, and the savings would be zero. He believed that the decision to make further environmentally oriented investments was a separate choice (and one that should be made much later) and, therefore, that to include such benefits (of a presumably later investment decision) in the project being considered today would be inappropriate.

[4]The company's capital-expenditure manual suggested the use of double-declining-balance (DDB) depreciation, even though other more aggressive procedures might be permitted by the tax code. The reason for this policy was to discourage jockeying for corporate approvals based on tax provisions that could apply differently for different projects and divisions. Prior to senior-management's approval, the controller's staff would present an independent analysis of special tax effects that might apply. Division managers, however, were discouraged from relying heavily on those effects. In applying the DDB approach, accelerated depreciation was used until the straight-line calculation gave a higher number at which point depreciation was calculated on a straight-line basis. The conversion to straight line was commonly done so that the asset would depreciate fully within its economic life.

[5]The corporate-policy manual stated that new projects should be able to sustain a reasonable proportion of corporate overhead expense. Projects that were so marginal as to be unable to sustain those expenses and also meet the other criteria of investment attractiveness should not be undertaken. Thus all new capital projects should reflect an annual pretax charge amounting to 3.5% of the value of the initial asset investment for the project.

the company and was responsible for managing the tank cars. Because of the project's increased throughput, the Transport Division would have to increase its allocation of tank cars to Merseyside Works. Currently, the Transport Division could make this allocation out of excess capacity, although doing so would accelerate from 2012 to 2010 the need to purchase new rolling stock to support the anticipated growth of the firm in other areas. The purchase was estimated to be GBP2 million in 2010. The rolling stock would have a depreciable life of 10 years,[6] but with proper maintenance, the cars could operate much longer. The rolling stock could not be used outside Britain because of differences in track gauge.

A memorandum from the controller of the Transport Division suggested that the cost of the tank cars should be included in the initial outlay of Merseyside Works' capital program. But Greystock disagreed. He told Morris:

> The Transport Division isn't paying one pence of actual cash because of what we're doing at Merseyside. In fact, we're doing the company a favor in using its excess capacity. Even *if* an allocation has to be made somewhere, it should go on the Transport Division's books. The way we've always evaluated projects in this company has been with the philosophy of "every tub on its own bottom"—every division has to fend for itself. The Transport Division isn't part of our own Intermediate Chemicals Group, so they should carry the allocation of rolling stock.

Accordingly, Greystock had not reflected any charge for the use of excess rolling stock in his preliminary DCF analysis, given in **Exhibit 20.2**.

The Transport Division and Intermediate Chemicals Group reported to separate executive vice presidents, who reported to the chairman and chief executive officer of the company. The executive vice presidents received an annual incentive bonus pegged to the performance of their divisions.

Concerns of the ICG Sales and Marketing Department

Greystock's analysis had led to questions from the director of sales. In a recent meeting, the director had told Greystock:

> Your analysis assumes that we can sell the added output and thus obtain the full efficiencies from the project, but as you know, the market for polypropylene is extremely competitive. Right now, the industry is in a downturn and it looks like an oversupply is in the works. This means that we will probably have to shift capacity away from Rotterdam toward Merseyside in order to move the added volume. Is this really a gain for Victoria Chemicals? Why spend money just so one plant can cannibalize another?

The vice president of marketing was less skeptical. He said that with lower costs at Merseyside Works, Victoria Chemicals might be able to take business from the plants of competitors such as Saône-Poulet or Vaysol. In the current severe recession,

---

[6]The transport division depreciated rolling stock using DDB depreciation for the first eight years and straight-line depreciation for the last two years.

competitors would fight hard to keep customers, but sooner or later the market would revive, and it would be reasonable to assume that any lost business volume would return at that time.

Greystock had listened to both the director and the vice president and chose to reflect no charge for a loss of business at Rotterdam in his preliminary analysis of the Merseyside project. He told Morris:

> Cannibalization really isn't a cash flow; there is no check written in this instance. Anyway, if the company starts burdening its cost-reduction projects with fictitious charges like this, we'll never maintain our cost competitiveness. A cannibalization charge is rubbish!

Concerns of the Assistant Plant Manager

Griffin Tewitt, the assistant plant manager and Morris's direct subordinate, proposed an unusual modification to Greystock's analysis during a late-afternoon meeting with Greystock and Morris. Over the past few months, Tewitt had been absorbed with the development of a proposal to modernize a separate and independent part of the Merseyside Works, the production line for ethylene-propylene-copolymer rubber (EPC). This product, a variety of synthetic rubber, had been pioneered by Victoria Chemicals in the early 1960s and was sold in bulk to European tire manufacturers. Despite hopes that this oxidation-resistant rubber would dominate the market in synthetics, EPC remained a relatively small product in the European chemical industry. Victoria Chemicals, the largest supplier of EPC, produced the entire volume at Merseyside Works. EPC had been only marginally profitable to Victoria Chemicals because of the entry by competitors and the development of competing synthetic-rubber compounds over the past five years.

Tewitt had proposed a renovation of the EPC production line at a cost of GBP1 million. The renovation would give Victoria Chemicals the lowest EPC cost base in the world and would improve cash flows by GBP25,000 ad infinitum. Even so, at current prices and volumes, the net present value (NPV) of this project was −GBP750,000. Tewitt and the EPC product manager had argued strenuously to the company's executive committee that the negative NPV ignored strategic advantages from the project and increases in volume and prices when the recession ended. Nevertheless, the executive committee had rejected the project, basing its rejection mainly on economic grounds.

In a hushed voice, Tewitt said to Morris and Greystock:

> Why don't you include the EPC project as part of the polypropylene line renovations? The positive NPV of the poly renovations can easily sustain the negative NPV of the EPC project. This is an extremely important project to the company, a point that senior management doesn't seem to get. If we invest now, we'll be ready to exploit the market when the recession ends. If we don't invest now, you can expect that we will have to exit the business altogether in three years. Do you look forward to more layoffs? Do you want to manage a shrinking plant? Recall that our annual bonuses are pegged to the size of this operation. Also remember that, in the last 20 years, no one from corporate has monitored renovation projects once the investment decision was made.

Concerns of the Treasury Staff

After a meeting on a different matter, Greystock described his dilemmas to Andrew Gowan, who worked as an analyst on Victoria Chemicals' treasury staff. Gowan scanned Greystock's analysis and pointed out:

> Cash flows and discount rate need to be consistent in their assumptions about inflation. The 10% hurdle rate you're using is a nominal target rate of return. The Treasury staff thinks this impounds a long-term inflation expectation of 3% per year. Thus Victoria Chemicals' real (that is, zero inflation) target rate of return is 7%.

The conversation was interrupted before Greystock could gain full understanding of Gowan's comment. For the time being, Greystock decided to continue to use a discount rate of 10% because it was the figure promoted in the latest edition of Victoria Chemicals' capital-budgeting manual.

Evaluating Capital-Expenditure Proposals at Victoria Chemicals

In submitting a project for senior management's approval, the project's initiators had to identify it as belonging to one of four possible categories: (1) new product or market, (2) product or market extension, (3) engineering efficiency, or (4) safety or environment. The first three categories of proposals were subject to a system of four performance "hurdles," of which at least three had to be met for the proposal to be considered. The Merseyside project would be in the engineering-efficiency category.

1. *Impact on earnings per share*: For engineering-efficiency projects, the contribution to net income from contemplated projects had to be positive. This criterion was calculated as the average annual earnings per share (EPS) contribution of the project over its entire economic life, using the number of outstanding shares at the most recent fiscal year-end (FYE) as the basis for the calculation. (At FYE2007, Victoria Chemicals had 92,891,240 shares outstanding.)

2. *Payback*: This criterion was defined as the number of years necessary for free cash flow of the project to amortize the initial project outlay completely. For engineering-efficiency projects, the maximum payback period was six years.

3. *Discounted cash flow*: DCF was defined as the present value of future cash flows of the project (at the hurdle rate of 10% for engineering-efficiency proposals) less the initial investment outlay. This net present value of free cash flows had to be positive.

4. *Internal rate of return*: IRR was defined as being the discount rate at which the present value of future free cash flows just equaled the initial outlay—in other words, the rate at which the NPV was zero. The IRR of engineering-efficiency projects had to be greater than 10%.

Conclusion

Morris wanted to review Greystock's analysis in detail and settle the questions surrounding the tank cars and the potential loss of business volume at Rotterdam. As

Greystock's analysis now stood, the Merseyside project met all four investment criteria:

1. Average annual addition to EPS = GBP0.022
2. Payback period = 3.8 years
3. Net present value = GBP10.6 million
4. Internal rate of return = 24.3%

Morris was concerned that further tinkering might seriously weaken the attractiveness of the project.

EXHIBIT 20.1 | Comparative Information on the Seven Largest Polypropylene Plants in Europe

	Plant Location	Year Plant Built	Plant Annual Output (in metric tons)	Production Cost per Ton (indexed to low-cost producer)
CBTG A.G	Saarbrün	1981	350,000	1.00
Victoria Chemicals	Liverpool	1967	250,000	1.09
Victoria Chemicals	Rotterdam	1967	250,000	1.09
Hosche A.G.	Hamburg	1977	300,000	1.02
Montecassino SpA	Genoa	1961	120,000	1.11
Saône-Poulet S.A.	Marseille	1972	175,000	1.07
Vaysol S.A.	Antwerp	1976	220,000	1.06
Next 10 largest plants			450,000	1.19

Source: Author analysis.

EXHIBIT 20.2 | Greystock's DCF Analysis of the Merseyside Project (financial values in millions of GBP)

Assumptions

Annual Output (metric tons)	250,000	Discount Rate	10.0%
Output Gain/Original Output	7.0%	Tax Rate	30%
Price/Ton (pounds sterling)	675	Investment Outlay (mill.)	12.0
Inflation Rate (prices and costs)	0.0%	Depreciable Life (years)	15
Gross Margin (ex. Deprec.)	12.50%	Salvage Value	0
Old Gross Margin	11.5%	WIP Inventory/Cost of Goods	3.0%
Energy Savings/Sales Yr. 1–5	1.25%	Months Downtime, Construction	1.5
Yr. 6–10	0.75%	Preliminary Engineering Costs	0.5
Yr. 11–15	0.0%	Overhead/Investment	3.5%

Year	Now	1 2008	2 2009	3 2010	4 2011	5 2012	6 2013	7 2014	8 2015	9 2016	10 2017	11 2018	12 2019	13 2020	14 2021	15 2022
1. Estimate of Incremental Gross Profit																
New Output (tons)		267,500	267,500	267,500	267,500	267,500	267,500	267,500	267,500	267,500	267,500	267,500	267,500	267,500	267,500	267,500
Lost Output—Construction	(33,438)															
New Sales (millions)		157.99	180.56	180.56	180.56	180.56	180.56	180.56	180.56	180.56	180.56	180.56	180.56	180.56	180.56	180.56
New Gross Margin		13.8%	13.8%	13.8%	13.8%	13.8%	13.3%	13.3%	13.3%	13.3%	13.3%	12.5%	12.5%	12.5%	12.5%	12.5%
New Gross Profit		21.72	24.83	24.83	24.83	24.83	23.92	23.92	23.92	23.92	23.92	22.57	22.57	22.57	22.57	22.57
Old Output		250,000	250,000	250,000	250,000	250,000	250,000	250,000	250,000	250,000	250,000	250,000	250,000	250,000	250,000	250,000
Old Sales		168.75	168.75	168.75	168.75	168.75	168.75	168.75	168.75	168.75	168.75	168.75	168.75	168.75	168.75	168.75
Old Gross Profit		19.41	19.41	19.41	19.41	19.41	19.41	19.41	19.41	19.41	19.41	19.41	19.41	19.41	19.41	19.41
Incremental Gross Profit		2.32	5.42	5.42	5.42	5.42	4.52	4.52	4.52	4.52	4.52	3.16	3.16	3.15	3.16	3.16
2. Estimate of Incremental WIP Inventory																
New WIP Inventory		4.09	4.67	4.67	4.67	4.67	4.70	4.70	4.70	4.70	4.70	4.74	4.74	4.74	4.74	4.74
Old WIP Inventory		4.48	4.48	4.48	4.48	4.48	4.48	4.48	4.48	4.48	4.48	4.48	4.48	4.48	4.48	4.48
Incremental WIP Inventory		−0.39	0.19	0.19	0.19	0.19	0.22	0.22	0.22	0.22	0.22	0.26	0.26	0.26	0.26	0.26
3. Estimate of Incremental Depreciation																
New Depreciation		1.60	1.39	1.20	1.04	0.90	0.78	0.68	0.59	0.55	0.55	0.55	0.55	0.55	0.55	0.55
4. Overhead		0.42	0.42	0.42	0.42	0.42	0.42	0.42	0.42	0.42	0.42	0.42	0.42	0.42	0.42	0.42
5. Prelim. Engineering Costs		0.50														
Pretax Incremental Profit		−0.20	3.61	3.80	3.96	4.10	3.32	3.42	3.51	3.55	3.55	2.20	2.20	2.20	2.20	2.20
6. Cash Flow Adjustments	−12.00															
Less Capital Expenditures																
Add Back Depreciation		1.60	1.39	1.20	1.04	0.90	0.78	0.68	0.59	0.55	0.55	0.55	0.55	0.55	0.55	0.55
Less Added WIP Inventory		0.39	−0.58	0.00	0.00	0.00	−0.03	0.00	0.00	0.00	0.00	−0.04	0.00	0.00	0.00	0.00
7. Free Cash Flow	−12.00	1.85	3.33	3.86	3.81	3.77	3.08	3.07	3.05	3.03	3.03	2.04	2.08	2.08	2.08	2.34

NPV = 10.57
IRR = 24.3%

Source: Created by author.

Victoria Chemicals PLC (B): The Merseyside and Rotterdam Projects[1]

James Fawn, executive vice president of the Intermediate Chemicals Group (ICG) of Victoria Chemicals, planned to meet with his financial analyst, John Camperdown, to review two mutually exclusive capital-expenditure proposals. The firm's capital budget would be submitted for approval to the board of directors in early February 2008, and any projects Fawn proposed for the ICG had to be forwarded to the CEO of Victoria Chemicals soon for his review. Plant managers in Liverpool and Rotterdam had independently submitted expenditure proposals, each of which would expand the polypropylene output of their respective plants by 7% or 17,500 tons per year.[2] Victoria Chemicals' strategic-analysis staff argued strenuously that a company-wide increase in polypropylene output of 35,000 tons made no sense but half that amount did. Thus Fawn could not accept *both* projects; he could sponsor only one for approval by the board.

Corporate policy was to evaluate projects based on four criteria: (1) net present value (NPV) computed at the appropriate cost of capital, (2) internal rate of return (IRR), (3) payback, and (4) growth in earnings per share. In addition, the board of directors was receptive to "strategic factors"—considerations that might be difficult to quantify. The manager of the Rotterdam plant, Elizabeth Eustace, argued vociferously that her project easily surpassed all the relevant quantitative standards and that it had

---

[1]The author wishes to acknowledge the helpful comments of Dr. Frank H. McTigue, the literary color of Anthony Trollope, and the financial support of the Citicorp Global Scholars Program.

[2]Background information on Victoria Chemicals and the polypropylene business is given in Robert F. Bruner, "Victoria Chemicals PLC (A): The Merseyside Project," UVA-F-1543 (Charlottesville, VA: Darden Business Publishing, 2008).

important strategic benefits. Indeed, Eustace had interjected those points in two recent meetings with senior management and at a cocktail reception for the board of directors. Fawn expected to review the proposal from Lucy Morris, manager of Merseyside Works, the Liverpool plant, at the meeting with Camperdown, but he suspected that neither proposal dominated the other on all four criteria. Fawn's choice would apparently not be straightforward.

The Proposal from Merseyside, Liverpool

The project for the Merseyside plant entailed enhancing the existing facilities and the production process. Based on the type of project and the engineering studies, the potential benefits of the project were quite certain. To date, Morris had limited her discussions about the project to conversations with Fawn and Camperdown. Camperdown had raised exploratory questions about the project and had presented preliminary analyses to managers in marketing and transportation for their comments. The revised analysis emerging from those discussions would be the focus of Fawn's discussion with Camperdown in the forthcoming meeting.

Camperdown had indicated that Morris's final memo on the project was only three pages long. Fawn wondered whether this memo would satisfy his remaining questions.

The Rotterdam Project

Elizabeth Eustace's proposal consisted of a 90-page document replete with detailed schematics, engineering comments, strategic analyses, and financial projections. The basic discounted cash flow (DCF) analysis presented in **Exhibit 21.1** shows that the project had an NPV of GBP15.5 million[3] and an IRR of 18.0%. Accounting for a worst-case scenario, which assumed erosion of Merseyside's volume equal to the gain in Rotterdam's volume, the NPV was GBP12.45 million.

In essence, Eustace's proposal called for the expenditure of GBP10.5 million over three years to convert the plant's polymerization line from batch to continuous-flow technology and to install sophisticated state-of-the-art process controls throughout the polymerization and compounding operations. The heart of the new system would be an analog computer driven by advanced software written by a team of engineering professors at an institute in Japan. The three-year-old process-control technology had been installed in several polypropylene production facilities in Japan, and although the improvements in cost and output had been positive on average, the efficiency gains had varied considerably across each of the production facilities. Other major producers were known to be evaluating this system for use in their plants.

Eustace explained that installing the sophisticated new system would not be feasible without also obtaining a continuous supply of propylene gas. She proposed obtaining this gas by pipeline from a refinery five kilometers away (rather than by railroad tank cars

---

[3]GBP = British pounds.

sourced from three refineries). Victoria Chemicals had an option to purchase a pipeline and its right-of-way for GBP3.5 million, which Eustace had included in her GBP10.5 million estimate for the project; then, for relatively little cost, the pipeline could be extended to the Rotterdam plant and refinery at the other end. The option had been purchased several years earlier. A consultant had informed Eustace that to purchase a right-of-way at current prices and to lay a comparable pipeline would cost approximately GBP6 million, a value the consultant believed was roughly equal to what it could be sold for at auction in case the plan didn't work out. The consultant also forecasted that the value of the right-of-way would be GBP40 million in 15 years.[4] This option was set to expire in six months.

Some senior Victoria Chemicals executives firmly believed that if the Rotterdam project were not undertaken, the option on the right-of-way should be allowed to expire unexercised. The reasoning was summarized by Jeffrey Palliser, chairman of the executive committee:

> Our business is chemicals, not land speculation. Simply buying the right-of-way with the intention of reselling it for a profit takes us beyond our expertise. Who knows when we could sell it, and for how much? How distracting would this little side venture be for Elizabeth Eustace?

Younger members of senior management were more willing to consider a potential investment arbitrage on the right-of-way.

Eustace expected to realize the benefit of this investment (i.e., a 7% increase in output) gradually over time, as the new technology was installed and shaken down and as the learning-curve effects were realized. She advocated a phased-investment program (as opposed to all at once) in order to minimize disruption to plant operations and to allow the new technology to be calibrated and fine-tuned. Admittedly, there was a chance that the technology would not work as well as hoped, but due to the complexity of the technology and the extent to which it would permeate the plant, there would be no going back once the decision had been made to install the new controls. Yet it was possible that the technology could deliver more efficiencies than estimated in the cash flows, if the controls reached the potential boasted by the Japanese engineering team.

Fawn recalled that the strategic factors to which Eustace referred had to do with the obvious cost and output improvements expected from the new system, as well as from the advantage of being the first major European producer to implement the new technology. Being the first to implement the technology probably meant a head start in moving

---

[4]The right-of-way had several commercial uses. Most prominently, the Dutch government had expressed an interest in using the right-of-way for a new high-speed railroad line. The planning for this line had barely begun, however, which suggested that land-acquisition efforts were years away. Moreover, government budget deficits threatened the timely implementation of the rail project. Another potential user was Medusa Communications, an international telecom company that was looking for pathways along which to bury its new optical-fiber cables. Power companies and other chemical companies or refineries might also be interested in acquiring the right-of-way.

down the learning curve toward reducing costs as the organization became familiar with the technology. Eustace argued:

> The Japanese, and now the Americans, exploit the learning-curve phenomenon aggressively. Fortunately, they aren't major players in European polypropylene, at least for now. This is a once-in-a-generation opportunity for Victoria Chemicals to leapfrog its competition through the exploitation of new technology.

In an oblique reference to the Merseyside proposal, Eustace went on to say:

> There are two alternatives to implementation of the analog process-control technology. One is a series of myopic enhancements to existing facilities, but this is nothing more than sticking one's head in the sand, for it leaves us at the mercy of our competitors who *are* making choices for the long term. The other alternative is to exit the polypropylene business, but this amounts to walking away from the considerable know-how we've accumulated in this business and from what is basically a valuable activity. Our commitment to analog controls makes it the right choice at the right time.

Fawn wondered how to take the technology into account in making his decision. Even if he recommended the Merseyside project over the Rotterdam project, it would still be possible to add the new controls to Merseyside at some point in the future. Practically speaking, Fawn believed the controls could be added in 2010, which would allow sufficient time to complete all the proposed capital improvements before embarking on the new undertaking. As with the Rotterdam project, it was expected that the controls would raise Merseyside's margin by 0.5% a year, to a maximum of 15%. The controls would not result in an incremental volume gain, however, as Merseyside would already be operating at its capacity of 267,500 tons. To obtain a supply of propylene gas at Merseyside, it would be necessary to enter into a 15-year contract with a local supplier. Although the contract would cost GBP0.4 million a year, it would obviate the need to build the proposed pipeline for Rotterdam, resulting in an investment at Merseyside of GBP7.0 million spread over three years.[5]

Lucy Morris, the plant manager at Merseyside, told James Fawn that she preferred to "wait and see" before entertaining a technology upgrade at her plant because there was considerable uncertainty in her mind as to how valuable, if at all, the analog technology would prove to be. Fawn agreed that the Japanese technology had not been tested with much of the machinery that was currently being used at Rotterdam and Merseyside. Moreover, he knew that reported efficiency gains had varied substantially across the early adopters.[6]

---

[5] If the Merseyside project were to begin two years later, the cost of the contract and the investment costs were expected to rise by the rate of inflation. Gas contracts were quoted in terms of the first-year cost but carried an inflation clause that raised the cost for each subsequent year by the inflation rate.

[6] Using Monte Carlo simulation, Morris had estimated that the cash returns from the Japanese technology had a standard deviation of 35%. The nominal risk-free rate of return was about 5.5%.

Conclusion

Fawn wanted to give this choice careful thought because the plant managers at Merseyside and Rotterdam seemed to have so much invested in their own proposals. He wished that the capital-budgeting criteria would give a straightforward indication of the relative attractiveness of the two mutually exclusive projects. He wondered by what rational analytical process he could extricate himself from the ambiguities of the present measures of investment attractiveness. Moreover, he wished he had a way to evaluate the primary technological difference between the two proposals: (1) the Rotterdam project, which firmly committed Victoria Chemicals to the new-process technology, or (2) the Merseyside project, which retained the flexibility to add the technology in the future.

EXHIBIT 21.1 | Analysis of Rotterdam Project (financial values in GBP millions)

Assumptions

Annual Output (metric tons)	250,000	Discount Rate	10.0%
Output Gain Per Year/Prior Year	2.0%	Depreciable Life (years)	15
Maximum Possible Output	267,500	Overhead/Investment	0.0%
Price/Ton (pounds sterling)	675	Salvage Value	0
Inflation (prices and costs)	0.0%	WIP Inventory/Cost of Goods Sold	3.0%
Gross Margin Growth Rate/Year	0.50%	Terminal Value of Right-of-Way	40
Maximum Possible Gross Margin	15.0%	Months Downtime, Construction	2008 — 5
Gross Margin	11.5%		2009 — 4
Tax Rate	30.0%		2010 — 3
Investment Outlay (millions)	Now — 3.5		2011 — 0
	2008 — 5		
	2009 — 1		
	2010 — 1		

Year	0 Now	1 2008	2 2009	3 2010	4 2011	5 2012	6 2013	7 2014	8 2015	9 2016	10 2017	11 2018	12 2019	13 2020	14 2021	15 2022
1. Estimate of Incremental Gross Profit																
New Output (tons)		255,000	260,100	265,302	267,500	267,500	267,500	267,500	267,500	267,500	267,500	267,500	267,500	267,500	267,500	267,500
Lost Output—Construction		(106,250)	(86,700)	(66,326)												
New Sales (Millions)		100.41	117.05	134.31	180.56	180.56	180.56	180.56	180.56	180.56	180.56	180.56	180.56	180.56	180.56	180.56
New Gross Margin		11.5%	12.0%	12.5%	13.0%	13.5%	14.0%	14.5%	15.0%	15.0%	15.0%	15.0%	15.0%	15.0%	15.0%	15.0%
New Gross Profit		11.55	14.05	16.79	23.47	24.38	25.28	26.18	27.08	27.08	27.08	27.08	27.08	27.08	27.08	27.08
Old Output		250,000	250,000	250,000	250,000	250,000	250,000	250,000	250,000	250,000	250,000	250,000	250,000	250,000	250,000	250,000
Old Sales		168.75	168.75	168.75	168.75	168.75	168.75	168.75	168.75	168.75	168.75	168.75	168.75	168.75	168.75	168.75
Old Gross Profit		19.41	19.41	19.41	19.41	19.41	19.41	19.41	19.41	19.41	19.41	19.41	19.41	19.41	19.41	19.41
Incremental Gross Profit		(7.86)	(5.36)	(2.62)	4.07	4.97	5.87	6.78	7.68	7.68	7.68	7.68	7.68	7.68	7.68	7.68
2. Estimate of Incremental Depreciation																
Yr. 1 Outlays		0.67	0.58	0.50	0.43	0.38	0.33	0.28	0.24	0.23	0.23	0.23	0.23	0.23	0.23	0.23
Yr. 2 Outlays			0.14	0.12	0.10	0.09	0.08	0.07	0.06	0.05	0.05	0.05	0.05	0.05	0.05	0.05
Yr. 3 Outlays				0.15	0.13	0.11	0.09	0.08	0.07	0.06	0.05	0.05	0.05	0.05	0.05	0.05
Total, New Depreciation		0.67	0.72	0.78	0.67	0.58	0.50	0.43	0.37	0.33	0.33	0.33	0.33	0.33	0.33	0.33
3. Overhead		0	0	0	0	0	0	0	0	0	0	0	0	0	0	0
4. Pretax Incremental Profit		(8.53)	(6.08)	(3.39)	3.40	4.39	5.38	6.35	7.31	7.35	7.35	7.35	7.35	7.35	7.35	7.35
5. Tax Expense		(2.56)	(1.82)	(1.02)	1.02	1.32	1.61	1.90	2.19	2.20	2.21	2.21	2.21	2.21	2.21	2.21
6. Aftertax Profit		(5.97)	(4.26)	(2.38)	2.38	3.08	3.76	4.44	5.12	5.14	5.15	5.15	5.15	5.15	5.15	5.15
7. Cash Flow Adjustments																
Add Back Depreciation		0.67	0.72	0.78	0.67	0.58	0.50	0.43	0.37	0.33	0.33	0.33	0.33	0.33	0.33	0.33
Less Added WIP Inventory		1.81	(0.42)	(0.44)	(1.19)	—	—	—	—	—	—	—	—	—	—	—
Less Capital Spending	(3.50)	(5.00)	(1.00)	(1.00)												
Terminal Value, Land																40.0
8. Free Cash Flow	(3.50)	(8.49)	(4.96)	(3.03)	1.86	3.68	4.29	4.90	5.51	5.47	5.47	5.47	5.47	5.47	5.47	45.60

DCF, Rotterdam = 15.50
IRR, Rotterdam = 18.0%

270

Year	0 Now	1 2008	2 2009	3 2010	4 2011	5 2012	6 2013	7 2014	8 2015	9 2016	10 2017	11 2018	12 2019	13 2020	14 2021	15 2022
9. Adjustment for Erosion in Merseyside Volume:																
Lost Merseyside Output		—	—	—	17,500	17,500	17,500	17,500	17,500	17,500	17,500	17,500	17,500	17,500	17,500	17,500
Lost Merseyside Revenue		—	—	—	11.81	11.81	11.81	11.81	11.81	11.81	11.81	11.81	11.81	11.81	11.81	11.81
Lost Merseyside Gross Profits		—	—	—	1.36	1.36	1.36	1.36	1.36	1.36	1.36	1.36	1.36	1.36	1.36	1.36
Lost Gross Profits After Taxes		—	—	—	0.95	0.95	0.95	0.95	0.95	0.95	0.95	0.95	0.95	0.95	0.95	0.95
Change in Merseyside Inventory		—	—	—	0.35	0.35	0.35	0.35	0.35	0.35	0.35	0.35	0.35	0.35	0.35	0.35
Total Effect on Free Cash Flow	**3.05**	—	—	—	(0.60)	(0.60)	(0.60)	(0.60)	(0.60)	(0.60)	(0.60)	(0.60)	(0.60)	(0.60)	(0.60)	(0.60)
DCF, Erosion Merseyside	(3.50)	(8.49)	(4.96)	(3.03)												
Cash Flows After Erosion					1.26	3.08	3.69	4.30	4.92	4.88	4.88	4.88	4.88	4.88	4.88	45.00
DCF, Rotterdam Adjusted for Full Erosion at Merseyside =	**12.45**															
IRR	16.5%															

Source: Created by author.

The Procter & Gamble Company: Investment in Crest Whitestrips Advanced Seal

It was May 2008, and Jackson Christopher, a financial analyst for the Procter & Gamble Company's (P&G) North America Oral Care (NAOC) group, hustled along a sunny downtown Cincinnati street on his way to work. NAOC's Crest teeth whitening group was considering the launch of an extension to its Whitestrips product, and the project had dominated most of his working hours. At least he avoided a long commute by living downtown.

The week before, the group had met to consider the merits of the proposed product, known as Crest Advanced Seal. Although openly intrigued by the concept, Angela Roman, the group's general manager (GM), was reserving judgment until she had a clearer picture of the idea and risks. She had tasked Christopher with putting together the economic perspective on Advanced Seal, an effort that had required a lot of work amalgamating all the different considerations and thinking through the financial implications. In the process, he had had to manage a lot of different constituencies. In short, it had been an interesting week, and with the follow-up meeting the next day, Christopher knew he needed to present some conclusions.

The Procter & Gamble Company

P&G was one of the world's premier consumer goods companies. Its 2007 total revenue exceeded $72 billion and came from almost every corner of the globe. P&G's wide range of brands focused on beauty, grooming, and household care and delivered

This case was prepared by Daniel Lentz (Procter & Gamble) and Michael J. Schill, Robert F. Vandell Research Associate Professor of Business Administration. The individuals and figures in this case have been fictionalized. All narrative details and economics are purely fictional and are not intended to be used for a real assessment of the Crest Whitestrips business. Copyright © 2012 by the University of Virginia Darden School Foundation, Charlottesville, VA. All rights reserved. *To order copies, send an e-mail to* sales@dardenbusinesspublishing.com. *No part of this publication may be reproduced, stored in a retrieval system, used in a spreadsheet, or transmitted in any form or by any means—electronic, mechanical, photocopying, recording, or otherwise—without the permission of the Darden School Foundation.*

a broad array of products from fragrances to batteries and medication to toothpaste (**Exhibit 22.1**).

P&G was an aggressive competitor in its market, seeking to deliver total shareholder returns in the top one-third of its peer group (**Exhibit 22.2**). Management achieved these returns by following a strategy to reach more consumers (by extending category portfolios vertically into higher and lower value tiers) in more parts of the world (by expanding geographically into category whitespaces) more completely (by improving existing products and extending portfolios into adjacent categories).

NAOC's portfolio consisted of seven different product lines: toothpaste, manual toothbrushes, power toothbrushes, oral rinses, dental floss, denture adhesives and cleansers, and teeth whitening strips. Leveraging the collective benefit of multiple products enabled P&G to focus on more complete oral health solutions for consumers. NAOC followed the corporate strategy by, among other things, expanding the global toothpaste presence under the Oral-B brand and to multiple adjacencies under the 3D White brand. At the heart of the portfolio, representing more than $5 billion in annual sales, was the Crest brand.

Crest Whitestrips and the context for Advanced Seal

Crest Whitestrips, an at-home tooth enamel whitening treatment launched in 2001, allowed consumers to achieve whitening results that rivaled far more expensive dental office treatments. Existing whitening toothpastes had worked by polishing surface stains from the tooth enamel, but they were unable to change the fundamental color of teeth. Whitestrips worked through a strip applied temporarily to the teeth, binding the product to surface enamel and actually whitening the layer of dentin beneath the enamel itself. The intrinsic whitening results were unique to the category.

On its introduction, Crest Whitestrips saw nearly $300 million in annual sales but virtually no growth in sales or profits after the first year (**Exhibit 22.3**). Multiple attempts at line extensions had failed to significantly improve results, only managing to breed skepticism in major customers. Competitors that entered the category either left shortly thereafter or encountered the same stagnant sales as had P&G. (**Exhibit 22.4** documents the category history.)

The commercial team believed that, to turn around the business's lackluster performance and win back trust and merchandising support, something fundamental had to change. Advanced Seal, the extension under consideration, was based on a new technology that prevented the strips from slipping out of position during use. Because the new product binded with teeth more reliably, the active ingredient was delivered more effectively, improving both the usage experience and the whitening results, which were superior to any existing product on the market. **Exhibit 22.5** provides the proposed packaging for the product.

With an extremely strong market share position (**Figure 22.1**), the Whitestrips team had to manage any new launch carefully; future success had to be as much a function of P&L accretion as of increasing competitive share. The business rarely saw

FIGURE 22.1 | Market share of the teeth whitening category, 2008.

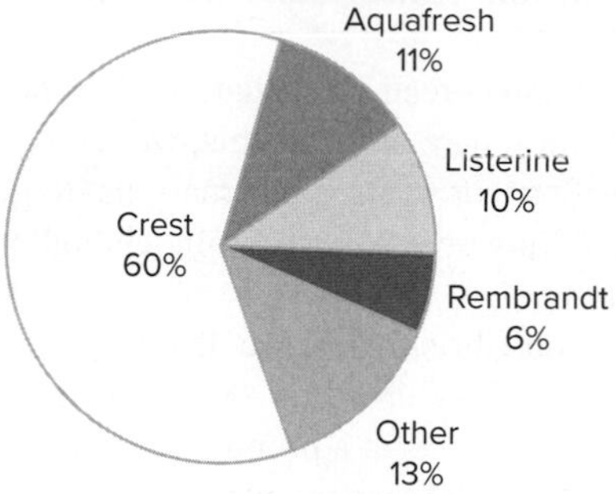

Source: Created by author

household penetration figures any higher than 3%[1], so there were plenty of new consumers to target.

Last Week's Meeting

The previous week, NAOC members had gathered in a conference room to consider the proposed launch of Advanced Seal. As the meeting had progressed, the group had strained to gauge the GM's reaction to the concept.

"I follow you so far," said Roman. "I have questions, but I don't want to derail you, Christina. Keep going."

Even among other brand managers, Christina Whitman was known for her energy and enthusiasm, which was saying something.

"Consumer research has been clear," Whitman asserted briskly. "The tendency of Whitestrips to slip off teeth is the number one barrier to repeat purchase and word-of-mouth recommendation. Advanced Seal's new technology will address this concern, providing a real jolt of energy to the whitening category and a strong sales lift in the process."

"We see pricing this innovation at the high end of our range, which should drive up trade in our portfolio and improve market share. The product improvement gives us creative advertising and positioning opportunities to leverage as well. We definitely think we should move forward."

Roman sat back in her chair and exhaled thoughtfully. "What's the downside scenario here, everyone?"

Hector Toro, the account executive, cleared his throat. "I'm worried about whether we can count on getting the merchandising support we'll need to get this off to a good start. For the product to catch on, we'll need to get out of the gates fast,

---

[1]*Household penetration* (HHP) tracked the percentage of a given market of households that had purchased a product within the last year. Whitestrips traditionally had very low HHP, whereas toothpaste had HHP of virtually 100%.

and a lot of retailers are still frustrated about the mediocre velocity of our last line extension. If they don't get behind this, it won't be successful no matter what we do."

Whitman agreed immediately. "To show them we're committed to pulling consumers to the oral care aisle for this, we really need to adequately fund marketing. We also need to allow for strong trade margins[2] to get us display space and offset the high carrying cost of this inventory. It's a much higher price point than buyers are used to carrying in inventory."

Jackson Christopher, the data floating in his head from hours of study, saw an opportunity to bring up some of his concerns. "That may not be as straightforward as it sounds. Pricing this at a premium is one thing, but can we price it high enough to cover the costs of the improvements?"

This was the first Roman had heard of this potential issue. "Say more about that. I agree with Christina in principle, but what are the preliminary economics we're looking at here?"

"Oh, we'll be able to price this up, for sure," he replied. "We could charge a 25% premium without having a precipitous drop in volume. The problem is that this product improvement will drive up our costs by almost 75%. That could easily dilute our margins. We could end up making less gross profit on this product than on our current Premium product line. If we're not careful, the more this product takes off, the worse off we'll be."

"But even so," Whitman interjected, "we're confident that we'll pick up so much incremental volume that we'll be net better off anyway." Whitman knew Christopher's concerns were valid but didn't want them to kill the idea prematurely.

"What do you think, Margaret?" asked Roman, turning to Margaret Tan, a market researcher.

"I think the real answer is probably somewhere in the middle," Tan replied. "I don't think we'll be able to price this high enough to offset the costs, but we probably will pick up a lot of new volume. Whether we'll be net better off depends on bringing in enough new users to the category to offset profit dilution from the cost structure."

Everyone was silent as Roman took a few moments to think it over. "Alright then," she said. "I'm OK to proceed at this point. I like the idea. We need to be looking for ways to delight our consumers. This product improvement really is huge for this consumer; we know that she's been complaining about Whitestrips slipping off her teeth for quite some time. But we need to find ways to meet her needs while preserving our core structural economics.

"If I'm following your logic, Christina, you're saying we'll sell enough incremental units to end up net better off, even with the margin dilution. That can happen sometimes, but I've been doing this long enough to know that's a risky strategy. That said, we need a jolt to drive top-line sales on this category. I may be willing to take that risk, but there must be enough of a top-line opportunity to make it interesting."

---

[2]*Trade margins* were the gross profit margins retailers made on any product they sold, the difference between the shelf price and the list price paid to product manufacturers. In general, the higher the shelf price (determined by the retailer), the higher the trade margin requirement to retailers.

She turned to Christopher. "I'm going to need you to set our baseline here. There are a lot of moving pieces, and I need you to paint the picture on how this comes together. Does this pay out for our business? Are we financially better off launching this product or not, what are the risks, what do we need to be thinking about as we design this? Work with marketing, sales, manufacturing, and market research to pull together the overall picture in the next week or so. We'll get back together and decide where to go from here."

Christopher agreed, and the meeting wrapped up.

Establishing a Base Case

Christopher's initial analysis established the expected price point for retailers at $22 per unit for Advanced Seal, compared to $18 and $13 per unit for P&G's Premium and Basic offering, respectively. Christopher had worked with his supply chain leaders to estimate the cost structure. The new technology would run at a cost of $5 per unit cost more than the current Premium product offering, such that the gross profit for Advanced Seal would be lower than for Premium. **Exhibit 22.6** provides the summary assessments that had coalesced regarding the unit price and cost for the Crest Whitestrips products.

The forecasting models suggested a base case annual forecast of 2 million units for Advanced Seal. The analysis also suggested that cannibalization of existing Crest Whitestrips products would be high, on the order of 50% to 60% for Premium units and 15% for Basic units. Such cannibalization rates meant that 65% to 75% of Advanced Seal's 2 million expected units was coming straight out of existing P&G sales.

Preliminary discussions around advertising spending indicated an expected launch budget of $6 million per year. He estimated that the cannibalized Premium and Basic products already received $4 million per year in advertising support that would no longer be required after the launch. This meant the group would have to spend an incremental $2 million in advertising to support the launch. He also needed to include $1 million per year for incremental selling, general, and administrative expenses.

Based on the amount of time R&D felt it would take a competitor to match the product innovation, Christopher expected a project life of four years, over which time annual unit sales were expected to be relatively constant. For this type of decision, P&G used an 8% discount rate and a 40% tax rate. Manufacturing partners expected to spend $4 million in capital expenditures and incur $1.5 million in one-time development expenses to get the project going. Regarding capital expenditure depreciation, he conferred with an accounting team, which recommended the five-year accelerated schedule for tax purposes and the straight-line schedule for reporting purposes.[3] Engineering indicated that the equipment likely would need to be replaced at the end of the project life, and they did not expect it to have any residual value.

Christopher also knew that he had to factor in any incremental working capital required to support the project. For the Whitestrips business, net working capital turnover

---

[3]Five-year accelerated depreciation specified by the U.S. tax authority (IRS) was calculated by multiplying the amount of investment by the following percentages for each respective year, 20% in Year 1, 32% in Year 2, 19.2% in Year 3, 11.52% in Year 4, 11.52% in Year 5, and 5.76% in Year 6.

typically ran at a rate of between 8 and 10 times.[4] The project would require that at least this amount be on hand prior to the market launch date. It was P&G's policy to model the recovery of any working capital investment at the end of the project life.

Proposal to Drive Revenue

Later that week, as Christopher rubbed his eyes to remove the imprint of a spreadsheet from his vision, Whitman popped her head into his cube. "I came to see where the steam was coming from. I guess from your ears."

Christopher chuckled. "The math isn't really complicated, but the results all depend on what you assume. I just need to make sure I think through everything the right way." He was getting close to wrapping up his work, but he knew that when Whitman came by unannounced and excited, it meant her creative wheels were turning and that she was looking for more advertising dollars.

"I had some great buzz-creation ideas that I think we can use for the launch," she said, her voice lowering. "I'm envisioning some digital campaigns that I think could go viral, and I'm also interested in expanding our initial media plan. We have such low household penetration numbers that, if we drive a change in launch plans, we could focus a great deal more on driving trial. According to Margaret, one problem with trial is that we're really at the high end of the price range. She thinks a small drop in price could really accelerate sales."

"That makes sense, assuming this consumer is as elastic as Margaret says. What kind of numbers are we talking about?"

"I'm going to need my starting advertising budget to go from $6 million to $7.5 million in Year 1. I can then go back to $6 million per year after that. Next, we reduce price by $1 to $21 for Advanced Seal. Margaret thinks those two effects will drive annual unit sales up 1.25 million to 3.25 million units per year."

"Sounds impressive. Let me take a look, and I'll let you know where we land."

"Thanks! We all know that Roman is looking for bigger revenue dollars from Whitestrips and my calculations suggest this will certainly deliver big revenue gains for the group."

Proposal to Minimize Cannibalization

The next day, Christopher thought he had figured out what he would recommend to Roman, and he had a good risk profile built for the team to design and sell against. Just as he was starting to relax, Tan entered his cube.

"This can't be good," Christopher said preemptively.

Tan sighed. "Yes and no. I've gone back and reworked the volume forecast for Christina's initiative. We have the potential for a more severe cannibalization problem than we originally thought. It's not certain, but there is greater likelihood that we end up sourcing more of the incremental volume from our current Premium products."

---

[4]The net working capital turnover ratio was defined as Revenue divided by Net Working Capital, where Net Working Capital was equal to Current Assets less Non-Interest-Bearing Current Liabilities.

"How much of an increase are we talking about here?"

"I expect the price reduction and extra advertising to expand the range of cannibalization rates on Premium to between 50% and 65%."

"All right, that might not be so bad. I need to look at the financials to be sure though."

"Well, in case it is, we've worked up an alternative strategy." Tan continued. "The alternative is to pivot to a more conservative position, to minimize cannibalization by reducing the launch advertising splash and focusing the marketing on untapped customers. In doing so, we'll have less of a broad appeal than we thought. More of a niche. We'd be prioritizing cannibalization over trial. Our thought was to also offset the gross profit differential by raising price to $23, giving Advanced Seal an $11 gross profit. It's clearly not what Christina was hoping for, but it's a choice that we have. Essentially, instead of dropping the price, raise it a little."

Together, they agreed on the final assumptions. The advertising budget would be reduced by $1 million each year, to $5 million. The sales model predicted that the effect on Advanced Seal units would be strong with unit sales declining to just 1 million per year. The changes would also reduce the cannibalization rate for Premium to a more certain rate of 45%.

The Recommendation

Christopher still needed to figure out how to convert all this data into a realistic P&L for the initiative and find the baseline net present value. Beyond that, he needed to determine what the team needed to do to mold this opportunity into a winning proposition for P&G shareholders. He agreed with Whitman that this was an exciting technology, but he had to make sure that any decision would give investors something to smile about.

EXHIBIT 22.1 | Procter & Gamble Brands

Beauty and Grooming

Always	Anna Sui	Aussie
Braun	Camay	Christina Aguilera Perfumes
Clairol Professional	CoverGirl	Crest
DDF	Dolce & Gabbana Cosmetics	Dolce & Gabbana Fragrances
Dunhill Fragrances	Escada Fragrances	Fekkai
Fusion	Ghost	Gillette
Gucci Fragrances	Hugo Boss Fragrances	Head & Shoulders
Herbal Essences	Ivory	Lacoste Fragrances
MACH3	Naomi Campbell	Natural Instincts
Nice 'n Easy	Nioxin	Olay
Old Spice	Oral-B	Pantene
Pert	Prestobarba/Blue	Puma
Rejoice	SK-II	Safeguard
Scope	Sebastian Professional	Secret
Tampax	Venus	Vidal Sassoon
Wella		

Household Care

Ace	Align	Ariel
Bold	Bounce	Bounty
Cascade	Charmin	Cheer
Comet	Dash	Dawn
Downy	Dreft Laundry	Duracell
Era	Eukanuba	Febreze
Gain	Iams	Joy
Luvs	Metamucil	Mr. Clean
Pampers	Pepto-Bismol	Prilosec OTC
Pringles	Puffs	Swiffer
Tide	Vicks	

EXHIBIT 22.2 | Value of $1 Invested in P&G Stock and the S&P 500 Index, 2001 to 2008

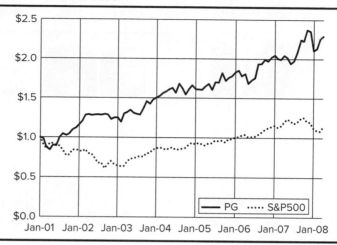

Data source: Yahoo! Finance.

EXHIBIT 22.3 | Crest Whitestrips' Revenue and After-Tax Profit Since 2001 Launch (in millions of dollars)

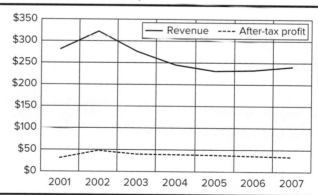

Note: Data is disguised.

EXHIBIT 22.4 | Whitening Category History

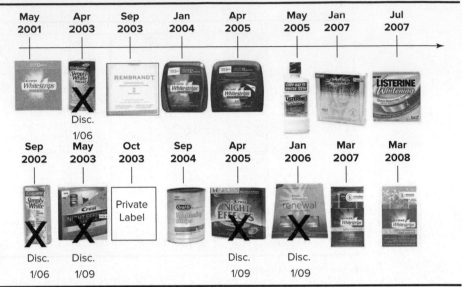

Image source: Procter & Gamble Company. Used with permission.

EXHIBIT 22.5 | Crest Whitestrips' Advanced Seal Packaging

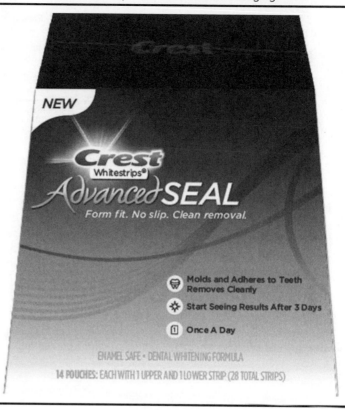

Image source: Procter & Gamble Company. Used with permission.

EXHIBIT 22.6 | Gross Profit Comparison

	Advanced Seal	Premium Product	Basic Product
Per unit revenue and costs			
Revenue	$22	$18	$13
Cost of goods sold expenses	$12	$7	$6
Gross profit	$10	$11	$7

Note: Data is disguised.

The Jacobs Division 2010

Richard Soderberg, financial analyst for the Jacobs Division of MacFadden Chemical Company, was reviewing several complex issues related to possible investment in a new product for the following year—2011. The product was a specialty coating material that qualified for investment according to company guidelines. But Jacobs Division Manager Mark Reynolds was fearful that it might be too risky. While regarding the project as an attractive opportunity, Soderberg believed that the only practical way to sell the product in the short run would place it in a weak competitive position over the long run. He was also concerned that the estimates used in the probability analysis were little better than educated guesses.

Company Background

MacFadden Chemical Company was one of the larger chemical firms in the world whose annual sales were in excess of $10 billion. Its volume had grown steadily at the rate of 10% per year throughout the 1980s until 1993; sales and earnings had grown more rapidly. Beginning in 1993, the chemical industry began to experience overcapacity, particularly in basic materials, which led to price cutting. Also, for firms to remain competitive, more funds had to be spent in marketing and research. As a consequence of the industry problems, MacFadden achieved only modest growth of 4% in sales in the 1990s and experienced an overall decline in profits. Certain shortages began developing in the economy in 2002, however, and by 2009, sales had risen 60% and profits over 100%, as a result of price increases and near-capacity operations. Most observers believed that the "shortage boom" would be only a short respite from the intensely competitive conditions of the last decade.

The 11 operating divisions of MacFadden were organized into three groups. Most divisions had a number of products centered on one chemical, such as fluoride, sulfur, or petroleum. The Jacobs Division was an exception.

This revised and updated case, based on "The Jacobs Division" by Professors Diana Harrington and Robert Vandell, was prepared by Professor Robert M. Conroy. It was written as a basis for class discussion rather than to illustrate effective or ineffective handling of an administrative situation. Copyright © 2003 by the University of Virginia Darden School Foundation, Charlottesville, VA. All rights reserved. *To order copies, send an e-mail to* sales@dardenbusinesspublishing.com. *No part of this publication may be reproduced, stored in a retrieval system, used in a spreadsheet, or transmitted in any form or by any means— electronic, mechanical, photocopying, recording, or otherwise—without the permission of the Darden School Foundation.*

It was the newest and—with sales of $100 million—the smallest division. Its products were specialty industrial products with various chemical bases, such as dyes, adhesives, and finishes, which were sold in relatively small lots to diverse industrial customers. No single product had sales over $5 million, and many had sales of only $500,000. There were 150 basic products in the division, each of which had several minor variations. Jacobs was one of MacFadden's more rapidly growing divisions—12% per year prior to 2009—with a 13% return on total net assets.

Capital Budgeting for New Projects

Corporate-wide guidelines were used for analyzing new investment opportunities. In the current environment, the long-term, risk-free rate was about 6%. At the firm level, the return criteria were 8% for cost-reduction projects, 12% for expansion of facilities, and 16% for new products or processes. Returns were measured in terms of discounted cash flows after taxes. Soderberg believed that these rates and methods were typical of those used throughout the chemical industry.

Reynolds tended, however, to demand higher returns for projects in his division, even though its earnings–growth stability in the past marked it as one of MacFadden's more reliable operations. Reynolds had three reasons for wanting better returns than corporate required. First, one of the key variables used in appraising management performance and compensation at MacFadden was the growth of residual income, although such aspects as market share and profit margins were also considered.[1] Reynolds did not like the idea of investing in projects that were close to the target rate of earnings embedded in the residual-income calculation.

Second, many new projects had high start-up costs. Even though they might achieve attractive returns over the long run, such projects hurt earnings performance in the short run. "Don't tell me what a project's discount rate of return is. Tell me whether we're going to improve our return on total net assets within three years," Reynolds would say. Third, Reynolds was skeptical of estimates. "I don't know what's going to happen here on this project, but I'll bet we overstate returns by 2% to 5%, on average," was a typical comment. He therefore tended to look for at least 4% more than the company standard before becoming enthusiastic about a project. "You've got to be hard-nosed about taking risk," he said. "By demanding a decent return for riskier opportunities, we have a better chance to grow and prosper."

Soderberg knew that Reynolds's views were reflected in decisions throughout the division. Projects that did not have promising returns, according to Reynolds's standards, were often dropped or shelved early in the decision process. Soderberg guessed that, at Jacobs Division, almost as many projects with returns meeting the company hurdle rates were abandoned as were ultimately approved. In fact, the projects that were finally submitted to Reynolds were usually so promising that he rarely rejected them. Capital projects from his division were accepted virtually unchanged, unless top management happened to be unusually pessimistic about prospects for business and financing in general.

---

[1] Residual income was the division's profit after allocated taxes minus a 10% capital charge on total assets after depreciation.

The Silicone-X Project

A new product was often under study for several years after research had developed a "test-tube" idea. The product had to be evaluated relative to market needs and competition. The large number of possible applications of any product complicated this analysis. At the same time, technological studies were undertaken to examine such factors as material sources, plant location, manufacturing-process alternatives, and economies of scale. While a myriad of feasible alternatives existed, only a few could be actively explored, and they often required outlays of several hundred thousand dollars before the potential of the project could be ascertained. "For every dollar of new capital approved, I bet we spend $0.30 on the opportunities," said Soderberg, "and that doesn't count the money we spend on research."

The project that concerned Soderberg at the moment was called Silicone-X, a special-purpose coating that added slipperiness to a surface. The coating could be used on a variety of products to reduce friction, particularly where other lubricants might imperfectly eliminate friction between moving parts. Its uniqueness lay in its hardness, adhesiveness to the applied surface, and durability. The product was likely to have a large number of buyers, but most of them could use only small quantities: Only a few firms were likely to buy amounts greater than 5,000 pounds per year.

Test-tube batches of Silicone-X had been tested both inside and outside the Jacobs Division. Comments were universally favorable, although $2.00 per pound seemed to be the maximum price that would be acceptable. Lower prices were considered unlikely to produce larger volume. For planning purposes, a price of $1.90 per pound had been used.

Demand was difficult to estimate because of the variety of possible applications. The division's market research group had estimated a first-year demand of 1 to 2 million pounds with 1.2 million pounds was cited as most likely. Soderberg said:

> They could spend another year studying it and be more confident, but we wouldn't find them more believable. The estimates are educated guesses by smart people. But they are also pretty wild stabs in the dark. They won't rule out the possibility of demand as low as 500,000 pounds, and 2 million pounds is not the ceiling.

Soderberg empathized with the problem facing the market-research group. "They tried to do a systematic job of looking at the most probable applications, but the data were not good." The market researchers believed that, once the product became established, average demand would probably grow at a healthy rate, perhaps 10% per year. But the industries served were likely to be cyclical with volume requirements swinging 20% depending on market conditions. The market researchers concluded, "We think demand should level off after 8 to 10 years, but the odds are very much against someone developing a cheaper or markedly superior substitute."

On the other hand, there was no patent protection on Silicone-X, and the technological know-how involved in the manufacturing process could be duplicated by others in perhaps as little as 12 months. "This product is essentially a commodity, and someone is certainly going to get interested in it when sales volume reaches $3 million," said Soderberg.

The cost estimates looked solid. Soderberg continued, "Basic chemicals, of course, fluctuate in purchase price, but we have a captive source with stable manufacturing costs. We can probably negotiate a long-term transfer price with Wilson [another MacFadden division], although this is not the time to do so."

Project Analysis

In his preliminary analysis, Soderberg used a discount rate of 20% and a project life of 15 years, because most equipment for the project was likely to wear out and need replacement during that time frame. He said:

> We also work with most likely estimates. Until we get down to the bitter end, there are too many alternatives to consider, and we can't afford probabilistic measures or fancy simulations. A conservative definition of most likely values is good enough for most of the subsidiary analyses. We've probably made over 200 present value calculations using our computer programs just to get to this decision point, and heaven knows how many quick-and-dirty paybacks.
>
> We've made a raft of important decisions that affect the attractiveness of this project. Some of them are bound to be wrong. I hope not critically so. In any case, these decisions are behind us. They're buried so deep in the assumptions, no one can find them, and top management wouldn't have time to look at them anyway.

With Silicone-X, Soderberg was down to a labor-intensive, limited-capacity approach and a capital-intensive method. "The analyses all point in one direction," he said, "but I have the feeling it's going to be the worst one for the long run."

The labor-intensive method involved an initial plant and equipment outlay of $900,000. It could produce 1.5 million pounds per year.

According to Soderberg:

> Even if the project bombs out, we won't lose much. The equipment is very adaptable. We could find uses for about half of it. We could probably sell the balance for $200,000, and let our tax write-offs cover most of the rest. We should salvage the working-capital part without any trouble. The start-up costs and losses are our real risks. We'll spend $50,000 debugging the process, and we'll be lucky to satisfy half the possible demand. But I believe we can get this project on stream in one year's time.

Exhibit 23.1 shows Soderberg's analysis of the labor-intensive alternative. His calculations showed a small net present value when discounted at 20% and a sizable net present value at 8%. When the positive present values were compared with the negative present values, the project looked particularly attractive.

The capital-intensive method involved a much larger outlay for plant and equipment: $3.3 million. Manufacturing costs would, however, be reduced by $0.35 per unit and fixed costs by $100,000, excluding depreciation. The capital-intensive plant was designed to handle 2.0 million pounds, the lowest volume for which appropriate equipment could be acquired. Since the equipment was more specialized, only $400,000 of this machinery could be used in other company activities. The balance probably had a salvage value of $800,000. It would take two years to get the plant on line, and the first year's operating volume was likely to be low—perhaps 700,000 pounds at the most. Debugging costs were estimated to be $100,000.

Exhibit 23.2 presents Soderberg's analysis of the capital-intensive method. At a 20% discount rate, the capital-intensive project had a large negative present value and thus appeared much worse than the labor-intensive alternative. But at an 8% discount rate, it looked significantly better than the labor-intensive alternative.

Problems in the Analysis

Several things concerned Soderberg about the analysis. Reynolds would only look at the total return. Thus, the capital-intensive project would not be acceptable. Yet, on the basis of the breakeven analysis, the capital-intensive alternative seemed the safest way to start. It needed sales of just 369,333 pounds to break even, while the labor-intensive method required 540,000 pounds (**Exhibit 23.3**).

Soderberg was concerned that future competition might result in price-cutting. If the price per pound fell by $0.20, the labor-intensive method would not break even unless 900,000 pounds were sold. Competitors could, once the market was established, build a capital-intensive plant that would put them in a good position to cut prices by $0.20 or more. In short, there was a risk, given the labor-intensive solution, that Silicone-X might not remain competitive. The better the demand proved to be, the more serious this risk would become. Of course, once the market was established, Jacobs could build a capital-intensive facility, but almost none of the labor-intensive equipment would be useful in such a new plant. The new plant would still cost $3.3 million, and Jacobs would have to write off losses on the labor-intensive facility.

The labor-intensive facility would be difficult to expand economically. It would cost $125,000 for each 200,000 pounds of additional capacity. It was only practical in 200,000-pound increments). In contrast, an additional 100,000 pounds of capacity in the capital-intensive unit could be added for $75,000.

The need to expand, however, would depend on sales. If demand remained low, the project would probably return a higher rate under the labor-intensive method. If demand developed, the capital-intensive method would clearly be superior. This analysis led Soderberg to believe that his breakeven calculations were somehow wrong.

Pricing strategy was another important element in the analysis. At $1.90 per pound, Jacobs could be inviting competition. Competitors would be satisfied with a low rate of return, perhaps 12%, in an established market. At a price lower than $1.90, Jacobs might discourage competition. Even the labor-intensive alternative would not provide a rate of return of 20% at any lower price. It began to appear to Soderberg that using a high discount rate was forcing the company to make a riskier decision than would a lower rate; it was also increasing the chance of realizing a lower rate of return than had been forecast.

Soderberg was not sure how to incorporate pricing into his analysis. He knew he could determine what level of demand would be necessary to encourage a competitor, expecting a 50% share and needing a 12% return on a capital-intensive investment, to enter the market at a price of $1.70, or $1.90, but this analysis did not seem to be enough.

Finally, Soderberg was concerned about the volatility of demand estimates on which he had based the analysis. He reviewed some analysts' reports and found some information on firms that were in businesses similar to Silicone-X. Based on those firms' stock market returns he estimated that the volatility of returns for this line of business was around 0.35.

Soderberg's job was to analyze the alternatives fully and to recommend one of them to Reynolds. On the simplest analysis, the labor-intensive approach seemed best. Even at 20%, its present value was positive. That analysis, however, did not take other factors into consideration.

EXHIBIT 23.1 | Analysis of Labor-Intensive Alternative for Silicone-X
(dollars in thousands, except per-unit data)

		Year				
	0	**1**	**2**	**3**	**4**	**5–15**
Investments						
Plant and equipment	$ 900					
Change in NWC		$ 140	$ 14	$ 15	$ 17	$ 20
Demand (thousands of pounds)		1,200	1,320	1,452	1,597	N.A.
Capacity (thousands of pounds)		600	1,500	1,500	1,500	1,500
Sales (thousands of pounds)		600	1,320	1,452	1,500	1,500
Sales price/unit		$1.90	$1.90	$1.90	$1.90	$1.90
Variable costs/unit						
Manufacturing		1.30	1.30	1.30	1.30	1.30
Marketing		0.10	0.10	0.10	0.10	0.10
Total variable cost/unit		1.40	1.40	1.40	1.40	1.40
Fixed costs						
Overhead		210	210	210	210	210
Depreciation		60	60	60	60	60
Start-up costs		50	0	0	0	0
Total fixed costs		320	270	270	270	270
Sales Revenue		$1,140	$2,508	$2,759	$2,850	$2,850
– Total Variable Costs		840	1,848	2,033	2,100	2,100
– Total Fixed Costs		320	270	270	270	270
Profit before taxes		(20)	390	456	480	480
– Taxes (tax rate = 50%)		10	(195)	(228)	(240)	(240)
Net operating profit after taxes (NOPAT)		(10)	195	228	240	240
Cash flow from operations						
+ Profit after taxes + depreciation		50	255	288	300	300
– Capital Expenditures	(900)	0	0	0	0	0
– Change in NWC		(140)	(14)	(15)	(17)	(20)
Free cash flow	$(900)	$ (90)	$ 241	$ 273	$ 283	280
Terminal value (year 15)						$ 381
N.A. = not available.						

Source: All exhibits created by case writer.

EXHIBIT 23.2 | Analysis of Capital-Intensive Alternative for Silicone-X
(dollars in thousands, except per-unit data)

	Year							
	0	1	2	3	4	5	6	7–15
Investments								
Plant and equipment	$ 1,900	$ 1,400						
Working capital			$ 160	$ 11	$ 17	$ 20	$ 24	$ 30
Demand (thousands of pounds)			1,320	1,452	1,597	1,757	1,933	2,125
Capacity (thousands of pounds)			700	2,000	2,000	2,000	2,000	2,000
Sales (thousands of pounds)			700	1,452	1,597	1,757	1,933	2,000
Sales price/unit			$1.90	$1.90	$1.90	$1.90	$1.90	$1.90
Variable cost/unit								
Manufacturing			0.85	0.85	0.85	0.85	0.85	0.85
Selling			0.20	0.20	0.20	0.20	0.20	0.20
Total variable cost/unit			1.05	1.05	1.05	1.05	1.05	1.05
Fixed costs								
Overhead			110	110	110	110	110	110
Depreciation			167	167	167	167	167	167
Start-up costs			100	0	0	0	0	0
Total fixed costs								
Sales Revenue			1,190	2,468	2,715	2,987	3,286	3,400
−Total Variable Costs			735	1,525	1,677	1,845	2,030	2,100
−Total Fixed Costs			377	277	277	277	277	277
Profit before taxes			8	522	601	689	786	823
−Taxes (50%)			(4)	(261)	(301)	(345)	(393)	(412)
Net operating profit after taxes (NOPAT)			4	261	301	345	393	412
Cash flow from operations								
(NOPAT + depreciation)			276	646	707	775	850	879
−Capital Expenditures	(1,900)	(1,400)	0	0	0	0	0	0
−Change in NWC			(160)	(11)	(17)	(20)	(24)	(30)
Free cash flow	$(1,900)	$(1,400)	$ 116	$ 635	$ 690	755	$ 826	849
Terminal value (year 15)								$1,384

EXHIBIT 23.3 | Breakeven Analysis for Silicone-X

	Labor-Intensive	Capital-Intensive
Normal ($1.90 price)		
Fixed costs		
Operations	$210,000	$110,000
Depreciation	60,000	167,000
Total	$270,000	$277,000
Sales price per unit	$1.90	$1.90
Variable cost per unit	$1.40	$1.05
Contribution per unit	0.50	0.85
Units to breakeven	540,000	325,882
Price competitive ($1.70 price)		
Contribution per unit	$0.30	$0.65
Units to break even	900,000	426,154

University of Virginia Health System: The Long-Term Acute Care Hospital Project

On the morning of March 2, 2006, Larry Fitzgerald knew he had to complete all the last-minute details for the board meeting the following day. Fitzgerald, the vice president for business development and finance for the University of Virginia Health System (U.Va. Health System), was eager to see the board's reaction to his proposal for a new long-term acute care (LTAC) hospital. His excitement was somewhat tempered that the board had rejected the LTAC hospital concept when Fitzgerald had first joined the U.Va. Health System in 1999. Since that time, however, the regulations regarding LTAC facilities had changed, which gave Fitzgerald reason to give the project another chance. The bottom line was that Fitzgerald thought that a LTAC hospital would improve patient care and, at the same time, bring more money into the U.Va. Health System.

As he looked at the memo on his desk from his analyst Karen Mulroney regarding the LTAC facility, Fitzgerald began to consider what guidance he could give her that would lead to the best possible proposal to present to the hospital's board of directors.

The U.Va. Health System

The University of Virginia (U.Va.) opened its first hospital in 1901, with a tripartite mission of service, education, and research. At its inception, the hospital had only 25 beds and 3 operating rooms, but by 2005, it had expanded to more than 570 beds and 24 operating rooms, with 28,000 admissions and 65,000 surgeries per year. This first hospital

This case was prepared by Nili Mehta (MBA '12) and Kenneth Eades, the Paul Tudor Jones Research Professor of Business Administration. It was written as a basis for class discussion rather than to illustrate effective or ineffective handling of an administrative situation. Some assumptions used for the analysis have been altered for pedagogical reasons. Copyright © 2012 by the University of Virginia Darden School Foundation, Charlottesville, VA. All rights reserved. *To order copies, send an e-mail to* sales@dardenbusinesspublishing.com. *No part of this publication may be reproduced, stored in a retrieval system, used in a spreadsheet, or transmitted in any form or by any means—electronic, mechanical, photocopying, recording, or otherwise—without the permission of the Darden School Foundation.*

was the only Level 1 trauma center in the area and provided care for Charlottesville residents as well as patients from across the state of Virginia and the Southeast.[1]

For each patient admitted, the hospital was reimbursed a predetermined amount by a private or public insurance company. For an open-heart surgery, for example, the hospital typically received $25,000 regardless of how many days a patient stayed in the hospital or which medications or interventions the patient needed during that time. But the cost to the hospital varied considerably based on length of stay and level of care received, which gave the hospital the incentive to help the patient recover and be discharged as quickly as possible.

Numerous studies showed that it was also in the patient's best interest to have a short stay in the hospital; longer stays put patients at risk for infections, morbidity, and mortality because there were more infectious diseases in hospitals than in patients' homes or other facilities. Lengthier hospital stays also compromised patient morale, which, in turn, was counterproductive to healing.

Like many hospital systems, U.Va.'s faced capacity issues due to its inadequate number of patient beds. The sooner it was able to discharge a patient, the sooner its staff could start caring for another; therefore, efficient patient turnover was beneficial to both patients and U.Va.

Before coming to the U.Va. Health System, Fitzgerald had been the CFO of American Medical International, a hospital ownership company that later became known as Tenet. His experience in the for-profit sector had convinced him that LTAC facilities brought value to a hospital system. Even though the idea of LTAC hospitals was relatively new in the nonprofit sector, Fitzgerald had pitched the idea for opening one when he first arrived at the U.Va. Health System in 1999. At that time, however, the regulatory system required a LTAC facility to be built within the original hospital structure. The project was rejected by the board partly because of anticipated disputes from medical service units within the hospital that would be asked to forfeit some beds to make room for the LTAC hospital. But in 2006, Fitzgerald still saw the advantages of having a LTAC facility and was certain he could justify building one within the U.Va. Hospital.

Fitzgerald knew it was critical to gain approval for adding an LTAC facility at the following day's board meeting, because the Centers for Medicare & Medicaid Services (CMS) had recently decided that, because LTAC hospitals were making so much money, they were partly responsible for driving up health care costs.[2] Reacting to this finding, the CMS had decided to put a moratorium on the establishment of new LTAC facilities beginning January 2007. For Fitzgerald, this meant that it was now or never to make his case for establishing an LTAC as part of the U.Va. Health System.

---

[1]Trauma centers were designated Level 1, 2, or 3. Level 1 centers provided the highest level of surgical care to patients.

[2]CMS was a federal agency within the U.S. Department of Health and Human Services that had a number of health-care–related responsibilities, including the determination of quality standards for long-term care facilities.

The Advantages of LTAC Hospitals

LTAC hospitals were designed to service patients who required hospital stays of 25 days or more and at least some acute care during that time. LTACs especially benefited patients who were diagnosed with infectious diseases and who needed to be weaned off ventilators, required pulmonary care or wound care, and who had critical care issues. It was often elderly patients who required these complex treatments, which were difficult to perform in a normal hospital setting.

LTAC hospitals were financially attractive to medical centers, because having one increased the amount of money available for patient care. Insurance companies reimbursed hospitals set amounts of money for each patient in its facility based on the patient's diagnosis, regardless of the time involved the patient's treatment and hospital stay. Yet if the patient was transferred to a LTAC facility, the hospital could bill insurance for the patient's stay in the hospital as well as for time spent in the LTAC. The LTAC facility also reduced patient care costs as the average daily hospital stay per patient cost more than $3,000 compared to only $1,500 per day for an LTAC.

Another advantage of an LTAC facility was that it helped address the capacity issues that the U.Va. Health System and most other hospital systems faced. By adding an LTAC facility, a hospital gained an additional 25 bed days for each patient transferred to the LTAC hospital. The average patient stay was five days in the hospital, compared to the average patient stay of 25 days in an LTAC facility. Therefore, by adding an LTAC facility, a hospital gained an additional 25 bed days for each patient transferred to the LTAC hospital. Thus, the hospital could take five more admissions for each patient transferred to an LTAC facility.

A stay in an LTAC facility had a number of advantages from the patient's perspective as well. The typical hospital setting was loud, the food could quickly become boring, and patients usually had to share rooms. Because the LTAC facility was essentially an extended-stay hospital, each patient had a private room, and the extended stay also helped a patient become more familiar with the caregivers. Fitzgerald remembered how, at one LTAC facility he had helped set up, a patient who was an avid bird watcher missed not seeing birds outside his window. To fix the problem, the staff climbed the tree outside his room and set up a bird feeder to allow him to enjoy his favorite pastime. This experience was not feasible within a regular hospital setting that often suffered from overcrowding of patients, understaffing, and an impersonal atmosphere. By contrast, patients were generally delighted with the atmosphere of an LTAC hospital with its attractive facilities, single rooms, fewer beds, and general lack of overcrowding. Higher patient morale meant a better rate of recovery and a lower rate of infection than in a typical hospital.

The U.Va. Health System comprised a large primary care network, a large hospital center, a community hospital in nearby Culpepper, a home health agency, a rehabilitation hospital, several nursing homes, an imaging center, and a physical therapy network. The LTAC facility would be another important part of the U.Va. Health System's network of care. Having all their medical care provided by U.Va. was advantageous for patients because it facilitated better communication between physicians through its electronic medical-records system.

Capital Investments at U.Va.

The U.Va. Health System's mission was to provide the highest quality health care service to the surrounding community while reinvesting in teaching and research. Unlike the for-profit hospitals that ultimately had to earn a return for shareholders, nonprofits such as the U.Va. Health System had to strike a balance across its various objectives. A typical for-profit hospital required a pretax profit margin of 15% to justify a capital investment, whereas a nonprofit could require a lower margin and still meet its objective of providing excellent clinical care.

During Fitzgerald's tenure, the U.Va. Health System had maintained an average net profit margin of 4.9%. The board of directors considered a margin of 3.0% to be the minimum needed to sustain the system. In order to be able to grow and develop the system, however, the board wanted a 5.0% profit margin as the minimum for new projects. The board reinvested any profits beyond the 5.0% level in the School of Medicine to support the U.Va. Health System's teaching and research missions.

When an investment proposal was brought forward, the board generally considered three distinct sources of funding: cash, debt, and leasing. When analyzing a project, a primary consideration for the board was to maintain an AA bond rating for the hospital. This was the highest rating a hospital could receive due to associated business risk. Maintaining the credit rating kept borrowing costs low and allowed the hospital to effectively compete for debt dollars in the future. On the other hand, the desire for an AA rating limited the total amount of debt the hospital could carry. Based on discussions with several banks about the LTAC project, Fitzgerald was confident that he could obtain the $15 million loan needed and that the added debt on the balance sheet would not jeopardize the U.Va. Health System's AA bond rating.

LTAC Project Analysis

Larry Fitzgerald looked at the memo and financial projections from his analyst (**Exhibits 24.1** and **24.2**) and realized that much work needed to be done before the board meeting the next day. But before he began to prepare his answers for Mulroney, he notified his assistant that she should expect a late addition to the paperwork for the board by early the next morning.

Fitzgerald was pleased that Mulroney had gathered working capital data and financial data from the for-profit hospital sector. But he was disappointed to see so many omissions in her projections on the eve of the board meeting. Fitzgerald was convinced that the LTAC facility would be profitable for the U.Va. Health System, but to get board approval, he would need to present an analysis that justified such a large undertaking. Because of the size and risk of the project, the LTAC hospital would need to have a profit margin well above the 5.0% level, and if it was to be debt-financed, he would need to show an adequate coverage of the interest expense. Finally, he would have to be ready to defend each of the assumptions used to create the financial projections, because the financial acumen varied significantly across the board members.

EXHIBIT 24.1 | Memo from Karen Mulroney

MEMO: Long-Term Acute Care Facility

Date: March 3, 2006

To: Larry Fitzgerald, Vice President of Business Development and Finance

From: Karen Mulroney, Analyst

Dear Mr. Fitzgerald,

After our meeting last week, I have developed the attached spreadsheet for the LTAC facility project. As you can see, I have most of the necessary assumptions in place to generate an operating profit, but more work needs to be done, and I have a few questions. What follows are my explanations about the key parts of the analysis.

VOLUME Metrics

We are assuming a 50-bed facility, which equals a capacity of 18,250 patient days. As with all LTAC facilities, the initial year is expected to have a low utilization rate (26%) until it is granted Medicare certification. Medicare will only provide certification if the facility can demonstrate that the average length of stay for patients is at least 25 days. If the facility is not certified, it will not be able to bill the LTAC rate for its patients on Medicare. Therefore, in the first year, we assume LTAC will be very selective by only admitting patients who are certain to stay for more than 25 days, which is why I have assumed 30 days as the average length of stay for Year 1. After the first year, I used 27 days, which is the national average length of stay for an LTAC facility patient.

For Year 2, I raised the utilization estimate to 60%, although a worst-case estimate is closer to 45%. For subsequent years, the utilization rate should increase 3% to 5% each year but will not be able to exceed 90% utilization. The utilization of the facility will be based on a number of factors including whether the facility is well received by the community, support from referring physicians, and hiring of hospitalists and nurses to ensure the facility runs smoothly and that patients receive exceptional care. Note that this version uses a 4% annual increase in the utilization, but we can easily reduce that if you want to see a more conservative scenario.

Total patient days for each year are computed as the utilization rate multiplied by the patient day capacity of 18,250 days. The next metric is the average patient census per day. Patient census measures how many patients the LTAC facility expects to serve on the average day. The average patient census is an important number because it is used to estimate how many full-time employees (FTEs) are needed to care for the patients. Due to the inefficiencies of the first year and based on the experiences of comparable LTAC facilities, we assume 4.8 FTEs are needed per occupied bed in the first year of operation. For subsequent years, we assume 3.5 FTEs will be needed as a reflection of operating at the efficiency level of an average LTAC facility.

EXHIBIT 24.1 | Memo from Karen Mulroney   *(continued)*

PAYER MIX metrics

Based on national trends and the local population demographics, we are confident that Medicare, Medicaid, and Indigent patients will represent 36%, 29%, and 2%, respectively, of our patient population. The "Commercial Payer Pool" and "Other"[1] were more difficult to estimate. The only information on this data is from for-profit hospital systems, and I am unsure if these numbers can be applied to a nonprofit organization such as U.Va. The data I found suggested commercial payers ranged from 20% to 28% of the mix with "Other" ranging from 5% to 13%.

NET REVENUE

Revenues for the LTAC facility are determined by patients' insurance policies. Medicare, Medicaid, Other, and Indigent categories are billed and paid per case. Those figures range from $28,000 to $38,000 per case. Commercial payers, however, pay based on the number days spent in the facility. Using current contracts and taking into account the mix of major commercial insurance carriers, we estimated an average billing rate of $2,800 per day.

I have also used historical data to estimate the annual billing rate increases for each of the payer categories, with commercial payers' rates increasing about 5% annually. Per our standard practice, net revenue is computed as total revenue less 1% to reflect noncollectable billings.

EXPENSES

Salaries, wages, and benefits for FTEs are estimated at $65,250 per employee with an increase of 3% per year, based on university and other local salary data. Supplies, drugs, and food for patient care are estimated as 19.3% of net revenues. Per your suggestion, I have included 9.0% of net revenues as the fees paid for managing the LTAC facility, which includes management salaries, billing, and overhead.

Operating expenses include utilities, minor equipment purchases and repairs, and legal and professional expenses. These costs were estimated to have a fixed component of $1.2 million and a variable component equal to approximately 8.5% of net revenues.

The land for the LTAC facility will be leased for $200,000 per year. We have several bids from construction companies, all of which are close to an all-in cost of $15 million to build the facility. About half the construction will occur prior to the first operating year, and the balance will be spent in the first half of Year 1.

---

[1]The "Other" category included out-of-pocket and foreign patients, who were always difficult to estimate.

EXHIBIT 24.1 | Memo from Karen Mulroney (*continued*)

Per your request, my final objective of the analysis is to compute a net present value and internal rate of return for the cash flows of the project. I recognize that in order to compute the cash flows, I will need to convert the above assumptions into revenues and costs, but first, I have a few questions:

1. It looks like we can get bank financing on the facility at 8.0%. This will be structured as a 30-year mortgage with monthly payments that include both principal and interest, which on an annual basis sum to $1.33 million. To calculate net profit, should I include the full amount as "interest expense," or should I segregate the interest and principal and only report the interest portion? When I worked in the for-profit world, we omitted interest expense because we wanted an "unlevered" cash flow (i.e., without financing cash flows). I assume that I should also compute an unlevered cash flow here for the NPV and IRR calculations, but I need to include interest expense to calculate a net profit, which I know the board wants to see.

2. Should I include depreciation of the facility as an expense? In my previous positions in manufacturing companies, we always viewed depreciation as a noncash flow, except for its impact upon taxes. Since this is a nonprofit entity that pays no taxes, would it be easier for me to just ignore depreciation?

3. You had instructed me to use 10 years as the time frame for the analysis, but the facility will last much longer, albeit with the benefit of significant renovations along the way. What should I show for cash flows after 10 years?

4. Are there any balance sheet effects for me to consider such as changes in working capital? Based on other LTAC facilities and the hospital, I would assume accounts receivable of 30 days, inventory of supplies, drugs, and food of 60 days, and accounts payable of 30 days. Would you be comfortable with these numbers?

5. What should I use as the discount rate to compute the NPV and to assess the IRR? I have compiled financial information for comparable publicly traded health care companies (**Exhibit 24.3**). I have also collected data about current yields on government and corporate bonds (**Exhibit 24.4**). Should I rely on these data to estimate a "market-based" cost of capital to use as the discount rate?

My notes from our January meeting indicate that you wanted this analysis completed by the end of February. I apologize for being late with this, but I have been busy analyzing the behavior of our receivables and payables balances for the hospital.

Any feedback you have on the attached projections would be greatly appreciated.

Sincerely,

Karen Mulroney
Analyst

EXHIBIT 24.2 | Karen Mulroney's LTAC Hospital Financial Projections

Assumptions

Number of Beds	50
Year 1 Utilization	26%
Year 2 Utilization	60%
Utilization Increase after Year 2	4%
Commercial Payer Mix	24%
Commercial Payer Billing per Day	$2,800
Operating Variable Expense	8.5%

VOLUME

	Year 1	Year 2	Year 3	Year 4	Year 5	Year 6	Year 7	Year 8	Year 9	Year 10
Patient Day Capacity	18,250	18,250	18,250	18,250	18,250	18,250	18,250	18,250	18,250	18,250
Utilization	26%	60%	64%	68%	72%	76%	80%	84%	88%	90%
Patient Days Used	4,745	10,950	11,680	12,410	13,140	13,870	14,600	15,330	16,060	16,425
Average Patient Census per Day	13	30	32	34	36	38	40	42	44	45
Average Length of Stay	30	27	27	27	27	27	27	27	27	27
Number of Patients per Year	158	406	433	460	487	514	541	568	595	608
Full-Time Employees/Census	4.8	3.5	3.5	3.5	3.5	3.5	3.5	3.5	3.5	3.5
Full-Time Employees	62	105	112	119	126	133	140	147	154	158

INSURANCE PAYERS

	MIX	Billing Rate		Annual Increase
Medicare	36%	$27,795	per case	0.0%
Medicaid	29%	$35,000	per case	1.3%
Commercial Payers	24%	$2,800	per day	5.0%
Other	9%	$38,500	per case	1.3%
Indigent	2%	$35,000	per case	1.3%

EXPENSES

			Annual Increase
Salary, Wage, Benefits	$65,250	per FTE	3%
Supplies, Drugs, Food	19.3%	of net rev	N.Ap.
Management Fees	9.0%	of net rev	N.Ap.
Operating Expenses (fixed)	$1,200,000		N.Ap.
Operating Expenses (variable)	8.5%	of net rev	N.Ap.
Land Lease (annual rate)	$200,000		3%
Construction	$15,000,000		N.Ap.

Source: Created by case writer.

EXHIBIT 24.3 I Financial Data of For-Profit Health Care Companies

	HCA Inc	Community Health	Health Management Associates	Manor Care	Triad Hospitals	Universal Health Services
Revenues (millions)	$24,475	$3,720	$3,580	$3,375	$4,805	$4,030
Assets (millions)	$5,222	$961	$997	$693	$1,458	$775
Total debt (millions)	$9,278	$1,810	$1,014	$857	$1,703	$532
Stock price ($/share)	$52.12	$39.73	$23.25	$39.49	$41.46	$49.03
Shares outstanding (millions)	452.7	88.5	247.2	78.7	84.8	54.6
Market cap (millions)	$23,593	$3,517	$5,747	$3,108	$3,517	$2,676
Bond rating	A	B	BB	BB	B	BB
Beta	0.60	0.60	0.70	0.80	0.60	0.60

• HCA Inc.—hospital management company; manages hospitals mainly in the Southeast and Texas.

• Community Health—operates general acute care hospitals in nonurban communities.

• Health Management Associates, Inc.—provides a range of general an acute care health services in nonurban communities.

• Manor Care—provider of health services with broad capabilities; operates skilled nursing facilities, subacute medical and rehabilitation units, outpatient rehab clinics, assisted living facilities, and acute care hospitals.

• Triad Hospitals—owns and manages health care facilities including hospitals and ambulatory surgery centers.

• Universal Health Services—owns and operates acute care and surgical hospitals, behavioral health centers, and surgery and radiation oncology centers.

Data source: Value Line, December 2005.

EXHIBIT 24.4 | U.S. Treasury and Corporate Bond Yields for March 2, 2006

U.S. Treasury Yields*	
1-year	4.77%
5-year	4.72%
10-year	4.72%
30-year	4.73%

Corporate Bond Yields**	
AAA	5.31%
AA	5.38%
A	5.45%
BBB	5.88%
BB	6.79%
B	7.57%

*Data source: http://federalreserve.gov/releases/h15/data.htm (accessed March 2006).

**Data source: Bloomberg, "Fair Market Curve Analysis," 10-Year Corporate Bonds, March 2, 2006.

Star River Electronics Ltd.

On July 5, 2015, her first day as CEO of Star River Electronics Ltd., Adeline Koh confronted a host of management problems. One week earlier, Star River's president and CEO had suddenly resigned to accept a CEO position with another firm. Koh had been appointed to fill the position—starting immediately. Several items in her in-box that first day were financial in nature, either requiring a financial decision or with outcomes that would have major financial implications for the firm. That evening, Koh asked to meet with her assistant, Andy Chin, to begin addressing the most prominent issues.

Star River Electronics and the Optical-Disc-Manufacturing Industry

Star River Electronics had been founded as a joint venture between Starlight Electronics Ltd., United Kingdom, and an Asian venture-capital firm, New Era Partners. Based in Singapore, Star River had a single business mission: to manufacture high-quality optical discs as a supplier to movie studios and video game producers.

When originally founded, Star River gained recognition for its production of compact discs (CD), which were primarily used in the music recording industry and as data storage for personal computers. As technological advances in disc storage and the movie and video game markets began to grow, Star River switched most of its production capacity to manufacturing DVD and Blu-ray discs and became one of the leading suppliers in the optical-disc-manufacturing industry.

Storage media had proven to be a challenging industry for manufacturers. The advent of the CD was the beginning of the optical storage media industry, which used laser light to read data, rather than reading data from an electromagnetic tape, such as a cassette tape. In the mid-1990s the CD replaced cassette tapes and became the standard media for music. CDs were also widely used for data storage in personal computers. What followed was a rapid growth in demand and production of CD discs that led to

This case is derived from materials originally prepared by Professors Robert F. Bruner, Robert Conroy, and Kenneth Eades. The firms and individuals in the case are fictitious. The financial support of the Darden Foundation and the Batten Institute is gratefully acknowledged. It was written as a basis for class discussion rather than to illustrate effective or ineffective handling of an administrative situation. Copyright © 2001 by the University of Virginia Darden School Foundation, Charlottesville, VA. All rights reserved. *To order copies, send an e-mail to sales@dardenbusinesspublishing.com. No part of this publication may be reproduced, stored in a retrieval system, used in a spreadsheet, or transmitted in any form or by any means—electronic, mechanical, photocopying, recording, or otherwise—without the permission of the Darden School Foundation.*

dramatic cost savings for users and tightening margins for manufacturers. Manufacturers struggled to keep pace with changing formats and quality enhancements that required substantial capital investments. As prices fell, many of the smaller producers failed or were acquired by larger, more cost-efficient competitors.

While CDs continued to be used by the music industry, the movie and video game industry required a much higher data density, which resulted in the development of the DVD (digital versatile disc). A DVD held 4.7 gigabytes (GB) of data compared to a CD with a capacity of 0.7 GB. As the entertainment industry evolved toward high-definition video, the Blu-ray format emerged as the standard video format because it offered up to 50 GB of capacity.

Star River Electronics was one of the few CD manufacturers that had been able to survive the many shakeouts created by the technological innovations in the industry. The challenge in 2015 for all disc manufacturers was the movement of music and video entertainment to online data streaming. Despite this challenge, however, Star River's volume sales had grown at a robust rate over the past two years. Sales to North America had suffered, but sales to emerging-market countries had more than compensated. Unit prices had declined because of price competition and the growing popularity of streaming. Many industry experts were predicting declining demand and further compression in margins in the CD and DVD segments, but stable-to-rising demand for Blu-ray discs over the next few years. Star River management believed that with its continued investment in production efficiency, the company was well positioned to grow its Blu-ray revenues enough to offset the continuing declines in its DVD and CD revenues over the next three to five years.

Financial Questions Facing Adeline Koh

That evening, Koh met with Andy Chin, a promising new associate whom she had brought along from New Era Partners. Koh's brief discussion with Chin went as follows:

KOH: Back at New Era, we looked at Star River as one of our most promising venture-capital investments. Now it seems that such optimism may not be warranted—at least until we get a solid understanding of the firm's past performance and its forecast performance. Did you have any success on this?

CHIN: Yes, the bookkeeper gave me these: the historical income statements (**Exhibit 25.1**) and balance sheets (**Exhibit 25.2**) for the last four years. The accounting system here is still pretty primitive. However, I checked a number of the accounts, and they look orderly. So I suspect that we can work with these figures. From these statements, I calculated a set of diagnostic ratios (**Exhibit 25.3**).

KOH: I see you have been busy. Unfortunately, I can't study these right now. I need you to review the historical performance of Star River for me, and to give me any positive or negative insights that you think are significant.

CHIN: When do you need this?

KOH: At 7:00 A.M. tomorrow. I want to call on our banker tomorrow morning and get an extension on Star River's loan.

CHIN: The banker, Mr. Tan, said that Star River was "growing beyond its financial capabilities." What does that mean?

KOH: It probably means that he doesn't think we can repay the loan within a reasonable period. I would like you to build a simple financial forecast of our performance for the next two years (ignore seasonal effects), and show me what our debt requirements will be at the fiscal years ending 2016 and 2017. I think it is reasonable to expect that Star River's sales will grow at 4% each year. Also, you should assume capital expenditures of SGD54.6 million[1] for DVD and Blu-ray manufacturing equipment, spread out over the next two years and depreciated over seven years. Use whatever other assumptions seem appropriate to you, based on your analysis of historical results. For this forecast, you should assume that any external funding is in the form of bank debt.

CHIN: But what if the forecasts show that Star River cannot repay the loan?

KOH: Then we'll have to go back to Star River's owners, New Era Partners and Star River Electronics United Kingdom, for an injection of equity. Of course, New Era Partners would rather not invest more funds unless we can show that the returns on such an investment would be very attractive and/or that the survival of the company depends on it. Thus, my third request is for you to examine what returns on book assets and book equity Star River will offer in the next two years and to identify the "key-driver" assumptions of those returns. Finally, let me have your recommendations regarding operating and financial changes I should make based on the historical analysis and the forecasts.

CHIN: The plant manager revised his request for a new packaging machine, which would add SGD1.82 million to the 2016 capital expenditures budget. He believes that these are the right numbers to make the choice between investing now or waiting three years to buy the new packaging equipment (see the plant manager's memorandum in **Exhibit 25.4**). The new equipment can save significantly on labor costs and will enhance the packaging options we can offer our customers. However, adding SGD1.82 million to the capex budget may not be the best use of our cash now. My hunch is that our preference between investing now versus waiting three years will hinge on the discount rate.

KOH: [laughing] The joke in business school was that the discount rate was always 10%.

CHIN: That's not what my business school taught me! New Era always uses a 40% discount rate to value equity investments in risky start-up companies. But Star River is well established now and shouldn't require such a high-risk premium. I managed to pull together some data on other Singaporean electronics companies with which to estimate the required rate of return on equity (see **Exhibit 25.5**).

KOH: Fine. Please estimate Star River's weighted average cost of capital and assess the packaging-machine investment. I would like the results of your analysis tomorrow morning at 7:00.

---

[1] SGD = Singaporean dollars.

EXHIBIT 25.1 | Historical Income Statements for Fiscal Year Ended June 30
(in SGD thousands)

	2012	2013	2014	2015
Sales	71,924	80,115	92,613	106,042
Operating expenses:				
Production costs and expenses	33,703	38,393	46,492	53,445
Admin. and selling expenses	16,733	17,787	21,301	24,633
Depreciation	8,076	9,028	10,392	11,360
Total operating expenses	58,512	65,208	78,185	89,438
Operating profit	13,412	14,907	14,428	16,604
Interest expense	3,487	3,929	6,227	7,614
Earnings before taxes	9,925	10,978	8,201	8,990
Income taxes*	2,430	2,705	1,925	2,220
Net earnings	7,495	8,273	6,276	6,770
Dividends to all common shares	2,000	2,000	2,000	2,000
Retentions of earnings	5,495	6,273	4,276	4,770

*The expected corporate tax rate was 24.5%.

Data source: Author estimates.

EXHIBIT 25.2 | Historical Balance Sheets for Fiscal Year Ended June 30
(in SGD thousands)

	2012	2013	2014	2015
Assets:				
Cash	4,816	5,670	5,090	5,795
Accounts receivable	22,148	25,364	28,078	35,486
Inventories	23,301	27,662	53,828	63,778
Total current assets	50,265	58,696	86,996	105,059
Gross property, plant & equipment	64,611	80,153	97,899	115,153
Accumulated depreciation	(4,559)	(13,587)	(23,979)	(35,339)
Net property, plant & equipment	60,052	66,566	73,920	79,814
Total assets	110,317	125,262	160,916	184,873
Liabilities and stockholders' equity:				
Short-term borrowings (bank)[1]	29,002	35,462	69,005	82,275
Accounts payable	12,315	12,806	11,890	13,370
Other accrued liabilities	24,608	26,330	25,081	21,318
Total current liabilities	65,925	74,598	105,976	116,963
Long-term debt2	10,000	10,000	10,000	18,200
Shareholders' equity	34,391	40,664	44,940	49,710
Total liabilities and stockholders' equity	110,316	125,262	160,916	184,873

[1] Short-term debt was borrowed from City Bank at an interest rate equal to Singaporean prime lending rate +1.5%. Current prime lending rate was 5.35%. The benchmark 10-year Singapore treasury bond currently yielded 2.30%.

[2] Two components made up the company's long-term debt. One was a SGD10 million loan that had been issued privately in 2010 to New Era Partners and to Star River Electronics Ltd., UK. This debt was subordinate to any bank debt outstanding. The second component was a SGD8.2 million public bond issuance on July 1, 2014, with a five-year maturity and a coupon of 5.75% paid semiannually. The bond had recently traded at a price of SGD97.

Data source: Monetary Authority of Singapore and author estimates.

EXHIBIT 25.3 | Ratio Analyses of Historical Financial Statements
Fiscal Year Ended June 30

	2012	2013	2014	2015
Profitability				
Operating margin	18.6%	18.6%	15.6%	15.7%
Tax rate	24.5%	24.6%	23.5%	24.7%
Return on sales	10.4%	10.3%	6.8%	6.4%
Return on equity	21.8%	20.3%	14.0%	13.6%
Return on assets	6.8%	6.6%	3.9%	3.7%
Leverage				
Debt/equity ratio	1.13	1.12	1.76	2.02
Debt/total capital	0.53	0.53	0.64	0.67
EBIT/interest	3.85	3.79	2.32	2.18
Asset Utilization				
Sales/assets	65.2%	64.0%	57.6%	57.4%
Sales growth rate	15.0%	11.4%	15.6%	14.5%
Assets growth rate	8.0%	13.5%	28.5%	14.9%
Days sales outstanding	112.4	115.6	110.7	122.1
Days payable outstanding	133.4	121.7	93.3	91.3
Days inventory outstanding	252.3	263.0	422.6	435.6
Liquidity				
Current ratio	0.76	0.79	0.82	0.90
Quick ratio	0.41	0.42	0.31	0.35

Data source: Author calculations.

EXHIBIT 25.4 | Lim's Memo regarding New Packaging Equipment

MEMORANDUM

TO: Adeline Koh, President and CEO, Star River Electronics
FROM: Esmond Lim, Plant Manager
DATE: June 30, 2015
SUBJECT: New Packaging Equipment

Although our packaging equipment is adequate at current production levels, it is terribly inefficient. The new machinery on the market can give us significant labor savings as well as increased flexibility with respect to the type of packaging used. I recommend that we go with the new technology. Should we decide to do so, the new machine can be acquired immediately. The considerations relevant to the decision are included in this memo.

Our current packaging equipment was purchased five years ago as used equipment in a liquidation sale of a small company. Although the equipment was inexpensive, it is slow, requires constant monitoring, and is frequently shut down for repairs. Since the packaging equipment is significantly slower than our production equipment, we routinely have to use overtime labor to allow packaging to catch up with production. When the packager is down for repairs, the problem is exacerbated and we may spend several two-shift days catching up with production. I cannot say that we have missed any deadlines because of packaging problems, but it is a constant concern around here and things would run a lot smoother with more reliable equipment. In fiscal 2016, we will pay about SGD15,470 per year for maintenance costs. The operator is paid SGD63,700 per year for his regular time, but he has been averaging SGD81,900 per year because of the overtime he has been working. The equipment is on the tax and reporting books at SGD218,400 and will be fully depreciated in three years (we are currently using the straight-line depreciation method for both tax and reporting purposes and will continue to do so). Because of changes in packaging technology, the equipment has no market value other than its worth as scrap metal. But its scrap value is about equal to the cost of having it removed. In short, we believe the equipment has no salvage value at all.

The new packager offers many advantages over the current equipment. It is faster, more reliable, more flexible with respect to the types of packaging it can perform, and will provide enough capacity to cover all our packaging needs in the foreseeable future. With suitable maintenance, we believe the packager will operate indefinitely. Thus, for the purposes of our analysis, we can assume that this will be the last packaging equipment we will ever have to purchase. Because of the anticipated growth at Star River, the current equipment will not be able to handle our packaging needs by the end of fiscal 2018. Thus, if we do not buy new packaging equipment by this year's end, we will have to buy it after three years anyway. Since the speed, capacity, and reliability of the new equipment will eliminate the need for overtime labor, we feel strongly that we should buy now rather than wait another three years.

The new equipment is priced at SGD1.82 million, which we would depreciate over 10 years at SGD182,000 per year. It comes with a lifetime factory maintenance contract that covers all routine maintenance and repairs at a price of SGD3,640 for the initial year. The contract stipulates that the price after the first year will be increased by the same percentage as the price increase of the new equipment. Thus if the manufacturer continues to increase the price of new packaging equipment at 5% per annum as it has in the past, the maintenance costs of the new equipment will rise by 5% also. We believe that this sort of regular maintenance should insure that the new equipment will keep operating in the foreseeable future without the need for a major overhaul.

Star River's labor and maintenance costs will continue to rise due to inflation at approximately 1.5% per year over the long term. Because the manufacturer of the packaging equipment has been increasing its prices at about 5% per year, we can expect to save SGD286,878 in the purchase price by buying now rather than waiting three years. The marginal tax rate for this investment would be 24.5%.

EXHIBIT 25.5 | Data on Comparable Companies

Name	Percent Sales from Optical Media Production	Price/Earnings Ratio	Beta	Book Debt/Equity	Book Value per Share	Market Price per Share	Number of Shares Outstanding (millions)	Last Annual Dividend per Share
Sing Studios, Inc.	20%	9.0	1.10	0.23	1.24	1.37	9.3	1.82
Wintronics, Inc.	95%	NMF	1.50	1.72	1.46	6.39	177.2	0.15
STOR-Max Corp.	90%	18.2	1.70	1.33	7.06	27.48	8.9	none
Digital Media Corp.	30%	34.6	1.20	0.00	17.75	75.22	48.3	none
Wymax, Inc.	60%	NMF	1.50	0.42	6.95	22.19	371.2	1.57

Note: NMF means not a meaningful figure. This arises when a company's earnings or projected earnings are negative.

Singapore's equity market risk premium could be assumed to be close to the global equity market premium of 6 percent, given Singapore's high rate of integration into global markets.

Data source: Author estimates.

Descriptions of Companies

Sing Studios, Inc.

This company was founded 60 years ago. Its major business activities had been production of original-artist recordings, management and production of rock-and-roll road tours, and personal management of artists. It entered the CD-production market in the 1980s, and only recently branched out into the manufacture of DVDs.

Wintronics, Inc.

This company was a spin-off from a large technology-holding corporation in 2001. Although the company was a leader in the production of optical media, it has recently suffered a decline in sales. Infighting among the principal owners has fed concerns about the firm's prospects.

STOR-Max Corp.

This company, founded only two years ago, had emerged as a very aggressive competitor in the area of DVD and Blu-ray production. It was Star River's major competitor and its sales level was about the same.

Digital Media Corp.

This company had recently been an innovator in the production of Blu-ray discs. Although optical-media manufacturing was not a majority of its business (film production and digital animation were its main focus), the company was a significant supplier to several major movie studios and was projected to become a major competitor within the next three years.

Wymax, Inc.

This company was an early pioneer in the CD and DVD industries. Recently, however, it had begun to invest in software programming and had been moving away from disc production as its main focus of business.

## PART 5

Management of the Firm's Equity: Dividends and Repurchases

Rockboro Machine Tools Corporation

On September 15, 2015, Sara Larson, chief financial officer (CFO) of Rockboro Machine Tools Corporation (Rockboro), paced the floor of her Minnesota office. She needed to submit a recommendation to Rockboro's board of directors regarding the company's dividend policy, which had been the subject of an ongoing debate among the firm's senior managers. Larson knew that the board was optimistic about Rockboro's future, but there was a lingering uncertainty regarding the company's competitive position. Like many companies following the "great recession" of 2008 and 2009, Rockboro had succeeded in recovering revenues back to prerecession levels. Unlike most other companies, however, Rockboro had not been able to recover its profit margins, and without a much-improved cost structure, it would be difficult for Rockboro to compete with the rising presence of foreign competition that had surfaced primarily from Asia. The board's optimism was fueled by the signs that the two recent restructurings would likely return Rockboro to competitive profit margins and allow the company to compete for its share of the global computer-aided design and manufacturing (CAD/CAM) market.

There were two issues that complicated Larson's dividend policy recommendation. First, she had to consider that over the past four years Rockboro shareholders had watched their investment return them no capital gain (i.e., the current stock price of $15.25 was exactly the same as it had been on September 15, 2011). The only return shareholders had received was dividends, which amounted to an average annual return of 2.9% and compared poorly to an annual return of 12.9% earned by the average stock over the same period.[1] The second complication was that the 2008 recession had prompted a number of companies to repurchase shares either in lieu of or in addition to paying a dividend. A share repurchase was considered a method for management and the board to signal confidence in their company and was usually greeted with a stock

[1]The average stock performance was measured by the performance of the S&P 500 index.

price increase when announced. Rockboro had repurchased $15.8 million of shares in 2009, but had not used share buybacks since then. Larson recognized, therefore, that her recommendation needed to include whether to use company funds to buy back stock, pay dividends, do both, or do neither.

Background on the Dividend Question

Prior to the recession of 2008, Rockboro had enjoyed years of consistent earnings and predictable dividend growth. As the financial crisis was unfolding, Rockboro's board decided to maintain a steady dividend and to postpone any dividend increases until Rockboro's future became more certain. That policy had proven to be expensive since earnings recovered much more slowly than was hoped and dividend payout rose above 50% for the years 2009 through 2011. To address the profit-margin issue, management implemented two extensive restructuring programs, both of which were accompanied by net losses. Dividends were maintained at $0.64/share until the second restructuring in 2014, when dividends were reduced by half for the year. For the first two quarters of 2015, the board declared no dividend. But in a special letter to shareholders, the board committed itself to resuming payment of the dividend "as soon as possible—ideally, sometime in 2015."

In a related matter, senior management considered embarking on a campaign of corporate-image advertising, together with changing the name of the corporation to "Rockboro Advanced Systems International, Inc." Management believed that the name change would help improve the investment community's perception of the company. Overall, management's view was that Rockboro was a resurgent company that demonstrated great potential for growth and profitability. The restructurings had revitalized the company's operating divisions. In addition, a newly developed software product promised to move the company beyond its machine- tool business into licensing of its state-of-the-art design software that provided significant efficiencies for users and was being well received in the market, with expectations of rendering many of the competitors' products obsolete. Many within the company viewed 2015 as the dawning of a new era, which, in spite of the company's recent performance, would turn Rockboro into a growth stock.

Out of this combination of a troubled past and a bright future arose Larson's dilemma. Did the market view Rockboro as a company on the wane, a blue-chip stock, or a potential growth stock? How, if at all, could Rockboro affect that perception? Would a change of name help to positively frame investors' views of the firm? Did the company's investors expect capital growth or steady dividends? Would a stock buyback affect investors' perceptions of Rockboro in any way? And, if those questions could be answered, what were the implications for Rockboro's future dividend policy?

The Company

Rockboro was founded in 1923 in Concord, New Hampshire, by two mechanical engineers, James Rockman and David Pittsboro. The two men had gone to school together and were disenchanted with their prospects as mechanics at a farm-equipment manufacturer.

In its early years, Rockboro had designed and manufactured a number of machinery parts, including metal presses, dies, and molds. In the 1940s, the company's large manufacturing plant produced armored-vehicle and tank parts and miscellaneous equipment for the war effort, including riveters and welders. After the war, the company concentrated on the production of industrial presses and molds, for plastics as well as metals. By 1975, the company had developed a reputation as an innovative producer of industrial machinery and machine tools.

In the early 1980s, Rockboro entered the new field of computer-aided design and computer-aided manufacturing (CAD/CAM). Working with a small software company, it developed a line of presses that could manufacture metal parts by responding to computer commands. Rockboro merged the software company into its operations and, over the next several years, perfected the CAM equipment. At the same time, it developed a superior line of CAD software and equipment that allowed an engineer to design a part to exacting specifications on a computer. The design could then be entered into the company's CAM equipment, and the parts could be manufactured without the use of blueprints or human interference. By the end of 2014, CAD/CAM equipment and software were responsible for about 45% of sales; presses, dies, and molds made up 40% of sales; and miscellaneous machine tools were 15% of sales.

Most press-and-mold companies were small local or regional firms with a limited clientele. For that reason, Rockboro stood out as a true industry leader. Within the CAD/CAM industry, however, a number of larger firms, including Autodesk, Inc., Cadence Design, and Synopsys, Inc., competed for dominance of the growing market.

Throughout the 1990s and into the first decade of the 2000s, Rockboro helped set the standard for CAD/CAM, but the aggressive entry of large foreign firms into CAD/CAM had dampened sales. Technological advances and significant investments had fueled the entry of highly specialized, state-of-the-art CAD/CAM firms. By 2009, Rockboro had fallen behind its competition in the development of user-friendly software and the integration of design and manufacturing. As a result, revenues had barely recovered beyond the prerecession-level high of $1.07 billion in 2008, to $1.13 billion in 2014, and profit margins were getting compressed because the company was having difficulty containing costs.

To combat the weak profit margins, Rockboro took a two-pronged approach. First, a much larger share of the research-and-development budget was devoted to CAD/CAM, in an effort to reestablish Rockboro's leadership in the field. Second, the company underwent two massive restructurings. In 2012, it sold three unprofitable business lines and two plants, eliminated five leased facilities, and reduced personnel. Restructuring costs totaled $98 million. Then, in 2014, the company began a second round of restructuring by refocusing its sales and marketing approach and adopting administrative procedures that allowed for a further reduction in staff and facilities. The total cost of the operational restructuring in 2014 was $134 million.

The company's recent financial statements (**Exhibits 26.1** and **26.2**) revealed that although the restructurings produced losses totaling $303 million, the projected results for 2015 suggested that the restructurings and the increased emphasis on new product development had launched a turnaround. Not only was the company becoming leaner, but also the investment in research and development had led to a breakthrough in Rockboro's

CAD/CAM software that management believed would redefine the industry. Known as the Artificial Intelligence Workforce (AIW), the system was an array of advanced control hardware, software, and applications that continuously distributed and coordinated information throughout a plant. Essentially, AIW allowed an engineer to design a part on CAD software and input the data into CAM equipment that controlled the mixing of chemicals or the molding of parts from any number of different materials on different machines. The system could also assemble and can, box, or shrink-wrap the finished product. As part of the licensing agreements for the software, Rockboro engineers provided consulting to specifically adapt the software to each client's needs. Thus regardless of its complexity, a product could be designed, manufactured, and packaged solely by computer. Most importantly, however, Rockboro's software used simulations to test new product designs prior to production. This capability was enhanced by the software's capability to improve the design based on statistical inferences drawn from Rockboro's large proprietary database.

Rockboro had developed AIW applications for the chemicals industry and for the oil- and gas-refining industries in 2014 and, by the next year, it would complete applications for the trucking, automobile-parts, and airline industries. By October 2014, when the first AIW system was shipped, Rockboro had orders totaling $115 million. By year-end 2014, the backlog had grown to $150 million. The future for the product looked bright. Several securities analysts were optimistic about the product's impact on the company. The following comments paraphrase their thoughts:

> The Artificial Intelligence Workforce system has compelling advantages over competing entries, which will enable Rockboro to increase its share of a market that, ignoring periodic growth spurts, will expand at a real annual rate of about 5% over the next several years.
>
> Rockboro's engineering team is producing the AIW applications at an impressive rate, which will help restore margins to levels not seen in years.
>
> The important question now is how quickly Rockboro will be able to sell licenses in volume. Start-up costs, which were a significant factor in last year's deficits, have continued to penalize earnings. Our estimates assume that adoption rates will proceed smoothly from now on and that AIW will have gained significant market share by year-end 2016.

Rockboro's management expected domestic revenues from the Artificial Intelligence Workforce series to total $135 million in 2015 and $225 million in 2016. Thereafter, growth in sales would depend on the development of more system applications and the creation of system improvements and add-on features. International sales through Rockboro's existing offices in Frankfurt, London, Milan, and Paris and new offices in Hong Kong, Shanghai, Seoul, Manila, and Tokyo were expected to help meet foreign competition head on and to provide additional revenues of $225 million by as early as 2017. Currently, international sales accounted for approximately 15% of total corporate revenues.

Two factors that could affect sales were of some concern to management. First, although Rockboro had successfully patented several of the processes used by the AIW system, management had received hints through industry observers that two strong competitors were developing comparable systems and would probably introduce them within the next 12 months. Second, sales of molds, presses, machine tools, and CAD/CAM equipment and software were highly cyclical, and current predictions about the strength of the United States and other major economies were not encouraging. As shown in **Exhibit 26.3**, real GDP (gross domestic product) growth was expected to expand to 2.9% by 2016, and industrial production, which had improved significantly for 2014 to 4.2% growth, was projected to decline in 2015 before recovering to 3.6% by 2016. Despite the lukewarm macroeconomic environment, Rockboro's management remained optimistic about the company's prospects because of the successful introduction of the AIW series.

Corporate Goals

A number of corporate objectives had grown out of the restructurings and recent technological advances. First and foremost, management wanted and expected revenues to grow at an average annual compound rate of 15%. With the improved cost structure, profit growth was expected to exceed top-line growth. A great deal of corporate planning had been devoted to the growth goal over the past three years and, indeed, second-quarter financial data suggested that Rockboro would achieve revenues of about $1.3 billion in 2015. If Rockboro achieved a 15% compound rate of revenue growth through 2021, the company would reach $3.0 billion in sales and $196 million in net income.

In order to achieve their growth objective, Rockboro management proposed a strategy relying on three key points. First, the mix of production would shift substantially. CAD/CAM with emphasis on the AIW system would account for three-quarters of sales, while the company's traditional presses and molds would account for the remainder. Second, the company would expand aggressively in the global markets, where it hoped to obtain half of its sales and profits by 2021. This expansion would be achieved through opening new field sales offices around the world, including Hong Kong, Shanghai, Seoul, Manila, and Tokyo. Third, the company would expand through joint ventures and acquisitions of small software companies, which would provide half of the new products through 2021; in-house research would provide the other half.

The company had had an aversion to debt since its inception. Management believed that a small amount of debt, primarily to meet working-capital needs, had its place, but anything beyond a 40% debt-to-equity ratio was, in the oft-quoted words of Rockboro cofounder David Pittsboro, "unthinkable, indicative of sloppy management, and flirting with trouble." Senior management was aware that equity was typically more costly than debt, but took great satisfaction in the company "doing it on its own." Rockboro's highest debt-to-capital ratio in the past 25 years (28%) had occurred in 2014 and was still the subject of conversations among senior managers.

Although 11 members of the Rockman and the Pittsboro families owned 13% of the company's stock and three were on the board of directors, management placed the interests of the outside shareholders first (**Exhibit 26.4**). Stephen Rockman, board chair and grandson of the cofounder, sought to maximize growth in the market value of the company's stock over time. At 61, Rockman was actively involved in all aspects of the company's growth. He dealt fluently with a range of technical details of Rockboro's products and was especially interested in finding ways to improve the company's domestic market share. His retirement was no more than four years away, and he wanted to leave a legacy of corporate financial strength and technological achievement. The Artificial Intelligence Workforce, a project that he had taken under his wing four years earlier, was finally beginning to bear fruit. Rockman now wanted to ensure that the firm would also soon be able to pay a dividend to its shareholders.

Rockman took particular pride in selecting and developing promising young managers. Sara Larson had a bachelor's degree in electrical engineering and had been a systems analyst for Motorola before attending graduate school. She had been hired in 2005, fresh out of a well-known MBA program. By 2014, she had risen to the position of CFO.

Dividend Policy

Before 2009, Rockboro's earnings and dividends per share had grown at a relatively steady pace (**Exhibit 26.5**). Following the recession, cost-control problems became apparent because earnings were not able to rebound to prerecession levels. The board maintained dividends at $0.64 per year until 2014 when the restructuring expenses led to the largest per-share earnings loss in the firm's history. To conserve cash, the board voted to pare back dividends by 50% to $0.32 a share—the lowest dividend since 1998. Paying any dividend with such high losses effectively meant that Rockboro had to borrow to pay the dividend. In response to the financial pressure, the directors elected to not declare a dividend for the first two quarters of 2015. In a special letter to shareholders, however, the directors declared their intention to continue the annual payout later in 2015.

In August 2015, Larson was considering three possible dividend policies to recommend:

- *Zero-dividend payout:* A zero payout could be justified in light of the firm's strategic emphasis on advanced technologies and CAD/CAM, which demanded huge cash requirements to succeed. The proponents of this policy argued that it would signal that the firm now belonged in a class of high-growth and high-technology firms. Some securities analysts wondered whether the market still considered Rockboro a traditional electrical-equipment manufacturer or a more technologically advanced CAD/CAM company. The latter category would imply that the market expected strong capital appreciation, but perhaps little in the way of dividends. Others cited Rockboro's recent performance problems. One questioned the "wisdom of ignoring the financial statements in favor of acting like a blue chip." Was a high dividend in the long-term interests of the company and its stockholders, or would the strategy backfire and make investors skittish?

- *40% dividend payout or a quarterly dividend of around $0.10 a share:* This option would restore the firm to an implied annual dividend payment of $0.40 a share, higher than 2014's dividend of $0.32, but still less than the $0.64 dividend paid in 2013. Proponents of this policy argued that such an announcement was justified by expected increases in orders and sales. Rockboro's investment banker suggested that the stock market would reward a strong dividend that would bring the firm's payout back in line with the 40% average within the electrical-industrial-equipment industry. Some directors agreed and argued that it was important to send a strong signal to shareholders, and that a large dividend (on the order of a 40% payout) would suggest that the company had conquered its problems and that its directors were confident of its future earnings. Finally, some older directors opined that a growth rate in the range of 10% to 20% should accompany a dividend payout of between 30% and 50%, but not all supported the idea of borrowing to fuel the growth and support that level of dividend.

Larson recalled a recently published study reporting that firms had increased their payout ratios to an average of 38% for Q2 2015, from a low of 27% in Q1 2011. Also, the trend since the recession was for more companies to pay dividends. For the S&P 500, about 360 companies paid dividends in Q1 2010 compared to 418 in Q2 2015.[2] Viewed in that light, perhaps the market would expect Rockboro to follow the crowd and would react negatively if Rockboro did not reinstitute a positive dividend-payout policy.

- *Residual-dividend payout:* A few members of the finance department argued that Rockboro should pay dividends only after it had funded all the projects that offered positive net present values (NPV). Their view was that investors paid managers to deploy their funds at returns better than they could otherwise achieve, and that, by definition, such investments would yield positive NPVs. By deploying funds into those projects and returning otherwise unused funds to investors in the form of dividends, the firm would build trust with investors and be rewarded through higher valuation multiples.

  Another argument in support of that view was that the particular dividend policy was "irrelevant" in a growing firm: any dividend paid today would be offset by dilution at some future date by the issuance of shares needed to make up for the dividend. This argument reflected the theory of dividends in a perfect market advanced by two finance professors, Merton Miller and Franco Modigliani.[3] To Sara Larson, the main disadvantage of this policy was that dividend payments would be unpredictable. In some years, dividends could even be cut to zero, possibly imposing negative pressure on the firm's share price. Larson was all too aware of Rockboro's own share-price collapse following its dividend cut. She recalled a study by another finance professor, John Lintner,[4] which found that firms' dividend payments tended to be "sticky" upward—that is, dividends would rise over time and rarely fall, and that mature, slower-growth firms paid higher dividends, while high-growth firms paid lower dividends.

In response to the internal debate, Larson's staff pulled together comparative information on companies in three industries—CAD/CAM, machine tools, and electrical-industrial equipment—and a sample of high- and low-payout companies (**Exhibits 26.6** and **26.7**).

---

[2] Birstingl, Andrew, "Aggregate Dividend Payments Continue to Rise in Q2." *Factset*, Sept. 28, 2015, http://www.factset.com/websitefiles/PDFs/dividend/dividend_9.28.15 (accessed Nov. 1, 2016).

[3] Merton H. Miller and Franco Modigliani, "Dividend Policy, Growth, and the Valuation of Shares," *Journal of Business* 34 (October 1961): 411–433.

[4] J. Lintner, "Distribution of Incomes of Corporations among Dividends, Retained Earnings, and Taxes," *American Economic Review* 46 (May 1956): 97–113.

To test the feasibility of a 40% dividend-payout rate, Larson developed a projected sources-and-uses-of-cash statement (**Exhibit 26.8**). She took an optimistic approach by assuming that the company would grow at a 15% compound rate, that margins would improve steadily, and that the firm would pay a dividend of 40% of earnings every year. In particular, the forecast assumed that the firm's net margin would gradually improve from 4.0% in 2015 to 6.5% in 2020 and 2021. The firm's operating executives believed that this increase in profitability was consistent with economies of scale and the higher margins associated with the Artificial Intelligence Workforce series.

Image Advertising and Name Change

As part of a general review of the firm's standing in the financial markets, Rockboro's director of investor relations, Maureen Williams, had concluded that investors misperceived the firm's prospects and that the firm's current name was more consistent with its historical product mix and markets than with those projected for the future. Williams commissioned surveys of readers of financial magazines, which revealed a relatively low awareness of Rockboro and its business. Surveys of stockbrokers revealed a higher awareness of the firm, but a low or mediocre outlook on Rockboro's likely returns to shareholders and its growth prospects. Williams retained a consulting firm that recommended a program of corporate-image advertising targeted toward guiding the opinions of institutional and individual investors. The objective was to enhance the firm's visibility and image. Through focus groups, the image consultants identified a new name that appeared to suggest the firm's promising new strategy: Rockboro Advanced Systems International, Inc. Williams estimated that the image-advertising campaign and name change would cost approximately $15 million.

Stephen Rockman was mildly skeptical. He said, "Do you mean to raise our stock price by 'marketing' our shares? This is a novel approach. Can you sell claims on a company the way Procter & Gamble markets soap?" The consultants could give no empirical evidence that stock prices responded positively to corporate-image campaigns or name changes, though they did offer some favorable anecdotes.

Conclusion

Larson was in a difficult position. Board members and management disagreed on the very nature of Rockboro's future. Some managers saw the company as entering a new stage of rapid growth and thought that a large (or, in the minds of some, any) dividend would be inappropriate. Others thought that it was important to make a strong public gesture showing that management believed that Rockboro had turned the corner and was about to return to the levels of growth and profitability seen prior to the last five to six years. This action could only be accomplished through a dividend. Then there was the confounding question about the stock buyback. Should Rockboro use its funds to repurchase stocks instead of paying out a dividend? As Larson wrestled with the different points of view, she wondered whether Rockboro's management might be representative of the company's shareholders. Did the majority of public shareholders own stock for the same reason, or were their reasons just as diverse as those of management?

EXHIBIT 26.1 | Consolidated Income Statements (dollars in thousands, except per-share data)

	2012	2013	2014	Projected 2015
Net sales	$1,287,394	$1,223,969	$1,134,956	$1,305,000
Cost of sales	811,121	752,186	748,319	824,625
Gross profit	476,273	471,782	386,638	480,375
Research and development	116,516	105,818	113,126	115,875
Selling, general, and administrative	344,957	335,450	346,511	317,250
Restructuring costs	98,172	0	134,116	0
Operating profit (loss)	(83,372)	30,515	(207,115)	47,250
Other income (expense)	(6,750)	1,598	(5,186)	(6,300)
Income (loss) before taxes	(90,122)	32,112	(212,301)	40,950
Income taxes (benefit)	1,861	12,623	(1,125)	13,923
Net income (loss)	($91,982)	$ 19,490	($211,176)	$ 27,027
Earnings (loss) per share	($3.25)	$ 0.69	($7.57)	$ 0.98
Dividends per share	$ 0.64	$ 0.64	$ 0.32	$ 0.39

Note: The dividends in 2015 assume a payout ratio of 40%.

Source: Author estimates.

EXHIBIT 26.2 | Consolidated Balance Sheets (dollars in thousands)

	2013	2014	Projected 2015
Cash and equivalents	$ 20,876	$ 33,345	$ 38,498
Accounts receivable	312,812	280,853	326,265
Inventories	345,513	305,832	325,832
Prepaid expenses	21,389	19,524	22,517
Other	33,276	31,071	31,500
Total current assets	733,865	670,625	744,611
Property, plant, and equipment	491,405	538,262	616,482
Less depreciation	251,121	275,229	308,295
Net property, plant, and equipment	240,284	263,033	308,187
Intangible assets	14,144	3,149	2,273
Other assets	23,585	26,532	26,954
Total assets	**$1,011,876**	**$963,338**	**$1,082,024**
Bank loans	$ 51,294	$ 107,018	$ 112,472
Accounts payable	54,674	51,359	56,291
Current portion of long-term debt	450	225	2,273
Accruals and other	194,061	242,450	274,521
Total current liabilities	300,479	401,051	445,556
Deferred taxes	25,479	20,654	24,789
Long-term debt	13,500	13,163	45,032
Deferred pension costs	67,185	96,488	105,240
Other liabilities	3,477	8,166	11,258
Total liabilities	410,120	539,520	631,874
Common stock, $1 par value	28,283	28,283	28,253
Capital in excess of par	161,811	161,861	161,834
Cumulative translation adjustment	(9,849)	30,312	40,485
Retained earnings	437,247	219,098	235,313
Less treasury stock at cost:	(15,735)	(15,735)	(15,735)
Total shareholders' equity	601,757	423,818	450,149
Total liabilities and equity	**$1,011,876**	**$963,338**	**$1,082,022**

Note: Projections assume a dividend-payout ratio of 40%.

Source: Author estimates.

EXHIBIT 26.3 I Economic Indicators and Projections (all numbers are percentages)

	2011	2012	2013	2014	Projected	
					2015	2016
Three-month Treasury bill rate	0.1%	0.1%	0.1%	0.1%	0.3%	1.2%
10-year Treasury note yield	2.8%	1.8%	2.4%	2.5%	2.2%	2.9%
AAA corporate bond rate	4.6%	3.7%	4.2%	4.2%	3.8%	4.6%
Percent change in:						
Real gross domestic product	1.6%	2.3%	2.2%	2.4%	2.3%	2.9%
Industrial production	3.3%	3.8%	2.9%	4.2%	0.5%	3.6%
Consumer price index	3.1%	2.1%	1.5%	1.6%	0.3%	2.2%

Data source: "Value Line Investment Survey," August 2015.

EXHIBIT 26.4 | Comparative Stockholder Data, 2004 and 2014 (in thousands of shares)

	2004		2014	
	Shares	Percentage	Shares	Percentage
Founders' families	3,585	13%	5,113	18%
Employees and families	5,516	20%	4,443	16%
Institutional investors				
Growth oriented	3,585	13%	1,602	6%
Value oriented	2,207	8%	3,409	12%
Individual investors				
Long term; retirement	10,205	37%	6,767	24%
Short term; trading oriented	1,379	5%	3,409	12%
Other; unknown	1,103	4%	3,153	11%
Total	27,578	100%	27,896	100%

Note: The investor-relations department identified these categories from company records. The type of institutional investor was identified from promotional materials stating the investment goals of the institutions. The type of individual investor was identified from a survey of subsamples of investors.

Source: Author estimates.

EXHIBIT 26.5 | Per-Share Financial and Stock Data[1]

Year	Sales/ share	EPS[2]	DPS[2]	CPS[2]	Stock price High	Stock price Low	Stock price Avg.	Avg. P/E	Payout ratio	Avg. yield	Shares outstanding (millions)
2000	$16.12	$1.19	$0.37	$2.03	$21.11	$10.18	$14.85	12.5	31%	2.5%	23.4
2001	15.00	1.28	0.39	2.14	21.23	8.20	13.50	10.5	30%	2.9%	24.1
2002	15.23	0.45	0.40	1.17	18.50	10.18	13.35	29.8	88%	3.0%	25.8
2003	16.37	0.86	0.42	1.65	22.48	12.17	18.36	21.4	48%	2.3%	27.1
2004	21.08	1.27	0.45	2.13	23.84	18.01	21.00	16.5	35%	2.1%	27.6
2005	24.93	1.90	0.47	2.86	26.70	18.25	22.73	11.9	25%	2.1%	28.0
2006	30.10	2.67	0.51	3.75	34.34	22.75	30.31	11.3	19%	1.7%	28.1
2007	34.59	3.07	0.59	4.22	44.13	32.66	38.29	12.5	19%	1.5%	28.2
2008	37.80	3.24	0.64	4.41	46.73	20.81	36.58	11.3	20%	1.7%	28.3
2009	26.61	0.75	0.64	1.52	33.00	15.52	25.07	33.5	86%	2.6%	28.0
2010	31.82	1.03	0.64	1.92	20.31	14.16	17.03	16.5	62%	3.8%	28.1
2011	41.94	1.29	0.64	2.04	18.42	13.36	16.27	12.6	50%	3.9%	28.1
2012	45.49	(3.25)	0.64	2.86	16.82	12.74	14.50	nmf	nmf	4.4%	28.3
2013	43.25	0.69	0.64	1.99	13.30	9.28	11.26	16.4	93%	5.7%	28.3
2014	40.68	(7.57)	0.32	(0.97)	14.03	11.85	13.00	nmf	nmf	2.5%	27.9

nmf = not a meaningful figure.

[1] Adjusted for a 3-for-2 stock split in January 1995 and a 50% stock dividend in June 2007.

[2] EPS = earnings per share; CPS = cash earnings per share; DPS = dividend per share.

Source: Author estimates.

EXHIBIT 26.6 | Comparative Industry Data

	Sales ($ millions)	Annual growth rate of cash flow[1]		Current payout ratio	Current dividend yield	Debt/ equity[2]	Insider ownership	P/E ratio
		Last 5 years	Next 3–5 years					
Rockboro Machine Tools Corp.	1,135	−1.5%	15.0%	nmf	0%	28.4%	34.3%	nmf
CAD/CAM companies (software and hardware)								
Autodesk, Inc.	2,512	3.0%	10.5%	0%	0%	33.7%	1.0%	nmf
Ansys, Inc.	941	14.5%	6.5%	0%	0%	0.0%	1.9%	23.0
Cadence Design	1,702	0.0%	10.0%	0%	0%	26.1%	3.2%	17.6
Mentor Graphics	1,244	43.0%	4.0%	0%	0%	18.1%	2.6%	16.9
PTC	1,357	8.5%	4.5%	0%	0%	68.7%	1.4%	26.4
Synopsys, Inc.	2,058	11.0%	7.5%	0%	0%	1.5%	1.4%	15.4
Electrical-industrial equipment manufacturers								
Emerson Electric Company	22,304	3.5%	3.5%	47%	3%	52.8%	0.8%	17.6
Hubbell Inc.	3,359	7.5%	6.0%	37%	2%	31.0%	1.3%	21.3
Rockwell Auto	6,624	12.5%	5.5%	39%	2%	34.1%	1.5%	19.9
Machine tool manufacturers								
Actuant Corp.	1,400	6.0%	5.5%	2%	0.1%	38.5%	3.7%	19.2
Lincoln Electric Holdings, Inc.	2,813	11.5%	3.5%	24%	1%	0.2%	3.3%	18.3
Milacron, Inc.	1,211	nmf	nmf	0%	0%	265.1%	0.0%	nmf
Snap-On Inc.	3,278	9.5%	8.5%	26%	2%	39.1%	3.4%	16.8

nmf = not a meaningful figure.

[1]Rockboro cash flow growth calculations use an adjusted cash flow for 2014 that omits the restructuring costs.

[2]Based on book values.

Data source: "Value Line Investment Survey," February 2016.

EXHIBIT 26.7 | Selected Healthy Companies with High- and Zero-Dividend Payouts

	Industry	Expected return on total capital (next 3–5 years)	Expected growth rate of dividends (next 3–5 years)	Current dividend payout	Current dividend yield	Expected growth rate of sales (next 3–5 years)	Current P/E ratio
High-Payout Companies							
Pfizer	Pharmaceutical	13.0%	6.0%	73.8%	3.6%	1.5%	21.1
Suburban Propane	Oil/gas pipeline—MLP[1]	8.0%	1.0%	212.1%	8.2%	1.5%	24.5
CenturyLink, Inc.	Telecommunications utility	5.5%	3.0%	86.4%	6.7%	3.0%	12.8
Southern Company	Electric utility	6.5%	3.0%	75.1%	4.8%	3.5%	16.5
Dow Chemical	Chemical manufacturing	10.5%	11.0%	46.0%	4.6%	7.0%	12.4
Ford Motor Co.	Auto manufacturer	7.5%	14.5%	43.1%	4.1%	2.5%	8.3
Zero-Payout Companies							
AutoZone	Auto parts	38.5%	0.0%	0.0%	0.0%	12.8%	19.7
Popeyes	Fried chicken fast food	21.0%	0.0%	0.0%	0.0%	14.5%	28.8
Manhatttan Assoc	Supply chain IT	27.5%	0.0%	0.0%	0.0%	10.0%	50.1
Biogen	Biotechnology	27.0%	0.0%	0.0%	0.0%	14.0%	16.6
Sirius XM	Entertainment radio	26.5%	0.0%	0.0%	0.0%	8.5%	26.4
Amazon.com, Inc.	Online retail	15.0%	0.0%	0.0%	0.0%	17.5%	nmf

[1]A master limited partnership (MLP) paid no corporate taxes. All income taxes were paid by shareholders on their share of taxable earnings.

Data source: "Value Line Investment Survey," August 2015.

EXHIBIT 26.8 | Projected Sources-and-Uses Statement Assuming a 40% Payout Ratio[1] (dollars in millions)

Assumptions:	2015	2016	2017	2018	2019	2020	2021	
Sales Growth Rate:	15%	15%	15%	15%	15%	15%	15%	
Net Income as % of Sales	2.1%	4.0%	5.0%	5.5%	6.0%	6.5%	6.5%	
Dividend Payout Ratio	40.0%	40.0%	40.0%	40.0%	40.0%	40.0%	40.0%	

Projections								Total
	2015	2016	2017	2018	2019	2020	2021	2015–21
Sales	$1,305	$1,501	$1,726	$1,985	$2,283	$2,625	$3,019	$14,444
Sources:								
Net income	27.0	60.0	86.3	109.2	137.0	170.6	196.2	786.4
Depreciation	33.9	39.0	44.9	51.6	59.4	68.3	78.5	375.6
Total	61.0	99.1	131.2	160.8	196.3	238.9	274.7	1,161.9
Uses:								
Capital expend.	65.3	75.0	86.3	99.3	102.7	118.1	135.9	682.6
Change in working capital	29.3	33.6	38.7	44.5	51.2	58.8	67.7	323.7
Total	94.5	108.7	125.0	143.7	153.9	177.0	203.5	1,006.3
Excess cash/(borrowing needs)	(33.6)	(9.6)	6.2	17.1	42.4	61.9	71.2	155.7
Dividend	10.8	24.0	34.5	43.7	54.8	68.3	78.5	314.6
After dividend Excess cash/(borrowing needs)	($44.4)	($33.6)	($28.3)	($26.6)	($12.3)	($6.3)	($7.3)	($158.9)

[1]This analysis ignores the effects of borrowing on interest expense.

Source: Author estimates.

EMI Group PLC

In this Internet age, the consumer is using music content more than ever before—whether that's playlisting, podcasting, personalizing, sharing, downloading or just simply enjoying it. The digital revolution has caused a complete change to the culture, operations, and attitude of music companies everywhere. It hasn't been easy, and we must certainly continue to fight piracy in all its forms. But there can be no doubt that with even greater commitment to innovation and a true focus on the consumer, digital distribution is becoming the best thing that ever happened to the music business and the music fan.

> **—Eric Nicoli, CEO, EMI Group[1]**

In early spring of 2007, Martin Stewart drove through the darkened streets of Kensington in West London. As chief financial officer (CFO) for global music giant EMI, Stewart already knew most of the news that would break at the company's April 18 earnings announcement. Annual underlying revenue for the company was down 16% to GBP 1.8 billion (British pounds). Earnings per share (EPS) had also dropped from 10.9 pence (p) in 2006 to −36.3p in FY2007 (fiscal year). Those disappointing numbers were roughly in line with the guidance Stewart had given investors in February. The performance reflected the global decline in music industry revenues, as well as the extraordinary cost of the restructuring program EMI was pursuing to realign its investment priorities and focus its resources to achieve the best returns in the future.

The earnings announcement would include an announcement of the dividend amount, which had not yet been determined. The board would meet soon to review EMI's annual results, and Stewart was to recommend an appropriate final dividend for the fiscal year.[2]

This case was written by Elizabeth W. Shumadine (MBA '01), under the supervision of Professor Michael J. Schill, based on public information. Funding was provided by the L. White Matthews Fund for Finance case writing. Copyright © 2008 by the University of Virginia Darden School Foundation, Charlottesville, VA. All rights reserved. *To order copies, send an e-mail to sales@dardenbusinesspublishing.com. No part of this publication may be reproduced, stored in a retrieval system, used in a spreadsheet, or transmitted in any form or by any means—electronic, mechanical, photocopying, recording, or otherwise—without the permission of the Darden School Foundation.* Rev. 2/09.

[1]International Federation of Phonographic Industry (IFPI), "IFPI: 07 Digital Music Report," January 2007.

[2]In the United Kingdom, companies typically declared dividends twice a year, first with the midyear results and second with the full-year results. Typically, EMI paid an interim dividend of 2p per share and a final dividend of 6p per share. In addition, both EMI's interim and final dividends were paid out to shareholders in the following fiscal year. In November 2006, EMI's board committed to paying the interim dividend of 2p per share following its 2007 fiscal midyear results with actual payment to shareholders expected in April 2007. Both the 2p interim dividend and the recommended final dividend would be reflected in the 2008 financial statements.

On an annual basis, EMI had consistently paid an 8p-per-share dividend to ordinary shareholders since 2002 (**Exhibit 27.1**). Now in light of EMI's recent performance, Stewart questioned whether EMI should continue to maintain what would represent a combined GBP 63-million annual dividend payment. Although omitting the dividend would preserve cash, Stewart appreciated the negative effect the decision might have on EMI's share price, which was currently at 227p. Stewart recognized that EMI faced considerable threat of a takeover. Although its board had recently been able to successfully reject an unsolicited 260p-per-share merger offer from U.S. rival Warner Music, there remained considerable outside interest in taking over EMI. It seemed that boosting EMI's share price was imperative if EMI was to maintain its independence.

EMI

With a storied history that included such names as the Beatles, the Beach Boys, Pink Floyd, and Duran Duran, it was not difficult to understand why EMI considered its current and historical catalog of songs and recordings among the best in the world. EMI, Warner Music Group, Sony BMG Music Entertainment, and Universal Music Group, collectively known as "the majors," dominated the music industry in the early 21st century and accounted for more than two-thirds of the world's recorded music and publishing sales.[3] **Exhibit 27.2** contains a list of the global top-10 albums with their respective record labels for the last four years.

Recorded music and music publishing were the two main revenue drivers for the music industry. EMI divided its organization into two corresponding divisions. EMI Music, the recorded-music side, sought out artists it believed would be long-term commercial recording successes. Each EMI record label marketed its artist's recordings to the public and sold the releases through a variety of retail outlets. EMI's extensive music catalog consisted of more than 3 million songs. Recorded-music division sales came from both new and old recordings with existing catalog albums constituting 30% to 35% of the division's unit sales. **Exhibit 27.3** contains a list of EMI's most successful recording artists in FY2007.

EMI Music Publishing focused not on recordings but on the songs themselves. Generally, there were three categories of publishing-rights ownership in the music industry: the lyric's author, the music's composer, and the publisher who acquired the right to exploit the song. These publishing-rights owners were entitled to royalties whenever and however their music was used. Music publishers categorized their revenue streams as mechanical royalties (sales of recorded music), performance royalties (performances of a song on TV, radio, at a live concert, or in other public venues such as bars), and synchronization royalties (use of a song in audiovisual works such as advertisements or computer games). EMI included a fourth category of royalties labeled "other," which included sales of sheet music and, increasingly, mobile ring tones and ring backs. Similar to the recorded-music division, the music-publishing division identified

---

[3]William B. Drewry, Jolanta Masojada, Nick Bertolotti, and Giasone Salati, "Global Music Industry, 'Just the Two of Us,'" Credit Suisse Equity Research, June 16, 2006. Sony BMG Music Entertainment was a joint venture owned by Sony Corporation and Bertelsmann. Universal Music was owned by Vivendi.

songwriters with commercial potential and signed them to long-term contracts. The division then assisted the songwriters in marketing their works to record companies and other media firms. EMI's current publishing catalog encompassed more than 1 million musical compositions. **Exhibit 27.3** includes a list of EMI's most-successful songwriters in FY2007. EMI's publishing business generated one-fourth of the total group revenue. Revenue in the publishing business was stable, and operating profits were positive.

In addition to seeking out and signing flourishing recording artists and songwriters to long-term agreements, both EMI divisions also expanded and enhanced their individual catalogs and artist rosters by strategic transactions. Two key acquisitions for EMI's recorded-music division were the 1955 acquisition of a leading American record label, Capitol Records, and the 1992 acquisition of Virgin Music Group, then the largest independent record label. Together the transactions added such key recording stars as Frank Sinatra, Nat King Cole, Janet Jackson, and the Rolling Stones. The music-publishing division similarly targeted existing publishing assets with large, proven commercial potential such as the purchase in various stages of Motown founder Berry Gordy's music catalog in 1997, 2003, and 2004.

Since the company's founding in 1897, EMI's model had been that of "constantly seeking to expand their catalog, with the hits of today forming the classics of tomorrow."[4] Both divisions pursued the goal of having the top-selling artists and songwriters and the deepest, most-recognized catalog assets. EMI welcomed technological innovations, which often drove increased music sales as consumers updated their music collections with the latest music medium (e.g., replacing an LP or cassette with the same recording on compact disc). But the latest technology, digital audio on the Internet, was different and revolutionary. Digital audio on the Internet demanded rethinking the business model of all the majors, including EMI.

Digital Audio and the Music Industry

Digital audio had been around since the advent of the compact disc (CD) in the early 1980s, but the 1990s combination of digital audio, Internet, and MP3 file format brought the music industry to a new crossroads. The MP3 format had nearly the same sound quality as CDs, but its small file size allowed it to be easily downloaded from the Internet, stored on a computer hard drive, and transferred to a digital audio player, generally referred to as an MP3 player.

Peer-to-peer file-sharing Internet services, most notably Napster, emerged in the late 1990s. First available in mid-1999, Napster facilitated the exchange of music files. The use of Napster's file-sharing program exploded, and Napster claimed 20 million users by July 2000. Napster's swift growth did not go unnoticed by the music industry. While the Recording Industry Association of America (RIAA) was eventually successful in using the court system to force Napster to remove copyrighted material, it did not stop peer-to-peer file sharing. New services were quickly developed to replace Napster. The International Federation of the Phonographic Industry (IFPI), an organization

---

[4]EMI Group PLC annual report, 2007.

representing the recording industry worldwide, estimated that almost 20 billion songs were downloaded illegally in 2005.

EMI was an early presence on the Internet in 1993. In 1999, EMI artist David Bowie's album, *hours . . .*, was the first album by a major recording artist to be released for download from the Internet. None of the record labels were prepared, however, for how quickly peer-to-peer file sharing would change the dynamics of the music industry and become a seemingly permanent thorn in the music industry's side. In the wake of Napster's demise, the music labels, including EMI, attempted various subscription services, but most failed for such reasons as cost, CD-burning restrictions, and incompatibility with available MP3 players. Only in the spring of 2003, when Apple launched its user-friendly Web site, iTunes Music Store, did legitimate digital-audio sales really take off in the United States, the world's largest music market. Apple began to expand iTunes globally in 2004 and sold its one-billionth download in February 2006. According to the IFPI, there were 500 legitimate on-line music services in more than 40 countries by the beginning of 2007, with $2 billion in digital music sales in 2006.

Despite the rise of legally downloaded music, the global music market continued to shrink due to the rapid decline in physical sales. Nielsen SoundScan noted that total album units sold (excluding digital-track equivalents) declined almost 25% from 2000 to 2006.[5] IFPI optimistically predicted that digital sales would compensate for the decrease in physical sales in 2006, yet in early 2007, IFPI admitted that this "holy grail" had not yet occurred, with 2006 overall music sales estimated to have declined by 3%.[6] IFPI now hoped digital sales would overtake the decline in physical sales in 2007. Credit Suisse's Global Music Industry Forecasts incorporated this view with a relatively flat music market in 2007 and minor growth of 1.1% to 1.5% in 2008 and 2009.[7] The Credit Suisse analyst also noted that the music industry's operating margins were expected to rise as digital sales became more significant and related production and distribution costs declined.[8] Lehman Brothers was more conservative, assuming a flat market for the next few years and commenting that the continued weakness in early 2007 implied that the "market could remain tough for the next couple of years."[9]

Many in the industry feared that consumers' ability to *unbundle* their music purchases—to purchase two or three favorite songs from an album on-line versus the entire album at a physical retail store—would put negative pressure on music sales for the foreseeable future. A Bear Stearns research report noted:

> While music consumption, in terms of listening time, is increasing as the iPod and other portable devices have become mass-market products, the industry has still not found a way of monetizing this consumption. Instead, growing piracy and the unbundling of the

---

[5]Brian Hiatt and Evan Serpick, "The Record Industry's Decline," RollingStones.com, June 19, 2007.

[6]International Federation of Phonographic Industry (IFPI), "IFPI: 07 Digital Music Report," January 2007.

[7]William B. Drewry, Jolanta Masojada, Dennis Sabo, and Ashish Gupta, "Warner Music Group," Credit Suisse Equity Research, February 9, 2007.

[8]Drewry, Masojada, Bertolotti, and Salati, "Global Music Industry, 'Just the Two of Us.'"

[9]Richard Jones and Tamsin Garrity, "EMI Group," Lehman Brothers Equity Research, February 15, 2007.

album, combined with the growing power of big retailers in the physical and iTunes in the digital worlds, have left the industry in a funk. There is no immediate solution that we are aware of on the horizon and in our view, visibility on sales remains poor.[10]

Recent Developments at EMI

The last few years had been incredibly difficult, particularly within EMI's recorded-music division, where revenues had declined 27% from GBP 2,282 million in 2001 to GBP 1,660 million in 2006. (**Exhibits 27.4** and **27.5** show EMI's financial statements through FY2007.) Fortunately, downloadable digital audio did not have a similar ruinous effect on the publishing division. EMI's publishing sales were a small buffer for the company's performance and hovered in a tight range of GBP 420 million to GBP 391 million during that period. CEO Eric Nicoli's address at the July 2006 annual general meeting indicated good things were in store for EMI in both the short term and the long term. Nicoli stressed EMI's exciting upcoming release schedules, growth in digital sales, and success with restructuring plans.

EMI's digital sales were growing and represented an increasingly large percentage of total revenues. In 2004, EMI generated group digital revenues of GBP 15 million, which represented just less than 1% of total group revenues. By 2006, EMI had grown the digital revenue to GBP 112 million, which represented 5.4% of total group revenues. The expected 2007 digital sales for EMI were close to 10% of group revenues.

Given the positive expectations for its 2007 fiscal year, financial analysts had expected EMI's recorded-music division to see positive sales growth during the year. EMI's surprising negative earnings guidance on January 12 quickly changed its outlook. EMI disclosed that the music industry and EMI's second half of the year releases had underperformed its expectations. While the publishing division was on track to achieve its goals, EMI's recorded-music division revenues were now expected to decline 6% to 10% from one year ago. The market and investor community reacted swiftly to the news. With trading volume nearly 10 times the previous day's volume, EMI's market capitalization ended up down more than 7%.

EMI further shocked the investment community with another profit warning just one month later. On February 14, the company announced that the recorded-music division's FY2007 revenues would actually decrease by about 15% year-over-year. EMI based its new dismal forecast on worsening market conditions in North America, where SoundScan had calculated that the physical music market had declined 20% in 2007. The investment community punished EMI more severely after this second surprise profit warning, and EMI's stock price dropped another 12%. British newspaper *The Daily Telegraph* reported shareholders were increasingly disgruntled with performance surprises. One shareholder allegedly said, "I think [Nicoli]'s a dead duck. [EMI] is now very vulnerable to a [takeover] bid, and Nicoli is not in any position to defend anything. I think the finance director [Martin Stewart] has also been tainted because it suggests they did not get to the bottom of the numbers." EMI analyst Redwan Ahmed of Oriel Securities also decried EMI management's recent news: "It's disastrous . . . they give themselves a big 6% to 10% range and a

---

[10]Nicholas Bell and Richard Gordon, CFA, "EMI," Bear Stearns International Limited European Equity Research, February 27, 2007.

month later say it's 15%. They have lost all credibility. I also think the dividend is going to get slashed to about 5p."[11] **Exhibit 27.6** contains information on EMI's shareholder profile.

As its fiscal year came to a close, EMI's internal reports indicated that its February 14 forecast was close to the mark. The recorded-music division's revenue was down, and profits were negative. The publishing-division revenue was essentially flat, and its division's margin improved as a result of a smaller cost base. The company expected underlying group earnings before interest, taxes, depreciation, and amortization (EBITDA), before exceptional items, to be GBP 174 million, which exceeded analysts' estimates. Digital revenue had grown by 59% and would represent 10% of revenue. EMI management planned to make a joint announcement with Apple in the next few days that it was going to be the first major music company to offer its digital catalog free from digital-rights management and with improved sound quality. The new format would sell at a 30% premium. EMI management expected this move would drive increased digital sales.

Management was pleased with the progress of the restructuring program announced with the January profit warning. The plan was being implemented quicker than expected and, accordingly, more cost savings would be realized in FY2008. The program was going to cost closer to GBP 125 million, as opposed to the GBP 150 million previously announced. Upon completion, the program was expected to remove GBP 110 million from EMI's annual cost base, with the majority of savings coming from the recorded-music division. The plan reduced layers in the management structure and encouraged the recorded-music and publishing divisions to work more closely together for revenue and cost synergies.[12] One headline-worthy change in the reorganization was the surprise removal of the recorded-music division head, Alain Levy, and Nicoli taking direct responsibility for the division.

The Dividend Decision

Since the board had already declared an interim dividend of 2p per share in November 2006, the question was whether to maintain the past payout level by recommending that an additional 6p final EMI dividend be paid. Considering EMI's struggling financial situation, there was good reason to question the wisdom of paying a dividend. **Exhibit 27.7** provides a forecast of the cash flow effects of maintaining the dividend, based on market-based forecasts of performance. Omitting the dividend, however, was likely to send a message that management had lost confidence, potentially accelerating the ongoing stock price decline—the last thing EMI needed to do.[13] (**Exhibit 27.9** depicts trends in the EMI share price from May 2000 to May 2006.)

---

[11]Alistair Osborne, "Nicoli 'a dead duck' as EMI issues new warning," *Daily Telegraph*, February 16, 2007.

[12]Restructuring efforts over the previous three years had collectively saved the company GBP 180 million annually; however, the result was a one-time implementation cost of GBP 300 million.

[13]Historically, there was strong evidence of significant negative stock-price reactions to dividend cancellations (see Balasingham Balachandran, John Cadle, and Michael Theobald, "Interim Dividend Cuts and Omissions in the U.K.," *European Financial Management* 2:1 (March 1996), 23–38, for a study using only British firms, and Roni Michaely, Richard Thaler, and Kent Womack, "Price Reactions to Dividend Initiations and Omissions: Overreaction of Drift?" *Journal of Finance*, 50, 2 (June 1995), 573–608, for a larger study using U.S. firms. Both academics and practitioners vigorously debated the impact of dividend policy. In fact, Nobel laureate economists had argued that dividend policy should maintain little relevance to investors. **Exhibit 27.8** contains a summary of Modigliani and Miller arguments.

Many believed that music industry economics were on the verge of turning the corner. A decision to maintain the historical 8p dividend would emphasize management's expectation of business improvement despite the disappointing recent financial news. Forecasts for global economic growth continued to be strong (**Exhibit 27.10**), and reimbursements to shareholders through dividends and repurchases were on the upswing among media peers (**Exhibit 27.11**).

As Stewart navigated his way home, the radio played another hit from a well-known EMI artist. Despite the current difficulties, Stewart was convinced there was still a lot going for EMI.

EXHIBIT 27.1 | Financial and Stock Data per Share (in pence)

| Fiscal Year End | Basic EPS | Underlying Diluted EPS | Dividend per Share | Stock Price[1] | | | Payout Ratio (%) Using | | Avg. Dividend Yield (%) | Wgtd. Avg. Shares Outstanding (millions) |
				High	Low	Average	Basic EPS	Underlying Dil. EPS		
2001	10.1	21.9	16.0	691.00	427.00	566.0	158	73	2.8	NA
2002	(25.5)	11.8	8.0	505.00	214.00	367.1	nmf	68	2.2	782.8
2003	29.3	15.7	8.0	365.00	80.00	194.7	27	51	4.1	784.0
2004	(9.1)	15.5	8.0	278.25	91.25	166.2	nmf	52	4.8	784.4
2005	9.6	13.1	8.0	281.25	191.00	236.1	83	61	3.4	785.6
2006	10.9	15.7	8.0	266.00	207.00	244.2	73	51	3.3	786.8
2007	(36.3)	5.8	2.0p + TBD	313.75	210.75	263.5	TBD	TBD	TBD	794.8

[1]Stock price data is for the fiscal year period. For example, 2007 data is from April 1, 2006 to March 31, 2007. Stock price data was available for 2001 only from May 15, 2000 to March 31, 2001.

Sources of data: Company Web site and Yahoo! Finance.

EXHIBIT 27.2 | Top-10 Albums for 2003 to 2006 (physical sales only)

	Artist	Album Title	Company
2006	1 Soundtrack	*High School Musical*	Walt Disney/Universal/**EMI**
	2 Red Hot Chili Peppers	*Stadium Arcadium*	Warner
	3 The Beatles	*Love*	**EMI**
	4 James Blunt	*Back to Bedlam*	Warner
	5 Justin Timberlake	*FutureSex/LoveSounds*	SonyBMG
	6 Beyoncé	*B'Day*	SonyBMG
	7 U2	*U2 18 Singles*	Universal
	8 Rascal Flatts	*Me and My Gang*	Lyric Street/Hollywood/Universal/**EMI**
	9 Il Divo	*Amore*	Universal
	10 Andrea Bocelli	*Amore*	Universal
2005	1 Coldplay	*X&Y*	**EMI**
	2 Mariah Carey	*The Emancipation Of Mimi*	Universal
	3 50 Cent	*The Massacre*	Universal
	4 Black Eyed Peas	*Monkey Business*	Universal
	5 Green Day	*American Idiot*	Warner
	6 Madonna	*Confessions on a Dance Floor*	Warner
	7 Kelly Clarkson	*Breakaway*	SonyBMG
	8 Eminem	*Curtain Call*	Universal
	9 James Blunt	*Back to Bedlam*	Warner
	10 Robbie Williams	*Intensive Care*	**EMI**
2004	1 Usher	*Confessions*	SonyBMG
	2 Norah Jones	*Feels Like Home*	**EMI**
	3 Eminem	*Encore*	Universal
	4 U2	*How To Dismantle An Atomic Bomb*	Universal
	5 Avril Lavigne	*Under My Skin*	SonyBMG
	6 Robbie Williams	*Greatest Hits*	**EMI**
	7 Shania Twain	*Greatest Hits*	Universal
	8 Destiny's Child	*Destiny Fulfilled*	SonyBMG
	9 Guns N' Roses	*Greatest Hits*	Universal
	10 Maroon 5	*Songs About Jane*	SonyBMG
2003	1 Norah Jones	*Come Away With Me*	**EMI**
	2 50 Cent	*Get Rich Or Die Tryin'*	Universal
	3 Linkin Park	*Meteora*	Warner
	4 Dido	*Life For Rent*	BMG
	5 Beyoncé Knowles	*Dangerously in Love*	Sony
	6 Coldplay	*A Rush of Blood to the Head*	**EMI**
	7 Evanescence	*Fallen*	Sony
	8 Britney Spears	*In The Zone*	BMG
	9 Avril Lavigne	*Let Go*	BMG
	10 Celine Dion	*One Heart*	Sony

Source of data: International Federation of Phonographic Industry (IFPI) Web site.

EXHIBIT 27.3 | EMI Top Recording and Publishing Successes in Fiscal Year 2007

Artist	Album Title	Unit Sales[1] (millions GBP)
The Beatles	*Love*	5.0
Norah Jones	*Not Too Late*	4.2
Corinne Bailey Rae	*Corinne Bailey Rae*	2.7
Robbie Williams	*Rudebox*	2.5
Keith Urban	*Love, Pain & The Whole Crazy Thing*	2.0
Lily Allen	*Alright, Still*	1.7
The Kooks	*Inside In/Inside Out*	1.6
RBD	*Celestial*	1.3
Joss Stone	*Introducing Joss Stone*	1.3
Utada Hikaru	*Ultra Blue*	1.3
Depeche Mode	*The Best of Depeche Mode Volume 1*	1.2
Janet Jackson	*20 Y.O.*	1.2
30 Seconds to Mars	*A Beautiful Lie*	1.2
Herbert Grönemeyer	*12*	1.1
Sarah Brightman	*Diva: The Singles Collection*	1.0
Gerard Rene-Gordon	*Toppers Kerst Album*	1.0
Bob Segar	*Face The Promise*	1.0
Iron Maiden	*A Matter of Life and Death*	0.9
Diam's	*Dans Ma Bulle*	0.8
Renaud	*Rouge Sang*	0.8

EMI Music Publishing's Most-Successful Songwriters of FY2007

Songwriter	Song
Amy Winehouse	*Rehab*
Beyoncé	*Irreplaceable*
Brad Paisley	*The World*
Death Cab for Cutie	*Soul Meets Body*
Enrique Iglesias	*Do You Know (Ping Pong Song)*
Good Charlotte	*Lifestyles of the Rich and Famous*
Hinder	*Lips of an Angel*
James Blunt	*Goodbye My Lover*
Jay-Z	*Show Me What You Got*
Kanye West	*Wouldn't Get Far*
Kelly Clarkson	*Never Again*
Ludacris	*Money Maker*
Natasha Bedingfield	*These Words*
Norah Jones	*Thinking About You*
Ozzy Osbourne	*I Don't Wanna Stop*
Panic! At The Disco	*I Write Sins Not Tragedies*
Pink	*U + Ur Hand*
Rob Thomas	*Lonely No More*
Take That	*Patience*
The Fray	*How To Save A Life*

[1]All sales figures are for the 12 months ended March 31, 2007. Unit sales include digital albums and digital track album equivalent.

Source of data: Company annual report.

EXHIBIT 27.4 | Consolidated Income Statements (in millions GBP, except per-share data)

	For Years Ended March 31,				
	2003	**2004**	**2005**	**2006**	**2007**
Underlying Revenue	2,175	2,121	2,001	2,080	1,752
Group profit from operations before exceptional items and amortization	255	249	225	251	151
Exceptional items	(21)	(138)	(18)	3	(307)
Amortization and impairment	(43)	(51)	(48)	(50)	(53)
Share of profit from associates and jv	1	(0)	1	1	2
Profit (loss) from operations	191	60	161	204	(207)
Exceptional items:					
(Losses) on disposal or closure of business	(25)	(40)			
Gains on disposal of PP&E and investments	235	24		2	50
Profit (loss) before finance charges	401	43	161	206	(157)
Finance charges	(77)	(96)	(62)	(88)	(107)
Profit (loss) before taxation	324	(53)	99	118	(264)
Taxation	(83)	(20)	(24)	(28)	(23)
Profit (loss) after taxation	241	(73)	75	90	(287)
Underlying EBITDA[1]	297	284	250	276	174
Underlying PBT[2]	179	163	141	159	63
Earnings per ordinary share:					
Basic	29.3p	(9.1)p	9.6p	10.9p	(36.3)p
Underlying diluted	15.7p	15.5p	13.1p	15.7p	5.8p
Dividend per ordinary share	8.0p	8.0p	8.0p	8.0p	2.0p + TBD
Net borrowings[3]	860	749	858	880	904
Interest cover[4]	3.9×	3.3×	2.9×	3.0×	1.9×
Dividend cover[5, 6]	2.0×	1.9×	1.6×	2.0×	TBD

[1]Underlying EBITDA is group profit from operations before depreciation, operating exceptional items and amortization.

[2]Underlying profit before taxes (PBT) is before exceptional items and amortization.

[3]Net borrowings is the sum of long-term and short-term borrowings including finance leases less cash, cash equivalents, and liquid funds investments.

[4]Interest cover is underlying EBITDA (before exceptional items) divided by finance charges (excluding nonstandard charges).

[5]Dividend cover is underlying diluted earnings per ordinary share divided by dividend declared per ordinary share.

[6]EMI noted the company targeted an ongoing dividend cover of 2.0× in its 2004 annual report.

Sources of data: Company annual reports and Web site.

EXHIBIT 27.5 | Consolidated Balance Sheets (in millions GBP)

	For the Years Ended March 31		
Assets	**2005**	**2006**	**2007**
Noncurrent assets			
Music copyrights and intangibles	405	389	306
Goodwill	35	43	29
Property, plant, and equipment	200	197	132
Investments in associates	9	9	8
Financial assets	57	56	20
Deferred taxation	30	23	12
Other receivables	7	4	4
	741	721	511
Current assets			
Inventories	28	37	30
Advances	336	330	218
Trade receivables	300	409	290
Corporation tax recoverable	21	17	16
Other receivables	110	110	101
Financial assets		0	0
Investments: liquid funds	2	2	2
Cash and cash equivalents	241	191	332
	1,038	1,096	988
Total assets	1,779	1,817	1,499
Liabilities			
Noncurrent liabilities			
Financial liabilities	1,162	1,150	1,317
Other payables	10	10	7
Deferred taxation	8	5	4
Pension provisions	100	31	42
	1,280	1,195	1,369
Current liabilities			
Financial liabilities	31	23	12
Other payables	1,060	1,149	1,045
Current tax liability	160	143	112
Other provisions for liabilities and charges	44	34	111
	1,295	1,348	1,280
Total liabilities	2,575	2,544	2,650
Equity			
Capital and reserves			
Share capital	111	111	112
Share premium account	447	448	455
Capital redemption reserve	496	496	496
Foreign exchange reserve	4	(17)	20
Other reserves	204	206	215
Retained earnings	(2,107)	(2,019)	(2,451)
Equity attributable to equity holders of the parent	(846)	(775)	(1,154)
Minority interests (equity)	49	49	3
Total equity	(796)	(727)	(1,151)

Sources of data: Company annual reports and Web site.

EXHIBIT 27.6 | Analysis of Ordinary Shareholdings on May 18, 2006

Categories of Shareholders		Number	Percentage	Total Shares Held by this Category	Percentage
Small	1 to 500 shares	9,720	50.0	1,923,604	0.2
	501 to 1,000 shares	4,243	21.8	3,100,499	0.4
	1,001 to 10,000 shares	4,648	23.9	10,864,585	1.4
	10,001 to 100,000 shares	434	2.2	15,502,961	2.0
	100,001 to 1,000,000 shares	291	1.5	101,194,240	12.8
Large	1,000,001 shares and over	123	0.6	660,339,675	83.3
Total		19,459 shareholders		792,925,564 shares	

Substantial Shareholders[1]	No. of Shares	Percentage of Capital Held
FMR Corp./Fidelity International Ltd.	114,065,999	14.39
Wellington Management Company, LLP	74,460,205	9.39
Deutsche Bank AG	49,278,472	6.21
HBOS plc/Insight Investment Management Ltd.	40,609,739	5.12
The Capital Group Companies, Inc.	40,512,803	5.11
Prudential plc group of companies	37,310,271	4.71
Legal & General Investment Management Ltd.	27,687,735	3.49

[1]Substantial shareholders are defined as owning three or more of ordinary shares and/or three or more of the voting rights of ordinary shares.

Source of data: Company annual reports.

EXHIBIT 27.7 | EMI Projected Sources-and-Uses Statement Assuming Annual 8.0p Dividend Is Maintained[1,2] (in GBP; end of year March 31)

Assumptions	2006	2007	2008 Est.	2009 Est.
Revenue growth			1.7	0.7
New equity issued	0.6	8.9	—	—
Share repurchases	0.5	5.5	0.0	0.0
Dividends	62.9	63.2	63.2	63.2
Financial Statements				
Revenue	2,079.9	1,751.5	1,781.3	1,793.7
Net income	90.0	(287.0)	(80.4)	26.3
Noncurrent assets	721	511	476	479
Current operating assets	903	654.6	821.0	857.0
Cash	193	333.4	191.0	177.5
Total assets	1,817	1,499	1,488	1,514
Debt obligations	1,150	1,317	1,442	1,494
Other noncurrent liabilities	46	52	52	52
Current liabilities	1,348	1,280	1,289	1,299
Total equity	(726)	(1,151)	(1,295)	(1,332)
Sources and Uses Statement				
Sources				
Net income	90.0	(287.0)	(80.4)	26.3
New equity issued	0.6	8.9	0.0	0.0
Other adjustments to equity	42.5	(77.6)	0.0	0.0
Increase in debt obligations	(12.0)	167.3	124.6	52.2
Increase in other NC liabilities	(72.6)	6.7	0.0	0.0
Increase in current liabilities	52.9	(68.1)	8.9	10.0
Total sources	101.4	(249.8)	53.1	88.5
Uses				
Increase in noncurrent assets	(19.9)	(210.9)	(34.1)	2.8
Increase in current operating assets	108.0	(248.2)	166.4	36.0
Increase in cash	(50.0)	140.6	(142.4)	(13.5)
Share repurchases	0.5	5.5	0.0	0.0
Dividends	62.9	63.2	63.2	63.2
Total uses	101.5	(249.8)	53.1	88.5

[1]The dividend use in 2007 reflects the 8.0p dividend declared in total for the fiscal year 2006, which was actually paid in the fiscal year 2007. The impact of the board's decision would be in the 2008 fiscal year.

[2]2008 and 2009 forecasts are from ABN AMRO Equity Research and case writer's estimates. Lehman Brothers forecasted net profit of GBP (110) million and GBP 81 million for 2008 and 2009, respectively.

Sources of data: Company annual reports and Web site; Bridie Barrett, Justin Diddams, and Paul Gooden, ABN AMRO Bank NV, "EMI, A Special Situation," February 16, 2007; Richard Jones and Tamsin Garrity, Lehman Brothers Equity Research, "EMI Group," February 15, 2007.

EXHIBIT 27.8 | Excerpt from Fischer Black's "The Dividend Puzzle"[1]

Why do corporations pay dividends? Why do investors pay attention to dividends?

Perhaps the answers to these questions are obvious. Perhaps dividends represent the return to the investor who puts his money at risk in the corporation. Perhaps corporations pay dividends to reward existing shareholders, and to encourage others to buy new issues of common stock at high prices. Perhaps investors pay attention to dividends because only through dividends or the prospect of dividends do they receive a return on their investment or the chance to sell their shares at a higher price in the future.

Or perhaps the answers are not so obvious. Perhaps a corporation that pays no dividends is demonstrating confidence that it has attractive investment opportunities that might be missed if it paid dividends. If it makes these investments, it may increase the value of the shares by more than the amount of the lost dividends. If that happens, its shareholders may be doubly better off. They end up with capital appreciation greater than the dividends they missed out on, and they find they are taxed at lower effective rates on capital appreciation than on dividends.

In fact, I claim that the answers to these questions are not obvious at all. The harder we look at the dividend picture, the more it seems like a puzzle, with pieces that just don't fit together. Suppose you are offered the following choice. You may have $2 today, and a 50–50 chance of $54 or $50 tomorrow. Or you may have nothing today, and a 50–50 chance of $56 or $52 tomorrow. Would you prefer one of these gambles to the other? Probably you would not. Ignoring such factors as the cost of holding the $2 and one day's interest on $2, you would be indifferent between these two gambles.

The choice between a common stock that pays a dividend and a stock that pays no dividend is similar, at least if we ignore such things as transaction costs and taxes. The price of the dividend-paying stock drops on the ex-dividend date by about the amount of the dividend. The dividend just drops the whole range of possible stock prices by that amount. The investor who gets a $2 dividend finds himself with shares worth about $2 less than they would have been worth if the dividend hadn't been paid, in all possible circumstances.

This, in essence, is the Miller–Modigliani theorem. It says that the dividends a corporation pays do not affect the value of its shares or the returns to investors, because the higher the dividend, the less the investor receives in capital appreciation, no matter how the corporation's business decision turns out. When we say this, we are assuming that the dividend paid does not influence the corporation's business decisions. Paying the dividend either reduces the amount of cash equivalents held by the corporation, or increases the amount of money raised by issuing securities.

If this theorem is correct, then a firm that pays a regular dividend equal to about half of its normal earnings will be worth the same as an otherwise similar firm that pays no dividends and will never pay any dividends. Can that be true? How can a firm that will never pay dividends be worth anything at all? Actually, there are many ways for the stockholders of a firm to take cash out without receiving dividends. The most obvious is that the firm can buy back some of its shares. Under the assumption of the Modigliani–Miller theorem, a firm has value even if it pays no dividends. Indeed, it has the same value it would have if it paid dividends.

[1]Fischer Black, "The Dividend Puzzle," *Journal of Portfolio Management* (Winter 1976).

EXHIBIT 27.9 | EMI Share Price Performance

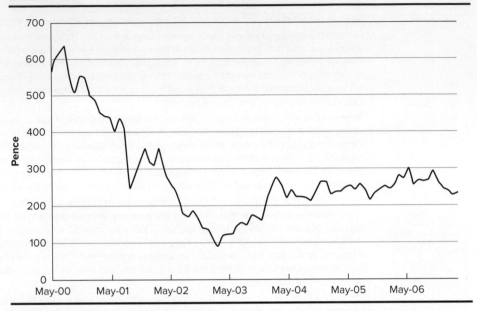

Source: Company annual reports and Web site

EXHIBIT 27.10 | Global Economic Indicators and Projections

Annual Growth Rate, Percentage

	Real GDP				Inflation			
	2005	2006	2007E	2008E	2005	2006	2007E	2008E
World	4.9	5.5	5.0	5.1	3.5	3.9	3.5	3.3
United States	3.2	3.3	2.6	3.3	3.4	3.2	1.9	2.3
Japan	3.2	3.5	2.0	2.5	(0.1)	0.1	0.2	0.5
EU 27	2.1	3.5	3.0	2.7	2.5	2.6	2.1	2.4
United Kingdom	1.9	2.7	2.7	2.1	2.1	2.3	1.9	2.0

Interest Rate Forecasts, Percentage

	3-Month Rates				10 Year Bond Yields			
	2005 avg.	2006 avg.	2007E avg.	2008E avg.	2005 avg.	2006 avg.	2007E avg.	2008E avg.
United States	3.51	5.20	5.23	5.38	4.24	4.79	4.49	5.24
Japan	0.05	0.30	0.74	1.03	1.39	1.76	1.62	1.98
Euro Zone	2.18	3.08	4.02	4.37	3.38	3.78	3.86	4.53
United Kingdom	4.80	4.85	5.44	4.91	4.40	4.50	4.58	5.18

Real Economy Forecasts

	Consumption Expenditure				Wage Growth			
	2005	2006	2007E	2008E	2005	2006	2007E	2008E
United States	3.5	3.2	3.3	3.1	2.8	3.9	3.8	4.0
Japan	3.5	3.2	2.0	3.0	0.2	0.8	0.7	1.2
Euro Zone	1.5	1.8	1.8	2.2	na	na	na	na
United Kingdom	1.4	2.1	2.5	2.0	4.1	4.1	4.4	4.0

Source of data: Société Générale Economic Research, "Global Economic Outlook," March 14, 2007.

EXHIBIT 27.11 | Comparative Global Media Data

	Data Currency	Fiscal Year End	Revenues (millions)	2006 Fiscal Year Operating Margin (%)	Net Profit Margin (%)	LT Debt/ Book Eq.	LT Debt/ Mkt. Eq.	Avg. P/E Ratio (X)
EMI Group plc	GBP	31-Mar	2,080	9.8	4.3	nmf	0.72	22.4
Bertelsmann[1]	EUR	31-Dec	19,297	9.7	12.6	0.97	na	na
Clear Channel	USD	31-Dec	7,067	31.8	9.8	0.91	0.42	22.2
Disney	USD	29-Sep	34,285	20.2	9.8	0.34	0.16	17.1
IAC/InterActiveCorp.	USD	31-Dec	6,278	15.7	3.1	0.10	0.08	48.9
News Corp.	USD	30-Jun	25,327	18.3	10.6	0.38	0.17	23.3
Sony Corporation	JPY	31-Mar	7,475,436	2.5	1.7	0.24	na	nmf
Time Warner	USD	31-Dec	44,224	27.3	11.6	0.58	0.42	14.9
Viacom	USD	31-Dec	11,467	28.1	12.9	1.06	0.27	18.5
Vivendi	EUR	31-Dec	20,044	21.8	13.0	0.22	na	12.2
Warner Music	USD	30-Sep	3,516	14.4	1.3	38.60	0.65	72.2
XM Satellite Radio	USD	31-Dec	933	nmf	nmf	nmf	0.29	nmf

	Data Currency	Share Repurchases (millions)[4] FY2004	FY2005	FY2006	Dividends Paid (millions)[4] FY2004	FY2005	FY2006
EMI Group plc	GBP	0	0	1	63	63	61
Bertelsmann[1]	EUR	0	0	0	324	287	120
Clear Channel	USD	1,841	1,070	1,371	256	343	383
Disney	USD	335	2,420	6,898	430	490	519
IAC/InterActiveCorp.	USD	430	1,848	983	0	0	0
News Corp.	USD	0	535	2,027	202	240	431
Sony Corporation	JPY	8,523	416	394	23,106	22,978	24,810
Time Warner	USD	0	2,141	13,660	0	466	876
Viacom[2]	USD	na	na	2,318	na	na	0
Vivendi	EUR	27	108	0	0	689	1,152
Warner Music[3]	USD	na	0	0	na	0	74
XM Satellite Radio	USD	0	0	0	0	0	0

	Average Dividend Yield (%)[5] FY2004	FY2005	FY2006	Payout Ratio (%)[6] FY2004	FY2005	FY2006
EMI Group plc	4.8	3.4	3.3	nmf	83	73
Bertelsmann[1]	na	na	na	27	28	5
Clear Channel	1.2	2.1	2.4	31	54	55
Disney	0.9	0.9	1.0	19	18	16
IAC/InterActiveCorp.	0.0	0.0	0.0	0	0	0
News Corp.	0.2	0.2	0.8	13	11	16
Sony Corporation	0.6	0.6	0.5	14	20	20
Time Warner	0.0	0.6	1.2	0	16	17
Viacom[2]	na	na	0.0	na	na	0
Vivendi	2.8	4.0	4.3	46	52	53
Warner Music[3]	na	0.0	2.9	na	0	168
XM Satellite Radio	0.0	0.0	0.0	0	0	0

[1]Bertelsmann is a private German company.

[2]Viacom split into two companies, Viacom and CBS Corporation, on December 31, 2005.

[3]Warner Music completed its initial public offering (IPO) in May 2005.

[4]Dividends-paid and share-repurchases data is sourced from the individual company's cash flow statement.

[5]Average dividend yield calculated as dividends declared per share for a year divided by the average annual price of the stock in the same year.

[6]Payout ratio calculated as the sum of all cash dividends declared but not necessarily yet paid for a company's fiscal year, divided by net profit for that year.

Sources of data: Value Line Investment Survey and company Web sites.

Autozone, Inc.

On February 1, 2012, Mark Johnson, portfolio manager at Johnson & Associates, an asset management company, was in the process of reviewing his largest holdings, which included AutoZone, an aftermarket auto-parts retailer. AutoZone shareholders had enjoyed strong price appreciation since 1997, with an average annual return of 11.5% (**Exhibit 28.1**). The stock price stood at $348, but Johnson was concerned about the recent news that Edward Lampert, AutoZone's main shareholder, was rapidly liquidating his stake in the company.

Since 1998, AutoZone shareholders had received distributions of the company's cash flows in the form of share repurchases. When a company repurchased its own shares, it enhanced earnings per share by reducing the shares outstanding, and it also served to reduce the book value of shareholders' equity (see AutoZone financial statements in **Exhibits 28.2, 28.3, 28.4,** and **28.5**). Johnson felt that Lampert was likely a driving force behind AutoZone's repurchase strategy because the repurchases started around the time Lampert acquired his stake and accelerated as he built up his position. Now that Lampert was reducing his stake, however, Johnson wondered if AutoZone would continue to repurchase shares or if the company would change its strategy and use its cash flows for initiating a cash dividend or reinvesting the cash in the company to grow its core business. In addition, given its large debt burden (**Exhibit 28.6**), AutoZone could choose to repay debt to improve its credit rating and increase its financial flexibility.

With AutoZone potentially changing its strategy for the use of its cash flows, Johnson needed to assess the impact of the change on the company's stock price and then decide whether he should alter his position on the stock.

The Auto Parts Business

Aftermarket auto-parts sales were split into Do-It-Yourself (DIY) and Do-It-For-Me (DIFM) segments. In the DIY segment, automobile parts were sold directly to vehicle

This case was prepared by Justin Brenner (MBA '12) under the supervision of Kenneth Eades, Paul Tudor Jones Research Professor of Business Administration. It was written as a basis for class discussion rather than to illustrate effective or ineffective handling of an administrative situation. The character of Mark Johnson and the Johnson & Associates company are fictional. Copyright © 2012 by the University of Virginia Darden School Foundation, Charlottesville, VA. All rights reserved. *To order copies, send an e-mail to* sales@dardenbusinesspublishing.com. *No part of this publication may be reproduced, stored in a retrieval system, used in a spreadsheet, or transmitted in any form or by any means—electronic, mechanical, photocopying, recording, or otherwise—without the permission of the Darden School Foundation.*

owners who wanted to fix or improve their vehicles on their own. In the DIFM segment, automobile repair shops provided the parts for vehicles left in their care for repair. DIY customers were serviced primarily through local retail storefronts where they could speak with a knowledgeable sales associate who located the necessary part. Because of their expertise in repairing vehicles, DIFM service providers generally did not require storefront access or the expertise of a sales associate. DIFM customers, however, were concerned with pricing, product availability, and efficient product delivery.

Sales in both segments were strongly related to the number of miles a vehicle had been driven. For the DIY segment, the number of late-model cars needing repair was also a strong predictor of auto-parts sales. As the age of a car increased, more repairs were required, and the owners of older cars were more likely to repair these senior vehicles themselves (**Exhibit 28.7**).

The number of miles a car was driven was affected by several economic fundamentals, the most important of which was the cost of gasoline. The number of older cars on the road increased during those times when fewer consumers bought new cars. New car purchases were subject to the same general economic trends applicable to most durable goods. As a result, in periods of strong economic growth and low unemployment, new car sales increased. Conversely, when the economy struggled and unemployment was high, fewer new cars were purchased, and older cars were kept on the road longer, requiring more frequent repairs.

Overall, when the economy was doing well, gas prices and new car sales both increased, decreasing the number of older cars on the road and also the amount of additional mileage accumulated. When the economy did poorly, gas prices and new car sales were more likely to be depressed, increasing the utilization of older cars and adding to their mileage. Because of these dynamics, auto-parts sales, especially in the DIY segment, were somewhat counter-cyclical.

The auto-parts business consisted of a large number of small, local operations as well as a few large, national retailers, such as AutoZone, O'Reilly Auto Parts, Advance Auto Parts, and Pep Boys. The national chains had sophisticated supply-chain operations to ensure that an appropriate level of inventory was maintained at each store while managing the tradeoff between minimizing inventory stock outs and maximizing the number of stock-keeping units (SKUs). This gave the large, national retailers an advantage because customers were more likely to find the parts they wanted at one of these stores. Counterbalancing the inventory advantage, however, was the expertise of sales associates, which allowed the smaller, local stores to enhance the customer service experience in DIY sales.

Recent Trends

In 2008, the U.S. economy had gone through the worst recession since the Great Depression, and the recovery that followed had been unusually slow. As a result, the auto-parts retail business enjoyed strong top-line growth. The future path of the U.S. economy was still highly uncertain as was the potential for a disconnect between GDP growth and gas price increases and between gas prices and miles driven. Furthermore, as auto-parts retailers operated with high-gross margins and significant fixed costs, profits varied widely with the level of sales, making the near-term earnings in the auto-parts retail segment particularly difficult to predict.

The auto-parts retail business experienced more competition as national retailers continued to expand their operations. Most of their expansion was at the expense of local retailers, but competition between major national retailers was heating up. If the economy strengthened and the auto-parts retail business was negatively affected by the replacement of older cars with new ones, competition between large, national retailers could make a bad situation worse.

Linked to high levels of industry competition and the expansion of the major retailers was the possibility that growth would eventually hit a wall if the market became oversaturated with auto-parts stores. Despite this concern, by 2012, AutoZone[1] management had stated that it was not seeing any signs of oversaturation, implying that expansion opportunities still remained.

The industry was also seeing an increase in sales via online channels as consumers enjoyed the flexibility of purchasing online and either picking up an order at the most convenient location or having it delivered to their doorstep. Given the high operating leverage provided by selling through online channels, especially given the preexisting supply chains that already were built for storefront operations, as well as the growth in this channel, the national retail chains continued to invest in their online solutions and looked at that channel for future earnings growth.

Finally, another trend was the expansion of the large, U.S. auto-parts retailers into adjacent foreign markets, such as Mexico, Canada, and Puerto Rico. Thus far, the national retail companies were successful using this strategy, but their ability to continue to succeed and prosper in these markets, as well as in new, attractive locations such as Brazil, was not yet a reality.

AutoZone

AutoZone's first store opened in 1979, under the name of Auto Shack in Forrest City, Arkansas. In 1987, the name was changed to AutoZone, and the company implemented the first electronic auto-parts catalog for the retail industry. Then in 1991, after four years of steady growth, AutoZone went public and was listed on the New York Stock Exchange under the ticker symbol AZO.

By 2012, AutoZone had become the leading retailer of automotive replacement parts and accessories in the United States, with more than 65,000 employees and 4,813 stores located in every state in the contiguous United States, Puerto Rico, and Mexico. AutoZone also distributed parts to commercial repair shops. In addition, a small but growing portion of AutoZone sales came through its online channel.

From the beginning, AutoZone had invested heavily in expanding its retail footprint via both organic and inorganic growth. It had also developed a sophisticated hub-and-feeder inventory system that kept the inventories of individual stores low as well as reduced the likelihood of stock outs. The expansion of its retail footprint had driven

---

[1] AutoZone Q1 2012 Earnings Call—"I haven't seen a market yet that was so saturated that we were challenged economically," Bill Rhodes, AutoZone chairman, president, and CEO.

top-line revenue growth. AutoZone's success in developing category-leading distribution capabilities had resulted in both the highest operating margin for its industry and strong customer service backed by the ability of its distribution network to supply stores with nearly all of the AutoZone products on a same-day basis (**Exhibit 28.8**).

AutoZone's management focused on after-tax return on invested capital (ROIC) as the primary way to measure value creation for the company's capital providers. As a result, while AutoZone management invested in opportunities that led to top-line revenue growth and increased margins, it also focused on capital stewardship. What resulted was an aggressively managed working capital at the store level through the efficient use of inventory as well as attractive terms from suppliers.

Starting in 1998, AutoZone had returned capital to its equity investors through share repurchases. Although share-repurchase programs were common among U.S. companies, the typical result was a modest impact on shares outstanding. AutoZone's consistent use of share repurchases, however, had resulted in a significant reduction of both the shares outstanding and the equity capital. In particular, shares outstanding had dropped 39% from 2007 to 2011, and shareholders' equity had been reduced to a negative $1.2 billion in 2011. The repurchases had been funded by strong operating cash flows and by debt issuance. The net result was that AutoZone's invested capital had remained fairly constant since 2007, which, combined with increased earnings, created attractive ROIC levels (**Exhibit 28.9**).

Operating Cash Flow Options

While AutoZone had historically repurchased shares with operating cash flow, Mark Johnson felt that Edward Lampert's reduced stake in the company could prompt management to abandon repurchases and use the cash flows for other purposes. For example, AutoZone could distribute cash flows through cash dividends, reinvest the cash flows back into the core business, or use the funds to acquire stores. The company could also invest further in its operational capabilities to stay on the leading edge of the retail auto-parts industry. Finally, given a negative book-equity position and a continually growing debt load, AutoZone might consider using its cash flows to pay down debt to increase its future financial flexibility.

Dividends versus Share Repurchases

Assuming that AutoZone decided to distribute some of its operating cash flows to shareholders, the company had the choice of distributing the cash through dividends, share repurchases, or some combination of the two. Dividends were seen as a way to provide cash to existing shareholders, whereas only those shareholders who happened to be selling their shares would receive cash from a share-repurchase program. On the other hand, dividends were taxed at the shareholder level in the year received, whereas if a share-repurchase program succeeded in increasing the share price, the nonselling shareholders could defer paying taxes until they sold the stock.[2]

---

[2]Current tax laws did allow for most dividends to be taxed at the same long-term capital gains rates, although this was not always the case, and the tax law regarding dividends was not certain going forward.

Dividends were also generally considered to be "sticky," meaning that the market expected a company to either keep its dividend steady or raise it each year. Because of this mindset, the implementation of a dividend or an increase of the dividend was usually interpreted by the market as a positive signal of the firm's ability to earn enough to continue paying the dividend far into the future. Conversely, any decrease in the dividend was normally viewed by the market as a very negative signal. Therefore, the stock price tended to change according to the dividend news released by the firm, which would be favorable for AutoZone shareholders so long as management was able to continue or increase the dividend each year.

Share repurchases were not viewed as sticky by the market because the amount of the repurchase often varied each year. The variance in the shares purchased might be caused by economic headwinds or tailwinds or differences in the quantity and size of investment opportunities that management believed would create shareholder value. Also, share repurchases were seen by some as a way to signal management's belief that the stock was undervalued and thus represented a good investment for the company.

Some companies chose to return shareholder capital through both dividends and share repurchases. In most of these cases, the company provided a stable but relatively small cash dividend and then repurchased shares at varying levels according to the circumstances each year. The benefit of this approach was to give shareholders the benefit of a sticky dividend while also receiving the price support of share repurchases.

Organic Growth

AutoZone could consider using its operating cash flow to increase the number of new stores it opened each year. Although the retail auto-parts industry was competitive and relatively mature, AutoZone's CEO had recently indicated that he did not see oversaturation of retail auto-parts stores in any of the company's markets.[3] Therefore, AutoZone could seize the opportunity to expand more rapidly and perhaps preempt competition from gaining a foothold in those markets.

Rapid expansion came with a number of risks. First, Johnson was not sure that AutoZone had the managerial capacity to expand that swiftly. The company's growth in recent years had been substantial as were the returns on investment, but it was not apparent if further growth would necessarily continue to create value. In addition, Johnson reasoned that the best retail locations were already covered and that remaining areas would have lower profitability. This could be exacerbated if AutoZone expanded into areas that were less well served by its distribution network.

Johnson thought that there were some very attractive overseas investment opportunities as evidenced by successful store openings in Mexico and Puerto Rico. AutoZone's 2011 annual report indicated work was underway to expand into Brazil over the next several years.[4] The company could increase its global presence by aggressively opening multiple stores in Brazil and other international locations. Hasty expansion into foreign markets, however, brought with it not only the risks of rapid store expansion but also the difficulties inherent in transferring and translating the domestically successful supply model.

---

[3] See footnote 1.

[4] AutoZone annual report, 2011.

Growth by Acquisition

Johnson noted that in 1998 AutoZone had acquired over 800 stores from competitors and reasoned that another way to swiftly increase revenues would be for AutoZone to acquire other auto-parts retail stores. While this strategy would require some postmerger integration investment, such stores would be productive much more quickly than greenfield stores and shorten the return time on AutoZone's investment. This was an interesting strategy, but Johnson also knew that industry consolidation (**Exhibit 28.10**) had removed most of the viable takeover targets from the market; therefore, it was unclear whether a merger of two of the large players would be allowed by the U.S. Department of Justice.

Debt Retirement

A final consideration was whether AutoZone might use part or all of its operating cash flows to retire some of the debt that the company had accumulated over the years. Much of the debt had been used to fund the share repurchases, but with a negative book-equity position and such a large debt position, Johnson wondered whether it was prudent to continue adding debt to the balance sheet. If AutoZone ran into trouble, it could struggle under the strain of making the interest payments and rolling over maturing debt. At some point, it was conceivable that AutoZone could lose its investment-grade credit rating,[5] which would only make future debt financing more difficult to secure and more expensive.

The Decision

Johnson had to decide what to do with his AutoZone investment. He was impressed with the company's history of strong shareholder returns and its leading position in the industry. Still he wondered if Lampert's reduced influence and the potential for less favorable economic trends for auto-parts retailers were enough uncertainty for him to consider selling some or all of his position in the stock. As an analyst, Johnson's first consideration regarding the value of a company was to determine how well management was using the operating cash flow to maximize value for shareholders. Based on the ROIC (**Exhibit 28.9**), AutoZone was earning high returns on the capital invested in the company, which was undoubtedly the primary driver of stock returns. The extent to which share repurchases had contributed to the stock's performance, however, was less clear.

How would the market react to the news that AutoZone was reducing or eliminating its share repurchases after years of consistently following that strategy? Did the market view AutoZone's share repurchases as a cash dividend or was it indifferent about whether cash flows were distributed by repurchasing shares or paying a cash dividend? In any case, Johnson wondered if any move away from repurchasing shares after so many years might cause the stock price to fall, regardless of how the cash flows were ultimately spent. Or would AutoZone's stock price continue to appreciate as it had in the past so long as it continued to produce strong cash flows?

---

[5]Moody's and S&P had consistently assigned investment-grade ratings of Baa and BBB, respectively, for AutoZone's senior unsecured debt.

EXHIBIT 28.1 | Edward Lampert's Position in AutoZone

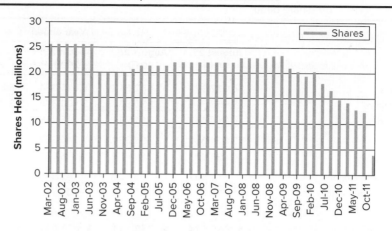

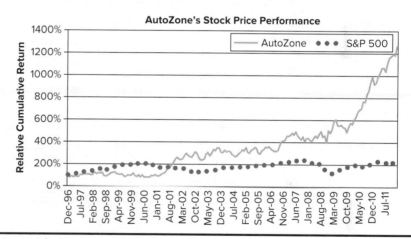

Data source: Bloomberg.

EXHIBIT 28.2 | AutoZone Income Statement (August FY, in thousands of dollars, except ratios and per-share data)

	Year ended				
	August 27, 2011	August 28, 2010	August 29, 2009	August 30, 2008	August 25, 2007
Net sales	$8,072,973	$7,362,618	$6,816,824	$6,522,706	$6,169,804
Cost of sales	3,953,510	3,650,874	3,400,375	3,254,645	3,105,554
Gross profit	4,119,463	3,711,744	3,416,449	3,268,061	3,064,250
SG&A	2,624,660	2,392,330	2,240,387	2,143,927	2,008,984
Operating profit	1,494,803	1,319,414	1,176,062	1,124,134	1,055,266
Interest expense, net	170,557	158,909	142,316	116,745	119,116
Income before income taxes	1,324,246	1,160,505	1,033,746	1,007,389	936,150
Income tax expense	475,272	422,194	376,697	365,783	340,478
Net income	**$ 848,974**	**$ 738,311**	**$ 657,049**	**$ 641,606**	**$ 595,672**
Wt. avg. shares for basic EPS	42,632	48,488	55,282	63,295	69,101
Effect of dilutive stock equivalents	971	816	710	580	743
Adj. wt. avg. shares for diluted EPS	43,603	49,304	55,992	63,875	69,844
Basic earnings per share	**$19.91**	**$15.23**	**$11.89**	**$10.14**	**$8.62**
Diluted earnings per share	**$19.47**	**$14.97**	**$11.73**	**$10.04**	**$8.53**
Other information:					
EBIT	$1,494,803	$1,319,414	$1,176,062	$1,124,134	$1,055,266
Depr. and Amort.	196,209	192,084	180,433	169,509	159,411
EBITDA	$1,691,012	$1,511,498	$1,356,495	$1,293,643	$1,214,677
EBITDA/Interest	**9.9x**	**9.5x**	**9.5x**	**11.1x**	**10.2x**

Data source: AutoZone annual reports.

EXHIBIT 28.3 | AutoZone Balance Sheet (August FY, in thousands of dollars)

	August 27, 2011	August 28, 2010	August 29, 2009	August 30, 2008	August 25, 2007
Assets					
Current assets:					
Cash and cash equivalents	$ 97,606	$ 98,280	$ 92,706	$ 242,461	$ 86,654
Accounts receivable	140,690	125,802	126,514	71,241	59,876
Merchandise inventories	2,466,107	2,304,579	2,207,497	2,150,109	2,007,430
Other current assets	88,022	83,160	135,013	122,490	116,495
Deferred income taxes	—	—	—	—	—
Total current assets	2,792,425	2,611,821	2,561,730	2,586,301	2,270,455
Property and equipment:					
Land	740,276	690,098	656,516	643,699	625,992
Buildings and improvements	2,177,476	2,013,301	1,900,610	1,814,668	1,720,172
Equipment	994,369	923,595	887,521	850,679	780,199
Leasehold improvements	275,299	247,748	219,606	202,098	183,601
Construction in progress	184,452	192,519	145,161	128,133	85,581
Gross property and equipment	4,371,872	4,067,261	3,809,414	3,639,277	3,395,545
Less: Accumulated depreciation and amortization	1,702,997	1,547,315	1,455,057	1,349,621	1,217,703
Net property and equipment	2,668,875	2,519,946	2,354,357	2,289,656	2,177,842
Goodwill	302,645	302,645	302,645	302,645	302,645
Deferred income taxes	10,661	46,223	59,067	38,283	21,331
Other long-term assets	94,996	90,959	40,606	40,227	32,436
Total assets	**$5,869,602**	**$5,571,594**	**$5,318,405**	**$5,257,112**	**$4,804,709**
Liabilities and Stockholders' Deficit					
Current liabilities:					
Accounts payable	$2,755,853	$2,433,050	$2,118,746	$2,043,271	$1,870,668
Accrued expenses and other	449,327	432,368	381,271	327,664	307,633
Income taxes payable	25,185	25,385	35,145	11,582	25,442
Deferred income taxes	166,449	146,971	171,590	136,803	82,152
Short-term borrowings	34,082	26,186	—	—	—
Total current liabilities	3,430,896	3,063,960	2,706,752	2,519,320	2,285,895
Long-term debt	3,317,600	2,882,300	2,726,900	2,250,000	1,935,618
Other long-term liabilities	375,338	364,099	317,827	258,105	179,996
Stockholders' deficit:					
Common stock, par: $0.01/share	441	501	579	636	713
Additional paid-in capital	591,384	557,955	549,326	537,005	545,404
Retained earnings	(643,998)	(245,344)	136,935	206,099	546,049
Accumulated other comprehensive loss	(119,691)	(106,468)	(92,035)	(4,135)	(9,550)
Treasury stock, at cost	(1,082,368)	(945,409)	(1,027,879)	(509,918)	(679,416)
Total stockholders' equity	(1,254,232)	(738,765)	(433,074)	229,687	403,200
Total liabilities and stockholders' equity	**$5,869,602**	**$5,571,594**	**$5,318,405**	**$5,257,112**	**$4,804,709**
Shares issued	44,084	50,061	57,881	63,600	71,250
Shares outstanding	40,109	45,107	50,801	59,608	65,960
Other information:					
Capital lease obligations	86,656	88,280	54,764	64,061	55,088

Data source: AutoZone annual reports.

EXHIBIT 28.4 | AutoZone Statement of Cash Flows (August FY, in thousands of dollars)

	Year ended				
	August 27, 2011	August 28, 2010	August 29, 2009	August 30, 2008	August 25, 2007
Cash flows from operating activities:					
Net income	$848,974	$738,311	$657,049	$641,606	$595,672
Adjustments to reconcile net income to net cash provided by operating activities:					
Depreciation and amortization of property and equipment	196,209	192,084	180,433	169,509	159,411
Amortization of debt origination fees	8,962	6,495	3,644	1,837	1,719
Income tax benefit from exercise of stock options	(34,945)	(22,251)	(8,407)	(10,142)	(16,523)
Deferred income taxes	44,667	(9,023)	46,318	67,474	24,844
Share-based compensation expense	26,625	19,120	19,135	18,388	18,462
Other	—	—	—	—	—
Changes in operating assets and liabilities:					
Accounts receivable	(14,605)	782	(56,823)	(11,145)	20,487
Merchandise inventories	(155,421)	(96,077)	(76,337)	(137,841)	(160,780)
Accounts payable and accrued expenses	342,826	349,122	137,158	175,733	186,228
Income taxes payable	34,319	12,474	32,264	(3,861)	17,587
Other, net	(6,073)	5,215	(10,626)	9,542	(1,913)
Net cash provided by operating activities	**1,291,538**	**1,196,252**	**923,808**	**921,100**	**845,194**
Cash flows from investing activities:					
Capital expenditures	(321,604)	(315,400)	(272,247)	(243,594)	(224,474)
Purchase of marketable securities	(43,772)	(56,156)	(48,444)	(54,282)	(94,615)
Proceeds from sale of marketable securities	43,081	52,620	46,306	50,712	86,921
Acquisitions	—	—	—	—	—
Disposal of capital assets	3,301	11,489	10,663	4,014	3,453
Net cash used in investing activities	**(318,994)**	**(307,447)**	**(263,722)**	**(243,150)**	**(228,715)**
Cash flows from financing activities:					
Net proceeds from commercial paper	134,600	155,400	277,600	(206,700)	84,300
Net proceeds from short-term borrowings	6,901	26,186	—	—	—
Proceeds from issuance of debt	500,000	—	500,000	750,000	—
Repayment of debt	(199,300)	—	(300,700)	(229,827)	(5,839)
Net proceeds from sale of common stock	55,846	52,922	39,855	27,065	58,952
Purchase of treasury stock	(1,466,802)	(1,123,655)	(1,300,002)	(849,196)	(761,887)
Income tax benefit from exercise of stock options	34,945	22,251	8,407	10,142	16,523
Payments of capital lease obligations	(22,781)	(16,597)	(17,040)	(15,880)	(11,360)
Other	(17,180)	—	(15,016)	(8,286)	(2,072)
Net cash used in financing activities	**(973,771)**	**(883,493)**	**(806,896)**	**(522,682)**	**(621,383)**
Effect of exchange rate changes on cash	553	262	(2,945)	539	—
Net (decrease) increase in cash and cash equivalents	(674)	5,574	(149,755)	155,807	(4,904)
Cash and cash equivalents at beginning of year	98,280	92,706	242,461	86,654	91,558
Cash and cash equivalents at end of year	$ 97,606	$ 98,280	$ 92,706	$242,461	$ 86,654
Supplemental cash flow information:					
Interest paid, net of interest cost capitalized	$155,531	$150,745	$132,905	$107,477	$116,580
Income taxes paid	$405,654	$420,575	$299,021	$313,875	$299,566
Assets acquired through capital lease	$ 32,301	$ 75,881	$ 16,880	$ 61,572	$ 69,325

Data source: AutoZone annual reports.

EXHIBIT 28.5 | AutoZone 2011 Statement of Stockholders' Equity (dollars in thousands)

(in thousands)	Common Shares Issued	Common Stock	Additional Paid-in Capital	Retained (Deficit) Earnings	Accumulated Other Comprehensive Loss	Treasury Stock	Total
Balance at August 28, 2010	50,061	501	$557,955	($245,344)	($106,468)	($945,409)	($738,765)
Net income				848,974			848,974
Pension liability adjustments, net of taxes of ($3,998)					(17,346)		(17,346)
Foreign currency translation adjustment					8,347		8,347
Unrealized loss adjustment on marketable securities, net of taxes of ($91)					(171)		(171)
Net losses on terminated derivatives					(5,453)		(5,453)
Reclassification of net losses on derivatives into earnings					1,400		1,400
Comprehensive income							835,751
Purchase of 5,598 shares of treasury stock						(1,466,802)	(1,466,802)
Retirement of treasury shares	(6,577)	(66)	(82,150)	(1,247,627)		1,329,843	—
Sale of common stock under stock options and stock purchase plan	600	6	55,840				55,846
Share-based compensation expense			24,794				24,794
Income tax benefit from exercise of stock options			34,945				34,945
Other				(1)			(1)
Balance at August 27, 2011	44,084	441	$591,384	($643,998)	($119,691)	($1,082,368)	($1,254,232)

Data source: AutoZone annual reports.

357

EXHIBIT 28.6 | AutoZone Capital Structure and Coverage Ratio

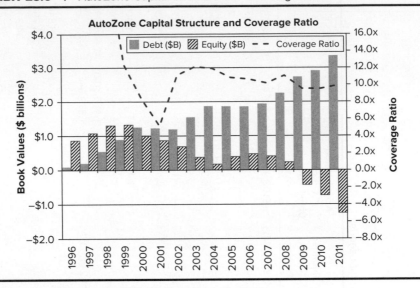

Note: Coverage ratio is defined as EBITDA divided by interest expense.

Data source: AutoZone annual reports.

EXHIBIT 28.7 | Miles Driven and Average Vehicle Age

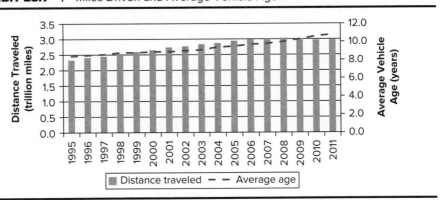

Data sources: U.S. Department of Transportation (miles driven) and Polk Research (vehicle age).

EXHIBIT 28.8 | Merchandise Listing (as of October 17, 2011)

Failure	Maintenance	Discretionary
A/C Compressors	Antlfreeze & Windshield Washer Fluid	Air Fresheners
Batteries & Accessories	Brake Drums, Rotors, Shoes & Pads	Cell Phone Accessories
Belts & Hoses	Chemicals, including Brake & Power	Drinks & Snacks
Carburetors	Steering Fluid, Oil & Fuel Additives	Floor Mats & Seat Covers
Chassis	Oil & Transmission Fluid	Mirrors
Clutches	Oil, Air, Fuel & Transmission Filters	Performance Products
CV Axles	Oxygen Sensors	Protectants & Cleaners
Engines	Paint & Accessories	Seat Covers
Fuel Pumps	Refrigerant & Accessories	Sealants & Adhesives
Fuses	Shock Absorbers & Struts	Steering Wheel Covers
Ignition	Spark Plugs & Wires	Stereos & Radios
Lighting	Windshield Wipers	Tools
Mufflers		Wash & Wax
Starters & Alternators		
Water Pumps		
Radiators		
Thermostats		

Data source: AutoZone annual report.

EXHIBIT 28.9 | Share Repurchases and ROIC 1996–2011

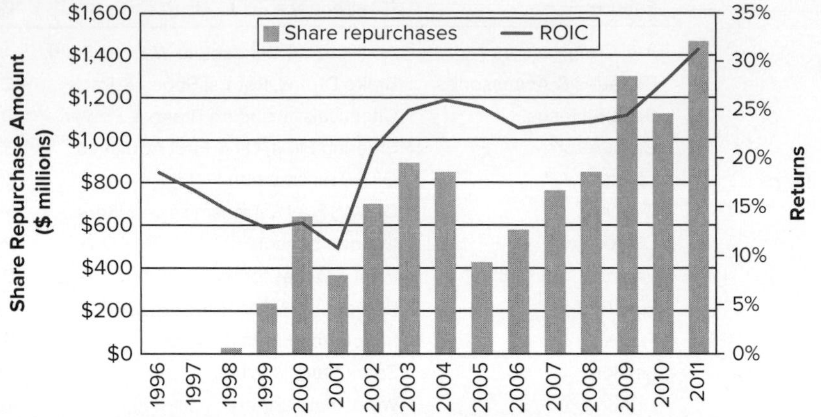

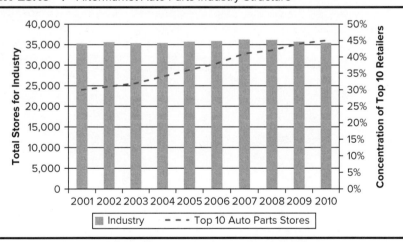

Note: ROIC is calculated as the sum of net income and tax-adjusted interest and rent expenses divided by the sum of average debt, average equity, six times rent expense (to approximate capitalizing rent), and average capital lease obligations.

Data source: AutoZone annual reports.

EXHIBIT 28.10 | Aftermarket Auto Parts Industry Structure

Note: The top 10 companies (stores) as of August 2010: AutoZone (4,728), O'Reilly Auto Parts (3,657), Advance Auto Parts (3,627), General Parts/CARQUEST (1,500), Genuine Parts/NAPA (1,035), Pep Boys (630), Fisher Auto Parts (406), Uni-Select (273), Replacement Parts (155), and Auto-Wares Group (128).

Data sources: *AAIA Factbook* and SEC filings.

## PART 6

Management of the Corporate Capital Structure

An Introduction to Debt Policy and Value

Many factors determine how much debt a firm takes on. Chief among them ought to be the effect of the debt on the value of the firm. Does borrowing create value? If so, for whom? If not, then why do so many executives concern themselves with leverage?

If leverage affects value, then it should cause changes in either the discount rate of the firm (that is, its weighted-average cost of capital) or the cash flows of the firm.

1. Please fill in the following:

	0% Debt/ 100% Equity	25% Debt/ 75% Equity	50% Debt/ 50% Equity
Book Value of Debt	—	$2,500	$5,000
Book Value of Equity	$10,000	$7,500	$5,000
Market Value of Debt	—	$2,500	$5,000
Market Value of Equity	$10,000	$8,350	$6,700
Pretax Cost of Debt	5.00%	5.00%	5.00%
After-Tax Cost of Debt	3.30%	3.30%	3.30%
Market Value Weights of			
Debt	0%	_____	
Equity	100%	_____	
Levered Beta	0.80	_____	
Risk-Free Rate	5.0%	5.0%	5.0%
Market Premium	6.0%	6.0%	6.0%
Cost of Equity	_____		
Weighted-Average Cost of Capital	_____		

(*continued*)

(continued)

	0% Debt/ 100% Equity	25% Debt/ 75% Equity	50% Debt/ 50% Equity
EBIT	$1,485	$1,485	$1,485
Taxes (@ 34%)			
EBIAT			
+ Depreciation	$500	$500	$500
− Capital exp.	($500)	($500)	($500)
+ Change in net working capital	—	—	—
Free Cash Flow			
Value of Assets (FCF/WACC)			

Why does the value of assets change? Where, specifically, do those changes occur?

2. In finance, as in accounting, the two sides of the balance sheet must be equal. In the previous problem, we valued the asset side of the balance sheet. To value the other side, we must value the debt and the equity, and then add them together.

	0% Debt/ 100% Equity	25% Debt/ 75% Equity	50% Debt/ 50% Equity
Cash flow to creditors:			
Interest	—	$125	$250
Pretax cost of debt	5.0%	5.0%	5.0%
Value of debt:			
(Int/K_d)			
Cash flow to shareholders:			
EBIT	$1,485	$1,485	$1,485
Interest	—	$125	$250
Pretax profit			
Taxes (@ 34%)			
Net income			
+ Depreciation	$500	$500	$500
− Capital exp.	($500)	($500)	($500)
+ Change in net working capital	—	—	—
− Debt amortization	—	—	—
Residual cash flow			
Cost of equity			
Value of equity (RCF/K_e)			
Value of equity plus value of debt			

As the firm levers up, how does the increase in value get apportioned between the creditors and the shareholders?

3. In the preceding problem, we divided the value of all the assets between two classes of investors: creditors and shareholders. This process tells us where the change in value is *going*, but it sheds little light on where the change is *coming from*. Let's divide the free cash flows of the firm into *pure business flows* and cash flows resulting from *financing effects*. Now, an axiom in finance is that you should discount cash flows at a rate consistent with the risk of those cash flows. Pure business flows should be discounted at the unlevered cost of equity (i.e., the cost of capital for the unlevered firm). Financing flows should be discounted at the rate of return required by the providers of debt.

	0% Debt/ 100% Equity	25% Debt/ 75% Equity	50% Debt/ 50% Equity
Pure Business Cash Flows:			
EBIT	$1,485	$1,485	$1,485
Taxes (@ 34%)	$505	$505	$505
EBIAT	$980	$980	$980
+ Depreciation	$500	$500	$500
− Capital exp.	($500)	($500)	($500)
+ Change in net working capital	—	—	—
Free Cash Flow	$980	$980	$980
Unlevered Beta	0.8	0.8	0.8
Risk-Free Rate	5.0%	5.0%	5.0%
Market Premium	6.0%	6.0%	6.0%
Unlevered WACC			
Value of Pure Business Flows: (FCF/Unlevered WACC)			
Financing Cash Flows			
Interest			
Tax Reduction			
Pretax Cost of Debt	5.0%	5.0%	5.0%
Value of Financing Effect: (Tax Reduction/Pretax Cost of Debt)			
Total Value (Sum of Values of Pure Business Flows and Financing Effects)			

The first three problems illustrate one of the most important theories in finance. This theory, developed by two professors, Franco Modigliani and Merton Miller, revolutionized the way we think about capital-structure policies.

The M&M theory says:

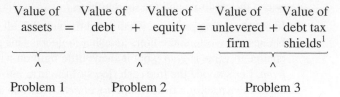

Value of   Value of   Value of   Value of   Value of
assets   =   debt   +   equity   = unlevered + debt tax
                                              firm   shields[1]

Problem 1   Problem 2   Problem 3

4. What remains to be seen, however, is whether shareholders are better or worse off with more leverage. Problem 2 does not tell us because there we computed total value of equity, and shareholders care about value *per* share. Ordinarily, total value will be a good proxy for what is happening to the price per share, but in the case of a relevering firm, that may not be true. Implicitly, we assumed that, as our firm in problems 1–3 levered up, it was repurchasing stock on the open market (you will note that EBIT did not change, so management was clearly not investing the proceeds from the loans into cash-generating assets). We held EBIT constant so that we could see clearly the effect of financial changes without getting them mixed up in the effects of investments. The point is that, as the firm borrows and repurchases shares, the total value of equity may decline, but the price per share may *rise*.

   Now, solving for the price per share may seem impossible because we are dealing with two unknowns—share price and the change in the number of shares:

$$\text{Share price} = \frac{\text{Market value of equity}}{\text{Original shares} - \text{Repurchased shares}}$$

But by rewriting the equation, we can put it in a form that can be solved:

$$\text{Share price} = \frac{\text{Original market value of equity} + \text{Value of financing effect}}{\text{Number of original shares}}$$

   Referring to the results of problem 2, let's assume that all the new debt is equal to the cash paid to repurchase shares. Please complete the following table:

	0% Debt/ 100% Equity	25% Debt/ 75% Equity	50% Debt/ 50% Equity
Total Market Value of Equity			
Cash Paid Out			
# Original Shares	1,000	1,000	1,000
Total Value Per Share			

---

[1]Debt tax shields can be valued by discounting the future annual tax savings at the pretax cost of debt. For debt, that is assumed to be outstanding in perpetuity, the tax savings is the tax rate, t, times the interest payment, $k \times D$. The present value of this perpetual savings is $tkD/k = tD$.

5. In this set of problems, is leverage good for shareholders? Why? Is levering/ unlevering the firm something that shareholders can do for themselves? In what sense should shareholders pay a premium for shares of levered companies?

6. From a macroeconomic point of view, is society better off if firms use more than zero debt (up to some prudent limit)?

7. As a way of illustrating the usefulness of the M&M theory and consolidating your grasp of the mechanics, consider the following case and complete the worksheet. On March 3, 1988, Beazer PLC (a British construction company) and Shearson Lehman Hutton, Inc. (an investment-banking firm) commenced a hostile tender offer to purchase all the outstanding stock of Koppers Company, Inc., a producer of construction materials, chemicals, and building products. Originally, the raiders offered $45 a share; subsequently, the offer was raised to $56 and then finally to $61 a share. The Koppers board asserted that the offers were inadequate and its management was reviewing the possibility of a major recapitalization.

   To test the valuation effects of the recapitalization alternative, assume that Koppers could borrow a maximum of $1,738,095,000 at a pretax cost of debt of 10.5% and that the aggregate amount of debt will remain constant in perpetuity. Thus, Koppers will take on additional debt of $1,565,686,000 (that is, $1,738,095,000 minus $172,409,000). Also assume that the proceeds of the loan would be paid as an extraordinary dividend to shareholders. **Exhibit 29.1** presents Koppers' book- and market-value balance sheets, assuming the capital structure before recapitalization. Please complete the worksheet for the recapitalization alternative.

EXHIBIT 29.1 | Koppers Company, Inc. (values in thousands)

	Before Recapitalization	After Recapitalization
Book Value Balance Sheets		
Net working capital	$ 212,453	_____
Fixed assets	601,446	_____
Total assets	813,899	_____
Long-term debt	172,409	_____
Deferred taxes, etc.	195,616	_____
Preferred stock	15,000	_____
Common equity	430,874	_____
Total capital	$ 813,899	_____
Market-Value Balance Sheets		
Net working capital	$ 212,453	_____
Fixed assets	1,618,081	_____
PV debt tax shield	58,619	_____
Total assets	1,889,153	_____
Long term debt	172,409	_____
Deferred taxes, etc.	—	_____
Preferred stock	15,000	_____
Common equity	1,701,744	_____
Total capital	$1,889,153	_____
Number of shares	28,128	_____
Price per share	$ 60.50	_____
Value to Public Shareholders		
Cash received	$ —	_____
Value of shares	$1,701,744	_____
Total	$1,701,744	_____
Total per share	$ 60.50	_____

M&M Pizza

Twenty-nine-year-old Moe Miller had recently been appointed managing director at M&M Pizza, a premium pizza producer in the small country of Francostan. As a third-generation director of M&M Pizza, Miller was anxious to make his mark on the company with which he had grown up. The business was operating well, with full penetration of the Francostani market, but Miller felt that the financial policies of the company were overly conservative. Despite generating strong and steady profitability of about F$125 million per year over recent memory, M&M Pizza's stock price had been flat for years, at about F$25 per share.[1]

His new office, Miller discovered, had an unobstructed view of the nearby marble quarry. How wonderfully irrelevant, he thought to himself as he turned to the financial analysis on his desk. With borrowing costs running at only 4%, he felt confident that recapitalizing the balance sheet would create sustained value for M&M owners. His plan called for issuing F$500 million in new company debt and using the proceeds to repurchase F$500 million in company shares. The plan would leave assets, profits, and operations of the business unchanged but allow M&M to borrow at the relatively low prevailing market yields on debt and increase dividends per share. Committed to raising the share price, Miller felt it was time to slice up the company's capital structure a little differently.

Francostan

The Mediterranean island nation of Francostan had a long tradition of political and economic stability. The country had been under the benevolent rule of a single family for generations. The national economy maintained few ties with neighboring countries, and trade was almost nonexistent. The population was stable, with approximately 12 million prosperous, well-educated inhabitants. The country was known for its exceptional IT and regulation infrastructure; citizens had unrivaled access to business and economic

---

[1]F$ = Franco dollars.

This case was prepared by Michael J. Schill, Associate Professor of Business Administration It was written as a basis for class discussion rather than to illustrate effective or ineffective handling of an administrative situation. Copyright © 2013 by the University of Virginia Darden School Foundation, Charlottesville, VA. All rights reserved. *To order copies, send an e-mail to* sales@dardenbusinesspublishing.com. *No part of this publication may be reproduced, stored in a retrieval system, used in a spreadsheet, or transmitted in any form or by any means—electronic, mechanical, photocopying, recording, or otherwise—without the permission of the Darden School Foundation.*

information. Economic policies in the country supported stability. Price inflation for the national currency, the Franco dollar, had been near zero for some time and was expected to remain so for the foreseeable future. Short- and long-term interest rates for government and business debt were steady at 4%. Occasionally, the economy experienced short periods of economic expansion and contraction.

The country's population was known for its high ethical standards. Business promises and financial obligations were considered fully binding. To support the country's practices, the government maintained no bankruptcy law, and all contractual obligations were fully and completely enforced. To encourage economic development, the government did not tax business income. Instead, government tax revenue was levied through personal income taxes. There was a law under consideration to alter the tax policy by introducing a 20% corporate income tax. To maintain business investment incentives under the plan, interest payments would be tax deductible.

The Recapitalization Decision

Miller's proposed recapitalization involved raising F$500 million in cash by issuing new debt at the prevailing 4% borrowing rate and using the cash to repurchase company shares.[2] Miller was confident that shareholders would be better off. Not only would they receive F$500 million in cash, but Miller expected that the share price would rise. M&M maintained a dividend policy of returning all company profits to equity holders in the form of dividends. Although total dividends would decline under the new plan, Miller anticipated that the reduction in the number of shares would allow for a net increase in the dividends paid per remaining share outstanding. With a desire to set the tone of his leadership at M&M, Miller wanted to implement the initiative immediately. The accounting office had provided a set of pro forma M&M financial statements for the coming year (**Exhibit 30.1**).

Based on a rudimentary knowledge of corporate finance, Miller estimated the current cost of equity (and WACC) for M&M with the current no-debt policy at 8% based on a market risk premium of 5% and a company beta of 0.8. Miller appreciated that, because equity holders bore the business risk, they deserved to receive a higher return. Nonetheless, from a simple comparison of the 8% cost of equity with the 4% cost of debt, equity appeared to be an expensive source of funds. To Miller, substituting debt for equity was a superior financial policy because it gave the company cheaper capital.[3] With other business inputs, the company was aggressive in sourcing quality materials and labor at the lowest available cost. Shouldn't M&M do the same for its capital?

---

[2]The recapitalization would change the number of shares outstanding for M&M from 62.5 million to 42.5 million.

[3]Miller's uncle, Mert, was highly skeptical of Miller's proposal. Uncle Mert claimed that substituting debt for equity capital shifted more business risk of the firm to equity holders, so they required higher returns. He countered that M&M's beta of 0.8 must increase in the following manner: Levered beta = (Unlevered beta) $\times [1 + (1 - t) \times D/E]$, where t is the corporate tax rate, D is the debt value, and E is the equity value. With the F$500 million share-repurchase proposal, Uncle Mert asserted that M&M's D/E ratio would become 0.471.

EXHIBIT 30.1 | Pro Forma Financial Statement (in millions of Franco dollars, except per-share figures)

Income Statement	
Revenue	1,500
Operating expenses	1,375
Operating profit	125
Net income	125
Dividends	125
Shares outstanding	62.5
Dividends per share	2.00

Balance Sheet	
Current assets	450
Fixed assets	550
Total assets	1,000
Book debt	0
Book equity	1,000
Total capital	1,000

Source: Created by case writer.

Structuring Corporate Financial Policy: Diagnosis of Problems and Evaluation of Strategies

This note outlines a diagnostic and prescriptive way of thinking about corporate financial policy. Successful diagnosis and prescription depend heavily on thoughtful creativity and careful judgment, so the note presents no cookie-cutter solutions. Rather, it discusses the elements of good *process* and offers three basic stages in that process:

Description: The ability to describe a firm's financial policies (which have been chosen either explicitly or by default) is an essential foundation of diagnosis and prescription. Part I of this note defines "financial structure" and discusses the design elements by which a senior financial officer must make choices. This section illustrates the complexity of a firm's financial policies.

Diagnosis: One develops a financial policy relative to the world around you, represented by three "benchmark" perspectives. You compare the financial policy for your firm to the benchmarks and look for opportunities for improvement. Part II of this note is an overview of three benchmarks by which you can diagnose problems and opportunities: (1) the expectations of investors, (2) the policies and behavior of competitors, and (3) the internal goals and motivations of corporate management itself. Other perspectives may also exist. Parts III, IV, and V discuss in detail the estimation and application of the three benchmarks. These sections emphasize artful homework and economy of effort by focusing on key considerations, questions, and information. The goal is to derive insights unique to each benchmark, rather than to churn data endlessly.

Prescription: Action recommendations should spring from the insights gained in description and diagnosis. Rarely, however, do unique solutions or ideas exist; rather, the typical chief financial officer (CFO) must have a *view* about competing suggestions. Part VI addresses the task of comparing competing proposals. Part VII presents the conclusion.

This technical note was prepared by Robert F. Bruner, University Professor, Distinguished Professor of Business Administration, and Dean Emeritus, and draws on collaborative work with Katherine L. Updike. Copyright © 1993 by the University of Virginia Darden School Foundation, Charlottesville, VA. All rights reserved. *To order copies, send an e-mail to* sales@dardenbusinesspublishing.com. *No part of this publication may be reproduced, stored in a retrieval system, used in a spreadsheet, or transmitted in any form or by any means—electronic, mechanical, photocopying, recording, or otherwise—without the permission of the Darden School Foundation.*

Part I: Identifying Corporate Financial Policy: The Elements of Its Design

You can observe a lot just by watching.
  —**Yogi Berra**

The first task for financial advisers and decision makers is to understand the firm's *current* financial policy. Doing so is a necessary foundation for diagnosing problems and prescribing remedies. This section presents an approach for identifying the firm's financial policy, based on a careful analysis of the *tactics* by which that policy is implemented.

The Concept of Corporate Financial Policy

The notion that firms *have* a distinct financial policy is startling to some analysts and executives. Occasionally, a chief financial officer will say, "All I do is get the best deal I can whenever we need funds." Almost no CFO would admit otherwise. In all probability, however, the firm has a more substantive policy than the CFO admits to. Even a management style of myopia or opportunism is, after all, a policy.

Some executives will argue that calling financing a "policy" is too fancy. They say that financing is reactive: it happens after all investment and operational decisions have been made. How can reaction be a policy? At other times, one hears an executive say, "Our financial policy is simple." Attempts to characterize a financial structure as reactive or simplistic overlook the considerable richness of choice that confronts the financial manager.

Finally, some analysts make the mistake of "one-size-fits-all" thinking; that is, they assume that financial policy is mainly driven by the economics of a certain industry and they overlook the firm-specific nature of financial policy. Firms in the same, well-defined industry can have very different financial policies. The reason is that financial policy is a matter of *managerial choice.*

"Corporate financial policy" is a set of broad *guidelines* or a preferred *style* to guide the raising of capital and the distribution of value. Policies should be set to support the mission and strategy of the firm. As the environment changes, policies should adapt.

The analyst of financial policy must come to terms with its ambiguity. Policies are guidelines; they are imprecise. Policies are products of managerial choice rather than the dictates of an economic model. Policies change over time. Nevertheless, the framework in this note can help the analyst define a firm's corporate financial policy with enough focus to identify potential problems, prescribe remedies, and make decisions.

The Elements of Financial Policy

Every financial structure reveals underlying financial policies through the following seven elements of financial-structure design[1]:

---

[1]For economy, this note will restrict its scope to these seven items. One can, however, imagine dimensions other than the ones listed here.

1. *Mix* of classes of capital (such as debt versus equity, or common stock versus retained earnings): *How heavily does the firm rely on different classes of capital? Is the reliance on debt reasonable in light of the risks the firm faces and the nature of its industry and technology?* Mix may be analyzed through capitalization ratios, debt-service coverage ratios, and the firm's sources-and-uses-of-funds statement (where the analyst should look for the origins of the new additions to capital in the recent past). Many firms exhibit a pecking order of financing: they seek to fulfill their funding needs through the retention of profits, then through debt, and, finally, through the issuance of new shares. *Does the firm observe a particular pecking order in its acquisition of new capital?*

2. *Maturity structure of the firm's capital:* To describe the choices made about the maturity of outstanding securities is to be able to infer the judgments the firm made about its priorities—for example, future financing requirements and opportunities or relative preference for refinancing risk[2] versus reinvestment risk.[3] A risk-neutral position with respect to maturity would be where the life of the firm's assets equals the life of the firm's liabilities. Most firms accept an inequality in one direction or the other. This might be due to ignorance or to sophistication: managers might have a strong internal "view" about their ability to reinvest or refinance. Ultimately, we want managers to maximize value, not minimize risk. The absence of a perfect maturity hedge might reflect managers' better-informed bets about the future of the firm and markets. Measuring the maturity structure of the firm's capital can yield insights into the bets that the firm's managers are apparently making. The standard measures of maturity are term to maturity, average life, and duration. *Are the lives of the firm's assets and liabilities roughly matched? If not, what gamble is the firm taking (i.e., is it showing an appetite for refunding risk or interest-rate risk)?*

3. *Basis of the firm's coupon and dividend payments:* In simplest terms, basis addresses the firm's preference for fixed or floating rates of payment and is a useful tool in fathoming management's judgment regarding the future course of interest rates. Interest-rate derivatives provide the financial officer with choices conditioned by caps, floors, and other structured options. Understanding management's basis choices can reveal some of the fundamental bets management is placing, even when it has decided to "do nothing." *What is the firm's relative preference for fixed or floating interest rates? Are the firm's operating returns fixed or floating?*

---

[2]Refinancing risk exists where the life of the firm's assets is *more* than the life of the firm's liabilities. In other words, the firm will need to replace (or "roll over") the capital originally obtained to buy the asset. The refinancing risk is the chance that the firm will be unable to obtain funds on advantageous terms (or at all) at the rollover date.

[3]Reinvestment risk exists where the life of the firm's assets is *less* than the life of the firm's liabilities. In other words, the firm will need to replace, or roll over, the investment that the capital originally financed. Reinvestment risk is the chance that the firm will be unable to reinvest the capital on advantageous terms at the rollover date.

4. *Currency* addresses the global aspect of a firm's financial opportunities: These opportunities are expressed in two ways: (a) management of the firm's exposure to foreign exchange-rate fluctuations, and (b) the exploitation of unusual financing possibilities in global capital markets. Exchange-rate exposure arises when a firm earns income (or pays expenses) in a variety of currencies. Whether and how a firm hedges this exposure can reveal the "bets" that management is making regarding the future movement of exchange rates and the future currency mix of the firm's cash flows. The financial-policy analyst should look for foreign-denominated securities in the firm's capital and for swap, option, futures, and forward contracts—all of which can be used to manage the firm's foreign-exchange exposure. The other way that currency matters to the financial-policy analyst is as an indication of the management's willingness to source its capital "offshore." This is an indication of sophistication and of having a view about the parity of exchange rates with security returns around the world. In a perfectly integrated global capital market, the theory of interest rate parity would posit the futility of finding bargain financing offshore. But global capital markets are not perfectly integrated, and interest rate parity rarely holds true everywhere. Experience suggests that financing bargains may exist temporarily. Offshore financing may suggest an interest in finding and exploiting such bargains. *Is the currency denomination of the firm's capital consistent with the currency denomination of the firm's operating cash flows? Do the balance sheet footnotes show evidence of foreign-exchange hedging? Also, is the company, in effect, sourcing capital on a global basis or is it focusing narrowly on the domestic capital markets?*

5. *Exotica:* Every firm faces a spectrum of financing alternatives, ranging from plain-vanilla bonds and stocks to hybrids and one-of-a-kind, highly tailored securities.[4] This element considers management's relative preference for financial innovation. Where a firm positions itself on this spectrum can shed light on management's openness to new ideas, intellectual originality and, possibly, opportunistic tendencies. As a general matter, option-linked securities often appear in corporate finance where there is some disagreement between issuers and investors about a firm's prospects. For instance, managers of high-growth firms will foresee rapid expansion and vaulting stock prices. Bond investors, not having the benefit of inside information, might see only high risk—issuing a convertible bond might be a way to allow the bond investors to capitalize the risk[5] and to enjoy the creation of value through growth in return for accepting a lower current yield. Also, the circumstances under which exotic securities were issued are often fascinating episodes in a company's history. *Based on past financings, what is the firm's appetite for issuing exotic securities? Why have the firm's exotic securities been tailored as they are?*

---

[4]Examples of highly tailored securities include exchangeable and convertible bonds, hybrid classes of common stock, and contingent securities, such as a dividend-paying equity issued in connection with an acquisition.

[5]In general, the call options embedded in a convertible bond will be more valuable depending on the greater the volatility of the underlying asset.

6. *External control:* Any management team probably prefers little outside control. One must recognize that, in any financial structure, management has made choices about subtle control trade-offs, including *who* might exercise control (for example, creditors, existing shareholders, new shareholders, or a raider) and the control *trigger* (for example, default on a loan covenant, passing a preferred stock dividend, or a shareholder vote). How management structures control triggers (for example, the tightness of loan covenants) or forestalls discipline (perhaps through the adoption of poison pills and other takeover defenses) can reveal insights into management's fears and expectations. Clues about external control choices may be found in credit covenants, collateral pledges, the terms of preferred shares, the profile of the firm's equity holders, the voting rights of common stock, corporate bylaws, and antitakeover defenses. *In what ways has management defended against or yielded to external control?*

7. *Distribution:* seeks to determine any patterns in (a) the way the firm markets its securities (i.e., acquires capital), and (b) the way the firm delivers value to its investors (i.e., returns capital). Regarding marketing, insights emerge from knowing where a firm's securities are listed for trading, how often the shares are sold, and who advises the sale of securities (the adviser that a firm attracts is one indication of its sophistication). Regarding the delivery of value, the two generic strategies involve dividends or capital gains. Some companies will pay low or no dividends and force their shareholders to take returns in the form of capital gains. Other companies will pay material dividends, even borrowing to do so. Still others will repurchase shares, split shares, and declare extraordinary dividends. Managers' choices about delivering value yield clues about management's beliefs regarding investors and the company's ability to satisfy investors' needs. *How have managers chosen to deliver value to shareholders, and with whose assistance have they issued securities?*

A Comparative Illustration

The value of looking at a firm's financial structure through these seven design elements is that the insights they provide can become a basis for developing a broad, detailed picture of the firm's financial policies. Also, the seven elements become an organizational framework for the wealth of financial information on publicly owned companies.

Consider the examples of FedEx Corporation (FedEx) and United Parcel Service, Inc. (UPS), both leading firms in the express-delivery industry. Sources such as Factset, Yahoo! Finance, and the Value Line Investment Survey distill information from annual reports and regulatory filings and permit the analyst to draw conclusions about the seven elements of each firm's financial policy. Drawing on the latest financial results as of 2016, analysts could glean the insights about the policies of FedEx and UPS from **Table 31.1**.

As **Table 31.1** shows, standard information available on public companies yields important contrasts in their financial policies. Note that the insights are *informed guesses*: neither of those firms explicitly describes its financial policies. Nonetheless, with practice and good information, the validity of the guesses can be high.

TABLE 31.1 | Financial Policies for FedEx Corporation and United Parcel Service, Inc.

Elements of Financial Policy	FedEx Corporation	United Parcel Service, Inc.
Mix	**Moderate debt** • Debt/assets = 30% • Debt/capital = 50% • Operating Income/Interest = 9.8 • Sold equity in none of previous three years. • Credit rating: BBB (S&P) and Baa2 reduced from Baa1 (Moody's) • Acquisitions financed with combinations of most likely cash and debt.	**Equity orientation** • Debt/assets = 36% • Debt/capital = 85% • Operating Income/Interest = 23.5 • Sold equity in none of previous three years. • Credit rating: A+ (S&P) and A1 reduced from Aa3 (Moody's) • Acquisition financing is undisclosed, cash and debt.
Maturity	**Medium to long** • Average life = 17.8 years • 16% from 0 to 4 years • 20% from 5 to 15 years • 63% more than 15 years	**More balanced: short to long** • Average life = 12 years • 43% from 0 to 4 years • 0% from 5 to 15 years • 37% more than 15 years
Basis	**Fixed rates** • 75% of debt is at a fixed rate	**Fixed rates** • 69% of debt is at a fixed rate
Currency	**Blend: US Dollars and Euros** • 75% Dollar-based financing • 25% Euro-based financing	**Blend: Dollars, Euros, Pounds (UK)** • 80% Dollar-based financing • 20% Euro- and Pound-based
Exotica	**Leases** • 0.5% capital leases/total debt • 129% projected operating lease payments/total debt	**Leases** • 3.4% capital leases/total debt • 9.2% projected operating lease payments/total debt
Control	**Favors large stockholders** • Debt unsecured and callable • Dispersed share ownership	**Significant controlling structure** • Debt unsecured and callable • Classified share structure. 'A' shares have 10 votes/share; 'B' shares have 1 vote/share.
Distribution	**Steady dividends** • Average payout: 15% **Share repurchases** • Active program: 150% of net income.	**Large dividends** • Average payout: 55% **Share repurchases** • Active program: 40% of net income.

Source: Created by author.

FedEx and UPS present different policy profiles. FedEx relies somewhat more on debt financing, with a longer maturity, greater commitment to operating leases, and a more aggressive program of returning cash to shareholders through dividends and share repurchases. UPS is somewhat more conservative (as reflected in its higher debt rating): a higher times-interest-earned ratio, a more balanced maturity structure, more reliance on capital leases and less on operating leases, larger return to shareholders through dividend payments, and a distinctive classified common equity structure that gives strong control rights to the holders of the "A" shares. The UPS "A" shares are held "primarily by UPS employees and retirees, as well as trusts and descendants of the Company's founders."[6]

Part II: General Framework for Diagnosing Financial-Policy Opportunities and Problems

Having parsed the choices embedded in the firm's financial structure, one must ask, "Were these the *right* choices?" What is "right" is a matter of the context and the clientele to which management must respond. A firm has many potential claimants.[7] The discussion that follows will focus on the perspectives of competitors, investors, and senior corporate managers.

1. *Does the financial policy create value?*

   From the standpoint of investors, the best financial structure will (a) maximize shareholder wealth, (b) maximize the value of the entire firm (i.e., the market value of assets), and (c) minimize the firm's weighted-average cost of capital (WACC). When those conditions occur, the firm makes the best trade-offs among the choices on each of the seven dimensions of financial policy. This analysis is all within the context of the *market* conditions.

2. *Does the financial policy create a competitive advantage?*

   Competitors should matter in the design of corporate financial policy. Financial structure can enhance or constrain competitive advantage mainly by opening or foreclosing avenues of competitive response over time. Thus, a manager should critically assess the strategic options created or destroyed by a particular financial structure. Also, assuming that they are reasonably well managed, competitors' financial structures are probably an indicator of good financial policy in a particular industry. Thus a manager should want to know how his or her firm's financial structure compares with the peer group. In short, this line of thinking seeks to evaluate the relative position of the firm in its competitive environment on the basis of financial structure.

3. *Does the financial policy sustain senior management's vision?*

   The internal perspective tests the appropriateness of a capital structure from the standpoint of the expectations and capacities of the corporate organization itself. The analyst begins with an assessment of corporate strategy and the resulting

---

[6]UPS annual report, 2015: 101.

[7]With a moment's reflection, the analyst will call up a number of claimants (stakeholders or clientele), whose interests the company might serve. Managers, customers, and investors are often the first to come to mind. Creditors (for example, bankers) often have interests that differ from those of the equity investors. Workers (and unions) often make tangible claims on the firm. Governments, through their taxing and regulatory powers, do so as well. One might extend the list to environmentalists and other social activists. The possibilities are almost limitless. For economy, this discussion treats only the three perspectives that yield the most insight about financial policy.

stream of cash requirements and resources anticipated in the future. The realism of the plan should be tested against expected macroeconomic variations, as well as against possible but unexpected financial strains. A good financial structure meets the classic maxim of corporate finance, "Don't run out of cash": in other words, the ideal financial structure adequately funds the growth goals and dividend payouts of the firm without severely diluting the firm's current equity owners. The concept of self-sustainable growth provides a straightforward test of this ideal.

The next three sections will discuss these perspectives in more detail. All three perspectives are unlikely to offer a completely congruent assessment of financial structure. The investor's view looks at the *economic* consequences of a financial structure; the competitor's view considers *strategic* consequences; the internal view addresses the firm's *survival and ambitions*. The three views ask entirely different questions. An analyst should not be surprised when the answers diverge.

Rather like estimating the height of a distant mountain through the haze, the analyst develops a concept of the best financial structure by a process of *triangulation*. Triangulation involves weighing the importance of each of the perspectives as each one *complements* the other rather than as it substitutes for the other, identifying points of consistency, and making artful judgments where the perspectives diverge.

The goal of this analysis should be to articulate concretely the design of the firm's financial structure, preferably in terms of the seven elements discussed in Part I. This exercise entails developing notes, comments, and calculations for every one of the cells of this analytical grid:

Elements of Financial Structure	Current Structure	Investor View	Competitor View	Internal View	Evaluation/ Comments
1. Mix					
2. Maturity					
3. Basis					
4. Currency					
5. Exotica					
6. External Control					
7. Distribution					

No chart can completely anticipate the difficulties, quirks, and exceptions that the analyst will undoubtedly encounter. What matters most, however, is the way of thinking about the financial-structure design problem that encourages both critical thinking and organized, efficient digestion of information.

Figure 31.1 summarizes the approach presented in this section. Good financial-structure analysis develops three complementary perspectives on financial structure, and then blends those perspectives into a prescription.

FIGURE 31.1 | Overview of Financial-Structure Analysis.

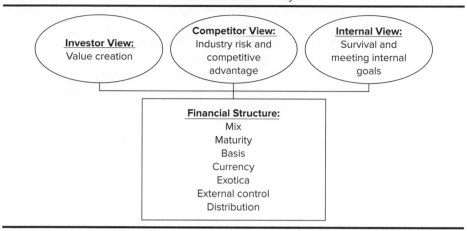

Source: Created by author.

Part III: Analyzing Financial Policy from the Investors' Viewpoint[8]

In finance theory, the investors' expectations should influence all managerial decisions. This theory follows the legal doctrine that firms should be managed in the interests of their owners. It also recognizes the economic idea that if investors' needs are satisfied after all other claims on the firm are settled, then the firm must be healthy. The investors' view also confronts the reality of capital market discipline. The best defense against a hostile takeover (or another type of intrusion) is a high stock price. In recent years, the threat of capital market discipline has done more than any academic theory to rivet the management's attention to *value creation*.

Academic theory, however, is extremely useful in identifying value-creating strategies. Economic value is held to be the present value of expected future cash flows discounted at a rate consistent with the risk of those cash flows. Considerable care must be given to the estimation of cash flows and discount rates (a review of discounted cash flow [DCF] valuation is beyond the scope of this note). Theory suggests that leverage can create value through the *benefits of debt tax shields* and can destroy value through the *costs of financial distress*. The balance of those costs and benefits depends upon specific capital market conditions, which are conveyed by the debt and equity costs that capital providers impose on the firm. Academic theory's bottom line is as follows:

> An efficient (i.e., value-optimizing) financial structure is one that simultaneously minimizes the weighted-average cost of capital and maximizes the share price and value of the enterprise.

---

[8]An excellent summary of the investors' orientation is found in Tim Koller, Marc Goedhart, and David Wessels, *Valuation: Measuring and Managing the Value of Companies*, 6th ed. (New York: Wiley, 2015).

The investors' perspective is a rigorous approach to evaluating financial structures: valuation analysis of the firm and its common stock under existing and alternative financial structures. The best structure will be one that creates the most value.

The phrase *alternative financial structures* is necessarily ambiguous, but should be interpreted to include a wide range of alternatives, including leveraged buyouts, leveraged recapitalizations, spin-offs, carve-outs, and even liquidations. However radical the latter alternatives may seem, the analyst must understand that investment bankers and corporate raiders routinely consider those alternatives. To anticipate the thinking of those agents of change, the analyst must replicate their homework.

Careful analysis does not rest with a final number, but rather considers a range of elements:

Cost of debt: The analysis focuses on yields to maturity and the spreads of those yields over the Treasury yield curve. Floating rates are always effective rates of interest.

Cost of equity: The assessment uses as many approaches as possible, including the capital asset pricing model, the dividend discount model, the financial leverage equation, the earnings/price model, and any other avenues that seem appropriate. Although it is fallible, the capital asset pricing model has the most rigor.

Debt/equity mix: The relative proportions of types of capital in the capital structure are important factors in computing the weighted-average cost of capital. All capital should be estimated on a *market value* basis.

Price/earnings ratio, market/book ratio, earnings before interest and taxes (EBIT) multiple: Comparing those values to the average levels of the entire capital market or to an industry group can provide an alternative check on the valuation of the firm.

Bond rating: The creditors' view of the firm is important. S&P and Moody's publish average financial ratios for bond-rating groups. Even for a firm with no publicly rated debt outstanding, a simple ratio analysis can reveal a firm's likely rating category and its current cost of debt.

Ownership: The relative mix of individual and institutional owners and the presence of block holders with potentially hostile intentions can help shed light on the current pricing of a firm's securities.

Short position: A large, short-sale position on the firm's stock can indicate that some traders believe a decline in share price is imminent.

To conclude, the first rule of financial-policy analysis is: *Think like an investor.* The investors' view assesses the value of a firm's shares under alternative financial structures and the existence of any strongly positive or negative perceptions in the capital markets about the firm's securities.

Part IV: Analyzing Financial Policy from a Competitive Perspective

The competitive perspective matters to senior executives for two important reasons. First, it gives an indication about (1) standard practice in the industry, and (2) the strategic position of the firm relative to the competition. Second, it implies rightly that finance can be a strategic competitive instrument.

The competitive perspective may be the hardest of the three benchmarks to assess. There are few clear signposts in industry dynamics, and, as most industries become increasingly global, the comparisons become even more difficult to make. Despite the difficulty of this analysis, however, senior executives typically give an inordinate amount of attention to it. The well-versed analyst must be able to assess the ability of the current policy (and its alternatives) to maintain or improve its competitive position.

This analysis does not proceed scientifically, but rather evolves iteratively toward an accurate assessment of the situation.[9] The steps might be defined as follows:

1. Define the universe of competitors.

2. Spread the data and financial ratios on the firm and its competitors in comparative fashion.

3. Identify similarities and, more importantly, differences. Probe into anomalies. Question the data and the peer sample.

4. Add needed information, such as a foreign competitor, another ratio, historical normalization, etc.

5. Discuss or clarify the information with the CFO or industry expert.

As the information grows, the questions will become more probing. What is the historical growth pattern? Why did the XYZ company suddenly increase its leverage or keep a large cash balance? Did the acquisition of a new line actually provide access to new markets? Are the changes in debt mix and maturity or in the dividend policy related to the new products and markets?

Economy of effort demands that the analyst begin with a few ratios and data that can be easily obtained (from annual reports and other sources). If a company is in several industries and does not have pure competitors, choose group-divisional competitors and, to the extent possible, use segment information to devise ratios that will be valid, which is to say, operating income to sales, rather than an after-tax equivalent). Do not forget information that may be outside the financial statements and may be critical to competitive survival, such as geographic diversification, research and development expenditures, and union activity. For some industries, other key ratios are

---

[9]An overview of industry and competitor analysis may be found in Michael Porter, *Competitive Strategy: Techniques for Analyzing Industries and Competitors* (New York: Free Press, 1998). An excellent survey of possible information sources on firms is in Leonard M. Fuld, *The New Competitor Intelligence: The Complete Resource for Finding, Analyzing, and Using Information about Your Competitors*, 2nd ed. (New York: Wiley, 1994).

available through trade groups, such as same-store sales and capacity analyses. Whatever the inadequacy of the data, the comparisons will provide direction for subsequent analysis.

The ratios and data to be used will depend on the course of analysis. An analyst could start with the following general types of measures with which to compare a competitor group:

1. *Size:* sales, market value, number of employees or countries, market share
2. *Asset productivity:* return on assets (ROA), return on invested capital, market to book value
3. *Shareholder wealth:* price/earnings (P/E), return on market value
4. *Predictability:* Beta, historical trends
5. *Growth:* 1- to 10-year compound growth of sales, profits, assets, and market value of equity
6. *Financial flexibility:* debt-to-capital, debt ratings, cash flow coverage, estimates of the cost of capital
7. *Other significant industry issues:* unfunded pension liabilities, postretirement medical benefit obligations, environmental liabilities, capacity, research and development expense to sales, percentage of insider control, etc.

One of the key issues to resolve in analyzing the comparative data is whether all the peer-group members display the same results and trends. Inevitably, they will not—which begs the question, why not? Trends in asset productivity and globalization have affected the competitors differently and elicited an assortment of strategic responses. These phenomena should stimulate further research.

The analyst should augment personal research efforts with the work of industry analysts. Securities analysts, consultants, academicians, and journalists—both through their written work and via telephone conversations—can provide valuable insights based on their extensive, personal contacts in the industry.

Analyzing competitors develops insights into the range of financial structures in the industry and the appropriateness of your firm's structure in comparison. Developing those insights is more a matter of qualitative judgment than of letting the numbers speak for themselves. For instance:

1. Suppose your firm is a highly leveraged computer manufacturer with an uneven record of financial performance. Should it unlever? You discover that the peer group of computer manufacturers is substantially equity financed, owing largely to the rapid rate of technological innovation and the predation of a few large players in the industry. The *strategic rationale* for low leverage is to survive the business and short product lifecycles. Yes, it might be good to unlever.

2. Suppose your firm is an airline that finances its equipment purchases with flotations of commercial paper. The average life of the firm's liabilities is 4 years, while the

average life of the firm's assets is 15 years. Should the airline refinance its debt using securities with longer maturity? You discover that the peer group of airlines finances its assets with leases, equipment-trust certificates, and project-finance deals that almost exactly match the economic lives of assets and liabilities. The *strategic rationale* for lengthening the maturity structure of liabilities is to hedge against yield-curve changes that might adversely affect your firm's ability to refinance, yet still leave its peer competitors relatively unaffected.

3. Here is a trickier example. Your firm is the last nationwide supermarket chain that is publicly held. All other major supermarket chains have gone private in leveraged buyouts. Should your firm lever up through a leveraged share repurchase? Competitor analysis reveals that other firms are struggling to meet debt service payments on already thin margins and that a major shift in customer patronage may be under way. You conclude that price competition in selected markets would trigger realignment in market shares in your firm's favor, because the competitors have little pricing flexibility. In that case, adjusting to the industry-average leverage would not be appropriate.

Part V: Diagnosing Financial Policy from an Internal Perspective

Internal analysis is the third major screen of a firm's financial structure. It accounts for the expected cash requirements and resources of a firm, and tests the consistency of a firm's financial structure with the profitability, growth, and dividend goals of the firm. The classic tools of internal analysis are the forecast cash flow, financial statements, and sources-and-uses of funds statements. The standard banker's credit analysis is consistent with this approach.

The essence of this approach is a concern for (1) the preservation of the firm's *financial flexibility*, (2) the *sustainability* of the firm's financial policies, and (3) the *feasibility* of the firm's strategic goals. For example, the firm's long-term goals may call for a doubling of sales in five years. The business plan for achieving that goal may call for the construction of a greenfield plant in year one, and then regional distribution systems in years two and three. Substantial working capital investments will be necessary in years two through five. How this growth is to be financed has huge implications for your firm's financial structure *today*. Typically, an analyst addresses this problem by forecasting the financial performance of the firm, experimenting with different financing sequences and choosing the best one, then determining the structure that makes the best foundation for that financing sequence. This analysis implies the need to maintain future financial flexibility.

Financial Flexibility

Financial flexibility is easily measured as the excess cash and unused debt capacity on which the firm might call. In addition, there may be other reserves, such as unused land or excess stocks of raw materials, that could be liquidated. All reserves that could be mobilized should be reflected in an analysis of financial flexibility. Illustrating with the narrower definition (cash and unused debt capacity), one can measure financial flexibility as follows:

1. Select a target minimum debt rating that is acceptable to the firm. Many CFOs will have a target minimum in mind, such as the BBB/Baa rating.

2. Determine the book value[10] debt/equity mix consistent with the minimum rating. Standard & Poor's, for instance, publishes average financial ratios, including debt/equity, that are associated with each debt-rating category.[11]

3. Determine the book value of debt consistent with the debt/equity ratio from step 2. This gives the amount of debt that would be outstanding, if the firm moved to the minimum acceptable bond rating.

4. Estimate financial flexibility using the following formula:

   Financial flexibility
      = Excess cash + (debt at minimum rating − current debt outstanding).

The amount estimated by this formula indicates the financial reserves on which the firm can call to exploit unusual or surprising opportunities (for example, the chance to acquire a competitor) or to defend against unusual threats (for example, a price war, sudden product obsolescence, or a labor strike).

Self-Sustainable Growth

A shorthand test for sustainability and internal consistency is the self-sustainable growth model. This model is based on one key assumption: over the forecast period, the firm sells no new shares of stock (this assumption is entirely consistent with the actual behavior of firms over the long run).[12] As long as the firm does not change its mix of debt and equity, the self-sustainable model implies that assets can grow only as fast as equity grows. Thus, the issue of sustainability is significantly determined by the firm's return on equity (ROE) and dividend payout ratio (DPO):

$$\text{Self-sustainable growth rate of assets} = \text{ROE} \times (1 - \text{DPO})$$

The test of feasibility of any long-term plan involves comparing the growth rate implied by this formula and the *targeted* growth rate dictated by management's plan. If the targeted growth rate equals the implied rate, then the firm's financial policies are in balance. If the implied rate exceeds the targeted rate, the firm will gradually become more liquid, creating an asset deployment opportunity. If the targeted rate exceeds the

---

[10]Ideally, one would work with market values rather than book values, but the rating agencies compute their financial ratios only on a book value basis. Because this analysis, in effect, mimics the perspective of the rating agencies, the analyst must work with book values.

[11]See *CreditWeek*, published by Standard & Poor's.

[12]From 1950 to 2015, only a very small percentage of the growth of the U.S. economy's business sector was financed by the sale of new common stock. The most significant sources were short-term liabilities, long-term liabilities, and retained earnings, in that order.

implied rate, the firm must raise more capital by selling stock, levering up, or reducing the dividend payout.

Management policies can be modeled finely by recognizing that ROE can be decomposed into various factors using two classic formulas:

DuPont system of ratios: $ROE = P/S \times S/A \times A/E$

P/S = profit divided by sales or net margin; a measure of profitability

S/A = sales divided by assets; a measure of asset productivity

A/E = assets divided by equity; a measure of financial leverage

Financial-leverage equation[13]: $ROE = ROTC + [(ROTC - K_d) \times (D/E)]$

$ROTC$ = return on total capital

K_d = cost of debt

D/E = debt divided by equity; a measure of leverage

Inserting either of those formulas into the equation for the self-sustainable growth rate gives a richer model of the drivers of self-sustainability. One sees, in particular, the importance of internal operations. The self-sustainable growth model can be expanded to reflect explicitly measures of a firm's operating and financial policies.

The self-sustainable growth model tests the internal consistency of a firm's operating and financial policies. *This model, however, provides no guarantee that a strategy will maximize value.* Value creation does not begin with growth targets; growth per se does not necessarily lead to value creation, as the growth-by-acquisition strategies of the 1960s and '70s abundantly illustrated. Also, the adoption of growth targets may foreclose other, more profitable strategies. Those targets may invite managers to undertake investments yielding less than the cost of capital. Meeting sales or asset growth targets can destroy value. Thus, any sustainable growth analysis must be augmented by questions about the value-creation potential of a given set of corporate policies. These questions include: (1) What are the magnitude and duration of investment returns as compared with the firm's cost of capital? and (2) With what alternative set of policies is the firm's share price maximized? With questions such as those, the investor orientation discussed in Part III is turned inward to double-check the appropriateness of any inferences drawn from financial forecasts of the sources-and-uses of funds statements and from the analysis of the self-sustainable growth model.

Part VI: What Is Best?

Any financial structure evaluated against the perspectives of investors, competitors, and internal goals will probably show opportunities for improvement. Most often, CFOs choose to make changes at the margin rather than tinkering radically with a financial

---

[13]This is the classic expression for the cost of equity, as originally presented in the work of the Nobel Prize winners, Franco Modigliani and Merton Miller.

structure. For changes large and small, however, the analyst must develop a framework for judgment and prescription.

The following framework is a way of identifying the trade-offs among "good" and "bad," rather than finding the right answer. Having identified the trade-offs implicit in any alternative structure, it remains for the CFO and the adviser to choose the structure with the most attractive trade-offs.

The key elements of evaluation are as follows:

Flexibility: the ability to meet unforeseen financing requirements as they arise— those requirements may be favorable (for example, a sudden acquisition opportunity) or unfavorable (such as the Source Perrier and the benzene scare). Flexibility may involve liquidating assets or tapping the capital markets in adverse market environments or both. Flexibility can be measured by bond ratings, coverage ratios, capitalization ratios, liquidity ratios, and the identification of salable assets.

Risk: the predictable variability in the firm's business. Such variability may be due to both macroeconomic factors (such as consumer demand) and industry- or firm-specific factors (such as product lifecycles, or strikes before wage negotiations). To some extent, past experience may indicate the future range of variability in EBIT and cash flow. High leverage tends to amplify those predictable business swings. The risk associated with any given financial structure can be assessed by EBIT–EPS (earnings per share) analysis, break-even analysis, the standard deviation of EBIT, and beta. In theory, beta should vary directly with leverage.[14]

Income: this compares financial structures on the basis of value creation. Measures such as DCF value, projected ROE, EPS, and the cost of capital indicate the comparative value effects of alternative financial structures.

Control: alternative financial structures may imply changes in control or different control constraints on the firm as indicated by the percentage distribution of share ownership and by the structure of debt covenants.

Timing: asks the question whether the current capital-market environment is the right moment to implement any alternative financial structure, and what the implications for future financing will be if the proposed structure is adopted. The current market environment can be assessed by examining the Treasury yield curve, the trend in the movement of interest rates, the existence of any windows in the market for new issues of securities, P/E multiple trends, etc. Sequencing considerations are implicitly captured in the assumptions

---

[14] This relationship is illustrated by the formula for estimating a firm's levered beta:

$$B_l = B_u \times [1 + (1 - t) \times D/E]$$

where: B_l = levered beta; B_u = unlevered beta; t = firm's marginal tax rate; and D/E = the firm's market value, debt-to-equity ratio.

underlying the alternative DCF value estimates, and can be explicitly examined by looking at annual EPS and ROE streams under alternative financing sequences.

This framework of flexibility, risk, income, control, and timing (FRICT) can be used to assess the relative strengths and weaknesses of alternative financing plans. To use a simple example, suppose that your firm is considering two financial structures: (1) 60% debt and 40% equity (i.e., debt will be issued), and (2) 40% debt and 60% equity (i.e., equity will be issued). Also, suppose that your analysis of the two structures under the investor, competitor, and internal-analysis screens leads you to make this basic comparison:

	60% Debt	**40% Debt**
Flexibility	A little low, not bad	High
	BBB debt rating	AA debt rating
	$50 million in reserves	$300 million in reserves
Risk	High	Medium
	EBIT coverage = 1.5	EBIT coverage = 3.0
Income	Good-to-high	Mediocre
	DCF value = $20/share	DCF value = $12/share (dilutive)
Control	Covenants tight	Covenants not restrictive
	No voting dilution	10% voting dilution
Timing	Interest rates low today	Equity multiples low today
	Risky sequence	Low-risk sequence for future

The 60% debt structure is favored on the grounds of income, control, and today's market conditions. The 40% debt structure is favored on the grounds of flexibility, risk, and the long-term financial sequencing. This example boils down to a decision between "eating well" and "sleeping well." It remains up to senior management to make the difficult choice between the two alternatives, while giving careful attention to the views of the investors, competitors, and managers.

Part VII: Conclusion

Description, diagnosis, and prescription in financial structuring form an iterative process. It is quite likely that the CFO in the eat-well/sleep-well example would send the analyst back for more research and testing of alternative structures. **Figure 31.2** presents an expanded view of the basic cycle of analysis and suggests more about the complexity of the financial-structuring problem. With time and experience, the analyst develops an intuition for efficient information sources and modes of analysis. In the long run, this intuition makes the cycle of analysis manageable.

FIGURE 31.2 | An Expanded Illustration of the Process of Developing a Financial Policy.

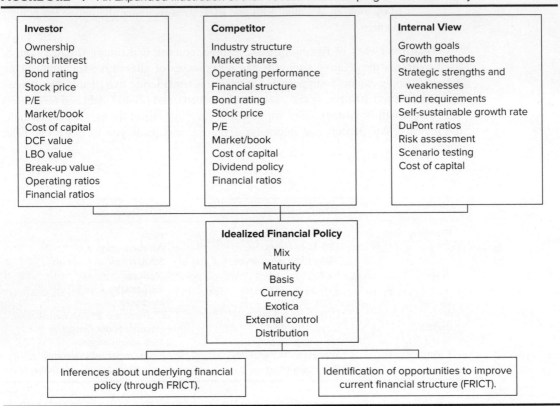

Investor

Ownership
Short interest
Bond rating
Stock price
P/E
Market/book
Cost of capital
DCF value
LBO value
Break-up value
Operating ratios
Financial ratios

Competitor

Industry structure
Market shares
Operating performance
Financial structure
Bond rating
Stock price
P/E
Market/book
Cost of capital
Dividend policy
Financial ratios

Internal View

Growth goals
Growth methods
Strategic strengths and
   weaknesses
Fund requirements
Self-sustainable growth rate
DuPont ratios
Risk assessment
Scenario testing
Cost of capital

Idealized Financial Policy

Mix
Maturity
Basis
Currency
Exotica
External control
Distribution

Inferences about underlying financial policy (through FRICT).

Identification of opportunities to improve current financial structure (FRICT).

Source: Created by author.

California Pizza Kitchen

Everyone knows that 95% of restaurants fail in the first two years, and a lot of people think it's "location, location, location." It could be, but my experience is you have to have the financial staying power. You could have the greatest idea, but many restaurants do not start out making money—they build over time. So it's really about having the capital and the staying power.
　　—Rick Rosenfield, Co-CEO, California Pizza Kitchen[1]

In early July 2007, the financial team at California Pizza Kitchen (CPK), led by Chief Financial Officer Susan Collyns, was compiling the preliminary results for the second quarter of 2007. Despite industry challenges of rising commodity, labor, and energy costs, CPK was about to announce near-record quarterly profits of over $6 million. CPK's profit expansion was explained by strong revenue growth with comparable restaurant sales up over 5%. The announced numbers were fully in line with the company's forecasted guidance to investors.

　　The company's results were particularly impressive when contrasted with many other casual dining firms, which had experienced sharp declines in customer traffic. Despite the strong performance, industry difficulties were such that CPK's share price had declined 10% during the month of June to a current value of $22.10. Given the price drop, the management team had discussed repurchasing company shares. With little money in excess cash, however, a large share repurchase program would require debt financing. Since going public in 2000, CPK's management had avoided putting any debt on the balance sheet. Financial policy was conservative to preserve what co-CEO Rick Rosenfeld referred to as staying power. The view was that a strong balance sheet would maintain the borrowing ability needed to support CPK's expected growth trajectory. Yet with interest rates on the rise from historical lows, Collyns was aware of the benefits of moderately levering up CPK's equity.

---

[1]Richard M. Smith, "Rolling in Dough; For the Creators of California Pizza Kitchen, Having Enough Capital Was the Key Ingredient to Success," *Newsweek*, June 25, 2007.

California Pizza Kitchen

Inspired by the gourmet pizza offerings at Wolfgang Puck's celebrity-filled restaurant, Spago, and eager to flee their careers as white-collar criminal defense attorneys, Larry Flax and Rick Rosenfield created the first California Pizza Kitchen in 1985 in Beverly Hills, California. Known for its hearth-baked barbecue-chicken pizza, the "designer pizza at off-the-rack prices" concept flourished. Expansion across the state, country, and globe followed in the subsequent two decades. At the end of the second quarter of 2007, the company had 213 locations in 28 states and 6 foreign countries. While still very California-centric (approximately 41% of the U.S. stores were in California), the casual dining model had done well throughout all U.S. regions with its family-friendly surroundings, excellent ingredients, and inventive offerings.

California Pizza Kitchen derived its revenues from three sources: sales at company-owned restaurants, royalties from franchised restaurants, and royalties from a partnership with Kraft Foods to sell CPK-branded frozen pizzas in grocery stores. While the company had expanded beyond its original concept with two other restaurant brands, its main focus remained on operating company-owned full-service CPK restaurants, of which there were 170 units.

Analysts conservatively estimated the potential for full-service company-owned CPK units at 500. Both the investment community and management were less certain about the potential for the company's chief attempt at brand extension, its ASAP restaurant concept. In 1996, the company first developed the ASAP concept in a franchise agreement with HMSHost. The franchised ASAPs were located in airports and featured a limited selection of pizzas and "grab-n-go" salads and sandwiches. While not a huge revenue source, management was pleased with the success of the airport ASAP locations, which currently numbered 16. In early 2007, HMSHost and CPK agreed to extend their partnership through 2012. But the sentiment was more mixed regarding its company-owned ASAP locations. First opened in 2000 to capitalize on the growth of fast casual dining, the company-owned ASAP units offered CPK's most-popular pizzas, salads, soups, and sandwiches with in-restaurant seating. Sales and operations at the company-owned ASAP units never met management's expectations. Even after retooling the concept and restaurant prototype in 2003, management decided to halt indefinitely all ASAP development in 2007 and planned to record roughly $770,000 in expenses in the second quarter to terminate the planned opening of one ASAP location.

Although they had doubts associated with the company-owned ASAP restaurant chain, the company and investment community were upbeat about CPK's success and prospects with franchising full-service restaurants internationally. At the beginning of July 2007, the company had 15 franchised international locations, with more openings planned for the second half of 2007. Management sought out knowledgeable franchise partners who would protect the company's brand and were capable of growing the number of international units. Franchising agreements typically gave CPK an initial payment of $50,000 to $65,000 for each location opened and then an estimated 5% of gross sales. With locations already in China (including Hong Kong), Indonesia, Japan, Malaysia, the Philippines, and Singapore, the company planned to expand its global reach to Mexico and South Korea in the second half of 2007.

Management saw its Kraft partnership as another initiative in its pursuit of building a global brand. In 1997, the company entered into a licensing agreement with Kraft Foods to distribute CPK-branded frozen pizzas. Although representing less than 1% of current revenues, the Kraft royalties had a 95% pretax margin, one equity analyst estimated.[2] In addition to the high-margin impact on the company's bottom line, management also highlighted the marketing requirement in its Kraft partnership. Kraft was obligated to spend 5% of gross sales on marketing the CPK frozen pizza brand, more than the company often spent on its own marketing.

Management believed its success in growing both domestically and internationally, and through ventures like the Kraft partnership, was due in large part to its "dedication to guest satisfaction and menu innovation and sustainable culture of service."[3] A creative menu with high-quality ingredients was a top priority at CPK, with the two co-founders still heading the menu-development team. **Exhibit 32.1** contains a selection of CPK menu offerings. "Its menu items offer customers distinctive, compelling flavors to commonly recognized foods," A Morgan Keegan analyst wrote.[4] While the company had a narrower, more-focused menu than some of its peers, the chain prided itself on creating craved items, such as Singapore Shrimp Rolls, that distinguished its menu and could not be found at its casual dining peers. This strategy was successful, and internal research indicated a specific menu craving that could not be satisfied elsewhere prompted many patron visits. To maintain the menu's originality, management reviewed detailed sales reports twice a year and replaced slow-selling offerings with new items. Some of the company's most recent menu additions in 2007 had been developed and tested at the company's newest restaurant concept, the LA Food Show. Created by Flax and Rosenfield in 2003, the LA Food Show offered a more upscale experience and expansive menu than CPK. CPK increased its minority interest to full ownership of the LA Food Show in 2005 and planned to open a second location in early 2008.

In addition to crediting its inventive menu, analysts also pointed out that its average check of $13.30 was below that of many of its upscale dining casual peers, such as P.F. Chang's and the Cheesecake Factory. Analysts from RBC Capital Markets labeled the chain a "Price–Value–Experience" leader in its sector.[5]

CPK spent 1% of its sales on advertising, far less than the 3% to 4% of sales that casual dining competitors, such as Chili's, Red Lobster, Olive Garden, and Outback Steakhouse, spent annually. Management felt careful execution of its company model resulted in devoted patrons who created free, but far more-valuable word-of-mouth marketing for the company. Of the actual dollars spent on marketing, roughly 50% was spent on menu-development costs, with the other half consumed by more typical

---

[2]Jeffrey D. Farmer, CIBC World Markets Equity Research Earnings Update, "California Pizza Kitchen, Inc.; Notes from West Coast Investor Meetings: Shares Remain Compelling," April 12, 2007.

[3]Company press release, February 15, 2007.

[4]Destin M. Tompkins, Robert M. Derrington, and S. Brandon Couillard, Morgan Keegan Equity Research, "California Pizza Kitchen, Inc.," April 19, 2007.

[5]Larry Miller, Daniel Lewis, and Robert Sanders, RBC Capital Markets Research Comment, "California Pizza Kitchen: Back on Trend with Old Management," September 14, 2006.

marketing strategies, such as public relations efforts, direct mail offerings, outdoor media, and on-line marketing.

CPK's clientele was not only attractive for its endorsements of the chain, but also because of its demographics. Management frequently highlighted that its core customer had an average household income of more than $75,000, according to a 2005 guest satisfaction survey. CPK contended that its customer base's relative affluence sheltered the company from macroeconomic pressures, such as high gas prices, that might lower sales at competitors with fewer well-off patrons.

Restaurant Industry

The restaurant industry could be divided into two main sectors: full service and limited service. Some of the most popular subsectors within full service included casual dining and fine dining, with fast casual and fast food being the two prevalent limited-service subsectors. Restaurant consulting firm Technomic Information Services projected the limited-service restaurant segment to maintain a five-year compound annual growth rate (CAGR) of 5.5%, compared with 5.1% for the full-service restaurant segment.[6] The five-year CAGR for CPK's subsector of the full-service segment was projected to grow even more at 6.5%. In recent years, a number of forces had challenged restaurant industry executives, including:

- Increasing commodity prices;
- Higher labor costs;
- Softening demand due to high gas prices;
- Deteriorating housing wealth; and
- Intense interest in the industry by activist shareholders.

High gas prices not only affected demand for dining out, but also indirectly pushed a dramatic rise in food commodity prices. Moreover, a national call for the creation of more biofuels, primarily corn-produced ethanol, played an additional role in driving up food costs for the restaurant industry. Restaurant companies responded by raising menu prices in varying degrees. The restaurants believed that the price increases would have little impact on restaurant traffic given that consumers experienced higher price increases in their main alternative to dining out—purchasing food at grocery stores to consume at home.

Restaurants not only had to deal with rising commodity costs, but also rising labor costs. In May 2007, President Bush signed legislation increasing the U.S. minimum wage rate over a three-year period beginning in July 2007 from $5.15 to $7.25 an hour. While restaurant management teams had time to prepare for the ramifications of this gradual increase, they were ill-equipped to deal with the nearly 20 states in late 2006 that passed anticipatory wage increases at rates higher than those proposed by Congress.

---

[6]Destin M. Tompkins, Robert M. Derrington, and S. Brandon Couillard, Morgan Keegan Equity Research, "California Pizza Kitchen, Inc.," April 19, 2007.

In addition to contending with the rising cost of goods sold (COGS), restaurants faced gross margins that were under pressure from the softening demand for dining out. A recent AAA Mid-Atlantic survey asked travelers how they might reduce spending to make up for the elevated gas prices, and 52% answered that food expenses would be the first area to be cut.[7] Despite that news, a Deutsche Bank analyst remarked, "Two important indicators of consumer health—disposable income and employment—are both holding up well. As long as people have jobs and incomes are rising, they are likely to continue to eat out."[8]

The current environment of elevated food and labor costs and consumer concerns highlighted the differences between the limited-service and full-service segments of the restaurant industry. Franchising was more popular in the limited-service segment and provided some buffer against rising food and labor costs because franchisors received a percentage of gross sales. Royalties on gross sales also benefited from any pricing increases that were made to address higher costs. Restaurant companies with large franchising operations also did not have the huge amount of capital invested in locations or potentially heavy lease obligations associated with company-owned units. Some analysts included operating lease requirements when considering a restaurant company's leverage.[9] Analysts also believed limited-service restaurants would benefit from any consumers trading down from the casual dining sub-sector of the full-service sector.[10] The growth of the fast-casual subsector and the food-quality improvements in fast food made trading down an increasing likelihood in an economic slowdown.

The longer-term outlook for overall restaurant demand looked much stronger. A study by the National Restaurant Association projected that consumers would increase the percentage of their food dollars spent on dining out from the 45% in recent years to 53% by 2010.[11] That long-term positive trend may have helped explain the extensive interest in the restaurant industry by activist shareholders, often the executives of private equity firms and hedge funds. Activist investor William Ackman with Pershing Square Capital Management initiated the current round of activist investors forcing change at major restaurant chains. Roughly one week after Ackman vociferously criticized the McDonald's corporate organization at a New York investment conference in late 2005, the company declared it would divest 1,500 restaurants, repurchase $1 billion of its stock, and disclose more restaurant-level performance details. Ackman advocated all those changes and was able to leverage the power of his 4.5% stake in McDonald's by using the media. His success did not go unnoticed, and other vocal minority investors aggressively pressed for changes at numerous chains including Applebee's, Wendy's,

---

[7]Amy G. Vinson and Ted Hillard, Avondale Partners, LLC, "Restaurant Industry Weekly Update," June 11, 2007.

[8]Jason West, Marc Greenberg, and Andrew Kieley, Deutsche Bank Global Markets Research, "Transferring Coverage–Reservations Available," June 7, 2007.

[9]As of July 1, 2007, CPK had $154.3 million in minimum lease payments required over the next five years with $129.6 million due in more than five years.

[10]Jeff Omohundro, Katie H. Willett, and Jason Belcher, Wachovia Capital Markets, LLC Equity Research, "The Restaurant Watch," July 3, 2007.

[11]Destin M. Tompkins, Robert M. Derrington, and S. Brandon Couillard, Morgan Keegan Equity Research, "California Pizza Kitchen, Inc.," April 19, 2007.

and Friendly's. These changes included the outright sale of the company, sales of noncore divisions, and closure of poor-performing locations.

In response, other chains embarked on shareholder-friendly plans including initiating share repurchase programs; increasing dividends; decreasing corporate expenditures; and divesting secondary assets. Doug Brooks, chief executive of Brinker International Inc., which owned Chili's, noted at a recent conference:

> There is no shortage of interest in our industry these days, and much of the recent news has centered on the participation of activist shareholders . . . but it is my job as CEO to act as our internal activist.[12]

In April 2007, Brinker announced it had secured a new $400 million unsecured, committed credit-facility to fund an accelerated share repurchase transaction in which approximately $300 million of its common stock would be repurchased. That followed a tender offer recapitalization in 2006 in which the company repurchased $50 million worth of common shares.

Recent Developments

CPK's positive second-quarter results would affirm many analysts' conclusions that the company was a safe haven in the casual dining sector. **Exhibits 32.2** and **32.3** contain CPK's financial statements through July 1, 2007. **Exhibit 32.4** presents comparable store sales trends for CPK and peers. **Exhibit 32.5** contains selected analysts' forecasts for CPK, all of which anticipated revenue and earnings growth. A Morgan Keegan analyst commented in May:

> Despite increased market pressures on consumer spending, California Pizza Kitchen's concept continues to post impressive customer traffic gains. Traditionally appealing to a more discriminating, higher-income clientele, CPK's creative fare, low check average, and high service standards have uniquely positioned the concept for success in a tough consumer macroeconomic environment.[13]

While other restaurant companies experienced weakening sales and earnings growth, CPK's revenues increased more than 16% to $159 million for the second quarter of 2007. Notably, royalties from the Kraft partnership and international franchises were up 37% and 21%, respectively, for the second quarter. Development plans for opening a total of 16 to 18 new locations remained on schedule for 2007. Funding CPK's 2007 growth plan was anticipated to require $85 million in capital expenditures.

The company was successfully managing its two largest expense items in an environment of rising labor and food costs. Labor costs had actually declined from 36.6% to 36.3% of total revenues from the second quarter of 2006 to the second quarter of 2007. Food, beverage, and paper-supply costs remained constant at roughly 24.5% of total

---

[12]Sarah E. Lockyer, "Who's the Boss? Activist Investors Drive Changes at Major Chains: Companies Pursue 'Shareholder-Friendly' Strategies in Response to Public Pressure," *Nation's Restaurant News*, April 23, 2007.

[13]Destin M. Tompkins and Robert M. Derrington, Morgan Keegan Equity Research, "California Pizza Kitchen, Inc.," May 11, 2007.

revenue in both the second quarter of 2006 and 2007. The company was implementing a number of taskforce initiatives to deal with the commodity price pressures, especially as cheese prices increased from $1.37 per pound in April to almost $2.00 a pound by the first week of July. Management felt that much of the cost improvements had been achieved through enhancements in restaurant operations.

Capital Structure Decision

CPK's book equity was expected to be around $226 million at the end of the second quarter. With a share price in the low 20s, CPK's market capitalization stood at $644 million. The company had recently issued a 50% stock dividend, which had effectively split CPK shares on a 3-for-2 shares basis. CPK investors received one additional share for every two shares of common stock held. Adjusted for the stock dividend, **Exhibit 32.6** shows the performance of CPK stock relative to that of industry peers.

Despite the challenges of growing the number of restaurants by 38% over the last five years, CPK consistently generated strong operating returns. CPK's return on equity (ROE), which was 10.1% for 2006, did not benefit from financial leverage.[14] Financial policy varied across the industry, with some firms remaining all equity capitalized and others levering up to half debt financing. **Exhibit 32.7** depicts selected financial data for peer firms. Because CPK used the proceeds from its 2000 initial public offering (IPO) to pay off its outstanding debt, the company completely avoided debt financing. CPK maintained borrowing capacity available under an existing $75 million line of credit. Interest on the line of credit was calculated at LIBOR plus 0.80%. With LIBOR currently at 5.36%, the line of credit's interest rate was 6.16% (see **Exhibit 32.8**).

The recent 10% share price decline seemed to raise the question of whether this was an ideal time to repurchase shares and potentially leverage the company's balance sheet with ample borrowings available on its existing line of credit. One gain from the leverage would be to reduce the corporate income-tax liability, which had been almost $10 million in 2006. **Exhibit 32.9** provides pro forma financial summaries of CPK's tax shield under alternative capital structures. Still, CPK needed to preserve its ability to fund the strong expansion outlined for the company. Any use of financing to return capital to shareholders needed to be balanced with management's goal of growing the business.

---

[14]By a familiar decomposition equation, a firm's ROE could be decomposed into three components: operating margin, capital turnover, and leverage. More specifically, the algebra of the decomposition was as follows:

$$\text{ROE} = \text{Profit} \div \text{Equity} = (\text{Profit} \div \text{Revenue}) \times (\text{Revenue} \div \text{Capital}) \times (\text{Capital} \div \text{Equity}).$$

EXHIBIT 32.1 | Selected Menu Offerings

Appetizers

Avocado Club Egg Rolls: A fusion of East and West with fresh avocado, chicken, tomato, Monterey Jack cheese, and applewood smoked bacon, wrapped in a crispy wonton roll. Served with ranchito sauce and herb ranch dressing.

Singapore Shrimp Rolls: Shrimp, baby broccoli, soy-glazed shiitake mushrooms, romaine, carrots, noodles, bean sprouts, green onion, and cilantro wrapped in rice paper. Served chilled with a sesame ginger dipping sauce and Szechuan slaw.

Pizzas

The Original BBQ Chicken: CPK's most-popular pizza, introduced in their first restaurant in Beverly Hills in 1985. Barbecue sauce, smoked gouda and mozzarella cheeses, BBQ chicken, sliced red onions, and cilantro.

Carne Asada: Grilled steak, fire-roasted mild chilies, onions, cilantro pesto, Monterey Jack, and mozzarella cheeses. Topped with fresh tomato salsa and cilantro. Served with a side of tomatillo salsa.

Thai Chicken: This is the original! Pieces of chicken breast marinated in a spicy peanut ginger and sesame sauce, mozzarella cheese, green onions, bean sprouts, julienne carrots, cilantro, and roasted peanuts.

Milan: A combination of grilled spicy Italian sausage and sweet Italian sausage with sautéed wild mushrooms, caramelized onions, fontina, mozzarella, and parmesan cheeses. Topped with fresh herbs.

Pasta

Shanghai Garlic Noodles: Chinese noodles wok-stirred in a garlic ginger sauce with snow peas, shiitake mushrooms, mild onions, red and yellow peppers, baby broccoli, and green onions. Also available with chicken and/or shrimp.

Chicken Tequila Fettuccine: The original! Spinach fettuccine with chicken, red, green, and yellow peppers, red onions, and fresh cilantro in a tequila, lime, and jalapeño cream sauce.

Source: California Pizza Kitchen Web site, http://www.cpk.com/menu (accessed on August 12, 2008).

EXHIBIT 32.2 | Consolidated Balance Sheets (in thousands of dollars)

	As of		
	1/1/06	**12/31/06**	**7/1/07**
Assets			
Current assets			
Cash and cash equivalents	$ 11,272	$ 8,187	$ 7,178
Investments in marketable securities	11,408		
Other receivables	4,109	7,876	10,709
Inventories	3,776	4,745	4,596
Current deferred tax asset, net	8,437	11,721	11,834
Prepaid income tax	1,428		8,769
Other prepaid expenses and other current assets	5,492	5,388	6,444
Total current assets	45,922	37,917	49,530
Property and equipment, net	213,408	255,382	271,867
Noncurrent deferred tax asset, net	4,513	5,867	6,328
Goodwill and other intangibles	5,967	5,825	5,754
Other assets	4,444	5,522	6,300
Total assets	$274,254	$310,513	$339,779
Liabilities and Shareholders' Equity			
Current liabilities			
Accounts payable	$ 7,054	$ 15,044	$ 14,115
Accrued compensation and benefits	13,068	15,042	15,572
Accrued rent	13,253	14,532	14,979
Deferred rent credits	4,056	4,494	5,135
Other accrued liabilities	9,294	13,275	13,980
Accrued income tax		3,614	9,012
Total current liabilities	46,725	66,001	72,793
Other liabilities	5,383	8,683	8,662
Deferred rent credits, net of current portion	24,810	27,486	32,436
Shareholders' equity:			
Common stock	197	193	291
Additional paid-in-capital	231,159	221,163	228,647
Accumulated deficit	(34,013)	(13,013)	(3,050)
Accumulated comprehensive loss	(7)		
Total shareholders' equity	197,336	208,343	225,888
Total liabilities and Shareholders' Equity	$274,254	$310,513	$339,779

Sources of data: Company annual and quarterly reports.

EXHIBIT 32.3 | Consolidated Income Statements (in thousands of dollars, except per-share data)

	Fiscal Year[1]				Three Months Ended	
	2003	2004	2005	2006	7/2/06	7/1/07
Restaurant sales	$356,260	$418,799	$474,738	$547,968	$134,604	$156,592
Franchise and other revenues	3,627	3,653	4,861	6,633	1,564	1,989
Total revenues	359,887	422,452	479,599	554,601	136,168	158,581
Food, beverage and paper supplies	87,806	103,813	118,480	135,848	33,090	38,426
Labor	129,702	152,949	173,751	199,744	49,272	56,912
Direct operating and occupancy	70,273	83,054	92,827	108,558	26,214	30,773
Cost of Sales	287,781	339,816	385,058	444,150	108,576	126,111
General and administrative	21,488	28,794	36,298	43,320	11,035	12,206
Depreciation and amortization	20,714	23,975	25,440	29,489	7,070	9,022
Pre-opening costs	4,147	737	4,051	6,964	800	852
Severance charges[2]	1,221					
Loss on impairment of PP&E	18,984		1,160			
Store closure costs		2,700	152	707		768
Legal settlement reserve		1,333	600			
Operating income	5,552	25,097	26,840	29,971	8,687	9,622
Interest income	317	571	739	718	287	91
Other income			1,105			
Equity in loss of unconsolidated JV	(349)	(143)	(22)			
Total other income (expense)	(32)	428	1,822	718	287	91
Income before income tax provision	5,520	25,525	28,662	30,689	8,974	9,713
Income tax provision (benefit)	(82)	7,709	9,172	9,689	2,961	3,393
Net income	$ 5,602	$ 17,816	$ 19,490	$ 21,000	$ 6,013	$ 6,320
Net income per common share:						
Basic	$ 0.30	$ 0.93	$ 1.01	$ 1.08	$ 0.20	$ 0.22
Diluted	$ 0.29	$ 0.92	$ 0.99	$ 1.06	$ 0.20	$ 0.21
Selected Operating Data:						
Restaurants open at end of period	168	171	188	205	193	213
Company-owned open at end of period[3]	137	141	157	176	162	182
Avg weekly full service rest. sales[3]	$ 54,896	$ 57,509	$ 62,383	$ 65,406	$ 65,427	$ 68,535
18-mo. comparable rest. sales growth[3]	3.4%	8.0%	7.5%	5.9%	4.8%	5.4%

Notes:

[1]For the years ended December 31, 2006, January 1, 2006, and January 2, 2005, December 28, 2003.

[2]Severance charges represent payments to former president/CEO and former senior vice president/senior development officer under the terms of their separation agreements.

[3]Data for company-owned restaurants.

Sources of data: Company annual and quarterly reports and quarterly company earnings conference calls.

EXHIBIT 32.4 | Selected Historical Comparable Store Sales (calendarized)

| | CY03 | CY04 | CY05 | CY06 | | | | CY07 |
				Q1	Q2	Q3	Q4	Q1
California Pizza Kitchen	3.4%	9.3%	6.4%	4.8%	5.9%	5.6%	6.9%	4.7%
Applebee's International, Inc.	4.1%	4.8%	1.8%	2.6%	-1.8%	-2.3%	-1.1%	-4.0%
BJ's Restaurants, Inc.	3.3%	4.0%	4.6%	6.8%	5.9%	5.3%	5.5%	6.9%
Brinker International[1]	2.1%	1.9%	3.2%	2.7%	-2.0%	-2.1%	-2.1%	-4.4%
The Cheesecake Factory, Inc.	0.7%	3.9%	1.7%	-1.3%	-0.8%	-1.6%	0.8%	0.4%
Chipotle Mexican Grill, Inc.	24.4%	13.3%	10.2%	19.7%	14.5%	11.6%	10.1%	8.3%
Darden Restaurants, Inc.—Red Lobster	0.0%	-3.9%	4.2%	1.6%	9.4%	-2.1%	0.7%	4.6%
Darden Restaurants, Inc.—Olive Garden	2.2%	4.7%	8.6%	5.7%	2.5%	2.9%	2.9%	1.0%
McCormick & Schmick's Seafood Restaurants, Inc.	1.1%	3.8%	3.0%	4.1%	2.8%	2.9%	2.0%	2.8%
Panera Bread Company	0.2%	2.7%	7.8%	9.0%	3.2%	2.8%	2.0%	0.0%
P. F. Chang's China Bistro	5.1%	3.0%	1.2%	1.3%	-1.0%	-0.5%	-0.9%	-2.5%
RARE—Longhorn Steakhouse	4.6%	5.0%	2.8%	3.7%	-0.4%	-0.3%	1.5%	-1.0%
Red Robin Gourmet Burgers	4.1%	7.5%	3.8%	4.8%	3.3%	0.8%	0.2%	-0.5%
Ruth's Chris Steak House, Inc.	1.4%	11.6%	10.4%	6.8%	6.0%	4.3%	7.4%	1.9%
Sonic Corporation	1.6%	7.0%	5.4%	5.5%	4.3%	4.0%	3.4%	2.0%
Texas Roadhouse, Inc.	3.5%	7.6%	5.6%	6.4%	1.2%	2.3%	3.3%	0.9%

Note:

[1]Brinker's comparable store sales were a blended rate for its various brands.

Source of data: KeyBanc Capital Markets equity research.

EXHIBIT 32.5 | Selected Forecasts for California Pizza Kitchen

Firm	Date of Report	Price Target	2007E		2008E		2009E	
			Revenues	EPS	Revenues	EPS	Revenues	EPS
Oppenheimer and Co. Inc.	4/9/07	$40	$652.9	$1.33	NA	NA	NA	NA
CIBC World Markets	4/12/07	37	647.5	1.29	755.1	1.57	NA	NA
KeyBanc Capital Markets	5/11/07	NA	NA	1.28	NA	1.55	NA	NA
RBC Capital Markets	5/11/07	37	650.7	1.31	753.1	1.59	878.2	1.90
Morgan Keegan & Co., Inc.	5/11/07	NA	644.2	1.33	742.1	1.58	NA	NA
MKM Partners	5/11/07	39	647.5	1.34	754.3	1.69	NA	NA

Source of data: Selected firms' equity research.

**EXHIBIT 32.6 | Stock Price Comparison

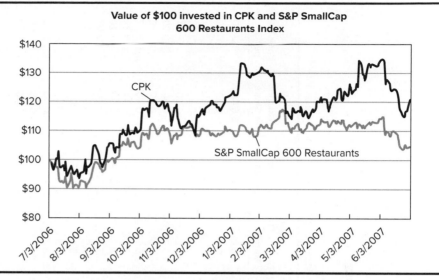

Value of $100 invested in CPK and S&P SmallCap
600 Restaurants Index

Note: Adjusted for the June 2007 50% stock dividend. With such a dividend, an owner of two shares of CPK stock was given an additional share. The effect was to increase CPK shares by one-third, yet maintain the overall capitalization of the equity.

Sources of data: Yahoo! Finance and Datastream.

EXHIBIT 32.7 | Comparative Restaurant Financial Data, 2006 Fiscal Year (in millions of dollars, except per-share data)

	Fiscal Year End Month	7/2/2007 Share Price	Revenue	EBITDA Margin	Net Profit Margin	Earnings per Share	Dividends per Share	Book Value per Share	Beta
California Pizza Kitchen	Dec.	$22.10	$55	10.7%	3.8%	$0.71	$ 0.00	$7.20	0.85
Applebee's International, Inc.	Dec.	24.28	1,338	15.9%	6.5%	1.17	0.20	6.49	0.80
BJ's Restaurants, Inc.	Dec.	20.05	239	9.6%	4.1%	0.41	0.00	7.78	1.05
Brinker International[1]	June	29.37	4,151	12.0%	4.7%	1.49	0.20	8.59	0.90
Buffalo Wild Wings, Inc.	Dec.	41.78	278	13.3%	5.8%	0.93	0.00	6.61	1.10
The Cheesecake Factory, Inc.	Dec.	24.57	1,315	12.2%	6.2%	1.02	0.00	9.09	1.00
Chipotle Mexican Grill, Inc.	Dec.	86.00	823	13.0%	5.0%	1.28	0.00	14.56	NA
Darden Restaurants, Inc.[2]	May	44.14	5,721	13.2%	5.9%	2.16	0.40	8.37	1.00
Frisch's Restaurants, Inc.	May	30.54	291	31.6%	3.1%	1.78	0.44	19.84	0.60
McCormick & Schmick's	Dec.	25.66	308	9.7%	4.3%	0.92	0.00	11.20	1.10
Panera Bread Company	Dec.	46.02	829	16.3%	7.2%	1.87	0.00	12.53	1.25
P.F. Chang's China Bistro	Dec.	35.37	938	10.5%	3.6%	1.24	0.00	11.41	1.10
RARE Hospitality Int'l Inc. [3]	Dec.	26.76	987	11.6%	5.1%	1.45	0.00	11.17	0.57
Red Robin Gourmet Burgers	Dec.	40.19	619	13.7%	4.9%	1.82	0.00	14.68	1.05
Ruth's Chris Steak House, Inc.	Dec.	16.80	272	15.6%	8.7%	1.01	0.00	2.93	NA
Sonic Corporation	Aug.	22.00	693	24.9%	11.4%	0.88	0.00	4.66	0.90
Texas Roadhouse, Inc.	Dec.	12.81	597	12.5%	5.7%	0.44	0.00	4.30	0.90

EXHIBIT 32.7 | Comparative Restaurant Financial Data, 2006 Fiscal Year (in millions of dollars, except per-share data) *(continued)*

	Current Assets	Current Liabilities	Total Debt	Share Equity	Debt/ Capital	Interest Coverage	Total Capital Turnover	Return on Capital	Return on Equity
California Pizza Kitchen	$ 38	$ 66	$ 0	$ 208	0.0%	NMF	2.7	10.1%	10.1%
Applebee's International, Inc.	105	187	175	487	26.5%	11.7	2.0	14.0%	18.0%
BJ's Restaurants, Inc.	96	36	0	203	0.0%	NMF	1.2	4.9%	4.9%
Brinker International[1]	242	497	502	1,076	31.8%	14.4	2.6	13.2%	18.0%
Buffalo Wild Wings, Inc.	75	26	0	116	0.0%	NMF	2.4	14.0%	14.0%
The Cheesecake Factory, Inc.	203	163	0	712	0.0%	NMF	1.8	11.4%	11.4%
Chipotle Mexican Grill, Inc.	179	61	0	474	0.0%	NMF	1.7	8.8%	8.7%
Darden Restaurants, Inc.[2]	378	1,026	645	1,230	34.4%	10.9	3.1	20.6%	27.5%
Frisch's Restaurants, Inc.	12	31	43	101	30.1%	5.9	2.0	7.9%	9.1%
McCormick & Schmick's	30	40	0	160	0.2%	NMF	1.9	8.3%	8.3%
Panera Bread Company	128	110	0	398	0.0%	NMF	2.1	15.1%	15.1%
P.F. Chang's China Bistro	65	104	19	290	6.2%	NMF	3.0	11.1%	11.5%
RARE Hospitality Int'l Inc.[3]	125	134	166	360	31.6%	29.2	1.9	9.8%	13.9%
Red Robin Gourmet Burgers	29	70	114	244	31.9%	7.7	1.7	9.3%	12.5%
Ruth's Chris Steak House, Inc.	26	59	68	68	50.0%	12.8	2.0	18.6%	34.9%
Sonic Corporation	43	78	159	392	28.9%	15.0	1.3	15.3%	20.1%
Texas Roadhouse, Inc.	53	78	36	319	10.2%	19.9	1.7	9.7%	10.7%

Notes:

[1]For the years ended December 31, 2006, January 1, 2006 and January 2, 2005, December 28, 2003.

[2]Severance charges represent payments tc former president/CEO and former senior vice president/senior development officer under the terms of their separation agreements.

[3]Data for company-owned restaurants.

Sources of data: Company annual and quarterly reports and conference calls.

EXHIBIT 32.8 | Interest Rates and Yields

| | U.S. Treasury Securities | | | | | | Corporate bonds (Moody's) | | Average Prime Lending | Average LIBOR 3-month |
| | Bills | | Notes & Bonds | | | | | | | |
	3-month	6-month	3-year	10-year	30-year		Aaa 3	Baa		
2000	5.85%	5.92%	6.22%	6.03%	5.94%		7.62%	8.36%	9.23%	6.55%
2001	3.45%	3.39%	4.09%	5.02%	5.49%		7.08%	7.95%	6.91%	3.63%
2002	1.62%	1.69%	3.10%	4.61%	—		6.49%	7.80%	4.67%	1.79%
2003	1.02%	1.06%	2.10%	4.01%	—		5.67%	6.77%	4.12%	1.22%
2004	1.38%	1.58%	2.78%	4.27%	—		5.63%	6.39%	4.34%	1.67%
2005	3.16%	3.40%	3.93%	4.29%	—		5.24%	6.06%	6.19%	3.63%
2006: Jan.	4.20%	4.30%	4.35%	4.42%	—		5.29%	6.24%	7.38%	4.68%
Feb.	4.41%	4.51%	4.64%	4.57%	4.54%		5.35%	6.27%	7.50%	4.82%
Mar.	4.51%	4.61%	4.74%	4.72%	4.73%		5.53%	6.41%	7.63%	4.99%
Apr.	4.59%	4.72%	4.89%	4.99%	5.06%		5.84%	6.68%	7.75%	5.15%
May.	4.72%	4.81%	4.97%	5.11%	5.20%		5.95%	6.75%	7.88%	5.23%
June	4.79%	4.95%	5.09%	5.11%	5.15%		5.89%	6.78%	7.13%	5.51%
July	4.96%	5.09%	5.07%	5.09%	5.13%		5.85%	6.76%	8.25%	5.49%
Aug.	4.98%	4.99%	4.85%	4.88%	5.00%		5.68%	6.59%	8.25%	5.40%
Sept.	4.82%	4.90%	4.69%	4.72%	4.85%		5.51%	6.43%	8.25%	5.37%
Oct.	4.89%	4.91%	4.72%	4.73%	4.85%		5.51%	6.42%	8.25%	5.37%
Nov.	4.95%	4.96%	4.64%	4.60%	4.69%		5.33%	6.20%	8.25%	5.37%
Dec.	4.85%	4.88%	4.58%	4.56%	4.68%		5.32%	6.22%	8.25%	5.36%
2007: Jan.	4.96%	4.94%	4.79%	4.76%	4.85%		5.40%	6.34%	8.25%	5.36%
Feb.	5.02%	4.97%	4.75%	4.72%	4.82%		5.39%	6.28%	8.25%	5.36%
Mar.	4.97%	4.90%	4.51%	4.56%	4.72%		5.30%	6.27%	8.25%	5.35%
Apr.	4.88%	4.87%	4.60%	4.69%	4.87%		5.47%	6.39%	8.25%	5.36%
May.	4.77%	4.80%	4.69%	4.75%	4.90%		5.47%	6.39%	8.25%	5.36%
June	4.63%	4.77%	5.00%	5.10%	5.20%		5.79%	6.70%	8.25%	5.36%

Sources of data: *Economic Report of the President* and Fannie Mae Web site.

EXHIBIT 32.9 | Pro Forma Tax Shield Effect of Recapitalization Scenarios (dollars in thousands, except share data; figures based on end of June 2007)

		Debt/Total Capital		
	Actual	**10%**	**20%**	**30%**
Interest rate [1]	6.16%	6.16%	6.16%	6.16%
Tax rate	32.5%	32.5%	32.5%	32.5%
Earnings before income taxes and interest[2]	30,054	30,054	30,054	30,054
Interest expense	0	1,391	2,783	4,174
Earnings before taxes	30,054	28,663	27,271	25,880
Income taxes	9,755	9,303	8,852	8,400
Net income	20,299	19,359	18,419	17,480
Book value:				
Debt	0	22,589	45,178	67,766
Equity	225,888	203,299	180,710	158,122
Total capital	225,888	225,888	225,888	225,888
Market value:				
Debt[3]	0	22,589	45,178	67,766
Equity[4]	643,773	628,516	613,259	598,002
Market value of capital	643,773	651,105	658,437	665,769

Notes:

[1]Interest rate of CPK's credit facility with Bank of America: LIBOR + 0.80%.

[2]Earnings before interest and taxes (EBIT) include interest income.

[3]Market values of debt equal book values.

[4]Actual market value of equity equals the share price ($22.10) multiplied by the current number of shares outstanding (29.13 million).

Source: Case writer analysis based on CPK financial data.

Dominion Resources: Cove Point

Scott Hetzer quickly shoved his notes and laptop into his briefcase and slipped on his suit jacket. Hetzer, the treasurer for Dominion Resources Inc. (Dominion), a major U.S. diversified producer and distributor of energy, was heading to meet with the company's investment bankers to discuss the impact of a large project upon Dominion's financing strategy for the next five years. The Cove Point liquefied natural gas (LNG) project would require $3.6 billion to build and represented one of the largest single capital investments in the company's 100-plus year history.

It was February 15, 2013, and the recent boom in hydraulic fracturing (fracking) had turned the U.S. natural gas market on its head, creating the opportunity to transform Cove Point from an importer of natural gas into primarily an exporter. In the company's 2012 annual report, CEO Thomas F. Farrell II highlighted the project by stating, "We firmly believe that incorporating liquefaction and export capability into our Cove Point LNG import terminal located on the Chesapeake Bay in Lusby, Maryland, can be beneficial both to you, our shareholders, and to gas producers operating in the eastern half of the U.S." The surging demand for LNG had allowed Dominion to sign long-term contracts for 100% of Cove Point's projected capacity, mitigating the project's financial risk. By mid-2014, Dominion expected to receive the final required permits from the regulatory authorities, such that the only remaining task was to revise the company's financing strategy from 2013 to 2017 to include the $3.6 billion investment.

After settling into the meeting room in Dominion's Richmond, Virginia, headquarters across from the team of bankers, Hetzer began, "Cove Point represents a terrific opportunity for all Dominion's stakeholders, but financing this sizable project clearly presents multiple financial challenges." Hetzer knew that determining the optimal mix of debt and equity would need to address the impact upon Dominion's credit ratings as well as regulators and Dominion's existing stock and debt holders.

This case was prepared by Stephen E. Maiden (MBA '01) and Professor Kenneth M. Eades. It was written as a basis for class discussion rather than to illustrate effective or ineffective handling of an administrative situation. Copyright © 2015 by the University of Virginia Darden School Foundation, Charlottesville, VA. All rights reserved. *To order copies, send an e-mail to* sales@dardenbusinesspublishing.com. *No part of this publication may be reproduced, stored in a retrieval system, used in a spreadsheet, or transmitted in any form or by any means—electronic, mechanical, photocopying, recording, or otherwise—without the permission of the Darden School Foundation.*

The Utilities Industry

While utilities had historically been considered a safe investment, the introduction of regulatory changes, new competition, demand fluctuations, and commodity price volatility over the last few decades had altered the landscape. No longer did big regional monopolies manage the entire industry from power generation to transmission and through to retail supply. The industry was now characterized by four segments: power generation, energy network operators, energy traders, and energy service providers.

The electric-utility industry provided indispensable energy to factories, commercial establishments, homes, and even most recreational facilities. According to the U.S. Department of Energy, 2012 U.S. electricity was generated by coal (37%), natural gas (30%), nuclear (19%), hydropower (7%), and other renewable energy (7%).[1] Lack of electricity caused not only inconvenience to the end users, but also economic loss for companies that suffered production reductions. Because of their importance to the economy, utilities were closely regulated by local and national authorities such as the State Corporation Commission in Virginia and the Federal Energy Regulatory Commission.

The Electricity Market

The demand for electricity had consistently grown along with the growth of the population and the economy. The U.S. Energy Information Administration (EIA) projected that 355 gigawatts of new electric generating capacity—more than 40% more than the industry currently supplied—would be needed by 2020.[2] Energy demand was dependent on numerous variables—particularly the climate such as an unusually cold winter or hot summer—that rendered determining short-term demand tricky, although long-term consumption growth was a sure thing. And demand for electricity changed from day to day and season to season, often adding pressure to the capacity-generating side or squeezing the revenue side of the industry.

This risk of large price swings began in 1996, when wholesale electricity prices were deregulated and prices were allowed to fluctuate with supply and demand. For example, although $10 to $20 per megawatt hour was average, demand spikes had led to prices as high as $5,000 or $10,000 per megawatt hour.[3] Utility managers and other energy buyers managed this risk by using forwards and futures options to hedge against unexpected price swings. Although the U.S. wholesale energy market had been deregulated, state regulatory authorities, such as a public service commission, still determined the prices a utility could charge its retail customers. The regulatory process was complex and prone to regulatory missteps and disputes between consumers, special interest groups, and political actors.[4]

[1]U.S. Energy Information Administration, "What Is U.S. Electricity Generation by Energy Source?," http://pbadupws.nrc.gov/docs/ML1408/ML14086A551.pdf (accessed Aug. 17, 2015).

[2]"Outlook for Energy," *Electric Perspectives*, 27 (March 1, 2002): 62–64.

[3]Investopedia, "The Industry Handbook: The Utilities Industry," http://www.investopedia.com/features/industryhandbook/utilities.asp (accessed Aug. 17, 2015).

[4]"The Industry Handbook: The Utilities Industry."

In addition to price regulatory authorities, environmental regulation affected power generation. The lead governmental agency, the Environmental Protection Agency (EPA), helped create and enforce compliance of the Clean Air Act among utilities. In an effort to limit air pollution and climate change, and to move toward a clean-energy economy, approvals for new power plants faced intense scrutiny.[5] Even with new technologies replacing old energy, such as clean coal or the cleaner alternative of natural gas or nuclear power, renewable energy source standards were often favored (i.e., biomass, biofuels, hydro, solar, and wind).

The Natural Gas Market

Natural gas was a fossil fuel found in deep underground rock formations. Industrially extracted to supply energy since 1825, by 2012 natural gas fueled 30% of U.S. electricity generation, up from 16% in 2000. For roughly 30 years, the increased growth in demand for natural gas had surpassed all other fossil fuels and was estimated to continue to grow.[6]

Much of the gas supply was being produced by fracking, which was an extraction method that combined horizontal drilling with hydraulic fracturing to remove natural gas from shale formations. Regulators predicted that, by 2040, 50% of total natural gas production in the United States would be shale gas.[7] As U.S. supply exceeded demand, the European market price grew until it was double that in the United States, and the Asian market price tripled (**Exhibit 33.1**).[8] And as technology allowed for more productivity and less expense around shale gas extracting, U.S. natural gas prices were expected to remain lower than in other regions of the world.[9]

To transport natural gas to the higher-priced markets required that the gas be converted to a liquid by cooling it to approximately −162°C (−260°F), which condensed the volume to only 1/600th of the volume of natural gas. The LNG was created at the exporting terminal and then regasified at the importing terminal. Most Asian economies were LNG dependent. Because of the global pricing disparity, by 2016, the United States was predicted to become a net exporter of natural gas exporting roughly 3 Tcf (trillion cubic feet) of natural gas per year by 2030.[10] Within 10 years, LNG exports were expected to increase to more than 6 Tcf per year.

Dominion Resources

With corporate roots dating back to the Colonial era, Dominion had become one of the largest producers and transporters of energy in the United States, providing electricity, natural gas, and related services in the eastern region of the United States (**Exhibit 33.2**).

[5]"The Industry Handbook: The Utilities Industry."

[6]Dominion Midstream Partners, LP, Form S-1, March 28, 2014, 86.

[7]Trefis Team, "Key Trends Impacting Natural Gas Prices in the U.S.," *Forbes/Investing*, January 2, 2014, http://www.forbes.com/sites/greatspeculations/2014/01/02/key-trends-impacting-natural-gas-prices-in-the-u-s/ (accessed Aug. 18, 2015).

[8]Trefis Team, "Key Trends Impacting Natural Gas Prices in the U.S."

[9]Trefis Team, "Key Trends Impacting Natural Gas Prices in the U.S."

[10]Trefis Team, "Key Trends Impacting Natural Gas Prices in the U.S."

Dominion's portfolio of assets included 23,600 megawatts of generating capacity; 6,400 miles of electric transmission lines; 57,000 miles of electric distribution lines; and 32,800 miles of natural gas transmission and distribution pipeline.[11] In 15 different states, the company supplied 6 million utility and retail energy clients and operated one of the nation's largest underground natural gas storage systems, totaling 947 billion cubic feet of storage capacity. In 2012, Dominion had grown into a $12 billion revenue company (**Exhibit 33.3**) with assets of $47 billion (**Exhibit 33.4**) and a $53 billion enterprise value composed of three primary business segments:

Generation (52% of earnings)—Dominion Generation managed the company's portfolio of merchant and regulated utility electric-power-generation assets along with its energy trading and marketing activities. The electric-generation mix included coal, nuclear, gas, oil, renewables, and purchased power.[12]

Energy (27% of earnings)—Dominion Energy managed the company's natural gas transmission, gathering, distribution, and storage pipeline, and a natural gas storage network, which was the largest in North America. Dominion Energy operated the Cove Point LNG facility on the Chesapeake Bay. At the time, Cove Point was limited to operating solely as an import and storage facility.[13]

Dominion Virginia Power (21% of earnings)—Dominion Virginia Power managed the company's "regulated electric distribution and electric-transmission operations in Virginia and northeastern North Carolina, as well as the nonregulated retail energy marketing and regulated and nonregulated customer service operations."[14] The company managed its 6,400 miles of electric transmission lines and 57,000 miles of distribution lines in this segment.

Before 2006, Dominion had been a highly regulated utility and a nonregulated exploration and production (E&P) oil and gas company. Because of the different risk profiles inherent in the two core businesses, investors held very different visions for the company. Investors who viewed the firm as a utility wanted Dominion to maximize cash flow, while those who owned it for its oil and gas production assets wanted the firm to increase investment in E&P in order to realize the value of its energy reserves. Some equity analysts thought this split in the investor base caused Dominion to be undervalued against both E&P and utility peers. From the standpoint of energy investors, Dominion was viewed as not being a big enough risk taker, while utility investors preferred a risk profile more similar to a stable, regulated utility.

When Farrell became CEO in 2007, he sold off billions of dollars of E&P oil and gas assets to create a business that would derive the majority of its earnings from regulated or "regulated-like" businesses. Under Farrell's leadership, Dominion grew investments in "regulated electric generation, transmission and distribution and regulated natural gas transmission and distribution infrastructure" in and near locations where it already conducted business.[15] In general, regulated rates were approved based on a

---

[11]Dominion Midstream Partners, LP, Form S-1, March 28, 2014, 96.

[12]Dominion Resources Form 10-K, 2013.

[13]Dominion Resources Form 10-K, 2013.

[14]Dominion Resources Form 10-K, 2013.

[15]Dominion Resources Form 10-K, 2013.

"cost-plus method" that set the price of the commodity high enough to cover the utility's operating costs as well as providing a sufficient return on equity (ROE) to attract capital. Thus to grow its earnings, Dominion sought investment opportunities in regulated/regulated-like businesses that would lock in future profits. The newly abundant supply of U.S. natural gas gave Dominion an opportunity with the Cove Point facility.

Because of the changing natural gas markets, Dominion had requested regulatory approval to convert and operate Cove Point as a bi-directional facility (i.e., to export as well as import LNG). Investor interest in the new potential use for Cove Point had buoyed Dominion's stock in recent months (**Exhibit 33.5**) as Wall Street analysts attempted to quantify the potential value of the opportunity.

Cove Point

Dominion acquired the Cove Point LNG terminal in 2002 for $217 million. In 2012, contracts related to the import, storage, and transportation of natural gas at Cove Point produced $293 million in revenues and $196.05 million in EBITDA. Anticipating the opportunity to export LNG, Dominion began renegotiating existing LNG import contracts in 2010 to free up pipeline and storage capacity utilization beginning in 2017. Subject to regulatory approvals and financing, Dominion planned to start construction on the project in 2014 and open the facilities by late 2017.

While the gas liquefied at Cove Point could be sourced from various places, the facility would offer direct access to the Marcellus and Utica shale plays, which were among the most productive natural gas basins in North America.[16] If approved, about 750 million standard cubic feet of inlet feed gas would be processed each day.[17] LNG would be produced through natural gas–fired turbines powering the main refrigerant compressors. The liquefaction facilities would "connect with the existing facility and share common facilities such as the LNG tanks, pumps, piping, and pier in order to support both importing and exporting LNG."[18]

Due to the robust global demand for natural gas, Dominion had been able to fully subscribe Cove Point's production capacity by signing 20-year agreements with two large investment-grade companies. Each company had contracted for half of Cove Point's LNG capacity and, in turn, had announced agreements to sell gas and power to other companies with the LNG supplied by Cove Point.[19] Under the service agreements, Dominion would not be responsible for inlet gas supply and would not be required to take ownership of any of the LNG. These agreements allowed Cove Point to mitigate commodity risk over the life of the contracts and positioned the project to fit within Dominion's "regulated-like" growth focus.

---

[16]Magnum Hunter Resources Corporation, Investor Presentation, July 2015, http://www.magnumhunterresources.com/MagnumHunterResources.pdf (accessed Aug. 18, 2015).

[17]"Dominion Announces Second-Quarter 2012 Earnings," Dominion Power press release, August 2012, https://www.dom.com/corporate/news/news-releases/131083 (accessed Aug. 18, 2015).

[18]"Dominion Cove Point," https://www.dom.com/covepoint (accessed Aug. 18, 2015).

[19]"Dominion Cove Point," https://www.dom.com/covepoint (accessed Aug. 18, 2015).

Meeting with Investment Bankers

After Scott Hetzer finished his opening statements, the investment bankers began their presentation by pointing out that Dominion compared well to other utilities in terms of credit rating, profitability, and capital structure (**Exhibit 33.6**). The discussion then turned to the costs and benefits of using an "all-debt" financing strategy versus a "debt-and-equity" strategy.

The bankers listed a variety of issues for Dominion to consider when choosing between these two strategies, which all were related to Dominion's access to capital in the future and the cost of that capital. As a capital intensive company, Dominion was frequently using the debt markets to raise money to either fund new investments or to refund outstanding debt that was maturing. Debt issuances occurred almost every year, whereas Dominion rarely accessed the equity market for funding. In fact, the last public issuances of equity occurred in the years 2002 and 2003, when the company issued 98 million shares to raise $2,395 million.[20]

A primary consideration was Dominion's credit rating, which would determine the interest rate Dominion would pay to borrow. A credit rating was assigned by rating agencies such as Standard and Poor's (S&P). S&P's current rating for Dominion was an A−, which S&P had assigned based on the combination of an "excellent" business risk and a "significant" financial risk. A variety of financial ratios were used to determine the level of financial risk. For utilities, the two core ratios were funds from operations (FFO)-to-debt and debt-to-EBITDA. The bankers judged that if debt-to-EBITDA were to persistently remain above 4.5 (currently 4.6) and if FFO-to-debt were to persistently fall below 13% (currently 13.6%), S&P would change Dominion's financial risk to "aggressive," which would result in a credit downgrade to BBB+. (See **Exhibit 33.7** for S&P's credit rating information.)

There were several costs to Dominion associated with a credit downgrade. First, Hetzer estimated that in the current interest rate environment, a downgrade to BBB+ would result in the borrowing rate being about 0.40% (40 basis points) higher. In addition, a BBB+ rating would be below Dominion's target rating of A. Dominion had committed to maintaining an A rating in order to be among the highest-rated utilities in the industry. A strong credit rating gave Dominion access to a larger market of lenders who wanted high-grade utility debt in their portfolios. Debt rated below the A level would make Dominion's risk profile less attractive to many institutional investors that currently held Dominion debt. Moreover, a downgrade would result in a price decline for Dominion's outstanding bonds that would compromise years of good relations with existing bondholders.

The bankers argued that Wall Street viewed Dominion as primarily a regulated business (i.e., equity analysts and shareholders were highly focused on Dominion's earnings per share (EPS) and dividend per share growth). Because utilities were regulated, the market viewed utility stocks as having a low-risk profile that allowed utilities to have consistent growth in EPS and distribute most of those earnings as dividends to the shareholders. Therefore, any interruption in the expected EPS growth would signal

---

[20]The shares issued were adjusted to reflect a 2-for-1 stock split on November 20, 2007.

that future earnings and dividends were less reliable, and the utility's stock price would suffer. Dominion had a strong record of EPS growth. From 1999 to 2012, the average compound growth rate had been 4.8%, which was due to the combination of good earnings and the reduction of shares outstanding. Beginning in 2006, Dominion used a series of stock repurchases to reduce the shares outstanding from 698 million in 2006 to 576 million in 2012. The bankers cautioned that an equity issuance would be a surprise to shareholders, and the resulting EPS dilution would likely prompt a significant share price decline. For example, if Dominion issued new shares at its current stock price of $55, raising $2 billion of equity would create a 6.3% dilution. In general, the bankers cautioned that with Dominion's stock trading at a price-to-earnings ratio (P/E) of 18 and 574 million shares outstanding, just a $0.10 reduction in EPS would result in a loss of $1 billion of market value for the company.

As the bankers finished their presentation, they assured Hetzer that Dominion would be able to raise enough money to refund all its debt coming due over the next five years plus finance all the expected capital expenditures, including Cove Point. The question, however, was whether Dominion wanted to rely solely upon the debt market or if the company should use the equity market for some portion of the external funds needed. To help understand the impact of the funding mix, Hetzer had asked his financial analysts to prepare a financial model (**Exhibit 33.8**) that estimated the amount of external financing needed and the impact upon the company's financial profile based on using debt as the sole source of external funding (**Exhibit 33.9**). To see the impact of issuing equity, Hetzer could simply input the equity amount in the "New Equity" row. Hetzer was meeting with Dominion's CFO the next morning and wanted to be ready with a specific financing plan that included the amount of equity issued, if any, and the timing of that issuance.

As another alternative to the funding problem, Hetzer could propose to cancel or postpone Cove Point. At $3.6 billion, Cove Point was an expensive undertaking. In fact, this single project represented 24% of Dominion's total capital expenditures for the next five years (**Exhibit 33.10**). Therefore, canceling Cove Point would reduce Dominion's funding needs enough to allow the company to raise all the funding with debt without jeopardizing the credit rating. On the other hand, the project was expected to contribute in excess of $200 million in net operating profit after tax by 2018 and create more than $600 million of value for the enterprise (**Exhibit 33.11**).

EXHIBIT 33.1 | Global Natural Gas Prices 1996–2013 ($ per million Btu)

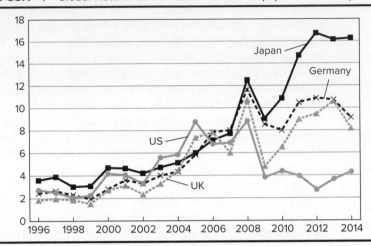

Data source: "BP Statistical Review of World Energy June 2015," https://www.google.com/?gws_rd=ssl#q=bp+stat
istical+review+of+world+energy+2015.

EXHIBIT 33.2 | Map of Power and Natural Gas Infrastructure

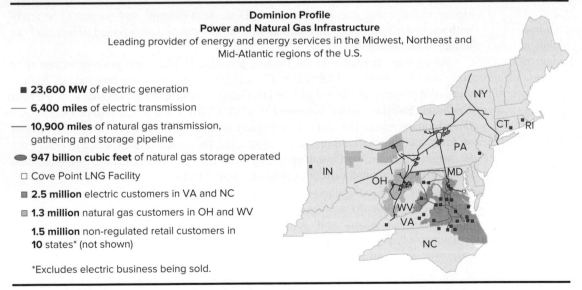

Dominion Profile
Power and Natural Gas Infrastructure
Leading provider of energy and energy services in the Midwest, Northeast and
Mid-Atlantic regions of the U.S.

■ **23,600 MW** of electric generation

— **6,400 miles** of electric transmission

— **10,900 miles** of natural gas transmission,
gathering and storage pipeline

⬤ **947 billion cubic feet** of natural gas storage operated

☐ Cove Point LNG Facility

■ **2.5 million** electric customers in VA and NC

■ **1.3 million** natural gas customers in OH and WV

1.5 million non-regulated retail customers in
10 states* (not shown)

*Excludes electric business being sold.

Source: Company document. Used with permission.

EXHIBIT 33.3 | Dominion Corporate Income Statements, 2011–2012 (non-GAAP)[1]
($ in millions except per share amounts)

	2011	2012
Operating revenue	$14,314	$12,762
Operating expenses		
Electric fuel and other energy-related purchases	4,152	3,650
Purchased electric capacity	454	387
Purchased gas	1,745	1,177
Other operations and maintenance	2,849	2,446
Depreciation, depletion, and amortization	1,068	1,148
Other taxes	545	551
Total operating expenses	10,813	9,359
Income from operations	3,501	3,403
Other income	176	159
EBIT	3,677	3,562
Interest and related charges	901	832
Income including noncontrolling interests before income taxes	2,776	2,730
Income tax expense	1,004	954
Net income including noncontrolling interests	1,772	1,776
Noncontrolling interests	18	27
Net income	$ 1,754	$ 1,749
Earnings per share	$ 3.05	$ 3.05
Avg shares outstanding, diluted	563.2	573.9
Dividends per share	$ 1.97	$ 2.11
GAAP Reconciliation		
Operating earnings (non-GAAP)*	1,754	1,749
Impairment of generation assets	(178)	(1,279)
Other items	(168)	(168)
Reported earnings (GAAP)	1,408	302

[1]"Dominion management believed non-GAAP operating earnings provided a more meaningful representation of the company's fundamental earnings power." Dominion Resource report: *"GAAP Reconciliation Operating Earnings to Reported 2007–2012,"* http://investors.dom.com/phoenix.zhtml?c=110481&p=irol-gaap.

Source: Company document. Used with permission.

EXHIBIT 33.4 | Dominion Corporate Balance Sheet, 2011–2012 ($ in millions)

Assets	2011	2012
Cash	$ 102	$ 248
Receivables	2,035	1,717
Inventory		
Materials and supplies	641	684
Fossil fuel	541	467
Gas stored	166	108
Other assets	1,945	1,916
Total current assets	5,430	5,140
Net property, plant, and equipment	29,670	30,773
Other assets	10,514	10,925
Total assets	$45,614	$46,838
Liabilities		
Securities due within one year	$ 1,479	$ 2,223
Short-term debt	1,814	2,412
Accounts payable	1,250	1,137
Accrued interest, payroll, and taxes	648	636
Derivative liabilities	951	510
Regulatory liabilities	243	136
Other	577	709
Total current liabilities	6,962	7,763
Long-term debt	15,675	15,478
Junior subordinated notes	1,719	1,373
Total long-term debt	17,394	16,851
Deferred credits and other liabilities	9,498	11,342
Total liabilities	33,854	35,956
Preferred stock	257	257
Total equity	11,503	10,625
Total liabilities and equity	$45,614	$46,838

Source: Company document. Used with permission.

EXHIBIT 33.5 | Dominion Stock Price versus Utility Index 2006–2013

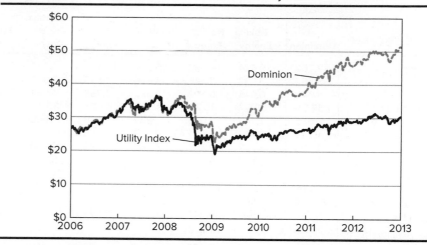

Source: Company document. Used with permission.

EXHIBIT 33.6 | Financial Data for Comparable Utility Companies (year-end 2012, $ in millions)

	Dominion	Duke Energy	NextEra Energy	Southern Co	Xcel Energy	American Electric Power	P.S. Enterprise Group	DTE Energy
Revenues	12,762	19,624	14,256	16,537	10,128	14,945	9,781	8,791
EBIT	3,562	3,693	3,641	4,608	1,829	2,810	2,434	1,400
EBITDA	4,745	6,648	5,159	6,395	2,755	4,592	3,488	2,395
EBITDA margin %	37.2%	33.9%	36.2%	38.7%	27.2%	30.7%	35.7%	27.2%
Interest expense	832	1,242	1,038	859	566	988	423	440
Net income	1,749	1,768	1,911	2,350	905	1,262	1,275	610
Earnings per share	$3.05	$3.07	$4.56	$2.67	$1.85	$2.60	$2.51	$3.55
Dividends per share	$2.11	$3.03	$2.40	$1.94	$1.07	$1.88	$1.42	$2.42
Total assets	46,838	113,856	64,439	63,149	31,141	54,367	31,725	26,339
Cash	248	1,757	329	635	82	279	379	187
Total debt	21,486	38,609	23,177	22,584	10,746	18,738	8,202	8,071
Book equity	10,625	40,941	39,245	19,004	8,874	15,237	17,468	7,411
Market data (2/15/13)								
Stock price	55	68	73	44	28	45	31	64
Shares (millions)	574	575	419	879	488	485	507	172
Market cap	31,519	39,135	30,392	38,773	13,730	21,892	15,765	11,080
Enterprise value (EV)	52,757	75,987	53,240	60,722	24,393	40,351	23,588	18,964
Beta	0.70	0.60	0.70	0.55	0.60	0.65	0.75	0.75
Financial ratios								
EV/EBITDA	11.1	11.4	10.3	9.5	8.9	8.8	6.8	7.9
Price/earnings	18.0	22.1	15.9	16.5	15.2	17.3	12.4	18.2
Dividend yield	3.8%	4.5%	3.3%	4.4%	3.8%	4.2%	4.6%	3.8%
Dividend payout	69%	99%	53%	73%	58%	72%	56%	68%
EBITDA/interest	5.7	5.4	5.0	7.4	4.9	4.6	8.2	5.4
Net debt/EBITDA	4.5	5.5	4.4	3.4	3.9	4.0	2.2	3.3
Total debt/capital	67%	49%	37%	54%	55%	55%	32%	52%
Market/Book	2.97	0.96	0.77	2.04	1.55	1.44	0.90	1.50
Debt/EV	41%	51%	44%	37%	44%	46%	35%	43%
Debt rating	A−	BBB+	BBB+	A	A−	BBB+	A−	A−

Sources: Company 10-K reports, Value Line, and case writer estimates.

EXHIBIT 33.7 | Standard and Poor's Credit Ratings Definitions and Benchmark Ranges for Cash Flow and Leverage Ratios of Medial Volatility Utilities

Standard & Poor's Credit Rating Definitions

AAA Extremely strong capacity to meet financial commitments. Highest rating.

AA   Very strong capacity to meet financial commitments.

A   Strong capacity to meet financial commitments, but somewhat susceptible to adverse economic conditions and changes in circumstances.

BBB Adequate capacity to meet financial commitments, but more subject to adverse economic conditions.

BB   Less vulnerable in the near term but faces major ongoing uncertainties to adverse business, financial, and economic conditions.

CCC Currently vulnerable and dependent on favorable business, financial, and economic conditions to meet financial commitments.

S&P Benchmark Ranges for Cash Flow and Leverage Ratios of Medial Volatility Utilities

	Core Ratios	
	FFO/Debt (%)	Debt/EBITDA (×)
Minimal	> 50	< 1.75
Modest	35–50	1.75–2.5
Intermediate	23–35	2.5–3.5
Significant	13–23	3.5–4.5
Aggressive	9–13	4.5–5.5
Highly leveraged	< 9	> 5.5

EBITDA: Earnings before interest, taxes, depreciation, and amortization.

Funds from Operations (FFO): EBITDA, minus net interest expense minus current tax expense.

Debt: All interest-bearing debt instruments plus finance leases minus surplus cash.

Data source: Standard & Poor's Ratings Services, "Corporate Methodology," November 19, 2013, Table 18: https://www.globalcreditportal.com/ratingsdirect/renderArticle.do?articleId=1306310&SctArtId=262128&from=CM&nsl_code=LIME&sourceObjectId=8314109&sourceRevId=12&fee_ind=N&exp_date=20240910-19:34:42

EXHIBIT 33.8 | Financial Planning Model: All-Debt Financing ($ in millions except per share amounts and ratios)

	Actual 2012	Estimates ⟶ 2013	2014	2015	2016	2017
Revenues	$12,762	$13,300	$13,830	$14,240	$14,667	$15,107
EBIT	3,562	3,987	4,229	4,460	4,683	5,097
Interest expense (4% of debt)	832	1,010	1,100	1,150	1,195	1,234
Pretax profit	2,730	2,977	3,129	3,310	3,488	3,863
Taxes (35%)	954	1,042	1,095	1,159	1,221	1,352
Net income	$ 1,749	$ 1,908	$ 2,007	$ 2,125	$ 2,240	$ 2,484
Dividends (67.5% payout)	$ 1,211	$ 1,288	$ 1,354	$ 1,434	$ 1,512	$ 1,677
Earnings per share	$ 3.05	$ 3.33	$ 3.50	$ 3.70	$ 3.90	$ 4.33
Shares outstanding	573.9	573.9	573.9	573.9	573.9	573.9
Net working capital (15.8% of Rev)	$ 2,012	$ 2,097	$ 2,180	$ 2,245	$ 2,312	$ 2,382
Net PPE	30,773	29,488	32,825	35,588	37,379	39,094
Capital expenditures (ex. Cove Pt)		3,570	3,080	2,450	2,900	3,200
Capital expenditures: Cove Point		1,130	1,120	850	400	100
Other assets	10,925	10,925	10,925	10,925	10,925	10,925
Total net assets	$43,710	$47,210	$50,130	$52,058	$53,916	$55,701
Existing debt less principal payments	$21,486	$18,868	$17,771	$16,582	$14,716	$12,637
New debt (balancing figure)		6,375	9,740	12,166	15,163	18,219
Other liabilities	10,465	10,465	10,465	10,465	10,465	10,465
Net worth	10,882	11,502	12,154	12,845	13,573	14,380
New equity (assumed)		0	0	0	0	0
Total liabilities and equity	$42,833	$47,210	$50,130	$52,058	$53,916	$55,701

Source: Case writer estimates.

EXHIBIT 33.9 | Financial Ratios and EPS for All-Debt Financing Strategy

	Actual 2012	Estimates ⟶ 2013	2014	2015	2016	2017
EBIT/Revenues	27.9%	30.0%	30.6%	31.3%	31.9%	33.7%
Return on Capital (%)	8.7%	8.9%	8.7%	8.7%	8.8%	9.3%
EBITDA Interest Coverage (x)	5.7	5.2	5.1	5.1	5.2	5.4
Funds from Operations/Debt (%)	13.6%	12.8%	12.3%	12.5%	12.6%	13.3%
Debt/EBITDA (x)	4.6	4.8	4.9	4.9	4.8	4.6
Debt/(Debt + Equity) (%)	66.4%	68.7%	69.4%	69.1%	68.8%	68.2%
Return on Equity (%)	15.5%	17.0%	17.0%	17.0%	17.0%	17.8%
Earnings per Share	$3.05	$3.33	$3.50	$3.70	$3.90	$4.33

Funds from operations: EBITDA, minus net interest expense minus current tax expense.

Debt: Gross financial debt (including items such as bank loans, debt capital market instruments, and finance leases) minus surplus cash.

Equity: Common equity and equity hybrids and minority interests.

Capital: Debt plus noncurrent deferred taxes plus equity.

Return on capital: EBIT/Average beginning-of-year and end-of-year capital.

Source: Case writer estimates.

EXHIBIT 33.10 | Dominion Resources Capital Expenditures 2013–2017 ($ in millions)

	2013	2014	2015	2016	2017	2013–2017
Maintenance	1,370	580	750	800	1,000	4,500
Growth (excluding Cove Point)	2,200	2,500	1,700	2,100	2,200	10,700
Cove Point	1,130	1,120	850	400	100	3,600
Total	4,700	4,200	3,300	3,300	3,300	18,800

Source: Case writer estimates.

EXHIBIT 33.11 | Cash Flows of Cove Point Liquefaction Project ($ in millions)

	2013	2014	2015	2016	2017	2018	2019	2020	2021
EBIT	$ 0	($38)	($78)	($103)	$ 63	$360	$368	$373	$ 378
Depreciation & Amortization	0	38	78	103	117	120	122	122	123
EBITDA	$ 0	$ 0	$ 0	$ 0	$180	$480	$490	$496	$ 502
Net Operating Profit after Tax	0	(23)	(47)	(62)	38	216	221	224	227
Change in Working Capital	0	0	0	0	(6)	(25)	(1)	(1)	(1)
Maintenance Capex	0	0	0	0	(4)	(17)	(19)	(21)	(23)
Liquefaction Capex	(1,130)	(1,120)	(850)	(400)	(100)	0	0	0	0
Free Cash Flow	($1,130)	($1,105)	($819)	($359)	$ 44	$294	$323	$325	$ 327
Terminal Value									$5,554
TOTAL Free Cash Flows	($1,130)	($1,105)	($819)	($359)	$ 44	$294	$323	$325	$5,881

Liquefaction project value:
Present-value cash flows = $614

Assumptions:	
WACC	8.0%
Terminal cash flow growth	2.0%
Terminal value 2021	$5,554
Operating expense/revenues	40%
Working capital/revenues	5%
Tax rate	40.0%

Source: Case writer estimates.

Nokia OYJ: Financing the WP Strategic Plan

I have learned we are standing on a burning platform.[1]
   —Stephen Elop, Nokia CEO

In January 2012, Stephen Elop reflected on his tumultuous first year and a half as president and CEO of Nokia. During that time, he had completed a review of the company's performance and strategic direction and been forced to admit to employees that they were "standing on a burning platform," threatened by intense competition in the mobile phone market (**Exhibit 34.1**).

In the preceding years, Nokia, the world's leading producer of mobile phones, had seen its market share and profits eroded by rival products such as Apple's iPhone and phones featuring Google's Android operating system. At the same time, its dominance in the larger, lower-priced phone segment had been threatened by competition from Samsung, LG, and ZTE. In February 2011, Elop had made his first major decision to correct the company's course, a broad strategic plan and partnership with Microsoft ("the plan") in which, among other initiatives, Windows would serve as Nokia's primary smartphone platform. Rather than quell the concerns as he had hoped, the plan's announcement had seemed only to raise more questions about the scope and timing of the transition involved.

Reinforcing those concerns, the company had reported a net loss of earnings in July 2011, which was followed by a downgrade of the company's credit rating the following month. In late 2011, the first Windows smartphones appeared in Europe and Asia (under the trade name Lumia), but the biggest challenge still awaited Nokia. Beginning

---

[1] "Full Text: Nokia CEO Stephen Elop's 'Burning Platform' Memo," *Wall Street Journal*, February 9, 2011, http://blogs.wsj.com/tech-europe/2011/02/09/full-text-nokia-ceo-stephen-elops-burning-platform-memo/ (accessed June 8, 2011).

in 2012, the new phones would roll out in the United States, the most important market for smartphones. Only after the rollout would Elop know whether his decision to join forces with Microsoft would improve Nokia's competive position.

It was left to Nokia's CFO Timo Ihamuotila to assess the firm's financing needs over the critical next two years. He estimated that the firm might need as much as (U.S. dollars) USD5.6 billion (equivalent to [euros] EUR4.3 billion) in external financing to see it through these years. At the moment, none of the alternatives to raise that amount of funding was particularly appealing. With its newly lowered credit rating, any new issue of debt would have to consider the impact of a potential loss of investment-grade rating. On the other hand, with the firm's stock price hovering near USD5 (EUR4) per share, an equity issue would raise concerns about share dilution and the negative signal it might send to the market. The firm had adequate cash reserves at the moment and, depite the decline in earnings, had maintained its dividend over the past few years. Ihamuotila would have to carefully assess these alternatives and devise a plan that would allow Nokia to complete its restructuring plan and give the firm a chance to put out the flames.

Company Background

Nokia began in 1865 as a paper company situated near the river Nokianvirta in Finland after which the company was named. It grew from a little-known company to be a leading mobile phone manufacturer in the 1990s, and by 2011, it was a global leader in mobile communications.[2] The company operated in more than 150 countries and had more than 130,000 employees. Nokia managed its operations across three operating segments: Devices and Services (D&S), Nokia Siemens Networks (NSN), and Location and Commerce (L&C). In 2011, D&S accounted for 62%, NSN for 36%, and L&C for 3% of its net sales.

The D&S segment comprised three business groups: mobile phones, multimedia, and enterprise solutions. It developed and managed the company's mobile devices portfolio and also designed and developed services and applications (apps) to customize mobile device users' experience.

NSN was a joint venture formed by combining Nokia's carrier networks business and Siemens's carrier-related operations for both fixed and mobile networks. It began operations on April 1, 2007, and although it was jointly owned by Nokia and Siemens, it was governed and consolidated by Nokia. NSN provided fixed and mobile network infrastructure, communications, and network service platforms to operators and service providers.

L&C was one of the main providers of comprehensive digital map information, mapping applications, and related location-based content services (i.e., GPS). It grew out of Nokia's $8 billion acquisition of NAVTEQ in July 2008.

---

[2]Nokia was formed from the merger of three Finnish companies: Nokia, a wood-pulp mill founded in 1865; Finnish Rubber Works, founded in 1898; and Finnish Cable Works, founded in 1912. In the early 1990s, the company made a strategic decision to focus on telecommunications and formed two main business groups: Nokia mobile phones and Nokia networks.

As recently as October 2007, Nokia's stock price had hit a six-year high of USD39.72 (EUR27.45) before falling to USD4.82 (EUR3.72) at the end of December 2011 (**Exhibit 34.2**). From that lofty performance of 2007, few could have imagined how quickly the company's fortunes would change.

Recent Financial Performance

Nokia's success historically had been rooted in its technical strength and reliability. Its products required a great deal of technical sophistication, and the company spent large amounts on R&D to maintain its edge. The company was credited with a number of "firsts" in the wireless industry and maintained intellectual property rights to over 10,000 patent families. In 2011, the company employed approximately 35,000 people in R&D, roughly 27% of its total work force, and R&D expenses amounted to EUR5.6 billion, or 14.5% of net sales. Few companies could match the scale of Nokia's R&D or the size of its distribution network—the largest in the industry, with over 850,000 points of sale globally.

Although Nokia's stock price performance was adversely affected by the global financial crisis in 2008–09, which weakened consumer and corporate spending in the mobile device market, its problems extended beyond that (**Exhibit 34.2**). Analysts estimated that only about 50% of Nokia's decline could be attributed to market conditions; the rest was said to be due to a loss of competitive position to established industry players and new entrants.[3] Since 2007, the firm had experienced a loss of market share in most of its core markets (**Exhibit 34.3**). The mobile phone market was broken into two segments: smartphones and mobile phones. Mobile phones had more basic functionality and generally sold at prices under EUR100. Smartphones had enhanced functionality and also higher average selling prices (ASPs). Traditionally, Nokia had concentrated on the mobile phone market, which helped facilitate its high market share in emerging markets. In 2007, mobile phones accounted for 86% of the firm's total handset production. For many years, this strategy had paid off because as late as 2007, smartphones made up only 10% of the total handset market. But since 2007, the growth in smartphones had accelerated so that by 2011, their share had increased to 30% of the market and accounted for 75% of total industry revenue.

Smartphones

Although Nokia introduced the first smartphone in 1996 (the Nokia 9000), since then, the market had become highly competitive. **Exhibit 34.4** details competitor offerings in the smartphone market and key features that differentiated their products. Nokia's smartphones featured the Symbian operating system (OS), which was introduced in 1998, as an open-source OS developed by several mobile phone vendors.[4] Symbian,

---

[3]"Downgrading Nokia to Market-Perform: Deteriorating Risk/Reward Profile—Things Now Depend Too Much on Symbian^3," Bernstein Research, April 26, 2010.

[4]Started in 1998, Symbian was originally a joint venture of some of the world's leading mobile phone vendors: Nokia, Ericsson, Motorola, and Psion. In December 2008, Nokia acquired the remaining 52% of Symbian's shares that it did not already own to expedite integration of the two companies in developing Nokia phones.

though reliable, proved to be an inflexible platform that had slow upgrade cycles and lacked an appealing user interface (UI).[5] The two most significant events for Nokia were the launch of Apple's iPhone in July 2007 and Google's Android system in October 2008. From a standing start, both products had made strong inroads in the marketplace and had captured significant market share from Nokia in just a few short years (**Exhibit 34.5**). Apple and Google were software companies that focused on ease of use and apps that enabled users to customize and personalize their phones. Nokia's origins were in manufacturing and engineering, and it had vertically integrated forward into software and design. Neither Apple nor Google manufactured their handsets, and analysts speculated about which trend would dominate the future smartphone market. One analyst said, "Nokia is not a software company. Apple is a software company, and what distinguishes the iPhone and the iPod Touch is their software. I think Nokia is just on the losing side."[6]

The Next Billion

Entry-level devices were one of the fastest-growing segments of the mobile phone market. With far fewer infrastructure requirements than traditional land lines, rural communities in emerging-market countries, such as China and India, were essentially skipping wired communications and moving straight to wireless networks. The same trend was also being observed in developed markets as individuals increasingly chose to rely on wireless phones and dropped land-line phones. It had taken until 2002, approximately 20 years after the first mobile phone was introduced, to achieve the first billion mobile phone subscribers but only 3 years to add the next billion subscribers, and 2 years for the next billion. As mobile phones were adopted globally, it took successively less time to add the next billion subscribers. In 2010, there were an estimated 3.2 billion people who lived within range of a mobile signal who did not own a mobile phone. Because Nokia had one of the widest product portfolios, with devices spanning from super-low-cost phones (<EUR50) to smartphones (+EUR300), and the most extensive distribution channel, it was well positioned to capture this growth.[7] But even with a strategy in place for the next billion, Nokia faced intense competition, particularly from Samsung, LG, and ZTE, which also had targeted phones at lower price points for these markets. Also troubling, the Asia-Pacific region saw a large increase in iPhone use in 2010, the strongest take-up of Apple devices in the world.

---

[5]In 2010, Nokia announced it would create a new Linux-based platform called MeeGo to be used in high-end smartphones and tablets, but as of year-end 2011, no products had yet rolled out under the new platform.

[6]Nick Bilton, "The Engineer-Driven Culture of Nokia," *New York Times*, February 11, 2011.

[7]Nokia planned to introduce a large number of low-priced smartphones in these high-growth markets, increasingly blurring the lines between market segments. In 2009, roughly 29% of its smartphone product portfolio featured phones in the EUR51 to EUR100 price range, and by 2011, it was estimated that this segment would grow to 44% and include new phones, comprising 11% of its product line, with prices below EUR50. Bernstein Research, analyst report, April 26, 2010.

Change at the Top

Throughout 2009, Nokia introduced a number of initiatives in response to the competitive pressures it faced. These included, among others, the opening of Ovi stores, one-stop shops for applications and content, similar to Apple's popular iTunes stores; introducing a new Linux-based operating system (MeeGo) and high-end tablets; placing an executive in charge of user-friendliness on the board; and pursuing several cost-cutting and restructuring measures. Despite its efforts, Nokia could not shake the perception that it was being upstaged by a "Cupertino competitor,"[8] and as global demand picked up in late 2009 and 2010, Nokia's performance was a notable laggard. In September 2010, Nokia's board asked long-term president and CEO Olli-Pekka Kallasvuo to step aside and replaced him with Stephen Elop, who was the first outsider and non-Finn (he was Canadian) to head the company.

Strategic Plan with Microsoft

During his first few months with the company, Elop carefully weighed three alternatives to be the firm's primary platform for smartphones: staying the course with Symbian/MeeGo, which meant building something new from MeeGo; adopting Android, which had volume share; or adopting Windows and becoming a key partner for Microsoft, which needed a hardware provider that would put it first.[9] On February 11, 2011, he announced the plan with Microsoft to build a new ecosystem with Windows Phone (WP) serving as Nokia's primary smartphone platform and a combined approach to capture the next billion in emerging growth markets. Main features of the plan included the following:

- Nokia delivering mapping and navigation capabilities to the WP ecosystem
- Microsoft bringing Bing search, apps, advertising, and social media to Nokia devices
- Both companies combining forces to develop apps and content for the WP platform
- Nokia's Ovi Store merging with Windows Marketplace
- Microsoft receiving a royalty from Nokia for each product shipped[10]
- Nokia contributing technical support, including hardware design, language support, and other help developing WP for a wider range of prices
- Nokia receiving payments from Microsoft to support marketing and development

Over the next few years, the Symbian platform would be gradually phased out as the WP platform was phased in. Underscoring the scope of this transition, in 2010, Symbian phones amounted to 104 million units (ASP EUR143.6), virtually all of

---

[8]J. Ewing and Olga Kharif, "Finns Strike Back—Nokia Takes Aim at Apple," *BusinessWeek*, August 28, 2009.

[9]Quentin Hardy, "Nokia CEO Paying to Be Microsoft's Future," *Forbes*, May 31, 2011.

[10]Google did not charge handset makers for its Android operating system or receive revenue from the sale of Android devices, but it did receive a small fee for app purchases and in-app advertising revenue generated from use of the devices. While nominally "free" to OEMs, Google controlled the timing and extent of upgrades.

Nokia's smart phone production (**Exhibit 34.3**). The plan would bolster Nokia's presence in North America (where individuals and businesses were familiar with Windows) while benefiting Microsoft in emerging markets (where Nokia was well known). Gross margins would be lower as a result of the royalty payments paid to Microsoft, but Nokia stood to gain from materially reduced R&D expenses and Microsoft's expected support for sales and marketing.[11]

Analysts were mixed on whether this plan would solve Nokia's problems. Some saw the plan as facilitating strong complementarities between the companies and eliminating the lagging Symbian/MeeGo product lines. Reducing the number of OS platforms and trimming its diverse product portfolio would improve focus and reduce the cost of maintaining multiple product lines. Other analysts were skeptical that the plan would halt Nokia's slide. In pursuing this plan, Nokia was all but admitting that Symbian had failed, and analysts feared a rapid fall-off in Symbian-based units during the transition. Further, as Nokia attempted to catch up in smartphones, other competitors would become stronger from a distribution and product perspective. Meanwhile, Microsoft itself was an unproven player in the mobile phone market. The market, too, seemed skeptical as Nokia's stock price declined 14% on announcement of the plan.

In the first months following the announcement of the plan, the skeptics' view seemed to prevail. Having announced that the company would cease support for Symbian phones after 2016, customers and app developers quickly turned their attention elsewhere, and Nokia suffered a more rapid decline in market share and profits than expected. As a result, in July 2011, the company reported a net loss of EUR368 million versus a net profit of EUR227 million a year earlier, and the loss widened considerably by year end. Prior to 2008, Nokia had issued relatively little long-term debt, but in response to the NAVTEQ acquisition and the global financial crisis in 2009, it raised EUR2.25 billion and another USD1.5 billion in debt at a rating of A. Citing severe weakening of the company's business position, in the summer of 2011, Moody's downgraded the company's debt two notches from A– to Baa2, and Fitch downgraded it to BBB–, the lowest notch before losing investment-grade.[12]

Overshadowed by questions about the transition were several positive developments that helped stabilize the situation. Beginning in November 2011, the first million units of Lumia 710 and 800 phones finally rolled out in Europe and Asia. In early 2012, the Lumia 900 won the presitigous Consumer Electronics Show award for "Best Smartphone of 2012."[13] Gartner Research, an influential commentator in the sector, predicted

---

[11]The net effect on Nokia's operating margins likely would depend on the sales of WP units. Microsoft's marketing and R&D support appeared to be relatively fixed, whereas the royalty paid by Nokia was on a per-unit basis (speculated to be between USD10 [EUR7.7] and USD14 [EUR11] per phone). In the fourth quarter of 2011, Nokia received its first quarterly "platform support" payment of USD250 million (EUR192 million), which would amount to $1 billion per year (EUR769 million). Microsoft did not disclose the royalty it charged other OEMs for WP 7, but reports suggested it was on the order of USD15 (EUR12) per device.

[12]S&P and Fitch followed a similar rating convention: Categories were denoted by capital letters and a + or − indicated better or worse credit strength within a category (e.g., AA+, AA, AA−). Moody's used a number to indicate relative credit strength within a category, with 1 being the highest and 3 the lowest (e.g., Aa1, Aa2, Aa3).

[13]Images and specifications of the Lumia 900 can be seen on Nokia's website: http://www.nokia.com/us-en/products/phone/lumia900/specifications/ (accessed May 2012).

that Nokia's WP units would be second in market share behind Android phones by 2015, displacing Apple as the current number two.[14] While Lumia phones did not yet rival the top Android or Apple phones, analysts viewed them as a significant improvement over Symbian phones.[15] The number of Windows apps materially improved over 2011 as developers showed renewed interest in the platform; this was also an important factor for the ecosystem that supported smartphones. By 2012, there were 60,000 Windows apps available compared with 460,000 for Apple and 320,000 for Android.[16] As the market narrowed to two OS platforms (Apple and Android), there was also growing consensus among procurers of mobile phones that a third competitor would be a positive development for the industry.

Over the course of 2011, the tough competitive environment also took its toll on Nokia's competitors. Research in Motion (RIM), a company with a strong platform among commercial users of mobile phones, fell behind in its product development and experienced significant losses in earnings and market share during 2011. Management turmoil at Ericsson frustrated attempts to gain market share. On August 15, 2011, after earlier slamming the Nokia–Microsoft merger, Google reversed course and announced plans to purchase Motorola Mobility, a financially struggling spin-off of Motorola, for $12.5 billion.[17] On October 5, 2011, the world was shaken by the death of Steve Jobs, the CEO and legendary founder of Apple. While analysts speculated about what the loss of his leadership might mean for the company longer term, consumers reacted favorably to the iPhone 4S, announced the day before his death. The Apple juggernaut seemed poised to continue, at least for the foreseeable future.

Implications for Financing

Nokia had always financed itself conservatively, and it fell to Nokia's CFO Timo Ihamuotila and his team to consider the implications of the plan on the firm's external financing requirements for 2012 and 2013. **Exhibits 34.6** and **34.7** give the historical income statement and balance sheet used as reference points to help prepare the forecasts. From these, the team chose initially to set cash and short-term securities at a minimum of 27% of sales, which reflected the average of Nokia's cash-to-sales ratio in the years outside of the global downturn (i.e., 2007, 2010, and 2011). In addition, the team wanted some cash reserves for acquisitions to be able to respond quickly to a changing competitive landscape as the firm had done with its acquisition of NAVTEQ in 2008. Information on Nokia's peers is given in **Exhibit 34.8**.

---

[14]"Gartner Says Android to Command Nearly Half of Worldwide Smartphone Operating System Market by Year-End 2012," April 7, 2011, http://www.gartner.com/it/page.jsp?id=1622614 (accessed May 2012).

[15]The same analysts also expressed concern that the Lumia 800 might be priced too expensively (EUR420) to compete in the marketplace, but the company planned more aggressive pricing for the Lumia 900.

[16]"Nokia: The Good and the Bad," Deutsche Bank analyst report, January 12, 2012.

[17]"Google Slams the Nokia + Microsoft deal, then buys Motorola Mobility?," Design Sojurn, August 27, 2011, http://www.designsojourn.com/google-slams-the-nokia-microsoft-deal-then-buys-motorola-mobility/ (accessed May 2012).

Nokia, like other technology companies, typically chose to maintain high cash balances to bolster perceptions of its financial strength. Bill Wetreich, a managing director at S&P, explained:

> Tech companies tend to self-impose high cash balances on themselves for a couple reasons. For one, a lot of cash is tied up in the business because they tend to self-fund working capital, R&D, etc., and don't make much use of commercial paper. Another reason is that they can miss a product cycle and need cash to see them through. You don't have to look very far to see examples of tech companies that miss a product cycle and have their financial strength rapidly disappear.[18]

Academics routinely prescribed more debt for these companies to take advantage of the tax savings on interest to lower the firm's cost of capital and to control agency costs by reducing the free cash flow at managers' discretion. The financial press simply called for higher dividends or share repurchases. In the meantime, companies appeared to reject those arguments and increased cash holdings, from an average cash-to-assets ratio of 10.5% in 1980 to 23.5% in 2006.[19] The secular increase in cash holdings seemed to suggest firms were responding to increased risk and using cash as some kind of buffer.

Given the uncertainty regarding Nokia's future market share, Ihamuotila forecasted a range of possible outcomes. **Exhibit 34.9** gives a forecast of Nokia's income statement by segment for 2012 and 2013 for one representative upside and downside scenario. He believed the downside scenario should be given greater weight for planning purposes given the firm's recent financial performance and the difficult transition ahead.

For Devices and Services (D&S), the largest division, the downside scenario recognized the continued significant loss of Symbian and overall Nokia market share, while under the upside scenario, sales stabilized and were predicted to exceed 2011 levels by 2013. Gross margins were expected to decline due to competitive price pressure, royalty payments to Microsoft, and aggressive pricing of Nokia phones, reflecting Elop's strategy for capturing market share. Under the downside scenario, these factors were expected to erode gross margins to 24% in the near term, while under the upside scenario, gross margins were projected at 26% over the next two years. Lower margins lead to lower adjusted operating profits in the pro formas, but these were partially offset by savings from restructuring efforts and Microsoft's support for R&D and marketing functions, with the upside scenario reflecting more and faster realization of savings.

Nokia Siemens Networks (NSN) announced a major restructuring effort in late 2011, which would result in significant near-term restructuring charges and a phase-out of less-profitable operations. Profits had been slow to materialize at NSN, and the downside scenario reflected continuing struggles for this division. Location and Commerce (L&C) had also been a disappointing performer (resulting in a significant write-down of goodwill in 2011), and the forecasts pointed to continued subpar performance.

---

[18]Case writer interview with Bill Wetreich, May 24, 2011.

[19]Thomas W. Bates, Kathleen M. Kahle, and René M. Stulz, "Why Do Firms Hold So Much More Cash Than They Used To?," *Journal of Finance* 64, no. 5 (2009): 1985–2022.

Based on the forecasted assumptions, in the event the downside scenario materialized, Nokia estimated it would need to raise EUR4.3 billion through 2013 (**Exhibit 34.10**).

Financing Alternatives

Ihamuotila and his team would have to carefully weigh the pros and cons of funding EUR4.3 billion through debt, equity, or a reduction in dividends or cash. Although some combination of these alternatives could be employed, the team chose to evaluate each separately to assess their relative impact on the firm's financial situation.

Issue Long-Term Debt

At its current rating, Nokia's debt was still investment-grade, but it did not want to risk a further deterioration in rating. Credits rated BBB–/Baa3 or higher were considered *investment-grade*, whereas those rated below that grade (BB+/Ba1 or lower) were considered *noninvestment-grade* and were often referred to as high-yield or junk debt. Some institutional investors (such as pension funds and charitable trusts) were limited in the amount of noninvestment-grade debt they could hold, and many individual investors also avoided it. For that reason, there was typically a large increase in spreads (i.e., the yield on debt over the yield on a comparable-maturity U.S. Treasury) when ratings dropped from investment- to noninvestment-grade (**Exhibit 34.11**). Currently, interest rates were at historic lows following rate reductions by the U.S. Federal Reserve and European Union monetary authorities in response to the financial crisis of 2008. As the global economy recovered, rates were expected to increase, but when that might happen and the extent of the increase were widely debated.

In addition, the ability to issue noninvestment-grade debt depended to a greater degree on the strength of the economy and on favorable credit market conditions compared with investment-grade debt. The high-yield debt market had grown significantly from its origins in the mid-1980s as a primary source of financing for leveraged buyouts to be a more diversified source of financing for many companies. For two decades, high-yield debt made up 20.5% of the total volume of debt raised, but in any given year, the percentage ranged from a low of 2.3% in 1991, a recessionary year, to highs above 29% in 2004 and 2005, before dropping to 8.8% in 2008 as the financial crisis took hold (**Exhibit 34.12**). Consequently, investment-grade debt was typically easier to raise in economic downturns when firms might have greater need to borrow.

Although Nokia's debt-to-equity ratio rose considerably from 2007 to 2011, when its cash position was factored in, it had negative net debt throughout this period. The ability to pay off its debt with cash seemed at odds with the notion of deteriorating creditworthiness. For the purposes of credit rating, the rating agencies did not look at leverage on a net debt (or net interest) basis. In their view, cash was at the discretion of management—a firm could have a high cash balance today but decide to do an acquisition, and the remaining cash might not be sufficient to pay off the debt when it matured. Credit ratings were therefore a combination of financial strength and business risk, which due to competitive pressures was currently high for Nokia. **Exhibit 24.13** provides credit metrics helpful in assessing the impact of a EUR4.3 billion debt issue on Nokia's credit rating.

Issue Equity

An equity issue would help support for the firm's existing debt and improve its credit rating. It also would provide the most flexible form of financing. But with the firm's share price at 5USD:4EUR, management was loath to raise EUR4.3 billion in new equity. It feared serious dilution of EPS and was concerned that the market might react negatively to an equity issue as a signal that management believed future earnings could deteriorate further.

Eliminate Dividends

Given the difficulty of making any external issue at this time, the team also considered eliminating the firm's dividend to fund the EUR4.3 billion. Over 2007 to 2011, Nokia had paid at least EUR0.40 dividends per share (DPS) despite the precipitous decline in earnings over the same period. Investors typically reacted negatively to reductions in dividends, and management worried about the implications of cutting dividends when its stock price was already so low. By comparison to the contractual obligations of debt, however, there was no legal requirement to pay dividends.

Reduce Cash

Finally, another alternative might be to reduce the cash balance of the firm to fund the entire EUR4.3 billion. Historically, Nokia had maintained high cash balances to preserve flexibility and financial strength. Some argued that if now was not the time to use the cash, when would be? On the other hand, RIM had chosen this course in dealing with its current difficulties, depleting 40% of its cash balance in 2011.

Decision

At the beginning of 2012, the members of the team had little visibility into what its financing needs might turn out to be. If they were prepared for the worst, they were confident more favorable outcomes could be managed. To the extent that not all of the funding was needed in a given year, the remainder could be held in cash, given Nokia's great need for flexibility and reserves.

Over its 145-year history, Nokia had survived many crises and reinvented itself numerous times to become a leading global mobile communications firm. As the plan with Microsoft unfolded over the next two years, the proud Finnish company would jump into the icy North Sea—which financing alternative would best prepare the company to survive this time?

EXHIBIT 34.1 | Elop's "Burning Platform" Memo to Employees, February 8, 2011

"There is a pertinent story about a man who was working on an oil platform in the North Sea. He woke up one night from a loud explosion, which suddenly set his entire oil platform on fire. In mere moments, he was surrounded by flames. Through the smoke and heat, he barely made his way out of the chaos to the platform's edge. When he looked down over the edge, all he could see were the dark, cold, foreboding Atlantic waters. As the fire approached him, the man had mere seconds to react. He could stand on the platform, and inevitably be consumed by the burning flames. Or, he could plunge 30 meters in to the freezing waters. The man was standing upon a "burning platform," and he needed to make a choice.

Over the past few months, I've shared with you what I've heard from our shareholders, operators, developers, suppliers and from you. Today, I'm going to share what I've learned and what I have come to believe. I have learned that we are standing on a burning platform. And, we have more than one explosion – we have multiple points of scorching heat that are fuelling a blazing fire around us.

Apple disrupted the market by redefining the smartphone and attracting developers to a closed, but very powerful ecosystem. Apple demonstrated that if designed well, consumers would buy a high-priced phone with a great experience and developers would build applications. They changed the game, and today, Apple owns the high-end range.

In about two years, Android came in at the high-end, they are now winning the mid-range, and quickly they are going downstream to phones under €100. Google has become a gravitational force, drawing much of the industry's innovation to its core.

[In] the low-end price range, manufacturers in the Shenzhen region of China produce phones at an unbelievable pace. By some accounts, this ecosystem now produces more than one third of the phones sold globally – taking share from us in emerging markets.

The battle of devices has now become a war of ecosystems. Our competitors aren't taking our market share with devices; they are taking our market share with an entire ecosystem. This means we're going to have to decide how we either build, catalyse, or join an ecosystem.

In the meantime, we've lost market share, we've lost mind share and we've lost time.

On Tuesday, Standard & Poor's informed that they will put our A long term and A-1 short term ratings on negative credit watch. This is a similar rating action to the one that Moody's took last week. Why are these credit agencies contemplating these changes? Because they are concerned about our competitiveness.

How did we get to this point? Why did we fall behind when the world around us evolved? This is what I have been trying to understand. I believe at least some of it has been due to our attitude inside Nokia. We had a series of misses. We haven't been delivering innovation fast enough. We're not collaborating internally.

Nokia, our platform is burning.

The burning platform, upon which the man found himself, caused the man to shift his behaviour, and take a bold and brave step into an uncertain future. He was able to tell his story. Now, we have a great opportunity to do the same.

Stephen

Source: Quoted passages from e-mail obtained by http://www.engadget.com/2011/02/08/nokia-ceo-stephen-elop-rallies-troops-in-brutally-honest-burnin/ and also reprinted in full at http://blogs.wsj.com/tech-europe/2011/02/09/full-text-nokia-ceo-stephen-elops-burning-platform-memo/ (accessed June 8, 2011).

EXHIBIT 34.2 | Cumulative Stock Returns on Nokia versus S&P500:
Jan. 2006–Dec. 2011

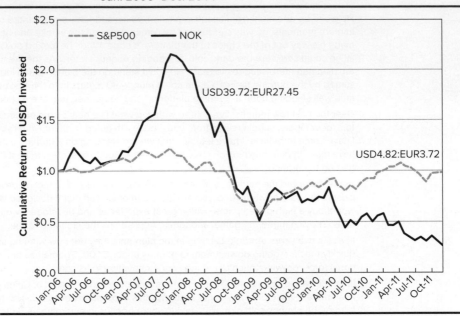

Nokia's shares were traded in U.S. dollars as an American Depositary Receipt on the New York Stock Exchange. Share prices were converted into euros at the daily exchange rate. Nokia's year-end 2011 share price was USD4.82:EUR3.72. The December 31, 2011, exchange rate was EUR1.2959 per U.S. dollar.

Data source: Center for Research in Security Prices (CRSP).

**EXHIBIT 34.3 | Nokia Market Share by Geographic Area and Mobile Device Volume
(units in millions)**

	2007 % of Area	2008 % of Area	2009 % of Area	2010 % of Area	2011 % of Area
Europe	27%	25%	25%	25%	21%
Middle East and Africa	17%	17%	18%	19%	23%
Greater China	16%	15%	17%	18%	16%
Asia-Pacific	26%	29%	29%	26%	29%
North America	4%	3%	3%	2%	1%
Latin America	9%	11%	9%	10%	11%
Smartphone Units	60	61	68	104	77
ASP (euros)			187	144	140
Mobile Device Units	377	407	364	349	340
ASP (euros)			64	64	57
Total Device Units	437	468	432	453	417
Global Market Share	**38%**	**39%**	**34%**	**32%**	**26%**

Data source: Nokia 20-F filings, 2007–11.

EXHIBIT 34.4 | Competing Smartphones and Operating System Platforms

	iPhone OSX	Blackberry OS	Android	Windows Mobile	Symbian
Major vendors subscribed	Apple	RIM	Dell, HTC, LG, ZTE, Motorola, Samsung, Sony Ericsson	HTC, LG, Motorola, Samsung, Sony Ericsson, ZTE	Nokia, LG, Samsung, Sony Ericsson
Date of first device launch (associated device)	June 29, 2007 (original iPhone)	March 4, 2002 (5810, first Java-based model)	Oct. 22, 2008 (HTC Dream/ T-Mobile G1)	April 19, 2000 (Under Pocket PC 2000)	June 19, 2001 (Nokia 9210, EPOC rel. 6)
Product orientation	Smart	Smart	Smart, midrange	Smart	Smart, midrange
Source model	Closed (with open-source app dev.)	Closed	Free and open	Closed (with open-source app dev.)	Open by Symbian ^ 2
Functional orientation and competitive advantage	Quick learning curve; consumer mind share victory: dominating app store distribution	E-mail, enterprise friendly; quick synchronization via BlackBerry enterprise server	Google, web; backed by open handset alliance	Resembles desktop experience; supports Windows Office	User interface and resource-conscious
Note to developers	Objective-C and closed, intuitive UI builder, big audience and mature payment system	Java dev. platform; good end-to-end security via BES, but not complex— apps friendly	Java dev. platform; with SDK readily available across major desktop OS, easy resource lookup	Visual Studio plus Net Compact Framework offers best of class commercial dev. environment	Big learning curve but not bound to a single programming language
Preinstalled app stores	iTunes, app store	BlackBerry World	Android Market	Windows Marketplace for Mobile	Ovi Store

Data source: "Nokia Corporation, Initiating Coverage," Wedbush research note, February 11, 2011.

EXHIBIT 34.5 | Smartphone Operating System and OEM Market Share

	2008A	2009A	2010A	2011*
OEM Shipment Market Share				
Nokia	36%	34%	29%	24%
Samsung	15%	19%	18%	18%
Motorola Mobility	8%	5%	2%	3%
LG	8%	10%	7%	5%
Ericsson	7%	5%	3%	2%
Apple	1%	2%	3%	4%
RIM	2%	3%	3%	3%
HTC	1%	1%	2%	3%
ZTE	1%	1%	2%	3%
All others	21%	20%	31%	34%
% that were Android-based	—	4%	22%	47%
Smartphone Operating System Share				
Symbian	52%	47%	38%	17%
RIM	17%	20%	16%	11%
Apple iOS	8%	14%	16%	15%
Android	1%	4%	23%	53%
Windows	12%	9%	4%	1%
Other OS	10%	6%	3%	3%
Nokia's Share Within Each Price Band				
≤ USD200			55%	34%
USD200–USD300			48%	28%
USD300–USD400			27%	12%
USD400–USD500			15%	3%
> USD500			3%	2%
Total			34%	18%

*Data through third quarter, September 2011.

Data sources: Gartner Research and company reports.

EXHIBIT 34.6 | Historical Income Statement (in millions of euros, except per share)

December 31,	2007	2008	2009	2010	2011
Net sales	51,058	50,710	40,984	42,446	38,659
Cost of sales	(33,754)	(33,337)	(27,720)	(29,629)	(27,340)
Gross profit	17,304	17,373	13,264	12,817	11,319
Research and development expenses	(5,647)	(5,968)	(5,909)	(5,863)	(5,612)
Selling and marketing expenses	(4,380)	(4,380)	(3,933)	(3,877)	(3,791)
Administrative and general expenses	(1,180)	(1,284)	(1,145)	(1,115)	(1,121)
Impairment of goodwill			(908)	0	(1,090)
Other income	2,312	420	338	476	221
Other expenses	(424)	(1,195)	510	(368)	(999)
Operating profit	7,985	4,966	1,197	2,070	(1,073)
Share of results of associated companies	44	6	30	1	(23)
Financial income and expenses	239	(2)	(265)	(285)	(102)
Profit before tax	8,268	4,970	962	1,786	(1,198)
Tax	(1,522)	(1,081)	(702)	(443)	(290)
Profit	6,746	3,889	260	1,343	(1,488)
Minority interest	459	99	631	507	324
Profit attributable to equity holders of the parent	7,205	3,988	891	1,850	(1,164)
Earnings per share					
Basic	1.85	1.07	0.24	0.50	−0.31
Diluted	1.83	1.05	0.24	0.50	−0.31
Cash dividends per share	0.53	0.40	0.40	0.40	0.40
Average shares outstanding					
Basic	3,885	3,744	3,705	3,709	3,710
Diluted	3,932	3,780	3,721	3,713	3,710
Gross margin (%)	33.9%	34.3%	32.4%	30.2%	29.3%
Operating margin (%)	15.6%	9.8%	2.9%	4.9%	−2.8%

Data source: Nokia 20-F filings.

EXHIBIT 34.7 I   Historical Balance Sheet (in millions of euros)

December 31,	2007	2008	2009	2010	2011
Assets					
Goodwill	1,384	6,257	5,171	5,723	4,838
Other intangible assets	2,736	4,157	2,905	1,968	1,406
Plant property and equipment	1,912	2,090	1,867	1,954	1,842
Deferred tax and other non-current assets	2,273	2,608	2,182	2,333	2,664
Total non-current assets	8,305	15,112	12,125	11,978	10,750
Inventories	2,876	2,533	1,865	2,523	2,330
Accounts receivable, net of allowances	11,200	9,444	7,981	7,570	7,181
Prepaid expenses, accrued income, and other current assets	3,465	5,673	4,894	4,777	5,042
Cash and short-term liquid investments	11,753	6,820	8,873	12,275	10,902
Total current assets	29,294	24,470	23,613	27,145	25,455
Total assets	**37,599**	**39,582**	**35,738**	**39,123**	**36,205**
Share capital	246	246	246	246	246
Share issue premium	644	442	279	312	362
Treasury shares, at cost	(3,146)	(1,881)	(681)	(663)	(644)
Translation differences and reserves	3,159	3,709	3,112	3,989	4,073
Retained earnings	13,870	11,692	10,132	10,500	7,836
Minority interests	2,565	2,302	1,661	1,847	2,043
Total equity	17,338	16,510	14,749	16,231	13,916
Long-term interest-bearing liabilities	203	861	4,432	4,242	3,969
Deferred tax and other long-term liabilities	1,082	1,856	1,369	1,110	876
Total non-current liabilities	1,285	2,717	5,801	5,352	4,845
Short-term debt	1,071	3,591	771	1,037	1,352
Other financial liabilities	0	924	245	447	483
Accounts payable	7,074	5,225	4,950	6,101	5,532
Accrued expenses	7,114	7,023	6,504	7,365	7,450
Provisions	3,717	3,592	2,718	2,590	2,627
Total shareholders' equity and liabilities	**37,599**	**39,582**	**35,738**	**39,123**	**36,205**

Data source: Nokia 20-F filings.

Exhibit 34.8 | Financial Information on Peer Companies (in millions of euros, except per share)

Company	Market Cap (millions of euros) 12/31/2011[2]	LT Issuer Credit Rating	Cash/ Assets	Cash/ Sales	Debt/Debt+ Equity	EBIT Interest Coverage	Debt/ EBITDA	EBIT Margin	DPS	EPS	Beta
Nokia	13,756	BBB	30%	28%	28%	9.6x	2.3	–3%	0.40	–0.31	1.6
Apple	289,506	NA	22%	24%	0%	NA	0.0	31%	0.00	20.66	1.3
Alcatel Lucent	2,724	B	18%	22%	55%	0.0x	3.3	1%	0.00	0.25	2.4
Ericsson	25,013	BBB+	29%	36%	18%	8.8x	1.0	8%	0.28	0.43	1.0
Motorola Mobility	9,005	NR	35%	26%	2%	–0.9x	0.5	–1%	0.00	–0.65	NA
Research in Motion	5,746	NR	9%	7%	1%	NA	NA	15%	0.00	3.27	1.7
Cisco	84,102	A+	51%	103%	26%	13.7x	1.5	18%	0.08	0.81	1.2
Google[1]	142,825	AA–	61%	118%	7%	211.1x	0.3	32%	0.00	22.89	1.1
Microsoft	175,518	AAA	46%	75%	17%	92.1x	0.4	39%	0.49	2.13	1.1
Qualcomm	60,520	NA	32%	80%	4%	42.8x	0.2	33%	0.62	2.01	1.0

[1]Google interest expense not reported; the immaterial amount is estimated by case writers.

[2]Market Cap information is from Yahoo! Finance. Financial data are on an as reported basis for most recent fiscal year-end. Cash includes short-term liquid investments. Dollar-per-euro exchange rate was 1.30 on December 31, 2011.

Notes: NA = not available, NR = not rated.

Data sources: S&P's Compustat and Mergent Online.

EXHIBIT 34.9 | Forecasted Income Statement (in millions of euros)

	2010A	2011A	Downside		Upside	
			2102E	2013E	2012E	2103E
D&S						
Sales	29,138	23,943	21,000	22,500	23,000	24,500
Year-over-year growth, %		−17.8%	−12.3%	7.1%	−3.9%	6.5%
Gross profit	8,773	6,640	5,040	5,513	5,980	6,370
Gross margin, %	30.1%	27.7%	24.0%	24.5%	26.0%	26.0%
Adjusted operating profit	3,162	1,577	525	1,013	1,150	1,960
Operating margin, %	10.9%	6.6%	2.5%	4.5%	5.0%	8.0%
NSN						
Sales	12,661	14,041	13,500	13,000	13,900	13,500
Adjusted operating profit	95	225	100	100	500	600
L&C						
Sales	1,003	1,091	900	900	1,200	1,200
Adjusted operating profit	265	204	250	250	300	300
Total Sales[1]	42,446	38,659	**35,170**	**36,170**	**37,870**	**38,970**
Total Adjusted Operating Profit[1]	3,203	1,825	**645**	**1,133**	**1,720**	**2,630**
Amortization	964	834	850	556	850	556
Goodwill impairment	—	1,090	0	0	0	0
Restructuring and other one-time costs	169	974	1,200	300	800	100
Operating Profit (reported)	2,070	(1,073)	**(1,405)**	**277**	**70**	**1,974**

[1]Total Sales and Total Operating Profits in 2010 (2011) include EUR356 (EUR416) and EUR319 (EUR181) in intercompany sales and profits, respectively. Projections subtract from EUR230 segment sales and EUR230 from operating profit each year to account for intercompany sales and profits.

Data sources: Case writer estimates, which are broadly consistent with range of analyst estimates; historical divisional sales and operating profit numbers from Oppenheimer Analyst Report, dated February 28, 2012; historical amortization and goodwill impairment from 20-F filings.

EXHIBIT 34.10 | Forecasted Balance Sheet (in millions of euros)

	Actual		Downside		Upside	
	2010A	**2011A**	**2012E**	**2013E**	**2012E**	**2013E**
Total Sales	42,446	38,659	**35,170**	**36,170**	**37,870**	**38,970**
Total Operating Profit (EBIT)	2,070	(1,073)	**(1,405)**	**277**	**70**	**1,974**
Financial income	110	170	95	98	102	105
Financial expense	254	255	224	224	224	224
Other financial expense	141	40	—	—	—	—
Profit before tax	1,786	(1,198)	(1,534)	150	(52)	1,855
Taxes (25%)	443	290	(384)	37	(13)	464
Minority losses	507	324	140	100	140	100
Net income to Nokia parent	1,850	(1,164)	**(1,011)**	**212**	**101**	**1,491**
Assets						
Goodwill, intangible, and other non-current assets	10,024	8,908	8,058	7,502	8,058	7,502
Plant property and equipment	1,954	1,842	1,842	1,842	1,842	1,842
Total non-current assets	11,978	10,750	**9,900**	**9,344**	**9,900**	**9,344**
Inventories	2,523	2,330	2,110	2,170	2,083	1,949
Accounts receivable, net of allowances	7,570	7,181	6,682	6,872	6,817	7,015
Prepaid expenses, accrued income, and other current assets	4,777	5,042	4,220	4,340	4,544	4,676
Cash and short-term liquid investments	12,275	10,902	9,496	9,766	10,225	10,522
Total assets	39,123	36,205	**32,409**	**32,493**	**33,569**	**33,505**
Common equity, net of retained earnings	5,731	6,080	6,080	6,080	6,080	6,080
Retained earnings	10,500	7,836	5,341	4,070	6,453	6,460
Total equity	16,231	13,916	**11,421**	**10,150**	**12,533**	**12,540**
Long-term interest-bearing liabilities	4,242	3,969	3,969	3,969	3,969	3,969
Other long-term liabilities	1,110	876	876	876	876	876
Total non-current liabilities	5,352	4,845	**4,845**	**4,845**	**4,845**	**4,845**
Short-term debt and other financial liabilities	1,484	1,835	—	—	—	—
Accounts payable	6,101	5,532	4,572	4,702	5,302	5,456
Accrued expenses, provisions, and other	9,955	10,077	8,265	8,500	8,899	9,158
Total shareholders' equity and liabilities	39,123	36,205	**29,103**	**28,197**	**31,579**	**31,999**
External Funds Needed		—	**3,305**	**4,296**	**1,989**	**1,506**
Other selected figures:						
Adjusted EBIT	3,203	1,825	645	1,133	1,720	2,630
EBITDA	3,841	489	145	1,533	1,620	3,230
Adjusted EBITDA	4,010	2,553	1,345	1,833	2,420	3,330

Data source: Case writer estimates based on company filings and analyst reports.

EXHIBIT 34.10 | Forecasted Balance Sheet (in millions of euros) (continued)

Assumptions for forecast	Actual					Downside		Upside	
	2007A	2008A	2009A	2010A	2011A	2012E	2013E	2012E	2013E
Forecasted as a percentage of sales:									
Inventories [1]	5.6%	5.0%	4.6%	5.9%	6.0%	6.0%	6.0%	5.5%	5.0%
Accounts receivable [2]	21.9%	18.6%	19.5%	17.8%	18.6%	19.0%	19.0%	18.0%	18.0%
Prepaid expenses, accrued income, and other current assets [3]	6.8%	11.2%	11.9%	11.3%	13.0%	12.0%	12.0%	12.0%	12.0%
Cash and cash equivalents [4]	23.0%	13.4%	21.6%	28.9%	28.2%	27.0%	27.0%	27.0%	27.0%
Accounts payable [4]	13.9%	10.3%	12.1%	14.4%	14.3%	13.0%	13.0%	14.0%	14.0%
Accrued expenses and provisions [5]	21.2%	20.9%	22.5%	23.5%	26.1%	23.5%	23.5%	23.5%	23.5%
Forecasts for other selected items: [6]									
Interest rate—cash and short-term liquid investments						1.0%	1.0%	1.0%	1.0%
Interest rate—short-term debt						1.0%	1.0%	1.0%	1.0%
Interest rate (avg.)—long-term debt						5.7%	5.7%	5.7%	5.7%
Income tax rate						25.0%	25.0%	25.0%	25.0%
Short-term debt [7]						0	0	0	0
Minority interest (losses) [8]						140	100	140	100
Amortization [8]						850	556	850	556
Depreciation						700	700	700	700
Capital expenditures [9]						700	700	700	700
Dividend per share [10]						0.40	0.40	0.40	0.40
Shares outstanding (millions)						3,710	3,710	3,710	3,710

[1] Sluggish demand keeps inventories at a higher percentage in the downside versus upside scenario.

[2] Accounts receivable are 19% of sales in the downside scenario but 18% in the upside scenario.

[3] Forecasted at the four-year average percentage of sales.

[4] Forecasted at the five-year average percentage of sales in the downside scenario and at a slightly higher rate in the upside scenario.

[5] Assumed 2011 was an outlier.

[6] Common equity and long-term liabilities are held constant.

[7] Short-term debt from 2011 is paid off.

[8] Amortization on intangible assets of EUR850 in 2012 and EUR556 in 2013 at which point the 2011 EUR1,406 million balance is fully amortized. The forecasts assume no new acquisitions so goodwill, intangibles, and other assets remain constant except for the above amortization.

[9] Capital expenditures are expected to roughly equal depreciation of EUR700 million.

[10] Assumes dividends remain the same as the past three years at EUR0.40 per share.

Data source: Case writer estimates based on company filings and analyst reports.

EXHIBIT 34.11 | Capital Market Rates
Aaa and Baa Spread over 10-Year U.S. Treasury Rate

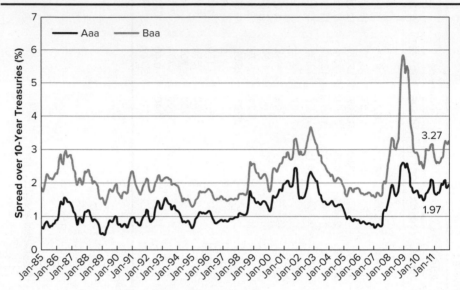

December 2011

Corporates (%)		U.S. Treasuries (%)	
Aaa	3.93	3-month	0.01
Aa	4.19	1-year	0.12
A	4.36	2-year	0.26
Baa	5.25	3-year	0.39
Ba	6.36	5-year	0.89
B	7.91	10-year	1.98
		20-year	2.67
		30-year	2.98
Exchange Rate	1.30		
(U.S. dollars per euro)			

Data source: St. Louis Federal Reserve Archival Federal Reserve Economic Data (ALFRED) database.

EXHIBIT 34.12 | Total Volume of Investment-Grade and High-Yield Debt Issued: 1991–2011

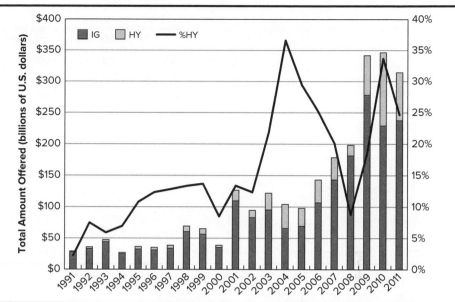

Note: Data all fixed-rate non-convertible debt issues with maturities of three years or more made by North American and European companies. "%HY" is the percentage of high-yield debt issued to total debt in a given year.

Data source: Thomson Reuters Security Data Corporation.

EXHIBIT 34.13 | Credit Metrics by Rating Category

Adjusted Key Industrial Financial Ratios Medians of Three-Year (2007–09) Averages						
Europe, Middle East, and Africa						
	AAA	AA	A	BBB	BB	B
EBIT interest coverage (x)[1]		14.9	6.4	4.4	3.2	1.3
Debt/EBITDA (x)[2]		0.7	1.7	2.4	3.0	5.0
Debt/(debt + equity) (%)[3]		28.4	34	42.5	51.5	69.4
No. of companies	0	9	51	101	58	43
United States						
	AAA	AA	A	BBB	BB	B
EBIT interest coverage (x)[1]	30.5	18.3	11.0	5.8	3.5	1.4
Debt/EBITDA (x)[2]	0.4	1.1	1.5	2.3	3.0	5.3
Debt/(debt + equity) (%)[3]	15.1	34.7	35.7	44.7	50.4	73.1
No. of companies	4	16	92	213	245	325
Companies in rating category (%)	0.3	2.2	12.4	27.1	26.2	31.8

Note: S&P defined the ratios on the book value of these items as follows:

[1]EBIT interest coverage = EBIT/interest expense

[2]Debt/EBITDA = (Short-term + Long-term debt)/(EBIT + depreciation and amortization)

[3]Debt/debt + equity = (Short-term debt + Long-term debt)/(Short-term debt + Long-term debt + Stockholders' equity)

Data source: S&P CreditStats "2009 Adjusted Key U.S. and European Industrial and Utility Financial Ratios," S&P Credit Research, August 20, 2010.

Kelly Solar

Jessica Kelly was learning to deal with disappointment. In early May of 2010 her start-up was poised to sell its designs and related patents to a large manufacturer of solar equipment. This was to be the culmination of two years of hard work developing a new product from a series of patents she had purchased through her fledgling company, Kelly Solar. That product, a major improvement in the reflector lenses used in solar power generation, had just proven out in a series of tests. But all her excitement turned to dread as she learned of a competing technology that promised to match all the advantages of the Kelly Solar designs. It was clear the equipment manufacturer would back only one of the technologies and the other would become worthless.

The Solar Energy Parts Business Opportunity

The "green technology" opportunity Jessica Kelly was exploring with Kelly Solar actually had its roots in her grandfather's "old technology" auto parts business. Jessica had spent many summers working in her grandfather's manufacturing facility, and when she graduated from college, her first job was in the accounting department of that business. After a few years, she obtained a business degree and began working for a small regional investment bank. She loved the bank job and advanced quickly, but she stayed close to her manufacturing roots and often dreamed about starting her own business. It all suddenly came together as she read an article about the use of Fresnel reflector technology in solar-energy power plants.[1]

Kelly was familiar with Fresnel lens technology; her grandfather's business had produced Fresnel lenses for the automobile industry for many years, and she had recently helped finance a small company called Lens Tech that was producing lenses for cars based on patents for a particular kind of high-density plastic. The Fresnel reflectors used in solar energy conversion were similar but on a much larger physical scale. As

---

[1]David R. Mills, "Advances in Solar Thermal Electricity Technology," *Solar Energy* 76 (2004): 19–31.

Kelly read the article on solar applications, she immediately realized that lenses built with high-density plastic could be very useful in the solar power industry. Certainly there was much additional work to be done to adapt the technology, and Kelly would need to secure certain patents and rights from Lens Tech, but she was convinced this application would be successful. One frantic year later, Kelly Solar had been formed and the patents acquired; Kelly pulled together the team she needed and began research and development in an old warehouse that, fittingly, was previously owned by her grandfather.

One thing that had attracted Kelly to this venture and facilitated the financing was the relative simplicity of the whole enterprise. Kelly was not interested in becoming the long-term manufacturer and distributor of the products Kelly Solar might develop. Her goal was to quickly prove the technology and then sell it to the industry's single dominant manufacturer. When Kelly started the business, the future could be effectively described as having two states. In one state, the technology would prove out and Kelly would secure a profitable sale of patents and processes. Given the market's size and the knowledge that her product, if successful, would be able to offer uniquely superior lenses at no extra cost relative to existing technology, she estimated that she could secure a payoff of $22 million. In the other state, the product would not prove out and, disappointing as it might be, the company would close down with no residual value.

By May of 2010, it was clear that the technology had proven successful. But the emergence of the competing technology created a new uncertainty. Only one of the two technologies would be backed by the manufacturer, and it was not clear which would be chosen. What had been a sure payoff of $22 million had turned into a gamble with equal odds of obtaining $22 million or closing down without any payoff at all.

Possible Improvements and Financing

One consolation was the possibility of making modifications that would effectively raise that probability that Kelly Solar's technology would be chosen. Lens Tech's technology offered some advantages over the competing technology related to the ability of the Kelly Solar lenses to be unaffected by high temperatures. Kelly had not initially chosen to buy the patents related to this characteristic because they would have provided no additional advantage over existing glass-based products in the market. With the competing plastic product, this was no longer the case. Kelly was sure that buying the patents and making the modifications would increase the odds of being selected to 70%.

Unfortunately, the modifications would require an additional investment of a hefty $3.20 million, much of that simply to buy the additional patents from Lens Tech. Kelly Solar had effectively used up its start-up funds and would have to seek new capital to develop the modifications. The initial investment in Kelly Solar had come from two sources. Kelly's grandfather had retired and sold his auto parts company and had given his granddaughter the funds she used to start Kelly Solar. These funds covered only a small portion of the needed research and development costs, and Kelly had secured the remaining funding from Scott Barkley, a local businessman with a history of lending to small innovation ventures. Barkley insisted that his investment be in the form of debt financing and that he would have to approve any dividend to Kelly, thereby guaranteeing that his claims would be paid in full before Kelly could receive any payout.[2] Kelly, on the other hand, reserved the right to determine exactly when the company would sell the rights to any products, thereby ensuring that Kelly would obtain her equity stake in a sale of technology. After substantial negotiation, Kelly and Barkley agreed upon a note that promised Barkley a single lump sum payment of $15 million at the start of 2011.

Given that the Kelly Solar designs had already proven out in tests and given that there was little development uncertainty related to the improvements, Kelly believed it would not be difficult to find new investors and she could certainly approach Barkley again. If necessary and with some effort, she could also obtain some additional money from her family. Of course, securing the initial funding had been expensive—legal and accounting fees associated with due diligence and drafting documents for the Barkley loan had totaled $400,000. Kelly expected that any new agreement or renegotiation of the existing agreement with Barkley would incur legal and accounting fees equal to $200,000.

Kelly realized that the next step was to inform Barkley as to recent developments and the possible additional investment. As disappointed as Kelly might be, she anticipated that Barkley would be even more upset. There had always been a chance that the firm would default on the promised debt payment, and this possibility was now substantially greater. But she hoped the conversation would go smoothly. The modifications were worth the investment. More important, she did not want a negative experience to dampen her enthusiasm as she began the hard work of implementing the modifications and pitching the product to its potential buyer. Whatever success they might achieve still depended a great deal on her.

---

[2]The agreement also specified that any additional debt would be subordinate to the debt owed to Barkley.

J. C. Penney Company

On Friday, February 8, 2013, J. C. Penney (JCP) CEO Ron Johnson was facing the unenviable task of turning around one of America's oldest and most prominent retailers. The past three years had seen variable financial results for the company (**Exhibit 36.1** through **Exhibit 36.4**) and the cash balance had gradually declined. According to Johnson, "as we execute our ambitious transformation plan, we are pleased with the great strides we made to improve J. C. Penney's cost structure, technology platforms and the overall customer experience. We have accomplished so much in the last twelve months. We believe the bold actions taken in 2012 will materially improve the Company's long-term growth and profitability."[1]

Despite Johnson's plans, there were rumors among Wall Street analysts that the company was facing significant liquidity issues and perhaps the possibility of bankruptcy. Sales and profits were continuing to decline and the dividend had been eliminated. Just two days earlier, a Wall Street equity analyst had recommended investors sell their JCP stock by stating, "Cash flow is weak and could become critical. At current burn rates—and absent any further asset sales—we estimate that J. C. Penney will be virtually out of cash by fiscal year-end 2013."[2] On top of that, JCP was dealing with allegations that the company was defaulting on its 7.4% debentures, which were due in 2037. Although JCP management had responded that the default allegations were invalid, the rumors of the company's liquidity problems continued to circulate and analysts wanted assurance that JCP had a financing plan in place in the event that an injection of cash became critical to the company's survival.

---

[1]"J. C. Penney Company, Inc., Reports 2012 Fiscal Fourth Quarter and Full Year Results," JCPenney.com, http://ir.jcpenney.com/phoenix.zhtml?c=70528&p=irol-newsCompanyArticle&ID=1790150&highlight (accessed Nov. 18, 2014).

[2]Sam Mamudi, "J. C. Penney's A (Strong) Sell, Says Maxim Group," Barron's, February 6, 2013, http://blogs.barrons.com/stockstowatchtoday/2013/02/06/j-c-penneys-a-strong-sell-says-maxim-group/ (accessed Nov. 18, 2014).

This public-sourced case was written by David Glazer (MBA '14) under the supervision of Kenneth M. Eades, Professor of Business Administration, and with the research assistance of Shachar Eyal (MBA '14). Copyright © 2014 by the University of Virginia Darden School Foundation, Charlottesville, VA. All rights reserved. *To order copies, send an e-mail to* sales@dardenbusinesspublishing.com. *No part of this publication may be reproduced, stored in a retrieval system, used in a spreadsheet, or transmitted in any form or by any means—electronic, mechanical, photocopying, recording, or otherwise—without the permission of the Darden School Foundation.*

History of J. C. Penney

In 1902, an ambitious 26-year-old man named James Cash Penney used his $500 savings account to open "The Golden Rule Store" in a one-room wooden building in Kemmerer, Wyoming. The store appealed to mining and farming families and was well known for its assortment of merchandise and exceptional customer service. By 1914, Penney had changed the company name to J. C. Penney and relocated headquarters to New York City. Penney was using private-label brands as a means to ensure a distinct level in quality, and the ability to control pricing and margins, which was not often the case when handling brand names.

By 1929, JCP had expanded to more than 1,000 stores and the company was listed on the New York Stock Exchange. The week after the company went public, however, the stock market crashed and the Great Depression began. Despite its dubious beginnings as a public company, JCP was able to prosper during the ensuing years by managing inventory levels and passing low prices on to consumers. By 1951, the company achieved the unprecedented sales level of $1 billion due partly to having eliminated the company's cash-only policy and introducing its first credit card. By 1968, sales exceeded $3 billion and the company had begun to see increased competition from small specialty stores that carried a specific range of merchandise. Nonetheless, with the help of its $1 billion catalog service and the launch of a women's fashion program, sales reached $11 billion by 1978.

In an effort to stay current with continued shifts in consumer trends and to solidify its identity, JCP launched a restructuring initiative in the early 1980s with the objective of transforming the company from a mass merchant to a national department store. JCP spent $1 billion to remodel its stores and announced in 1983 that it would begin to phase out its auto-service, appliance, hardware, and fabrics merchandising in favor of emphasizing apparel, home furnishings, and leisure lines. Despite these changes, JCP continued to face challenges of being perceived as being a middle-ground retailer; consumers were favoring either luxury merchants or discounters. As part of the effort to revamp JCP's image, the company named a new CEO, Allen Questrom, in 2000. Questrom was known as a "retailing turnaround artist," and had made his name leading famous department stores—including Federated Department Stores, Macy's, and Barneys—out of bankruptcy.[3] Questrom competed a second round of restructuring that included store closings, layoffs, a conversion to a centralized merchandising system, and large divestitures of noncore units (insurance and Eckerd Drug). The results for 2004 were promising: the company reported $584 million in net profits.

Having succeeded in his turnaround efforts, Questrom stepped down and was replaced by Mike Ullman. Considered a branding expert, Ullman ushered in a new era of higher-end fashion as JCP signed large exclusive deals with big brands such as Liz Claiborne and makeup retailer Sephora. Ullman successfully grew online sales and, in 2007, instituted an aggressive expansion plan for new store openings and to expand

---

[3] Ann Zimmerman, "Seeking Turnaround, J. C. Penney Hires Questrom as Designer CEO," *Wall Street Journal*, July 28, 2000, http://online.wsj.com/news/articles/SB965313356651209377 (accessed Nov. 18, 2014).

the net income margin to 15%. Despite these efforts, the credit crisis and economic downturn of 2008 to 2011 provided an extra set of challenges as growing consumer frugality allowed "off-price" competitors such as Kohl's to further erode JCP's sales and margins.[4]

Bill Ackman Takes a Stake

After each of the first two quarters of 2010, Ullman lowered sales and earnings guidance. After a disappointing Q2 earnings report, JCP's stock price dropped to a low for the year of $19.82 per share. In the days following, activist investor Bill Ackman, founder of Pershing Square Management, began buying JCP shares. Ackman was well known for his activism tactics with companies such as Wendy's, Target, and Barnes & Noble, wherein he had successfully pressured management into making decisions that he believed benefited shareholder interests. For example, in 2006, Ackman managed to convince Wendy's management to sell its subsidiary Tim Hortons doughnut chain through an IPO.[5] In 2012, Ackman persuaded Burger King's private equity owners to postpone a planned IPO in order to begin merger negotiations with a publicly traded shell company.[6]

By early October 2010, Ackman's position in JCP was close to 40 million shares, which represented a 16.8% stake in the company and was worth approximately $900 million.[7] By February 2011, when asked about his investment in JCP, Ackman responded that it had "the most potential of any company in his portfolio."[8] Furthermore, he believed that the stock was being valued cheaply at only five times EBITDA and that the company's 110 million square feet of property was "some of the best real estate in the world."[9] Ackman also disclosed that he was interested in changing the operations of the company and that he would be joining the board of directors.[10] Later in February, when JCP released its results for 2010, it appeared that Ackman had once again picked a winner. Not only had earnings beaten expectations, but based on the company's strong

---

[4]Jay P. Pederson, *The International Directory of Company Histories*, volume 91 (Michigan: St. James Press, 2008), 263–272.

[5]Rob Cox, "Burger King Wins Support Where Wendy's Didn't in Tim Hortons Deal," New York Times, August 26, 2014, http://dealbook.nytimes.com/2014/08/26/burger-king-wins-support-where-wendys-didnt-in-tim-hortons-deal/?_r=0 (accessed Nov. 24, 2014).

[6]Michael J. De La Merced, "Ackman's Influence on Burger King's Future," *New York Times*, April 4, 2014, http://dealbook.nytimes.com/2012/04/04/ackmans-influence-on-burger-kings-future/ (accessed Nov. 19, 2014).

[7]"Bill Ackman Starts New Activist Position in J. C. Penney (JCP)," *Market Folly* (blog), October 8, 2010, http://www.marketfolly.com/2010/10/bill-ackman-starts-new-activist.html (accessed Feb. 18, 2014).

[8]Jonathan Chen, "Two Investment Legends at the Harbor Investment Conference (GGP, HHC, HOE, C, GS)," Benzinga.com, February 4, 2011, http://www.benzinga.com/trading-ideas/long-ideas/11/02/836605/two-investment-legends-at-the-harbor-investment-conference-ggp (accessed Nov. 19, 2014).

[9]Chen.

[10]Roger Nachman, "A Penney for Your Portfolio?" Minyanville.com, February 25, 2011, http://www.minyanville.com/investing/articles/jc-penney-stock-investment-strategy-trading/2/25/2011/id/33025?refresh=1 (accessed Feb. 18, 2014).

cash position of $2.6 billion, Ullman announced that JCP would commence a $900 million buyback program:

> Our performance in 2010 reflects the strides we have made to deliver on our operating goals and position J. C. Penney as a retail industry leader. This was particularly evident in the fourth quarter when the actions we took during the year—including new growth initiatives and improvements across our merchandise assortments, redefining the jcp.com experience and driving efficiencies across our company—enabled us to achieve sales, market share and profitability growth that surpassed our expectations, and to establish a share buyback plan which will return value to our shareholders.[11]

Management Changes

Despite Ullman's successful 2010 and Q1 2011 results, he announced he would be stepping down as CEO. Although Ullman retained his position as executive chairman, Ron Johnson of Apple Inc.'s retail stores was hired as the new CEO. Johnson's success at Apple had been well documented. The *New York Times* described him as the man at Apple who had "turned the boring computer sales floor into a sleek playroom filled with gadgets."[12] In an interview following the announcement, Johnson stated, "My lifetime dream has been to lead one of the large great retailers, to reimagine what it could be. In the U.S., the department store has a chance to regain its status as the leader in style, the leader in excitement. It will be a period of true innovation for this company." Ackman conveyed confidence in the management change by saying, "Ron Johnson is the Steve Jobs of the retail industry."[13]

JCP investors echoed Ackman's optimism as the stock rallied 17% upon the announcement of Johnson's appointment. JCP's board had created a compensation package to incentivize Johnson's performance that included a base salary of $375,000 and a performance-based bonus of $236,000. The board also awarded Johnson $50 million of restricted stock to offset the Apple stock options Johnson had forfeited when he accepted the JCP position.[14] Through the rest of 2011, Johnson continued to make headlines by recruiting high-profile executives for his management team. The most noteworthy was the CMO, Michael Francis, who had held the same position at Target. Francis received a base salary of $1.2 million and $12 million as a "sign-on cash bonus."[15] In addition to Francis, Johnson hired Daniel Walker as his chief talent officer for $8 million and Michael Kramer as COO for $4 million in cash and $29 million in restricted stock.

---

[11]Nachman.

[12]Stephanie Clifford and Miguel Helft, "Apple Stores Chief to Take the Helm at J. C. Penney." *New York Times*, June 14, 2011, http://www.nytimes.com/2011/06/15/business/economy/15shop.html (accessed Feb. 20, 2014).

[13]Clifford and Helft.

[14]Clifford and Helft.

[15]Tyler Durden, "JC Penney President Mike Francis Came, Saw, Collected $10 Million, and Quit Nine Months Later," *Zero Hedge* (blog), June 18, 2012, http://www.zerohedge.com/news/jc-penney-president-mike-francis-came-saw-collected-10-million-and-quit-nine-months-later (accessed Feb. 20, 2014).

Results for Q3 2011 were disappointing: sales declined 4.8% compared to Q3 2010 and earnings fell to a $143 million loss.[16] As JCP entered 2012 in a tenuous financial position, Johnson responded by announcing a "fair-and-square" pricing strategy that eliminated all promotions in favor of "everyday, regular prices."[17] Having run 590 separate promotions in 2011, Johnson argued, "We want customers to shop on their terms, not ours. By setting our store monthly and maintaining our best prices for an entire month, we feel confident that customers will love shopping when it is convenient for them, rather than when it is expedient for us."[18]

The new pricing strategy was met with skepticism. Pricing consultant Rafi Mohammed wrote in the *Harvard Business Review* that "J. C. Penney lacks the differentiation to make this pricing strategy successful. J. C. Penney's products are fairly homogenous. When selling a relatively undifferentiated product, the only lever to generate higher sales is discounts. Even worse, if competitors drop prices on comparable products, J. C. Penney's hands are tied—it is a sitting duck that can't respond."[19]

By Q1 2012, JCP's financial condition was showing signs of rapid deterioration as sales dropped 20% relative to Q1 2011 and losses hit 75 cents per share.[20] Johnson announced a 10% reduction of the work force and that the dividend that had been paid since 1987 would be discontinued. The dividend cut was a clear signal to Wall Street that the company was experiencing significant liquidity concerns. As retail equities analyst Brian Sozzi observed, "The dividend cut makes you lose shareholder support. And it also makes you wonder, [does JCP] have the balance sheet to fund this massive transformation of the business over the next two to three years?"[21]

In June 2012, with sales declining and the share price sliding toward $20 a share, Johnson's key hire, CMO Francis, resigned. After only nine months at the company, Francis left with a $12 million bonus in his pocket.

Liquidity Issues

At the end of Q2 2012, JCP's capital structure was relatively strong. With $3.1 billion in debt and a market capitalization of $6.5 billion, JCP had a debt-to-capital ratio of 33%, only slightly higher than the average of 30% for its competitors (**Exhibit 36.5**).

---

[16]"J. C. Penney Company, Inc. Reports Third Quarter Financial Results," JCPenney.com, November 14, 2011, http://ir.jcpenney.com/phoenix.zhtml?c=70528&p=irol-newsCompanyArticle&ID=1629772 (accessed Nov. 19, 2014).

[17]"J. C. Penney's Transformation Plans Revealed at Launch Event in New York City," JCPenney.com, January 25, 2012, http://ir.jcpenney.com/phoenix.zhtml?c=70528&p=irol-newsArticle&ID=1652614&highlight (accessed Feb. 21, 2014).

[18]http://ir.jcpenney.com/phoenix.zhtml?c=70528&p=irol-newsArticle&ID=1652614&highlight.

[19]Rafi Mohammed, "Understanding J. C. Penney's Risky New Pricing Strategy," *Harvard Business Review*, http://blogs.hbr.org/2012/01/understanding-jc-penneys-risky (accessed Feb. 26, 2014).

[20]"J. C. Penney Company, Inc. Reports 2012 First Quarter Results," JCPenney.com, May 15, 2012, http://ir.jcpenney.com/phoenix.zhtml?c=70528&p=irol-newsArticle&ID=1696183 (accessed Nov. 19, 2014).

[21]Phil Wahba, "J. C. Penney Posts Loss, Sales Tumble; Cuts Dividend," Reuters, May 15, 2012, http://www.reuters.com/article/2012/05/15/us-jcpenney-idUSBRE84E1DA20120515 (accessed Feb. 26, 2014).

The company's debt included secured and unsecured bonds and a short-term credit facility (revolver) that was secured by JCP's credit card receivables, accounts receivable, and inventory. JPC had traditionally made limited use of the revolver and had not drawn upon it during 2012. As was true for most short-term credit facilities, JCP's was designed primarily to finance seasonal inventories and receivables around the holiday season. The credit limit of the revolver was $1.5 billion.

By Q3 2012, the company's diminishing cash balance had become evident (**Exhibit 36.6**)—it had only $525 million in cash. Analysts began to question the company's long-term stability. For example, prior to the company's 2012 annual earnings announcement, JPMorgan Chase & Co. equity analysts wrote:

> We increasingly question JCP's ability to self-fund its transformation on [free cash flow] generation alone. We view a draw on the revolver as increasingly likely in 1H13. Despite recent actions geared toward capital preservation, JCP will likely require $1B of capital this year to continue its transformation at the pace initially discussed.[22]

The release of the full-year results proved to be worse than expected: JCP lost $985 million for 2012 and Q4 earnings alone were $1.71-per-share below analyst expectations. When compared to prior Q4 cash balances of $2.6 billion in 2010 and $1.5 billion in 2011, JCP's cash balance of $930 million for 2012 confirmed that the analyst community had good reason for concern. An analysis of the sources and uses of cash for 2012 revealed that JCP's large operating losses were draining the company of cash, and were it not for the reduction of inventories and sales of "other assets," JCP's cash could have fallen critically close to zero (**Exhibit 36.7**).

Johnson had a variety of actions he could take to meet the demand for cash flow. First, he could manage cash flow by stretching payables and reducing inventories. Both of these working-capital components were significant cash flow determinants for most large retailers. If the internally generated cash flow proved inadequate, he could turn to JCP's credit facility, which had $1.5 billion of available credit. By design, however, the revolver was a short-term source of funds that the banks could choose to not renew if they perceived that JCP was using the revolver as permanent financing. If JCP had to seek permanent financing, Johnson could access either the debt market or the equity market. The prospect, however, of issuing debt was no more appealing than issuing equity. The debt would likely carry a non-investment-grade credit rating with a coupon rate of approximately 6.0% (**Exhibit 36.8**). Given that the stock was currently selling at $19.80 per share, a much larger share issuance would be required than if it had occurred just one year earlier, when the stock was selling at $42 per share (**Exhibit 36.9**).

---

[22]Matthew Boss, Anne McCormick, and Michael Joyce, "Sales to Return, but Bark > Bite; Checks Point to Feb 1 Shops Delayed w/ Spring RFID Launch Scaled Back," JPMorgan Chase & Co. Equity Research, February 1, 2013.

EXHIBIT 36.1 I   Income Statements 2010–2012 (in millions of dollars, except per-share data)

	2012	2011	2010
Total revenue	12,985	17,260	17,759
Cost of revenue	8,919	11,042	10,799
Gross profit	4,066	6,218	6,960
Selling general and administrative	4,535	5,251	5,358
Non recurring	298	451	255
Others	543	518	515
Total operating expenses	5,376	6,220	6,128
Operating income or loss	(1,310)	(2)	832
Income from continuing operations			
Total other income/expenses net	0	0	9
Earnings before interest and taxes	(1,310)	(2)	823
Interest expense	226	227	231
Income before tax	(1,536)	(229)	592
Income tax expense	(551)	(77)	203
Net income	(985)	(152)	389
Wt. avg. shares for basic EPS—basic	219.2	217.4	236.4
Weighted average shares—diluted	219.2	217.4	238.0
Basic earnings per share	($4.49)	($0.70)	$1.64
Diluted earnings per share	($4.49)	($0.70)	$1.63

Data source: All exhibits, unless otherwise specified, include data sourced from J. C. Penney annual reports.

EXHIBIT 36.2 | Balance Sheets 2010–2012 (in millions of dollars)

	2012	2011	2010
Assets			
Current assets			
Cash and cash equivalents	930	1,507	2,622
Inventory	2,341	2,916	3,213
Prepaid and other	412	658	535
Total current assets	**3,683**	**5,081**	**6,370**
Property, plant, and equipment	5,353	5,176	5,231
Other assets	745	1,167	1,467
Total assets	**9,781**	**11,424**	**13,068**
Liabilities			
Current liabilities			
Merchandise accounts payable	1,162	1,022	1,133
Other accounts payable	1,380	1,503	1,514
Short-term and current long-term debt	26	231	—
Total current liabilities	**2,568**	**2,756**	**2,647**
Long-term debt	2,956	2,871	3,099
Other liabilities	698	899	670
Deferred long-term liability charges	388	888	1,192
Total liabilities	**6,610**	**7,414**	**7,608**
Stockholders' equity			
Common stock	110	108	118
Retained earnings	380	1,412	2,222
Capital surplus	3,799	3,699	3,925
Other stockholder equity	(1,118)	(1,209)	(805)
Total stockholder equity	**3,171**	**4,010**	**5,460**
Total liabilities and stockholders' equity	**9,781**	**11,424**	**13,068**

EXHIBIT 36.3 | Quarterly Income Statements, 2011 and 2012 (in millions of dollars, except per-share data)

	Q4 2012	Q3 2012	Q2 2012	Q1 2012	Q4 2011	Q3 2011	Q2 2011	Q1 2011
Total revenue	3,884	2,927	3,022	3,152	5,425	3,986	3,906	3,943
Cost of revenue	2,960	1,975	2,018	1,966	3,788	2,497	2,409	2,348
Gross profit	924	952	1,004	1,186	1,637	1,489	1,497	1,595
Operating expenses								
Selling, general and administrative	1,209	1,087	1,050	1,160	1,343	1,242	1,243	1,281
Depreciation and amortization	157	133	128	125	135	127	128	128
Other	303	(112)	9	127	232	291	45	25
Total operating expenses	1,669	1,108	1,187	1,412	1,710	1,660	1,416	1,434
Operating income	(745)	(156)	(183)	(226)	(73)	(171)	81	161
Interest expense	57	55	58	56	57	55	57	58
Income before tax	(802)	(211)	(241)	(282)	(130)	(226)	24	103
Income tax expense	(250)	(88)	(94)	(119)	(43)	(83)	10	39
Net income	(552)	(123)	(147)	(163)	(87)	(143)	14	64
Wt. avg. shares for basic EPS—basic	219.5	219.4	219.3	218.3	217.4	213.3	216	229.2
Weighted average shares—diluted	219.5	219.4	219.3	218.3	217.4	213.3	216	231.7
Basic earnings per share	($2.51)	($0.56)	($0.67)	($0.75)	($0.40)	($0.67)	$0.06	$0.28
Diluted earnings per share	($2.51)	($0.56)	($0.67)	($0.75)	($0.40)	($0.67)	$0.06	$0.28

EXHIBIT 36.4 | Quarterly Balance Sheets 2011–2012 (in millions of dollars)

	Q4 2012	Q3 2012	Q2 2012	Q1 2012	Q4 2011	Q3 2011	Q2 2011	Q1 2011
Assets								
Current assets								
Cash and cash equivalents	930	525	888	839	1507	1085	1551	1767
Inventory	2,341	3,362	2993	3084	2916	4376	3572	3408
Other current assets	412	743	855	759	658	649	528	458
Total Current Assets	**3,683**	**4,630**	**4,736**	**4,682**	**5,081**	**6,110**	**5,651**	**5,633**
Property, plant, and equipment	5,353	5,493	5,153	5,126	5,176	5,242	5,237	5,226
Other assets	745	767	923	1,231	1,167	1,399	1,541	1,515
Total assets	**9,781**	**10,890**	**10,812**	**11,039**	**11,424**	**12,751**	**12,429**	**12,374**
Liabilities								
Current liabilities								
Merchandise accounts payable	1,162	1,408	1,015	984	1,022	1,831	1,386	1,274
Other accounts payable	1,380	1,344	1,219	1,222	1,503	1,404	1,381	1,396
Short-term and current long-term debt	26	22	250	231	231	231	0	0
Total current liabilities	**2,568**	**2,774**	**2,484**	**2,437**	**2,756**	**3,466**	**2,767**	**2,670**
Long-term debt	2,956	2,943	2901	2,871	2,871	2,871	3,099	3,099
Other liabilities	698	885	852	871	899	740	644	646
Deferred long-term liability charges	388	786	904	924	888	1,152	1,216	1,208
Total liabilities	**6,610**	**7,388**	**7,141**	**7,103**	**7,414**	**8,229**	**7,726**	**7,623**
Stockholders' equity								
Common stock	110	110	109	109	108	107	107	108
Retained earnings	380	932	1,057	1,204	1,412	1,541	1,728	1,819
Capital surplus	3,799	3789	3,782	3,767	3,699	3,619	3,605	3,587
Other stockholder equity	(1,118)	(1,329)	(1,277)	(1,144)	(1,209)	(745)	(737)	(763)
Total stockholder equity	**3,171**	**3,502**	**3,671**	**3,936**	**4,010**	**4,522**	**4,703**	**4,751**
Total liabilities and stockholders' equity	**9,781**	**10,890**	**10,812**	**11,039**	**11,424**	**12,751**	**12,429**	**12,374**

EXHIBIT 36.5 I   Capital Structure of J. C. Penney and Competitors (in millions of dollars as of June 30, 2012)

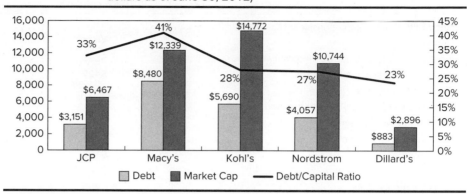

Debt includes all short-term and long-term interest-bearing debt. Operating leases are included in debt as six times the reported rental expense for the year.

Equity is computed on a market-value basis (i.e., market cap = stock price × shares outstanding).

EXHIBIT 36.6 I   Cash Balances: Q1 2010–Q4 2012 (in millions of dollars)

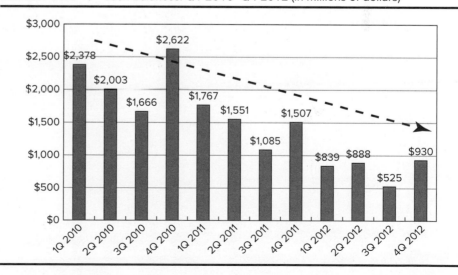

EXHIBIT 36.7 | Sources and Uses of Cash for 2012 (in millions of dollars)

	SOURCES of Cash:	USES of Cash:
Net profit/Loss + Comprehensive income/Loss	—	$894
Depreciation	$543	—
Increase/Decrease in net working capital	$838	—
Increase/Decrease in other assets	$422	—
Capital expenditures	—	$720
Decrease/Increase in other and deferred liabilities	—	$701
Net issuance/Retirement of debt	—	$120
Net issuance/Retirement of equity	—	—
Stock compensation	$102	—
Dividends	—	$47
TOTAL sources/Uses	**$1,905**	**$2,482**
Beginning cash balance	$1,507	
+ Sources of cash	$1,905	
– Uses of cash	($2,482)	
Ending cash balance	$930	

Source: Case writer estimates.

EXHIBIT 36.8 | Credit Rating History and Debt Yields J. C. Penney Long-Term Unsecured Senior Debt

Moody's		S&P	
4/1/2009	Ba1	4/16/2009	BB
5/18/2010	Ba1	4/7/2010	BB+
8/10/2012	Ba3	7/11/2012	B+

Moody's and Standard & Poor's (S&P) were the two largest credit rating agencies. Credit ratings were based on the assessment of the likelihood that the issuer would meet its financial obligation. The rating of a company's long-term unsecured senior debt was a key measure because such debt represented an important source of financing. The debt rating symbols for Moody's and S&P were as follows:

	Moody's	S&P	
↑	AAA	AAA	Extemely strong capacity to meet financial obligations
ǀ	Aa	AA	Very strong capacity to meet financial obligations
ǀ	A	A	Strong capacity to meet financial obligations
Investment Grade	Baa	BBB	Adequate capacity to meet financial obligation
Speculative Grade	Ba	BB	Substantial credit risk
ǀ	B	B	High credit risk
ǀ	Caa	CCC	Very high credit risk
ǀ	Ca	CC	Near default: some prospect of recovery of principal and interest
↓	C	C	Near default: little prospect of recovery of principal and interest
Default	D	D	

S&P ratings could be modified by the addition of a plus (+) or minus (−) sign to show relative standing within the major rating categories. Similarly, Moody's used numerical modifiers: 1 represented a plus, 2 was neutral, and 3 represented a minus. For example, Moody's "Baa1" was analogous to S&P's "BBB+."

Examples of interest rates as of December 31, 2012, for 10-year corporate bonds were 3.44% for BBB-rated debt, 4.89% for BB-rated debt, and 5.88% for B-rated debt.

Data sources: Bloomberg, Moodys.com, StandardandPoors.com.

EXHIBIT 36.9 | Stock Price Performance: January 2011–February 2013

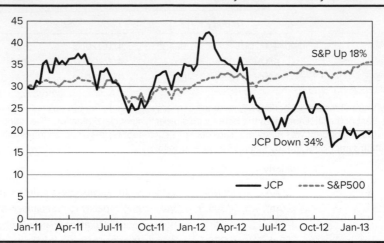

Data source: Yahoo! Finance.

Horizon Lines, Inc.

Even a small leak will sink a great ship[1]
—**Benjamin Franklin**

By April 1, 2011, the Horizon Lines 2010 annual report had been published with a statement from newly appointed CEO Stephen Fraser, explaining that the company expected to be in technical default on its debt. During the previous 50 years, Horizon Lines (Horizon) had revolutionized the global economy with the invention of containerized shipping to become the largest U.S. domestic ocean carrier. By the beginning of 2007, however, Horizon was unprofitable, and its losses had increased each year since (**Exhibit 37.1**). As negative earnings mounted, so did Horizon's debt burden: current liabilities had nearly quadrupled by the end of 2010 (**Exhibits 37.2** and **37.3**). The company had also suffered two major setbacks in the past six months: the loss of a key strategic alliance and $65 million in criminal and civil fines.

Management's reaction had been to conserve cash by cutting the common dividend for 2010 by more than half and then eliminating it completely beginning in the first quarter of 2011. Investors responded accordingly; the company's stock price dropped from $5 per share at the start of 2011 to a recent price of $0.85. Bondholders also were concerned as the market price of the convertible notes had fallen to $0.80 on the dollar, raising the yield on the notes to more than 20% (**Exhibit 37.4**).

Price Fixing in Puerto Rico

In October 2008, three Horizon executives and two executives from its competitor Sea Star Line pled guilty to crimes related to price fixing. A U.S. Department of Justice investigation revealed that for nearly six years, Horizon and Sea Star Line had colluded to fix prices, rig bids, and allocate customers. All five executives were sentenced to

---

[1]From Benjamin Franklin's "The Way to Wealth" essay written in 1758.

This case was prepared by Daniel Hake (MBA '12) under the direction of the Paul Tudor Jones Research Professor Kenneth M. Eades. All information about Horizon Lines was drawn from public sources. Some dates and amounts have been changed for pedagogical reasons. It was written as a basis for class discussion rather than to illustrate effective or ineffective handling of an administrative situation. Copyright © 2012 by the University of Virginia Darden School Foundation, Charlottesville, VA. All rights reserved. *To order copies, send an e-mail to* sales@dardenbusinesspublishing.com. *No part of this publication may be reproduced, stored in a retrieval system, used in a spreadsheet, or transmitted in any form or by any means—electronic, mechanical, photocopying, recording, or otherwise—without the permission of the Darden School Foundation.*

prison time, and Horizon began a long period of litigation that culminated in February 2011 when Horizon pleaded guilty to one felony count of violating the Sherman Antitrust Act. The court imposed a fine of $45 million to be paid out over the next five years.[2] On top of the criminal penalties, nearly 60 civil class-action lawsuits had also been filed against Horizon, which prompted the company to report a $20 million expense for legal settlements in 2009. In 2011, Horizon would begin payments on the criminal fine and expected to close out the civil claims with a payment of $11.8 million.

As a result of the legal difficulties, Horizon's board of directors announced that Chairman, President, and CEO Chuck Raymond would be leaving the company, and Stephen Fraser, a board member, would assume the roles of president and CEO.

The Jones Act

Consistent with most sectors in the transportation industry, shipping was greatly affected by government regulations. For almost a century, the U.S. domestic shipping market had been regulated by Section 27 of the Merchant Marine Act of 1920, more commonly known as the Jones Act.[3] The federal statute applied to maritime commerce traveling in U.S. waters between ports located on the U.S. mainland and in Alaska, Hawaii, and Puerto Rico. The law's purpose was to support the U.S. maritime industry by requiring that all goods transported by water between U.S. ports be carried on ships constructed and flagged in the United States.

In the last few decades, however, the economic conditions of the industry, in particular high labor rates in the United States, caused Jones Act vessels to have higher construction, maintenance, and operation costs than foreign vessels. This prompted critics to claim that the regulations were outdated and protectionist and that they hindered free trade and priced U.S. shipbuilders out of the international market. But the law had continued to receive political support from every U.S. president since Woodrow Wilson, who had originally signed it into law. In reference to the current political climate, Horizon's 2010 annual report stated: "The ongoing war on terrorism has further solidified political support for the Jones Act, as a vital and dedicated U.S. merchant marine cornerstone for strong homeland defense, as well as a critical source of trained U.S. mariners for wartime support."[4]

Despite the extra costs associated with the Jones Act, it also created an attractive competitive landscape for existing container ship operators in the market. Although container shipping between ports in the contiguous United States was no longer competitive with inland trucking, Jones Act carriers had been able to maintain an operating advantage on trade routes between the U.S. mainland, Alaska, Hawaii, and Puerto Rico. As of 2008, only 27 vessels, 19 of which were built before 1985, were qualified by the Jones Act. The high capital investments and long delivery lead times associated with

---

[2]Horizon's payment schedule was $1 million due immediately, $1 million at the end of year one, $3 million at the end of year two, $5 million at the end of year three, $15 million at the end of year four, and $20 million at the end of year five.

[3]Named after the bill's sponsor, U.S. Senator Wesley Jones.

[4]Horizon Lines annual report, 2010.

building a new containership created high barriers for new entrants. These barriers also caused the domestic market to be less fragmented and less vulnerable to overcapacity.

The Maersk Partnership

A major drawback of the Jones Act market was that very few goods were shipped back to the continental United States, leading to a severe imbalance in container utilization. This was particularly significant for Hawaii and Guam, because ships returning to the mainland had to travel a long distance with mostly empty containers. To alleviate this problem, Horizon entered into a strategic alliance with A.P. Moller-Maersk in the 1990s to share container space along the Hawaii and Guam lane. Under the terms of the agreement, Horizon used its vessels to ship a portion of its cargo in Maersk-owned containers on westbound routes. The cargo would be unloaded in Hawaii or Guam, and the empty containers would then be shipped to ports in China and Taiwan instead of directly back to the United States. After the vessels arrived in Asia, Maersk replaced the empty containers with loaded containers for Horizon to carry back to the West Coast of the United States.

This alliance was so beneficial that in 2006, Horizon entered into a long-term lease agreement with Ship Finance International Limited to charter five container vessels not qualified by the Jones Act to travel on its Asia-Pacific route. Horizon was obligated to charter each ship for 12 years from the date of delivery at an annual rate of $6.4 million per vessel. The economic conditions changed with the global recession of 2008, however, causing overcapacity in the international shipping market, which led to container freight rates falling significantly. Horizon's profitability also fell, due partly to top-line reductions but also to escalating fuel costs. Although Horizon was locked into its long-term lease until 2018–19, Maersk was only committed until December 2010, at which time the company elected to exit the alliance.

Shortly after termination of the partnership, Horizon attempted to cover its lease obligations by starting its own trans-Pacific shipping service. Unfortunately, by March 2011, freight rates continued to decline, and fuel costs continued to increase. Projections for the remainder of the year showed that eastbound freight rates would drop 35%, while the average price of fuel would increase 40%, which put the Pacific route into a significant operating-loss position.

Pushed by mounting operating losses, Horizon management decided to save money by shutting down its unprofitable routes in the Pacific and holding all five non-Jones Act vessels pier-side in a reduced operational state. Although Horizon would continue to incur leasing costs for those vessels for another eight or nine years, it eliminated most of the operating costs associated with the Pacific routes.

The Debt Structure

In 2007, when the future of the shipping business seemed bright and Horizon's stock was trading at an all-time high, the company completed a major round of refinancing to consolidate its debt into two sources. The first was a senior secured credit agreement that used all Horizon-owned assets as collateral. The senior credit facility included a

$125 million term loan and a $100 million five-year revolving credit facility provided by a lending group of major banks. The second source was $330 million of unsecured, 4.25% convertible senior notes which, like the term loan, matured in 2012. The notes were primarily held by three large mutual fund companies: Legg Mason, Pioneer Investment Management, and Angelo Gordon & Co. **Exhibit 37.5** provides the details of Horizon's debt structure.

Both the senior credit facility and the 4.25% convertible notes carried covenants that specified a maximum leverage ratio and a minimum interest coverage ratio.[5] By the time 2010 results were released, the company's poor earnings performance plus its payments for the criminal fine and the civil settlements made it apparent that the company would be unlikely to satisfy these covenants during 2011. Tripping a debt covenant would put the company in technical default, giving debt holders the right to call the loan (i.e., demand immediate and full payment of the principal outstanding). Unless Horizon could negotiate a change to the covenants to remove the default, it would almost certainly have to seek the protection of the bankruptcy courts because it would be impossible to raise new debt or equity under such dire circumstances.

Although Horizon was not expected to miss an interest payment the following quarter, future interest and principal payments would be accelerating and would place an increasing strain on Horizon's ability to meet its cash obligations, regardless of whether the company satisfied the debt covenants. For example, the $125 million term loan required Horizon to make quarterly principal payments of $4.7 million through September 2011, at which point the principal payments escalated to $18.4 million until August 2012 when the loan matured. Interest payments on the senior credit facility were due semiannually (February and August) and averaged about 4.6%. The convertible notes carried a low coupon rate of 4.25%, but the $330 million principal would also be due in August 2012. **Exhibit 37.6** provides management's report of interest, principal, and other contractual obligations for 2011 and beyond. **Exhibit 37.7** shows current interest rates for government and corporate debt obligations.

Restructuring Options

On the operational side, in addition to shutting down the Pacific routes, Horizon had made attempts to reduce headcount, but this had had little impact, since much of the work force was protected by unions. The next step would be to divest underperforming business units or sell the entire business to a strategic buyer. Given the high barriers to entry for the domestic market and the general view that container traffic was relatively stable, finding a buyer was feasible, but finding a buyer that would pay a reasonable price would be difficult to execute in the near term. The net effect was that Horizon was expecting poor performance for 2011 as operating costs were rising, and shutting down

---

[5]The interest coverage ratio was defined as Adjusted EBITDA/Cash Interest, and the leverage ratio was computed as Senior Secured Debt/Adjusted EBITDA (annualized). Between the credit facility and the convertible notes, the tightest covenant requirements were a minimum interest coverage ratio of 2.75× for each quarter of 2011 and a maximum leverage ratio of 3.25× for each quarter of 2011. The use of Adjusted EBITDA in the covenants was the result of a negotiation with the holders of the convertible notes after the $45 million of criminal fines casued a covenant to be breached.

the Pacific routes would add to those expenses for 2011. Longer term, the reduced operations were expected to decrease Horizon's revenues for 2012, but they would also allow the company to show positive EBIT starting in 2013 (**Exhibit 37.8**).

Realistically, the only viable alternative to avoid a default in 2011 was for Horizon to restructure its capital structure. For a financial restructuring, there were three basic options available to Stephen Fraser and his management team.

Option 1: Issue new equity

A straightforward way to inject capital into the business would be to issue new shares of common stock. Horizon could use the funds from the new stock offering to pay down its debt obligation and give the business additional capital to grow the Jones Act side of the business. This was relatively easy and required no negotiations with existing debt holders.

Option 2: File for Chapter 11

As a U.S. business, Horizon had the option of filing for protection under Chapter 11 of the U.S. Bankruptcy code.[6] Fraser could file immediately and rely on the bankruptcy judge to oversee the reorganization. Normally, the judge would request a plan of reorganization (POR) from management that specified how the company needed to be changed in order to emerge from Chapter 11 as an economically viable entity. The primary purpose of the POR was to present a blueprint of how to restructure the balance sheet to a manageable level of interest and principal payments. This meant that many of the debt claimants were asked to accept new securities that summed to less than the face value of their claim.

The amount of the *haircut* would depend upon the seniority of the claim. For example, a senior secured lender might receive full cash payment for its claim, whereas a junior unsecured lender might receive a combination of new debt and equity representing $0.40 on the dollar of the face value of the original debt. The judge would not allow senior claimants to take a larger haircut than any junior claimant, nor would the judge entertain a POR that was unlikely to receive the voting approval of all the impaired claimants. If the judge thought a POR was fair to all claimants and provided a viable capital structure for the company going forward, he or she could overrule a dissenting class of claimants in order to force a solution. In this regard, the judge played the role of mediator in a negotiation process that often involved many revisions to the POR before being accepted by all parties, or the judge exercised the right to *cram down* the plan in order to enact it.

A Chapter 11 bankruptcy was designed to give a failing company the best possible chance to restructure and continue operating as a viable enterprise. The courts served the purpose of intervening with bill collectors to protect the company from being forced to liquidate in order to make an interest or principal payment. The theory was that it was better to have an orderly reorganization within the court system that resulted in a viable

---

[6]Matthias Hild, "A Managerial Primer on the U.S. Bankruptcy Code," UVA-QA-0633 (Charlottesville, VA: Darden Business Publishing, 2008) reviews Chapter 11 bankruptcy rules.

company that could continue to pay its suppliers and employees than to allow the company to disintegrate in the chaos of a feeding frenzy of its creditors. Companies continued to operate normally while in Chapter 11, so most customers were not aware of the reorganization process. If the company needed additional capital to grow the business, it could simply increase the size of the new debt and equity offerings as part of the POR.

Option 3: Restructure the debt directly

This approach had the same objective as using Chapter 11. Negotiating a deal directly with the debt holders, however, had the advantage of being faster, and it avoided court costs. The typical Chapter 11 process took months or years to resolve and resulted in large legal fees for both company and claimants. To be successful, Horizon would need to exchange its existing debt for a combination of new notes and common shares. The swap would give the existing debt holders a reduced claim on the company, but it would be a claim that was much more likely to be serviced. At the same time, Horizon could ask creditors to accept a new set of covenants and a longer maturity to alleviate the short-term cash-flow crunch it currently faced. The net effect would be to lengthen the maturity of the outstanding debt plus reduce the overall amount of debt outstanding and therefore reduce the level of interest payments.

As part of the restructuring, Horizon also needed to receive new capital to pay off the senior credit facility and help grow the Jones Act business. The new capital could come from issuing shares to the public in addition to the shares distributed to the existing debt holders to satisfy their claims on the company. Horizon could also raise the capital by issuing new debt. Regardless of whether the new capital was debt or equity, it would be expensive and reflect the high risk associated with Horizon. For example, given the low stock price, it would require a large number of new shares to raise a meaningful amount of equity money. Also for such a risky situation, any new lender would require collateral for the debt plus an interest rate in the range of 10% to 15%.

Restructuring had several disadvantages. First, it would be unlikely that Horizon could successfully include any claimants other than the senior creditors. Like most companies with strong unions, Horizon offered a defined-benefit pension plan to its employees, and that plan was underfunded. A Chapter 11 proceeding could result in a reduction of the benefits paid to employees, which would reduce the company's own mandatory contributions to the plan. But such changes were very difficult to enact outside of the court system, so if Horizon opted to restructure its debt directly, it would need to focus solely on the claims of the senior credit facility and the convertible bonds. A second disadvantage was that a voluntary restructuring created a risk for the claimants. In particular, if Horizon were to declare bankruptcy shortly after the restructuring, the Chapter 11 proceedings would start from the newly restructured claims. Therefore, if debt holders had agreed to accept equity in lieu of all or part of their original debt claim, the courts would view the reduced debt claim as the relevant claim for the Chapter 11 proceedings. Once a claimant voluntarily agreed to a reduction of its original claim, that claim was gone forever.

Stephen Fraser was not in an enviable position. Regardless of the option he chose, the company's success was not guaranteed. Moreover, with the covenant default approaching, it was time to "right the ship," but a poor choice by Fraser at this point could take his company down and his career along with it.

EXHIBIT 37.1 | Consolidated Statement of Operations, December 31, 2008–10
(in thousands of U.S. dollars)

	2010	2009	2008
Operating Revenue	1,162,505	1,124,215	1,270,978
Operating expense			
Cost of services (excluding depreciation expense)	989,923	922,959	1,047,871
Depreciation and amortization	44,475	44,307	44,537
Amortization of vessel drydocking	15,046	13,694	17,162
Selling, general and administrative	83,232	97,257	103,328
Legal settlements	31,770	20,000	0
Miscellaneous expense and charges	3,909	3,710	12,018
Total operating expense	1,168,355	1,101,927	1,224,916
Operating (loss) income	(5,850)	22,288	46,062
Interest expense, net	(40,117)	(38,036)	(39,923)
Income tax and other (expense) benefit	(332)	(10,659)	4,214
Loss from discontinued operations	(11,670)	(4,865)	(12,946)
Net loss	**(57,969)**	**(31,272)**	**(2,593)**
Basic and diluted loss per share	(1.88)	(1.03)	(0.09)
Dividends declared per share	0.20	0.44	0.44

Data source: Horizon Lines annual report, 2010.

EXHIBIT 37.2 | Consolidated Balance Sheet Statements, December 31, 2009–10
(in thousands of U.S. dollars)

	2010	2009
Assets		
Cash	2,751	6,419
Accounts receivable, net of allowance	111,887	115,069
Materials and supplies	29,413	30,254
Other current assets	21,638	30,059
Total current assets	165,689	181,801
Property and equipment, net	194,657	192,624
Goodwill and intangible assets, net	394,973	419,008
Other long-term assets	30,438	25,678
Total assets	**785,757**	**819,111**
Liabilities		
Accounts payable	43,413	42,372
Current portion of long-term debt*	508,793	18,750
Other accrued liabilities	115,895	115,697
Total current liabilities	668,101	176,819
Long-term debt, net of current portion*	7,530	496,105
Deferred rent, taxes and other liabilities	70,334	44,909
Total liabilities	745,965	717,833
Common stock**	345	341
Treasury stock, 3,800 shares at cost	(78,538)	(78,538)
Additional paid in capital	193,266	196,900
Accumulated deficit	(75,281)	(17,425)
Total stockholders' equity	39,792	101,278
Total liabilities and stockholders' equity	**785,757**	**819,111**

*Includes capital lease.

**Common stock, $0.01 par value, 100,000 shares authorized, 34,546 shares issued and 30,746 shares outstanding on December 26, 2010, and 34,091 shares issued and 30,291 shares outstanding on December 20, 2009.

Data source: Horizon Lines annual report, 2010.

EXHIBIT 37.3 | Consolidated Cash Flow Statements, December 31, 2008–10
(in thousands of U.S. dollars)

	2010	2009	2008
Cash flows from operating activities			
Net (loss) income from continuing operations	(46,299)	(26,407)	10,353
Adjustments			
Depreciation	23,777	24,002	24,232
Amortization of intangibles	20,698	20,305	20,305
Amortization of vessel drydocking	15,046	13,694	17,162
Impairment charge	2,655	1,867	6,030
Restructuring charge	2,057	787	3,126
Amortization of deferred financing costs	3,412	2,947	2,693
Deferred income taxes	148	10,617	(4,153)
Gain on equipment disposals	(47)	(154)	(24)
Gain on sale of interest in joint venture	(724)	0	0
Loss on early modification/extinguishment of debt	0	50	0
Accretion on convertible notes	11,060	10,011	8,901
Stock-based compensation	2,122	3,096	3,651
Accounts receivable, net	1,301	13,710	7,931
Materials and supplies	807	(6,739)	7,636
Other current assets	(1,148)	1,247	23
Accounts payable	1,041	910	1,434
Accrued liabilities	5,581	(767)	(5,653)
Vessel rent	(3,898)	(4,874)	(4,883)
Vessel dry-docking payments	(19,159)	(14,735)	(13,913)
Accrued legal settlements	26,770	15,000	0
Other assets/liabilities	(768)	(3,486)	3,506
Net cash provided by operating activities	**44,432**	**61,081**	**88,357**
Cash flows from investing activities			
Purchases of equipment	(16,298)	(12,931)	(38,639)
Proceeds from the sale of interest in joint venture	1,100	0	0
Proceeds from sale of equipment	454	1,237	500
Net cash used in investing activities	**(14,744)**	**(11,694)**	**(38,139)**
Cash flows from financing activities			
Borrowing under revolving credit facility	108,800	64,000	78,000
Payments on revolving credit facility	(108,800)	(84,000)	(80,000)
Payments of long-term debt	(18,750)	(7,968)	(6,538)
Dividend to stockholders	(6,281)	(13,397)	(13,273)
Payment of financing costs	(75)	(3,492)	(139)
Common stock issued under employee stock purchase plan	111	104	38
Payments on capital lease obligation	(124)	0	(81)
Purchase of treasury stock	0	0	(29,330)
Proceeds from exercise of stock options	0	0	13
Net cash used in financing activities	**(25,119)**	**(44,753)**	**(51,310)**
Net change in cash from continuing operations	4,569	4,634	(1,092)
Net change in cash from discontinued operations	(8,237)	(3,702)	303
Net change in cash	**(3,668)**	**932**	**(789)**
Cash at beginning of year.	6,419	5,487	6,276
Cash at end of year.	2,751	6,419	5,487

Data source: Horizon Lines annual report, 2010, (F-5).

EXHIBIT 37.4 | Horizon Lines (HRZ) Stock Price and Convertible Notes Price

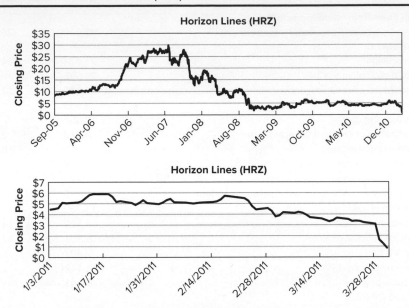

Recent Closing Prices and Yields for March 2011

	Mar. 29	Mar. 30	Mar. 31
Common stock ($ per share)	1.62	1.27	0.85
4.25% convertible notes (per $100 face value)	91.1	90.0	80.0
4.25% convertible notes (yield to maturity)	10.8%	10.9%	20.4%

Data sources: Yahoo! Finance, NYSE, and author estimates.

EXHIBIT 37.5 | Debt Structure* (in thousands of U.S. dollars)

	2010	2009
Term loan**	93,750	112,500
Revolving credit facility**	100,000	100,000
4.25% convertible senior notes***	313,414	302,355
Capital lease obligations	9,159	—
Total long-term debt	516,323	514,855

*Both the senior credit facility and the 4.25% convertible notes carried covenants that specified a maximum leverage ratio and a minimum interest coverage ratio. The interest coverage ratio was defined as Adjusted EBITDA/Cash Interest, and the leverage ratio was computed as Senior Secured Debt/Adjusted EBITDA (annualized). Between the credit facility and the convertible notes, the tightest covenant requirements were a minimum interest coverage ratio of 2.75x for each quarter of 2011 and a maximum leverage ratio of 3.25x for each quarter of 2011. For purposes of the covenants, EBITDA was adjusted to report legal settlements on a cash basis.

**The senior credit facility is provided by a lending group of major banks and is composed of the term loan and the revolving credit facility and is secured by substantially all of the assets of the company. Interest payments on the revolver are variable and are based on the three-month London Inter-Bank Offered Rate (LIBOR) plus 3.25%. Through the use of an interest rate swap, the term loan bears interest at a fixed rate of 4.52% per annum. The weighted average interest rate for the facility was 4.6% at the end of 2010. Remaining quarterly principal payments for the term loan are specified as $4.7 million through September 30, 2011, and $18.8 million until final maturity on August 8, 2012.

***The notes are unsecured and mature on August 15, 2012. The aggregate principal amount of $330 million for the notes is recorded net of original issue discount. Each $1,000 of principal is convertible into 26.9339 shares of Horizon's common stock, which is the equivalent of $37.13 per share. The notes were primarily held by three large mutual fund companies: Legg Mason, Pioneer Investment Management, and Angelo Gordon & Co.

Data sources: Horizon Lines 10-K filing, 2010, and author estimates.

EXHIBIT 37.6 | Contractual Obligations, 2011 and Beyond
(in thousands of U.S. dollars)

	2011	2012	2013	2014	2015	2016	After 2016	Total Obligations
Principal and operating lease obligations								
Senior credit facility*	18,750	175,000						193,750
4.25% convertible senior notes*	—	330,000						330,000
Operating leases	100,373	105,681	105,681	67,770	67,770	67,770	143,035	658,080
Capital lease	1,629	1,307	1,307	756	756	756	2,647	9,158
Subtotal	120,752	611,988	106,988	68,526	68,526	68,526	145,682	1,190,988
Cash interest obligations**								
Senior credit facility	8,913	8,050						16,963
4.25% convertible senior notes	14,025	14,025						28,050
Capital lease	857	620	620	262	262	262	277	3,160
Subtotal	23,795	22,695	620	262	262	262	277	48,173
Legal settlements**	12,767	4,000	5,000	15,000	20,000			56,767
Other commitments	14,932	119	100					15,151
Total obligations	172,246	638,802	112,708	83,788	88,788	68,788	145,959	1,311,079

*Horizon has announced that it expects a covenant default on its debt. The company has until May 21, 2011, to obtain a waiver from the debt holders, which if not received could result in the holders' demanding acceleration of all principal and interest payments. In addition, due to cross-default provisions, such a default could lead to the acceleration of the maturity of all the company's scheduled principal and interest payments.

**Interest payments on the term loan portion of the senior credit facility are fixed via an interest rate swap at 4.52%. Interest payments on the revolver portion of the senior credit facility are variable and are computed as LIBOR plus 3.25%. The weighted average interest rate for the facility was 4.6% at the end of 2010. Interest on the 4.25% convertible senior notes is fixed and is paid semiannually on February 15 and August 15 of each year, until maturity on August 15, 2012.

***Legal settlement for 2011 consists of a $1 million charge for the $45 million criminal fines and $11.767 million as final settlement of the civil lawsuits. The civil settlement was originally recorded as $20 million in 2009, of which $5 million was paid immediately, and the remainder was eventually settled as $11.767 million.

Data sources: Horizon Lines 10-K filing, 2010, and author estimates.

EXHIBIT 37.7 | Interest Rates for March 31, 2011
U.S. Treasury Yields

U.S. Treasury Yields	
1-Year	0.19%
10-Year	3.17%
Corporate Yields	
6-Month LIBOR	0.41%
Prime	3.25%
AAA	4.14%
AA	4.35%
A	4.49%
BBB	4.99%
BB	6.52%
B	7.94%

Data source: Yahoo! Finance.

EXHIBIT 37.8 | Operating Cash Flow Projections for 2011–15
(in thousands of U.S. dollars)

	2010	2011E	2012E	2013E	2014E	2015E
Operating Revenue*	1,162,505	1,220,630	915,473	942,937	971,225	1,000,362
Operating expense						
Cost of services (excluding depreciation expense)	989,923	1,074,155	778,152	782,638	786,692	800,289
Depreciation and amortization	59,521	59,521	59,521	59,521	59,521	59,521
Selling, general and administrative	83,232	87,394	65,545	67,512	69,537	71,623
Other charges	3,909	4,000	4,000	4,000	4,000	4,000
Total operating expense	1,136,585	1,225,069	907,218	913,670	919,750	935,433
EBIT (before legal settlements)	25,920	(4,439)	8,255	29,267	51,475	64,928
– Legal settlements (cash basis)	(5,000)	(12,767)	(4,000)	(5,000)	(15,000)	(20,000)
Adjusted EBIT	20,920	(17,206)	4,255	24,267	36,475	44,928
Adjusted EBITDA**	80,441	42,315	63,776	83,788	95,996	104,449
Assumptions:						
Cost of services/revenue	85%	88.0%	85.0%	83.0%	81.0%	80.0%
SG&A/revenue	7%	7.2%	7.2%	7.2%	7.2%	7.2%
Revenue growth		5.0%	−25.0%	3.0%	3.0%	3.0%
EBIT/revenue	1.8%	−1.4%	0.5%	2.6%	3.8%	4.5%

*Revenues for 2012 and beyond reflect the shutdown of unprofitable routes in the Pacific.

**Cash flow projections are computed using an "adjusted" EBITDA for which legal settlements are recorded on an expected cash basis. In contrast, GAAP requires EBIT to be computed based on settlement charges computed as the present value of the future payments and reported in the year of the settlement. Specifically, Horizon reported $31.77 million as legal settlements for 2010, which represented the present value of the $45 million to be received over the ensuing five years. Legal settlement for 2011 consists of a $1 million charge for the $45 million criminal fines and $11.767 million as final settlement of the civil lawsuits. Debt covenants use adjusted EBITDA for the leverage and interest coverage ratios.

Source: Author estimates.

Analysis of Financing Tactics: Leases, Options, and Foreign Currency

Baker Adhesives

In early June 2006, Doug Baker met with his sales manager Alissa Moreno to discuss the results of a recent foray into international markets. This was new territory for Baker Adhesives, a small company manufacturing specialty adhesives. Until a recent sale to Novo, a Brazilian toy manufacturer, all of Baker Adhesives' sales had been to companies not far from its Newark, New Jersey, manufacturing facility. As U.S. manufacturing continued to migrate overseas, however, Baker would be under intense pressure to find new markets, which would inevitably lead to international sales.

Doug Baker was looking forward to this meeting. The recent sale to Novo, while modest in size at 1,210 gallons, had been a significant financial boost to Baker Adhesives. The order had used up some raw-materials inventory that Baker had considered reselling at a significant loss a few months before the Novo order. Furthermore, the company had been running well under capacity and the order was easily accommodated within the production schedule. The purpose of the meeting was to finalize details on a new order from Novo that was to be 50% larger than the original order. Also, payment for the earlier Novo order had just been received and Baker was looking forward to paying down some of the balance on the firm's line of credit.

As Baker sat down with Moreno, he could tell immediately that he was in for bad news. It came quickly. Moreno pointed out that since the Novo order was denominated in Brazilian reais (BRL), the payment from Novo had to be converted into U.S. dollars (USD) at the current exchange rate.[1] Given exchange-rate changes since the time Baker Adhesives and Novo had agreed on a per-gallon price, the value of the payment was substantially lower than anticipated. More disappointing was the fact that Novo was unwilling to consider a change in the per-gallon price for the follow-on order. Translated into dollars, therefore, the new order would not be as profitable as the original order had initially appeared. In fact, given further anticipated changes

---

[1]The Brazilian currency is referred to as *real* in the singular (as in "the Brazilian real") and *reais* in the plural (as in "sales are denominated in reais").

in exchange rates the new order would not even be as profitable as the original order had turned out to be!

Adhesives Market

The market for adhesives was dominated by a few large firms that provided the vast bulk of adhesives in the United States and in global markets. The adhesives giants had international manufacturing and sourcing capabilities. Margins on most adhesives were quite slim since competition was fierce. In response, successful firms had developed ever more efficient production systems which, to a great degree, relied on economies of scale.

The focus on scale economies had left a number of specialty markets open for small and technically savvy firms. The key to success in the specialty market was not the efficient manufacture of large quantities, but figuring out how to feasibly and economically produce relatively small batches with distinct properties. In this market, a good chemist and a flexible production system were key drivers of success. Baker Adhesives had both. The business was started by Doug Baker's father, a brilliant chemist who left a big company to focus on the more interesting, if less marketable, products that eventually became the staple of Baker Adhesives' product line. While Baker's father had retired some years ago, he had attracted a number of capable new employees, and the company was still an acknowledged leader in the specialty markets. The production facilities, though old, were readily adaptable and had been well maintained.

Until just a few years earlier, Baker Adhesives had done well financially. While growth in sales had never been a strong point, margins were generally high and sales levels steady. The company had never employed long-term debt and still did not do so. The firm had a line of credit from a local bank, which had always provided sufficient funds to cover short-term needs. Baker Adhesives presently owed about USD180,000 on the credit line. Baker had an excellent relationship with the bank, which had been with the company from the beginning.

Novo Orders

The original order from Novo was for an adhesive Novo was using in the production of a new line of toys for its Brazilian market. The toys needed to be waterproof and the adhesive, therefore, needed very specific properties. Through a mutual friend, Moreno had been introduced to Novo's purchasing agent. Working with Doug Baker, she had then negotiated the original order in February (the basis for the pricing of that original order is shown in **Exhibit 38.1**). Novo had agreed to pay shipping costs, so Baker Adhesives simply had to deliver the adhesive in 55-gallon drums to a nearby shipping facility.

The proposed new order was similar to the last one. As before, Novo agreed to make payment 30 days after receipt of the adhesives at the shipping facility. Baker anticipated a five-week manufacturing cycle once all the raw materials were in place. All materials would be secured within two weeks. Allowing for some flexibility, Moreno believed payment would be received about three months from order placement; that was about how long the original order took. For this reason, Moreno expected receipt of payment on the new order, assuming it was agreed upon immediately, somewhere around September 5, 2006.

Exchange Risks

With her newfound awareness of exchange-rate risks, Moreno had gathered additional information on exchange-rate markets before the meeting with Doug Baker. The history of the dollar-to-real exchange rate is shown in **Exhibit 38.2**. Furthermore, the data in that exhibit provided the most recent information on money markets and an estimate of the expected future (September 5, 2006) spot rates from a forecasting service.

Moreno had discussed her concerns about exchange-rate changes with the bank when she had arranged for conversion of the original Novo payment.[2] The bank, helpful as always, had described two ways in which Baker could mitigate the exchange risk from any new order: hedge in the forward market or hedge in the money markets.

Hedge in the forward market

Banks would often provide their clients with guaranteed exchange rates for the future exchange of currencies (forward rates). These contracts specified a date, an amount to be exchanged, and a rate. Any bank fee would be built into the rate. By securing a forward rate for the date of a foreign-currency-denominated cash flow, a firm could eliminate any risk due to currency fluctuations. In this case, the anticipated future inflow of reais from the sale to Novo could be converted at a rate that would be known today.

Hedge in the money markets

Rather than eliminate exchange risk through a contracted future exchange rate, a firm could make any currency exchanges at the known current spot rate. To do this, of course, the firm needed to convert future expected cash flows into current cash flows. This was done on the money market by borrowing "today" in a foreign currency against an expected future inflow or making a deposit "today" in a foreign account so as to be able to meet a future outflow. The amount to be borrowed or deposited would depend on the interest rates in the foreign currency because a firm would not wish to transfer more or less than what would be needed. In this case, Baker Adhesives would borrow in reais

---

[2]Though Baker Adhesives had a capable accountant, Doug Baker had decided to let Alissa Moreno handle the exchange-rate issues arising from the Novo order until they better understood the decisions and tradeoffs that needed to be made.

against the future inflow from Novo. The amount the company would borrow would be an amount such that the Novo receipt would exactly cover both principal and interest on the borrowing.

After some discussion and negotiation with the bank and bank affiliates, Moreno was able to secure the following agreements: Baker Adhesives' bank had agreed to offer a forward contract for September 5, 2006, at an exchange rate of 0.4227 USD/BRL. An affiliate of the bank, located in Brazil and familiar with Novo, was willing to provide Baker with a short-term real loan, secured by the Novo receivable, at 26%.[3] Moreno was initially shocked at this rate, which was more than three times the 8.52% rate on Baker's domestic line of credit; however, the bank described Brazil's historically high inflation and the recent attempts by the government to control inflation with high interest rates. The rate they had secured was typical of the market at the time.

The Meeting

It took Doug Baker some time to get over his disappointment. If international sales were the key to the future of Baker Adhesives, however, Baker realized he had already learned some important lessons. He vowed to put those lessons to good use as he and Moreno turned their attention to the new Novo order.

---

[3]Note that the loan from the bank affiliate was a 26% annual percentage rate for a three-month loan (the bank would charge exactly 6.5% on a three-month loan, to be paid when the principal was repaid). The effective rate over three months was, therefore, 6.5%. The 8.52% rate for Baker's line of credit was an annual percentage rate based on monthly compounding. The effective monthly rate was, therefore, $8.52\% \div 12 = 0.71\%$, which implies a $(1.0071)^3 - 1 = 2.1452\%$ effective rate over three months.

EXHIBIT 38.1 | Novo Price Calculation on Initial Order
(figures in U.S. dollars unless otherwise specified)

Labor	6,000
Materials	32,500
Manufacturing overhead	4,000
Administrative overhead	2,000
Total costs	44,500
Profit margin (12%)	6,068
Cost plus profit margin in dollars	50,568
Conversion (USD/BRL)	0.4636
Cost plus markup (BRL)	109,077
Amount (gallons)	1,210
Quoted price per gallon (BRL)	90.15

Notes:

The exchange rate used in the calculation was obtained from the *Wall Street Journal.*

Overhead was applied based on labor hours.

The raw materials expense was based on the original cost (book value) of the materials.

The rounded price of BRL90.15 per gallon was used in negotiations with Novo. Thus, for the final order, Novo was billed a total of BRL90.15 × 1,210 = BRL109,081.50.

Source: Created by case writer.

EXHIBIT 38.2 | Exchange Rate and Money-Market Information

Exchange rates for the real as of June 5, 2006 (USD/BRL)	
Bid on real	0.4368
Ask for real	0.4371
Consensus forecast bid for September 5, 2006	0.4234
Consensus forecast ask for September 5, 2006	0.4239
Standard deviation of monthly exchange-rate changes	
2005	3.36%
Year to date 2006	6.53%
Interbank rates (annual effective rates)	
Brazil	19.47%
United States	5.08%

Data source: *Wall Street Journal.*

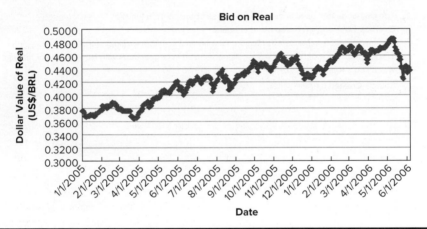

Source: Created by case writer.

Vale SA

Headquartered in Brazil but with a global presence, Vale SA was the world's largest producer of iron ore and second-largest producer of nickel. The company had continued growing rapidly despite the global economic downturn that had begun in 2007 and, by April 2010, was in need of (U.S. dollars) USD1.0 billion of additional capital. This issue was intended to support organic growth, particularly with respect to investments in its fertilizer business. Historically, Vale issued bonds in U.S. dollars, but the conditions in global capital markets suggested that the firm should consider borrowing in other currencies. In particular, the company was considering an eight-year bond that could be priced close to par at a coupon rate of 4.375% in euros, 5.475% in British pounds, or 5.240% in U.S. dollars.

Early 2010 was a good time for companies to issue debt if they were able. Central banks across the globe had been keeping interest rates at record lows for an extended period to support economic recovery, and this, in turn, would lower the real cost of borrowing. Other market conditions favored Vale and suggested an issue denominated in euros or British pounds to take advantage of interest in Vale credit from investors in Europe and Great Britain, respectively. First, companies in emerging markets were viewed favorably since their economies had recovered more quickly than developed economies, and investors therefore viewed them as more financially sound. This was particularly true of Latin America. Second, the market had little interest in issues by European or British companies. In fact, investors had abandoned European assets in general due to concerns about the European economy, and this had resulted in a depreciation of the euro against major currencies. Similarly, a high level of UK debt relative to the British pound combined with political uncertainty around the parliamentary elections had depressed interest in British assets.

Given the high cost of local-currency borrowing in Brazil and the fact that many of the commodities it sold were priced in U.S. dollars, Vale had traditionally looked to U.S. dollar debt markets.[1] Certainly, going global with its financing was the right thing

---

[1]The Brazilian government benchmark overnight rate had averaged close to 14% over the prior five years and, though declining recently, was still close to 11%.

This case was prepared by Associate Professor Marc Lipson with the assistance of Vahid Gholampour (MBA '12). It was written as a basis for class discussion rather than to illustrate effective or ineffective handling of an administrative situation. Copyright © 2011 by the University of Virginia Darden School Foundation, Charlottesville, VA. All rights reserved. *To order copies, send an e-mail to* sales@dardenbusinesspublishing.com. *No part of this publication may be reproduced, stored in a retrieval system, used in a spreadsheet, or transmitted in any form or by any means—electronic, mechanical, photocopying, recording, or otherwise—without the permission of the Darden School Foundation.*

to do. Still, at the time, it also seemed that markets other than the United States might look attractive.

Vale SA

Vale was founded by the Brazilian government in 1974 and privatized in 1997. A focus on mining became Vale's prevailing strategy after its privatization. The firm sold its steel and wood pulp businesses between 2000 and 2007. Vale acquired several iron ore manufacturing companies during that period and gained control of 85% of Brazil's 300 million tons of annual iron ore production by 2007. The company also invested in the iron transportation infrastructure: Vale owned three major railway concessions, 800 locomotives, and more than 35,000 freight cars and either owned or operated six ports.[2]

Much of the Vale mining business was concentrated on iron and in Brazil. To mitigate the impact of iron ore price changes on its revenue and net income and to diversify globally, Vale launched a diversification program in 2001. The share of nonferrous metals, including aluminum, alumina, copper, cobalt, gold, and nickel, increased as a fraction of Vale's revenue from 7% in 2000 to 30.7% in 2009. Global acquisitions included Canico Resource Corp. (a Canadian nickel company), AMCI Holdings Inc. (an Australian coal-mining company), and Inco Limited (Canada's second-largest mining company). The acquisition of Inco for USD18.9 billion was the largest acquisition ever made by a Brazilian company. By 2009, over half of Vale's revenue (56.9%) came from Asia; Brazil, the Americas excluding Brazil, and Europe accounted for 15.3%, 8.7%, and 16.9% of the revenue, respectively.

The firm experienced strong growth from 2005 to 2009. Revenue increased at a compound annual growth rate (CAGR) of 17.5%, and earnings per share rose at a CAGR of 7%. For the same period, capital spending averaged 360% of depreciation, and dividends increased at a CAGR of 18.9%. Vale's consolidated financial results are presented in **Exhibit 39.1** and **Exhibit 39.2**.

Global Markets

The financial crisis that sparked the global recession starting in 2007 had only slightly abated by the start of 2010. The weak global economy had forced central banks to loosen their monetary policy and governments to use stimulus plans to prevent further slowdown in major economies around the world. As a result, several European countries were dealing with huge fiscal deficits and high levels of debt relative to GDP.[3] The fiscal situation in emerging markets was exactly the opposite. Most emerging markets were running trade surpluses and had average debt-to-GDP ratios of 30%. Those markets were expected to grow faster than industrial countries' markets should the global

---

[2]Vale SEC 20-F filings, 2000–09.

[3]Riva Froymovich, "PIMCO Embraces Emerging-Market Corporate Debt," *Wall Street Journal*, April 26, 2010.

economy recover. In particular, Latin American economies were well positioned for growth, and some sovereign debts traded at rates favorable to highly rated European corporates.[4]

Emerging economies were also appealing to investors, since they provided geographic diversification and offered high return in a very low interest rate environment. In fact, investors were selling highly rated sovereign debt and buying riskier emerging-market corporate bonds.[5] The fact that emerging-market governments didn't need excessive external financing generated substantial demand for high-quality corporate debt. The overall situation created a good place for large emerging-market companies to tap global bond markets.

Major central banks had slashed short-term interest rates to near zero in response to the global recession. With treasury interest rates at historically low levels, investors looked increasingly to riskier assets for higher returns. As a result, corporate bonds looked quite attractive. In 2009, large European companies had raised substantial funds, largely to boost cash reserves. **Figure 39.1** shows quarterly government bond yields by government, and **Figure 39.2** shows credit spreads for corporate issues (BBB-rated issuers) by currency. **Exhibit 39.3** provides interest rates and exchange rates by maturity for the U.S. dollar, euro, and British pound, as well as data on spot exchange rates.

Investors across the globe were big buyers of emerging-market corporate bonds. Emerging-market issuers were glad to access these global capital flows given the high local currency borrowing rates. For example, nominal and real interest rates in Brazil were still higher than those of comparably rated countries. Even though credible fiscal and monetary policy in Brazil suggested that the gap between Brazilian interest rates and rates in developed countries would narrow, observers expected an aggressive

FIGURE 39.1 | Quarterly government bond yields.

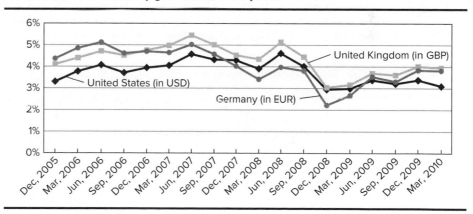

Data source: Bloomberg.

---

[4]Sid Verma, "Latin American Debt: Backed by Popular Demand," *Emerging Markets*, March 23, 2010, http://www.emergingmarkets.org (accessed Oct. 26, 2010).

[5]Riva Froymovich, "In Emerging-Market Debt, the Riskier the Better," *Wall Street Journal*, January 23, 2010.

FIGURE 39.2 | Quarterly credit spreads for corporate issues (BBB-rated issuers) by currency.

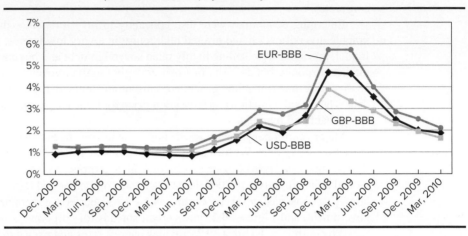

Data source: Bloomberg.

tightening following a robust recovery and were concerned about inflation due to increases in commodity prices. **Figure 39.3** shows quarterly historic inflation rates for the Brazilian real, euro, U.S. dollar, and British pound. The general consensus was that over the next five years, inflation rates would remain high at about 8.0% for the Brazilian real, would drop to about 3.1% for the British pound, and would rise slightly to about 2.8% and 2.1% for the U.S. dollar and euro, respectively.

FIGURE 39.3 | Quarterly inflation rates by currency.

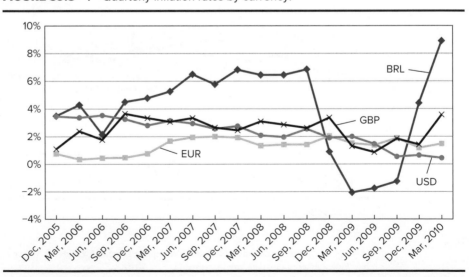

Data source: Bloomberg.

FIGURE 39.4 | Monthly exchange rates.

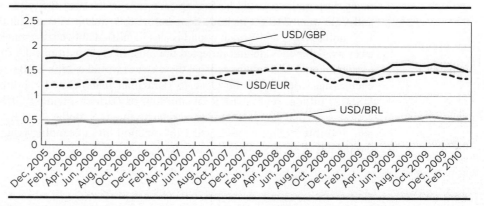

Data source: Bloomberg.

The spike in inflation for the British pound in the last quarter had raised some concerns about possible changes in the value of the pound relative to other developed countries. Further fueling concern was the low real rate or return on 10-year government securities given the recent inflation figure. While some argued that the inflation number was anomalous, others pointed to structural issues in the British economy and concerns that the Bank of England would not aggressively pursue its inflation targets.

Over the previous eight years, most major currencies had appreciated against the dollar. The financial crisis in 2008 reversed the trend as a flight to safety caused significant appreciation of the U.S. dollar. The depreciation of the U.S. dollar started over again in 2009, but the euro had recently been under pressure for sovereign debt concerns, and capital had flowed to emerging markets.[6] (**Figure 39.4** shows monthly exchange rates.)

Vale Capital Structure

Vale was a disciplined borrower. The firm had maintained an average debt-to-equity ratio of 47.6% from 2007 to 2009. Given that sufficient debt capital was often difficult to obtain in Brazilian reais, that the real rates on those borrowings were relatively high when the debt could be obtained, and that most of Vale's revenues were denominated in U.S. dollars, the company had traditionally issued bonds in U.S. dollars. Detailed information on Vale's outstanding debt is provided in **Exhibit 39.4**. Whereas the global demand for emerging-market corporate debt certainly suggested a Vale debt issue would be well received and priced at an attractive yield, the complicated state of global capital markets made the choice of currency difficult. It was clear the company should consider other alternatives along with the U.S. dollar.

---

[6]Jamus Lim and Monsoor Dailami, "Two Distinct Windows on Recent Emerging Market Currency Movements," Prospects for Development (blog), http://blogs.worldbank.org/prospects/two-distinct-windows-for-recent-emerging-market-currency-movements (accessed Oct. 26, 2010).

At this point, the firm needed to make a choice and proceed. There was concern that many corporations would be issuing securities in the next few years to roll over debt, and Vale wanted to get its issue done before this "maturity wall" hit the markets.[7] The U.S. dollar, euro, and British pound issues identified above represented typical alternatives available to Vale and reflected the most likely conditions the firm would face in each market. It was anticipated that these issues would carry a BBB+ rating. The size of each issue would generate close to (Brazilian reais) BRL1.8 billion, equivalent to USD1.0 billion, (euros) EUR750 million, or (British pounds) GBP700 million. Of course, any loan would be evaluated relative to a U.S. dollar loan. By way of comparison, **Exhibit 39.5** provides current information on outstanding issues by comparable companies in each of the three currencies.

---

[7]Nelson D. Schwartz, "Corporate Debt Coming Due May Squeeze Credit," *New York Times,* March 15, 2010.

EXHIBIT 39.1 I Income Statement (in millions of U.S. dollars)

	Year Ended December 31				
	2005	**2006**	**2007**	**2008**	**2009**
Revenue	14,581	21,188	36,373	30,464	27,814
Cost of goods sold	6,996	9,710	16,896	13,887	15,898
	7,585	11,478	19,477	16,577	11,916
Selling and general	694	913	1,431	1,562	1,359
Other operating expenses	645	1,167	1,581	3,181	2,997
	6,246	9,398	16,465	11,834	7,560
Interest expense (income)	414	817	(155)	853	662
Other nonoperating income (expense)	107	(194)	(533)	(1,317)	1,901
	5,939	8,387	16,087	9,664	8,799
Taxes	1,015	1,585	3,979	287	2,824
Minority interest	(445)	(519)	(873)	(187)	(97)
Net income	4,479	6,283	11,235	9,190	5,878

Data source: Vale 20-F filings, 2000–09.

EXHIBIT 39.2 | Balance Sheet Statement (in millions of U.S. dollars)

	As of December 31				
	2005	2006	2007	2008	2009
Cash	1,159	4,574	1,195	10,716	7,582
Receivables	1,851	3,720	4,028	3,438	3,377
Inventory	1,387	2,979	4,076	4,183	3,391
Other current assets	993	1,436	2,580	5,872	7,590
	5,390	12,709	11,879	24,209	21,940
Property, plant, and equipment	14,484	36,309	51,647	47,719	66,047
Goodwill	0	0	0	3,328	4,118
Other long-term assets	2,736	8,530	11,114	4,976	8,685
	22,610	57,548	74,640	80,232	100,790
Accounts payable	1,151	2,416	2,411	2,266	2,207
Short-term debt	0	0	0	469	370
Current portion long-term debt	1,482	1,712	1,887	683	3,042
Other current liabilities	2,370	3,657	6,565	4,629	4,369
	5,003	7,785	10,863	8,047	9,988
Long-term debt	3,888	21,522	18,222	18,438	20,719
Minority interest	1,265	2,807	2,630	2,626	3,330
Other long-term liabilities	2,137	7,143	10,895	9,543	11,846
	12,293	39,257	42,610	38,654	45,883
Common equity	10,317	18,291	32,030	41,578	54,907
	22,610	57,548	74,640	80,232	100,790

Data source: Vale 20-F filings, 2000–09.

EXHIBIT 39.3 | Interest Rates and Exchange Rates as of April 30, 2010

	U.S. Dollar	Euro	British Pound
Spot rate (in U.S. dollars)		1.3739 (USD/EUR)	1.5296 (USD/GBP)
Interest rates by maturity (%)*			
1-year	0.492	1.100	1.154
2-year	1.084	1.471	1.657
3-year	1.690	1.825	2.277
4-year	2.206	2.138	2.798
5-year	2.636	2.419	3.177
6-year	2.987	2.669	3.493
7-year	3.264	2.885	3.782
8-year	3.486	3.071	4.054
Other 10-year yields (%)			
Government (U.S., Germany, UK)	3.826	3.092	3.939
AAA corporate	4.588	3.828	4.753
BBB corporate	5.930	4.969	5.562

*Interest rates are zero-curve fixed-to-floating swap rates appropriate for pricing currency forward rates and indicative of prevailing interbank market rates for the given maturities.

Data sources: U.S. Federal Reserve Board and Datastream.

EXHIBIT 39.4 | Vale's Debt Outstanding as of December 31, 2009

Maturity Date	Coupon	Offer Date	Amount (in millions of U.S. dollars)	Currency	Offering Price	Offering YTM
May-15-2012	7.750	May-08-2002	400	U.S. dollar	99.917	7.762
Jun-15-2012	6.750	Jul-07-2009	292	U.S. dollar	100.000	6.750
Jun-15-2012	6.750	Jul-07-2009	649	U.S. dollar	100.000	6.750
Aug-15-2013	9.000	Oct-27-2003	282	U.S. dollar	98.386	9.250
Aug-15-2013	9.000	Aug-01-2003	300	U.S. dollar	98.386	9.250
Nov-20-2013	Floating rate	Nov-20-2006	2,316	Brazillian real	Floating rate	Floating rate
Mar-15-2014	6.125	May-05-2004	150	U.S. dollar	100.000	6.125
Oct-15-2015	5.700	Sep-23-2003	300	U.S. dollar	99.978	5.702
Jan-11-2016	6.250	Jan-05-2006	1,000	U.S. dollar	99.970	6.254
Jan-23-2017	6.250	Nov-16-2006	1,250	U.S. dollar	99.267	6.347
Sep-15-2019	5.625	Sep-08-2009	1,000	U.S. dollar	99.232	5.727
Mar-14-2023	1.000	Apr-29-2003	273	U.S. dollar	91.381	1.500
Sep-15-2032	7.200	Sep-18-2002	400	U.S. dollar	99.552	7.237
Jan-17-2034	8.250	Jan-09-2004	500	U.S. dollar	98.904	8.350
Nov-21-2036	6.875	Nov-16-2006	2,500	U.S. dollar	98.478	6.997
Nov-10-2039	6.875	Nov-03-2009	1,000	U.S. dollar	98.564	6.990
Mar-14-2052	3.500	Apr-29-2003	227	U.S. dollar	100.000	3.500

Data source: Capital IQ.

EXHIBIT 39.5 | Select Outstanding Debt Issues of Comparable Companies

Ticker	Company Name	Currency	Headquarters	Maturity Date	YTM on Apr-30-2010	Moody's Rating	S&P Rating	Coupon
XTA	Xstrata plc	U.S. dollar	Switzerland	Jun-01-2017	5.432	Baa2	BBB	5.500
AA	Alcoa Inc.	U.S. dollar	United States	Jun-01-2018	5.548	Baa3	BBB–	6.500
MT	ArcelorMittal	U.S. dollar	Luxembourg	Jun-01-2018	5.217	Baa3	BBB	6.125
VMC	Vulcan Materials Co.	U.S. dollar	United States	Jun-01-2018	5.353	Baa2	BBB	7.000
RIOLN	Rio Tinto plc	U.S. dollar	UK/Australia	Jul-01-2018	4.580	Baa1	BBB+	6.500
ABX	Barrick Gold Corp.	U.S. dollar	United States	Sep-01-2018	4.702	Baa1	A–	6.800
AA	Alcoa Inc.	U.S. dollar	United States	Feb-01-2019	6.608	Baa3	BBB–	5.720
AAI	Anglo American	U.S. dollar	United Kingdom	Apr-01-2019	5.317	Baa1	BBB	9.375
MT	ArcelorMittal	Euro	Luxembourg	Jun-01-2016	4.634	Baa3	BBB	9.375
AAL	Anglo American	Euro	United Kingdom	Dec-01-2016	4.584	Baa1	BBB	4.375
XTA	Xstrata	Euro	Switzerland	Jun-01-2017	4.522	Baa2	BBB	5.250
GASSM	Gas Natural	Euro	Spain	Feb-01-2018	4.580	Baa2	BBB	4.125
GOGLN	Go-Ahead Group plc	British pound	United Kingdom	Sep-01-2017	5.385	Baa3	BBB–	5.375
REEDLN	Reed Elsevier	British pound	UK/Netherlands	Dec-01-2017	4.869	Baa1	BBB+	7.000
TLM	Talisman Energy Inc.	British pound	United States	Dec-01-2017	5.007	Baa2	BBB	6.625
TITIM	Telecom Italia Group	British pound	Italy	Dec-01-2017	5.421	Baa2	BBB	7.375
AALLN	Anglo American	British pound	United Kingdom	May-01-2018	5.353	Baa1	BBB	6.875
XTA	Xstrata	British pound	Switzerland	May-01-2020	5.896	Baa2	BBB	7.375

Data sources: Datastream and case writer estimates.

J&L Railroad

It was Saturday, April 25, 2009, and Jeannine Matthews, chief financial officer at J&L Railroad (J&L), was in the middle of preparing her presentation for the upcoming board of directors meeting on Tuesday. Matthews was responsible for developing alternative strategies to hedge the company's exposure to locomotive diesel-fuel prices for the next 12 months. In addition to enumerating the pros and cons of alternative hedging strategies, the board had asked for her recommendation for which strategy to follow.

Fuel prices had always played a significant role in J&L's profits, but management had not considered the risk important enough to merit action. During February as the board reviewed the details of the company's performance for 2008, they discovered that, despite an increase of $154 million in rail revenues, operating margin had shrunk by $114 million, largely due to an increase in fuel costs (**Exhibits 40.1** and **40.2**). Having operating profit fall by 11% in 2008 after it had risen 9% in 2007 was considered unacceptable by the board, and it did not want a repeat in 2009.

Recently in a conversation with Matthews, the chairman of the board had expressed his personal view of the problem:

> Our business is running a railroad, not predicting the strength of an oil cartel or whether one Middle East nation will invade another. We might have been lucky in the past, but we cannot continue to subject our shareholders to unnecessary risk. After all, if our shareholders want to speculate on diesel fuel prices, they can do that on their own; but I believe fuel-price risk should *not* be present in our stock price. On the other hand, if the recession continues and prices drop further, we could increase our profit margins by not hedging.

Diesel-fuel prices had peaked in early July 2008 but then had trended downward as a result of the worldwide recession and softening demand. By January 2009, diesel-fuel prices had fallen to their lowest level since early 2005. At February's meeting, the board had decided to wait and see how the energy markets would continue to react to the recession and softening demand. By March, however, oil and diesel-fuel prices had begun to rebound, so the board charged Matthews with the task of proposing a hedging policy at the meeting on April 28.

This disguised case was revised and updated by Rick Green based on an earlier version adapted from a Supervised Business Study written by Jeannine Lehman under the direction of Professor Kenneth Eades. Funding was provided by the L. White Matthews Fund for finance case writing. Copyright © 1994 by the University of Virginia Darden School Foundation, Charlottesville, VA. All rights reserved. *To order copies, send an e-mail to* sales@dardenbusinesspublishing.com. *No part of this publication may be reproduced, stored in a retrieval system, used in a spreadsheet, or transmitted in any form or by any means—electronic, mechanical, photocopying, recording, or otherwise—without the permission of the Darden School Foundation.* Rev. 4/17.

It was industry practice for railroads to enter into long-term contracts with their freight customers, which had both good and bad effects. On the positive side, railroads could better predict available resources by locking in revenues in advance. On the negative side, fixed-price contracts limited railroads' profit margins and exposed them to potentially large profit swings if any of their costs changed. In this regard, diesel fuel was a particularly troublesome cost for railroads, because it represented a large cost item that also was difficult to predict due to the volatility of fuel prices.

An ideal solution to the fuel-price risk would be for railroads to enter into long-term fixed-price contracts with their fuel suppliers. A fixed-price contract with suppliers when combined with the fixed-price contracts with freight customers would serve to steady future profits. Moreover, by contracting with fuel suppliers to deliver all of J&L's fuel needs at a fixed price, management could be assured of meeting its fuel budget numbers at year's end. At times, fuel suppliers had agreed to such contracts, but over the years, J&L had not been satisfied with the results. The problem was that when fuel prices had risen substantially, many suppliers walked away from their commitments leaving J&L with a list of three unattractive options:

1. *Force compliance*: J&L could take the supplier to court to enforce the contract; however, many suppliers were thinly capitalized, which meant that the legal action against them could put them into bankruptcy. As a result, J&L might get little or nothing from the supplier and yet would be saddled with significant legal fees.

2. *Negotiate a new price*: This usually meant that J&L would agree to pay at or near the current market price, which was equivalent to ignoring the original contract; plus it set a bad precedent for future contracts.

3. *Walk away and buy the fuel on the open market from another supplier*: This choice avoided "rewarding" the supplier for defaulting on its contract but was functionally equivalent to never having the contract in the first place.

Based on this history, J&L's board decided to "assume the fuel suppliers are not the answer to our fuel price problem." The board then asked Matthews to explore other alternatives to manage the fuel risk and preserve J&L's relationships with the fuel suppliers.

Mathews had determined that, if J&L were to hedge, it could choose between two basic strategies. The first was to do the hedging in-house by trading futures and options contracts on a public exchange. This presented a number of tradeoffs, including the challenge of learning how to trade correctly. The second was to use a bank's risk management products and services. This would cost more but would be easier to implement. For either alternative, she would need to address a number of important details, including how much fuel to hedge and how much risk should be eliminated with the hedge.

Railroad Industry

Railroads hauled record amounts of freight in 2006 and 2007 and began to encounter capacity constraints. In 2008, the industry hauled nearly 2-billion tons of freight, although rail traffic declined due to weakness in the economy. The transportation of coal was by far the number one commodity group carried. Other significant commodity groups were chemicals, farm products, food, metallic ores, nonmetallic minerals, and lumber, pulp, and paper products.

Freight and unit trains had expanded the industry since deregulation in the 1980s. Rail carriers served as long-distance haulers of *intermodal* freight, carrying the freight containers for steamship lines, or trailers for the trucking industry. *Unit* train loads were used to move large amounts of a single commodity (typically 50 or more cars) between two points using more efficient locomotives. A unit train would be used, for example, to move coal between a coal mine and an electric generating plant.

Several factors determined a railroad's profitability: government regulation, oligopolistic competition within the industry, and long-term contracts with shippers and suppliers. The railroad industry had a long history of price regulation; the government had feared the monopolistic pricing that had driven the industry to the brink of ruin in the 1970s. Finally recognizing the intense competition among most rail traffic, Congress passed the Staggers Rail Act of 1980, allowing railroads to manage their own assets, to price services based on market demand, and earn adequate revenues to support their operations. America's freight railroads paid almost all of the costs of tracks, bridges, and tunnels themselves. In comparison, trucks and barges used highways and waterways provided and maintained by the government.

After the Staggers Act was passed, railroad fuel efficiency rose 94%. By 2009, a freight train could move a ton of freight 436 miles on a single gallon of locomotive diesel fuel, approximately four times as far as it could by truck. The industry had spent considerable money on the innovative technology that improved the power and efficiency of locomotives and produced lighter train cars. Now, a long freight train could carry the same load as 280 trucks while at the same time producing only one-third the greenhouse-gas emissions.[1]

Market share was frequently won or lost solely on the basis of the price charged by competing railroads. Although rarely more than two or three railroads competed for a particular client's business, price competition was often fierce enough to prohibit railroads from increasing freight prices because of fuel-price increases. But, as fuel prices during 2008 climbed higher and faster than they had ever done before, there was some discussion in the railroad industry regarding the imposition of fuel surcharges when contracts came up for renewal. So far, however, none of the major carriers had followed up the talk with action.

J&L Railroad

J&L Railroad was founded in 1928 when the Jackson and Lawrence rail lines combined to form one of the largest railroads in the country. Considered a Class I railroad, J&L operated approximately 2,500 miles of line throughout the West and the Midwest. Although publicly owned, J&L was one of the few Class I railroads still managed by the original founding families. In fact, two of the family members still occupied seats on its

---

[1]Association of American Railroads, http://www.freightrailworks.org.

board of directors. During the periods 1983–89, 1996–99, and 2004–08, J&L had invested significant amounts of capital into replacing equipment and refurbishing roadways. These capital expenditures had been funded either through internally generated funds or through long-term debt. The investment in more efficient locomotives was now paying off, despite the burden of the principal and interest payments.

J&L had one of the most extensive intermodal networks, accounting for approximately 20% of revenues during the last few years, as compared to the Class I industry average of 10%. Transportation of coal, however, had accounted for only 25% to 30% of freight revenues. With the projected increase in demand for coal from emerging economies in Asia, management had committed to increase revenues from coal to 35% within three years. That commitment was now subject to revision due to slowing global economic activity and the recent fall in energy prices.

Exchange-Traded Contracts

J&L's exposure to fuel prices during the next 12 months would be substantial. Matthews estimated that the company would need approximately 17.5 million gallons of diesel fuel per month or 210 million gallons for the coming year. This exposure could be offset with the use of heating oil futures and option contracts that were traded on the New York Mercantile Exchange (NYMEX) (**Exhibits 40.3** and **40.4**). NYMEX did not trade contracts on diesel fuel, so it was not possible to hedge diesel fuel directly. Heating oil and diesel fuel, however, were both distillates of crude oil with very similar chemical profiles and highly correlated market prices (**Exhibit 40.5**). Thus, heating-oil futures were considered an excellent hedging instrument for diesel fuel.

Futures allowed market participants to contract to buy or sell a commodity at a future date at a predetermined price. If market participants did not want to buy a commodity today based on its *spot price*, the current market price, they could use the futures market to contract to buy it at a future date at the futures price. A futures price reflected the market's forecast of what the spot price was expected to be at the contract's maturity date. Many factors influenced the spot price and futures prices, both of which changed constantly depending on the market news. As illustrated in **Exhibit 40.3**, the current market conditions were such that the futures market was expecting price to trend up from the spot of $1.36 to an average of $1.52 over the next 12 months.

A trader who wanted to buy a commodity would take a "long" position in the contract, whereas a seller would take a "short" position. Because J&L's profits fell when fuel prices increased, the company could offset its exposure by taking long positions in heating-oil futures. For example, instead of waiting two months to buy fuel on the open market at the going price, J&L could enter into the July futures contract on April 25 to buy heating oil at $ 1.4138/gallon (**Exhibit 40.3**). Therefore, when the contract matured in two months,[2] J&L would end up buying heating oil at exactly $1.4138/gallon regardless of the price of heating oil at the time. This could work for or against J&L depending

---

[2]NYMEX futures expired on the last trading day of the previous month; therefore, the July futures matured on June 30, 2009.

on whether prices rose or fell during the two months. For example, if at maturity of the contract, heating oil was selling at $1.4638, J&L would have benefited by $.05/gallon by owning the futures. If heating oil was selling for $1.3638 at maturity, J&L would have lost $.05/gallon on the futures. In either case, however, J&L would pay exactly $1.4138 per gallon.

Fuel producers or distributors who wanted to fix their selling price would take a short position in the fuel futures. Alternatively, the seller might be a speculator who believed that the spot price of fuel at maturity would end up being lower than the current futures price. In either case, futures was a zero-sum game because one party's gain exactly equals the other party's loss. As long as the futures price was an unbiased estimate of the future spot price, the *expected* payoff at maturity was zero for both the long and short side of the contract. Thus, although the buyer and seller were required to pay a modest fee to the exchange to enter a futures contract, no money was exchanged between buyers and sellers at the outset. If the futures price increased over time, the buyer would collect, and if the futures price decreased, the seller would collect. When the contract matured, it was rare for the buyer to request physical delivery of the commodity, rather the vast majority of contracted futures were cash settled.

NYMEX futures created a few problems for J&L management. First, because J&L would have to use heating-oil contracts to hedge its diesel-fuel exposure, there would be a small amount of risk created by the imperfect match of the prices of the two commodities. This "basis," however, was minimal owing to the high correlation historically between the two price series. Of greater concern was that NYMEX contracts were standardized with respect to size and maturity dates. Each heating-oil futures contract was for the delivery of 42,000 gallons and matured on the last business day of the preceding month. Thus, J&L faced a maturity mismatch because the hedge would only work if the number of gallons being hedged was purchased specifically on the day the futures contract matured. In addition, J&L faced a size mismatch because the number of gallons needed in any month was unlikely to equal an exact multiple of 42,000 gallons.

Some institutional features of NYMEX futures contracts had to be considered as well. NYMEX futures were "marked to market" daily, which meant that every investor's position was settled daily, regardless of whether the position was closed or kept open. Daily marking-to-market limited the credit risk of the transaction to a single day's movement of prices. To further reduce the credit risk, the exchange required margin payments as collateral. When a contract was initially opened, both parties were required to post an initial margin equal to approximately 5% or less of the contract value. At the end of each trading day, moneys were added or subtracted from the margin account as the futures trader's position increased or decreased in value. If the value of the position declined below a specified maintenance level, the trader would be required to replenish the margin to its initial margin level. Thus, the combination of daily marking-to-market and the use of margins effectively eliminated any credit risk for exchange-traded futures contracts. Still, the daily settlement process created a cash-flow risk because J&L might have to make cash payments well in advance of the maturity of a contract.

In addition to futures contracts, it was possible to buy NYMEX options on the futures. A call option gave the buyer the right, but not the obligation, to go long on the underlying commodity futures at a given price (the strike price) on or before the expiration date. A *put* option gave the buyer the right to go short on the futures at the strike price. The typical futures option expired a few days prior to the expiration of the underlying futures contract to give the counterparties time to offset their positions on the futures exchange. Options were offered at a variety of strike prices and maturities (**Exhibit 40.4**). Unlike the underlying futures contract, puts and calls commanded a market price called the *premium*. A call premium increased as the spread of the futures price over the strike price increased, whereas a put premium increased as the spread of the strike price over the futures price increased. The premiums of both puts and calls were higher for options with more time to maturity. Thus, unlike the futures, option buyers had to pay the premium to buy the contract in addition to both buyer and seller paying a fee for the transaction.

The Risk-Management Group at Kansas City National Bank

Walt Bernard, vice president of the risk management group of Kansas City National Bank, (KCNB) had recently given a presentation to J&L senior management in which he described the wide range of risk-management products and techniques available to protect J&L's profit margin. Each technique used a particular financial product to hedge by various degrees J&L's exposure to diesel-fuel price changes. The products offered by KCNB were completely financial in design (i.e., no actual delivery of the commodity took place at maturity). To hedge diesel fuel, KCNB offered No. 2 heating-oil contracts, the same commodity traded on the NYMEX. Also similar to trading on the NYMEX, working with KCNB meant that J&L could continue to do business as usual with its suppliers and perform its hedging activities independently.

The primary risk-management products offered by KCNB were commodity swaps, caps, floors, and collars (see **Exhibit 40.6** for cap and floor quotes). KCNB's instruments were designed to hedge the *average* price of heating oil during the contract period. By contrast, NYMEX futures and options were contracts designed against the spot price in effect on the last day of the contract. In a commodity swap, the bank agreed to pay on the settlement date if the average price of heating oil was above the agreed-upon swap price for the year. Conversely, J&L would have to pay the bank if the average price was below the contracted swap price. Thus, a swap was essentially a custom-fit futures contract, with KCNB rather than NYMEX carrying the credit risk. Because the swap was priced on the average heating-oil price, settlement occurred at the end of the swap (12 months in J&L's case) rather than daily as with NYMEX futures. In addition, KCNB would not require J&L to post a margin but would charge a nominal up-front fee as compensation for accepting J&L's credit risk. KCNB was currently quoting the 12-month swap price for heating oil as $1.522/gallon.

KCNB also offered commodity options, referred to as caps, floors, and collars. A *cap* was essentially a call option; a *floor* was a put option; and a *collar* was the combination of a cap and a floor. For a cap, KCNB agreed to pay the excess of the realized average fuel price over the cap's "strike price." If the average fuel price never reached the strike price, KCNB would pay nothing. As for any option, J&L would need to pay KCNB a premium for the cap. The cap premium varied according to how far the strike price was above the expected price. If the strike was close to the expected price implied by the futures contracts, J&L would have to pay a relatively high premium. If J&L was willing to accept some risk by contracting for a strike price that was significantly higher than the expected average price, the premium would be smaller. In any case, the cap would allow J&L to take advantage of price decreases and yet still be protected from price increases above the cap's strike price.

A commodity collar was used to limit the movement of prices within the range of the cap and floor strike prices. By choosing a collar, J&L would be selling a floor while simultaneously buying a cap. KCNB agreed to pay the excess, if any, of the average heating-oil price over the cap strike price. Conversely, J&L would have to pay if the average price fell below the floor strike price. Collars could be designed to have a minimal up-front cost by setting the cap and floor strike prices so that the revenue derived from selling the floor exactly offset the premium for buying the cap. If J&L management wanted to guard against prices rising above a certain price (the cap's strike price) but were willing to give up the benefit of prices falling below a certain level (the floor's strike price), a collar could be the logical choice.

Matthews's Choice

Jeannine Matthews had decided to recommend that J&L hedge its fuel costs for the next 12 months, at least to some extent. Her analysis revealed that despite using more efficient equipment, the cost of fuel as a percentage of revenues had increased every year since 2001 (**Exhibit 40.7**). The immediate questions to be answered were: How much fuel should be hedged, and how should the hedge be structured?

Bernard had presented Matthews with a myriad of possibilities, each of which provided some degree of profit protection. A commodity swap, for example, could be used to completely fix the price of fuel for the next year. If the price of diesel fuel ended up falling below the swap price, however, the hedge would be more of an embarrassment than a benefit to Matthews. Defending a newly initiated hedging policy would be difficult if J&L's profits lagged those of other railroads because of a failure to capture lower fuel costs.

Then there was the issue of how much fuel to hedge. If the economy experienced a slowdown, J&L would experience a drop in rail loads, which would result in using less than the 210 million gallons currently expected. If the hedge was constructed based on more fuel than needed, it was conceivable that J&L could end up paying to settle its position with the bank for fuel that it could not use. At the same time, it was also possible that the economy would pick up, and J&L would end up having to buy a significant amount of fuel on the open market without the benefit of a hedge.

Instead of a swap, Matthews could use a cap to eliminate the risk of high fuel prices. This would seem to alleviate the problem of over- or under-hedging because the cap would only be exercised if it was profitable (i.e., if prices rose beyond the cap's strike price). At that point, J&L would prefer to have been over-hedged because the company would get a higher payoff from the cap. The biggest concern about the cap strategy was that the price of heating oil might not rise high enough to trigger the cap, in which case the premium paid for the cap would have only served to reduce profits with no offsetting benefits. Another alternative was to enter into a collar, which could be structured to have a zero cost; however, a collar carried a hidden cost because it gave up the savings if fuel prices happened to fall below the floor's strike price.

Matthews knew that it was important for her to keep in mind that all of KCNB's product could be mimicked using NYMEX futures and options. In fact, maybe there was a creative way to combine NYMEX securities to give J&L a better hedge than provided by KCNB's products. Regardless of what she recommended, Matthews realized that she needed to devise a hedging strategy that would give J&L the maximum benefit at the lowest cost and would not prove to be an embarrassment for her or J&L.

EXHIBIT 40.1 | Consolidated Income Statement, 2006–08 (in millions of dollars) December 31

	2008	2007	2006
Revenues by market group:			
Coal	$1,080	$ 871	$ 857
Merchandise	1,907	1,954	1,878
Intermodal	714	722	725
Total operating revenues	3,701	3,547	3,461
Expenses:			
Compensation and benefits	987	939	970
Purchased service and rent	588	571	581
Fuel	603	430	403
Depreciation	296	285	271
Materials and other	313	294	295
Total operating expenses	2,787	2,519	2,520
Operating income:	914	1,028	941
Other income	40	34	55
Interest expense, net	(163)	(162)	(175)
Income (loss) before income taxes:	791	900	820
Income tax provision	(297)	(310)	(276)
Net income	$ 494	$ 589	$ 545

Source: Main Street Trading data.

EXHIBIT 40.2 | Consolidated Balance Sheets, 2007–08 (in millions of dollars) December 31

Assets	2008	2007
Current assets:		
Cash	$ 227	$ 76
Receivable net	320	347
Materials and suppliers, at average cost	71	65
Deferred income taxes, current	55	70
Other current assets	62	58
Total current assets	735	616
Properties:		
Investment	654	726
Property, road and structures, net	8,184	7,940
Other assets	101	336
Total assets	$9,674	$9,618
Liabilities and shareholders' equity		
Current liabilities:		
Accounts payable	$ 419	$ 419
Current portion of long-term debt	96	75
Income taxes payable	81	87
Other accrued expenses	178	136
Total current liabilities	774	717
Long-term debt	2,275	2,207
Deferred income taxes	2,344	2,366
Other liabilities and reserves	747	750
Total liabilities	6,140	6,040
Shareholders' equity:		
Common stock	135	140
Additional paid-in capital	618	539
Accumulated other comprehensive income (loss)	(347)	(147)
Retained income	3,128	3,046
Total shareholders' equity	3,534	3,578
Total liabilities and shareholders' equity	$9,674	$9,618

Source: Main Street Trading data.

EXHIBIT 40.3 | NYMEX Heating Oil Exchange Futures (in dollars per gallon) April 24, 2009

Month	Last
May '09	$1.368
Jun '09	$1.386
Jul '09	$1.414
Aug. '09	$1.443
Sep '09	$1.472
Oct '09	$1.502
Nov '09	$1.533
Dec '09	$1.563
Jan '10	$1.593
Feb '10	$1.614
Mar '10	$1.626
Apr '10	$1.629
May '10	$1.638

Spot = $1.360

Each heating-oil futures contract was for the delivery of 42,000 gallons and matured on the last business day of the preceding month (e.g., the June 2009 contract expires May 29, 2009).

Source: New York Mercantile Exchange data.

EXHIBIT 40.4 | NYMEX Heating Oil Call Option Premiums (in dollars per gallon) April 24, 2009

Strike Price	Aug. '09 Calls	Oct. '09 Calls	Dec. '09 Calls	Feb. '10 Calls	May '10 Calls
1.36	0.196	0.265	0.326	0.376	0.394
1.40	0.175	0.244	0.303	0.353	0.371
1.45	0.151	0.219	0.277	0.326	0.344
1.50	0.131	0.196	0.253	0.301	0.319
1.55	0.113	0.176	0.230	0.277	0.295
1.60	0.098	0.158	0.210	0.255	0.272
1.65	0.084	0.142	0.192	0.235	0.252
1.70	0.072	0.127	0.175	0.216	0.233
Expiry date	7/28/2009	9/25/2009	11/24/2009	1/26/2010	4/27/2010
Days to expiry	95	154	215	278	369
Futures price	$1.443	$1.502	$1.563	$1.614	$1.638
Treasury yield	0.11%	0.17%	0.31%	0.38%	0.49%

Source: Main Street Trading data.

EXHIBIT 40.5 | Diesel Fuel versus Heating Oil Prices (in dollars per gallon) January 2007 to March 2009

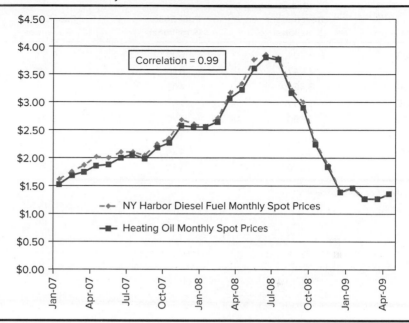

Source: Graph created by case writer using data from Energy Information Association.

EXHIBIT 40.6 | KCNB Cap and Floor Prices (in dollars per gallon) April 24, 2009

Strike Price	1-Year Cap	1-Year Floor
1.40	0.201	0.079
1.45	0.172	0.101
1.50	0.147	0.125
1.55	0.125	0.152
1.60	0.105	0.182
1.65	0.088	0.215
1.70	0.073	0.250

Note: Cap and floors prices are based on the average daily closing price of heating fuel for one year.

Data Source: Company documents.

EXHIBIT 40.7 | Fuel Costs 2001–2008

Year	Rail Revenues ($ millions)	Fuel Costs ($ millions)	Fuel Costs/ Revenues	Gallons (millions)
2008	3,701	603	16.3%	205.1
2007	3,547	430	12.1%	205.6
2006	3,461	403	11.6%	216.6
2005	3,137	285	9.1%	170.0
2004	2,690	220	8.2%	191.2
2003	2,379	189	7.9%	216.1
2002	2,307	126	5.5%	179.4
2001	2,270	152	6.7%	206.4

Data Source: Company documents.

WNG Capital LLC

WNG succeeds because we create value for all our stakeholders. Our model allows both airlines and investors to achieve their financial objectives.
   —**Michael Gangemi, CEO WNG Capital LLC**[1]

In late 2013, Wenbo Su, an analyst at WNG Capital LLC (WNG), a U.S.-based asset management firm, was reviewing the terms of a proposed transaction for his employer. WNG specialized in aviation leases, and Su was evaluating the terms of a proposed purchase and leaseback deal with a small private airline based in the United Kingdom. The essence of the transaction would be to transform the airline from being the owner of certain aircraft in its fleet to being the lessee of the aircraft for 12 months (through the end of 2014). WNG would be the new owner of the equipment and would act as the lessor in the deal. The airline would have full use of the aircraft, but would not own the aircraft or have use of the aircraft after the end of the lease. The cash flows to all parties were complicated, and Su planned to conduct a thorough analysis of the proposed lease terms before making a recommendation to WNG's CEO, Michael Gangemi.

WNG was established in 2009 as an operating lessor of used commercial aircraft manufactured by Airbus Group and Boeing Corporation. The company had offices in Dallas, Boston, and Dublin, Ireland, where Su worked. Since its first investment in 2011, the firm had invested approximately $805 million in 54 aircraft using special-purpose entities (SPEs). The small firm of 15 employees had global reach, with leases to 34 airlines operating in 22 countries around the world. At the time of the proposed deal, the firm was managing 41 aircraft valued in excess of $735 million in four SPEs. In its marketing materials, WNG informed potential investors that it sought an unlevered, pretax net-annual internal rate of return (IRR) on invested capital of 11% to 14%.

---

[1]Author interviews with Michael Gangemi between July 1, 2016, and January 25, 2017.

The challenge of analyzing and setting lease terms was not new to Su, who was aware that the aircraft-leasing market was both small and competitive. Beyond structuring a deal that was profitable for both WNG and its investors, Su understood the importance of reputation in such a small market. A deal that proved too costly for an airline could cost the firm future deals not only with that airline but also with others. Protecting the firm's reputation in the industry was as important as protecting the firm's capital; and structuring a deal that benefited WNG, its investors, and the airline presented an interesting challenge given the opaque nature of older aircraft values.

Aviation Industry

The aviation industry launched on December 17, 1903, in Kill Devil Hills, North Carolina, when inventors Wilbur and Orville Wright successfully piloted their heavier-than-air machine on four flights ranging from 12 to 59 seconds. Within 11 years of this historic event, the commercial airline business had begun, and it quickly evolved into an industry dominated by regulation. Routes and fares were controlled by governments, and airlines competed on food and service, including frequency of flights. Fares were high and the load factor—the percentage of seats filled—was low because the price of air travel was beyond the reach of many.

The passage of the 1978 Airline Deregulation Act in the United States ushered in a new age, making it possible for smaller regional economy airlines, such as Southwest Airlines, to enter the U.S. market. Ticket prices fell and air travel increased. The European market deregulated several years later, and new airlines such as Ryan Air and EZJet emerged to offer travelers low-cost flights between the United Kingdom and the European continent. Following deregulation, air travel became affordable for many and passenger air travel grew. **Exhibit 41.1** shows the historical growth in global air traffic from 1974 through 2015. Growth in the industry, measured in revenue passenger kilometers (RPK)[2] was forecast to continue its growth at an average annual rate of 4.5% from 2011 to 2030, comparable to the 4.6% growth recorded from 1995 to 2010.[3]

Deregulation reduced government control of routes and fares but had little impact on the regulations governing aircraft safety. Regulations required that aircraft demonstrate "airworthiness" through a certification process. The process included registering the aircraft, followed by intensive physical and records inspection. Once a certificate had been issued, the aircraft operator was required to keep detailed records for each aircraft, documenting each flight hour and flight cycle (defined as a take-off and landing), as well as all maintenance performed on the aircraft, to prove continued airworthiness.

The development of widespread fatigue damage (WFD) was a major safety issue for aircraft with high hour and cycle counts. To reduce the risk of passenger injury,

---

[2]RPK = the number of revenue-paying passengers multiplied by the number of kilometers flown during the period.

[3]International Civil Aviation Organization, Air Transport in Figures: Economic Development at a Glance, "Global Air Transport Outlook to 2030," 14, http://www.icao.int/sustainability/documents/AirTransport-figures.pdf, (accessed Feb. 1, 2017).

regulations required increasingly frequent airframe inspections for airframes with high hour and cycle counts and specific service actions to preclude the onset of WFD. Each airframe was tested for its limits of validity (LOV), defined as the period of time (in cycles, hours, or both) up to which WFD would not occur. The LOV set the operational limits of the airframe's maintenance program and thus defined the airframe's usable life. Separate regulations governed aircraft engines, which were unaffected by WFD.

To meet the regulations, aircraft and their parts had to be tracked by both their age and flight cycles. The records, referred to as back-to-birth traceability, or "trace," had to be available to the FAA, as well as the next owner/operator of the aircraft. Without complete trace from original delivery of an aircraft and its related parts, the owner could not prove the aircraft's airworthiness, and the aircraft could not be operated commercially. Parts lacking complete trace had zero residual value. Detailed recordkeeping, therefore, was vital to maintaining the value of an aircraft.[4]

Two manufacturers, U.S.-based Boeing and France-based Airbus, dominated the aircraft industry. Each offered a wide range of aircraft, from small single-aisle to large wide-body aircraft. Among the most popular for leasing were short- to medium-range, narrow-body commercial jet aircraft, and the most popular of these was the Boeing 737. Originally introduced in 1967, the 737 design developed into a family of 10 models, each with the capacity to transport 85 to 215 passengers. Since its inception, Boeing had delivered more than 7,700 of the narrow-bodied jets to airlines around the globe.[5] More than 4,100 remained in service, used by more than 500 airlines, servicing 1,200 destinations in 190 countries.[6]

In 1981, Boeing introduced the 757, a slightly larger aircraft. The mid-size, narrow-body twin-engine jet aircraft was intended for short- to medium-range routes and could carry up to 295 passengers for a maximum of 4,100 nautical miles. The larger capacity, however, came at the expense of fuel efficiency, and only 1,049 of the 757 aircraft were built before production ended in 2004.

Airbus introduced the A320 in 1984. A close competitor of the 737, the A320 also developed into a family of multiple models, accommodating as many as 220 passengers. Since its introduction, Airbus had built more than 7,100 of the A320 family. Together, the 737 and the A320 numbered more than 11,600 aircraft in service, representing approximately 58% of the worldwide fleet. The retirement age for narrow-body aircraft averaged approximately 25 years.[7] Prices for new aircraft ranged from $32 million to $114 million, and each manufacturer had a backlog of orders in the thousands.

---

[4]FAA Aircraft Certification website, http://www.faa-aircraft-certification.com/standard-airworthiness-certification.html (accessed Feb. 1, 2017).

[5]Boeing Corporation, http://www.boeing.com/commercial/#/orders-deliveries (accessed Dec. 6, 2016).

[6]Guy Norris, "The 737 Story: Little Wonder," Flight Global, February 7, 2006, https://www.flightglobal.com/news/articles/the-737-story-little-wonder-204505/ (accessed Dec. 7, 2016).

[7]Dick Forsberg, "Avolon World Fleet Forecast 2014–2033," September 2014, http://avolon.aero/wp/wp-content/uploads/2014/09/WFF_2014.pdf (accessed Feb. 1, 2017).

Aircraft Financing

For an airline to buy and own an aircraft required a significant capital investment. Leasing aircraft, however, improved an airline's financial flexibility by improving its liquidity position and balance sheet. In addition, leasing aircraft improved an airline's operating flexibility by allowing it to respond to short- and medium-term fluctuations in demand, as well as changes in technology and route structures, without capital-intensive investments. Over the course of its 25-year economic life, an aircraft could be leased multiple times, with the owner/lessor retaining the residual-value risk until the aircraft was either sold or retired and converted to parts. Overall, operating leases were attractive to airlines because of the low capital outlay, flexibility for fleet planning, increased access to new or improved technology, shortened delivery times, and the elimination of residual-value risk.[8]

As illustrated in **Exhibit 41.2,** aircraft leasing gained momentum following deregulation. In the face of increasing competition, many airlines pursued leasing aircraft to maintain as much liquidity as possible. For smaller start-up airlines, leasing offered an additional benefit: established leasing companies were able to access bank lines of credit and the capital markets at lower costs than the start-ups could.

Capital versus Operating Leases

WNG followed U.S. accounting rules and Su was familiar with the existing rules regarding both capital and operating leases. Operating leases were generally perceived to have a number of financial advantages for a lessee, but to qualify as an operating lease meant that it could not meet any of the criteria of a capital lease. According to the Financial Accounting Standards Board (FASB) Statement No. 13, a lease was considered a capital lease if any of the following four criteria were true.[9]

1. Ownership of the asset transferred to the lessee by the end of the lease term.
2. The lease contained a bargain-purchase option, whereby the lessee paid below fair market value for the property at the end of the lease.
3. The lease term was equal to 75% or more of the economic life of the property.
4. The present value of the lease payments over the lease term was equal to or greater than 90% of the fair market value of the leased property at the beginning of the lease.

In a capital lease, the FASB required that the lessee include both the asset (the property) and the corresponding liability (the lease) on its balance sheet. At the end of

---

[8] Avolon Holdings Limited, Form F-1 Registration Statement, December 1, 2014, 89, https://www.sec.gov/Archives/edgar/data/1610128/000119312514428456/d739557df1a.htm (accessed Feb. 1, 2017).

[9] Statement of Financial Accounting Standards No. 13: "Accounting for Leases," Financial Accounting Standards Board, November 1976, 7–9.

the lease term, the lessee retained ownership of the property. Importantly, capital-lease payments were not tax-deductible expenses, but depreciation expenses associated with the asset could be deducted by the lessee and, as the owner, the lessee bore the risk of any changes in the asset's value, including depreciation.

Operating leases were treated significantly differently in terms of ownership and thus balance-sheet impact. Under an operating lease, the lessor retained ownership of the leased property and included the property as an asset on its balance sheet. The lessee enjoyed the use of the property for the term of the lease without having reported the asset on its balance sheet. The lessee recorded lease payments as ordinary business expenses, deductible from taxable income. At the conclusion of the lease term, physical control of the leased property returned to the lessor.

Under the existing rules, long-term leases—more than 12 months—were not reported as liabilities on the balance sheet. Earlier in the year, the International Accounting Standards Board (IASB) and the FASB had published an exposure draft outlining proposed changes to the accounting for leases, including a requirement that lessees would recognize assets and liabilities for leases of more than 12 months. The accounting boards believed that the proposed changes would provide investors with "greater transparency about . . . exposure to credit risk and asset risk."[10] If approved, Su recognized that the proposed rules would have a significant impact on the financial statements of airlines and could affect WNG's business model. Su also knew that such changes would take years to implement, since the IASB and FASB had been studying the issue since 2006.

Special-Purpose Entities (SPEs)

Financial institutions often created legal entities known as SPEs to meet specific or temporary objectives. Often structured as a limited liability company (LLC) or a limited liability partnership (LLP), an SPE isolated the parent company from the financial and reputational risk of a large project. SPEs could also be used to hide debt, which could strengthen the balance sheet, or ownership, which could obscure relationships between entities. When used to hold a single asset with permits and contract rights (e.g., a power plant or an aircraft), SPEs simplified transfer of the asset. When registered in low-tax jurisdictions, such as Ireland, SPEs offered tax advantages. Ireland had become popular for aircraft finance and leasing activities because of its favorable tax legislation and treaties. Under Irish tax legislation, SPEs could be liable for a corporate tax rate of up to 25%, but with appropriate structuring the SPE's taxable profit would be minimal. In addition, Ireland had negotiated bilateral tax treaties with the majority of countries where aircraft were operated. Under these treaties, lease payments made to Irish registered owners were not subject to the host-country withholding taxes that otherwise applied to lease income.

---

[10]"IASB and FASB Propose Changes to Lease Accounting," Financial Accounting Standards Board press release, May 16, 2013, http://www.fasb.org/cs/ContentServer?pagename=FASB%2FFASBContent_C%2FNewsPage&cid=1176162614474 (accessed Feb. 1, 2017).

The Lease Proposal

The deal being reviewed by Su was the purchase and leaseback of three Boeing 757–200 aircraft, each with two Rolls-Royce engines and all related maintenance and technical records (**Exhibit 41.3** lists the equipment). The deal also included two spare engines and the related maintenance and technical records. The two engines would be sold as is without a full QEC (Quick Engine Change).[11] Under the terms of the initial agreement as detailed in the Letter of Intent (LOI), WNG would establish an SPE as the purchaser and lessor of the equipment. On the delivery date, December 15, 2013, the SPE would make payment of $15 million for the three aircraft and two spare engines. Under the proposed terms of the lease, the lessee would make rent payments of $325,000 at the beginning of each of the 12 months, and the lessee would be responsible for all maintenance, insurance, and taxes on the aircraft during the lease.

The deal involved some potential wrinkles. First, Su needed to consider the adequacy of the maintenance and technical records associated with the equipment. Su was already aware that some of the equipment lacked complete back-to-birth traceability based on information provided by the seller. Prior to signing the LOI, the seller had disclosed complete back-to-birth traceability on one complete set of landing gear, partial traceability on another set, and no back-to-birth traceability on a third. The purchase price of $15 million reflected the lack of full traceability for the landing gear. The LOI specified that if the airline were to provide proof of full traceability for the landing gear prior to closing, the purchase price would be increased to $15.5 million. Given that the seller had proactively disclosed the missing trace for the landing gear, Su was hoping that the full inspection results would confirm that the remaining equipment had full traceability. In the event that this proved too optimistic, the LOI provided an opportunity to renegotiate terms. The LOI specified that both the purchase price and rental payments were subject to further negotiation if inspections revealed missing trace for any equipment other than the landing gear.

Another potential wrinkle was that the deal was for 757s rather than the more common 737s, which could affect WNG's options for the aircraft at the end of the lease. The 757 was a versatile aircraft that was popular with pilots because of its more powerful engines and ability to fly in any weather. In addition to its larger capacity, the 757 had a longer range and could be used for trans-Atlantic flights.[12] Even so, the 757 was not as popular among airlines as the 737, primarily because the larger size made it much more expensive to operate. The higher operating costs suppressed overall demand for the aircraft, making the used 757 market much smaller and much less active than the 737 market. **Exhibit 41.4** shows the capacity and operating costs of narrow-body jets in the short-haul sector.

At the end of an initial lease, WNG was usually able to re-lease rather than part out its aircraft. Historically, more than 80% of WNG's deals resulted in re-leasing the aircraft, either to the current lessee or another airline. Ultimately WNG would sell the

---

[11] Rolls-Royce defined QEC as a basic engine plus electrical, fuel, oil, and air systems.

[12] The 757 shared the same cockpit layout as the wide-body 767, so flight crews trained on one aircraft could be certified on the other without additional training.

aircraft, or, if the airframe were near the end of its operating life based on the LOV, WNG might sell the airframe and lease or sell the engines and other major components, including the landing gear and the auxiliary power unit. Another, less likely option was a freighter conversion. Aircraft that did not justify further investment to meet the airworthiness requirements for passenger transport were sometimes converted to freight-carrying aircraft. Such a conversion required extensive airframe investment. Federal Express operated 70 converted 757 freighters at the time WNG was considering this investment.

WNG had used published aircraft-appraisal valuations to determine the proposed $15 million purchase price for the 757s and engines. To estimate the residual value—the market value of the equipment at the end of the lease—Su had used comparable appraisal valuations and engine values based upon expected engine life at lease expiry. Those valuations suggested a residual value of approximately $14 million. However, Su knew that the market for 757s was far less robust than the market for more popular aircraft and that finding a buyer in a timely fashion was often very difficult, unless the seller was willing to reduce the asking price by up to 20%. Also, when he considered the age of the 757s and their LOV, Su doubted that selling the aircraft to another operator would be a viable option when the lease expired.

The most likely option in Su's view was to re-lease the equipment to another operator, and for this there was a reasonably healthy market. He expected that when the lease expired at the end of 2014, the aircraft and engines would have up to three years of remaining operating life, and he surmised that the equipment could be re-leased at the same monthly rental rate. Su estimated that the most likely outcome for WNG would be that the equipment would be on lease for 80% of the time during the last three years of operating life, after which WNG would realize $3 million for each aircraft, including parts and engines.

Finally, Su considered the lessee. The airline was far less creditworthy than WNG's typical client. It had suffered significant losses in recent years and was heavily in debt, which made Su wonder about the risks of entering into a deal with a heavily indebted and financially challenged counterparty. Would the airline be able to meet its financial obligations to WNG? On the plus side, the airline had completed several sale-and-leaseback deals in the past 18 months, which had substantially improved its balance sheet. The question for Su was whether WNG's usual IRR of 11% to 14% would be sufficient compensation for either WNG or WNG's investors. Therefore, to reflect the higher risk, Su had chosen to use a required annual return of 20% to evaluate the deal.

The Side Letter

As Su began reviewing all the documents of the deal, he learned that the final inspections had just been completed and WNG had discovered more problems with the condition of the equipment. At the time of the LOI, WNG had assumed that all the engines were serviceable and the trace would be intact for all the equipment except the landing gear. To Su's chagrin, the most recent inspections revealed that one of the two spare engines was not serviceable, and a long list of additional equipment lacked back-to-birth traceability. To deal with these revelations, WNG would draft and send a "side letter" to the airline, detailing the inspection results and specifying revisions to the terms in the LOI. The first item in the side letter would be a reduction of the purchase price by $750,000 as compensation for the unserviceable engine.

The inspection team had estimated the value of the items missing trace documentation as "at least US$1.4 million." To compensate for the missing traces, WNG was seeking two adjustments to the LOI terms: a reduction in the purchase price by $1.4 million and an increase in the monthly rent by $140,000 (10% of the $1.4 million). The additional rent would serve as an incentive for the seller/lessee to locate and provide as many of the records as possible and as quickly as possible. If and when the missing documentation was located and provided, the additional 10% in rent for those items would no longer apply. Also, if the airline were to agree to re-lease the equipment beyond 2014, the additional 10% in rent would no longer apply.

As Su reviewed the proposed terms of the side letter, it was clear to him that the revisions to the purchase price and the additional rent would have a substantial impact on the value of the lease to WNG. He wondered about the value of the unserviceable engine. Su was aware that a used modern jet engine contained precious metals such as cadmium and palladium that would have some small value in the scrap market. If the engine could be sold for parts, it could be worth in the neighborhood of $50,000, but since the engine was unserviceable, Su was assuming a residual/salvage value of zero for the analysis.

Like the purchase price, Su's estimate of the residual value would have to be adjusted for the unserviceable engine and the missing trace. Su estimated that a reduction of the appraisal value by $1.4 million would approximate the impact of the missing trace. If anything, however, the missing trace would make finding a buyer even more difficult than he had originally thought. The prospect of searching for a buyer for months and months made it all the more likely to Su that WNG would follow a re-leasing strategy to stretch out the cash flows for the equipment.

With these issues in mind, Su had begun to create a model for computing the net present value (NPV) and IRR of the cash flows. Because of the tax advantages of the SPE structure, Su conducted his analyses with a zero marginal tax rate. Included in the specific cash flows of the deal (**Exhibit 41.5**) were the purchase price and rental rates agreed upon in the LOI, plus the adjustments to the purchase price and the additional rent demanded in the side letter. Su wondered whether the airline would be able to locate the missing records, and if not, whether the extra rent would become unaffordable. Maybe it would be better to propose a larger reduction of the purchase price and smaller additional rent payments. Most importantly, however, Su wondered whether this deal would be profitable for WNG.

EXHIBIT 41.1 | Global Air Transport: Billions of Passengers Carried 1970–2015

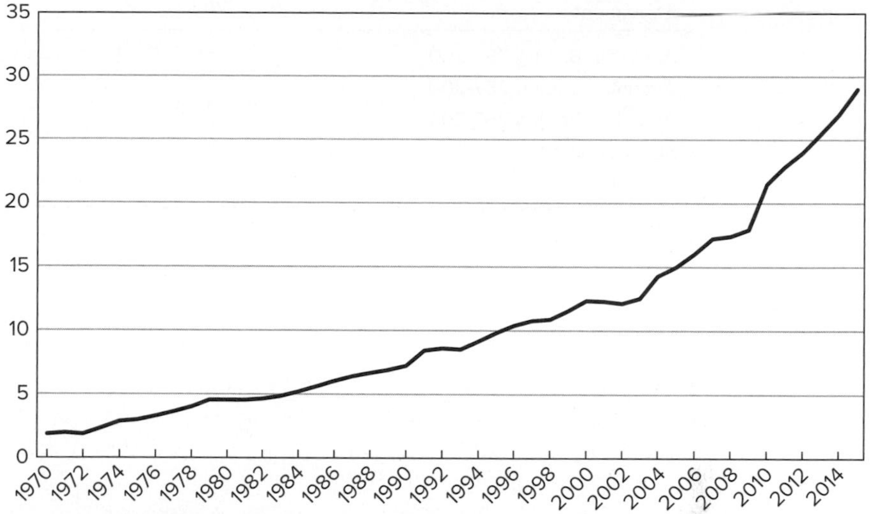

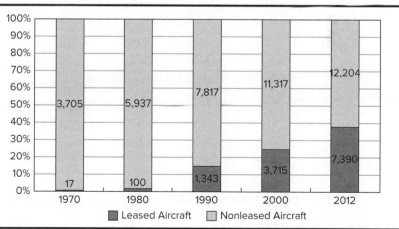

Source: Created by author from data provided by the World Bank from the International Civil Aviation Organization, Civil Aviation Statistics of the World, and ICAO staff estimates, http://data.worldbank.org/indicator/ IS.AIR.PSGR (accessed Feb. 3, 2017).

EXHIBIT 41.2 | Growth of Leased Aircraft 1970–2012

Sources: Created by author using Boeing Corporation data from Avolon Holdings Limited, Form F-1 Registration Statement, December 1, 2014, 90, https://www.sec.gov/Archives/edgar/data/1610128/000119312514428456/ d739557df1a.htm (accessed Feb. 3, 2017) and "Aircraft Leasing—A Promising Investment Market for Institutional Investors," KGAL Group, 3, http://www.kgal-group.com/fileadmin/kgal/documents/pdf_WhitePaper/KGAL_White-Paper_Aircraft-Leasing.pdf (accessed Feb. 3, 2017).

EXHIBIT 41.3 | Equipment to be Purchased and Leased Back

Equipment	Rolls-Royce Engine
Aircraft 1: Boeing 757-200	(2) RB211-535E4
Aircraft 1: Boeing 757-200	(2) RB211-535E4
Aircraft 1: Boeing 757-200	(2) RB211-535E4
Spare Engine 1	(1) RB211-535E4
Spare Engine 2	(1) RB211-535E4

Source: Created by author.

EXHIBIT 41.4 | Aircraft Capacity and Trip Costs of Selected Aircraft in the Short-Haul Sector 1,000 nautical miles (1,900 km)

Aircraft type	757-200	737-900ER	737-800	737-700	A321-200	A320	A319
Maximum take-off weight (lbs)	255,000	187,700	174,200	154,500	205,000	169,800	166,450
Seats	190	177	160	128	180	150	124
Available Seat Miles	190,000	177,000	160,000	128,000	180,000	150,000	124,000
Fuel burn-USG*	2,805	2,350	2,100	1,700	2,200	1,915	1,791
Fuel cost @ $1.60/USG	4,488	3,760	3,360	2,720	3,520	3,064	2,866
Fuel cost/Available seat mile	$ 0.0236	$ 0.0212	$ 0.0210	$ 0.0213	$ 0.0196	$ 0.0204	$ 0.0231
Maintenance cost $/FH**	1,140	662	632	602	652	637	617
Maintenance cost-$	2,887	1,677	1,601	1,534	1,652	1,614	1,573
Flightcrew cost-$	965	910	910	910	910	910	910
Flight attendant cost-$	1,455	1,273	1,091	732	1,273	1,091	732
Landing and navigation cost-$	1,129	922	868	823	973	856	852
Total cash direct operating costs-$	10,924	8,542	7,830	6,719	8,328	7,535	6,933
Cash direct operating costs/Seat-$	57	48	49	53	46	50	56
Lease rate-$	350,000	385,000	350,000	320,000	390,000	350,000	310,000
Trip lease cost-$	4,000	4,400	4,000	3,654	4,457	4,000	3,539
Total trip cost-$	14,924	12,942	11,830	10,373	12,785	11,535	10,472
Trip cost/seat-$	79	73	74	81	71	77	84
Unit cost (Cost per Available Seat Mile)	$ 0.0785	$ 0.0731	$ 0.0739	$ 0.0810	$ 0.0710	$ 0.0769	$ 0.0844

*USG = U.S. gallons.

**FH = flight hour.

Data source: "Analysing the Options for 757 Replacement," *Aircraft Commerce*, no. 42, August/September 2005, 29.

EXHIBIT 41.5 | Summary of Cash-Flow Assumptions

Letter of intent (LOI) terms:	
Lease expiry	15-Dec-14
Purchase price	$15,000,000
Monthly rent*	$ 325,000
Side letter adjustments:	
Published value of unserviceable engine	($ 750,000)
Published value of items missing trace	($ 1,400,000)
Adjusted purchase price	$12,850,000
Additional rent of items missing trace (10% of value)	$ 140,000
Analyst assumptions:	
1-year residual value (at time of LOI)	$14,000,000
Haircut to residual value for unserviceable engine	($ 750,000)
Haircut to residual value for missing trace	($ 1,400,000)
Revised estimate of residual value	$11,850,000
Tax rate	0.0%
Annual required rate of return	20.0%

*Rent is due at the beginning of each month with the first payment due at closing

Source: Author estimates.

Mogen, Inc.

On January 10, 2006, the managing director of Merrill Lynch's Equity-Linked Capital Markets Group, Dar Maanavi, was reviewing the final drafts of a proposal for a convertible debt offering by MoGen, Inc. As a leading biotechnology company in the United States, MoGen had become an important client for Merrill Lynch over the years. In fact, if this deal were to be approved by MoGen at $5 billion, it would represent Merrill Lynch's third financing for MoGen in four years with proceeds raised totaling $10 billion. Moreover, this "convert" would be the largest such single offering in history. The proceeds were earmarked to fund a variety of capital expenditures, research and development (R&D) expenses, working capital needs, as well as a share repurchase program.

The Merrill Lynch team had been working with MoGen's senior management to find the right tradeoff between the conversion feature and the coupon rate for the bond. Maanavi knew from experience that there was no "free lunch," when structuring the pricing of a convertible. Issuing companies wanted the conversion price to be as high as possible and the coupon rate to be as low as possible; whereas investors wanted the opposite: a low conversion price and a high coupon rate. Thus, the challenge was to structure the convert to make it attractive to the issuing company in terms of its cost of capital, while at the same time selling for full price in the market. Maanavi was confident that the right balance in the terms of the convert could be found, and he was also confident that the convert would serve MoGen's financing needs better than a straight bond or equity issuance. But, he needed to make a decision about the final terms of the issue in the next few hours, as the meeting with MoGen was scheduled for early the next morning.

Company History

Founded in 1985 as MoGen (Molecular Genetics) the company was among the first in the biotechnology industry to deliver on the commercial promises of emerging sciences, such as recombinant DNA and molecular biology. After years of research, MoGen emerged with two of the first biologically derived human therapeutic drugs, RENGEN and MENGEN, both of which helped to offset the damaging effects from chemotherapy

This case was prepared by Alex Holsenbeck (MBA '08), under the supervision of Professor Kenneth M. Eades. It was written as a basis for class discussion rather than to illustrate effective or ineffective handling of an administrative situation. Copyright © 2008 by the University of Virginia Darden School Foundation, Charlottesville, VA. All rights reserved. *To order copies, send an e-mail to* sales@dardenbusinesspublishing.com. *No part of this publication may be reproduced, stored in a retrieval system, used in a spreadsheet, or transmitted in any form or by any means—electronic, mechanical, photocopying, recording, or otherwise—without the permission of the Darden School Foundation.*

for cancer patients undergoing treatment. Those two MoGen products were among the first "blockbuster" drugs to emerge from the nascent biotechnology industry.

By 2006, MoGen was one of the leading biotech companies in an industry that included firms such as Genentech, Amgen, Gilead Sciences, Celgene, and Genzyme. The keys to success for all biotech companies were finding new drugs through research and then getting the drugs approved by the U.S. Food and Drug Administration (FDA). MoGen's strategy for drug development was to determine the best mode for attacking a patient's issue and then focusing on creating solutions via that mode. Under that approach, MoGen had been able to produce drugs with the highest likelihood of both successfully treating the patient as well as making the company a competitive leader in drug quality. In January 2006, MoGen's extensive R&D expenditures had resulted in a portfolio of five core products that focused on supportive cancer care. The success of that portfolio had been strong enough to offset other R&D write-offs so that MoGen was able to report $3.7 billion in profits in 2005 on $12.4 billion in sales. Sales had grown at an annual rate of 29% over the previous five years, and earnings per share had improved to $2.93 for 2005, compared with $1.81 and $1.69 for 2004 and 2003, respectively (**Exhibits 42.1** and **42.2**).

The FDA served as the regulating authority to safeguard the public from dangerous drugs and required extensive testing before it would allow a drug to enter the U.S. marketplace. The multiple hurdles and long lead-times required by the FDA created a constant tension with the biotech firms who wanted quick approval to maximize the return on their large investments in R&D. Moreover, there was always the risk that a drug would not be approved or that after it was approved, it would be pulled from the market due to unexpected adverse reactions by patients. Over the years, the industry had made progress in shortening the approval time and improving the predictability of the approval process. At the same time, industry R&D expenditures had increased 12.6% over 2003 in the continuing race to find the next big breakthrough product.

Like all biotech companies, MoGen faced uncertainty regarding new product creation as well as challenges involved with sustaining a pipeline of future products. Now a competitive threat of follow-on biologics or "biosimilars" began emerging. As drugs neared the end of their patent protection, competitors would produce similar drugs as substitutes. Competitors could not produce the drug exactly, because they did not have access to the original manufacturer's molecular clone or purification process. Thus, biosimilars required their own approval to ensure they performed as safely as the original drugs. For MoGen, this threat was particularly significant in Europe, where several patents were approaching expiration.

Funding Needs

MoGen needed to ensure a consistent supply of cash to fund R&D and to maintain financial flexibility in the face of uncertain challenges and opportunities. MoGen had cited several key areas that would require approximately $10 billion in funding for 2006:

1. *Expanding manufacturing and formulation, and fill and finish capacity*: Recently, the company had not been able to scale up production to match increases in demand for certain core products. The reason for the problem was that MoGen outsourced most of its formulation and fill and finish manufacturing processes,

and these offshore companies had not been able to expand their operations quickly enough. Therefore, MoGen wanted to remove such supply risks by increasing both its internal manufacturing capacity in its two existing facilities in Puerto Rico as well as new construction in Ireland. These projects represented a majority of MoGen's total capital expenditures that were projected to exceed $1 billion in 2006.

2. *Expanding investment in R&D and late-stage trials*: Late-stage trials were particularly expensive, but were also critical as they represented the last big hurdle before a drug could be approved by the FDA. With 11 late-stage "mega-site" trials expected to commence in 2006, management knew that successful outcomes were critical for MoGen's ability to maintain momentum behind its new drug development pipeline. The trials would likely cost $500 million. MoGen had also decided to diversify its product line by significantly increasing R&D to approximately $3 billion for 2006, which was an increase of 30% over 2005.

3. *Acquisition and licensing*: MoGen had completed several acquisition and licensing deals that had helped it achieve the strong growth in revenues and earnings per share (EPS). The company expected to continue this strategy and had projected to complete a purchase of Genix, Inc., in 2006 for approximately $2 billion in cash. This acquisition was designed to help MoGen capitalize on Genix's expertise in the discovery, development, and manufacture of human therapeutic antibodies.

4. *The stock repurchase program*: Due to the highly uncertain nature of its operations, MoGen had never issued dividends to shareholders but instead had chosen to pursue a stock repurchase program. Senior management felt that this demonstrated a strong belief in the company's future and was an effective way to return cash to shareholders without being held to the expectation of having a regular dividend payout. Due to strong operational and financial performance over the past several years, MoGen had executed several billion dollars worth of stock repurchases, and it was management's intent to continue repurchases over the next few years. In 2005, MoGen purchased a total of 63.2 million shares for an aggregate $4.4 billion.[1] As of December 31, 2005, MoGen had $6.5 billion remaining in the authorized share repurchase plan, of which management expected to spend $3.5 billion in 2006.

With internally generated sources of funds expected to be $5 billion (net income plus depreciation), MoGen would fall well below the $10 billion expected uses of funds for 2006. Thus, management estimated that an offering size of about $5 billion would cover MoGen's needs for the coming year.

Convertible Debt

A convertible bond was considered a hybrid security, because it had attributes of both debt and equity. From an investor's point of view, a convert provided the safety of a bond plus the upside potential of equity. The safety came from receiving a fixed income

---

[1]Through various share repurchase programs authorized by the board of directors, MoGen had repurchased $4.4 billion, $4.1 billion, and $1.8 billion of MoGen common stock in 2005, 2004, and 2003, respectively.

stream in the form of the bond's coupon payments plus the return of principal. The upside potential came from the ability to convert the bond into shares of common stock. Thus, if the stock price should rise above the conversion price, the investor could convert and receive more than the principal amount. Because of the potential to realize capital appreciation via the conversion feature, a convert's coupon rate was always set lower than what the issuing company would pay for straight debt. Thus, when investors bought a convertible bond, they received less income than from a comparable straight bond, but they gained the chance of receiving more than the face value if the bond's conversion value exceeded the face value.

To illustrate, consider a convertible bond issued by BIO, Inc., with a face value of $1,000 and a maturity of five years. Assume that the convert carries a coupon rate of 4% and a conversion price of $50 per share and that BIO's stock was selling for $37.50 per share at the time of issuance. The coupon payment gives an investor $40 per year in interest (4% × $1,000), and the conversion feature gives investors the opportunity to exchange the bond for 20 shares (underlying shares) of BIO's common stock ($1,000 ÷ $50). Because BIO's stock was selling at $37.50 at issuance, the stock price would need to appreciate by 33% (conversion premium) to reach the conversion price of $50. For example, if BIO's stock price were to appreciate to $60 per share, investors could convert each bond into 20 shares to realize the bond's conversion value of $1,200. On the other hand, if BIO's stock price failed to reach $50 within the five-year life of the bond, the investors would not convert, but rather would choose to receive the bond's $1,000 face value in cash.

Because the conversion feature represented a right, rather than an obligation, investors would postpone conversion as long as possible even if the bond was well "in the money." Suppose, for example, that after three years BIO's stock had risen to $60. Investors would then be holding a bond with a conversion value of $1,200; which is to say, if converted they would receive the 20 underlying shares worth $60 each. With two years left until maturity, however, investors would find that they could realize a higher value by selling the bond on the open market, rather than converting it. For example, the bond might be selling for $1,250; $50 higher than the conversion value. Such a premium over conversion value is typical, because the market recognizes that convertibles have unlimited upside potential, but protected downside. Unlike owning BIO stock directly, the price of the convertible bond cannot fall lower than its bond value—the value of the coupon payments and principal payment—but its conversion value could rise as high as the stock price will take it. Thus, as long as more upside potential is possible, the premium price will exist, and investors will have the incentive to sell their bonds, rather than convert them prior to maturity.[2]

Academics modeled the value of a convertible as the sum of the straight bond value plus the value of the conversion feature. This was equivalent to valuing a convert as a bond plus a call option or a warrant. Although MoGen did not have any warrants outstanding, there was an active market in MoGen options (**Exhibit 42.3**). Over the past five years, MoGen's stock price had experienced modest appreciation with considerable variation (**Exhibit 42.4**).

---

[2]If BIO paid a dividend on its stock and if the dividend cash flow exceeded the coupon payment, investors might convert prior to maturity in order to capture the higher cash flow afforded by owning the stock.

MoGen's Financial Strategy

As of December 31, 2005, the company had approximately $4 billion of long-term debt on the books (**Exhibit 42.5**). About $2 billion of the debt was in the form of straight debt with the remaining $1.8 billion as seven-year convertible notes. The combination of industry and company-specific risks had led MoGen to keep its long-term debt at or below 20% of total capitalization. There was a common belief that because of the industry risks, credit-rating agencies tended to penalize biotech firms by placing a "ceiling" on their credit ratings. MoGen's relatively low leverage, however, allowed it to command a Standard and Poor's (S&P) rating of A+, which was the highest rating within the industry. Based on discussions with S&P, MoGen management was confident that the company would be able to maintain its rating for the $5 billion new straight debt or convertible issuance. For the current market conditions, Merrill Lynch had estimated a cost to MoGen of 5.75%, if it issued straight five-year bonds. (See **Exhibit 42.6** for capital market data.)

MoGen's seven-year convertible notes had been issued in 2003 and carried a conversion price of $90.000 per share. Because the stock price was currently at $77.98 per share, the bondholders had not yet had the opportunity to exercise the conversion option.[3] Thus, the convertibles had proven to be a low-cost funding source for MoGen, as it was paying a coupon of only 1.125%. If the stock price continued to remain below the conversion price, the issue would not be converted and MoGen would simply retire the bonds in 2010 (or earlier, if called) at an all-in annual cost of 1.125%.[4] On the other hand, if the stock price appreciated substantially by 2010, then the bondholders would convert and MoGen would need to issue 11.1 shares per bond outstanding or approximately 20 million new shares. Issuing the shares would not necessarily be a bad outcome, because it would amount to issuing shares at $90 rather than at $61, the stock price at the time of issuance.[5]

Since its initial public offering (IPO), MoGen had avoided issuing new equity, except for the small amounts of new shares issued each year as part of management's incentive compensation plan. The addition of these shares had been more than offset, however, by MoGen's share repurchase program, so that shares outstanding had fallen from 1,280 million in 2004, to 1,224 million in 2005. Repurchasing shares served two purposes for MoGen: (1) It had a favorable impact upon EPS by reducing the shares outstanding; and (2) It served as a method for distributing cash to shareholders. Although MoGen could pay dividends, management preferred the flexibility

---

[3]Like most convertibles, MoGen's seven-year notes were callable. This meant that MoGen had the right to buy back the bonds at a given call price at a 10% or 15% premium over face value. The call provision was often used as a means to force the bondholders to convert their bonds into stock. For example, assume a bond was callable at "110" (10% over face value) and the underlying stock price had appreciated so that the bond price had risen to a 20% premium over face value. If the company called the bond at 110, investors would choose to convert, to keep the 20% premium rather than accept the 10% call premium from the company.

[4]Interest expense for convertibles was tax deductible just like interest on straight bonds. Thus, the 1.125% coupon rate would represent an after-tax cost of about 0.78%, for a 40% tax rate. Convertible bondholders had no voting rights prior to converting the bonds into equity.

[5]The impact of conversion was reported in fully *diluted* earnings per share that was computed using the potential shares outstanding, including shares issued in the event of a conversion.

of repurchasing shares. If MoGen were to institute a dividend, there was always the risk that the dividend might need to be decreased or eliminated during hard times which, when announced, would likely result in a significant drop of the stock price.

Merrill Lynch Equity-Linked Origination Team

The U.S. Equity-Linked Origination Team was part of Merrill Lynch's Equity Capital Markets Division that resided in the Investment Banking Division. The team was the product group that focused on convertible, corporate derivative, and special equity transaction origination for Merrill Lynch's U.S. corporate clients. As product experts, members worked with the industry bankers to educate clients on the benefits of utilizing equity-linked instruments. They also worked closely with derivatives and convertible traders, the equity and equity-linked sales teams, and institutional investors including hedge funds, to determine the market demand for various strategies and securities. Members had a high level of expertise in tax, accounting, and legal issues. The technical aspects of equity-linked securities were rigorous, requiring significant financial modeling skills, including the use of option pricing models, such as Black-Scholes and other proprietary versions of the model used to price convertible bonds. Within the equities division and investment banking, the team was considered one of the most technically capable and had proven to be among the most profitable businesses at Merrill Lynch.

Pricing Decision

Dar Maanavi was excited by the prospect that Merrill Lynch would be the lead book runner of the largest convertible offering in history. At $5 billion, MoGen's issue would represent more than 12% of the total proceeds for convertible debt in the United States during 2005. Although the convert market was quite liquid and the Merrill Lynch team was confident that the issue would be well received, the unprecedented size heightened the need to make it as marketable as possible. Maanavi knew that MoGen wanted a maturity of five years, but was less certain as to what he should propose regarding the conversion premium and coupon rate. These two terms needed to be satisfactory to MoGen's senior management team while at the same time being attractive to potential investors in the marketplace. **Exhibit 42.7** shows the terms of the offering that had already been determined.

Most convertibles carried conversion premiums in the range of 10% to 40%. The coupon rates for a convertible depended upon many factors, including the conversion premium, maturity, credit rating, and the market's perception of the volatility of the issuing company's stock. Issuing companies wanted low coupon rates and high conversion premiums, whereas investors wanted the opposite: high coupons and low conversion premiums. Companies liked a high conversion premium, because it effectively set the price at which its shares would be issued in the future. For example, if MoGen's bond was issued with a conversion price of $109, it would represent a 40% conversion premium over its current stock price of $77.98. Thus, if the issue were eventually converted, the number of MoGen shares issued would be 40% less than what MoGen would have issued at the current stock price. Of course, a high conversion premium also carried with it a lower probability that the stock would ever reach the conversion price. To compensate investors for this reduced upside potential, MoGen would need to offer a higher coupon rate. Thus, the challenge for Maanavi was to find the right combination of conversion premium and coupon rate that would be acceptable to MoGen management as well as desirable to investors.

There were two types of investor groups for convertibles: fundamental investors and hedge funds. Fundamental investors liked convertibles, because they viewed them as a safer form of equity investment. Hedge fund investors viewed convertibles as an opportunity to engage in an arbitrage trading strategy that typically involved holding long positions of the convertible and short positions of the common stock. Companies preferred to have fundamental investors, because they took a longer-term view of their investment than hedge funds. If the conversion premium was set above 40%, fundamental investors tended to lose interest because the convertible became a more speculative investment with less upside potential. Thus, if the conversion premium were set at 40% or higher, it could be necessary to offer an abnormally high coupon rate for a convertible. In either case, Maanavi thought a high conversion premium was not appropriate for such a large offering. It could work for a smaller, more volatile stock, but not for MoGen and not for a $5 billion offering.

Early in his conversations with MoGen, Maanavi had discussed the accounting treatment required for convertibles. Recently, most convertibles were being structured to use the "treasury stock method," which was desirable because it reduced the impact upon the reported fully diluted EPS. To qualify for the treasury stock method the convertible needed to be structured as a net settled security. This meant that investors would always receive cash for the principal amount of $1,000 per bond, but could receive either cash or shares for the excess over $1,000 upon conversion. The alternative method of accounting was the if-converted method, which would require MoGen to compute fully diluted EPS, as if investors received shares for the full amount of the bond when they converted; which is to say the new shares equaled the principal amount divided by the conversion price per share. The treasury stock method, however, would allow MoGen to report far fewer fully diluted shares for EPS purposes because it only included shares representing the *excess* of the bond's conversion value over the principal amount. Because much of the issue's proceeds would be used to fund the stock repurchase program, MoGen's management felt that using the treasury stock method would be a better representation to the market of MoGen's likely EPS, and therefore agreed to structure the issue accordingly (see "conversion rights" in **Exhibit 42.7**).

In light of MoGen management's objectives, Maanavi decided to propose a conversion premium of 25%, which was equivalent to conversion price of $97.000.[6] MoGen management would appreciate that the conversion premium would appeal to a broad segment of the market, which was important for a $5 billion offering. On the other hand, Maanavi knew that management would be disappointed that the conversion premium was not higher. Management felt that the stock was selling at a depressed price and

---

[6]Although the conversion premium would be determined in advance of the issuance, the conversion price would be determined based on the stock price on the issuance day. For example, a 25% conversion premium would lead to a conversion price of $100, if MoGen's stock price were to rise to $80 on the date of issuance.

represented an excellent buy. In fact, part of the rationale for having the stock repurchase program was to take advantage of the stock price being low. Maanavi suspected that management would express concern that a 25% premium would be sending a bad signal to the market: a low conversion premium could be interpreted as management's lack of confidence in the upside potential of the stock. For a five-year issue, the stock would only need to rise by 5% per year to reach the conversion price by maturity. If management truly believed the stock had strong appreciation potential, then the conversion premium should be set much higher.

If Maanavi could convince MoGen to accept the 25% conversion premium, then choosing the coupon rate was the last piece of the pricing puzzle to solve. Because he was proposing a mid-range conversion premium, investors would be satisfied with a modest coupon. Based on MoGen's bond rating, the company would be able to issue straight five-year bonds with a 5.75% yield. Therefore, Maanavi knew that the convertible should carry a coupon rate noticeably lower than 5.75%. The challenge was to estimate the coupon rate that would result in the debt being issued at exactly the face value of $1,000 per bond.

EXHIBIT 42.1 | Consolidated Income Statements
(in millions of dollars, except per share)

	2005	2004	2003
Total Revenues	**$12,430**	**$10,550**	**$8,356**
Operating expenses:			
Cost of sales	2,082	1,731	1,341
Research and development	2,314	2,028	1,655
Write-off of acquired research and development	0	554	0
Selling, general, and administrative	2,790	2,556	1,957
Amortization of acquired intangible assets	347	333	336
Other items, net	49	0	(24)
Total operating expenses	7,582	7,202	5,265
Operating Income	**4,848**	**3,348**	**3,091**
Interest expense, net	20	47	82
Income before income taxes	4,868	3,395	3,173
Provision for income taxes	1,194	1,032	914
Net income	**$3,674**	**$2,363**	**$2,259**
Earnings per share:			
Basic	$2.97	$1.86	$1.75
Diluted	$2.93	$1.81	$1.69
Shares used in calculation of earnings per share (millions):			
Basic	1,236	1,271	1,288
Diluted	1,258	1,320	1,346

EXHIBIT 42.2 | Consolidated Balance Sheets
(in millions of dollars)

	2005	2004	2003
Current Assets			
Cash and short-term investments	5,255	5,808	5,123
Receivables	1,769	1,461	1,008
Inventories	1,258	888	713
Other current assets	953	1,013	558
Total current assets	9,235	9,170	7,402
Long-Term Assets			
Net property, plant, and equipment	5,038	4,712	3,799
Intangible assets and goodwill	14,237	14,558	14,108
Other assets	787	781	804
Total Assets	29,297	29,221	26,113
Current Liabilities			
Current portion of long-term debt	–	1,173	–
Accounts payable	596	507	327
Other accrued liabilities	2,999	2,477	2,129
Total current liabilities	3,595	4,157	2,456
Long-Term Liabilities			
Long-term debt	3,957	3,937	3,080
Deferred taxes and other	1,294	1,422	1,188
Total liabilities	8,846	9,516	6,724
Shareholders' Equity			
Common capital ($0.0001 par value)	0.122	0.126	0.128
Capital surplus	23,561	22,078	19,995
Retained earnings	(3,110)	(2,373)	(606)
Total Shareholders' Equity	20,451	19,705	19,389
Total Liabilities and Shareholders' Equity	29,297	29,221	26,113
Common shares outstanding (millions)	1,224	1,260	1,284

EXHIBIT 42.3 | MoGen Option Data: January 10, 2006
(MoGen closing stock price = $77.98)

	Exercise Date	Days to Maturity	Exercise Price	Closing Price	Open Interest	Volume
Call	4/22/2006	102	$75	$6.60	3,677	52
Call	4/22/2006	102	$80	$3.85	6,444	98
Call	1/20/2007	375	$75	$10.70	6,974	143
Call	1/20/2007	375	$80	$7.75	9,790	3
Put	4/22/2006	102	$75	$2.70	9,529	10
Put	4/22/2006	102	$80	$5.00	8,512	5
Put	1/20/2007	375	$75	$4.65	5,175	10
Put	1/20/2007	375	$80	$6.90	4,380	0

EXHIBIT 42.4 | MoGen Stock Price for 2001 to 2005

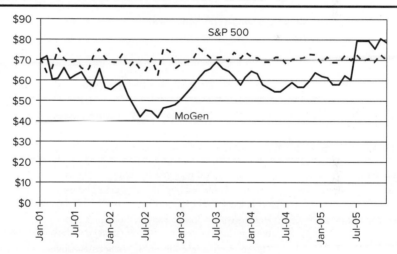

Performance Summary for 2001 to 2005

	MoGen	S&P 500
Five-year appreciation	12.2%	−8.6%
Annual appreciation (average)	2.4%	−1.7%
Annualized volatility	27.0%	14.9%

EXHIBIT 42.5 | Long-Term Debt as of December 31, 2005
(in millions of dollars)

1.125% convertible notes due in 2010	$1,759
4.85% notes due 2014	1,000
4.00% notes due 2009	998
6.5% debt securities due 2007	100
8.1% notes due 2097	100
Total borrowings	$3,957

EXHIBIT 42.6 | Capital Market Data for January 2006

U.S. Government Yields	
Treasury bill (1-year)	4.45%
Treasury note (5-year)	4.46%
Treasury bond (20-year)	4.65%
Corporate Long-Term Bond Yields	
Aaa	5.29%
Aa	5.45%
A	5.79%
Baa	6.24%

EXHIBIT 42.7 | Selected Terms of Convertible Senior Notes

Notes offered	$5,000,000,000 principal amount of Convertible Senior Notes due February 1, 2011.
Interest and payment dates	The annual interest rate of _____ would be payable semiannually in arrears in cash on January 1 and July 1 of each year, beginning July 1, 2006.
Conversion rights	Holders will be able to convert their notes prior to the close of business on the business day before the stated maturity date based on the applicable conversion rate.
	The conversion rate will be _____ shares of common stock per $1,000 principal amount. This is equivalent to a conversion price of _____ per share of common stock.
	Upon conversion, a holder will receive an amount in cash equal to the lesser of (i) the principal amount of the note, and (ii) the conversion value. If the conversion value exceeds the principal amount of the note on the conversion date, MoGen will deliver cash or common stock or a combination of cash and common stock for the conversion value in excess of $1,000.
Ranking	The notes will rank equal in right of payment to all of MoGen's existing and future unsecured indebtedness and senior in right to payment to all of MoGen's existing and future subordinated indebtedness.
Use of proceeds	We estimate that the net proceeds from this offering will be approximately $4.9 billion after deducting estimated discounts, commissions, and expenses. We intend to use the net proceeds for our share repurchase program as well as for working capital and general corporate purposes.

## PART 8

Valuing the Enterprise: Acquisitions and Buyouts

Methods of Valuation for Mergers and Acquisitions

This note addresses the methods used to value companies in a merger and acquisitions (M&A) setting. It provides a detailed description of the discounted-cash-flow (DCF) approach and reviews other methods of valuation, such as market multiples of peer firms, book value, liquidation value, replacement cost, market value, and comparable transaction multiples.

Discounted-Cash-Flow Method

Overview

The DCF approach in an M&A setting attempts to determine the *enterprise value*, or value of the company, by computing the present value of cash flows over the life of the company.[1] Because a corporation is assumed to have infinite life, the analysis is broken into two parts: a forecast period and a terminal value. In the *forecast period*, explicit forecasts of free cash flow that incorporate the economic costs and benefits of the transaction must be developed. Ideally, the forecast period should comprise the interval over which the firm is in a transitional state, as when enjoying a temporary competitive advantage (i.e., the circumstances wherein expected returns exceed required returns). In most circumstances, a forecast period of five or ten years is used.

The *terminal value* of the company, derived from free cash flows occurring after the forecast period, is estimated in the last year of the forecast period and capitalizes the

---

[1]This note focuses on valuing the company as a whole (i.e., the enterprise). An estimate of equity value can be derived under this approach by subtracting interest-bearing debt from enterprise value. An alternative method not pursued here values the equity using residual cash flows, which are computed as net of interest payments and debt repayments plus debt issuances. Residual cash flows must be discounted at the cost of equity.

This technical note was prepared by Susan Chaplinsky, Professor of Business Administration, and Michael J. Schill, Associate Professor of Business Administration, with the assistance of Paul Doherty (MBA '99). Portions of this note draw on an earlier note, "Note on Valuation Analysis for Mergers and Acquisitions" (UVA-F-0557). Copyright © 2000 by the University of Virginia Darden School Foundation, Charlottesville, VA. All rights reserved. *To order copies, send an e-mail to* sales@dardenbusinesspublishing.com. *No part of this publication may be reproduced, stored in a retrieval system, used in a spreadsheet, or transmitted in any form or by any means—electronic, mechanical, photocopying, recording, or otherwise—without the permission of the Darden School Foundation.*

present value of all future cash flows beyond the forecast period. To estimate the terminal value, cash flows are projected under a steady-state assumption that the firm enjoys no opportunities for abnormal growth or that expected returns equal required returns following the forecast period. Once a schedule of free cash flows is developed for the enterprise, the weighted average cost of capital (WACC) is used to discount them to determine the present value. The sum of the present values of the forecast period and the terminal value cash flows provides an estimate of company or enterprise value.

Review of DCF basics

Let us briefly review the construction of free cash flows, terminal value, and the WACC. It is important to realize that these fundamental concepts work equally well when valuing an investment project as they do in an M&A setting.

Free cash flows: The free cash flows in an M&A analysis should be the expected incremental operating cash flows attributable to the acquisition, before consideration of financing charges (i.e., prefinancing cash flows). Free cash flow equals the sum of net operating profits after taxes (NOPAT), plus depreciation and noncash charges, less capital investment and less investment in working capital. NOPAT captures the earnings after taxes that are available to all providers of capital. That is, NOPAT has no deductions for financing costs. Moreover, because the tax deductibility of interest payments is accounted for in the WACC, such financing tax effects are also excluded from the free cash flow, which is expressed in Equation 43.1.

$$FCF = NOPAT + Depreciation - CAPEX - \Delta NWC, \tag{1}$$

where:

- *NOPAT* is equal to *EBIT (1 − t)*, where *t* is the appropriate marginal (not average) cash tax rate, which should be inclusive of federal, state, local, and foreign jurisdictional taxes.[2]

- *Depreciation* is noncash operating charges including depreciation, depletion, and amortization recognized for tax purposes.

- *CAPEX* is capital expenditures for fixed assets.

- ΔNWC is the increase in net working capital defined as current assets less the non-interest-bearing current liabilities.[3]

The cash-flow forecast should be grounded in a thorough industry and company forecast. Care should be taken to ensure that the forecast reflects consistency with firm strategy as well as with macroeconomic and industry trends and competitive pressure.

---

[2]EBIT = earnings before interest and tax.

[3]The net working capital should include the expected cash, receivables, inventory, and payables levels required for the operation of the business. If the firm currently has excess cash (more than is needed to sustain operations), for example, the cash forecast should be reduced to the level of cash required for operations. Excess cash should be valued separately by adding it to the enterprise value.

The forecast period is normally the years during which the analyst estimates free cash flows that are consistent with creating value. A convenient way to think about value creation is whenever the return on net assets (RONA)[4] exceeds the WACC.[5] RONA can be divided into an income statement component and a balance sheet component:

$$RONA = NOPAT/Net\ Assets$$

$$= NOPAT/Sales \times Sales/Net\ Assets$$

In this context, value is created whenever earnings power increases (NOPAT/Sales) or when asset efficiency is improved (Sales/Net Assets). In other words, analysts are assuming value creation whenever they allow the profit margin to improve on the income statement and whenever they allow sales to improve relative to the level of assets on the balance sheet.

Terminal value: A terminal value in the final year of the forecast period is added to reflect the present value of all cash flows occurring thereafter. Because it capitalizes all future cash flows beyond the final year, the terminal value can be a large component of the value of a company, and therefore deserves careful attention. This can be of particular importance when cash flows over the forecast period are close to zero (or even negative) as the result of aggressive investment for growth.

A standard estimator of the terminal value (TV) in the final year of the cash-flow forecast is the constant growth valuation formula **(Equation 43.2).**

$$Terminal\ Value = FCF^{Steady\ State} \div (WACC - g), \tag{2}$$

where:

- $FCF^{Steady\ State}$ is the steady-state expected free cash flow for the year after the final year of the cash-flow forecast.
- *WACC* is the weighted average cost of capital.
- g is the expected steady-state growth rate of $FCF^{Steady\ State}$ in perpetuity.

The free-cash-flow value used in the constant growth valuation formula should reflect the steady-state cash flow for the year after the forecast period. The assumption of the formula is that in steady state, this cash flow will grow in perpetuity at the steady-state growth rate. A convenient approach is to assume that RONA remains constant in perpetuity; that is, both profit margin and asset turnover remain constant in perpetuity. Under this assumption, the analyst grows all financial statement line items (i.e., revenue, costs, assets) at the expected steady-state growth rate. In perpetuity, this assumption makes logical sense in that if a firm is truly in steady state, the financial statements should be growing, by definition, at the same rate.

---

[4]In this context, we define net assets as total assets less non-interest-bearing current liabilities or equivalently as net working capital plus net fixed assets. A similar relationship can be expressed using return on capital (ROC). Because the uses of capital (working capital and fixed assets) equal the sources of capital (debt and equity), it follows that RONA (return on net assets) equals ROC and, therefore, ROC = NOPAT/(Debt + Equity).

[5]WACC is discussed later in this note as the appropriate discount rate used for the free cash flows.

Discount rate: The discount rate should reflect the weighted average of investors' opportunity cost (WACC) on comparable investments. The WACC matches the business risk, expected inflation, and currency of the cash flows to be discounted. In order to avoid penalizing the investment opportunity, the WACC also must incorporate the appropriate target weights of financing going forward. Recall that the appropriate rate is a blend of the required rates of return on debt and equity, weighted by the proportion of the firm's market value they make up (Equation 43.3).

$$WACC = W_d k_d (1 - t) + W_e k_e, \tag{3}$$

where:

- k_d is the required yield on new debt: It is yield to maturity.
- k_e is the cost of equity capital.
- W_d, W_e are target percentages of debt and equity (using market values of debt and equity).[6]
- t is the marginal tax rate.

The costs of debt and equity should be going-forward market rates of return. For debt securities, this is often the yield to maturity that would be demanded on new instruments of the same credit rating and maturity. The cost of equity can be obtained from the Capital Asset Pricing Model (CAPM) (Equation 43.4).

$$k_e = R_f + \beta(R_m - R_f), \tag{4}$$

where:

- R_f is the expected return on risk-free securities over a time horizon consistent with the investment horizon. Most firm valuations are best served by using a long maturity government bond yield.
- $R_m - R_f$ is the expected market risk premium. This value is commonly estimated as the average historical difference between the returns on common stocks and long-term government bonds. For example, Ibbotson Associates estimated that the geometric mean return between 1926 and 2007 for large capitalization U.S. equities between 1926 and 2007 was 10.4%. The geometric mean return on long-term government bonds was 5.5%. The difference between the two implies a historical market-risk premium of about 5.0%. In practice, one observes estimates of the market risk premium that commonly range from 5% to 8%.
- β, or beta, is a measure of the systematic risk of a firm's common stock. The beta of common stock includes compensation for business and financial risk.

---

[6] Debt for purposes of the WACC should include all permanent, interest-bearing debt. If the market value of debt is not available, the book value of debt is often assumed as a reasonable proxy. The shorter the maturity of the debt and the closer the correspondence between the coupon rate and required return on the debt, the more accurate the approximation.

The M&A Setting

No doubt, many of these concepts look familiar. Now we must consider how they are altered by the evaluation of a company in an M&A setting. First, we should recognize that there are two parties (sometimes more) in the transaction: an acquirer (buyer or bidder) and a target firm (seller or acquired). Suppose a bidder is considering the potential purchase of a target firm and we must assess whether the target would be a good investment. Some important questions arise in applying our fundamental concepts:

1. *What are the potential sources of value from the combination? Does the acquirer have particular skills or capabilities that can be used to enhance the value of the target firm? Does the target have critical technology or other strengths that can bring value to the acquirer?*

   Potential sources of gain or cost savings achieved through the combination are called *synergies*. Baseline cash-flow projections for the target firm may or may not include synergies or cost savings gained from merging the operations of the target into those of the acquirer. If the base-case cash flows do not include any of the economic benefits an acquirer might bring to a target, they are referred to as *stand-alone* cash flows. Examining the value of a target on a stand-alone basis can be valuable for several reasons. First, it can provide a view of what the target firm is capable of achieving on its own. This may help establish a floor with respect to value for negotiating purposes. Second, construction of a stand-alone DCF valuation can be compared with the target's current market value. This can be useful in assessing whether the target is under- or overvalued in the marketplace. Given the general efficiency of markets, however, it is unlikely that a target will be significantly over- or undervalued relative to the market. Hence, a stand-alone DCF valuation allows analysts to calibrate model assumptions to those of investors. By testing key assumptions relative to this important benchmark, analysts can gain confidence that the model provides a reasonable guide to investors' perception of the situation.

2. *What is the proper discount rate to use?*

   The discount rate used to value the cash flows of the target should compensate the investor/acquiring firm for the risk of the cash flows. Commonly, the cost of capital of the target firm provides a suitable discount rate for the stand-alone and merger cash flows. The cost of capital of the target firm is generally more appropriate as a discount rate than the cost of capital of the acquiring firm because the target cost of capital generally better captures the risk premium associated with bearing the risk of the target cash flows than does the cost of capital of the acquiring firm. If the target and acquirer are in the same industry, they likely have similar business risk. Because in principle the business risk is similar for the target and the acquirer, either one's WACC may be justifiably used. The use of the target's cost of capital also assumes that the target firm is financed with the optimal proportions of debt and equity and that these proportions will continue after the merger.

   Additional information on the appropriate discount rate can be obtained by computing the WACCs of firms in the target's industry. These estimates can be summarized by taking the average or median WACC. By using the betas and financial structures of firms engaged in this line of business, a reliable estimate of the business risk and optimal financing can be established going forward.

Sometimes an acquirer may intend to increase or decrease the debt level of the target significantly after the merger—perhaps because it believes the target's current financing mix is not optimal. The WACC still must reflect the business risk of the target. A proxy for this can be obtained from the unlevered beta of the target firm's equity or an average unlevered beta for firms with similar business risk. The target's premerger unlevered beta must then be relevered to reflect the acquirer's intended postmerger capital structure.

To unlever a firm beta, one uses the prevailing tax rate (T) and the predeal debt-to-equity ratio (D/E) of the firm associated with the beta estimate (β_L) to solve Equation 43.5:

$$\beta_u = \beta_L/[1 + (1 - T)D/E]. \tag{5}$$

Next, one uses the unlevered beta estimate (β_u) or average unlevered beta estimate (if using multiple firms to estimate the unlevered beta) to relever the beta to the new intended debt-to-equity ratio (D/E^*) (Equation 43.6):

$$\beta'_L = \beta_u[1 + (1 - T)D/E^*] \tag{6}$$

The result is a relevered beta estimate (β'_L) that captures the business risk and the financial risk of the target cash flows.

The circumstances of each transaction will dictate which of these approaches is most reasonable. Of course, if the target's business risk somehow changes because of the merger, some adjustments must be made to all of these approaches on a judgment basis. The key concept is to find the discount rate that best reflects the business and financial risks of the target's cash flows.

3. *After determining the enterprise value, how is the value of the equity computed?*

This is a straightforward calculation that relies upon the definition of enterprise value as the value of cash flows available to *all* providers of capital. Because debt and equity are the sources of capital, it follows that enterprise value (V) equals the sum of debt (D) and equity (E) values (Equation 43.7):

$$V = D + E. \tag{7}$$

Therefore, the value of equity is simply enterprise value less the value of existing debt (Equation 43.8):

$$E = V - D, \tag{8}$$

where debt is the market value of all interest-bearing debt outstanding at the time of the acquisition. For publicly traded targets, the value of the share price can be computed by simply dividing the equity value by the number of shares of stock outstanding.

4. *How does one incorporate the value of synergies in a DCF analysis?*

Operating synergies are reflected in enterprise value by altering the stand-alone cash flows to incorporate the benefits and costs of the combination. Free cash flows that include the value an acquirer and target can achieve through combination are referred to as *combined* or *merger* cash flows.

If the acquirer plans to run the acquired company as a stand-alone entity, as in the case of Berkshire Hathaway purchasing a company unrelated to its existing holdings (e.g., Dairy Queen), there may be little difference between the stand-alone and merger cash flows. In many strategic acquisitions, however, such as the Pfizer/Wyeth and InBev/Fujian Sedrin Brewery mergers, there can be sizable differences.

How the value of these synergies is split among the parties through the determination of the final bid price or premium paid is a major issue for negotiation.[7] If the bidder pays a premium equal to the value of the synergies, all the benefits will accrue to target shareholders, and the merger will be a zero net-present-value investment for the shareholders of the acquirer.

Example of the DCF Method

Suppose Company A has learned that Company B (a firm in a different industry but in a business that is strategically attractive to Company A) has retained an investment bank to auction the company and all of its assets. In considering how much to bid for Company B, Company A starts with the cash-flow forecast of the stand-alone business drawn up by Company B's investment bankers shown in **Table 43.1.** The discount rate used to value the cash flows is Company B's WACC of 10.9%. The inputs to WACC, with a market risk premium of 6%, are shown in **Table 43.2.**

On a stand-alone basis, the analysis in **Table 43.1** suggests that Company B's enterprise value is $9.4 million.

Now suppose Company A believes it can make Company B's operations more efficient and improve its marketing and distribution capabilities. In **Table 43.3,** we incorporate these effects into the cash-flow model, thereby estimating a higher range of values that Company A can bid and still realize a positive net present value (NPV) for its shareholders. In the merger cash-flow model of the two firms in **Table 43.3,** Company B has added two percentage points of revenue growth, subtracted two percentage points from the COGS[8]/Sales ratio, and subtracted one percentage point from the SG&A/Sales ratio relative to the stand-alone model. We assume that all of the merger synergies will be realized immediately and therefore should fall well within the five-year forecast period. The inputs to target and acquirer WACCs are summarized in **Table 43.3.**

Because Company A and Company B are in different industries, it is not appropriate to use Company A's WACC of 10.6% in discounting the expected cash flows. Despite the fact that after the merger, Company B will become part of Company A, we do not use Company A's WACC because it does not reflect the risk associated with the merger cash flows. In this case, one is better advised to focus on "where the money is going, rather than where the money comes from" in determining the risk associated with the transaction. In other words, the analyst should focus on the target's risk and financing (not the buyer's risk and financing) in determining the appropriate discount rate. The discount rate should reflect the expected risk of the cash flows being priced and not necessarily the source of the capital.

---

[7]The premium paid is usually measured as: (Per-Share Bid Price—Market Price for Target Shares Before Merger) ÷ Market Price for Target Shares Before Merger.

[8]Cost of Goods Sold.

TABLE 43.1 | Valuation of Company B as a stand-alone unit. (assume that Company A will allow Company B to run as a stand-alone unit with no synergies)

Revenue growth	6.0%		Steady state growth		5.9%	
COGS	55%		WACC		10.9%	
SG&A	20%		Tax rate		39%	
Net working capital (NWC)	22%					

	Year 0	Year 1	Year 2	Year 3	Year 4	Year 5	Year 6 Steady State
Revenues ($ thousands)	9,750	10,000	10,600	11,236	11,910	12,625	13,370
COGS		5,500	5,830	6,180	6,551	6,944	
Gross profit		4,500	4,770	5,056	5,360	5,681	
SG&A		2,000	2,120	2,247	2,382	2,525	
Depreciation		1,000	1,000	1,000	1,000	1,000	
EBIT		1,500	1,650	1,809	1,978	2,156	
Less taxes		(585)	(644)	(706)	(771)	(841)	
NOPAT		915	1,007	1,103	1,207	1,315	1,393
Add: depreciation		1,000	1,000	1,000	1,000	1,000 }	(664)
Less: capital expenditures		(1,250)	(1,250)	(1,250)	(1,250)	(1,250) }	
Less: increase in NWC		(55)	(132)	(140)	(148)	(157)	(164)
= Free cash flow		610	625	713	809	908	565
Terminal value						11,305	
Free Cash Flows + Terminal Value		610	625	713	809	12,213	
Enterprise Value PV$_{10.9\%}$ (FCF) =	9,396						
NWC (22% Sales)	2,145	2,200	2,332	2,472	2,620	2,777	2,941
NPPE (+ CAPEX − Depr. each year)	10,000	10,250	10,500	10,750	11,000	11,250	11,914
Operating margin [NOPAT/Sales]		9.2%	9.5%	9.8%	10.1%	10.4%	10.4%
PPE turnover [Sales/NPPE]		0.98	1.01	1.05	1.08	1.12	1.12
RONA [NOPAT/(NWC+NPPE)]		7.3%	7.8%	8.3%	8.9%	9.4%	9.4%

Year 6 Steady-State Calculations:

Sales = Year 5 Sales × (1 + Steady-State Growth) = 12,625 × 1.059 = 13,370
NOPAT = Year 5 NOPAT × (1 + Steady-State Growth) = 1,315 × 1.059 = 1,393
NWC = Year 5 NWC × (1 + Steady-State Growth) = 2,777 × 1.059 = 2,941
NPPE = Year 5 NPPE × (1 + Steady-State Growth) = 11,250 × 1.059 = 11,914
Increase in NPPE = Capital Expenditures less Depreciation = 11,250 − 11,914 = −664
Year 5 Terminal Value = Steady-State FCF ÷ (WACC − Steady-State Growth) = 565 ÷ (0.109 − 0.059) = 11,305

Notice that the value with synergies, $15.1 million, exceeds the value as a stand-alone entity by $5.7 million. In devising its bidding strategy, Company A would not want to offer the full $15.1 million and concede all the value of the synergies to Company B. At this price, the NPV of the acquisition to Company A is zero. The existence

TABLE 43.2 | Inputs to WACC.

	Bidder Co. A	Target Co. B
Bond rating	A	BBB
Yield to maturity of bonds—k_d	7.2%	7.42%
Tax rate	39.0%	39.0%
After-tax cost of debt—$k_d(1-t)$	4.39%	4.53%
Beta	1.05	1.20
Cost of equity—k_e	12.18%	13.08%
Debt as % of capital—W_d	20.0%	25.0%
Equity as % of capital—W_e	80.0%	75.0%
10-year treasury bond yield	5.88%	5.88%
Market risk premium	6.0%	6.0%
WACC	10.6%	10.9%

of synergies, however, allows Company A leeway to increase its bid above $9.4 million and enhance its chances of winning the auction.

Considerations for Terminal Value Estimation

In the valuation of both the stand-alone and merger cash flows, the terminal value contributes the bulk of the total cash-flow value (if the terminal value is eliminated, the enterprise value drops by about 75%). This relationship between terminal value and enterprise value is typical of firm valuation because of the ongoing nature of the life of a business. Because of the importance of the terminal value in firm valuation, the assumptions that define the terminal value deserve particular attention.

In the stand-alone Company B valuation in **Table 43.1,** we estimated the terminal value using the constant-growth valuation model. This formula assumes that the business has reached some level of steady-state growth such that the free cash flows can be modeled to infinity with the simple assumption of a constant growth rate. Because of this assumption, it is important that the firm's forecast period be extended until such a steady state is truly expected.[9] The terminal-value growth rate used in the valuation is 5.9%. In this model, the analyst assumes that the steady-state growth rate can be approximated by the long-term risk-free rate (i.e., the long-term Treasury bond yield). Using the risk-free rate to proxy for the steady-state growth rate is equivalent to assuming that the expected long-term cash flows of the business grow with the overall economy (i.e., nominal expected growth rate of GDP). Nominal economic

---

[9]The steady state may only be accurate in terms of expectations. The model recognizes that the expected terminal value has risk. Businesses may never actually achieve steady state due to technology innovations, business cycles, and changing corporate strategy. The understanding that the firm may not actually achieve a steady state does not preclude the analyst from anticipating a steady-state point as the best guess of the state of the business at some point in the future.

TABLE 43.3 | Valuation of Company B with synergies.
(assume that Company B merges with Company A and realizes operational synergies)

Revenue growth	8.0%			Steady state growth		5.9%
COGS	53%			WACC		10.9%
SG&A	19%			Tax rate		39%
Net working capital (NWC)	22%					

	Year 0	Year 1	Year 2	Year 3	Year 4	Year 5	Year 6 Steady State
Revenues ($ in thousands)	9,750	10,000	10,800	11,664	12,597	13,605	14,408
COGS		5,300	5,724	6,182	6,676	7,211	
Gross profit		4,700	5,076	5,482	5,921	6,394	
SG&A		1,900	2,052	2,216	2,393	2,585	
Depreciation		1,000	1,000	1,000	1,000	1,000	
EBIT		1,800	2,024	2,266	2,527	2,809	
Less taxes		(702)	(789)	(884)	(986)	(1,096)	
NOPAT		1,098	1,235	1,382	1,542	1,714	1,815
Add: depreciation		1,000	1,000	1,000	1,000	1,000 ⎫	(664)
Less: capital expenditures		(1,250)	(1,250)	(1,250)	(1,250)	(1,250) ⎬	
Less: increase in NWC		(55)	(176)	(190)	(205)	(222) ⎭	(177)
= Free cash flow		793	809	942	1,086	1,242	974
Terminal value						19,490	
Free Cash Flows + Terminal Value		793	809	942	1,086	20,732	
Enterprise Value PV$_{10.9\%}$ (FCF) =	15,140						
NWC (22% sales)	2,145	2,200	2,376	2,566	2,771	2,993	3,170
NPPE (+ CAPEX – Depr. each year)	10,000	10,250	10,500	10,750	11,000	11,250	11,914
Operating margin [NOPAT/Sales]		11.0%	11.4%	11.9%	12.2%	12.6%	12.6%
PPE turnover [Sales/NPPE]		0.98	1.03	1.09	1.15	1.21	1.21
RONA [NOPAT/(NWC+NPPE)]		8.8%	9.6%	10.4%	11.2%	12.0%	12.0%

Year 6 Steady-State Calculations:

Sales = Year 5 Sales × (1 + Steady-State Growth) = 13,605 × 1.059 = 14,408
NOPAT = Year 5 NOPAT × (1 + Steady-State Growth) = 1,714 × 1.059 = 1,815
NWC = Year 5 NWC × (1 + Steady-State Growth) = 2,993 × 1.059 = 3,170
NPPE = Year 5 NPPE × (1 + Steady-State Growth) = 11,250 × 1.059 = 11,914
Increase in NPPE = Capital Expenditures less Depreciation = 11,250 − 11,914 = −664
Year 5 Terminal Value = Steady-State FCF ÷ (WACC − Steady-State Growth) = 974 ÷ (0.109 − 0.059) = 19,490

growth contains a real growth component plus an inflation rate component, which are also reflected in long-term government bond yields. For example, the Treasury bond yield can be decomposed into a real rate of return (typically between 2% and 3%) and expected long-term inflation. Because the Treasury yield for our example is 5.9%, the implied inflation is between 3.9% and 2.9%. Over the long term, companies should experience the same real growth and inflationary growth as the economy on average, which justifies using the risk-free rate as a reasonable proxy for the expected long-term growth of the economy.

Another important assumption is estimating steady-state free cash flow that properly incorporates the investment required to sustain the steady-state growth expectation. The steady-state free-cash-flow estimate used in the merger valuation in **Table 43.3** is $974,000. To obtain the steady-state cash flow, we start by estimating sales in Equation 43.9:[10]

$$Sales^{Steady\ State} = Sales^{Year\ 5} \times (1+g) = 13{,}605 \times 1.059 = 14{,}408 \qquad (9)$$

Steady state demands that all the financial statement items grow with sales at the same steady-state rate of 5.9%. This assumption is reasonable because in steady state, the enterprise should be growing at a constant rate. If the financial statements did not grow at the same rate, the implied financial ratios (e.g., operating margins or RONA) would eventually deviate widely from reasonable industry norms.

The steady-state cash flow can be constructed by simply growing all relevant line items at the steady-state growth rate as summarized in **Tables 43.1** and **43.3**. To estimate free cash flow, we need to estimate the steady-state values for NOPAT, net working capital, and net property, plant, and equipment. By simply multiplying the Year 5 value for each line item by the steady-state growth factor of 1.059, we obtain the steady-state Year 6 values.[11] Therefore, to estimate the steady-state change in NWC, we use the difference in the values for the last two years **(Equation 43.10)**:

$$\Delta NWC^{Steady\ State} = NWC^{Year\ 5} - NWC^{Steady\ State} = 2{,}993 - 3{,}170 = -177 \qquad (10)$$

This leaves depreciation and capital expenditure as the last two components of cash flow. These can be more easily handled together by looking at the relation between sales and net property, plant, and equipment where NPPE is the accumulation of capital expenditures less depreciation. **Table 43.3** shows that in the steady-state year, NPPE has increased to 11,914. The difference of NPPE gives us the net of capital expenditures and depreciation for the steady state (Equation 43.11):

$$\Delta NPPE^{Steady\ State} = NPPE^{1995} - NPPE^{Steady\ State} = 11{,}250 - 11{,}914 = -664. \qquad (11)$$

Summing the components gives us the steady-state free cash flow (Equation 43.12):

$$\begin{aligned} FCF^{Steady\ State} &= NOPAT^{steady\ state} + \Delta NPPE^{steady\ state} + \Delta NWC^{steady\ state} \qquad (12) \\ &= 1{,}815 \qquad\qquad -664 \qquad\qquad\quad -176 \\ &= 974.^{12} \end{aligned}$$

---

[10] Note that **Tables 43.1** and **43.3** summarize the steady-state calculations.

[11] Alternatively, we can compute NOPAT using Year 5's NOPAT/Sales ratio of 12.6% or net working capital using the same 22% of sales relation used throughout the analysis. As long as the ratios are constant and linked to the steady-state sales value, the figures will capture the same-steady state assumptions.

[12] Note that we can demonstrate that the cash-flow estimation process is consistent with the steady-state growth. If we were to do these same calculations using the same growth rate for one more year, the resulting FCF would be 5.9% higher (i.e., $974 \times 1.059 = 1{,}031$).

Therefore, by maintaining steady-state growth across the firm, we have estimated the numerator of the terminal value formula that gives us the value of all future cash flows beyond Year 5 (Equation 43.13):

$$Terminal\ Value^{Year\ 5} = FCF^{Steady\ State} \div (WACC - g)$$
$$= 974 \div (0.109 - 0.059) = 19{,}490. \qquad (13)$$

The expression used to estimate steady-state free cash flow can be used for alternative assumptions regarding expected growth. For example, one might also assume that the firm does not continue to build new capacity but that merger cash flows grow only with expected inflation (e.g., 3.9%). In this scenario, the calculations are similar but the growth rate is replaced with the expected inflation. Even if capacity is not expanded, investment must keep up with growth in profits to maintain a constant expected rate of operating returns.

Finally, it is important to acknowledge that the terminal value estimate embeds assumptions about the long-term profitability of the target firm. In the example in **Table 43.3,** the implied steady-state RONA can be calculated by dividing the steady-state NOPAT by the steady-state net assets (NWC + NPPE). In this case, the return on net assets is equal to 12.0% [1,815 ÷ (3,170 + 11,914)]. Because in steady state the profits and the assets will grow at the same rate, this ratio is estimated to remain in perpetuity. The discount rate of 10.9% maintains a benchmark for the steady-state RONA. Because of the threat of competitive pressure, it is difficult to justify in most cases a firm valuation wherein the steady-state RONA is substantially higher than the WACC. Alternatively, if the steady-state RONA is lower than the WACC, one should question the justification for maintaining the business in steady state if the assets are not earning the cost of capital.

Market Multiples as Alternative Estimators of Terminal Value

Given the importance attached to terminal value, analysts are wise to use several approaches when estimating it. A common approach is to estimate terminal value using market multiples derived from information based on publicly traded companies similar to the target company (in our example, Company B). The logic behind a market multiple is to see how the market is currently valuing an entity based on certain benchmarks related to value rather than attempting to determine an entity's inherent value. The benchmark used as the basis of valuation should be something that is commonly valued by the market and highly correlated with market value. For example, in the real estate market, dwellings are frequently priced based on the prevailing price per square foot of comparable properties. The assumption made is that the size of the house is correlated with its market value. If comparable houses are selling at $100 per square foot, the market value for a 2,000-square-foot house is estimated to be $200,000. For firm valuation, current or expected profits are frequently used as the basis for relative market multiple approaches.

Suppose, as shown in **Table 43.4,** that there are three publicly traded businesses that are in the same industry as Company B: Company C, Company D, and Company E. The respective financial and market data that apply to these companies are shown in

TABLE 43.4 | Comparable companies to target company.

	Company C	Company D	Company E
Industry	Industry Z	Industry Z	Industry Z
Stage of growth	Mature	Mature	High Growth
EBIT ($ in thousands)	$ 3,150	$ 2,400	$ 750
Net earnings	1,500	1,500	150
Equity value	14,000	11,400	3,000
Debt value	2,800	3,000	3,500
Enterprise value	$16,800	$14,400	$6,500
Enterprise Value/EBIT	5.3	6.0	8.7
Equity Value/Net Earnings	9.3	7.6	20.0

Table 43.4. The enterprise value for each comparable firm is estimated as the current share price multiplied by the number of shares outstanding (equity value) plus the book value of debt. Taking a ratio of the enterprise value divided by the operating profit (EBIT), we obtain an EBIT multiple. In the case of Company C, the EBIT multiple is 5.3 times, meaning that for every $1 in current operating profit generated by Company C, investors are willing to pay $5.3 of firm value. If Company C is similar today to the expected steady state of Company B in Year 5, the 5.3-times-EBIT multiple could be used to estimate the expected value of Company B at the end of Year 5, the terminal value.[13]

To reduce the effect of outliers on the EBIT multiple estimate, we can use the information provided from a sample of comparable multiples. In sampling additional comparables, we are best served by selecting multiples from only those firms that are comparable to the business of interest on the basis of business risk, economic outlook, profitability, and growth expectations. We note that Company E's EBIT multiple of 8.7 times is substantially higher than the others in **Table 43.4.** Why should investors be willing to pay so much more for a dollar of Company E's operating profit than for a dollar of Company C's operating profit? We know that Company E is in a higher growth stage than Company C and Company D. If Company E profits are expected to grow at a higher rate, the valuation or capitalization of these profits will occur at a higher level or multiple. Investors anticipate higher future profits for Company E and consequently bid up the value of the respective capital.[14]

Because of Company E's abnormally strong expected growth, we decide that Company E is not a good proxy for the way we expect Company B to be in Year 5.

---

[13]We assume in this example that current multiples are the best proxies for future multiples. If there is some reason to believe that the current multiple is a poor or biased estimate of the future, the market multiples must be adjusted accordingly. For example, if the current profits are extraordinarily small or large, a multiple based on such a distorted value will produce an artificial estimate of the expected future value. A more appropriate multiple will use a nondistorted or "normalized" profit measure.

[14]See **Appendix** for an example of the relationship between market multiples and the constant-cash-flow growth model.

We choose, consequently, to not use the 8.7-times-EBIT multiple in estimating our terminal value estimate. We conclude instead that investors are more likely to value Company B's operating profits at approximately 5.7 times (the average of 5.3 and 6.0 times). The logic is that if investors are willing to pay 5.7 times EBIT today for operating profit of firms similar to what we expect Company B to be in Year 5, this valuation multiple will be appropriate in the future. To estimate Company B's terminal value based on our average EBIT multiple, we multiply the Year 5 stand-alone EBIT of $2.156 million by the average comparable multiple of 5.7 times. This process provides a multiple-based estimate of Company B's terminal value of $12.2 million. This estimate is somewhat above the constant-growth-based terminal value estimate of $11.3 million.

Although the importance of terminal value motivates the use of several estimation methods, sometimes these methods yield widely varying values. The variation in estimated values should prompt questions on the appropriateness of the underlying assumptions of each approach. For example, the differences in terminal value estimates could be due to:

- A forecast period that is too short to have resulted in steady-state performance.

- The use of comparable multiples that fail to match the expected risk, expected growth, or macroeconomic conditions of the target company in the terminal year.

- An assumed constant growth rate that is lower or higher than that expected by the market.

The potential discrepancies motivate further investigation of the assumptions and information contained in the various approaches so that the analyst can "triangulate" to the most appropriate terminal-value estimate.

In identifying an appropriate valuation multiple, one must be careful to choose a multiple that is consistent with the underlying earnings stream of the entity one is valuing. For example, one commonly used multiple based on net earnings is called the price–earnings, or P/E, multiple. This multiple compares the value of the equity to the value of net income. In a valuation model based on free cash flow, it is typically inappropriate to use multiples based on net income because these value only the equity portion of the firm and assume a certain capital structure.[15] Other commonly used multiples that are appropriate for free-cash-flow valuation include EBITDA (earnings before interest, tax, depreciation, and amortization), free cash flow, and total capital multiples.

Although the market-multiple valuation approach provides a convenient, market-based approach for valuing businesses, there are a number of cautions worth noting:

1. *Multiples can be deceptively simple.* Multiples should provide an alternative way to triangulate toward an appropriate long-term growth rate and not a way to avoid thinking about the long-term economics of a business.

2. *Market multiples are subject to distortions due to market misvaluations and accounting policy.* Accounting numbers further down in the income statement (such

---

[15]Only in the relatively rare case of a company not using debt would the P/E ratio be an appropriate multiple.

as net earnings) are typically subject to greater distortion than items high on the income statement. Because market valuations tend to be affected by business cycles less than annual profit figures, multiples can exhibit some business-cycle effects. Moreover, business profits are negative; the multiples constructed from negative earnings are not meaningful.

3. *Identifying closely comparable firms is challenging.* Firms within the same industry may differ greatly in business risk, cost and revenue structure, and growth prospects.

4. *Multiples can be computed using different timing conventions.* Consider a firm with a December 31 fiscal year (FY) end that is being valued in January 2005. A trailing EBIT multiple for the firm would reflect the January 2005 firm value divided by the 2004 FY EBIT. In contrast, a current-year EBIT multiple (leading or forward EBIT multiple) is computed as the January 2005 firm value divided by the 2005 EBIT (expected end-of-year 2006 EBIT).[16] Because leading multiples are based on expected values, they tend to be less volatile than trailing multiples. Moreover, leading and trailing multiples will be systematically different for growing businesses.

Transaction multiples for comparable deals

In an M&A setting, analysts look to comparable transactions as an additional benchmark against which to assess the target firm. The chief difference between transaction multiples and peer multiples is that the former reflects a "control premium," typically 30% to 50%, that is not present in the ordinary trading multiples. If one is examining the price paid for the target equity, transactions multiples might include the Per-Share Offer Price ÷ Target Book Value of Equity per Share, or Per-Share Offer Price ÷ Target Earnings per Share. If one is examining the total consideration paid in recent deals, one can use Enterprise Value ÷ EBIT. The more similarly situated the target and the more recent the deal, the better the comparison will be. Ideally, there would be several similar deals in the past year or two from which to calculate median and average transaction multiples. If there are, one can glean valuable information about how the market has valued assets of this type.

Analysts also look at premiums for comparable transactions by comparing the offer price to the target's price before the merger announcement at selected dates, such as 1 day or 30 days before the announcement. A negotiator might point to premiums in previous deals for similarly situated sellers and demand that shareholders receive "what the market is paying." One must look closely, however, at the details of each transaction before agreeing with this premise. How much the target share price moves upon the announcement of a takeover depends on what the market had anticipated before the announcement. If the share price of the target had been driven up in the days or weeks before the announcement on rumors that a deal was forthcoming, the control premium may appear low. To adjust

---

[16]Profit figures used in multiples can also be computed by cumulating profits from the expected or most recent quarters.

for the "anticipation," one must examine the premium at some point before the market learns of (or begins to anticipate the announcement of) the deal. It could also be that the buyer and seller in previous deals are not in similar situations compared with the current deal. For example, some of the acquirers may have been financial buyers (leveraged buyout [LBO] or private equity firms) while others in the sample were strategic buyers (companies expanding in the same industry as the target.) Depending on the synergies involved, the premiums need not be the same for strategic and financial buyers.

Other Valuation Methods

Although we have focused on the DCF method, other methods provide useful complementary information in assessing the value of a target. Here, we briefly review some of the most popularly used techniques.

Book value

Book-value valuation may be appropriate for firms with commodity-type assets valued at market, stable operations, and no intangible assets. Caveats are the following:

- This method depends on accounting practices that vary across firms.
- It ignores intangible assets such as brand names, patents, technical know-how, and managerial competence.
- It ignores price appreciation due, for instance, to inflation.
- It invites disputes about types of liabilities. For instance, are deferred taxes equity or debt?
- Book-value method is *backward-looking*. It ignores the positive or negative operating prospects of the firm and is often a poor proxy for market value.

Liquidation value

Liquidation value considers the sale of assets at a point in time. This may be appropriate for firms in financial distress or, more generally, for firms whose operating prospects are highly uncertain. Liquidation value generally provides a conservative lower bound to the business valuation. Liquidation value will depend on the recovery value of the assets (e.g., collections from receivables) and the extent of viable alternative uses for the assets. Caveats are the following:

- It is difficult to get a consensus valuation. Liquidation values tend to be highly appraiser-specific.
- It relies on key judgment: How finely one might break up the company? Group? Division? Product line? Region? Plant? Machines?
- Physical condition, not age, will affect values. There can be no substitute for an on-site assessment of a company's real assets.
- It may ignore valuable intangible assets.

Replacement-cost value

In the 1970s and early 1980s, an era of high inflation in the United States, the U.S. Securities and Exchange Commission required public corporations to estimate replacement values in their 10-K reports. This is no longer the case, making this method less useful to U.S. firms, but it is still useful to international firms, for which the requirement continues. Caveats are the following:

- Comparisons of replacement costs and stock market values ignore the possible reasons for the disparity: overcapacity, high interest rates, oil shocks, inflation, and so on.

- Replacement-cost estimates are not highly reliable, often drawn by simplistic rules of thumb. Estimators themselves (operating managers) frequently dismiss the estimates.

Market value of traded securities

Most often, this method is used to value the equity of the firm (E) as Stock Price × Outstanding Shares. It can also be used to value the enterprise (V) by adding the market value of debt (D) as the Price per Bond × Number of Bonds Outstanding.[17] This method is helpful if the stock is actively traded, followed by professional securities analysts, and if the market efficiently impounds all public information about the company and its industry. It is worth noting the following:

- Rarely do merger negotiations settle at a price below the market price of the target. On average, mergers and tender offers command a 30% to 50% premium over the price one day before the merger announcement. Premiums have been as high as 100% in some instances. Often the price increase is attributed to a "control premium." The premium will depend on the rarity of the assets sought after and also on the extent to which there are close substitutes for the technology, expertise, or capability in question; the distribution of financial resources between the bidder and target; the egos of the CEOs involved (the hubris hypothesis); or the possibility that the ex ante target price was unduly inflated by market rumors.

- This method is less helpful for less well-known companies that have thinly or intermittently traded stock. It is not available for privately held companies.

- The method ignores private information known only to insiders or acquirers who may see a special economic opportunity in the target company. Remember, the market can efficiently impound only *public* information.

---

[17]Since the market price of a bond is frequently close to its book value, the book value of debt is often used as a reasonable proxy for its market value. Conversely, it is rare that book value per share of equity is close enough to its market price to serve as a good estimate.

Summary Comments

The DCF method of valuation is superior for company valuation in an M&A setting because it:

- Is not tied to historical accounting values. It is forward-looking.
- Focuses on cash flow, not profits. It reflects noncash charges and investment inflows and outflows.
- Separates the investment and financing effects into discrete variables.
- Recognizes the time value of money.
- Allows private information or special insights to be incorporated explicitly.
- Allows expected operating strategy to be incorporated explicitly.
- Embodies the operating costs and benefits of intangible assets.

Virtually every number used in valuation is *measured with error*, either because of flawed methods to describe the past or because of uncertainty about the future. Therefore:

- No valuation is "right" in any absolute sense.
- It is appropriate to use several scenarios about the future and even several valuation methods to limit the target's value.

> Adapt to diversity: It may be easier and more accurate to value the divisions or product lines of a target, rather than to value the company as a whole. Recognize that different valuation methods may be appropriate for different components.

> Avoid analysis paralysis: Limit the value quickly. Then if the target still looks attractive, try some sensitivity analysis.

Beyond the initial buy/no buy decision, the purpose of most valuation analysis is to support negotiators. Knowing value boundaries and conducting sensitivity analysis enhances one's flexibility to respond to new ideas that may appear at the negotiating table.

APPENDIX

Methods of Valuation for Mergers and Acquisitions

Description of Relationship between Multiples of Operating Profit and Constant Growth Model

One can show that cash-flow multiples such as EBIT and EBITDA are economically related to the constant growth model. For example, the constant growth model can be expressed as follows:

$$V = \frac{FCF}{WACC - g}$$

Rearranging this expression gives a free-cash-flow multiple expressed in a constant growth model:

$$\frac{V}{FCF} = \frac{1}{WACC - g}$$

This expression suggests that cash-flow multiples are increasing in the growth rate and decreasing in the WACC. In the following table, one can vary the WACC and growth rate to produce the implied multiple.

		WACC		
		8%	10%	12%
Growth	0%	12.5	10.0	8.3
	2%	16.7	12.5	10.0
	4%	25.0	16.7	12.5
	6%	50.0	25.0	16.7

Medfield Pharmaceuticals[1]

Susan Johnson, founder and CEO of Medfield Pharmaceuticals, had planned to spend the first few weeks of 2011 sorting out conflicting recommendations for extending the patent life of the company's flagship product, Fleximat, which was scheduled to go off patent in two years. With only three other products in Medfield's lineup of medications, one of which had only just received U.S. Food and Drug Administration (FDA) approval, strategic management of the company's product pipeline was of paramount importance. But a recent $750 million offer to purchase the company had entirely shifted her focus.

The offer was not a complete surprise. The pharmaceutical industry landscape had changed considerably since Johnson, formerly a research scientist, had founded Medfield 20 years earlier. Development costs were rising, patents were running out, and new breakthroughs seemed ever more difficult to obtain. The industry was now focused on mergers and acquisitions, restructuring, and other strategies for cost-cutting and survival. Smaller firms like Medfield were being gobbled up by the major players all the time. Companies with approved products or products in the later stages of development, such as Medfield, were especially likely targets.

While she no longer owned a controlling interest in the firm and could not force a particular decision, Johnson recognized that as CEO, founder, and largest single investor, she would be expected to offer an opinion and that her opinion would be extremely influential. It was also clear that determining the value of the company, and therefore whether the offer was reasonable, would necessitate a careful review of the company's existing and potential future products, and no one understood these as well as Johnson.

Of course, for Johnson, this was more than simply a financial decision. She believed strongly, as did other employees, particularly among the research staff, that Medfield was engaged in work that was important, and she took great pride in the firm's accomplishments. Medfield's corporate culture was explicitly oriented toward the end goal of improving patients' health, as evidenced by its slogan: "We Bring Wellness." This was an

---

[1]Except where otherwise noted, general statistics and information about the pharmaceutical industry come from Plunkett Research, http://www.plunkettresearch.com.

This case was prepared by Marc L. Lipson, Associate Professor of Business Administration; Jared D. Harris, Assistant Professor of Business Administration; and Jenny Mead, Senior Researcher. It was written as a basis for class discussion rather than to illustrate effective or ineffective handling of an administrative situation. Copyright © 2011 by the University of Virginia Darden School Foundation, Charlottesville, VA. All rights reserved. *To order copies, send an e-mail to* sales@dardenbusinesspublishing.com. *No part of this publication may be reproduced, stored in a retrieval system, used in a spreadsheet, or transmitted in any form or by any means—electronic, mechanical, photocopying, recording, or otherwise—without the permission of the Darden School Foundation.*

important value that Johnson had consciously and specifically built into the firm's culture. Both Johnson's parents were doctors and ran a small family-oriented practice that they had taken over from Johnson's maternal grandfather in the town where Johnson was raised. The idea of bettering lives through medicine was one Johnson had grown up with.

Current Product Lines

The company had experienced excellent growth over the years and in 2009 had 290 employees, total sales of $329 million (primarily in the United States), and a net income of $58 million. See **Exhibits 44.1** and **44.2** for financial information. The company manufactured and sold three primary drugs; all but one had substantial patent life remaining. Two were for pain management and the third was for auto-immune diseases. A fourth drug, also for pain management, had been approved and was ready for distribution. Due to its strong marketing and sales force, Medfield enjoyed an excellent reputation with both physicians and hospitals.

The company's leading seller—responsible for 64% of its revenues—was Fleximat. Fleximat was a drug used to treat pain and swelling in patients with ulcerative colitis, rheumatoid arthritis, and Crohn's disease, an ongoing disorder that caused painful inflammation of the digestive tract. Fleximat had proved to be much more effective than competing sulfa-based drugs (such as sulfasalazine) in treating those patients—particularly juveniles—who had an inadequate response to conventional therapies for Crohn's disease. Fleximat, however, had only two years remaining on its patent.

The other three products were as follows:

- *Lodamadal* was an extended-release tablet for once-daily treatment of moderate to severe pain in patients requiring continuous, around-the-clock opioid therapy for an extended period of time. It was in the class of medications called opiate agonists, which worked by changing the way the body sensed pain. This drug accounted for 12% of Medfield's revenues. Lodamadal had five years remaining on its patent.

- *Orsamorph* was a morphine sulfate sustained-release tablet designed to treat more intense pain. This was a popular drug in hospitals and accounted for 24% of revenues. Orsamorph had fourteen years remaining on its patent.

- *Reximet* treated acute migraines. Reximet, which would begin selling in 2012, was a single tablet containing sumatriptan succinate, a 5-HT 1B/1D agonist, and naproxen sodium, a non-steroidal anti-inflammatory drug. Reximet had proved effective in treating arthritis and joint pain. It would have a full twenty-year patent life.

The Pharmaceutical Industry

Globally, the pharmaceutical industry was a powerhouse, generating billions in revenues. The U.S. pharmaceutical manufacturing industry, at the core of the global business, had historically enjoyed high profits. Yearly, from 1995 through 2002, it was the most profitable industry in the United States, and drug manufacturers had experienced three times more profitability than the median of all *Fortune* 500 companies in 2004.[2]

---

[2]Haiden A. Huskamp, "Prices, Profits, and Innovation: Examining Criticisms of New Psychotropic Drugs' Value," *Health Affairs* 25, no. 3 (2006).

Drug companies made money by bringing "blockbuster" drugs to market, relying on the period during which they were protected by patent to make significant revenues and focusing on mass-market drugs that treated a wide variety of ailments. Traditional pharmaceutical companies, several of which had existed since the 19th century, discovered and created new drugs using organic chemistry and natural compounds, but biotechnology companies—which used gene-splicing to produce their drugs—had been on the rise since the mid-1970s. These companies often created "orphan drugs" that focused on rare diseases affecting a small percentage of the population.[3]

In 2009, the pharmaceutical industry had approximately 1,500 companies with combined annual revenues of $200 billion. At the top of the drug-company pile were Abbott, Bristol-Myers Squibb, Eli Lilly and Company, Johnson & Johnson, Pfizer, and Merck. More than 80% of pharmaceutical revenue was brought in by the 50 largest companies.

But the pharmaceutical industry had found itself at a crossroads as the first decade of the 21st century wound down. With the economic downturn, impending health-care-reform legislation, and many drugs losing their patents, drug companies had to determine how best to boost their bottom line. Most alarming to many of the major pharmaceutical companies was the imminent expiration of patents; estimates were that from 2009 to 2016, losses from these expirations would benefit generics to the tune of $140 billion.[4] As a result, the large pharmaceuticals were turning to various options to stay viable, including restructuring, cutting internal R&D, adding biologics,[5] building generic units, entering emerging markets, and looking at M&A. Many large companies were bulking up their products by buying or licensing drugs from other companies or acquiring smaller outfits.

New drug approvals had also taken a dive. In 2009, there were only 25 new drugs[6] that received approval from the Center for Drug Evaluation and Research at the FDA. In contrast, during the mid-1990s, more than twice that number had been approved. The cost of bringing a drug to market was high: The latest figure (2005) was $1.3 billion, as compared with $802 million in 2001, $300 million in 1991, and $100 million in 1979. In general, only 2 in 10 approved medicines recouped R&D costs.

The pharmaceutical industry—particularly in the 1990s and in the first decade of the 21st century—had come under criticism both from the public and the government, not only for the high price of branded drugs, but also for some of its tactics and strategies. Various manufacturers were accused of, among other things, withholding data from the FDA; manipulating certain data to achieve specific results (as Merck was accused of doing with Vioxx); hiring physician opinion leaders at great cost to promote its products; lavishing gifts, meals, and other luxuries on physicians in an attempt to get

---

[3]An example of an orphan drug was Rituxan, which had been developed by Genentech and Biogen to treat people suffering from non-Hodgkin's lymphoma—a relatively small market.

[4]Ian Mawhinney, "2020: A New Drug Delivery Landscape," *Drug Discovery and Development* 12, no. 10 (December 2009): 32.

[5]Biologics were created using biological processes, such as T-cell activation or stimulation of blood components, rather than chemical synthesis.

[6]This number refers to traditional pharmaceuticals, which were discovered via organic chemistry; there were nine approvals of biologics in 2009.

them to prescribe a particular drug; and promoting drugs for off-label use. Drug companies had become the whipping posts for practically everyone, from presidents to consumer activists to the general public.

The Generic Equation

U.S. patent policy gave drug manufacturers a 20-year protection from the date of the original patent (usually filed early in the research process), plus 14 years from the date of FDA approval. Once the patent expired, the medication was fair game and other companies could make generic forms of it. In the United States, the modern system of generics came into being in 1984, after passage of the Drug Price Competition and Patent Term Restoration Act (or the Hatch-Waxman Act), which significantly changed the pharmaceutical patent landscape. The legislation's purpose was to ensure that generics were more widely available and to ensure adequate incentives for investing in the development of new drugs. The act expedited the process of generics reaching the market by letting manufacturers file an abbreviated new drug application with the FDA. The act also granted concessions to the brand manufacturers, allowing them to increase the patent time.

Generics were, on average, 50% to 75% cheaper than the branded drug, and in many cases, the price difference was much bigger. This disparity benefited consumers tremendously but had the opposite effect on name-brand pharmaceutical firms. Sales of blockbuster drugs could plunge 80% or more the first year after a generic competitor entered the market. In 2009, the generics' share of the market was 74%, compared with 49% in 2000. In 2008, generics manufacturers Teva Pharmaceuticals and Mylan Laboratories topped the list of producers of dispensed prescriptions in the United States at 494.2 million and 307.7 million, respectively, beating out Pfizer and Merck.[7] Of that top ten, six were generics manufacturers.

Generics received a big boost in 2006, when Wal-Mart pharmacies, primarily to fight mail-order pharmacies, began offering deeply discounted generic brands for a flat $4 per month. Other large chains with pharmacies (e.g., Kroger, Target, and Walgreens) jumped on the $4 generic bandwagon. The popularity of these programs led to still-deeper discounts and even some free medication over the following years. Wal-Mart offered 90-day supplies of some generic drugs for $10, and grocery chain Publix offered free generic antibiotics for up to 14 days. Competition was fierce among manufacturers of generic drugs, resulting in heavy discounting.

Given this change in the competitive landscape, toward the end of the first decade of the 21st century, many major pharmaceutical companies were branching out by producing generics, not only of their own brands but also those of other companies. This represented an attempt to introduce a subtle form of differentiation into the mostly cost-leader-focused generics market; brand-name companies that produced generics could charge slightly more for the promise of quality, as opposed to no-name generic producers, whose selling point was rock-bottom prices. Among others, Pfizer (with its generics

---

[7]Business Monitor International, "Competitive Landscape," *United States Pharmaceuticals & Healthcare Report Q1 2010*, 62.

division Greenstone), Schering-Plough (which created a generic subsidiary, Warrick Pharmaceuticals), Novartis, Sanofi-Aventis, and GlaxoSmithKline were manufacturing copycat drugs from other companies; the latter two targeted non-U.S. markets. Obviously, independent generic manufacturers were not pleased with this practice.

Fleximat Strategies

As Johnson considered the state of the industry and Medfield's specific situation, her attention increasingly focused on Fleximat—the firm's core product but biggest source of uncertainty. Aside from simply letting Fleximat's patent lapse and losing sales to the inevitable generic substitutes, Johnson knew the company had several possible alternative actions. Of these, Johnson believed four approaches stood out:

1. Launch a renewed marketing effort. This would include becoming more aggressive in Medfield's current tactics. Johnson was well aware of how successful AstraZeneca's commercials for Nexium had been, which featured apparently suicidal people standing on cliffs, desperate for heartburn relief, and diners at fancy restaurants (mis)hearing a waiter describe the gastric distress that would follow after they ate their meals.

2. Engage in evergreening tactics. This essentially would allow the firm to maintain the benefits of patents through aggressive litigation. For example, a manufacturer could "stockpile" patent protections by taking out many separate patents (each good for 20 years), legitimate or not, on various components or attributes of one of its products. Components covered could include the color of the medication, a particular chemical reaction when the drug is taken and metabolized, or dose amounts. The firm would then defend these with legal actions that would impede the development and sale of generics.

3. Manufacture the generic form of Fleximat in-house. Medfield could also partner with a large generic manufacturer. This would be the easiest approach and would lead to the widest use of Fleximat by patients, but it would generate little in the way of financial benefits to the firm.

4. Reformulate Fleximat. This was the practice of "reinventing" a drug to "improve" it and thus stave off the generics. It meant reconfiguring the medication so it was different enough for FDA approval and a new patent, although this often could be done without substantially changing the medication itself. Methods to extend the patent life of the compound could include slightly changing the formulation, dosage, or labeling. See **Exhibit 44.3** for examples of drug reformulation.

Of these four alternatives, reformulation struck Johnson as likely the most beneficial to Medfield; however, there were notable risks. The most famous reformulation controversy had been the case of AstraZeneca's Nexium (a.k.a. "the purple pill"). AstraZeneca (AZ) released the patented heartburn drug Prilosec in 1981. It was one of the company's biggest blockbuster drugs. As patent expiration loomed, AZ got FDA approval in February 2001 for the reformulation of Prilosec into a newly patented drug called Nexium, also a heartburn prescription and very similar to Prilosec. AZ then ceased promoting Prilosec and began aggressively pushing Nexium. Two years later, the FDA approved an over-the-counter (OTC) version of Prilosec, which had exclusivity in the OTC market until 2006.

As a result of this reformulation, Walgreen Company sued AstraZeneca for antitrust violations, claiming the pharmaceutical company had deliberately switched "the market from its heartburn prescription drug Prilosec just as that patent was about to expire to its newly approved drug Nexium, which had a fresh patent."[8] Walgreen's lawsuit alleged that AZ manipulated the market, taking the emphasis off Prilosec, which had generic competition, and placing it on Nexium, which had a patent until 2014 and no generic competition, and that in doing so, the company eliminated choices for patients. Furthermore, Walgreen argued that there was little difference between Prilosec and Nexium and that AZ's switching of them was exclusionary and violated the Sherman Antitrust Act. Walgreen also claimed that AZ was guilty of further exclusionary action when it introduced the OTC version of Prilosec and received a three-year exclusivity grant from the FDA. In addition, Walgreen contended that AstraZeneca engaged in prohibited exclusionary conduct when it introduced Prilosec OTC and obtained an FDA grant of exclusivity for three years.

Ultimately, all five complaints in the lawsuit were dismissed for "failure to state a claim," and the federal district court judge asserted, among other things, that instead of having taken away drug choices, as Walgreen claimed, AZ had created additional choices (Prilosec OTC and Nexium). The court also made the point that antitrust laws do not evaluate the quality of a particular drug—whether superior or inferior; new products could only affect the market share if customers preferred them. Finally, the court did not find that AZ had interfered with Walgreen's freedom to compete; in other words, the court found that AZ was not guilty of illegal antitrust activity. While there was only one study that demonstrated superiority of Nexium, it had been sponsored by AstraZeneca.[9]

Nevertheless, while not considered racketeering in the courts, the process of reformulation came under increasing public scrutiny. According to author Malcolm Gladwell, Nexium had become a "symbol of everything that is wrong with the pharmaceutical industry":

> The big drug companies justify the high prices they charge—and the extraordinary profits they enjoy—by arguing that the search for innovative, life-saving medicines is risky and expensive. But Nexium is little more than a repackaged version of an old medicine. And the hundred and twenty dollars a month that AstraZeneca charges isn't to recoup the costs of risky research and development; the costs were for a series of clinical trials that told us nothing we needed to know, and a half-billion-dollar marketing campaign selling the solution to a problem we'd already solved.[10]

[8]"Prilosec/Nexium Antitrust Claims Dismissed: No Antitrust Violation for Introducing New Drugs to the Market," *Judicial View*, https://www.judicialview.com/Court-Cases/Antitrust/Prilosec-Nexium-Antitrust-Claims-Dismissed/No-Antitrust-Violation-for-Introducing-New-Drugs-to-the-Market/5/2666 (accessed September 1, 2011).

[9]Esomeprazole (Nexium) provided improved acid control versus omeprazole (Prilosec) in patients with symptoms of gastroesophageal reflux disease.

[10]Malcolm Gladwell, "High Prices: How to Think About Prescription Drugs," *New Yorker*, October 25, 2004, 86.

Furthermore, in a front-page article that first revealed AZ's initiative to reformulate its expiring medication, the *Wall Street Journal* concluded that "the Prilosec pattern, repeated across the pharmaceutical industry, goes a long way to explain why the nation's prescription drug bill is rising an estimated 17% a year even as general inflation is quiescent.[11]

The Value of Medfield

As Johnson sat down to contemplate the acquisition offer, she began to look at the company's portfolio of drugs in a new light. Rather than therapies for ailments, they were sources of cash flow. Fortunately, whereas the R&D process was notoriously unpredictable, once a product was approved, the future was relatively clear. This future could be summarized as follows:

- For 20 years, the product would be patent-protected, and from the initial sales level, sales would grow at about 2% a year. When the patent expired, sales would decline 50% in each of the following three years and then would have effectively negligible sales in the fourth year.

- The direct cost of sales would be 23%.

- Direct marketing costs were 27% of revenue and Medfield typically spent 19% of revenue on future R&D.

- The company estimated other general and administrative expenses would be about 4% of sales. A large portion of this expense category was tied directly or indirectly to sales and little of the cost was reasonably classified as fixed.

- Capital expenditures were typically close to depreciation levels so that net changes in plant and equipment associated with a given product could be ignored. Similarly, net working capital tended to be very small and could be ignored.

- The marginal tax rate for the firm was 32% and Johnson estimated that 8.5% was a reasonable discount rate (cost of capital) for this industry.

Johnson had recently requested a forecast of the firm's financials based on approved products. This forecast (**Exhibit 44.4**) included a forecast for Reximet starting with initial sales of $80 million. This forecast was generated largely as a tool for examining the prospects associated with products already in existence and to allow her to gauge the possible impact of Fleximat going off patent. Clearly, the forecast did not include the operating effects of adding new products to the lineup. While generated for an alternate purpose, the forecast was built from the assumptions listed above, and Johnson wondered if this forecast could also form a reasonable basis for valuing the company.

As Johnson contemplated her analysis, she immediately recognized that she needed to reach some decision regarding extending the patent life of Fleximat. The simplest and most obvious approach was to reformulate the drug. Her research team was reasonably

---

[11]Gardiner Harris, "Prilosec's Maker Switches Users To Nexium, Thwarting Generics," *Wall Street Journal*, June 6, 2002, 1.

certain that if it focused its efforts on changing the shape of the pill and applying an easier-to-swallow coating, a reformulation push in 2011 and 2012 at a cost of $35 million a year would likely generate a suitable reformulation. This reformulation would very likely leave the pharmacology of the medication unchanged. Of course, getting users to opt for the reformulation would require a strong marketing campaign above what was typical. She estimated the firm would have to spend $25 million annually for five years starting in 2011 (the first year getting the market ready for the reformulation) to ensure the success of the reformulation. A reformulation would not, of course, prevent some erosion in sales. Johnson estimated that when the patent expired in 2013, the drug would still see a 50% decline in sales, but after that, sales would grow at 2% a year for eight years. After that eight-year period, she reasonably expected that sales would dissipate in a manner similar to drugs going off patent (three years of 50% declines before dissipating entirely).

Big Decisions

Johnson had started the company with a simple mission: to find and develop medicines that would make lives better. Fleximat, she knew, had brought untold relief to children suffering from Crohn's disease, and this was particularly important to her because her nephew had Crohn's disease and Johnson had witnessed the incurable, chronic disease firsthand. For this reason, she wondered how the potential sale of the company might transform Medfield. The focus on making lives better, she hoped, would remain unchanged since the effectiveness of Medfield's drugs was the core source of its demand. She also expected the research staff and structures would be only slightly altered given that the team she had put together was quite effective; whereas a typical firm might have to spend $50 million for five years to develop a new product such as Reximet, her team could probably do it for $35 million a year.[12]

It was clear to Johnson that this offer was a great opportunity for her to exit the business on a high note. Given that Medfield was about to roll out Reximet and that it had two other products with substantial patent lives remaining, the company was a good catch for a potential buyer. Johnson also realized that the state of early-stage product development at Medfield was quite weak at the time. None of its new products was in late-stage trials. The fact was that the offer would leave her extremely wealthy and it would afford her a graceful exit from her venture. Of course, in deference to the many other owners, she had to put aside her own cares and evaluate the offer in the spirit of a financial transaction. This was a big decision—likely the largest of her life.

---

[12] Research costs at Medfield were lower, and development times were shorter than they were for the typical large pharmaceutical company given that Medfield targeted small markets; Medfield was not seeking the next blockbuster drug.

EXHIBIT 44.1 | Medfield Pharmaceuticals Annual Income Statement[1]
(in thousands of dollars)

	2007	2008	2009	2010
Revenue	223,721	261,253	300,556	329,203
Cost of goods sold	55,788	65,724	75,241	76,472
Gross profit	167,933	195,529	225,315	252,731
SG&A expenses	71,586	82,446	97,542	105,166
Research and development	42,175	54,078	57,535	62,457
	113,761	136,524	155,077	167,623
Earnings before interest and taxes	54,172	59,005	70,238	85,108
Interest	984	1,385	1,403	1,457
	53,188	57,620	68,835	83,651
Income taxes	16,457	18,982	22,495	25,875
Net income	36,731	38,638	46,340	57,776

Note: The company has negligible depreciation and amortization.

[1]All exhibits were created by the case writer.

EXHIBIT 44.2 | Medfield Pharmaceuticals Balance Sheet
(in thousands of dollars)

	2007	2008	2009	2010
Cash	21,465	28,227	29,542	32,251
Receivables	28,815	39,568	39,117	41,927
Inventory	24,704	24,316	27,859	30,559
	74,984	92,111	96,518	104,737
Property and equipment	102,977	118,553	127,498	129,171
Other assets	45,937	49,312	61,569	67,718
	223,898	259,976	285,585	301,626
Accounts payable	25,187	26,460	27,070	30,142
Accrued expenses	39,236	52,634	55,256	59,850
Current LTD	2,882	3,373	3,801	4,501
	67,305	82,467	86,127	94,493
LTD	17,069	23,609	25,278	26,850
Equity	139,524	153,900	174,180	180,283
	223,898	259,976	285,585	301,626

EXHIBIT 44.3 | Drug Reformulation Methods

AstraZeneca	To create Nexium, AstraZeneca cut Prilosec in half and changed its color (modest change, basically repackaging) and thus maintained a patented brand.
GlaxoSmithKline	As GlaxoSmithKline lost its patent on Paxil, an antidepressant, the company developed a new version (Paxil CR) that patients took just once a day, rather than twice. (Even though a Paxil generic weakened sales of Paxil CR, the company stuck with the extended-release version because it was a better fit for people with depression, who tended not to take their medication.)
Eli Lilly and Company	As Eli Lilly's patent expired on the antidepressant Prozac, the company introduced Prozac Weekly (again, easier and more efficient for patients with depression). Nonetheless, the $182 million sales of Prozac Weekly paled in comparison to the $2 billion sales that the daily Prozac, when patented, had brought in.
Schering-Plough	Schering-Plough launched Clarinex, a tweaked version of Claritin, its blockbuster antihistamine, the same year that Claritin lost patent protection. Schering-Plough also beat the generic companies at their own game by launching Claritin as an OTC drug within days of losing its patent. (Nonetheless, though Claritin was making $3 billion in sales when it lost patent exclusivity, the combined OTC Claritin and Clarinex sales were $1 billion—only a third of peak [and patented] prescription Claritin sales.)
Pfizer	Pfizer created an under-the-tongue version of Xanax (formerly just a pill), which provided faster delivery into the system, thus changing the method of delivery.
Elan	Drugmaker Elan used Nanocrystal technology for a 600% improvement in the bioavailability of compounds that dissolved poorly in water. Patients would still take the medication orally, but it allowed for a lower required dosage, smaller and more convenient dosage forms, and faster rates of absorption. For example, Elan reformulated Bristol-Myers Squibb's liquid Megace so it was not so thick and so that HIV/AIDS patients could drink less of it and more easily. Novartis created a patch delivery system with the Alzheimer's drug Exelon.

EXHIBIT 44.4 | Financial Forecast Based on Existing Products (in millions of dollars, unless otherwise noted)

	2010	2011	2012	2013	2014	2015	2016	2017	2018	2019
Costs of Sales	23.0%									
Research	19.0%									
Direct Marketing General and Admin.					27.0%					
					4.0%					
Taxes							32.0%			
Discount Rate							8.5%			
Fleximat										
Sales	210.56	214.77	219.07	109.53	54.77	27.38				
Cost of sales	47.46	49.40	50.39	25.19	12.60	6.30				
Lodamadal										
Sales	39.67	40.47	41.28	42.10	42.94	43.80	21.90	10.95	5.48	
Cost of sales	10.55	9.31	9.49	9.68	9.88	10.07	5.04	2.52	1.26	
Orsamorph										
Sales	78.97	80.55	82.16	83.80	85.48	87.19	88.93	90.71	92.52	94.37
Cost of sales	18.46	18.53	18.90	19.27	19.66	20.05	20.45	20.86	21.28	21.71
Reximet										
Sales			80.00	81.60	83.23	84.90	86.59	88.33	90.09	91.89
Cost of sales			18.40	18.77	19.14	19.53	19.92	20.32	20.72	21.14
Total sales	329.20	335.79	422.50	317.04	266.42	243.27	197.43	189.99	188.09	186.27
Cost of sales	76.47	77.23	97.18	72.92	61.28	55.95	45.41	43.70	43.26	42.84
Research	62.46	63.80	80.28	60.24	50.62	46.22	37.51	36.10	35.74	35.39
Direct marketing	91.22	90.66	114.08	85.60	71.93	65.68	53.31	51.30	50.78	50.29
General and administrative	13.94	13.43	16.90	12.68	10.66	9.73	7.90	7.60	7.52	7.45
	85.11	90.66	114.08	85.60	71.93	65.68	53.31	51.30	50.78	50.29
Taxes	27.15	29.01	36.50	27.39	23.02	21.02	17.06	16.41	16.25	16.09
NOPAT	57.96	61.65	77.57	58.21	48.91	44.66	36.25	34.88	34.53	34.20

American Greetings

This year American Greetings is demonstrating to naysayers that the greeting card space is not dead. The company has accelerated top-line [growth] through a combination of organic growth and acquisitions, and year-to-date revenues are trending well ahead of our forecast. However, the growth has come at a cost that is also far greater than we had anticipated . . . In Q3 marketing, spending increased by a surprising $10 million . . . The company also accelerated investment spending in the digital space to support the growth of recently launched cardstore.com. In addition, [American Greetings] has incurred . . . incremental expenses this year to roll out new doors in the dollar-store channel.

—**Jeff Stein, Managing Director, Northcoast Research**

It was New Year's Day 2012, and the weather was unseasonably warm in Cleveland, Ohio, headquarters for American Greetings Corporation (AG). But while temperatures were up, the same could not be said of AG's share price, which had been cut in half over the previous several months to a year-end closing price of $12.51 **(Exhibit 45.1)**.

At times of low equity valuation, AG management historically had turned to share buybacks. With current valuation levels, management was considering going into the market with a $75 million repurchase program. The repurchase was to be funded from AG's operating profit and cash reserves. The decision hinged on how the future of the enterprise was expected to play out. If the share price reasonably reflected bleak prospects for AG, management should preserve cash for future needs. If, on the other hand, AG stock was simply temporarily out of favor, the buyback plan presented a prudent defensive strategy.

American Greetings

With $1.7 billion in revenue, AG was the second-largest greeting card publisher in the United States. To meet the changing times, AG sold greeting cards as both paper products through traditional retail channels and electronic products through a number of company websites. In addition to gift cards, AG marketed gift wrap, candles, party goods, candles, and other giftware. To strengthen its business, the company owned and maintained the following major brands: American Greetings, Carlton Cards, Gibson, Recycled Paper Greetings, Papyrus, and DesignWare. AG owned the rights to a variety of popular characters, including Strawberry Shortcake, the Care Bears, Holly Hobbie, the Get Along Gang, and the Nickelodeon characters. The company was able to generate additional revenue by licensing the rights to these characters. Overall, management positioned AG as a leader in social expression products that assisted "consumers in enhancing their relationships to create happiness, laughter, and love."[1]

The company had a long affiliation with the founding Sapirstein family. Shortly after immigrating to the United States in 1905, Jacob Sapirstein, a Polish entrepreneur, launched a business distributing German manufactured postcards in Cleveland with the help of his young family. Eventually the business leadership was passed on to Jacob's oldest son, Irving Stone, then to Irving's son-in-law, Morry Weiss. In 2003, Morry's sons, Zev and Jeffrey Weiss, were appointed as CEO and president, respectively. Morry Weiss continued to serve as chairman.

Despite the strong family affiliation, AG was widely held in the public equity markets, with more than 11,000 shareholders, including large positions by such institutional investors as the British investment fund MAM Investments (10.6% of AG shares) and U.S. funds Dimensional Fund Advisors (10.5%), BlackRock (7.9%), and LSV Asset Management (6.7%). Dividend payments to investors had been on an upward trend in recent years, rising from 12 cents per share in 2004 to 56 cents in 2010.

Exhibits 45.2 and **45.3** provide AG's detailed financial statements. Since AG's fiscal year ended in February, the figures for 2011, for example, included results through February 2012, so remained estimates for the remaining two months.

Greeting Cards

Two players, Hallmark and AG, dominated the U.S. greetings card industry. Hallmark, privately held by the Hall family, was the larger of the two, with total worldwide revenue at $4 billion. From its headquarters in Kansas City, Missouri, Hallmark had aggressively expanded its business internationally with operations in more than 100 countries. Hallmark maintained licensing agreements with independent Hallmark Gold Crown retail stores that marketed Hallmark products and owned ancillary businesses such as Crayola (the crayon maker) and the Hallmark Channel cable network. Other card companies, such as Avanti Press, Blyth, CSS Industries, and Deluxe had found successful niches in the $6 billion U.S. greeting card market.

Mintel, the industry analyst firm, maintained that the overall greeting card market had contracted by 9% since 2005 and that the contraction would continue (**Exhibit 45.4**). Mintel's best-case scenario called for a 4% market decline over the next four years; its worst-case called for a 16% decline. The market contraction was thought to be driven by the substitution for greeting cards of other forms of social expression products, due to the ease of such alternative forms as smart phones, electronic social networking, and digital imaging, the last of which affected the traditional Christmas card market in particular. The rapid expansion of social media networks such as Facebook provided even

---

[1]Company website.

stronger challenges to electronic cards. An industry survey found that the social media substitution was particularly acute in a younger demographic (**Exhibit 45.5**). Analysts expected the trend to continue as the ease of digital communication substituted for traditional forms of social expression.

The industry had responded to the substantive technological shift with important market innovations. Both Hallmark and AG had created an extensive collection of electronic cards that made it easy for customers to send cards electronically. Card manufacturers maintained websites that allowed consumers to purchase paper greeting cards on the Internet via computer or smart phone and have the physical cards delivered directly to the recipient. Kiosks had been placed in retail stores that allowed customers to create custom cards. Distribution had expanded to build a substantive presence in the expanding dollar-store retail channel, where greeting cards were reported to be a top-selling item.

Despite the trends, large numbers of people continued to buy greeting cards. In a recent survey, 52% of U.S. respondents had purchased a greeting card in the past three months. This figure was down from 59% who had responded affirmatively in 2006.[2]

Valuation

With an end-of-year close of $12.51 per share, AG's PE ratio was at 6 times, its enterprise value to EBITDA ratio at 3.5 times, and its market-to-book ratio was below 1. All these valuation ratios were at the bottom of AG's group of comparable companies. **Exhibit 45.6** contains financial details and business descriptions for the AG-comparable group. AG's management believed its valuation suggested an opportunity, but low levels also demonstrated substantial concern by the capital market regarding the prospects of the company. For example, equity analysts at Standard and Poor's maintained a hold recommendation on the stock, claiming the following:

> We see [AG's 2012] sales increasing 2.5% to $1.73 billion. . . . We see demand benefitting from increased promotional spending in a more stable economic environment as the company pursues growth within the discount distribution channel . . . acquisitions . . . [and] international sales . . . We expect margins to narrow . . . reflecting a shift in customer mix toward the discount channel, increasing marketing costs to spur demand, distribution expansion costs, and expenses related to plans to move AG's headquarters building. While we believe channel migration will result in a permanent negative margin shift, we do not believe transition costs related to expanded distribution efforts will be a factor in the long term.[3]

Orly Seidman, a Value Line analyst, held a more optimistic view, expecting steady margins and steady long-term growth:

> The company has been improving the product pipeline. Management should continue to follow consumer and societal trends to better brand its offerings. It has shifted its focus from its core segment to pursue noncard merchandise. Product innovation, stronger retail

---

[2]Greeting Cards and E-Cards—U.S.: February 2011, Mintel report, February 2011.

[3]American Greetings Corp., Standard & Poor's stock report, December 27, 2011.

partnerships, and sell-diversified portfolio ought to drive customer interest in its goods. Technological enhancements will likely remain key to its long-term approach. Over the past few quarters, [AG] rolled out several complementary interactive products (i.e., mobile apps) and should continue to bolster its digital position.[4]

It was clear that there was substantial disagreement regarding the future growth trajectory and operating margins for the company. Over the past several years, revenue growth had been near to below zero. In 2011, however, revenue growth was anticipated to be more than 7% (**Exhibit 45.7**). Similarly, operating margins, which had been abnormally low two to five years previously, had improved to 9% recently. The marginal tax rate for AG income was 39%.

A bullish view held that AG would be able to maintain operating margins at 9% and achieve long-term ongoing revenue growth of 3%. A bearish view held that AG's prospective revenue growth would be near zero into the future and that margins would continue to erode to a long-term rate of 5%. The expectation was that recent investments and ongoing electronic product substitution would generate some future working capital efficiency for AG, but there was little evidence that fixed asset turnover would improve. **Exhibit 45.8** details the specific assumptions for the two scenarios.

Management understood that returns and growth were challenging to achieve in early 2012. Yields on U.S. Treasury bills and bonds were at historic lows of 0.1% and 2.8%, respectively (**Exhibit 45.9**). In such an environment, investors would richly reward returns of even small magnitudes.

---

[4]Orly Seidman, *American Greetings*, Value Line investment survey, November 11, 2011.

EXHIBIT 45.1 | American Greetings Share Price (monthly close)

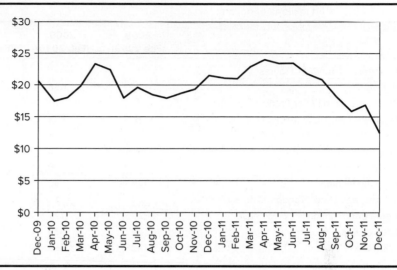

Data source: Yahoo! Finance.

EXHIBIT 45.2 | American Greetings Income Statement, December 2011[1]
(in millions of dollars)

	2008 (Feb 2009)	2009 (Feb 2010)	2010 (Feb 2011)	2011E (Feb 2012)
Total American Greetings Figures				
Total Revenue	1,691	1,636	1,593	1,677
Material, Labor, and Other Pruduction Costs	810	713	682	743
Selling, Distribution, and Marketing Expenses	619	508	478	526
Administrative and General Expenses	226	276	261	258
Goodwill and Other Intangible Asset Impairments	290	0	0	0
Other Operating Expenses	1	0	3	(6)
Operating Income	(253)	139	175	157
Net Interest and Other Nonoperating Expenses	22	18	19	28
Income Before Income Tax Expense	(275)	121	156	129
Income Tax Expense	(47)	39	69	47
Net Income	(228)	82	87	82
Earnings Per Share (Basic)	(4.89)	2.07	2.18	2.22
Dividends per Share	0.60	0.36	0.56	0.60
By Business Unit				
Operating Segment Net Sales				
North American Social Expression Products	1,095	1,235	1,191	1,215
International Social Expression Products	271	254	262	344
Retail Operations	179	12		
AG Interactive	83	80	78	68
Operating Segment Earnings				
North American Social Expression Products	70	236	218	148
International Social Expression Products	(78)	17	20	20
Retail Operations	(19)	(35)		
AG Interactive	(162)	11	14	14
Total Revenue by Product Category				
Everyday Greeting Cards	704	764	753	823
Seasonal Greeting Cards	357	369	377	408
Gift Packaging	240	221	223	239
Other Revenue	44	38	32	32
All Other Products	345	244	207	176

Data sources: Company accounts; management and case writer estimates.

[1]Fiscal year ends February of subsequent year.

EXHIBIT 45.3 | American Greetings Balance Sheet[1] (in millions of dollars)

	2009 (Feb 2010)	2010 (Feb 2011)	2011E (Feb 2012)
Cash and Cash Equivalents	138	216	172
Trade Accounts Receivable	136	120	130
Inventories	164	180	190
Prepaid Expenses	148	128	131
Other Current Assets	94	72	54
Total Current Assets	679	716	677
Net Property, Plant, and Equipment and Other Assets	850	832	859
Total Assets	1,529	1,547	1,536
Debt Due within One Year	1	0	0
Accounts Payable	95	87	87
Other Current Liabilities	272	245	255
Current Liabilities	369	332	343
Long-Term Debt	329	233	235
Other Liabilities	196	219	206
Shareholders' Equity	636	763	752
Total Liabilities and Shareholders' Equity	1,529	1,547	1,536

Data sources: Company accounts; management and case writer estimates.

[1]Fiscal year ends February of subsequent year.

EXHIBIT 45.4 | Total U.S. Greeting Cards Sales (Actual and Forecast)

	Sales at current prices	
	in millions of dollars	% annual change
2005	6,537	
2006	6,420	−1.8
2007	6,285	−2.1
2008	6,266	−0.3
2009	6,149	−1.9
2010	5,935	−3.5
2011 (est.)	5,838	−1.6
2012 (est.)	5,711	−2.2
2013 (est.)	5,596	−2.0
2014 (est.)	5,478	−2.1
2015 (est.)	5,359	−2.2

Data source: Mintel, based on U.S. Census Bureau, Economic Census.

EXHIBIT 45.5 | Feelings about e-Cards: Usage Change among 2,000 Respondents, October 2010

	All	By Age Category					
		18–24	25–34	35–44	45–54	55–64	65+
In the last year, I have sent more e-cards than I used to.	22%	17%	26%	20%	22%	21%	24%
In the last year, I have sent fewer e-cards than I used to because I send greetings over social networking sites such as Facebook.	20%	26%	27%	21%	19%	15%	13%

Data source: Mintel.

EXHIBIT 45.6 | Comparable Firms, End of 2011 (in millions of dollars except share price)

	Share Price	Shares Outstanding	Total Cash	Total Debt	Enterprise Value	Revenue	EBITDA	EBITDA Multiple*
American Greetings	12.51	38.3	86	235	714	1,660	204	3.5
Blyth	56.80	8.2	182	101	568	984	48	11.7
Consolidated Graphics	48.28	10.2	7	197	692	1,050	122	5.6
CSS Industries	19.92	9.7	10	0	194	453	30	6.5
Deluxe	22.76	50.9	31	742	1,901	1,420	359	5.3
Hallmark	NA	NA	NA	NA	NA	4,100	NA	NA
Lancaster Colony	69.34	27.3	162	0	1,890	1,090	156	12.2
Meredith	32.65	44.8	26	250	1,712	1,350	240	7.1
Scholastic	29.97	31.1	114	215	1,145	1,950	189	6.0

	ROA	ROE	Beta	Bond Rating**
American Greetings	7%	11%	1.63	BB+
Blyth	4%	9%	1.60	B
Consolidated Graphics	5%	10%	1.45	BB
CSS Industries	4%	2%	1.36	
Deluxe	13%	55%	1.85	B
Hallmark	NA	NA	NA	
Lancaster Colony	14%	19%	0.42	
Meredith	7%	15%	1.75	BB
Scholastic	6%	8%	1.04	BB−

Data sources: Yahoo! Finance, Standard & Poor's, Mergent.

*EBITDA miltiple is defined as Enterprise Value divided by EBITDA

**The ratings for Cons. Graphics and Meredith are estimated by case writer.

Blyth	Global marketer of candles, gourmet foods, weight management products, holiday cards, photo albums, and houseware products
Consolidated Graphics	Provides commercial printing services in North America, including brochures, shareholder communications, trading cards, calendars, catalogs, and greeting cards
CSS Industries	Designs, produces, and sells social expression products in North America, including greeting cards, gift wrapping, Valentine cards, Halloween costumes, and stationery
Deluxe	Provides printed products to financial institutions and small businesses worldwide, including forms, checks, envelopes, and greeting cards
Lancaster Colony	Manufactures and markets specialty foods, glassware, and candles in the United States
Meredith	Licenses brands and publishes magazines (e.g., *Better Homes and Gardens, Ladies' Home Journal, FamilyFun*) in the United States
Scholastic	Publishes and distributes children's books and other media in the United States

Data source: Case writer descriptions.

EXHIBIT 45.7 | American Greetings Operating Performance

	2005	2006	2007	2008	2009	2010	2011
Revenue Growth	0%	−7%	−1%	−5%	−3%	−2%	7%
Operating Margin	8%	2%	5%	−1%	6%	9%	9%

Note: Fiscal year ends February of subsequent year.

Data source: Company financial statements.

EXHIBIT 45.8 | Financial Forecast Assumptions

	Actual	Forecast			
	2011	2012	2013	2014	2015
Bullish Scenario					
Revenue Growth	5.3%	1.0%	1.5%	2.0%	2.5%
Operating Margin	9.4%	9.0%	9.0%	9.0%	9.0%
Net Working Capital Turnover	5.02	6.00	6.50	7.00	7.50
Fixed Asset Turnover	1.95	1.95	1.95	1.95	1.95
Bearish Scenario					
Revenue Growth	5.3%	0.0%	0.0%	0.0%	0.0%
Operating Margin	9.4%	8.0%	7.0%	6.0%	5.0%
Net Working Capital Turnover	5.02	6.00	6.50	7.00	7.50
Fixed Asset Turnover	1.95	1.95	1.95	1.95	1.95

Note: The ratios are defined in the following manner: Revenue Growth is the annual percentage change in total revenue, Operating Margin is operating income divided by total revenue, Net Working Capital Turnover is total revenue divided by net working capital where net working capital is current assets less current liabilities, Fixed Asset Turnover is total revenue divided by net PP&E and other assets.

Data source: Case writer estimates.

EXHIBIT 45.9 | Capital Market Data

	Yield
30-Day Treasury Bill	0.1%
10-Year Treasury Bond	2.8%

10-Year Corporate Bonds of Industrial Companies

AAA	2.8%
AA	2.9%
A+	3.2%
A	3.3%
A−	3.5%
BBB+	3.8%
BBB	4.1%
BBB−	4.6%
BB+	5.8%
BB	6.5%
BB−	6.5%
B+	6.8%
B	8.4%
B−	9.0%

Historical Market Risk Premium	
Equity Market Index Less Government Debt	5.5%

	5-Year Forecast
U.S. Real GDP Annual Growth Rate	3.3%
U.S. GDP Annual Deflator Rate	1.8%
Consumer Price Index Annual Rate	2.2%

Data sources: Bloomberg, Value Line Investment Survey, and case writer estimates.

Ferrari: The 2015 Initial Public Offering

The Ferrari is a dream—people dream of owning this special vehicle, and for most people it will remain a dream apart from those lucky few.

—Enzo Ferrari, Founder, Ferrari

It was October 20, 2015, the day before what was anticipated to be the first day of public trading for the stock of legendary Italian sports car company Ferrari NV (Ferrari). Sergio Marchionne, chairman of Ferrari and CEO of its parent company, Fiat Chrysler Automobiles NV (FCA), had announced a year previously that FCA would be spinning off Ferrari into a separately traded company. As an independent company, the shares of Ferrari (under the aptly named ticker symbol RACE) would be listed on the New York Stock Exchange (NYSE), with an eventual listing in Milan. Marchionne's plan was to sell 10% of Ferrari's shares in an initial public offering (IPO), and the money raised in the offering would go to FCA.

The worth of the Ferrari shares had been the subject of fierce debate among analysts and investors, especially after FCA set an initial price range of USD48 to USD52 per share in early October.[1] Following the road-show meetings with potential investors in both Europe and the United States, Marchionne knew there was strong demand for the 17.175 million shares that would be offered for sale in the IPO. If the offer price was set too low, FCA would leave money on the table, which suggested pricing the deal at the top of the initial range or beyond. However, if the offer price was set too high, poor first-day trading returns would sour the investor's initial experience with the company. It was time now for Marchionne—in negotiation with lead bank UBS—to set the price at which the company's IPO shares would be offered to investors that evening.

---

[1] USD = U.S. dollars, EUR= euros.

This case was prepared by Michael J. Schill, Professor of Business Administration, and Jenny Craddock, Senior Case Writer. It was written as a basis for class discussion rather than to illustrate effective or ineffective handling of an administrative situation. Copyright © 2017 by the University of Virginia Darden School Foundation, Charlottesville, VA. All rights reserved. *To order copies, send an e-mail to* sales@ dardenbusinesspublishing.com. *No part of this publication may be reproduced, stored in a retrieval system, used in a spreadsheet, or transmitted in any form or by any means—electronic, mechanical, photocopying, recording, or otherwise—without the permission of the Darden School Foundation.*

Ferrari—A Background[2]

The history of Ferrari, the business, was inextricably linked to Ferrari, the man. Enzo Ferrari, born to a lower-middle-class family in Modena, Italy, in 1898, felt a powerful draw to racing from a young age. He moved to Turin to work for Fiat after the First World War only to have his application hurtfully rejected. He eventually landed an assistant job at a new automobile manufacturer nearby, and it was there that he competed in his first race in 1919. Despite his passion for racing, he was not immediately successful; he finished fourth. Enzo Ferrari joined the team of racecar maker Alfa Romeo as a test driver, and his role soon grew to include racing Alfa Romeos on behalf of the company and selling cars to wealthy clients around northern Italy. Over the years, he raced his way to multiple victories and built a large dealership from which he sold and serviced Alfa cars. In the late 1920s, Alfa Romeo encountered financial difficulties and shut down its involvement in the racing circuit.

Unable to be around cars and not race them, Enzo Ferrari founded his own racing *scuderia* ("stable" or "team") in 1929—Scuderia Ferrari. Over the ensuing years he continued to run both his dealership and Scuderia Ferrari (which Alfa Romeo frequently used to represent the company at races). Alfa Romeo eventually bought 80% of Scuderia Ferrari and returned the management of the racing program to company headquarters. Following the acquisition, Enzo Ferrari realized that he would never achieve his ambition of running Alfa Romeo's racing program and left the company in 1939 after two decades of service. The parting agreement forbade him from racing or using the name Scuderia Ferrari for the next four years, so he returned to one of his old scuderia buildings in Modena the next year and established his own manufacturing firm while waiting out the racing ban.

However, with Italy's involvement in the Second World War, Mussolini's fascist government forced Enzo Ferrari to focus his manufacturing operation on building aircraft engines for the war rather than cars. When Allied forces bombed the factory, Enzo Ferrari moved his operations from Modena to Maranello. After the war, Enzo Ferrari debuted his first Ferrari racecar, which quickly won a high-profile race in Turin in front of Italy's elite. Before long, members of European society were contacting Ferrari for cars of their own. The following year Ferrari's car designers finished a nonracing road car. During the following decade these handmade cars, produced in batches of 10, became the prize of every car enthusiast in Europe and North America, with a client list including kings, princes, and members of America's wealthiest families.

Despite his commercial business success, Enzo Ferrari's single focus continued to be racing. Throughout the 1950s and 1960s, he used the profits from his sports car sales to fund competition in Grand Prix and Formula 1 races. Enzo Ferrari was so present on the racing circuit that he became Italy's national symbol of motor racing. His negligence toward road car production (and the ensuing design and production flaws) became evident, and Ferrari sales declined throughout the 1960s.

Refusing to cut costs and miss races, Enzo Ferrari sought external funds to keep the company afloat. He went to Fiat for help, an ironic turn following his longtime disdain for

---

[2]The background on Ferrari is partially drawn from Drew D. Johnson, ed., *International Directory of Company Histories: Volume 146* (Detroit: St James Press, 2013). Thomas Derdak, "Ferrari S.p.A," pp 140–146.

Fiat. In 1969, Fiat purchased 50% of Ferrari shares and took control of all road car production. Ferrari retained ownership in the remaining 50% and continued to manage the racing operation. Fiat's efforts to modernize the factory and update the manufacturing process paid off, and by 1980, annual road car production reached 2,000, more than double what it had been prior to Fiat's involvement. At the time of Enzo Ferrari's death in 1988, Fiat's stake in Ferrari was 90%, with the remaining 10% held by the Ferrari family.

Ferrari—The Car Business

After Ferrari's death, his namesake company entered a period of aimlessness and decline—annual sales consisted of only 2,000 cars in the early 1990s. In 1992, Fiat hired Luca Cordero di Montezemolo, a marketing maven who had once worked as both an assistant to Enzo Ferrari and later as the Ferrari team leader, as chairman of Ferrari. Montezemolo wasted no time in making sweeping changes at the automaker. The product line grew from two outdated models to nine new ones and a commitment to engineering excellence was instilled.

A key aspect of Montezemolo's quality and branding strategy over the period from 1992 to 2014 involved holding production volumes below demand in order to instill a perception of exclusivity. In 2014, for example, Ferrari sold just 7,255 cars compared to the nearly 40,000 cars sold by FCA's sister company, Maserati.[3] The restricted production created long waiting lists, but customers who were designated as preferred customers due to their regular purchases were allowed to bypass the waiting list. This policy prompted many buyers to regularly purchase Ferrari cars just to stay on the preferred customer list. Ferrari also produced limited-edition "halo" cars that were exclusively sold to a select group of loyal customers. One notable such offering was the roofless F60 America, which was announced in 2014; only 10 of the USD2.5 million roadsters were produced and all were sold in advance of the cars' actual production, with commitments based simply on a full-scale maquette. The limited production policy ensured high resale value. For example, in August 2014 Bonhams auctioned a 1962 Ferrari GTO for a jaw-dropping USD38 million.[4] Montezemolo believed that the waiting list and limited-edition model policies promoted the Ferrari brand without jeopardizing customer satisfaction. Ferrari had recently been named the most powerful brand in the world by Brand Finance, the intangible-asset-valuation consultancy.

By 2014, Montezemolo's restricted-volume strategy was creating increased tension with the leadership at Ferrari's parent company, FCA. In September, Marchionne, who was business-school educated and had long pushed Ferrari management to increase volume, asked Montezemolo to leave the company. On his way out, Montezemolo reportedly said that Ferrari was now American, and that statement wasn't meant as a compliment.[5] After Montezemolo left, Marchionne stepped in as chairman and immediately pushed for higher volume—particularly to China and the Middle East. Marchionne indicated that Ferrari shipment volume would rise to 9,000 units by 2019. He maintained that the volume increase

---

[3]*Ward's Automotive Yearbook* (Southfield, MI: Penton Media, 2016).

[4]Mark Ewing, "Ferrari at the Crossroads," *Forbes*, December 15, 2014: 106–108.

[5]Ewing.

was justified by both "growing demand in emerging markets" and "demographic changes as the size and spending capacity of target clients." By maintaining restricted volumes in Europe and the Americas, Marchionne believed Ferrari could maintain its levels of perceived exclusivity and preserve the value of brand, even with a higher vehicle output. **Exhibit 46.1** provides Ferrari historical data on shipments by car model.

In 2015, the company had four sports cars and two grand touring cars in production, in addition to a half-dozen limited-edition vehicles (see **Exhibit 46.2** for descriptions of the current product line). Ferrari's brand power was such that the average car selling price exceeded USD267,000, and Ferrari was one of the most profitable companies in the global auto-manufacturing industry, with operating margins far greater than industry average. **Exhibits 46.3** and **46.4** provide financial statement information for Ferrari.

In addition to its revenue from car, engine, and parts sales, Ferrari maintained a steady stream of income, totaling roughly 15% of yearly sales, from its sponsorships and licensing activities, a line of business that was developed under Montezemolo's leadership. Not only did Ferrari lend its name to its Formula 1 racing team and collect on those sponsorship agreements and shared revenues with the Formula 1 World Championship commercial revenue, but, starting in the mid-1990s, the company also licensed its brand power and iconic prancing horse logo to a "select number of producers and retailers of luxury and lifestyle goods" ranging from watches and sportswear to perfume and video games.[6] Ferrari launched its first retail store in 2002, and by 2015, the company sold Ferrari-branded merchandise through 32 franchised or company-owned Ferrari stores and on its website. In 2010, the first Ferrari theme park, Ferrari World, opened in Abu Dhabi and featured the world's fastest roller coaster—Formula Roussa. Ferrari management believed there were ongoing opportunities to expand the company's brand presence further "in attractive and growing lifestyle categories . . . including sportswear, watches, accessories, consumer electronics and theme parks, which . . . [would] enhance the brand experience of . . . loyal clients and Ferrari enthusiasts."[7]

FCA

The formation of FCA resulted from the merger of Fiat, the leading Italian car manufacturer, which had been founded in 1899, and Chrysler, the third-largest U.S. auto company, which had been founded in 1925. The two companies partially merged in 2009, as Fiat hoped to expand its exposure beyond a struggling European market and Chrysler hoped to use Fiat's technology to build more fuel-efficient, smaller cars to sell in North America. Over the next few years, Fiat bought additional stakes in Chrysler before assuming full ownership in early 2014, in the midst of a highly competitive year for the global automotive sector.

FCA was currently the world's seventh-largest automaker. With operations in approximately 40 countries, FCA designed, manufactured, distributed, and sold vehicles for both the mass market (under the Abarth, Alfa Romeo, Chrysler, Dodge, Fiat, Fiat

---

[6]Ferrari prospectus.

[7]Ferrari prospectus.

Professional, Jeep, Lancia, and Ram brands) and the luxury market (under the Maserati and Ferrari brands). Despite its broad portfolio of vehicles, FCA received disproportionate benefits from its luxury automotive sector—FCA's luxury brand division provided 21% of 2014's EBIT despite just 5% of revenue. **Exhibit 46.5** provides operating details on FCA's car portfolio.

Facing a range of competitive and economic threats in 2014, Marchionne announced a five-year business plan. The plan sought to aggressively reorganize the company over the period from 2014 to 2018 by focusing on strengthening, differentiating, and globalizing FCA's portfolio of brands and standardizing production architecture for multiple brands to increase productivity. Soon after the plan was announced and just weeks after Montezemolo's exit, Marchionne announced the intended separation of Ferrari from FCA. The plan provided that FCA would sell 17.175 million shares in an IPO, with the proceeds going to FCA. Several months after the IPO, FCA would spin off the 80% of Ferrari stock it held. The spin-off entailed simply distributing FCA holdings in Ferrari to the existing FCA shareholders as a stock dividend. Following the spin-off, 90% of Ferrari shares would be publicly traded and the other 10% retained by the Ferrari family. FCA saw the upcoming Ferrari IPO and spin-off as having several purposes.

1. Generate a large cash payment to FCA through the sale of the IPO shares, while simultaneously transferring some of FCA's debt to Ferrari (Ferrari debt was expected to be EUR2.3 billion after the deal).

2. Promote and extend the value of Ferrari's brand among the world's premier luxury lifestyle companies.

3. Allow Ferrari direct access to sources of equity and debt capital on favorable terms.

4. Attract American investors by listing on the NYSE—historically one of Ferrari's most important product markets.

5. Attract and reward technical and management talent by allowing them to have direct ownership in Ferrari.

6. Unlock "hidden value" that shareholders were not currently attributing to FCA share values under the consolidated structure. While the entire FCA group (including Ferrari) was trading for a market capitalization of EUR21 billion, Marchionne believed that both Ferrari and the rest of FCA would trade for much more than that if the companies traded independently.

The Premium Car Industry

The premium car industry historically included a wide range of entry points. In order to categorize the industry further, some analysts divided the sector into a normal premium segment and a super luxury segment.[8] Normal premium brands included Audi (owned by Volkswagen), Mercedes (owned by Daimler), BMW, and Japanese luxury brands

---

[8] Christian Breitsprecher et al., "Premium Car Makers—the Sweetest Piece of the Pie," *Macquarie*, January 6, 2014: 42.

Lexus and Infiniti. The super luxury brands included lower-volume makers such as Ferrari, Rolls-Royce (owned by BMW), Porsche, Bentley, and Bugatti (all three owned by Volkswagen), all of which shared a historic European legacy as a key component of their branding power.

Some argued that Ferrari's business was closer to such luxury-good firms as Hermès or Prada than that of car manufacturers. These firms maintained similarly high-margin, low-volume, and low-volatility business models. While the level of Ferrari's capital investment was much higher than that required of most luxury goods firms, Ferrari spent substantially less on advertising and used Formula 1 as its marketing tool. **Exhibit 46.6** provides capital market and financial data for car-related companies and luxury brands.

In 2015, the premium car industry exhibited continued strength in its traditional markets in the developed world while also enjoying growing demand from China, the world's single-largest automotive market.[9] WardsAuto claimed that the annual growth of units of the Chinese luxury car sales had exceeded 20% over the past five years and now exceeded 1.5 million units per year.[10] While the global car market expanded by 3.5% in 2014, the premium sector enjoyed considerably more gains. For example, in 2014 BMW Group sold over 1.8 million BMW-brand cars and over 4,000 Rolls-Royce–brand cars, up 9.5% and 11.9%, respectively, from the previous year.

The IPO Process

The process of going public—selling publicly traded equity for the first time—was an arduous undertaking that, at a minimum, required about three months. (**Table 46.1** provides a timetable for a typical IPO.)

Before initiating the equity-issuance process, private firms needed to fulfill a number of prerequisites: generate a credible business plan; gather a qualified management team; create an outside board of directors; prepare audited financial statements, performance measures, and projections; and develop relationships with investment bankers, lawyers, and accountants. Frequently, firms held "bake-off" meetings to discuss the equity-issuance process with various investment banks before selecting a lead underwriter. Important considerations when choosing an underwriter included the proposed compensation package, track record, analyst research support, distribution capabilities, and aftermarket market-making support. After the firm satisfied the prerequisites, the equity-issuance process began with a meeting of all the key participants (management, underwriters, accountants, and legal counsel for both the underwriters and the issuing firm) to plan the process and reach agreement on specific terms. Throughout the process, additional meetings could be called to discuss problems and review progress.

Following the initiation of the equity-issuance process, the company was commonly prohibited from publishing information outside the prospectus. The company could continue established, normal advertising activities, but any increased publicity designed to raise awareness of the company's name, products, or geographical presence

---

[9]Breitsprecher et al.: 31.

[10]Mike Dean, Alexander Haissl, and Fei Teng, "European Autos 2015 Outlook," Credit Suisse, January 9, 2015.

TABLE 46.1 | Timetable for typical U.S. IPO (in days).

Prior to Day 1: Organizational "all-hands" meeting	1	2	3	4	5	6	7
	8	9	10	11	12	13	14	**1–14: Quiet period**

15–44: Due diligence
Underwriter interviews management, suppliers, and customers; reviews financial statements; drafts preliminary registration statement. Senior management of underwriter gives OK on issue.

15	16	17	18	19	20	21
22	23	24	25	26	27	28
29	30	31	32	33	34	35
36	37	38	39	40	41	42

45: Registration (announcement) — 43 44 45 46 47 48 49

50: Prospectus (*red herring*) — 50 51 52 53 54 55 56

45–75: SEC review period
SEC auditor reviews for compliance with SEC regulations. Underwriter assembles syndicate and initiates road show.

57 58 59 60 61 62 63
64 65 66 67 68 69 70
71 72 73 74 75 76 77

76–89: Road show
Preliminary price range set. Underwriters, issuing firm's management present deal to institutional investors, build book of purchase orders.

76–89:
Letters of comment received from SEC; amendments filed with SEC.

78 79 80 81 82 83 84

90: Effective date; shares offered — 85 86 87 88 89 90 91   **91: Trading begins**

92 93 94 95 96 97 98   **98: Settlement**

Source: Created by author based on industry standards.

---

in order to create a favorable attitude toward the company's securities could be considered illegal. This requirement was known as the "quiet period."

The underwriter's counsel generally prepared a letter of intent that provided most of the terms of the underwriting agreement but was not legally binding. The underwriting agreement described the securities to be sold, set forth the rights and obligations of the various parties, and established the underwriter's compensation. Because the underwriting agreement was not signed until the offering price was determined (just before distribution began), both the firm and the underwriter were free to pull out of the agreement any time before the offering date. If the firm did withdraw the offer, the letter of intent generally required the firm to reimburse the underwriter for direct expenses.

Selling securities required a registration process with the government's security regulatory agency. In the United States, the Security and Exchange Commission (SEC) called for preparation of the prospectus (part I of the registration statement), answers to specific questions, copies of the underwriting contract, company charter and bylaws, and a specimen of the security (included in part II of the registration statement), all of which required considerable attention from the parties on the offering firm's team. One of the important features of the registration process was the performance of due-diligence procedures by the company and the bankers. Due diligence referred to the process of providing reasonable grounds that there was nothing in the registration statement that was significantly untrue or misleading and was motivated by the liability of all parties to the registration statement for any material misstatements or omissions. Due-diligence procedures involved such things as reviewing company documents, contracts, and tax returns; visiting company offices and facilities; soliciting "comfort letters" from company auditors; and interviewing company and industry personnel.

During this period, the lead underwriter began to form the underwriting syndicate, which comprised a number of investment banks that agreed to buy portions of the offering at the offer price less the underwriting discount. The underwriting discount provided the bulk of compensation for the underwriter as it paid a discounted price for the IPO shares and then turned around and sold them for the full offering price. In addition to the syndicate members, dealers were enlisted to sell a certain number of shares on a "best-effort" basis. The dealers received a fixed reallowance, or concession, for each share sold. The selling agreement provided the contract to members of the syndicate, granted power of attorney to the lead underwriter, and stipulated (a) the management fee that each syndicate member was required to pay the lead underwriter, (b) the share allocations, and (c) the dealer reallowances or concessions. Because the exact terms of the agreement were not specified until approximately 48 hours before selling began, the agreement did not become binding until just before the offering. The original contract specified a range of expected compensation levels; the selling agreement was structured so that the contract became binding when it was orally approved via telephone by the syndicate members after the effective date.

The SEC review process started when the registration statement was filed and the statement was assigned to a branch chief of the Division of Corporate Finance. As part of the SEC review, the statement was given to accountants, attorneys, analysts, and industry specialists. The SEC review process was laid out in the Securities Act of 1933, which according to its preamble aspired to "provide full and fair disclosure of the character of securities sold in interstate commerce." Under the Securities Act, the registration statement became effective 20 days after the filing date. If, however, the SEC found anything in the registration statement that was regarded as materially untrue, incomplete, or misleading, the branch chief sent the registrant a letter of comment detailing the deficiencies. Following a letter of comment, the issuing firm was required to correct and return the amended statement to the SEC. Unless an acceleration was granted by the SEC, the amended statement restarted the 20-day waiting period.

While the SEC was reviewing the registration statement, the underwriter was engaged in book-building activities, which involved surveying potential investors to construct a schedule of investor demand for the new issue. To generate investor interest, the preliminary offering prospectus or "red herring" (so called because the prospectus was required to have the words "preliminary prospectus" on the cover in red ink) was printed and offered to potential investors. During this period, underwriters generally organized a one- to two-week "road show" tour, which enabled managers to discuss their investment plans, display their management potential, and answer questions from financial analysts, brokers, and institutional investors in locations across the country or abroad.

Finally, companies could place "tombstone ads" in various financial periodicals announcing the offering and listing the members of the underwriting syndicate.

By the time the registration statement was ready to become effective, the underwriter and the offering firm's management negotiated the final offering price and the underwriting discount. The negotiated price depended on perceived investor demand and current market conditions (e.g., price multiples of comparable companies, previous offering experience of industry peers). Once the underwriter and the management agreed on the offering price and discount, the underwriting agreement was signed, and the final registration amendment was filed with the SEC. The company and the underwriter generally asked the SEC to accelerate the final pricing amendment, which was usually granted immediately by phone. The offering was then ready for public sale. The final pricing and acceleration of the registration statement typically happened within a few hours.

During the morning of the effective day, the lead underwriter confirmed the selling agreement with the members of the syndicate. Following confirmation of the selling agreement, selling began. Members of the syndicate sold shares of the offering through oral solicitations to potential investors. Because investors were required to receive a final copy of the prospectus with the confirmation of sale, and the law allowed investors to back out of purchase orders upon receipt of the final prospectus, the offering sale was not realized until underwriters actually received payment. Underwriters would generally cancel orders if payment was not received within five days of the confirmation.

SEC Rule 10b-7 permitted underwriters to engage in price-stabilization activities for a limited period during security distribution. Under this rule, underwriters often posted stabilizing bids at or below the offer price, which provided some price stability during the initial trading of an IPO.

The offering settlement, or closing, occurred 7 to 10 days after the effective date, as specified in the underwriting agreement. At this meeting, the firm delivered the security certificates to the underwriters and dealers, and the lead underwriter delivered the prescribed proceeds to the firm. In addition, the firm traditionally delivered an updated comfort letter from its independent accountants. Following the offering, the underwriter generally continued to provide valuable investment-banking services by distributing research literature and acting as a market maker for the company.

Pricing the Ferrari IPO

As the date of the Ferrari IPO approached, an active debate around the appropriate valuation for Ferrari continued to make waves in the investment community. **Exhibit 46.7** contains samples of analyst and reporter opinions on the value of the shares. **Exhibit 46.8** provides a base-case financial forecast for Ferrari based on Marchionne's volume-expansion forecast. The cost of capital had been estimated to be 5.0% in euro based on market data for comparable companies. This figure was consistent with the relatively low risk that analysts associated with Ferrari's expected cash flows. Although Ferrari was incorporated in the Netherlands, because the company headquarters and operations were in Italy, Ferrari profits would be taxed in Italy at a tax rate of 38%.

The number of Ferrari shares outstanding was to increase from 172 million before the offering to 189 million after the offering.[11] To facilitate trading in U.S. dollars on the NYSE, U.S.-dollar Ferrari certificates would be authorized for trading in the United States based on euro-denominated Ferrari shares held in trust. The trust would facilitate transfer of all dividends and voting privileges between the certificate holder and the company as if the certificate were equivalent to the underlying share. This arrangement was common in the United States to allow the shares of non-U.S. companies to trade on U.S. exchanges.

The level of comparable price multiples played an important role in the valuation of IPO firms, but for Ferrari there were no perfect "pure plays" (publicly traded companies that were solely in the exact same business). World IPO volume was down from 2014, but European IPO volume was up. Back in March, Autotrader, the British website for buying and selling used cars, had gone public at an enterprise-to-EBITDA multiple of 26 times. In June, the American producer of wearable activity trackers, Fitbit, had priced its IPO at 21 times EBITDA. Last week, the large British payment-processing company Worldpay had gone public at 19 times EBITDA. Concurrently, it was expected that Poste Italiane, Italy's postal service, would price its IPO at a multiple of 8 times EBITDA. The only related auto manufacturer transaction was the 2012 acquisition of Aston Martin by a private equity firm that had occurred at an EBITDA multiple of 9.9 times. But Aston Martin had been poorly performing and unprofitable at the time of the acquisition and had a much lower brand loyalty than Ferrari. **Exhibit 46.9** provides prevailing capital market information.

The current interest reports suggested that investor interest in the Ferrari IPO was so high that the deal was expected to be as much as 10 times oversubscribed. Indeed, following the road show in Europe the previous week, UBS claimed that the book was well oversubscribed. These signals left Marchionne wondering if pricing the stock within range might leave money on the table.

The contrasting view, however, held that pricing too high would send a message of imprudence to the investment community and risk losing subsequent upsurges in price. Some analysts had, after all, expressed concern that Ferrari might struggle as an independent entity because of its small scale. Others worried that once Ferrari as a public company, management would be pushed to think more about numbers and sales than preserving brand exclusivity.

---

[11]Since FCA, rather than Ferrari, would receive the cash proceeds of the offering, the appropriate number of shares to consider in pricing the company was the post-money shares of 189 million.

EXHIBIT 46.1 | Ferrari Car Shipments

	Full Year			First Half of Year	
	2012	2013	2014	2014	2015
By model type					
Sports cars					
V8	4,274	3,944	3,651	2,077	1,581
V12	481	1,401	1,565	900	645
Total	4,755	5,345	5,216	2,977	2,226
GT cars					
V8	1,589	1,219	1,645	454	1,280
V12	1,061	436	394	237	188
Total	2,650	1,655	2,039	691	1,468
By geography					
Europe, Middle East, and Africa					
United Kingdom	686	686	705	408	456
Germany	755	659	616	353	214
Switzerland	366	350	332	181	155
Italy	318	206	243	132	139
France	330	273	253	138	129
Middle East	423	472	521	232	185
Rest of EMEA	825	663	604	349	320
Total EMEA	3,703	3,309	3,274	1,793	1,598
Americas					
Americas	2,208	2,382	2,462	1,199	1,287
Asia Pacific					
Greater China	789	572	675	289	261
Rest of APAC	705	737	844	387	548
Total APAC	1,494	1,309	1,519	676	809
Total	7,405	7,000	7,255	3,668	3,694

Source: Ferrari prospectus.

Middle East includes the United Arab Emirates, Saudi Arabia, Bahrain, Lebanon, Qatar, Oman, and Kuwait.

Rest of Europe, Middle East, and Africa (EMEA) includes Africa and the other European markets not separately identified.

Americas includes the United States of America, Canada, Mexico, the Caribbean, and Central and South America.

Greater China includes China, Hong Kong, and Taiwan.

Rest of Asia Pacific (APAC) mainly includes Japan, Australia, Singapore, Indonesia, and South Korea.

EXHIBIT 46.2 | Ferrari Car Models in October 2015

Sports Cars

458 Italia

The 458 Italia is a two-seater sports car with a 570 hp mid-rear mounted V8 engine, launched in 2009. Its longitudinally-mounted engine is influenced by Ferrari's Formula 1 racing technology, and has been engineered to reach 9,000 rpm, a first on an eight cylinder road car. The 458 Italia is designed as a pure sports car, for drivers seeking spirited performance on and off the track. The cabin features a reinterpretation of Ferrari's traditional sports car interior themes, with clean and simple yet innovative components. The redesigned and intuitive ergonomics have resulted in a completely driver-oriented layout. We discontinued production of the 458 Italia, which is being replaced by the 488 GTB, in May 2015.

488 GTB

Our latest sports car, the 488 GTB a two seater berlinetta with a 670 hp mid-rear mounted V8 engine, is replacing the 458 Italia. It was launched in March 2015, 40 years after we unveiled our first ever mid-rear-engined V8 model (the 308 GTB). Its large signature air intake scallop evokes the original 308 GTB and is divided into two sections by a splitter. Designed for track-level performance, the 488 GTB can also provide enjoyment to non-professional drivers for everyday use. Accelerating from 0-200 km/h in only 8.3 seconds, its new 3902 cc V8 turbo engine is at top of the class for power output, torque and response times. In the cabin, the seamless integration of the new satellite control clusters, angled air vents and instrument panel heightens the sense that the cockpit is completely tailored around the driver, leading to an extremely sporty yet comfortable ambiance.

458 Spider

Launched in 2011, the 458 Spider is a two seat coupe with a 570 hp mid-rear mounted V8 engine and is the world's first mid-rear-engine car with a retractable hard top. If offers the full experience of sports car driving, especially on mixed and challenging surfaces, but aims to cater to those who do not need to constantly push their car to the limit on the track. Unlike the 458 Italia, the engine air intakes have been moved to the rear spoiler, close to the gearbox, clutch and oil radiators. Like the 458 Italia and the 458 Speciale (see below), the Spider draws inspiration from Formula 1 single-seaters, and has been made 12 percent more aerodynamic than its convertible predecessors, such as the F430. Among its other awards, it was named 2012's "Best of the Best" convertible by the Robb Report (a prominent luxury periodical). We currently expect to stop producing the 458 Spider by the end of July 2015.

F12berlinetta

Launched in 2012, the F12berlinetta is equipped with a 740 hp V12 engine. It is the most powerful high performance Ferrari sports car ever built. Built around evolved transaxle architecture with cutting-edge components and control systems, it sets a new standard in aerodynamics and handling. Though conceived as a performance automobile, the F12berlinetta is capable of both high speed and long-distance driving.

Grand Touring (GT) Cars

California T

The California T, which followed the great success of our 2008 California model, is equipped with a 560 hp V8 turbo engine. Launched in 2014, it is the only GT car in the segment to combine a retractable hard top, rear seats and a ski passage to the spacious trunk. Its new turbocharged V8 engine comes with a variable boost management system. This makes it the only turbo engine in the world with close to no turbo lag. It also features a revised rear and interior design and a 15 percent reduction in fuel consumption compared to its predecessor.

FF

Launched in 2011, the FF, our first four-wheel drive model, is equipped with a 660 hp V12 engine. Among its main innovations, the FF features the patented lightweight 4RM system, which transmits torque to all four wheels, thus allowing a 50 percent saving in weight compared to a traditional four-wheel drive system and a lower center of gravity to be maintained. Part of our GT class, the FF features an elegant two door, four seat sporting layout, and the best cabin and luggage space and occupant comfort in its class.

EXHIBIT 46.2 | Ferrari Car Models in October 2015   (*continued*)

Special Series Cars

458 Speciale

The 458 Speciale was launched in 2013 and features a 605 hp V8 engine. It is aimed at clients willing to trade some on board comfort for a more track focused car. With a Ferrari-patented special active aerodynamics designed by the Ferrari Design Centre and Pininfarina, it is currently our most aerodynamic road car. Building on the integration of Formula 1 technology, on-track handling is enhanced by Ferrari's Side Slip Angle Control (SSC) system, which employs an algorithm to analyze the car's side slip, compare it to the car's projected trajectory and work with the electronic differential to instantly change the torque distribution between the rear wheels. The Speciale is available as a two seat coupe. We currently expect to stop producing the 458 Speciale by October 2015.

458 Speciale A

The 458 Speciale A (equipped with a 605 hp V8 engine) debuted at the 2014 Paris Auto Show and features the most powerful naturally aspirated V8 engine ever produced for a Ferrari spider. It is the latest variant of the 458 models, and celebrates the remarkable success of this line. It adopts the innovative retractable hard top that has become a signature of Ferrari spiders and features significantly improved combustion, mechanical and volumetric efficiency. The 499 models produced come as a two seat coupe. We currently expect to stop producing the 458 Speciale A by November 2015.

Limited Edition Supercars, Fuoriserie and One-Offs

LaFerrari

Launched in 2013, LaFerrari is the latest in our line of supercars. Planned for a total production run of just 499 cars, LaFerrari is our first car with hybrid technology. Alongside its powerful rear-wheel drive layout V12 engine (which generates 800 hp), the hybrid system comprises two electric motors and a special battery consisting of cells developed by the Scuderia Ferrari where the F138 KERS technology was pioneered. Because the battery generates an additional 163 hp, LaFerrari has a combined total of 963 hp. LaFerrari's HY-KERS system is designed to achieve seamless integration and rapid communication between the V12 and electric motor, thus blending extreme performance with maximum efficiency. Thanks to the hybrid technology, LaFerrari generates almost 50 percent more horsepower than the Enzo, its predecessor, and 220 hp more than the F12, our most powerful car to date. Acceleration: 0 to 200 km/h in less than 7 seconds. 0 to 300 km/h in 15 seconds.

F60 America

The F60 America, a V12 open air roadster, celebrates our 60 years in the United States and is available to U.S. clients only. It combines two of our American clients' great passions—the modified V12 engine and open-top driving. The exterior is finished in North American Racing Team livery, with special 60th anniversary prancing horse badges adorning the wheel arches. Inside, the F60America features bespoke cabin trim, with the driver's side finished in red and the passenger side in black—a nod to our historic competition cars. We have pre-sold ten F60s, with scheduled production and delivery between 2015 and 2016.

Sergio

The Sergio is a 605 hp V8 2-seater *barchetta* named after Sergio Pininfarina. The car celebrates the spirit and core values of the historic company on the 60th anniversary of its collaboration with Ferrari. The Sergio's performance and dynamics are designed for excellence even when pushed to the limits. Based on the 458 Spider, it retains the latter's technological content as well as all of the functional aspects of its cockpit. It is powered by the latest 605 hp model of Ferrari's naturally aspirated 4,497 cubic centimeter V8 engine, which has won multiple categories of the International Engine of the Year award from Engine Technology International magazine in three of the last four years. This power unit also guarantees a 0 to 100 km/h acceleration in just three seconds. We produced six Sergio cars, all of which have been sold and will be dispatched to our clients by the end of 2015.

One-Offs

Finally, in order to meet the varying needs of our most loyal and discerning clients, we also from time to time produce one-off models. While based on the chassis and equipped with engines of one of the current range models for registration purposes, these cars reflect the exact exterior and interior design and specifications required by the clients, and are produced as a single, unique car.

Source: Ferrari prospectus.

EXHIBIT 46.3 | Ferrari Income Statement (millions of euro)

	2012	2013	2014	First Half 2015
Sales				
Cars and spare parts[1]	1,695	1,655	1,944	1,007
Engines[2]	77	188	311	121
Sponsorship, commercial and brand[3]	385	412	417	212
Other[4]	69	80	91	46
Total sales	2,225	2,335	2,762	1,387
Cost of sales excluding dep and amort	961	964	1,217	592
Depreciation and amortization expense	238	270	289	130
Selling, general, and admin. expense	243	260	300	152
Research and development	431	479	541	291
Other operating expense	17	−2	26	4
Operating income (EBIT)	335	364	389	218
Net financial income (Expense)	−1	3	9	−27
Profit before tax	335	366	398	191
Income tax expense	101	120	133	65
Net profit	233	246	265	126
Capital expenditures	258	271	330	151

Source: Company prospectus.

[1] Includes the net revenues generated from shipments of our cars, including any personalization revenue generated on these cars and sales of spare parts.

[2] Includes the net revenues generated from the sale of engines to Maserati for use in their cars, and the revenues generated from the rental of engines to other Formula 1 racing teams

[3] Includes the net revenues earned by our Formula 1 racing team through sponsorship agreements and our share of the Formula 1 World Championship commercial revenues and net revenues generated through the Ferrari brand, including merchandising, licensing and royalty income.

[4] Primarily includes interest income generated by the Ferrari Financial Services group and net revenues from the management of the Mugello racetrack.

EXHIBIT 46.4 | Ferrari Balance Sheet (millions of euro)

	31-Dec-2013	31-Dec-2014	30-Jun-2015
Cash and cash equivalents	798	1,077	258
Trade receivables	206	184	154
Receivables from financing activities	863	1,224	1,181
Inventories	238	296	352
Other current assets	115	64	100
Total current assets	2,219	2,845	2,045
Investments and other financial assets	37	47	48
Deferred tax assets	42	112	149
Property, plant, and equipment	568	585	589
Intangible assets[1]	242	265	283
Goodwill	787	787	787
Total assets	3,895	4,641	3,900
Trade payables	486	536	578
Current tax payables	104	110	182
Other current liabilities	475	774	836
Total current liabilities	1,065	1,420	1,595
Long-term debt	317	510	2,267
Other liabilities	197	233	239
Total equity	2,316	2,478	−201
Total liabilities and equity	3,895	4,641	3,900

Source: Company prospectus.

[1]Costs incurred for car project development are recognized as asset following the conditions of IAS38. Capitalized development costs are amortized on a straight-line basis over the estimated life of the model (generally four to eight years).

EXHIBIT 46.5 | FCA Car Shipments by Brand (thousands of units)

	2013	2014
Mass-market vehicle brands		
NAFTA (U.S., Canada, Mexico)	2,100	2,500
LATAM (Latin America)	900	800
APAC (Asia Pacific)	200	300
EMEA (Europe, Middle East, Africa)	1,100	1,200
Total	4,300	4,800
Maserati	20	40
Ferrari	7	7

Source: Created by author from data found in the FCA 2014 annual report.

Mass-market brands: Abarth, Alfa Romeo, Chrysler, Dodge, Fiat, Fiat Professional, Jeep, Lancia, and Ram.

EXHIBIT 46.6 | Data for Comparable Companies (in millions of euros)

	Total Revenue	Capital Expend	EBITDA	Projected Growth Rate	Market Value of Equity	Total Debt	Cash
Auto manufacturers							
BMW	80,401	6,099	16,426	6.1%	56,562	77,506	7,688
Daimler	129,872	6,307	18,514	6.9%	77,906	86,689	15,543
Fiat Chrysler	96,090	8,121	8,271	4.6%	18,657	33,724	23,601
Ford Motor	108,619	5,626	8,537	10.1%	52,925	98,484	25,743
General Motors	117,554	8,946	6,674	4.5%	46,554	38,710	24,391
Honda Motor	96,196	6,374	12,730	6.9%	51,128	52,483	11,427
Hyundai Motor	63,924	3,385	7,233	6.8%	33,631	40,802	19,547
Kia Motors	33,730	1,446	2,800	1.6%	16,977	3,535	5,502
Nissan Motor	82,101	11,432	10,879	6.2%	40,013	51,796	6,698
Peugeot	53,607	2,428	3,318	7.0%	12,230	21,914	10,521
Renault	41,055	2,703	3,967	8.9%	23,096	36,299	14,049
Tata Motors	33,811	4,100	5,647	5.5%	16,701	10,952	7,125
Tesla Motors	2,411	731	9	94.9%	26,400	2,051	1,590
Toyota Motor	196,622	24,233	30,260	3.2%	186,069	147,344	40,497
Volkswagen	202,458	16,613	23,048	3.5%	52,916	139,021	34,143
Luxury brands							
Burberry Group	3,221	199	745	2.6%	7,691	90	865
Cie Financiere	10,410	708	2,902	3.1%	38,986	3,093	8,553
Hermes International	4,119	279	1,478	6.8%	35,297	41	1,481
LVMH Moet Hennessy	30,638	1,848	7,027	2.1%	80,731	9,243	4,648
Prada	3,552	362	954	1.9%	8,772	519	720
Tiffany & Co.	3,248	189	819	4.7%	9,125	989	648

Data source: FactSet; the projected growth rate is obtained based on Value Line Investment Survey (August–October 2015) and author estimates.

Figures as of end of 2014, except Equity Value, which is as of October 2015. The projected growth rate is equal to the 5-year compound annual growth rate of operating profits from 2014 actuals to 2019 forecast.

EXHIBIT 46.7 | Selected Quotations from Analysts and Reporters

"Indications of interest [in Ferrari] have been high . . . with some reports stating that the deal could be as much as 10 times oversubscribed . . . The indications of interest and the valuation cited yesterday's media reports certainly confirm our thesis that Ferrari deserves a luxury goods stock multiple."

—Richard Hilgert, "Daimler AG," Morningstar Equity Research, October 1, 2015.

"Fiat wants its crown jewel to fetch a high price . . . yet this pricey offer, plus the burdens of maintaining Ferrari's specialness, could end up repelling investors . . . Though Ferrari's operating margin is higher than its peers, thanks to the high price of its products, it has been stuck between 14% and 16% since 2010 . . . .Ferrari shares are [pricey], at 36 times last year's earnings at the midpoint of their IPO range."

—Abheek Bhattacharya, "Ferrari IPO: Why This Engine Runs Too Rich," *Wall Street Journal,* October 20, 2015.

"Ferrari isn't geared to the auto cycle and has exceptionally high pricing power, with strong cash conversion and brand value. As such, we think it could also be valued in line with the top end of luxury goods companies."

—Alexander Haissl and Fei Teng, "European Auto OEMs," Credit Suisse, July 15, 2015.

"The Chief Executive of UBS recently . . . [said] that it was 'almost impossible to think that the Ferrari IPO can't be successful."

—FT reporters, "Red Faces as Banker Revs up Ferrari IPO," *Financial Times,* October 9, 2015.

"The demand for Ferrari shares has significantly surpassed the amount offered in the luxury sports carmaker's US IPO, and the final price might exceed the top end of the initial price range by 20%."

—"Ferrari IPO Demand Well Above Offer, Final Price Might Jump 20%," *SeeNews Italy,* October 19, 2015.

"We believe Ferrari will struggle as an independent entity given a lack of scale."

—Mike Dean, Alexander Haissl, and Fei Teng, "European Autos 2015 Outlook," Credit Suisse, January 9, 2015.

"Ferrari has pricing power, however, Ferrari's products sell at a similar price to comparable products. Ferrari is not "hard" luxury. Its products need updating and refreshing."

—George Galliers, Chris McNally, and Arndt Ellinghorst, "Ferrari," Evercore, November 16, 2015.

"In our view, the success and desirability of Ferrari's road cars lies precisely in their exclusivity. We do not think that Montezemolo arbitrarily imposed the 7,000 unit cap on Ferrari production back in May 2013, but rather that this represented the apex of the supply/demand price maximization equation . . . A decision to produce significantly more might drive Ferrari into lower and less rarefied segments where completion is much more acute from extremely well capitalized manufacturers."

—Stephen Reitman, Erwann Dagorne, and Philippe Barrier, "FCA—Analysing the Ferrari IPO and FCA Thereafter," Societe Generale, July 29, 2015.

EXHIBIT 46.8 | Ferrari Forecast (millions of euro, except as noted)

	2014	2015	2016	2017	2018	2019
Assumptions						
Growth in cars shipped	3.6%	7.0%	5.0%	4.0%	4.0%	3.0%
Growth in revenue/car		5.0%	5.0%	5.0%	5.0%	5.0%
Growth in engine revenue		3.0%	3.0%	3.0%	3.0%	3.0%
Growth in other revenue		3.0%	6.0%	6.0%	6.0%	6.0%
Operating margin—Cars	12.5%	13.0%	13.5%	14.0%	14.0%	14.0%
Operating margin—Engines	9.1%	10.0%	10.0%	10.0%	10.0%	10.0%
Operating margin—All other revenue	24.9%	25.0%	27.0%	28.0%	30.0%	30.0%
Net working capital turnover	1.9	2.0	2.1	2.2	2.2	2.2
Net fixed asset turnover	3.2	3.2	3.3	3.5	3.7	3.8
Deprec and amort/PPE	34%	34%	34%	34%	34%	34%
Financial forecast						
Car shipments (000s)	7.26	7.76	8.15	8.48	8.82	9.08
Avg revenue per car (Euro 000s)	268	281	295	310	326	342
Car revenue	1,944	2,184	2,408	2,629	2,871	3,105
Engine revenue	311	320	330	340	350	361
All other revenue	507	523	554	587	623	660
Total revenue	2,762	3,027	3,292	3,556	3,844	4,126
Operating profit—Cars	243	284	325	368	402	435
Operating profit—Engines	28	32	33	34	35	36
Operating profit—All other revenue	126	131	150	164	187	198
Total operating profit	398	447	508	567	624	669
Net working capital	1,425	1,513	1,568	1,617	1,747	1,875
Net PP&E and int. assets	851	932	998	1,016	1,039	1,086
Dep and amort	289	317	339	345	353	369

Source: Created by author based on author estimates.

EXHIBIT 46.9 I Capital Markets Data (October 19, 2015)

Government Bond Yields (Italy)	
1 year	0.23%
10 year	1.70%

Corporate Bonds	
	Euro
AAA	1.91%
AA	1.99%
A	2.30%
BBB	3.43%
BB	4.98%
B	6.79%

Exchange Rate	
USD/EUR	1.1375

Source: Created by author based on data from ADB Analisi Data Borsi, Merrill Lynch, and author estimates.

Rosetta Stone: Pricing the 2009 IPO

We are changing the way the world learns languages.
—**Tom Adams**

It was mid-April 2009. Tom Adams, president and CEO of Rosetta Stone, Inc. (Rosetta Stone), the language learning software company, reached for his iPhone to contact Phil Clough of private equity fund ABS Capital. Adams and Clough had been discussing plans to take Rosetta Stone public for some time. The wait was finally over.

In the wake of the 2008 financial crisis, the market for initial public offerings (IPOs) evaporated. By early spring the market was showing its first encouraging signs. Just a week prior, Chinese online videogame developer Changyou.com had listed on the NASDAQ at a price to EBITDA of 6.5 times followed by a one-day jump of 25%, and the online college Bridgeport Education was currently circulating its plans to go public at a range of 10 to 12 times EBITDA.

Having received preliminary approval of its registration filings with the U.S. Securities and Exchange Commission (SEC), Rosetta Stone was authorized to sell 6.25 million shares, a 30% stake in the company. **Exhibits 47.1** and **47.2** provide financial statements from Rosetta Stone's IPO prospectus, required by the SEC to inform investors about the details of the equity offering. Half of the shares were to be new shares and the other half were shares to be sold by existing shareholders. Rosetta Stone management had circulated an estimated price range of $15 to $17 per share, representing a price to EBITDA of about 8 times. Demand for the shares was strong, and some analysts believed that Rosetta Stone was leaving money on the table. Yet with world financial and product markets still in turmoil, there was a strong case to be made for prudence.

This case was written by Associate Professor Michael J. Schill with the assistance of Suprajj Papireddy (MBA '10), Tom Adams (Rosetta Stone), and Phil Clough (MBA '90 and ABS Capital). It was written as a basis for class discussion rather than to illustrate effective or ineffective handling of an administrative situation. Copyright © 2009 by the University of Virginia Darden School Foundation, Charlottesville, VA. All rights reserved. *To order copies, send an e-mail to* sales@dardenbusinesspublishing.com. *No part of this publication may be reproduced, stored in a retrieval system, used in a spreadsheet, or transmitted in any form or by any means—electronic, mechanical, photocopying, recording, or otherwise—without the permission of the Darden School Foundation.*

Economic Conditions

The previous year had been a dramatic one for the world economy. Prices on global credit and equity markets had been in free fall. The U.S. equity market was down more than 50% from its peak in October 2007 (see **Exhibit 47.3** for details of the recent price history of U.S. equity market returns in total and for select industries). The collapse of world financial markets had preceded deterioration in economic activity worldwide, including dramatic shifts in real estate values, unemployment levels, and discretionary consumer spending. The severity of economic conditions had prompted massive intervention by world governments with dramatic policy changes, particularly by the U.S. federal government. The economic and political conditions were frequently compared with those of the Great Depression of the 1930s. With the crisis in full swing, investors had flocked to U.S. Treasuries for security, pushing down yields on these instruments to historic lows (see **Exhibit 47.4**). Heightened investor risk aversion had expanded the risk premium for all securities. The general market risk premium was currently estimated at 6.5% or 8.5%, respectively, depending on whether long-term or short-term government yields were used in estimating the risk-free rate.

In February and March of 2009, there had been some evidence of improvement in financial and economic conditions. Wholesale inventories were in decline. New-home sales were beginning to rise. The equity market had experienced a rally of more than 20% in recent weeks. Yet many money managers and analysts worried that such economic green shoots were only a temporary rally in a longer-running bear market. There was strong concern that the magnitude of government spending would spur inflation in the U.S. dollar. GDP growth was still negative, corporate bankruptcy rates and unemployment were at historic highs, and many believed the economic void was just too big for a quick recovery to be feasible. A *Wall Street Journal* survey of U.S. economists suggested that the economy was expected to generate positive growth in the last half of 2009.[1] In contrast, a survey of U.S. corporate executives stated that less than one-third of respondents expected to see an economic upturn in 2009.[2] The debate regarding the economic future of the world economy raged on.

Rosetta Stone

In the 1980s, Allen Stoltzfus, an economics professor, real estate agent, and history buff, was frustrated with his slow progress in mastering the Russian language. He was enrolled in a conventional classroom Russian course but found it much less effective than the process he had used to learn German while living in Germany years before. Seeking to produce a more natural language learning method, Stoltzfus envisioned using computer technology to simulate the way people learn their native language—with pictures and sounds in context. Rather than learning the language by translating one language to another, his approach would be to use electronic technology to encourage

---

[1] Phil Izzo, "Obama, Geithner Get Low Grades from Economists," *Wall Street Journal*, March 11, 2009.

[2] "Economic Conditions Snapshot, March 2009: McKinsey Global Survey Results," *McKinsey Quarterly,* March 2009.

people to think in the target language from the beginning. He sought the aid of his brother-in-law, John Fairfield, who had received graduate training in computer science. Together they explored the concept of how a computer could be made to facilitate language learning. Stoltzfus and Fairfield founded Fairfield Language Technologies in Harrisonburg, Virginia, in 1992. The emergence of CD-ROM technology in the 1990s made the project feasible. The company released its first retail language training software product in 1999 under the name Rosetta Stone.[3]

The Rosetta Stone series of CD-ROMs provided users an effective way of learning new languages. The software utilized a combination of images, text, and sound to teach various vocabulary terms and grammatical functions intuitively by matching images with the spoken word. Following the way children learn their first language, the company called this method of teaching languages the *Dynamic Immersion* method: "dynamic" because digital technology and the teaching method powerfully engaged the learner in an interactive learning process, and "immersion" because learners anywhere, from any language background, started at the very beginning and studied exclusively in the target language. A recent research study provided scientific evidence that the language test scores of students that completed 55 hours of Rosetta Stone training performed comparably to those who had completed an entire semester of a good quality college language course.[4] Rosetta Stone users were broadly satisfied with the experience and regularly recommended the software to others.

After focusing initially on school and government sales, the company began aggressively pursuing the retail market in 2001. Following the death of Stoltzfus in 2002, the company hired an outsider, 31-year-old Tom Adams, as chief executive. Adams brought an international dimension to the small-town, rural company: A native of Sweden who had grown up in England and France, he was fluent in Swedish, English, and French. He had studied history at Bristol University in the UK and had earned an MBA from INSEAD in France. Prior to arriving in Harrisonburg, Adams had been a commodity merchant in Europe and China.

Adams got right to work by entering new markets and scaling up the current business; from 2004 to 2005, the revenues of the company nearly doubled, from $25 million to $48 million. Acknowledging the need for capital and professional support as the company expanded, Adams solicited a capital infusion from the private equity market. In 2006, two firms, ABS Capital Partners and Norwest Equity Partners, made major equity investments in the company. As part of the recapitalization, the name of the company was changed from Fairfield Language Technologies to Rosetta Stone, Inc., to match the signature product. Over the ensuing two years, revenue continued to expand aggressively, rising to $81 million in 2006, $137 million in 2007, and $210 million in 2008. Since Adams's arrival, the compound annual growth rates of Rosetta Stone's

---

[3]The name *Rosetta Stone* referred to a black basalt tablet discovered in 1799 by a French engineer in Napoleon's army near the Egyptian town of Rosetta. The tablet contained an inscription of a single text in three languages—two Egyptian scripts (hieroglyphic and demotic) and ancient Greek—thus enabling 19th century scholars to decipher Egyptian scripts conclusively for the first time.

[4]Roumen Vesselinov, "Measuring the Effectiveness of Rosetta Stone," working paper, City University of New York, January 2009.

revenue and operating profit were at 70% and 98%, respectively, and the company employed over 1,200 people. By early 2009, Rosetta Stone was the most recognized language learning software brand in the world. Millions of language learners in more than 150 countries were using the Rosetta Stone software. The company offered self-study language learning solutions in 31 languages to its customers. (**Exhibit 47.5** lists the language training software currently offered by the company.) In 2008, approximately 80% of Rosetta Stone revenue was accounted for by retail consumers, 20% by institutions. Institutional customers included educational institutions, government and military institutions, commercial institutions, and not-for-profit institutions.

In a few short years, Rosetta Stone had successfully developed a strong brand; its kiosks with bright yellow boxes had become an institution in U.S. airports, and its print advertising in travel publications included a popular print ad of a young farm boy holding a Rosetta Stone box, the copy reading, "He was a hardworking farm boy. She was an Italian supermodel. He knew he would have just one chance to impress her." The unaided awareness of the Rosetta Stone brand was more than seven times that of any other language learning company in the United States. Leveraging a strong brand, steady customer base, and diverse retail network, Rosetta Stone had maintained positive profitability in 2008 despite the severe economic downturn and, in both average orders of bundled products and services and in units sold, even had experienced increases.

The company expanded its product line by increasing the number of languages and levels offered and broadened the language learning experience by introducing Rosetta Studio and Rosetta World. Rosetta Studio allowed each Rosetta Stone learner to schedule time to chat with other learners and with a native-speaking coach to facilitate language practice, motivation, and confidence. Rosetta World connected a virtual community of language learners to practice their skills through a collection of games and other dynamic conversation opportunities. Adams envisioned a substantial growth trajectory for the company with a multitude of ways to leverage its novel learning technology and expand its geographic reach. With a fixed development cost, Adams expected the strategy to continue to increase company operating margins and expand revenue, but he recognized that, as the company continued to show strong profit and growth, the incentive for competition to attempt to gain market share would intensify. **Exhibit 47.6** provides three video excerpts of an interview with Adams in which he describes the future of Rosetta Stone.

Industry Overview

The worldwide language learning industry was valued at more than $83 billion, of which more than $32 billion was for self-study learning, according to a Nielsen survey. The U.S. market, from which Rosetta Stone generated 95% of its revenue, was estimated to be more than $5 billion for total language learning and $2 billion for self-study learning. The total language learning market was expected to expand as proficiency in multiple languages was becoming increasingly important due to trends in globalization and immigration. The self-study market, particularly through electronic delivery, was expected to dominate the industry expansion given that self-study was increasingly accepted by language learning and travel enthusiasts.

The language learning industry had historically been dominated by specialized language schools that taught languages through conventional classroom methods. The largest player in the market was privately held Berlitz International. Berlitz taught languages in its classrooms using the Berlitz Method of Language Instruction, which advocated immersion in the target language, among other things, and according to company literature, offered programs and services through more than 470 centers in more than 70 countries. Auralog, a French company, was another important competitor in the industry. Both Berlitz and Auralog offered electronic software packages that provided quality language training software.

As had the Rosetta World product, businesses such as LiveMocha, Babalah, and Palabea had also adopted a social media approach, connecting language learners through the Internet, but these sites tended to be secondary enrichment sources for language learners.

Major software companies with deep pockets represented the most important potential threat. Although the novelty of Rosetta Stone's approach shielded it from many of the existing players in the industry, the entry of a company such as Apple or Microsoft into the language learning market had the potential to thwart Rosetta Stone's aspiration of dominating global language learning.

The IPO Process[5]

The process of *going public*—selling publicly traded equity for the first time—was an arduous undertaking that, at a minimum, required about three months. (**Table 47.1** provides a timetable for the typical IPO. **Exhibit 47.6** links to video of Adams describing the specific ways Rosetta Stone management prepared the company to go public.)

Before initiating the equity-issuance process, private firms needed to fulfill a number of prerequisites: generate a credible business plan; gather a qualified management team; create an outside board of directors; prepare audited financial statements, performance measures, and projections; and develop relationships with investment bankers, lawyers, and accountants. Frequently, firms held "bake-off" meetings to discuss the equity-issuance process with various investment banks before selecting a lead underwriter. Important characteristics of an underwriter included the proposed compensation package, track record, analyst research support, distribution capabilities, and aftermarket market-making support.

After the firm satisfied the prerequisites, the equity-issuance process began with a meeting of all the key participants (management, underwriters, accountants, and legal counsel for both the underwriters and the issuing firm) to plan the process and reach agreement on specific terms. Throughout the process, additional meetings could be called to discuss problems and review progress.

---

[5]This section draws from Michael C. Bernstein and Lester Wolosoff, *Raising Capital: The Grant Thornton Guide for Entrepreneurs* (Chicago: Irwin Professional Publishing, 1995); Frederick Lipman, *Going Public* (Roseville, CA: Prima, 1994); Coopers and Lybrand, *A Guide to Going Public*, 2nd ed. (New York: Coopers & Lybrand, 1997); and Craig G. Dunbar, "The Effect of Information Asymmetries on the Choice of Underwriter Compensation Contracts in IPOs" (PhD diss., University of Rochester, n.d.).

TABLE 47.1. | Timetable for typical U.S. IPO (in days).

	1–7	8–14					
Prior to Day 1: Organizational "all-hands" meeting	1 2 3 4 5 6 7						**1–14: Quiet period**
	8 9 10 11 12 13 14						
15–44: Due diligence Underwriter interviews management, suppliers, and customers; reviews financial statements; drafts preliminary registration statement. Senior management of underwriter gives OK on issue.	15 16 17 18 19 20 21						
	22 23 24 25 26 27 28						
	29 30 31 32 33 34 35						
	36 37 38 39 40 41 42						
45: Registration (announcement)	43 44 **45** 46 47 48 49						**45–75: SEC review period** SEC auditor reviews for compliance with SEC regulations. Underwriter assembles syndicate and initiates road show.
50: Prospectus (*red herring*)	**50** 51 52 53 54 55 56						
	57 58 59 60 61 62 63						
	64 65 66 67 68 69 70						
	71 72 73 74 75 76 77						**76–89: Road show** Preliminary price range set. Underwriters, issuing firm's management present deal to institutional investors, build book of purchase orders.
76–89: Letters of comment received from SEC; amendments filed with SEC.	78 79 80 81 82 83 84						
90: Effective date; shares offered	85 86 87 88 89 **90** 91						**91: Trading begins**
	92 93 94 95 96 97 **98**						**98: Settlement**

Source: Created by author based on industry standards

Following the initiation of the equity-issuance process, the SEC prohibited the company from publishing information outside the prospectus. The company could continue established, normal advertising activities, but any increased publicity designed to raise awareness of the company's name, products, or geographical presence in order to create a favorable attitude toward the company's securities could be considered illegal. This requirement was known as the *quiet period*.

The underwriter's counsel generally prepared a letter of intent that provided most of the terms of the underwriting agreement but was not legally binding. The underwriting agreement described the securities to be sold, set forth the rights and obligations of the various parties, and established the underwriter's compensation. Because the underwriting agreement was not signed until the offering price was determined (just before distribution began), both the firm and the underwriter were free to pull out of the agreement any time before the offering date. If the firm did withdraw the offer, the letter of intent generally required the firm to reimburse the underwriter for direct expenses.

The SEC required that firms selling equity in a public market solicit the market's approval. The filing process called for preparation of the prospectus (Part I of the registration statement), answers to specific questions, copies of the underwriting contract, company charter and bylaws, and a specimen of the security (all included in Part II of the registration statement), all of which required the full attention of all parties on the offering firm's team.

One of the important features of the registration process was the performance of due-diligence procedures. *Due diligence* referred to the process of providing reasonable grounds that there was nothing in the registration statement that was significantly untrue or misleading and was motivated by the liability of all parties to the registration statement for any material misstatements or omissions. Due-diligence procedures involved such things as reviewing company documents, contracts, and tax returns; visiting company offices and facilities; soliciting "comfort letters" from company auditors; and interviewing company and industry personnel.

During this period, the lead underwriter began to form the underwriting *syndicate*, which comprised a number of investment banks that agreed to buy portions of the offering at the offer price less the underwriting discount. In addition to the syndicate members, dealers were enlisted to sell a certain number of shares on a "best-efforts" basis. The dealers received a *fixed reallowance*, or concession, for each share sold. The selling agreement provided the contract to members of the syndicate, granted power of attorney to the lead underwriter, and stipulated (a) the management fee that each syndicate member was required to pay the lead underwriter, (b) the share allocations, and (c) the dealer reallowances or concessions. Because the exact terms of the agreement were not specified until approximately 48 hours before selling began, the agreement would not become binding until just before the offering. The original contract specified a range of expected compensation levels; the selling agreement was structured so that the contract became binding when it was orally approved via telephone by the syndicate members after the effective date.

The SEC review process started when the registration statement was filed and the statement was assigned to a branch chief of the Division of Corporate Finance. As part of the SEC review, the statement was given to accountants, attorneys, analysts, and industry specialists. The SEC review process was laid out in the Securities Act of 1933, which according to its preamble aspired to "provide full and fair disclosure of the character of securities sold in interstate commerce." Under the Securities Act, the registration statement became effective 20 days after the filing date. If, however, the SEC found anything in the registration statement that was regarded as materially untrue, incomplete, or misleading, the branch chief sent the registrant a *letter of comment* detailing the deficiencies. Following a letter of comment, the issuing firm was required to correct and return the amended statement to the SEC. Unless an acceleration was granted by the SEC, the amended statement restarted the 20-day waiting period.

While the SEC was reviewing the registration statement, the underwriter was engaged in "book-building" activities, which involved surveying potential investors to construct a schedule of investor demand for the new issue. To generate investor interest, the preliminary offering prospectus or "red herring" (so called because the prospectus was required to have the words *preliminary prospectus* on the cover in red ink) was printed and offered to potential investors. During this period, underwriters generally organized a one- to two-week "road show" tour, which enabled managers to discuss their investment plans, display their management potential, and answer questions from financial analysts, brokers, and institutional investors in locations across the country or abroad. Finally, companies could place "tombstone ads" in various financial periodicals announcing the offering and listing the members of the underwriting syndicate.

By the time the registration statement was ready to become effective, the underwriter and the offering firm's management negotiated the final offering price and the underwriting discount. The negotiated price depended on perceived investor demand and current market conditions (e.g., price multiples of comparable companies, previous offering experience of industry peers). Once the underwriter and the management agreed on the offering price and discount, the underwriting agreement was signed, and the final registration amendment was filed with the SEC. The company and the underwriter generally asked the SEC to accelerate the final pricing amendment, which was usually granted immediately by phone. The offering was now ready for public sale. The final pricing and acceleration of the registration statement typically happened within a few hours.

During the morning of the effective day, the lead underwriter confirmed the selling agreement with the members of the syndicate. Following confirmation of the selling agreement, selling began. Members of the syndicate sold shares of the offering through oral solicitations to potential investors. Because investors were required to receive a final copy of the prospectus with the confirmation of sale, and the law allowed investors to back out of purchase orders upon receipt of the final prospectus, the offering sale was not realized until underwriters actually received payment. Underwriters would generally cancel orders if payment was not received within five days of the confirmation.

SEC Rule 10b-7 permitted underwriters to engage in price stabilization activities for a limited period during security distribution. Under this rule, underwriters often posted stabilizing bids at or below the offer price, which provided some price stability during the initial trading of an IPO.

The *offering settlement*, or closing, occurred seven to ten days after the effective date, as specified in the underwriting agreement. At this meeting, the firm delivered the security certificates to the underwriters and dealers, and the lead underwriter delivered the prescribed proceeds to the firm. In addition, the firm traditionally delivered an updated comfort letter from its independent accountants. Following the offering, the underwriter generally continued to provide valuable investment-banking services by distributing research literature and acting as a market maker for the company.

Pricing the Rosetta Stone IPO

Adams had a preference for a strong balance sheet and cash position for the company. As a private company, corporate investment was limited by the amount of capital the company could borrow from private sources. With constrained resources, Adams was concerned that Rosetta Stone was an attractive takeover target for a company with the needed resources. Led by Phil Clough at ABS Capital, the private equity investors were anxious to recognize the gains achieved through the Rosetta Stone investment.

In March, the board had discussed the matter and yielded the IPO decision to Adams. Despite the uncertainty of taking a relatively young company public in the most volatile markets in decades, Adams was inclined to move forward with the deal. The fourth quarter financials continued to show impressive performance, with a 53% expansion in revenue despite the global economic contraction. (**Exhibit 47.7** details the historical financial performance of the company along with historical internally generated values of Rosetta Stone shares.) Advisors at Morgan Stanley had shared their view that Rosetta Stone was one of only a handful of companies that currently had a shot at a successful IPO. Senior management had been preparing the systems and organization of the company for public company status for years. Adams saw the IPO event as significant opportunity to establish business credibility and build the Rosetta Stone brand in a global marketplace. His decision was to launch.

Over the following week or two, senior management and bankers visited prospective investors on the east and west coasts of the United States and in Europe. The investor response was highly enthusiastic, with investors commonly asking to "max out" their allocation in the deal. By the end of the road show, Morgan Stanley reported that the book was more than 25 times oversubscribed, meaning that the underwriters maintained orders for 25 shares for every Rosetta Stone share being offered in the deal.

Adams was delighted that many investors appeared to share his vision of Rosetta Stone's unique capacity to play a substantial role in the global language learning market. Such a trajectory implied revenue growth rates of 20% to 35% for some time. Other analysts were more skeptical, predicting revenue growth of around 15% for the next five years and then tapering down to a long-term growth rate of 3% to 4%. Adams believed that the operating leverage in the organization allowed margins to continue to improve for some time; others believed that competitive pressure would soon drive margins down. (**Exhibit 47.8** provides one view of how the financials were expected to play out in the years to come.) In the debt market, Rosetta Stone faced a prevailing borrowing rate of about 7.5%. The marginal corporate tax rate for the company was 38%. **Exhibit 47.9** details the current ownership structure of the company and details the new shares to be sold in the offering, which would grow the total number of shares outstanding from 17.2 million to 20.3 million.[6]

Comparable multiples played an important role in the valuation of IPO firms. **Exhibit 47.10** provides financial data on a broad set of industry comparable firms. Adams liked K12 Inc. as a comparable match, but acknowledged that no other firm perfectly matched Rosetta Stone's business strategy, skill set, risk profile, or growth potential. Still, there was some debate regarding whether Rosetta Stone would be positioned as a technology company or an educational company. See **Exhibit 47.6** for a link to video excerpts of Adams and Clough discussing this topic.

---

[6]To avoid the dilution of the value of securities of pre-IPO investors, it was appropriate in pricing IPO shares to divide the total premoney equity value of the firm by the premoney shares outstanding. In the case of Rosetta Stone, the number of premoney shares outstanding was 17.19 million. Since the pre-IPO investors held claim on the ongoing business, a valuation based on the ongoing business represented a premoney valuation. Valuations based on postmoney shares required adding the value of the new IPO shares to the ongoing business valuation prior to dividing by the postmoney shares.

EXHIBIT 47.1 | Rosetta Stone Income Statement (in thousands of dollars)[1]

	2004	2005	2006	2007	2008
Revenue	$25,373	$48,402	$91,570	$137,321	$209,380
Cost of revenue	3,968	8,242	12,744	20,687	28,676
Gross profit	21,405	40,160	78,826	116,634	180,704
Operating expenses:					
Sales and marketing	11,303	22,432	46,549	65,437	93,384
Research and development	1,833	2,819	8,158	12,893	18,387
Acquired in-process research and development	0	0	12,597	0	0
General and administrative	6,484	8,157	16,732	29,786	39,577
Lease abandonment	0	0	0	0	1,831
Transaction-related expenses	0	0	10,315	0	0
Total operating expenses	19,620	33,408	94,351	108,116	153,179
Income from operations	1,785	6,752	−15,525	8,518	27,525
Other income and expense:					
Interest income	84	38	613	673	454
Interest expense	0	0	−1,560	−1,331	−891
Other income	120	134	63	154	239
Interest and other income (expense), net	204	172	−884	−504	−198
Income before income taxes	1,989	6,924	−16,409	8,014	27,327
Income tax expense (benefit)	66	143	−1,240	5,435	13,435
Net income	1,923	6,781	−15,169	2,579	13,892
Preferred stock accretion	0	0	−159	−80	0
Net income attributable to common stockholders	$1,923	$6,781	−$15,328	$2,499	$13,892

Data source: Rosetta Stone preliminary prospectus (Form S-1/A, filed March 17, 2009), U.S. SEC.

[1] Depreciation and amortization expense was reported as $6.5, $7.8, and $7.1 million, respectively, for 2006, 2007, and 2008.

EXHIBIT 47.2 | Rosetta Stone Balance Sheet (in thousands of dollars)

	As of December 31	
Assets	**2007**	**2008**
Cash and cash equivalents	$22,084	$30,660
Accounts receivable	11,852	26,497
Inventory, net	3,861	4,912
Prepaid expenses and other current assets	3,872	6,598
Deferred income taxes	848	2,282
Total current assets	42,517	70,949
Property and equipment, net	13,445	15,727
Goodwill	34,199	34,199
Intangible assets, net	13,661	10,645
Deferred income taxes	6,085	6,828
Other assets	469	470
Total assets	110,376	138,818
Liabilities and stockholders' equity		
Accounts payable	4,636	3,207
Accrued compensation	4,940	8,570
Other current liabilities	11,421	21,353
Deferred revenue	12,045	14,382
Current maturities of long-term debt	3,400	4,250
Total current liabilities	36,442	51,762
Long-term debt	9,909	5,660
Deferred revenue	894	1,362
Other long-term liabilities	6	963
Total liabilities	47,251	59,747
Commitments and contingencies	5,000	0
Common stock outstanding	51,038	56,038
Additional paid-in capital	8,613	10,814
Accumulated income (loss)	−1,470	12,422
Accumulated other comprehensive loss	−56	−203
Total stockholders' equity	58,125	79,071
Total liabilities and stockholders' equity	$110,376	$138,818

Data source: Rosetta Stone prospectus.

EXHIBIT 47.3 | Value of $1 invested in January 1998

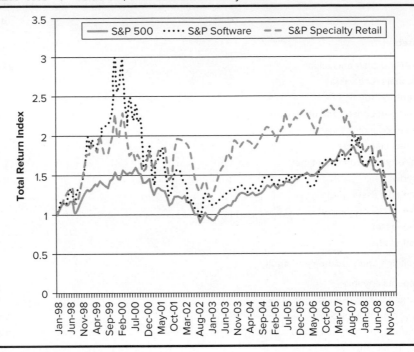

Source: Created by author using data from Morningstar.

EXHIBIT 47.4 | U.S. Yield Curve Data (in percent)

Date	Yields				
	3-month	**1-year**	**5-year**	**10-year**	**30-year**
1/30/2009	0.24	0.51	1.85	2.87	3.58
2/27/2009	0.26	0.72	1.99	3.02	3.71
3/31/2009	0.21	0.57	1.67	2.71	3.56
4/1/2009	0.22	0.58	1.65	2.68	3.51
4/2/2009	0.22	0.59	1.74	2.77	3.57
4/3/2009	0.21	0.60	1.87	2.91	3.70
4/6/2009	0.20	0.60	1.90	2.95	3.73
4/7/2009	0.20	0.60	1.87	2.93	3.72
4/8/2009	0.18	0.59	1.83	2.86	3.66
4/9/2009	0.18	0.60	1.90	2.96	3.76

Data source: U.S. Department of the Treasury.

EXHIBIT 47.5 | Language Coverage of Rosetta Stone Products (2008)

	Instructional software			Audio companion		
	Level 1	Level 2	Level 3	Version 1	Version 2	Version 3
Arabic	●	●	●	●		●
Chinese (Mandarin)	●	●	●	●		●
Danish	●				●	
Dutch	●	●	●	●		●
English (UK)	●	●	●	●		●
English (U.S.)	●	●	●	●		●
Farsi (Persian)	●	●	●	●		●
French	●	●	●	●		●
German	●	●	●	●		●
Greek	●	●	●	●		●
Hebrew	●	●	●	●		●
Hindi	●	●	●	●		●
Indonesian	●				●	
Irish	●	●	●			●
Italian	●	●	●	●		●
Japanese	●	●	●	●		●
Korean	●	●	●	●		●
Latin	●				●	
Pashto	●				●	
Polish	●	●	●	●		●
Portuguese (Brazil)	●	●	●	●		●
Russian	●	●	●	●		●
Spanish (Latin America)	●	●	●	●		●
Spanish (Spain)	●	●	●	●		●
Swahili	●				●	
Swedish	●	●	●	●		●
Tagalog	●	●			●	
Thai	●	●			●	
Turkish	●				●	
Vietnamese	●				●	
Welsh	●				●	

Data source: Rosetta Stone prospectus.

EXHIBIT 47.6 | Video Exhibit Links

Video Exhibit 47.1. What is the future for Rosetta Stone?
Interview with Tom Adams, CEO, Rosetta Stone, Inc.

(http://www.youtube.com/watch?v=FjxZ6VhWPBw)

Video Exhibit 47.2. What does it take to go public?
Interview with Tom Adams, CEO, Rosetta Stone, Inc.

(http://www.youtube.com/watch?v=QVl9NNgmT7U)

Video Exhibit 47.3. What kind of business is Rosetta Stone?
Interview with Tom Adams, CEO, Rosetta Stone, Inc. and
Phil Clough, Managing General Partner, ABS Capital Partners

(http://www.youtube.com/watch?v=Lnilib9UJx0)

EXHIBIT 47.7 | Rosetta Stone Historical Financial Performance, 2006 to 2008
(in thousands of dollars except percent and share value)

	2006	2007	2008
Revenue	91,570	137,321	209,380
Revenue growth	89%	50%	52%
EBITDA	1,290	16,318	34,625
EBITDA margin	1.4%	11.9%	16.5%
Total debt		13,309	9,910
Total equity		58,125	79,071
Total capital		71,434	88,981
Capital turnover		1.92	2.24
Return on capital		11.9%	30.9%
Estimated share value[1]	$6.08	$11.19	$17.49

[1]Estimated by Rosetta Stone board of directors based on multiple of EBITDA for industry comparables.

EXHIBIT 47.8 | Financial Forecast for Rosetta Stone (in millions of dollars)

	2008A	2009E	2010E	2011E	2012E	2013E	2014E	2015E	2016E	2017E	2018E
Revenue growth	52.5%	35.0%	35.0%	30.0%	25.0%	23.0%	21.0%	18.0%	13.0%	10.0%	5.0%
Gross margin	86.3%	86.0%	86.0%	85.0%	84.0%	83.0%	82.0%	81.0%	80.0%	79.0%	78.0%
SGA exp / revenue	63.5%	63.5%	63.5%	63.0%	63.0%	62.5%	62.5%	62.5%	62.5%	62.5%	62.5%
R&D exp / revenue	8.8%	9.0%	9.0%	8.5%	8.5%	8.5%	8.5%	8.0%	8.0%	8.0%	8.0%
Capital expenditures	7.0	5.0	8.0	9.0	9.5	10.0	11.0	11.0	9.0	8.0	5.0
NPPE turnover	13.5	15.0	15.2	15.4	15.6	15.8	16.0	16.2	16.4	16.8	17.3
NWC turnover	8.9	9.0	9.0	9.0	8.5	8.5	8.0	8.0	8.0	8.0	8.0
Revenue	209.4	282.7	381.6	496.1	620.1	762.7	922.9	1,089.0	1,230.6	1,353.6	1,421.3
Gross profit	180.7	243.1	328.2	421.7	520.9	633.1	756.8	882.1	984.5	1,069.4	1,108.6
SGA expense	133.0	179.5	242.3	312.5	390.7	476.7	576.8	680.6	769.1	846.0	888.3
R&D expense	18.4	25.4	34.3	42.2	52.7	64.8	78.4	87.1	98.4	108.3	113.7
EBIT	29.4	38.2	51.5	67.0	77.5	91.5	101.5	114.3	116.9	115.1	106.6
Net working capital	23.4	31.4	42.4	55.1	73.0	89.7	115.4	136.1	153.8	169.2	177.7
Net PPE	15.7	18.8	25.1	32.2	39.7	48.3	57.7	67.2	75.0	80.6	82.2

Source: Author analysis.

EXHIBIT 47.9 | Principal and Selling Stockholders
(in thousands except percent)

Name of beneficial owner	Shares owned prior to offering		Shares offered in IPO
Entities affiliated with ABS Capital Partners	7,556.1	44.0%	1,889.6
Norwest Equity Partners VIII	4,940.0	28.7%	1,235.4
Tom Adams (President, CEO)	743.7	4.3%	
Eric Eichmann (COO)	146.3	0.9%	
Brian Helman (CFO)	91.0	0.5%	
Gregory Long (CPO)	106.2	0.6%	
Michael Wu (General Counsel)	45.5	0.3%	
Patrick Gross (Director)	20.7	0.1%	
John Coleman (Director)	16.2	0.1%	
Laurence Franklin (Director)	16.2	0.1%	
Other owners	3,507.6	20.4%	
New IPO shares			3,125.0
Total shares	17,189.5		6,250.0

Source: Rosetta Stone prospectus.

EXHIBIT 47.10 | Financial Data for Industry Comparables[1]

	Recent Price	Number of shares (in millions)	Debt (in millions)	Beta	Revenue growth	Income growth	Price/EPS 2008	Price/EPS 2009	EV/EBITDA 2008	EV/EBITDA 2009
For-profit education										
Apollo Group, Inc.	63.81	160.15	0.0	0.60	15%	491%	19.2	14.5	9.7	7.2
American Public Education Inc.	37.56	18.06	0.0	NA	55%	54%	42.4	29.3	20.5	13.8
Corinthian Colleges, Inc.	16.88	86.45	31.9	0.75	16%	78%	28.7	18.1	11.6	7.8
Career Education Corp.	21.05	90.09	1.7	0.70	−2%	9%	19.5	20.0	6.8	6.8
Capella Education	50.34	16.69	0.0	0.55	20%	32%	31.5	23.4	13.4	10.3
Strayer Education	168.01	13.88	0.0	0.55	25%	24%	33.2	25.8	17.8	14.1
DeVry Inc.	42.47	71.64	20.0	0.55	17%	33%	23.2	17.5	12.5	9.6
ITT Educational Services Inc.	101.6	38.56	150.0	0.60	17%	45%	19.0	13.6	10.1	7.4
K12 Inc.	15.29	28.86	13.7	NA	61%	44%	18.3	35.4	13.4	8.7
Grand Canyon Education, Inc.	14.72	45.47	32.1	NA	62%	126%	NA	24.3	30.2	11.5
New Oriental Ed. & Tech. Group, Inc.	50.33	149.19	0.0	1.20	43%	−3%	32.9	24.5	23.8	17.2

Data source: SEC filings, Value Line Investment Survey, and other analyst reports.

[1]The reported multiples are based on the same valuation numerator but with 2008 actual profits or 2009 expected profits, respectively.

EXHIBIT 47.10 | Financial Data for Industry Comparables (continued)

	Recent Price	Number of shares (in millions)	Debt (in millions)	Beta	Revenue growth	Income growth	Price/EPS 2008	Price/EPS 2009	EV/EBITDA 2008	EV/EBITDA 2009
Internet										
Activision Blizzard, Inc.	$10.03	1,359	$0.0	NA	124%	340%	18.5	17.2	6.9	6.9
Amazon.com, Inc.	74.71	429	74.0	1.10	29%	24%	53.8	47.9	27.1	23.6
Dice Holdings Inc.	3.2	62.21	60.2	NA	9%	2%	12.3	25.7	4.5	6.9
drugstore.com, Inc.	1.3	97.36	2.1	1.65	8%	63%	NA	NA	NA	91.1
eBay	14.32	1,287.81	0.0	1.15	11%	−22%	12.8	17.1	7.0	8.1
Google	379.5	315.25	0.0	0.90	31%	9%	23.6	20.7	13.2	11.3
GSI Commerce	14.93	47.93	195.9	1.15	29%	−2%	NA	NA	12.2	10.6
TechTarget Inc.	2.38	41.75	0.0	1.45	20%	−117%	NA	NA	8.8	11.3
WebMD Health Corp.	25.58	57.58	0.0	0.85	15%	114%	45.8	46.0	18.1	16.4
Electronic Arts Inc.	19.16	322	0.0	0.90	15%	55%	NA	24.1	NA	11.5
Yahoo! Inc.	14.02	1,393.35	0.0	1.00	3%	−78%	32.6	37.3	10.2	10.3
Software										
Adobe Systems	23.64	524.27	350.0	1.20	13%	−41%	14.9	22.9	8.6	12.6
ArcSight Inc.	14.15	31.5	0.0	NA	34%	509%	NA	52.8	39.2	21.8
Intuit	25.35	320.53	998.1	0.90	15%	9%	19.5	16.2	9.2	7.9
Microsoft	18.83	8891	0.0	0.80	18%	−32%	10.2	12.0	5.9	6.8
Omniture	13.54	75.05	13.2	1.30	107%	37%	NA	NA	16.4	9.6
Salesforce.com	37.36	122.43	0.0	1.20	44%	93%	NA	57.7	35.0	20.7
Symantec	16.47	819.92	1,766.0	0.90	5%	−234%	9.4	9.5	4.7	4.9
McAfee Inc.	34.49	153.72	0.0	1.00	22%	77%	26.1	24.1	12.3	10.1
Vmware Inc.	29.6	389.86	450.0	NA	42%	62%	27.1	33.9	21.0	23.8

Data source: SEC filings, Value Line Investment Survey, and other analyst reports.

EXHIBIT 47.10 | Financial Data for Industry Comparables   *(continued)*

For-Profit Education	
Apollo Group, Inc.	Education programs for working adults at the high school, undergraduate, and graduate levels, online and on-campus through subsidiaries.
American Public Education Inc.	Online postsecondary education degree programs and certificate programs including national security, military studies, intelligence, homeland security, criminal justice, technology, business administration and liberal arts; primarily serves military and public service communities.
Corinthian Colleges, Inc.	Private, for-profit postsecondary education degree programs in health care, electronics, and business.
Career Education Corporation	North American private, for-profit postsecondary education in information technologies, visual communication and design technologies, business studies, and culinary arts.
Capella Education Company	Online postsecondary education services company; doctoral, master's and bachelor's programs through their subsidiary.
Strayer Education, Inc.	Holding company of Strayer University, which offers undergraduate and graduate degree programs in business administration, accounting, information technology, education, and public administration to working adults.
DeVry, Inc.	North American higher education programs, offering associate, bachelor's and master's degree programs in technology; health care technology; business, and management; also offers online secondary education to school districts and medical education.
ITT Educational Services, Inc.	Technology-based postsecondary degree programs in the United States.
K12 Inc.	Technology-based education company; proprietary curriculum, software and educational services created for online delivery to students in kindergarten through 12th grade.
Grand Canyon Education, Inc.	Online undergraduate and graduate degree programs in education, business, and health care.
New Oriental Education & Technology Group, Inc.	Foreign language training and test preparation courses in the United States and the People's Republic of China; development and distribution of primary and secondary educational content and technology.

Data source: Adapted from company sources.

EXHIBIT 47.10 | Financial Data for Industry Comparables   *(continued)*

	Internet
Activision Blizzard, Inc.	Interactive entertainment software and peripheral products.
Amazon.com, Inc.	Diversified online retailer with emphasis on books.
Dice Holdings Inc.	Career services and recruiting.
drugstore.com, Inc.	Online drugstore.
eBay Inc.	Online trading community.
Google Inc.	Web-based search engine and global technology company.
GSI Commerce, Inc.	E-commerce business developer/operator.
TechTarget	Industry-specific portal operator.
WebMD Health Corp.	Health information services for consumers, physicians, health care professionals, employers, and health plans.
Electronic Arts Inc.	Interactive entertainment software and peripheral products.
Yahoo! Inc.	Internet media company providing web navigation, aggregated information content, communication services, and commerce.

	Software
Adobe Systems Incorporated	Computer software products and technologies.
ArcSight, Inc.	Security and compliance management solutions.
Intuit Inc.	Business and financial management software solutions.
Microsoft Corporation	Operating system software, server application software, business and consumer applications software, software development tools, and Internet/intranet software; also video game consoles and digital music entertainment devices.
Omniture, Inc.	Online business optimization software.
Salesforce.com, Inc.	Application services that permit sharing of on-demand customer information.
Symantec Corporation	Security, storage, and systems management solutions.
McAfee Inc.	Computer security solutions.
VMware Inc.	Virtual infrastructure solutions.

Data source: Adapted from company sources.

Sun Microsystems

Oracle will be the only company that can engineer an integrated system-application to disk—where all the pieces fit together so the customers do not have to do it themselves . . . Our customers benefit as their systems integration costs go down while system performance, reliability and security go up.

—Larry Ellison, CEO, Oracle Corporation[1]

It was the first time in the last two weeks that Margaret Madison, a member of Oracle's corporate development team, had not stayed in the office until two in the morning. At the close of business earlier that day, Friday, April 17, 2009, Oracle had put in an offer of $7.38 billion, or $9.50 per share, to acquire Sun Microsystems. Only nine months into her position, Madison, a recent MBA graduate, had found herself to be a member of Oracle's valuation team, assessing a potential merger with Sun. The journey, however, was not over yet. Sun had a number of potential suitors, IBM standing prominently among them, and Madison and her colleagues expected IBM to counter Oracle's offer.

Oracle, a California-based business software company, was one of the world's largest and most reputable sellers of database management systems and other related software. With $23.6 billion in annual revenue, the company was a leviathan, led forward with lightning speed by the only CEO Oracle had ever had, Larry Ellison. Sun was nothing to scoff at either. Once the darling of Silicon Valley, it had fallen on tough times but was still competitive. Sun had started as a hardware and servers producer, but over the years, it had established a solid position in the software industry with its Java programming language, Solaris operating system, and MySQL database management software. Combining these two companies had the potential to create the Wal-Mart of the enterprise software industry. Ellison "had a vision for creating an end-to-end vendor [that] clients go to for all their technology" needs.[2]

---

[1]"Oracle Buys Sun," Oracle Corporation press release, April 20, 2009.

[2]Jerry Hirsch and Alex Pham, "With IBM Out, Oracle Jumps in to Buy Sun for $7.4 Billion," *Los Angeles Times,* April 21, 2009.

This case was prepared by Eric Varney (MBA '10) and Assistant Professor of Business Administration Elena Loutskina. It was written as a basis for class discussion rather than to illustrate effective or ineffective handling of an administrative situation. Copyright © 2010 by the University of Virginia Darden School Foundation, Charlottesville, VA. All rights reserved. *To order copies, send an e-mail to* sales@dardenbusinesspublishing.com. *No part of this publication may be reproduced, stored in a retrieval system, used in a spreadsheet, or transmitted in any form or by any means—electronic, mechanical, photocopying, recording, or otherwise—without the permission of the Darden School Foundation.*

Oracle's bid of $9.50 per share was more than a 40% premium over Sun's $6.69 closing price that day. But only a few weeks prior, IBM—Oracle's chief rival in the $15 billion database software business—had offered $9.40 per share for Sun. The talks had stalled due to antitrust concerns, employment contracts, and the final price, which opened a window of opportunity for Oracle to step in and ensure that Sun did not fall into a competitor's hands.

Oracle had been on a successful shopping spree over the past several years. The ability to acquire 10% margin companies and turn them into 40% margin companies had distinguished Ellison and his team as ruthless cost-cutters who planned ahead well before making purchases. As a member of the corporate development team, Madison knew that better than anyone else. She had spent the last few weeks carefully poring over every part of Sun's financials, business lines, R&D figures, and personnel expenditures. Today was a break from the 20-hour work days, the sight of empty Chinese food cartons, documents strewn across the table, and weary-eyed bankers. Today had been a better day, but only delivered brief respite to the team. All the questions they had worked on so diligently still remained. Had they considered everything? Was the final offer appropriate? If competitors upped their bids, how much more could Oracle offer?

Competitive Landscape

The technology industry had historically comprised three sectors: hardware, software and services, and storage and peripherals. In 2008, revenue generated by these three segments was $411 billion,[3] $2,239 billion,[4] and $160 billion,[5] respectively. In total, the value of the industry was roughly $2.8 trillion, or about one-fifth of U.S. GDP.

The computer hardware market consisted of personal computers (PCs) (roughly half of sales), servers, mainframes, and workstations (**Exhibit 48.1**). Although customer loyalty was relatively low, brand awareness was high, which somewhat restricted new entry into the market. Business customers were typically tied to specific hardware manufacturers through long-term contracts, which led to significant switching costs. Individuals were less fettered and had minimal switching costs, but only represented a small percentage of the market. Computer hardware was a necessity for individuals and businesses alike, making demand strong and consistent.[6] With weak rivalry among players, the market had enjoyed a healthy 4.8% growth over the previous few years and was expected to grow at the same pace until 2013.

The software and services segment was the largest part of the IT industry. The industry was peppered with thousands of competitors large and small, young and mature,

---

[3]Datamonitor, "Global Computer Hardware: Industry Profile," December 2008.

[4]Datamonitor, "Global Software & Services: Industry Profile," March 2009.

[5]Datamonitor, "Global Computer Storage & Peripherals: Industry Profile," March 2009.

[6]Major producers of computer hardware included Dell, Hewlett-Packard (HP), Sun, IBM, and Apple. Some (e.g., Dell and HP) were fairly diversified and offered a swath of hardware products. Others (e.g., Sun and IBM) marketed their products almost exclusively to business customers. Apple was unique because it dealt mainly with retail customers.

fun and serious. It offered a wide array of products ranging from heavyweight software, such as Microsoft Windows, to small applications; services also ran the gamut, ranging from large-scale consulting products to small projects, such as website development and design for local businesses. Some competitors had a large Internet presence (e.g., Google or YouTube), whereas other niche players operated small tools, such as online surveys (**Exhibit 48.2**). Only the heavyweights enjoyed some customer loyalty. Major software and services providers—Microsoft, IBM, HP, and Oracle—had stable and rather predictable revenues and notable market share (**Exhibit 48.3**). This software and services segment outpaced the hardware and storage and peripherals segments, growing at 12.2% annually between 2004 and 2008, and it was expected to maintain a healthy annual growth rate of 10.4% until 2013.[7]

The smallest segment—computer storage and peripherals—included data storage components, computer processors, and other peripherals (e.g., printers). The market was dominated by storage devices, such as hard drives. Combined, HP, Toshiba, and IBM commanded about half of the market. Historic sales growth rates of storage and peripherals mirrored that of the computer hardware segment.

In the 1990s, the IT industry resembled a tiered cake, with one or two heavyweights controlling each tier. These tiers were essentially technology swim lanes with little competition from other firms. For example, Cisco controlled the networking hardware market; Sun and HP were known for manufacturing servers. The business software segment belonged to SAP, while Oracle led in databases. IBM, a longtime hardware company, had moved into consulting and services. Everyone knew that HP laptops ran Windows operating systems but used Toshiba hard drives. Commercial clients bought Sun servers and ran Oracle database management software. There was relatively little overlap between these rival giants.[8]

At the dawn of the new millennium, the industry started to change. Lines between segments were becoming blurred; former allies encroached on each other's turf, and customers were forced to deal with fewer suppliers. The success of Apple's concept of a one-stop shop for consumers to acquire hardware, software, and even peripherals with a tightly controlled distribution channel forced large technology companies to reconsider their strategic approaches to business development. "The maturing tech industry has set giant companies on a collision course, as once-disparate technologies take on new capabilities in a 'convergence' of computers, software and networking."[9] Companies such as Apple and Dell moved away from PC manufacturing to other consumer devices, such as mobile phones, printers, and cameras. By the end of 2008, Apple, a long-standing competitor in the PC segment, derived only one-third of its total revenue from computers and laptops.[10] But simple deviation from historical products was a drop in the bucket. Battles were breaking out all across the industry. In 2009, Cisco, a manu-

---

[7]"Global Software & Services: Industry Profile," March 2009.

[8]"Mr. Ellison Helps Himself," *Economist,* April 23, 2009.

[9]Ben Worthen and Justin Scheck, "As Growth Slows, Ex-Allies Square Off in a Tech Turf War," *Wall Street Journal,* March 16, 2009, A1

[10]Apple, Inc., annual report, 2008.

facturer of networking hardware, announced it would start building its own servers, thus stepping into the territory of its longtime ally HP, which dominated the server market. HP itself took aggressive steps to compete with IBM in the technological outsourcing segment by acquiring Electronic Data Systems in 2008. Microsoft attempted to take over Yahoo, thereby eyeing Google's domain. Dell was rumored to be in the final stages of developing a "data-center management software that [would] compete with existing offerings by HP, IBM and others."[11] Oracle was on a long-term shopping spree expanding from database management software to an array of products. (See **Exhibit 48.4** for company descriptions and **Exhibit 48.5** for sales growth.)

"In the past, when big tech companies crossed over into others' businesses, they often dismissed it as 'co-opetition,' meaning they planned to compete in some areas and cooperate in others."[12] With healthy growth of the technology industry and consumer hunger for new gadgets, there was plenty of revenue to go around. But the financial crisis, beginning in 2007, changed the landscape. The looming recession shrunk sales all across the industry and forced technology companies to explore every opportunity for extra revenue.

Oracle

In 1977, Larry Ellison, Bob Miner, and Ed Oates, three twentysomething software engineers, left Ampex Inc. to start a new venture, Software Development Laboratories.[13] Ellison became the head of the fledgling firm. Within a year, the team had designed the first relational database management system (RDBMS) under the code name "Oracle." Early adopters of the technology included government, military, and intelligence entities (including the U.S. Central Intelligence Agency) and innovative businesses, such as Bell Telephone Laboratories. The original product and all the following versions of Oracle capitalized heavily on the revolution of electronic record keeping that hit U.S. corporations in the 1970s. By 2009, all large U.S. corporations without exception were using database management products in every aspect of their business: back office, front office, client relationships, Internet, and so on. Every set of records that companies kept required a database server and an application that would search through data quickly and efficiently providing managers with information on demand. Both the software for keeping the data in an easily accessible format and the tools to speedily search through that data were Oracle's bread and butter. Every heartbeat of a corporation, every step it took involved a database management system: payroll, sales, supply chain decisions, and travel reimbursements, to name a few.

Oracle's relationships with clients did not stop at merely developing and distributing the RDBMS software. The company provided continued support to its clients through constant improvements in its software, customized customer support and

---

[11]Worthen and Scheck.

[12]Worthen and Scheck.

[13]Justin Rohrlich, "Rags to Riches CEOs: Larry Ellison," *Minyanville.com,* November 18, 2009, http://www.minyanville.com/businessmarkets/articles/oracle-ibm-ellison-ampex-sdl-billionaire/11/18/2009/id/25369 (accessed November 2, 2010).

training, and on-site installation and tune-up of the applications to a particular client's needs. Oracle targeted high-end customers because it had a lot to offer them. Apart from being the best among competitors in data access speed, Oracle also provided best-in-class data security protection. Its early versions could be installed and used on any type of computer, running any operating system. This was a revolutionary move that catapulted Oracle's sales early on.

Oracle went public in 1986 on the NASDAQ. Although its journey had not been smooth at all times, Ellison had always managed to turn the company around. He had a vision to create a company that would dominate the "desktop of business users" market. As early as the 1980s, Oracle had aimed to create customized applications for business users built upon the core product: Oracle RMDBS. Over time, the company had gained significant presence in developing applications for supply chain management, manufacturing, financials, project systems, market management, and human resources, which were highly popular among Oracle's customers.[14]

By 2000, Oracle sales had topped $10 billion. Despite a dip in sales during the dotcom bubble, Oracle had remained highly profitable. For a brief period, Ellison was the wealthiest man in the world. Oracle's success continued into the new millennium. Between 2000 and 2005, the top line grew annually at 2.9%, operating profit increased at 5.5%, and the margin improved by nearly 400 basis points. These healthy profits led to a significant accumulation of cash, which in turn allowed Oracle, under Ellison's leadership, to become a serial acquirer.

Since 2005, Oracle had spent more than $30 billion on over 50 bolt-on acquisitions (see **Exhibit 48.6** for select transactions), only a few of which were intended to refine and innovate Oracle's core database product line. Other acquisitions had allowed Oracle to aggressively move into new areas that would complement its current offerings and allow it to compete in the middleware, applications, and industry-specific software arenas. The most transformational move was in the applications space, where Oracle had snapped up PeopleSoft, Siebel, and Hyperion, all of which provided enterprise management solutions.[15] Oracle's 2008 acquisition of BEA Systems, a middleware company that utilized service-oriented architecture infrastructure to better link databases and software applications, was notable because it provided Oracle with additional flexibility to link all the products in its portfolio.[16] By early 2009, Oracle had become the biggest supplier of commercial software.

Sun Microsystems

Sun Microsystems, Inc., established in 1982 by three Stanford graduate students, built desktop computers and workstations. Sun entered the market at a time when pairing proprietary hardware, operating systems, and software was the norm. Sun broke new

---

[14]Michael Abbey, *Oracle 9i: A Beginner's Guide,* (Berkeley, CA: McGraw-Hill, 2002).

[15]Oracle Corporation, "Oracle Corporate Timeline," http://www.oracle.com/timeline/index.html (accessed November 2, 2010).

[16]"Oracle to Acquire BEA Systems," Oracle Corporation press release, January 16, 2008.

ground with its UNIX-based Solaris, which made its computers compatible with many other software and hardware products available on the market.[17] Sun's success, similar to Oracle, was attributed to rapid computerization of the companies' records where new workstations rapidly replaced the behemoth "minicomputers." From 1985 to 1989, Sun grew at average annual rate of 145%, reaching the status of fastest-growing company in America. The next step in Sun's stardom was due to its development, in 1989, of a new chipset based on scalable performance architecture (SPARC). Sun's SPARCs enhanced existing products by allowing it to create the smallest and fastest workstations on the market at the time. Combining the high-quality hardware with excellent on- and off-site customer service was a recipe for success.

Alongside the best-in-its-class workstations, Sun had been the proud owner of the Solaris operating system, which successfully competed with Microsoft Windows in the corporate world and was treasured by many in the industry. In 1995, the company had also developed the Java programming language, which customers universally loved and had become an industry standard for developing software for web applications. Virtually all PCs and eventually mobile phones required Java, which Sun licensed for a small fee. In 1997, Oracle converted to Sun's Java programming language, thus allowing its applications to be easily used by web developers. Oracle had also adopted the Linux operating system.

Sun went public in 1986 with a solid product offering dominated by its hardware sales. It had thrived until the turn of the century, when competition and market trends had turned against the company. After an altercation with Microsoft in the late 1990s, Sun was forced to make Java and Solaris available to users gratis. The burst of the dot-com bubble had hit Sun hard by almost annihilating its high-end hardware sales to the financial sector. The economic downturn following the dot-com bust had forced financial conglomerates to cut costs and move to lower-end hardware offered by Sun's competitors.[18] Companies had also started to shy away from the SPARC proprietary chip line favoring more widely used chips from Intel and Advanced Micro Devices. Sun's product mix had begun to move from predominantly hardware to a mix of hardware, software, and services, but waning hardware sales were not offset by gains in other offerings.[19]

Sun tried to leverage its acclaimed software systems to boost hardware sales by making Java (and later Solaris) an open-source platform in 2007. Open-source software allowed developers to adjust the platform to their specifications and thus provided a greater ability to adapt systems to a variety of tasks. The rationale for changing was to compete with Symbian and Microsoft in the mobile phone market and to increase the number of

---

[17]"Sun Microsystems, Inc., Company History," http://www.fundinguniverse.com/company-histories/Sun-Microsystems-Inc-Company-History.html (accessed November 2, 2010).

[18]Matthew Karnitschnig, "IBM in Talks to Buy Sun in Bid to Add to Web Heft," *Wall Street Journal,* March 18, 2009.

[19]Sun Microsystems, Inc., Form 10-K, September 27, 1999. In 1999, Sun generated $9.6 billion in revenue from its hardware segment, while software and services added $1.6 billion. Ten years later, in 2009, Sun's business mix had changed dramatically; the Systems and Services segments were expected to generate $6.7 and $4.7 billion in revenue, respectively.

users. Sun had also expected this move would lead to greater adoption of the Solaris platform in the corporate world and drive hardware sales in uncaptured markets.[20] In reality, these moves failed to garner the sales Sun had anticipated. Sun was losing consumers on the high end to IBM and on the low end to Dell and HP, and nothing seemed to be able to change the trend.[21] In January 2008, Sun decided to move in yet another direction by announcing it would acquire MySQL AB for $1 billion. The company's core product was open-source database management software, touted as the world's most popular. MySQL was widely used by companies, such as Facebook, that ran websites on thousands of servers. By adding MySQL, Sun had hoped to find new outlets for its existing product lines and also to distribute MySQL through current channels.[22]

All the efforts to revive the once-glorious company were undermined by the financial crisis in 2007. In 2008, facing a banking industry on the brink of collapse and finding themselves unable to borrow to finance their immediate needs, companies reined in capital expenditures; naturally, computer and software updates were put on the back burner. In November 2008, well into the swing of the crisis, Sun announced plans to reduce its work force by approximately 15%.[23] Sales in 2009 were expected to drop by 17.5% from $13.9 billion to about $11.4 billion. Sun was expected to record a charge of $1.5 billion for goodwill impairment. The company that once had a reputation for turning laboratory successes into profits was headed into a tailspin. At that point, company management started to look for a potential suitor.

Oracle Eyes Sun

Ellison was one of those suitors who believed in the future of Sun as a part of Oracle. In his opinion, many smaller companies were doomed due to slowing revenue growth and the desire by clients to work with fewer suppliers. Armed with a respected management team and a war chest of more than $8 billion in cash,[24] Oracle aggressively pursued acquisition. Oracle had followed Sun for some time, hoping to capitalize on Sun's misfortunes by getting specific assets or the entire company at a deflated price (**Exhibit 48.7**). On March 12, 2009, Oracle contacted Sun about acquiring some assets. Within a week, while Sun was mulling Oracle's offer, a rumor surfaced that IBM was considering taking over Sun. On April 6, 2009, news broke that IBM and Sun had been in serious merger talks for more than a month. But the negotiations did not end in a deal, and Oracle did not wait long to step in. After all, the combination of Oracle's databases and Sun's servers had driven both companies' sales for much of 1990s. Both companies formed a united front against Microsoft, exploiting Solaris and Java as foundations for business software.

---

[20]Connie Guglielmo, "Sun Makes Java Free, Expands Mobile-Phone Software," *Bloomberg Online*, Bloomberg, May 8, 2007.

[21]Morningstar, "Sun Microsystems, Inc.," *Morningstar*, October 31, 2008.

[22]"Sun to Acquire MySQL." Sun Microsystems, Inc., press release, January 16, 2008.

[23]"What's Next after IBM-Sun Merger Talks Fizzle?," *EE Times Asia*, April 8, 2009.

[24]Oracle Corporation, Form 10-Q, February 28, 2009.

Ellison's stated vision was to transform Oracle into the Apple for the business customer by delivering high-quality, seamlessly integrated consumer products where software and hardware components were developed in conjunction, thus minimizing the customer setup process.

Strategically, the merger would combine Oracle's dominant position in the software space with Sun's expertise in hardware and networking (**Exhibit 48.8**). The move also added the prized Java, MySQL, and Solaris platforms to Oracle's portfolio. The cannibalization of software products, though possible, was expected to be minimal. Although core Oracle products and MySQL were both database management systems, they appealed to different customers and were not in competition: Oracle could sell its software to the high-end clients while effectively serving smaller clients well. The corporate development team was sure that Oracle could capitalize on Sun's customer base and service contracts. The move made perfect sense strategically; the only matter to be determined was the price. That's where Madison and her valuation team stepped in.

Fortunately, Madison had already collected plenty of information needed to put a price on Sun; she had gathered it when Oracle had first showed interest. She had market data for comparable companies (**Exhibit 48.9**), the appropriate yields (**Exhibit 48.10**), balance sheets for both Sun and Oracle (**Exhibits 48.11** and **48.12**, respectively), and historic financials for Oracle (**Exhibit 48.13**). With Oracle entering into a confidentiality agreement with Sun, she had also received access to proprietary information. Madison and her team had spent a great deal of time looking at Sun's historical record and carefully developed projections for its future performance as a standalone company (**Exhibit 48.14**), which she knew would be the cornerstone of crafting a firm valuation.

The next step was to determine how much extra value Oracle could generate by making Sun's operations more efficient, cutting outdated and inefficient products and departments, streamlining remaining product lines, and introducing new synergistic systems. Knowing that a significant percentage of anticipated merger synergies were never realized historically, Madison and her team were fairly conservative with their estimates.

Cost cutting was the easy part. Having restructured and implemented lean operations in a line of past acquisitions, Madison and her colleagues were pros at trimming the fat. They knew Oracle could reduce Sun's staff by 20% to 25%, slash SG&A expenses by 22% to 32%, and allocate a significant amount for other restructuring costs. Estimating sales forecasts, potential new product lines, and software licensing was a completely different story, which necessitated bringing the marketing, sales, and R&D people on board.

First of all, Oracle team members expected Sun to initially lose some customers as a result of the merger. They knew that uncertainty of product offerings would push some customers to delay purchases and some to switch to competitors. After all, nobody wanted to buy an expensive piece of computer equipment only to find later that it would not be supported by the new owners of the company. Another issue was the lower-end customers that Oracle had never dealt with before. The marketing team expected these customers to hesitate to buy from Oracle for fear of being pushed into buying more expensive products. Marketing specialists knew that rivals would use similar arguments in aggressively pursuing Sun's clients. The only thing Oracle could do on this front was to minimize the extent of customer attrition. Oracle's marketing department was already working on a plan to reassure low- and high-end customers alike of continued service.

The second order of business was Sun's precious software. Although the open-source software could be downloaded free of charge, customers could elect to pay for product support and updates. The software had been particularly attractive during the recession. Market surveys, which Oracle had quietly conducted, suggested that customers might be open to paying a small fee for software downloads. The quality of Sun's software was so well known and appreciated by the market that the Oracle team was certain to increase its revenue stream from software licensing. The bigger source of revenue, however, was in the potential new products at the intersection of Sun and Oracle technologies. After all, most of Oracle's systems were built using Java and ran on the Solaris operating system.

The R&D team brainstormed on combining Oracle's products and Sun's hardware and software. Oracle had a long-standing plan to build Exadata machines that could handle both online transactions and data warehousing. Initially, the company had planned to use HP's hardware, but the opportunities Sun offered were too good to miss. Oracle engineers were positive that combining Oracle software with FlashWire technology, which Sun possessed, and then putting it on Sun hardware, could create a transaction-processing database machine. This machine would be twice as fast as its predecessor and, with high probability, much faster than machines produced by its closest rival, IBM.

When Madison put a bottom line to the dollar value of all the potential synergies the merger could generate, the numbers were rather impressive. But the merger would also be costly. The team's calculations suggested that integration charges would be close to $1.1 billion in aggregate, with most (about $750 million) incurred in 2010. It also anticipated an initial loss in operating income of about $45 million, due to loss of customers and/or delayed purchases. Cost cutting, licensing income, new products, and the addition of the "integrated application-to-disk" service had the potential to boost operating profit by as much as $900 million per year. Preferring to remain conservative, Madison assumed that such synergies would kick in gradually over a three-year time horizon starting in 2011.

The Decision

As Madison drove from San Francisco to her Redwood City, California, office the following morning, she wondered if her teammates had accounted for everything. She knew they were conservative in most of the financial projections, but they remained merely estimates. If rivals such as IBM placed a competitive bid for Sun over the weekend, Madison's team and manager would go over the estimates yet again, evaluating every aspect of the due diligence Oracle conducted in its effort to acquire Sun.

EXHIBIT 48.1 | Global Computer Hardware Sales

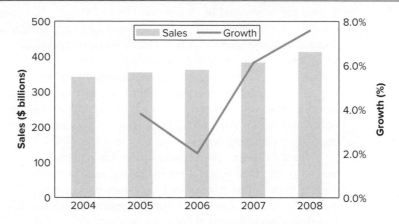

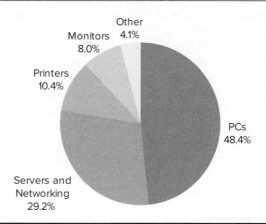

Data source: Datamonitor, "Global Computer Hardware: Industry Profile," December 2008.

EXHIBIT 48.2 I   Global Software & Services Sales

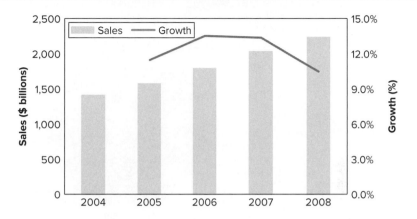

Global Software & Services Sales: 2004–08

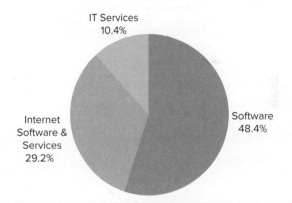

Global Software & Services Sales by Product: 2008

IT Services
10.4%

Internet
Software &
Services
29.2%

Software
48.4%

Data source: Datamonitor, "Global Software & Services: Industry Profile," March 2009.

EXHIBIT 48.3 | Global Software & Services Sales by Share, 2008

Global Software & Services Sales by Share:2008

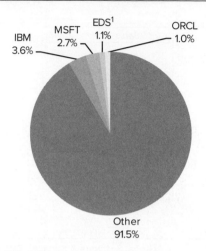

[1]EDS was acquired by HP in 2008

Data source: Datamonitor, "Global Software & Services: Industry Profile," March 2009.

EXHIBIT 48.4 | IT Industry Companies

Primarily Hardware	Description	Key Products	Notable Acquisitions
Advanced micro devices	Develops and manufactures semiconductors and microprocessors	x86 microprocessors, microprocessors for computers and servers	*ATI Technologies (2006)
Apple	Designs, manufactures, and markets personal computers, related software and mobile communication and entertainment devices	Macintosh computers, iPhones, iPods, music related products	
Dell	Offers a wide range of computers and related products	Desktop and laptop computers, software and peripherals, servers	*EqualLogic (2008)
EMC	Provides enterprise storage systems, software, networks, and services	Information storage, VMware	
Hewlett-Packard	Provides imaging and printing systems, computing systems, and information technology for business and home	Consulting services, enterprise storage and servers, personal computers, digital cameras, printers and ink	*Compaq (2002) *EDS (2008)
Intel	Designs and manufactures computing and communications components and platforms	Microprocessors, chipsets, mother-boards, platforms	
International Business Machines	Offers computer solutions through the use of advanced information technology	Consulting services, middleware, servers, laptops	
NetApp	Provides storage and data management solutions	Filers	
Sun Microsystems	Provides products, services, and support for building and maintaining network computing environments	Enterprise systems and services; storage and software platforms Java, Solaris, and MySQL	*MySQL (2008)
Primarily Software			
Adobe Systems	Develops, markets and supports computer software products and technology	Creative solutions, Acrobat	
Microsoft	Develops, manufactures, licenses, sells and supports software products	Windows, business and server software, gaming and handheld devices	
Novell	Provides network and Internet directory software and services	Enterprise networking software	
Oracle	Supplies software for enterprise information management	Relational databases, middleware software, applications, related services	*PeopleSoft (2005) *Siebel Systems (2006) *Hyperion Solutions (2007) *BEA Systems (2008)
Red Hat	Develops and provides open source software and services	Linux	

Sources: Industry reports and Bloomberg.

EXHIBIT 48.5 | Relative Sales Growth, 2000–08

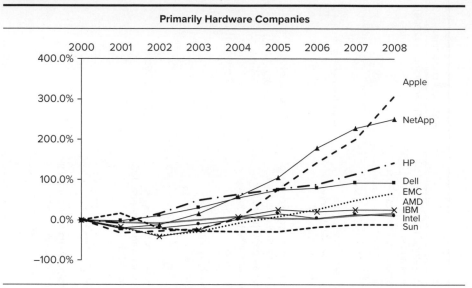

Primarily Hardware Companies

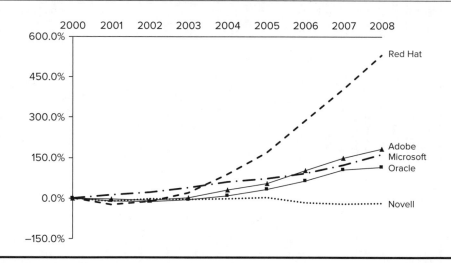

Primarily Software Companies

Data source: Compustat.

EXHIBIT 48.6 | Selected Acquisitions Completed by Oracle, 2005–08

Target	Completion Date	Deal Size ($MM)	Product Category	Core Products
PeopleSoft	January 2005	10,300.0	Applications	Human resource management systems and customer relationship management software
Retek Inc.	April 2005	630.0	Industry Solutions	Management software for the retail industry
G-Log	September 2005	N/A	Industry Solutions	Logistics and transportation management software
Siebel Systems Inc.	January 2006	5,946.5	Applications	Customer relationship management, business intelligence and data integration software
360 Commerce	January 2006	N/A	Industry Solutions	Open-store and multichannel solutions software
Portal Software Inc.	April 2006	233.7	Industry Solutions	Billing and revenue management solutions for communications and media industry
Mantas Inc.	October 2006	122.6	Industry Solutions	Fraud and compliance software for financial institutions
Stellent Inc.	November 2006	398.7	Middleware	Content management software solutions
MetaSolv Inc.	October 2006	217.7	Industry Solutions	Customer relationship software for the communications industry
Hyperion Solutions Corp.	March 2007	3,292.1	Applications	Performance management software
Agile Software Corp.	May 2007	480.1	Applications	Product life cycle software for the industrial products, electronics and high-tech, and life science industries
BEA Systems Inc.	January 2008	8,056.0	Middleware	Enterprise infrastructure software
Skywire Software LLC	June 2008	N/A	Industry Solutions	Web-based insurance, financial and enterprise management software
Primavera Software Inc.	October 2008	N/A	Applications	Project, program, and portfolio management software

Source: SDC Platinum.

EXHIBIT 48.7 | Relative Stock Performance, January 3, 2006 to April 16, 2009

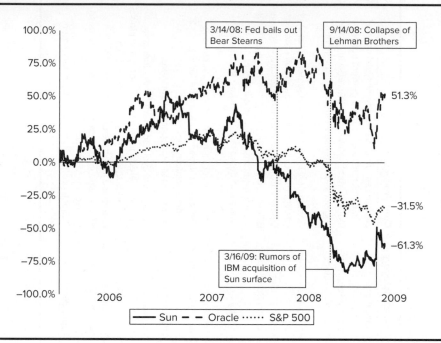

Data sources: Yahoo! Finance and Wharton Research Database Service.

EXHIBIT 48.8 | Comparing Oracle and Sun Microsystems (in billions of U.S. dollars)

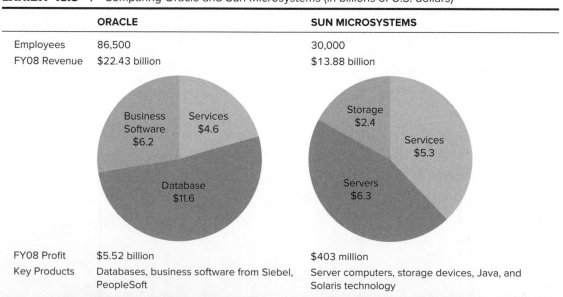

	ORACLE	**SUN MICROSYSTEMS**
Employees	86,500	30,000
FY08 Revenue	$22.43 billion	$13.88 billion
FY08 Profit	$5.52 billion	$403 million
Key Products	Databases, business software from Siebel, PeopleSoft	Server computers, storage devices, Java, and Solaris technology

Data source: Don Clark and Ben Worthen, "Oracle Snatches Sun, Foiling IBM," *Wall Street Journal,* April 21, 2009.

EXHIBIT 48.9 | IT Companies' Financial Data (market data as of April 17, 2009)

	Ticker	Stock Price ($)	Shares Out (MM)	Market Cap ($MM)	BV Debt ($MM)	Levered Beta	Bond Rating	Cash and Investments ($MM)	LTM Sales ($MM)	LTM EBIT ($MM)	LTM EBITDA ($MM)	LTM Earnings ($MM)
Primarily hardware												
Advanced micro devices	AMD	3.56	609	2,168	4,988	2.19	B	933	5,808	(1,955)	(732)	(3,098)
Apple	AAPL	123.42	889	109,713	—	1.11	—	24,490	37,096	7,984	8,739	5,728
Dell	DELL	11.06	1,944	21,505	2,011	1.12	A2	9,546	61,101	3,190	3,959	2,478
EMC	EMC	12.81	2,041	26,142	3,404	1.39	—	6,446	14,876	1,569	2,626	1,346
Hewlett-Packard	HPQ	36.30	2,416	87,708	20,458	1.25	A2	10,140	118,697	10,354	14,175	8,050
Intel	INTC	15.60	2,562	39,967	1,988	1.20	A1	8,840	37,586	8,954	13,570	5,292
International Business Machines	IBM	101.27	1,343	136,052	33,925	0.93	A1	12,907	103,630	16,715	22,165	12,334
NetApp	NTAP	17.59	330	5,808	1,265	1.80	—	2,604	3,464	116	286	101
Sun Microsystems	JAVA	6.69	739	4,941	1,257	1.73	Ba1	3,061	13,438	(2,231)	(1,757)	n/a
Primarily software												
Adobe Systems	ADBE	24.70	524	12,944	350	1.32	—	2,018	3,476	961	1,231	809
Microsoft	MSFT	19.20	8,896	170,795	2,000	0.99	Aaa	31,447	61,981	22,128	24,485	17,232
Novell	NOVL	3.94	343	1,353	122	1.50	B1	1,067	940	10	55	(15)
Oracle	ORCL	19.06	5,046	96,180	11,238	1.27	A2	12,624	23,630	8,406	10,291	5,739
Red Hat	RHT	18.32	190	3,482	—	1.20	BB	663	628	80	119	85

Data Sources: Yahoo! Finance, Moody's, Bloomberg, and company filings.

EXHIBIT 48.10 | Relevant Security Yields, April 2009

Corporate Bond Yields	
AAA	5.50%
AA	5.77%
A+	6.27%
A	6.35%
A−	6.50%
BBB+	7.54%
BBB	7.62%
BBB−	8.64%
BB+	11.42%
BB	11.49%
BB−	11.70%
B+	13.28%
B	14.70%
B−	15.46%
U.S. Treasury Yields	
180-Day	0.34%
1-Year	0.54%
3-Year	1.22%
5-Year	1.71%
10-Year	2.82%
30-Year	3.66%

Data sources: Mergent Bond Record, U.S. Treasury, and Ibbotson Associates.

EXHIBIT 48.11 | Sun Microsystems Historical and Projected Balance Sheet
(in millions of U.S. dollars)

	Fiscal Year-End June 30		
	2007	2008	2009E
Assets			
Current assets			
Cash[1]	3,620	2,272	1,876
Marketable debt securities	2,322	1,038	1,185
Net receivables	2,964	3,019	2,258
Inventory	524	680	566
Deferred prepaid taxes[2]	200	216	188
Other current assets	1,058	1,218	995
Total current assets	10,688	8,443	7,068
Property, plant, and equipment, net	1,504	1,611	1,616
Goodwill	2,514	3,215	1,743
Intangible assets	633	565	269
Other noncurrent assets	499	506	536
Total assets	**15,838**	**14,340**	**11,232**
Liabilities and equity			
Current liabilities			
Accounts payable including accrued payroll	2,222	2,121	1,600
Short/Current long-term debt	1	—	554
Deferred taxes[2]	2,047	2,236	2,341
Other current liabilities including warranty reserve	1,182	1,311	1,126
Total current liabilities	5,451	5,668	5,621
Long-term debt	1,264	1,265	695
Deferred long-term charges[2]	659	683	635
Other noncurrent liabilities[3]	1,285	1,136	976
Total liabilities	8,659	8,752	7,927
Stockholders' equity			
Common stock	6,987	7,391	7,582
Treasury stock	(311)	(2,726)	(2,569)
Retained earnings	189	430	(2,055)
Other stockholders' equity	314	493	347
Total stockholders' equity	7,179	5,588	3,305
Total liabilities and equity	**15,838**	**14,340**	**11,232**

[1](Sun Microsystems') long-term strategy is to maintain a minimum amount of cash and cash equivalents in subsidiaries for operational purposes and to invest the remaining amount of our cash in interest-bearing and highly liquid cash equivalents and marketable debt securities.

[2]Deferred taxes and related accounts are not expected to vary with sales or continue to accumulate as a company growth.

[3]Includes deferred settlement income from Microsoft as of June 30, 2009, 2008, 2007, and 2006, long-term tax liabilities as of June 30, 2009, 2008, 2007, and 2006, and long-term restructuring liabilities.

Data sources: Company filings and case writer estimates.

EXHIBIT 48.12 | Oracle Historical and Projected Balance Sheet (in millions of U.S. dollars)

	Fiscal Year-End May 31		
	2007	2008	2009E
Assets			
Current assets			
Cash and cash equivalents	7,020	11,043	12,624
Net receivables	4,589	5,799	4,430
Inventory	—	—	—
Other current assets	1,274	1,261	1,527
Total current assets	12,883	18,103	18,581
Property, plant, and equipment, net	1,603	1,688	1,922
Goodwill	13,479	17,991	18,842
Intangible assets	5,964	8,395	7,269
Other noncurrent assets	643	1,091	802
Total assets	**34,572**	**47,268**	**47,416**
Liabilities and equity			
Current liabilities			
Accounts payable	315	383	271
Short/Current long-term debt	1,358	1,001	1,001
Other current liabilities	7,714	8,645	7,877
Total current liabilities	9,387	10,029	9,149
Long-term debt	6,235	10,235	9,237
Deferred long-term charges	1,121	1,218	480
Other noncurrent liabilities	910	2,761	3,460
Total liabilities	17,653	24,243	22,326
Stockholders' equity			
Common stock	10,293	12,446	12,980
Treasury stock	—	—	—
Retained earnings	6,223	9,961	11,894
Other stockholders' equity	403	618	216
Total stockholders' equity	16,919	23,025	25,090
Total liabilities and equity	**34,572**	**47,268**	**47,416**

Data sources: Company filings and case writer estimates.

EXHIBIT 48.13 | Oracle Historical and Projected Income Statement (in millions of U.S. dollars)

	Fiscal Year-End May 31		
	2007	2008	2009E
Software revenues	14,211	17,843	18,877
Services revenues	3,785	4,587	4,375
Net revenue	17,996	22,430	23,252
Selling, general, and administrative	8,790	10,468	10,217
Research and development	2,195	2,741	2,767
Amortization of intangible assets	878	1,212	1,713
Other operating expense	159	165	234
Total operating expense	12,022	14,586	14,931
Operating income	5,974	7,844	8,321
Income tax on operations	1,709	2,316	2,380
Net operating profit after tax	4,265	5,528	5,941
Effective corporate tax rate	28.6%	29.5%	28.6%

Data Sources: Company filings and case writer estimates.

EXHIBIT 48.14 | Sun Microsystems Historical and Projected Income Statement (in millions of U.S. dollars)

					Fiscal Year-End June 30				
	2007	2008	2009E	2010E	2011E	2012E	2013E	2014E
Net revenue	13,873	13,880	11,449	12,665	13,047	13,526	13,885	14,243
Cost of sales	7,608	7,425	6,718	7,685	7,583	7,735	7,889	8,075
Gross margin	6,265	6,455	4,731	4,980	5,464	5,791	5,996	6,168
Selling, general, and administrative	3,851	3,955	3,461					
Research and development	2,008	1,834	1,648					
Impairment of goodwill	—	—	1,460					
Other operating expense	97	294	398					
Total operating expense	5,956	6,083	6,967	4,839	4,992	5,121	5,249	5,372
Operating income	309	372	(2,236)	141	472	670	747	796
Depreciation and amortization	517	476	474	536	456	470	487	500
as % of prior year PP&E	34.4%	29.5%	29.3%	30.0%	30.0%	30.0%	30.0%	30.0%
Net PP&E	1,504	1,611	1,616	1,520	1,566	1,623	1,666	1,709
as % of sales	10.8%	11.6%	14.1%	12.0%	12.0%	12.0%	12.0%	12.0%

Data Sources: Company filings and case writer estimates.

644

Carter International

Chris Smith had only joined the corporate finance team of the prestigious hotel concern Carter International (Carter) four weeks ago in early 2016, but was already advising the CEO in critical matters. Just that morning he had received a memo request (**Exhibit 49.1**) to provide analysis related to a possible acquisition of Hope Enterprises (Hope) and a change in capital structure. With some reassurance that he knew the basics of financial management, it was time to get to work.

Carter International

Carter had a long history in the hotel business. The Carter name was recognized internationally as synonymous with quality accommodations. Its flagship hotels were the Carter-Plaza in New York, the Carter-Beverly in Los Angeles, California, and the Carter-Ashelworth and Carter-Westminster in London. Carter owned and operated additional hotel properties in Australia, Great Britain, New Zealand, Turkey, and the United States, and two casino properties in Las Vegas, Nevada. In total, Carter maintained 79,000 rooms with an average occupancy of 71%. Management had previously sought to sell off Carter's gambling segment, but the new management team was now pushing to increase Carter's participation in this growth segment.

Carter's new president and CEO, Jane Scarret, had recently taken over from long-time CEO Francis Carter-Hellman, a member of one of Carter's founding families. Carter-Hellman remained the chair, and 25% of Carter's 45 million shares of stock was owned by officers and directors (some of whom were family members). Scarret was well regarded in the financial community. According to one analyst, Scarret brought "the reputation of an astute finance person who would be able to create value-enhancing initiatives for the company." Carter's recent share price of $100 seemed to reflect this market confidence in Scarret.

This fictional case was prepared by Michael J. Schill, Professor of Business Administration. It was based on Robert S. Harris and Kenneth M. Eades, "Hope Enterprises," UVA-F-1219 (Charlottesville, VA: Darden Business Publishing, 1998). It was written as a basis for class discussion rather than to illustrate effective or ineffective handling of an administrative situation. Copyright © 2016 by the University of Virginia Darden School Foundation, Charlottesville, VA. All rights reserved. *To order copies, send an e-mail to* sales @dardenbusinesspublishing.com. *No part of this publication may be reproduced, stored in a retrieval system, used in a spreadsheet, or transmitted in any form or by any means—electronic, mechanical, photocopying, recording, or otherwise—without the permission of the Darden School Foundation.*

The hotel industry had experienced strong performance as of late. An equity analyst summarized the state of the industry in the United States:

> Demand for rooms stateside are apt to remain favorable in 2016, as economic expansion and high employment augurs well for leisure and corporate travel. Although companies will be hard pressed to continue to increase average daily rates at a pace comparable to those of recent years, high occupancy levels should give lodgers more pricing power. There is a caveat. Six straight years of auspicious operating conditions have resulted in greater hotel construction activity, with sector behemoths Marriott International and Hilton World-wide accounting for a significant portion of the sector's development pipeline.[1]

Some acquisition activity in the industry was in progress. Marriott had recently announced an offer to purchase rival Starwood Hotels for $12 billion, representing an enterprise-value-to-EBITDA ratio of about 9.5 times.

The Gaming Industry

The worldwide gaming industry had experienced spectacular growth over the past 30 years, but its future was less certain. The ongoing aging of the population in developed markets meant that a growing portion of the population was looking for relatively passive activities with attractive amenities. Increasingly, the public found casino gambling to be an acceptable form of entertainment. In the United States, access to legalized gambling had increased greatly since the 1980s as states and localities looked to stimulate both business and tax revenues. There was some concern about saturation in the gaming markets, and that increased competition would bring margin compression. Some evidence showed that newer casinos had been failing financially.

Internet gambling had grown dramatically in popularity over the past 20 years. The U.S. government regulated Internet gambling, and both interstate and international transactions remained illegal. Gambling activity in gaming ventures in Las Vegas continued to be strong. Internationally, there had been massive investment and success in Macao, and currently most of the world's largest casinos were located in that special administrative region of China. With the recent tightening of Chinese government regulation, it was clear that gaming demand in Macao was softening. The reduced attendance was particularly evident among the high-roller gamblers. The market contraction in Macao had had a particularly strong effect on those firms that were heavily invested there. Stock prices for gaming companies that were heavily invested in Macao (i.e., Las Vegas Sands and Wynn Resorts) were down 20% to 50% in the past year. **Exhibit 49.2** provides financial summary data on the participants in both the hotel and gaming industries.

Some observers believed that the gaming industry was ripe for consolidation. There were rumors that gaming companies as well as hotel concerns were on the hunt for gaming acquisitions as the industry was reaching maturity. Analysts believed that adequate capital resources would be critical to companies that were going to see their way through this new phase of the casino business.

---

[1] Dominic B. Silva, "Hotel/Gaming Industry," Value Line Publishing, February 2016.

Hope Enterprises

Hope owned and operated three world-class casino-hotel resorts in Atlantic City and Las Vegas, a dockside casino and hotel in Florence, Mississippi, and a riverboat casino in New Orleans, Louisiana. **Exhibits 49.3** and **49.4** provide financial information on Hope. According to one analyst:

> Hope is considered a prime acquisition target because of the strategic location of its holdings and the kind of customers it attracts. The company controls two casinos in Atlantic City, a market that was ignored by some major gambling companies for years but is now booming, prompting a scramble to acquire key locations there. Hope also controls a Las Vegas casino, and its properties serve midmarket gamblers who usually do not patronize high-roller casinos such as Carter's Las Vegas Palace.

Increasingly analysts suggested that independent casino businesses like Hope needed to partner with larger hotel concerns to remain viable.

Deal Considerations

From early on, Scarret had made it very evident that she wanted Carter to be an important player in the casino business. The question was not whether Carter would make a gaming acquisition but rather when and who. Although Hope represented an attractive deal candidate, Smith knew that there were other targets under consideration.

Yesterday a team had begun investigating the economics of Hope and how the merged entities might look. Overall, the view of the group was that growth in the industry would continue to keep ahead of broad economic growth for the next five years and then ease down to pace with the general economy in the years beyond. A contracting of economic expectations was a theme for the beginning of 2016. World stock markets were down as investors processed the economic uncertainty associated with depressed commodity prices (oil prices were at a 10-year low), a slowing of the Chinese economy (Chinese GDP growth was at a five-year low), and a volatile U.S. presidential election. **Exhibit 49.5** provides information on financial market conditions.

The motivations for the deal were several. First, Hope looked like a bargain. The stock price had continued to drift down during the past year and now traded at a price-to-earnings ratio of under 10 times. Second, Hope was well run. Hope management was well respected in the industry. An acquisition would allow Carter to retain a talented management team. But this would not be a business-turnaround acquisition. Third, Hope was small. Hope's small size meant that Carter could add value by providing scale opportunities on both the cost and revenue sides. The team thought Hope's margins would be substantially improved by taking advantage of Carter's existing expertise in the industry and exploiting several scale economies. It also believed that revenue would be accelerated for the next few years by leveraging Carter's brand, its loyalty program, and its reservation system into greater customer volume, although not necessarily higher prices. The merger was expected to keep Hope's balance sheet largely unaffected. Hope's cash balance, while large, was about normal for a well-run gaming company and was not expected to be altered. The team didn't expect to see any material merger efficiencies across Hope's assets.

There was some debate regarding whether Carter should use debt or equity to finance the $1 billion of cash that was expected to be needed for the acquisition. Joakim Nilsen, a longtime member of the company's treasury staff, noted that there was significant pride and borrowing-cost advantage in Carter's credit rating. Carter's A rating was the highest credit rating among all the major U.S. hotel companies, and Pearson was concerned that the credit rating would be compromised if the $1 billion payment was made using debt financing.

On the other hand, Trishala Shankar, the newest and youngest member of the treasury staff, argued that Carter was far too conservative in its use of debt capital and claimed that an acquisition provided an excellent opportunity for Carter to better leverage its balance sheet. Initial discussions with Carter's investment bank provided a sense of the borrowing terms for a five-year $1 billion Carter bond. The bank expected the offering would be issued at par if the coupon was set at either 4.7% in U.S. dollars or 4.3% in British pounds. Shankar believed strongly enough about the need to use more debt capital that she recommended that, even if the Hope acquisition fell through, Carter proceed with the debt issuance and use the proceeds to repurchase shares. Her primary argument was based on the ability of debt to shield the company from its high 40% tax rate.

The team recognized that other suitors for Hope might appear, and that Carter would need to be thoughtful in its bidding strategy. It was thought there were other potential acquirers for which the synergy gains with Hope were expected to be even larger than what might be achieved with Carter. Maybe the lack of bidding activity suggested that Hope was in fact overpriced. Alternatively, Hope had traded for more than $30 a share a few years before the recent slide that led to the current $15 price. Could Hope's stock price rebound if Carter didn't act now? With 65 million shares outstanding for Hope, such a change in price represented a large swing in value.[2]

To be successful and with such an important decision on the line, Chris Smith knew that he needed more than hope.

---

[2]Hope's equity beta had been recently estimated at 1.45.

EXHIBIT 49.1 I   E-mail Message from Jane Scarret to Chris Smith

TO: Chris Smith

FROM: Jane Scarret

SUBJECT: Hope Enterprises

DATE: February 1, 2016

As we discussed yesterday, the operating committee will be meeting tomorrow to consider an acquisition offer for Hope Enterprises. Please draft a recommendation covering the issues below. Thanks for doing this. I look forward to your thoughts. Jane

Top of mind questions:

1. Hope's stock price is down substantially. Do you think $15 represents an abnormal buying opportunity? Please use the seven-year forecast we discussed yesterday as a base case in your valuation (**Exhibit 49.6**).

2. Quantify the value that Carter brings to Hope. The purpose of your valuation is to educate the team on figures that will be helpful in developing a bidding strategy. There is a consensus that Hope would get a healthy bump in both revenue growth and operating margin. The view is that an acquired Hope would achieve:

    •   Annual revenue growth expansion of five percentage points starting in 2017 (e.g., revenue growth in 2017 expanding from 7% in the base case to 12% in the merger scenario. Future years would get similar bumps in revenue growth.)

    •   A 30% to 50% reduction in Hope's general and administrative expenses starting in 2017.

    There is some discussion about whether these gains should be included beyond 2021. We would appreciate your perspective on the value implications of this decision. Also, how important is the realization of each of these two gains in the value of the merger?

3. Assuming we make an all-cash offer, we will have to do some external financing. How should the team think about the choice of debt versus equity financing? Should we rethink Carter's capital structure mix?

4. Niles Bardsley talked to our investment bankers who suggested we fund the deal with five-year U.S. dollar bonds at 4.7%. As an intriguing alternative, the bankers said that the five-year borrowing rate would be less in British pounds at 4.3%. I generally don't consider financing operations in currencies other than U.S. dollars, but I'd like you to consider whether you find British pound debt to be advantageous.

EXHIBIT 49.2 | Financial Summary Data on Companies in the Hotel and Gaming Industry (financial statement data as of 2015 in millions)

Company	Hotel Rooms (thousands)	Gaming Space (thousands of sq. ft.)	Operations
Las Vegas Sands	20	1,900	Casino resorts in Macao, Singapore, and United States.
MGM Resorts	52	2,200	15 casino resorts in the United States and a stake in a casino in Macao.
Penn National Gaming	3	NA	26 gaming facilities in United States. Company facilities feature 26,000 gaming machines.
Wynn Resorts	1	300	Casino resorts in the United States and Macao.
Choice Hotels	500		Hotels under the Comfort Inn, Comfort Suites, Quality, Clarion, Sleep Inn, Econo Lodge, Rodeway Inn, MainStay Suites names.
Hilton Worldwide	715		Hotel and resorts worldwide under the Hilton, Conrad, Embassy Suites, Hilton Garden Inn, Hampton Inn, and Homewood Suites names.
Hyatt Hotels	155		Hotel, resort, and vacation housing worldwide.
Marcus	NA		Operates hotels, resorts, and movie theatres in the United States.
Marriott International	714		Operates or franchises hotels and resorts worldwide under the Marriott, Courtyard, Residence Inn, Ritz Calrton, and Renaissance names.
Starwood Hotels	350		Hotels under the Sheraton, Le Meridien, Westin, St. Regis, and W names.
Wyndham Worldwide	NA		Hotels under the Wyndham, Ramada, Days Inn, and Super 8 names. Also a major operator of vacation time-share properties.

EXHIBIT 49.2 | (continued)

Gaming	Revenue	Total Debt	Market Equity	Book Equity	EBITDA Margin	EBIT Margin	Interest Expense	Beta	Bond Rating
Las Vegas Sands	$11,688	$9,128	$32,518	$6,930	41.3%	32.8%	$275	1.35	Baa
MGM Resorts	$9,250	$12,821	$10,697	$5,840	32.5%	23.5%	$850	1.65	B
Gaming	$2,825	$1,261	$1,134	$645	33.5%	27.5%	$70	1.40	B
Wynn Resorts	$4,105	$8,780	$6,369	–$50	32.0%	24.0%	$420	1.75	B
Hotels									
Choice Hotels	$845	$818	$2,434	–$380	30.4%	29.0%	$39	0.85	Ba
Hilton Worldwide	$11,430	$10,193	$18,315	$5,220	29.0%	23.0%	$550	1.20	B
Hyatt Hotels	$4,325	$1,377	$5,224	$4,000	20.7%	13.5%	$45	1.10	Baa
Marcus	$488	$242	$580	$ 346	28.1%	20.2%	$12	1.05	—
International	$14,530	$4,304	$15,996	–$3,460	11.5%	10.5%	$165	1.10	Baa
Starwood Hotels	$3,045	$2,140	$10,478	$1,310	42.9%	33.5%	$100	1.00	Baa
Worldwide	$5,500	$5,183	$7,540	$1,300	27.9%	23.5%	$110	1.25	B
Carter International	$1,500	$742	$4,500	$1,574	29.2%	25.0%	$37	1.00	A

Sources: Value Line Investment Survey, *Mergent Bond Record*, and author estimates.

EXHIBIT 49.3 | Income Statement for Hope Enterprises
(dollars in millions, except per-share figures)

	2014	2015
Revenue		
Casino	460.8	493.1
Rooms	112.0	119.9
Food and beverage	111.2	118.8
Other	92.2	96.9
Gross Revenue	776.2	828.7
Promotional Allowances	−38.1	−40.8
Net Revenue	738.1	787.9
Expenses		
Casino	177.9	188.6
Rooms	42.0	45.0
Food and Beverage	89.3	94.8
Other	46.1	51.0
General and Administrative	156.2	162.0
Depreciation and Amortization	42.4	45.3
Total Expenses	553.9	586.7
Operating Income	184.2	201.2
Interest Expenses	55.7	44.4
Income before Taxes	128.5	156.8
Provision for Income Taxes	38.1	44.3
Net Income	90.4	112.5

Source: Created by author.

EXHIBIT 49.4 | Balance Sheet for Hope Enterprises (dollars in millions)

	Dec 2014	Dec 2015
Assets		
Cash and cash equivalents	63.6	67.8
Receivables less allowance for doubtful accounts	35.3	36.9
Deferred income-tax benefits	12.1	13.1
Prepayments and other	12.9	14.5
Inventories	10.3	10.8
Total current assets	134.3	143.0
PP&E, net	893.8	954.5
Deferred costs and other	40.3	42.4
Other assets	165.5	161.8
Total assets	1,233.8	1,301.7
Liabilities and stockholders' equity		
Accounts payable	27.8	33.5
Construction payables	14.8	16.4
Accrued expenses	71.1	79.0
Current portion of long-term debt	12.5	9.4
Total current liabilities	126.3	138.4
Long-term debt	702.9	693.5
Other liabilities	18.2	22.7
Deferred income taxes	12.9	14.4
Total liabilities	860.3	869.0
Common stock	32.7	32.7
Additional paid-in capital	214.4	214.4
Retained earnings	126.3	185.6
Total stockholders' equity	373.5	432.7
Total liabilities and stockholders' equity	1,233.8	1,301.7

Source: Created by author.

EXHIBIT 49.5 | Financial Market Conditions

Market Bond Yields—January 2016		
	USD	**GBP**
Maturity	**Government Bond Yields**	
1 year	0.47%	0.23%
2 year	0.67%	0.34%
3 year	0.78%	0.47%
4 year	0.98%	0.55%
5 year	1.16%	0.77%
30 year	2.75%	2.37%
Corporate Bond Yields		
Aaa	3.97%	
Aa	4.16%	
A	4.38%	
Baa	5.46%	
Ba	6.10%	
B	6.90%	

Market Risk Premium

Consensus premium used within Carter	5.0%

Foreign Exchange Rates

US Dollar to British Pound (USD/GBP)	1.44

Economic Indicators for the United States

	Five Year Forecast
Annual real GDP growth	2.9%
Annual GDP Deflator (Inflation)	2.7%
National Unemployment Rate	5.0%

Sources: Bloomberg, Value Line Investment Survey, and author estimates.

EXHIBIT 49.6 | Financial Projections for Hope Enterprises (dollars in millions)

	2016	2017	2018	2019	2020	2021	2022
Revenue growth	7%	7%	7%	7%	6%	5%	3%
Cost of goods sold/revenue	0.50	0.51	0.52	0.53	0.54	0.56	0.58
General and admin/revenue	0.20	0.20	0.20	0.20	0.20	0.20	0.20
NWC turnover	55.5	58.8	62.5	66.5	66.5	66.5	66.5
PPE turnover	0.86	0.90	0.95	0.97	0.97	0.97	0.97
Revenue	843	902	965	1,033	1,095	1,150	1,184
Cost of goods sold	422	460	502	547	591	644	687
Depreciation expense	51	54	57	57	58	60	63
Gross profit	371	388	406	428	446	446	434
General and admin	169	180	193	207	219	230	237
Operating profit	202	208	213	222	227	216	198

Note: NWC turnover is defined as Revenue/Net Working Capital; PPE turnover is defined as Revenue/Net PPE.

Source: Created by author.

DuPont Corporation: Sale of Performance Coatings

In January 2012, Ellen Kullman, CEO and chairman of DuPont, was reviewing an internal report on the company's Performance Coatings division. A month earlier, she had dismissed rumors that the business was up for sale after reports had surfaced that the company had hired Credit Suisse to seek potential buyers for it. Kullman stated that the business would be given a "chance" to see if it could meet certain performance targets, saying: "From a performance standpoint we will give them a chance to see if they can get there. If any of our businesses can't obtain their targets, obviously we will look at alternatives."[1] For several years, the business, which produced paint for the auto and trucking industries, had struggled with low demand and high raw-material costs that had hurt profits. During her tenure as CEO, Kullman had attempted to move DuPont away from commodity chemicals to a specialty chemical and science–focused products business. It was no longer clear whether DuPont Performance Coatings (DPC) fit her strategic vision for the firm. Still, the issue was what course would produce the greatest value for shareholders. She had called for an internal review of the business that fall to assess its value to DuPont compared to what outside parties might pay for it. Those reports were now complete, and she would have to decide whether to retain the business or sell it and, if so, at what price.

History of DuPont

E. I. du Pont de Nemours and Company was one of the longest continually operating companies in the United States. It traced its origin to a French émigré, Eleuthère Irénée (E. I.) du Pont, who had studied chemistry and who, at age 14, had written a paper on

---

[1]Stefan Baumgarten, "DuPont CEO Slams News Media Over Reports of Coatings Business Sale," ICIS News, December 13, 2011.

This case was prepared by Susan Chaplinsky, Tipton P. Snavely Professor of Business Administration, and Felicia Marston, Professor of Commerce, McIntire School of Commerce, with the assistance of Brett Merker, Research Assistant. It was written as a basis for class discussion rather than to illustrate an effective or ineffective handling of an administrative situation. Copyright © 2014 by the University of Virginia Darden School Foundation, Charlottesville, VA. All rights reserved. *To order copies, send an e-mail to* sales@dardenbusinesspublishing.com. *No part of this publication may be reproduced, stored in a retrieval system, used in a spreadsheet, or transmitted in any form or by any means—electronic, mechanical, photocopying, recording, or otherwise—without the permission of the Darden School Foundation.*

gunpowder. In 1799, his family fled revolutionary France, and in 1802, he founded a company in Delaware, at the urging of Thomas Jefferson, to manufacturer gunpowder.[2] From its origins in gunpowder, in the 1880s, the company pioneered the manufacture of dynamite. At the turn of the 20th century, the chemistry of nitrocellulose, critical to explosives, began to spawn early innovations in plastics, lacquers, films, and fibers. In 1911, the U.S. government, citing antitrust reasons, forced DuPont to break up its monopoly gunpowder business. Notwithstanding this, the company made enormous profits during World War I, which it used to diversify into other businesses. By 2011, DuPont was among the world's largest chemical companies; it had $38 billion in sales and operations in 90 countries. Among its most well-known products were nylon (introduced in 1935), Tyvek (used in construction), Kevlar (a protection product), and Teflon (a protective surface). **Exhibit 50.1** shows the evolving nature of DuPont's businesses since its founding.

Kullman's Watch

Kullman joined DuPont in 1988 as a marketing manager after starting her career at GE. Within DuPont, she had a reputation for making businesses grow, a legacy she attributed to her father, who was a landscaper. In 1998, she launched a safety consulting business, which later became the Safety & Protection business, which boasted sales approaching $4 billion in 2011. She was named DuPont's CEO in January 2009 and, later that same year, chairman. That year was a difficult one for the company because its performance was closely tied to the broader economy, which had fallen into a recession. Shortly after her appointment as CEO, in February 2009, DuPont's stock price fell below $19, a multiyear low (**Exhibit 50.2**). In response to the downturn, Kullman cut costs, laid off 4,500 employees, and continued to transition the company from a commodity chemical business to a specialty chemical and science–driven business. Commodity chemicals typically were cyclical, and intense priced-based competition kept margins low. By moving toward specialty chemicals and more customized products based on DuPont's research and development (R&D), Kullman hoped to focus the company on higher-growth and -margin businesses.

As part of this plan, the company acquired Danisco, a leading food ingredient and enzyme company, for $7.1 billion in January 2011. It was the second-largest acquisition in company history, smaller only than the 1999 acquisition of Pioneer Hi-Bred International, a maker of genetically modified seeds. With the shift taking place away from the "Old DuPont" to a more specialty-focused company, the drivers of growth over the next few years were likely to be Agriculture, Nutrition & Health, Performance Chemicals, and the nascent Industrial Biosciences businesses. Kullman saw the firm's

---

[2]Du Pont's gunpowder company was capitalized at $36,000, with 18 shares worth $2,000 each, a portion of which was used to purchase a site on Brandywine Creek for $6,740. Jefferson advised du Pont of the new nation's need for gunpowder and gave him his first order, calling the agreement between the two a "handshake that built a country," from E. I. du Pont de Nemours and Company, "DuPont—200 Years of Service to the U.S. Government in Times of Need."

future increasingly at the core of industrial biotechnology; the company was positioned to compete in agriculture, nutrition, and advanced materials. She articulated her direction for the firm in the 2010 annual report:

> We have attractive growth opportunities supported by market-driven science and fueled by global megatrends associated with population growth. We are allocating resources to drive the highest growth opportunities . . . Global population will pass the 7 billion mark in 2011 and exceed 9 billion people by 2050—or about 150,000 more people on the planet every day. This will translate into critical needs in the areas of feeding the world, reducing our dependence on fossil fuels and keeping people and the environment safe—the megatrends that are driving our science and innovation. . . .[3]

With her push to match the company's focus to these megatrends, DuPont's business units were evaluated to determine whether they fit this vision and could meet the company's performance goals. The company had publicly stated that its longer-term performance goals were to achieve 7% sales growth annually and 12% earning margins. The firm had eight separate business units: Agriculture (24% of 2011 sales), Performance Chemicals (21%), Performance Materials (18%), Performance Coatings (11%), Safety & Protection (10%), Electronics & Communications (8%), Nutrition & Health (6%), and Industrial Biosciences (2%). Based on 2011 revenue, Agriculture had grown to be DuPont's largest business (**Exhibit 50.3**). Although there was some unevenness in growth over the past two years, most of DuPont's divisions had been able to grow sales in line with the 7% goal. This was also true of DPC, which, in rebounding from the lows of 2009, had grown sales by 12.5% in 2011, but the growth rate in sales over the next two years was expected to be only 3% to 5% (**Exhibit 50.4**). More concerning was that its profit margins were the lowest among the eight businesses. All of this suggested that DPC would have to significantly improve its growth and profitability to meet DuPont's performance goals.

Performance Coatings

DPC was formed in March 1999 when Herberts GmbH and DuPont Automotive Finishes merged.[4] Its products included high-performance liquid and powder coatings for motor vehicle original equipment manufacturers (OEMs), the motor vehicle aftermarket (refinishing), and general industrial applications, such as coatings for heavy equipment, pipes and appliances, and electrical insulation.[5] DPC employees liked to say that the products they made didn't make cars go faster, they just made them look good going faster. From 2007 to 2011, sales had grown at a –0.3% cumulative average growth rate (CAGR) and profits had declined at a –6.0% CAGR (**Exhibit 50.5**). Due to the

---

[3]DuPont, "Letter to Shareholders," *2010 Annual Review*, 2011, 2.

[4]DuPont had been a supplier of paint to the U.S. auto industry since its infancy, providing paint to General Motors in the 1920s. Herberts, a subsidiary of Hoechst, was acquired for $1.9 billion, making the combined firms the largest supplier of automotive finishes in the world. At the time, 80% of Herberts's operations were in Europe, while 75% of DuPont's business was in North America.

[5]Sales to OEMs included all vehicles (e.g., cars, trucks, buses, and motorcycles).

company's exposure to the auto sector, sales and earnings had been adversely affected by the 2008 and 2009 downturn. In 2011, the company posted stronger revenue growth of 12.5%, but most of this was attributed to price increases, which were unlikely to continue. Notwithstanding the pickup in sales, operating margins remained muted because of rising input costs. Nearly 50% of the key raw-material inputs (e.g., hydrocarbon solvents and organic pigments) were tied to crude oil prices, which had risen since the middle of 2010 due to tight supply and improving economic conditions.

Key competitive factors in its business included technology and technical expertise, product innovation and quality, breadth of product line, service, and price. In most industrial applications, the coating itself was only a small part of total production costs (e.g., 10% to 15%), and most customers were willing to pay more for technologically advanced coatings if it reduced application costs (e.g., labor). The industry in general was also not highly capital-intensive—capital expenditures and R&D were relatively small in comparison to the variable costs of production.

DPC held the number-four position in the global industrial coatings market, where it faced strong competition in all the business verticals that made up the industry (**Exhibit 50.6**). The market was highly fragmented: two companies—PPG Industries and Akzo Nobel N.V., each with sales greater than $10 billion—together accounted for 25% of industry sales. Seventeen firms had sales between $1 billion and $10 billion, the range of DPC's sales, which accounted for 45% of sales. The remainder of sales came from over 60 additional firms. Given the increased pressures for cutting costs and finding higher-growth opportunities, over the last six years, the industry had been consolidating; the market share of the six top companies increased from 28% in 2005 to 35% in 2011.[6] The top-10 global competitors controlled 60% to 75% of the sales in U.S. and European markets. To varying degrees, all the top competitors saw opportunities for growth in the less saturated Asia-Pacific and Latin American markets.

Relative to peers, DPC's strengths were in refinishing and the vehicle OEM market. In 2011, the vehicle aftermarket accounted for 43% of the division's sales, down from 53% of sales in 2009. The decline in refinishing was of concern because its profit margins tended to be higher than those in the vehicle OEM market. Of the $7 billion global refinishing market, PPG and DuPont were the market leaders—each had approximately a 28% market share—followed by Akzo Nobel (17% market share). Sales to motor vehicle OEMs accounted for 37% of DPC's 2011 sales, and DPC held the number-three market position in the OEM paint market behind PPG and BASF SE.

The two key drivers of revenue for these businesses were miles driven and vehicle sales. Miles driven was correlated with the incidence of collisions, which affected the demand for paint from refinishing, and sales of vehicles generated demand for paint from OEMs (**Exhibit 50.7**). Trends in the refinishing market were generally steady to negative. In the past several years, the number of miles driven in the United States had tapered off, resulting in fewer collisions. Potentially offsetting this trend was an expected increase in miles driven—and relatedly, collisions—outside the United States.

---

[6]Buckingham Research Group, *PPG Industries: "Other" Industrial Coatings Review*, May 21, 2012.

Also reducing the demand for paint was a significant dropoff in the number of damaged cars that were refinished. This was due to more damaged cars being written off ("totaled") and insurance companies imposing higher deductibles such that damaged cars more frequently went without repair. In the United Kingdom, for example, an estimated 7% of damaged cars were written off in 2010 compared to 5% in 2000; that translated to 80,000 fewer cars requiring repair (and paint) every year.[7] Further, advances in the quality of paint used by OEMs made it more durable and resistant to scratches and weathering.

The OEM market had experienced a sharp decline in global motor vehicle production in 2009 that had since begun to recover (**Exhibit 50.8**). In 2011, North American vehicle production (13.5 million units) still fell short of its 2007 level (15.5 million units). Over the past decade, most of the growth in vehicle production had taken place in countries outside the United States, particularly in emerging markets. For example, between 2000 and 2010, China and India had experienced an astonishing 763% and 344% increase, respectively, in vehicle manufacturing. DPC's existing customer base was heavily concentrated in Detroit, but North America accounted for only 27% of its revenues. As vehicle manufacturing continued to grow outside North America, DPC's revenues would likely expand in those markets.

DPC's overall revenues were closely tied to GDP growth, which was expected to be 1% to 2% in 2012–13 in the United States, largely flat in Europe, and more positive but erratic in emerging markets. Most analysts expected that emerging-market growth coupled with unprecedented fleet aging would spur a recovery in vehicle sales on the order of 3% to 5% per year.[8] Increases in sales, however, did not necessarily translate into higher profits for several reasons. First, the OEM profit margins were set by multiyear contracts with vehicle manufacturers, which made it difficult for paint suppliers to quickly pass on raw-material price increases. By comparison, the margins in refinishing were primarily based on claims paid by insurance companies, which left consumers less price sensitive to repair costs. Second, growing concerns about lead, the high cost of treating airborne emissions and solid hazardous waste generated by paint operations, and new regulations covering the global chemical industry in Europe were all expected to increase environmental compliance costs gradually over time.

Although a bullish scenario could be concocted for DPC, industry trends suggested that stable to modest improvement was the more likely course for the business over the next several years. As part of the internal review, DuPont attempted to assess DPC's value if it remained a division of the company. DuPont's internal targets for DPC were annual revenue growth of 3% to 5% and operating margins of 10% to 12%. Given DPC's mixed track record of performance, the internal review set targets at 4% for growth and 10% for margins, the low end of the targeted range. Other assumptions underlying the stand-alone valuation were incorporated into the analysis itself (**Exhibit 50.9**) and together yielded a value of approximately $4 billion for the division.

[7]Morgan Stanley, "E. I. du Pont de Nemours & Co.," analyst report, February 13, 2012.
[8]Morgan Stanley, 5.

Potential Buyers

When news surfaced in late October 2011 that DuPont was seeking a potential buyer for DPC, companies including PPG, BASF, Akzo Nobel, and Valspar Corporation were mentioned as prospective strategic buyers. For all but BASF, a potential purchase price of $4 billion would be a sizable transaction to complete (**Exhibit 50.10**). In response to a question about his company's potential interest, Valspar CEO Gary E. Hendrickson said that DPC was "a little too big a bite for us."[9] Although the $4 billion price tag would also be large in the current environment for private equity (PE) firms, Blackstone, Advent International, KKR & Co., Onex Corporation, and Clayton, Dubilier & Rice were all reportedly considering bids or had already made inquiries about the division.[10] The interest from PE firms was not surprising, given that buyout firms were sitting on record levels of "dry powder" cumulatively totaling over $400 billion at the end of 2011. A large portion of that was concentrated in buyout funds with 2006 and 2007 vintage years. In those years, buyout funds had raised record amounts of capital but had found it difficult to invest in the ensuing crisis years. As these funds neared the end of their investment periods, their general partners were under increasing pressure to find investments.

A leveraged buyout (LBO) was the purchase of a firm facilitated by large amounts of debt financing. In an LBO, the PE firm or sponsor would arrange debt financing for the deal and contribute the balance of financing with equity from one or more of its funds. Because of the anticipated higher debt load, PE firms generally looked for firms that could readily service the debt. Target characteristics might include steady and predictable cash flows, assets that provided good collateral for debt, or non-core assets that could be sold to pay down debt. Debt support (and returns) could also be bolstered if the targets had opportunities to grow EBITDA by increasing sales or cutting costs. For similar reasons, sponsors looked for mature firms that did not seemingly require large amounts of additional capital expenditures or R&D. Most sponsors also looked for a strong management team because they typically were not hands-on operators and had to rely on the target's management to run day-to-day operations.

Of course, to make a good return, the sponsor had to increase the target's value above its purchase price over a typically four- to five-year period, after which it would seek to exit the investment. Sponsors in PE deals generally looked to three factors to drive returns in their investee companies: benefits from the use of leverage, growth in EBITDA, and multiple arbitrage (i.e., buy at a low multiple and sell at a high multiple).

Benefits of Leverage

One benefit of leverage was that interest on debt was tax deductible and therefore the cost of debt was lower than the cost of equity. As a result, increasing leverage could produce interest tax shields that enhanced the company's value. The use of leverage

---

[9]Doug Cameron, "Valspar: DuPont Coatings Business Too Big a Bite for Us to Buy," *Wall Street Journal*, May 14, 2012.

[10]At the same time, DuPont hired Greenhill & Co. to handle the sale of a smaller part of the business that handled coatings for tractors and playground equipment. Zachary R. Mider and Jeffrey McCracken, "DuPont Is Said to Weigh $4 Billion Sale of Auto-Paint Unit," Bloomberg, October 28, 2011.

could also help augment a sponsor's returns, because for a given price paid for the business, more debt financing directly translated to a smaller equity contribution. All else equal, the smaller the equity base, the higher the return. Additionally, as equity holders, the sponsors received their share of the difference between the selling price (i.e., enterprise value of the firm at exit) and the equity value remaining after the debt and other senior claims were paid off. In a highly leveraged company, a relatively small increase in the firm's enterprise value could lead to a substantial increase in the sponsor's equity value. But high leverage also increased the sponsor's risk, since, analogously, a relatively small decline in enterprise value could materially reduce the value of its equity. High leverage could also be instrumental in driving returns for another reason—high interest and principal payments helped focus management's attention on improving performance and operating efficiency to generate cash for debt service.

DPC as a stand-alone company was expected to be all equity financed, and therefore the use of leverage was a potential source of value for PE sponsors. Sponsors typically spoke to bankers ahead of a deal to gauge how much debt might be available to finance the transaction. The total financing that would have to be raised depended on how much the sponsors paid for the target. Given its size, DPC would be considered a large buyout, which was generally defined as a deal above $1 billion in size. The number of large buyouts had declined precipitously from 98 deals in 2007 to just 10 in 2009, before clawing back to 36 deals in 2011 (**Exhibit 50.11**). The pressure to put money to work and the resulting pickup in number of deals had increased median purchase price multiples (PPMs) to 9.0× in 2011, almost as high as their peak of 9.5× in 2008. Not unrelatedly, the increase in PPMs coincided with easing in the credit markets as the markets moved further away from the financial crisis. Total debt-to-EBITDA multiples contracted sharply, from 7.6× in 2007 to 3.3× in 2009, necessitating a large increase in equity contributions from the sponsors. Thereafter, there had been a significant increase in debt availability: the median debt multiple expanded to 6.2× in 2011. Over 2010–11, large buyouts had been approximately 60% debt financed on average. If current trends held, it appeared that PE firms would have generous amounts of debt financing available, on the order of 5.5× to 6.0× EBITDA for a potential purchase of DPC.

Growth in EBITDA

Growth in EBITDA created value by improving the target's operations by undertaking measures such as product expansions, cost reductions, and add-on acquisitions. In assessing the opportunity for growth in EBITDA, PE firms routinely conducted extensive due diligence to develop improvement plans after they gained control of a company. A first step in this process was often to compare the target's performance to that of close competitors. Because PPG's industrial and performance coatings business segments directly competed with DPC, it was DPC's closest peer. Compared with DPC, PPG had projected slightly stronger sales growth and had achieved higher margins. PPG's mix of products accounted for some of the difference, but DPC's lower margins were mostly the result of higher costs and overhead. Based on this assessment and other due diligence, sponsors might reasonably expect to increase DPC's sales growth by 1% to 2% and improve its operating margins by 200 to 250 basis points.

DPC was led by DuPont veteran John McCool, 58, who was well regarded in the industry. McCool had held a variety of leadership positions since joining DuPont's Textile Fibers department in 1976. Kullman named McCool president in 2010 after he had served as vice president for DPC's Europe, Middle East, and Africa (EMEA) operations. She had given him the specific charge to turn the division's performance around. All the PE firms that were contemplating a bid for DPC would have to evaluate McCool and his team to see if they had the requisite skills to head the new company. If the current team was found wanting, the sponsors would have to be prepared to replace management as part of their plans.

Multiple Arbitrage

Multiple arbitrage arose when a sponsor received a higher PPM at exit for a target than it paid for it. All else equal, the higher the entry PPM, the lower the chances of a sponsor achieving multiple arbitrage. At a stand-alone value of approximately $4 billion, it looked as if DPC's potential buyers would have to pay on the order of 7× projected EBITDA for the company. Exit opportunities could arise from an IPO, sale to a strategic buyer, or sale to another PE fund (secondary buyout). Over the period 2006 to 2011, sales to strategic buyers had been the most frequent mode of exit by PE firms (**Exhibit 50.12**). Due to the growth in the size of the PE sector, however, secondary buyouts were a strong second to them. IPOs had fallen off as exit vehicles, in part due to uncertain market conditions accompanying the financial crisis and its aftermath. Because strategic buyers likely had greater opportunity for operating synergies with a target company, they were commonly thought to pay more for a target than financial buyers. Based on the PPMs of recent exits, however, the average PPM for exits to secondary buyouts was somewhat higher than the average PPM of exits to strategic buyers (**Exhibit 50.12**). Based on the current valuation of PPG and potential market expansion, sponsors might look to achieve 7.5× to 8.0× EBITDA at exit for DPC, given improvements in margins and growth as a private firm.

Decision

If Ellen Kullman decided to divest DPC, she would put in motion an auction for the division. At that point, DuPont would provide detailed information about the target and invite interested parties to bid. As part of that process, she would likely set a minimum price for bidders. Her stand-alone valuation suggested that the division was worth nearly $4 billion to DuPont. She would then need to assess how much potential additional value could be obtained, both separately and jointly, from EBITDA growth, multiple arbitrage, and the use of leverage to give her some idea of the potential range of values that bidders might offer. Relative to that, she knew that sponsors would likely seek higher returns to justify the greater financial risk from the use of leverage. Although financial buyers naturally sought the highest possible internal rate of return (IRR), in the current environment of tough competition, they often had to settle for IRRs of 20%. With that in mind, she would formulate her minimum required bid to ensure that shareholders' interests were served no matter what decision she reached about DPC.

EXHIBIT 50.1 | History and Outlook of Business

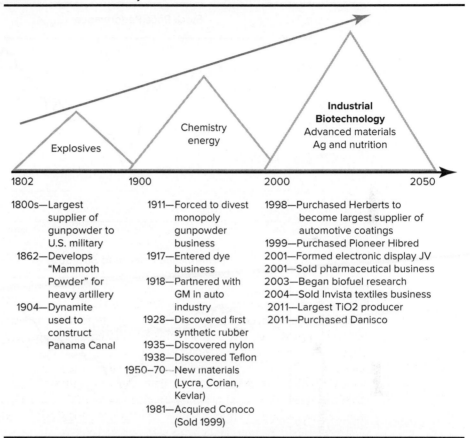

1802   1900   2000   2050

1800s—Largest   1911—Forced to divest   1998—Purchased Herberts to
     supplier of   monopoly   become largest supplier of
     gunpowder to   gunpowder   automotive coatings
     U.S. military   business   1999—Purchased Pioneer Hibred
1862—Develops   1917—Entered dye   2001—Formed electronic display JV
     "Mammoth   business   2001—Sold pharmaceutical business
     Powder" for   1918—Partnered with   2003—Began biofuel research
     heavy artillery   GM in auto   2004—Sold Invista textiles business
1904—Dynamite   industry   2011—Largest TiO2 producer
     used to   1928—Discovered first   2011—Purchased Danisco
     construct   synthetic rubber
     Panama Canal   1935—Discovered nylon
                1938—Discovered Teflon
           1950–70—New materials
                 (Lycra, Corian,
                 Kevlar)
           1981—Acquired Conoco
                 (Sold 1999)

Data Source: Macquarie Research, "E. I. du Pont de Nemours & Co.," analyst report, January 26, 2012, adapted by case writers.

EXHIBIT 50.2

Stock Price Performance

Performance Relative to S&P 500

Data Source: Yahoo! Finance.

EXHIBIT 50.3 | Business Segment Performance (dollars in millions)

Segment Sales	2009	2010	2011	Year-over-Year Growth 2009	2010	2011
Agriculture	$ 7,069	$ 7,845	$ 9,166	7.9%	11.0%	16.8%
Electronics and communications	1,918	2,764	3,173	−10.7%	44.1%	14.8%
Nutrition and health	1,218	1,240	2,460	−13.2%	1.8%	98.4%
Performance chemicals	4,964	6,322	7,794	−14.5%	27.4%	23.3%
Performance coatings	3,429	3,806	4,281	−21.4%	11.0%	12.5%
Performance materials	4,768	6,287	6,815	−25.3%	31.9%	8.4%
Safety and protection	2,811	3,364	3,934	−24.4%	19.7%	16.9%
Industrial biosciences			705			
Other	158	194	40			
Total segment sales	26,335	31,822	38,368			
Elimination of transfers	(226)	(317)	(407)			
Net sales	$26,109	$31,505	$37,961	−14.5%	20.7%	20.5%

Pretax Operating Income*	2009	2010	2011	Segment Margins 2009	2010	2011
Agriculture	$1,160	$1,293	$1,527	16.4%	16.5%	16.7%
Electronics and communications	87	445	355	4.5%	16.1%	11.2%
Nutrition and health	64	62	44	5.3%	5.0%	1.8%
Performance chemicals	547	1,081	1,923	11.0%	17.1%	24.7%
Performance coatings	69	249	271	2.0%	6.5%	6.3%
Performance materials	287	994	973	6.0%	15.8%	14.3%
Safety and protection	260	454	500	9.2%	13.5%	12.7%
Industrial biosciences			(1)			−0.1%
Pharmaceuticals (discontinued)	1,037	489	289			
Other	(169)	(206)	(235)			
Total pretax operating income	$3,342	$4,861	$5,646	12.8%	15.4%	14.9%

*After significant items.

Data Source: Company reports.

EXHIBIT 50.4 | Sales Growth Forecasts for Business Units

	Est. Sales Growth (2012–14)	Major Products	Sales as % of Product	Major Industry	Sales as % of Industry
Agriculture	10%	Corn seeds	47%	Seeds	68%
		Soybean seeds	15%	Chemicals	32%
		Herbicides	13%		
Performance chemicals	12%	White pigments (TiO$_2$)	47%	Industrials and chemicals	36%
		Fluoroproducts	34%	Construction	31%
		ChemSolutions	19%	Specialties	18%
Performance materials	4%	Engineering resins	46%	Transportation	37%
		Ethylene co-polymers	23%	Industrial	18%
		Elastomers	9%	Packaging	14%
Performance coatings	3%–5%	Refinish coatings	43%	Vehicle aftermarket	43%
		OEM coatings	31%	Vehicle OEM	37%
		Ind. liquid and powder coatings	26%	General industrial	15%
Safety and protection	7%	Aramids products	39%	Industrial	54%
		Tyvek/Typar	26%	Consumer	20%
		Safety consulting and training	16%	Construction materials	12%
Electronics and communications	6%	Photovoltaic materials	39%	Photovoltaics	39%
		Electronic materials	25%	Consumer electronics	18%
		Printing, packaging materials	18%	Advanced printing	18%
Nutrition and health	15%	Food ingredients	100%	Food ingredients	100%
Industrial biosciences	29%	Biomaterials—enzymes	100%	Bioprocessing	100%

Data Source: Company data, Macquarie Research, "E. I. du Pont de Nemours & Co.," analyst report, January 26, 2012, and case writer estimates.

EXHIBIT 50.5 | Performance Coatings Historical Performance (dollars in millions)

	2007	2008	2009	2010	2011	5-year CAGR
Net sales	$4,347	$4,360	$3,428	$3,806	$4,281	−0.3%
Year-over-year growth		0.3%	−21.4%	11.0%	12.5%	
Pretax operating income	366	−8	69	255	268	−6.0%
Margin	8.4%	−0.2%	2.0%	6.7%	6.3%	
Depreciation and amortization	107	111	123	105	104	
Research and development	71	69	56	48	46	
Capital expenditures	126	91	55	74	80	
Segment net assets	2,607	2,226	2,018	2,047	2,107	
Sales by industry						
Aftermarket (refinishing)			53%	44%	43%	
Vehicle OEM			28%	36%	37%	
General industrial			14%	14%	15%	
Other			5%	6%	5%	
Sales by region						
North America			26%	27%	27%	
Asia-Pacific			12%	13%	13%	
Europe, Middle East, and Africa			46%	44%	43%	
Latin America			16%	18%	17%	

Data Source: Company Databooks, various years.

EXHIBIT 50.6 | Global Competitive Position in Industrial Coatings Market

	Global Position	Architectural	Industrial	Protective and Marine	Refinishing	Auto OEM	Packaging	Aerospace
End market sales (billions)	$95.0	$40.9	$24.7	$12.4	$6.7	$5.7	$2.9	$1.9
% of end market sales	100%	43%	26%	13%	7%	6%	3%	2%
Peer ranking:								
Akzo Nobel	1	1	1	1	3		3	2
PPG	2	3	2	2	1	1	2	1
Sherwin-Williams	3	2	4+	4+	4+			4+
DuPont	**4**		**4+**		**2**	**3**		
Valspar	5	4+	3		4+		1	
BASF	6	4+	4+		4+	2		

A blank cell indicates "no participation" in business vertical.

Penetration Rates of Top Global Competitors by Region

	Percent of Sales of Top-10 Competitors
U.S. and Canada	75%
EMEA	60%
Asia-Pacific	30%
Latin America	30%

Data Source: Buckingham Research Group, *PPG Industries: "Other" Industrial Coatings Review*, May 21, 2012.

EXHIBIT 50.7 | Trends Affecting Paint Demand in Vehicle Aftermarket

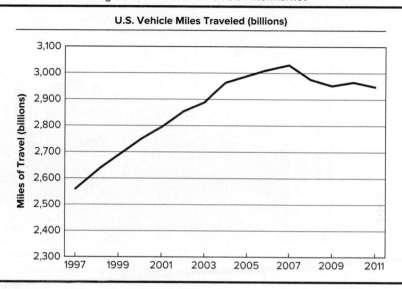

U.S. Vehicle Miles Traveled (billions)

Data Source: U.S. Federal Highway Administration, Highway Statistics.

U.S. Motor Vehicle Accidents per Million

Data Source: National Safety Council.

EXHIBIT 50.8 | Trends Affecting Paint Demand from Vehicle Manufacturers

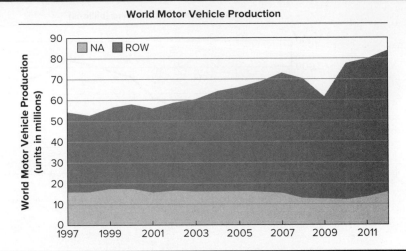

World Motor Vehicle Production

Notes: NA = North America (United States, Canada, and Mexico); ROW = Rest of World.

World Production of Vehicles, 2000 and 2010.

	2000	2010	% Change
North America	**17,699**	**12,177**	**–31%**
United States	12,800	7,761	–39%
Canada	2,964	2,071	–30%
Mexico	1,935	2,345	21%
Asia-Oceania	**17,928**	**40,900**	**128%**
Japan	10,144	9,625	–5%
China	2,069	18,263	783%
India	796	3,537	344%
South Korea	3,115	4,272	37%
Europe	**20,275**	**19,822**	**–2%**
France	3,348	2,229	–33%
Germany	5,527	5,906	7%
Italy	1,738	838	–52%
Spain	3,032	2,388	–21%
United Kingdom	1,814	1,393	–23%
South America	**2,076**	**4,464**	**115%**

Data Source: Organisation Internationale des Constructeurs d'Automobiles (OICA) production statistics.

EXHIBIT 50.9 | Stand-Alone Valuation (dollars in millions)

PPG Industries

Metric	Actual 2011	Projected	
		2012E	2013E
Sales growth (%)	10.9%	4.1%	4.3%
EBIT margin (Pretax)	11.2%	11.0%	12.0%
EV/EBITDA 2012 (x)	7.3		

DuPont Performance Coatings

Metric	2011A	Closing	2012E	2013E	Projected 2014E	2015E	2016E
Sales growth (%)	12.5%		4.0%	4.0%	4.0%	4.0%	4.0%
Depreciation and amortization	$104		$115	$118	$122	$125	$130
EBIT margin (Pretax)	6.3%		10.0%	10.0%	10.0%	10.0%	10.0%
Tax rate[1]	25%		25%	25%	25%	25%	25%
Capital expenditures	$80		$115	$122	$132	$144	$150
Net working capital (%)			15.0%	15.0%	15.0%	15.0%	15.0%
Terminal EBITDA multiple (x)[2]							7.0
Debt/EBITDA 2012 (x)	N/A						
Debt							
Blended interest rate on debt	6.75%						
Unlevered cost of equity[3]	11.2%						

EXHIBIT 50.9 | Stand-Alone Valuation (*continued*)

		Closing	2011A	2012E	2013E	2014E	2015E	2016E
	APV Analysis							
Net sales			$4,281	$4,452	$4,630	$4,816	$5,008	$5,208
EBITDA			$372	$560	$581	$604	$626	$651
Depreciation and amortization			$104	$115	$118	$122	$125	$130
Pretax operating income (EBIT)			$268	$445	$463	$482	$501	$521
Interest expense				$0	$0	$0	$0	$0
Earnings before taxes				$445	$463	$482	$501	$521
Taxes				($111)	($116)	($120)	($125)	($130)
Net income				$334	$347	$361	$376	$391
Increase in net working capital				($26)	($27)	($28)	($29)	($30)
Capital expenditures				($115)	($122)	($132)	($144)	($150)
Residual (levered) cash flow				$308	$317	$323	$327	$341
Unlevered free cash flow (FCF)				$308	$317	$323	$327	$341
Terminal value								$4,738
Unlevered FCF, including TV				$308	$317	$323	$327	$5,079
Enterprise value (EV)		$3,970						
Interest tax shield								
PV tax shield		$3,970						
EV with tax shield								

Data Sources: Historical information for DPC is from DuPont company Databooks. Projections are case writer estimates. PPG's enterprise value is based on prices at the end of January 2012. PPG's projections are based on Buckingham Research Group analyst report, *PPG Industries: "Other" Industrial Coatings Review*, May 21, 2012.

Notes to stand-alone model:

[1] DPC's estimated average tax rate of 25% is lower than the U.S. marginal corporate tax rate as a result of international operations taxed at lower rates.

[2] Assumed forward exit multiple for Terminal Value is based on projected EBITDA growth in 2017 and is below PPG's multiple because of lower margins and slightly lower growth.

[3] Unlevered Cost of Equity (k_u) is based on PPG's estimated unlevered beta of 1.2, a normalized 4% long-term U.S. Treasury rate, and a 6% market risk premium.

EXHIBIT 50.10 | Financial Characteristics of Potential Strategic Buyers (fiscal-year-end values in millions, except multiples and percentages)

	Market Capitalization 12/31/2011	Revenues	EBITDA	Total Debt	Total Debt/ EBITDA	5-Year Stock Performance	1-Year Stock Performance
Akzo Nobel N.V.	$11,837	$18,972	$2,311	4,585	2.0x	NA	−21.0%
BASF SE	$66,702	$95,482	$15,205	16,972	1.1x	−5.4%	−12.8%
PPG industries	$12,893	$14,885	$2,141	3,682	1.7x	30.0%	−0.7%
Sherwin-Williams	$9,263	$8,766	$956	993	1.0x	40.4%	6.6%
Valspar	$3,637	$3,953	$513	1,057	2.1x	41.0%	13.0%

Data Source: Financial data are from Capital IQ; stock price performance is based on CRSP data.

EXHIBIT 50.11 | Buyout Deals

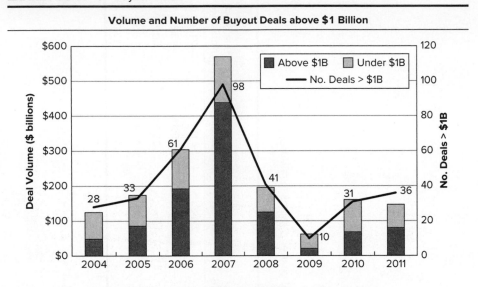

Volume and Number of Buyout Deals above $1 Billion

Debt, Equity, and Purchase Price Multiples for Buyout Deals

Medians	2004	2005	2006	2007	2008	2009	2010	2011
Total Debt/EBITDA	5.3	5.0	5.9	7.6	4.4	3.3	4.6	6.2
Equity/EBITDA	2.3	3.2	3.1	1.2	5.0	3.2	2.7	2.8
Purchase Price/EBITDA	7.6	8.2	9.0	8.8	9.4	6.5	7.3	9.0

Data Source: PitchBook, *Annual Private Equity Breakdown 2012.*

EXHIBIT 50.12   I   Private Equity Exits

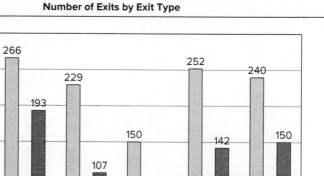

Number of Exits by Exit Type

☐ Strategic Buyer   ▨ PE-Backed IPO   ▨ Secondary Buyouts

Exit Multiple by Exit Type

Medians	2006	2007	2008	2009	2010	2011	Average
Strategic buyer	9.5	10.9	9.5	8.0	8.5	8.7	9.2
PE-backed IPOs	5.8	11.7	10.8	7.4	7.2	5.1	8.0
Secondary buyouts	11.0	6.9	9.8	12.4	9.4	9.6	9.9

Data Source: PitchBook and Grant Thornton, *Private Equity Exits Report, 2012 Annual Edition.*

Outreach Networks: First Venture Round

Phillip P. "Pete" Perez, CEO and founder of OutReach Networks, Inc. (ORN), was evaluating an offer in November 2011 that he had recently received from a venture capital (VC) firm. Perez had founded ORN in 2007 and had served as its CEO ever since. Prior to that, he had worked as a wireless engineer at Qualcomm, Inc., where, while researching broadband connectivity and signal strength issues, he had discovered an unlicensed radio frequency (RF) spectrum that could extend wireless signals across a much broader area than the licensed spectrum could. He believed he could design a product that could tap this unlicensed spectrum and provide Internet access to areas that currently had little or no access. With this idea in mind, he had cashed out his Qualcomm options and founded ORN.

Currently, he was ORN's largest stockholder and owned 75% of the company. The VC firm, Everest Partners, had a successful track record developing technology companies; it had offered to invest $30 million, which would significantly enhance ORN's ability to grow and pursue several promising market opportunities that would otherwise take far longer to develop. While Perez was pleased to have the offer, he was concerned that the valuation offered by the VC firm was too low. Everest Partners had offered $30 million in exchange for 30% of the company. He believed that amount of funding should be worth no more than 15% of the company based on its profitability and success without VC funding.

The Company

OutReach Networks sold wireless networking products and solutions for the unlicensed RF spectrum, including high-performance radios, antennas, and management tools. It targeted populations that had little or no Internet access. In 2011, it was estimated that only about 25% of the world's population had access to the Internet. Even in developed countries such as the United States, where approximately 70% of the population could access broadband, the remaining 30% had limited or no access. Providing universal

---

access was feasible from a technological perspective, and after 15 years, urban areas had achieved a high degree of access, but reaching the rest of the population had proven difficult. In developed economies, the main challenge was boosting the speeds of installed telephone and cable connections, whereas in emerging economies, the challenge was reaching users in any form.

The so-called "last mile" from core networks to individual homes had been bridged by a range of proposed technologies, each expensive to implement. Traditionally, service providers had favored wired networking solutions to connect end users to the Internet. Over time, consumers' bandwidth needs increased and fiber had replaced copper, leading to expensive buildouts and long lead times. These two factors had limited the deployment of wired access networks in underserved and underpenetrated areas in both developed and emerging markets. As a result, wireless solutions were gaining traction as a cost-effective way to address last-mile connectivity in these markets.

Using commodity hardware coupled with proprietary software, ORN solutions greatly reduced the up-front capital expenditures required to build out a last-mile network, enabling Internet service to be provided to a wide range of currently underserved or poorly served markets. Traditionally, Wi-Fi carriers had been large, deep-pocketed companies (e.g., AT&T, Comcast), but ORN's products had sparked the growth of entrepreneurial wireless Internet service providers (WISPs). Typically, a WISP started because broadband connectivity was needed where it currently did not exist or the existing service was poor or expensive. Decreases in equipment costs had lowered barriers to entry, allowing these entrepreneurial-minded ISPs to enter. WISPs needed elevated sites for their equipment as well as access to commercial-grade Internet. With that, and about $5,000 of ORN gear, individuals with basic networking skills could build a network that covered 100 subscribers. WISP customers could realize 15 Mbps to 20 Mbps download speeds, compared to DSL, which topped out at 3 Mbps to 4 Mbps. It was estimated that with as few as 20 customers spending $50 per month on service, the hardware cost, including the customer premise equipment (CPE), could be covered in the first five months of operations.

The idea for ORN grew out of Perez's experience at Qualcomm, where he researched issues of broadband connectivity and the strength of wireless signals. He learned through this process that the U.S. Federal Communications Commission (FCC) permitted Wi-Fi signals ranging from 13 dBm to over 20 dBm, which greatly increased the effective range of an 802.11 signal.[1] The 802.11 signal utilized spectrum formally known as the industrial, scientific, and medical bands and fell in the unlicensed RF spectrum.[2] It had two main advantages—it was free and available in ample supply. Because WISPs did not have to rent access infrastructure or obtain and resell service from incumbent operators, they avoided having to negotiate costly access from these providers and were able to achieve a highly competitive cost structure. These advantages resulted in a growing community of WISPs, which fueled the use of ORN equipment.

---

[1] The abbreviation "dBm" stood for for the power ratio in decibels (dB) referenced to one milliwatt (m). It was used in radio, microwave, and fiber optic networks as a convenient measure of the absolute power of signal strength.

[2] 802.11 wireless networks used electromagnetic (EM) waves to transmit data between devices with a specific frequency. There was a wide spectrum of EM waves that included visible light, infrared, ultraviolet, and radio waves. This unlicensed part of the radio spectrum was used by 802.11. Source: Elizabeth Dafne Di Rocco, "Physics of 802.11 Wireless Networks," University of Ljubljana, May 13, 2009.

In 2007, when Perez realized no one was using this spectrum commercially, he cashed out $50,000 in Qualcomm options and designed a radio card that extended the range of Wi-Fi equipment. Over the course of 2008, he experimented with several prototypes designed to overcome significant performance challenges to signal quality (e.g., dynamic spectrum noise, device interference, and outdoor obstacles). Revenues had grown exponentially from $9 million in 2009, the company's first full year of operations, to $63 million in 2011 (**Exhibit 51.1**).

Unusual for a start-up, ORN had been profitable from the beginning for several reasons. First, the company employed an indirect sales model selling through various channels that responded to demand from a growing community of WISP users. This eliminated the cost of direct-sales efforts, such as building a sales force, and limited its marketing costs. As a testament to its lean operations, the company had fewer than 100 total employees in 2011. As a result, operating margins in the vicinity of 30% had been achieved starting in 2010 and were projected to remain at that level in future years. The downside of this was that ORN had limited visibility into future sales, making it more difficult to predict future operating results and limited means to spur sales should the need arise. The second reason for early profitability was that ORN's simple product designs allowed for outsourcing of their manufacture, eliminating large outlays for property, plant, and equipment and reducing capital expenditures.

Funding Opportunity

Due to ORN's profitability, Perez had never sought VC funding. That was not to say that he was unfamiliar with venture capital. Early on, when he was developing his prototype, he presented at several VC conferences for young companies. At one such conference, he met Jeff Chalmers of Everest Partners, who had more than 20 years' experience investing in IT companies. Chalmers had been intrigued with ORN's concept from the beginning. In 2008, he offered to invest in ORN, but Perez had refused the offer. The two had kept in touch over the years and, recently, Chalmers made the case again for VC funding. He proposed that Everest Partners invest $30 million in ORN in exchange for 30% of the company. Only 31% of the company's revenues came from sales in North America, and in the future, its growth was expected to be in markets outside of North America (**Figure 51.1**).

FIGURE 51.1 | Geographic distribution of 2011 revenues.

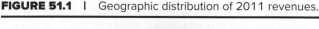

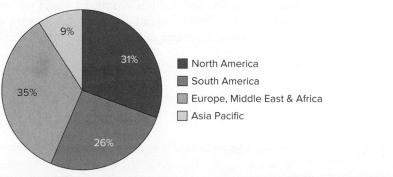

Data Source: Company documents.

The additional funds would allow ORN to scale its operations and penetrate international markets more quickly. Based on discussions with Perez and his CFO, Chalmers had prepared a set of projections for what ORN could achieve with the funding and Everest Partners' help (**Exhibit 51.1**). Chalmers also put together a set of publicly traded comparables—ones he thought any investor might look at in judging ORN's value (**Exhibit 51.2**). Because he followed this sector closely, he was aware of several private companies that were developing products similar to those ORN was working on. Although he believed ORN had superior technology, he stressed to Perez the need to scale quickly and create a more formidable barrier to future entrants.

Aside from funding, given the firm's success to date, Chalmers thought an initial public offering (IPO) might be feasible in the next several years, in which case the company's lean management team would raise investor concerns about the loss of key personnel. Chalmers offered that Everest Partners, and its large network of contacts, could be helpful in building out ORN's management team. ORN also had developed state-of-the-art equipment but had not been aggressive in patenting its technology and proprietary software. Chalmers suggested that before going public, the company should seek to protect its intellectual property, and Everest Partners had experience to draw on in doing this.

Although he had turned down VC funding earlier, at this point in his firm's development, Perez thought it might be valuable, and he saw merit in many of Chalmers's points. As the firm had grown, he found himself increasingly stretched in many directions and worried he might not be prioritizing his efforts effectively. ORN was closely held: Perez held 75% of the firm, CFO Ray Reynolds held 15%, and the remaining 10% was held by other senior executives and employees.[3] His small management team had been successful at the firm's current scale, but it would have to grow to meet future demands. He knew by reputation that Everest Partners would be the lead investor and actively assist ORN. Everest Partners' investment criteria also fit well with his own view and goals for ORN. It looked for: (1) a unique proprietary advantage, (2) a large market opportunity, (3) creativity, (4) scalability and defensibility, and (5) management that wanted to change the world.

Despite his good relationship with Chalmers and Everest Partners, Perez had trouble understanding how it could demand 30% of his company—even allowing for the fact that VCs typically looked for a 40% to 60% compounded return. When he expressed this concern, Chalmers responded that $30 million was large in relation to a typical Series A funding and that this investment would represent a significant portion of the fund's $350 million in capital. He noted that over the previous two years, first-round investments in IT companies had averaged around $5 million.

---

[3]These percentages were based on the company having 50 million shares of equity outstanding in November 2011.

The Decision

Pete Perez wondered how Everest Partners had arrived at its offer for ORN. Based on his own calculations, he thought a 15% stake would be more appropriate, especially in light of the profitable nature and strong growth prospects of the company. But even if he heavily discounted the projected free cash flows (to 50% of their projected values), he obtained a much higher valuation for ORN than Everest Partners had offered.

What rationale had Everest Partners used in making its offer? Was it just trying to "squeeze" him? Did the low valuation simply reflect the industry norm? Would another VC firm yield a higher offer? Still, Perez thought, everything had its price, and at some point, it gets to be real money—in this case his own. Should he accept Chalmers's offer, try to negotiate a higher valuation, approach other VC firms, or turn down the offer and VC funding altogether?

EXHIBIT 51.1 | Financial Performance and Projections (dollars in millions)

		2009	2010	2011	2012P	2013P	2014P	2015P	2016P	2017P
Revenue		$9.00	$22.00	$63.00	$137.00	$198.00	$260.00	$335.00	$425.00	$525.00
Year-on-year growth			*144%*	*186%*	*117%*	*45%*	*31%*	*29%*	*27%*	*24%*
COGS		$4.20	$10.90	$37.20	$82.40	$117.10	$153.40	$194.30	$242.30	$290.00
Gross Profit		$4.80	$11.10	$25.80	$54.60	$80.90	$106.60	$140.70	$182.70	$235.00
Operating Expenses		$2.79	$4.32	$8.50	$15.76	$20.78	$29.90	$41.85	$57.35	$77.15
EBITDA		$2.01	$6.78	$17.30	$38.84	$60.12	$76.70	$98.85	$125.35	$157.85
Depreciation and Amortization		$0.05	$0.11	$0.32	$0.69	$0.99	$1.30	$1.68	$2.13	$2.63
EBIT		$1.97	$6.67	$16.99	$38.16	$59.13	$75.40	$97.18	$123.23	$155.23
EBIT margin		*21.83%*	*30.32%*	*26.96%*	*27.85%*	*29.86%*	*29.00%*	*29.01%*	*28.99%*	*29.57%*
Interest Expense		$0.00	$0.00	$0.00	$0.00	$0.00	$0.00	$0.00	$0.00	$0.00
Profit before Taxes		$1.97	$6.67	$16.99	$38.16	$59.13	$75.40	$97.18	$123.23	$155.23
Taxes	30%	$0.59	$2.00	$5.10	$11.45	$17.74	$22.62	$29.15	$36.97	$46.57
Net Income		$1.38	$4.67	$11.89	$26.71	$41.39	$52.78	$68.02	$86.26	$108.66
Capital Expenditures					$1.00	$1.45	$1.90	$2.45	$3.10	$3.83
Increase in Net Working Capital					$6.00	$8.67	$11.39	$14.67	$18.61	$22.99
Free Cash Flow					$20.39	$32.26	$40.80	$52.58	$66.67	$84.46

Source: Case writer estimates.

EXHIBIT 51.2 | Comparable Company Valuation Data (dollars in millions)

Company Name (Ticker)	Market Capitalization	Revenue	Revenues, 1Yr Growth %	EBITDA Margin %	Total Debt/ Capital %	TEV/Forward EBITDA	Forward P/E	Beta
Acme Packet, Inc. (APKT)	$2,244	$295	45.6%	30.1%	—	13.7x	24.3x	1.50
Aruba Networks, Inc. (ARUN)	$2,258	$433	48.2%	3.0%	—	13.3x	31.5x	1.95
Aviat Networks, Inc. (AVNW)	$108	$463	3.9%	0.2%	7.6%	4.2x	21.3x	1.35
Cisco Systems (CSCO)	$100,206	$43,724	4.7%	25.3%	26.3%	6.4x	10.3x	1.20
Mean	$26,204	$11,229	25.6%	14.6%	17.0%	9.4x	21.8x	1.50
Median	$2,251	$448	25.2%	14.1%	17.0%	9.9x	22.8x	1.43

Notes: Valuation multiples as of November 2011. The 10-year U.S Treasury rate was assumed to be 5% and the market risk premium 6.0%.

Company Descriptions:

Acme Packet provided session delivery network solutions that enabled the delivery of voice, video, data, and unified communications services and applications across Internet protocol (IP) networks.

Aruba Networks, incorporated in 2002, was a provider of next-generation network access solutions for the mobile enterprise. Its products unified wired and wireless network infrastructures into one seamless access solution for corporate headquarters, mobile business professionals, and remote workers.

Aviat Networks designed, manufactured, and sold wireless networking products, solutions, and services in North America and internationally. It offered point-to-point digital microwave transmission systems for first- and last-mile access, middle mile/backhaul, and long-distance trunking applications. It also provided broadband wireless access base stations and customer premises equipment.

Cisco Systems designed, manufactured, and sold IP-based networking and other products related to the communications and IT industry worldwide. It offered routers that interconnected public and private IP networks for mobile, data, voice, and video applications, and switching products, which provided connectivity to end users, workstations, IP phones, access points, and servers.

Data source: Capital IQ.

Sanofi-Aventis's Tender Offer for Genzyme

On the foggy morning of October 5, 2010, Henri Termeer, the chairman and CEO of Genzyme Corporation, drove to the firm's headquarters in Cambridge, Massachusetts. Termeer usually spent his early mornings working from the indoor garden on top of the building, but on that day he went straight to his office, grabbing a cup of coffee on his way. One thing was on his mind—the letter he had received from the CEO of Sanofi-Aventis (Sanofi) announcing the company's intention to commence a tender offer for Genzyme (**Exhibit 52.1**).

Termeer had been Genzyme's CEO for more than 25 years, leading its growth from an entrepreneurial venture to one of the country's top five biotechnology firms. Yet the past two years presented a significant test. Genzyme was just recovering from an unexpected contamination in 2009 at its major production facility in Allston, Massachusetts, which had led to shutting down the plant and limiting the supply of life-sustaining drugs for Genzyme's patients. As a result of the economic and reputational damages, the company's stock had plummeted before rebounding as a result of the news of the tender offer (**Exhibit 52.2**). When compared to the industry and the overall stock market during the previous decade, however, the stock had performed very well (**Exhibit 52.3**). The recent downturn in the stock price had attracted activist investors, which resulted in Genzyme entering into a cooperation agreement with Relational Investors and subsequently fending off a proxy battle with Carl Icahn.[1] But Termeer fully understood that together the two activists controlled a substantive position of Genzyme shares and wanted to exit their positions at a gain (**Exhibit 52.4**).

---

[1]See Rick Green, Kenneth Eades, and Pedro Matos, "Genzyme and Relational Investors: Science and Business Collide?," UVA-F-1660 (Charlottesville, VA: Darden Business Publishing, 2011).

This public-sourced case was prepared by Dmitriy Aleyev (MBA '14) and Chong Xu (MBA '14), under the supervision of Kenneth M. Eades, Professor of Business Administration; and Pedro Matos, Associate Professor of Business Administration. It was written as a basis for class discussion rather than to illustrate effective or ineffective handling of an administrative situation. Copyright © 2014 by the University of Virginia Darden School Foundation, Charlottesville, VA. All rights reserved. *To order copies, send an e-mail to* sales@dardenbusinesspublishing.com. *No part of this publication may be reproduced, stored in a retrieval system, used in a spreadsheet, or transmitted in any form or by any means—electronic, mechanical, photocopying, recording, or otherwise—without the permission of the Darden School Foundation.*

Sanofi, the leading French pharmaceutical company, had approached Genzyme as a potential acquisition at the start of the summer. After a few rounds of negotiating, Termeer and his board publicly rejected Sanofi's cash offer of $69 per share on August 29, 2010.[2] The letter from Sanofi's CEO conveyed frustration with Termeer's unwillingness "to engage in constructive discussions" (**Exhibit 52.1**) and announced that Sanofi would be circumventing Termeer by taking the $69 tender offer directly to Genzyme's shareholders.

A biotech veteran, Termeer was familiar with M&A activity in the industry. In fact, Genzyme itself had grown to become a diversified business through a series of acquisitions (**Exhibit 52.5**).[3] A fervent believer in Genzyme and its mission, Termeer thought the Sanofi offer significantly undervalued Genzyme for a number of reasons. First, the market was just beginning to see the evidence that Genzyme had turned the corner on its production problems. Also, Termeer knew that there were many promising new drugs in the company's pipeline that would add to an already successful portfolio of drugs. A meeting of Genzyme's board of directors was scheduled for October 7, 2010, and he needed to prepare a proposal for Genzyme's response to the tender offer.

Genzyme

Genzyme began in 1981 with the goal of developing drugs that would cure enzyme deficiency conditions that caused severe suffering for those affected. Because these diseases typically affected a small percentage of the world's population, drugs used to treat them were considered to be "orphan drugs." In the United States, orphan status was given to drugs that cured diseases affecting fewer than 200,000 people. In order to give pharmaceutical companies an incentive to develop drugs for such rare diseases, the Orphan Drug Act (1983) gave orphan drugs distinct legal and economic advantages.[4]

Genzyme was one of the first biotechnology companies to exploit the benefits provided by the Orphan Drug Act. Since its founding, the company started developing the drugs against rare genetic diseases such as lysosomal storage diseases (LSDs), in which patients lacked enzymes that removed and recycled proteins, causing harmful deposits to accumulate in organs. Because of the limited number of patients, the extensive R&D required, and the complex manufacturing process, the cost of these drugs often exceeded $200,000 per patient per year.[5] For example, Genzyme's leading product

[2]"Timeline: Sanofi's Quest for U.S. Biotech Genzyme," Reuters, February 15, 2011 http://www.reuters.com/article/2011/02/16/us-genzyme-sanofi-timeline-idUSTRE71E62U20110216 (accessed Oct. 12, 2015).

[3]Geoffrey Gagnon, "So, This Is What a Biotech Tycoon Looks Like," *Boston*, June 2008.

[4]All drugs were granted a 20-year patent protection in the United States, but that protection began as soon as the patent was filed. Due to the time-intensive process required by the FDA to approve a new drug, many drugs reached the market with only a few years of patent protection remaining. Orphan drugs were granted an exclusive right that guaranteed seven years of selling the drug without competition. In addition, orphan drug companies received a 50% tax credit for expenditures incurred during the clinical testing phase. See Enrique Seoane-Vasquez, Rosa Rodriguez-Monguio, Sheryl L. Szeinbach, and Jay Visaria, "Incentives for Orphan Drug Research and Development in the United States," *Orphanet Journal of Rare Diseases* 3, 33 (2008).

[5]Matthew Herper, "The World's Most Expensive Drugs," *Forbes*, February 22, 2010.

was Cerezyme, an enzyme replacement therapy used to treat Gaucher's disease. Gaucher's was a rare disease (affecting 1 out of 100,000 people) that could be life-threatening and was caused by a deficiency in the enzyme glucocerebrosidase. This deficiency led to a variety of symptoms, including anemia, spleen and liver enlargement, and bone deterioration. Though people with a mild case could have normal life expectancies, children whose illness began during infancy generally did not live longer than two years. Originally approved by the United States Food and Drug Administration (FDA) in 1991, Cerezyme generated $1.23 billion in sales in 2008 (**Exhibit 52.6**), almost 30% of Genzyme's total revenue, prior to the 2009 manufacturing problems.[6]

The strategy of focusing on rare diseases had worked exceptionally well for Genzyme. By 2009, the company had become the third-largest biotech company in the world, employing more than 11,000 people and selling drugs in more than 90 countries. With annual revenue of over $4 billion in 2009, the company's market capitalization was above $13 billion by year-end. The company's stock price had been increasing since the summer amid shareholder-friendly initiatives, including the recent sale of a genetics unit for $921 million and the announcement of a share buyback program.

Genzyme divided its business into five reporting units (see **Exhibit 52.6**): Genetic Diseases (GD), which included treatments against genetic and chronic diseases such as LSDs; Cardiometabolic and Renal (CR), which included treatments against cardiovascular and chronic renal disease; Biosurgery (BI), which included biotherapeutics and biomaterial products used in surgical areas; Hematologic Oncology (HO), which included treatments for cancer and multiple sclerosis (MS); and Other Products, which included diagnostic products, transplant products, and bulk pharmaceuticals.

In addition to the products in the market, Genzyme also had a robust pipeline of products under development (**Exhibit 52.7**). Some of the late-stage potential drugs were widely considered to have very high market potential. For example, an MS drug called alemtuzumab (previously marketed under the name Campath) showed promise to become the most efficacious drug against this inflammatory central-nervous-system disease, and some analysts suggested it had the potential, upon FDA approval, to bring more than $12 billion in revenue through 2020.

Genzyme's impressive sales growth during the last two decades suffered a setback on March 2, 2009, when Genzyme disclosed an FDA warning letter that identified manufacturing deficiencies at the company's Allston plant. To address the problem, Genzyme had to shut down the plant in June 2009 to clean up a virus contamination. The stoppage resulted in a shortage of Cerezyme and Fabrazyme, two drugs that accounted for more than 40% of Genzyme revenue in 2008. As the cleanup operation dragged on, the supply of these two drugs continued to suffer. This forced doctors to ration these life-saving drugs to patients, which in turn caused numerous patient complaints and sour patient relationships. As a result of the cleanup costs, the shutdown, and lost sales associated with the contamination, Genzyme's sales growth was arrested and operating income suffered (see **Exhibit 52.8** for Genzyme's financials).

---

[6]Genzyme SEC form 10-K, 2009.

The Pharmaceutical Industry

The pharmaceutical industry developed and marketed drugs licensed as medications. Given the importance of proper research and safety measures, the industry was heavily regulated. In the United States, the drug approval process was tightly controlled by the FDA. **Exhibit 52.9** details the typical drug R&D and FDA approval process.

In order to successfully complete an FDA approval process, every drug needed to go through years or decades of intensive scientific laboratory research. After being identified as a worthy candidate, the drug compound was first tested on animals during its preclinical stage, and then tested on human subjects in subsequent clinical studies. Clinical trials usually ran for several years, and only about 5% to 10% of drugs ultimately received FDA approval after the trials.[7] Not surprisingly, the pharmaceutical industry's R&D spending as a percentage of revenues was among the highest of any U.S. industry group.[8] The lengthy drug-development process required not only significant costs but also precious time. Most drugs were protected by patents, but the patent application was filed very early in the drug-discovery process, and it took, on average, four to five years to get patent approval. Although the typical patent life was 20 years, by the time a drug went through the preclinical, clinical, and FDA approval stages, there were usually fewer than 10 years of patent life left to market the drug.[9]

Given the long development cycle, high R&D costs, and risks associated with the high failure rate, many companies adopted a blockbuster-drug model by targeting diseases and drug compounds that were more likely to bring in big sales quickly. After spending billions of dollars during the decade-long R&D process, pharmaceutical companies needed to recoup their investments. Increasingly, pharmaceutical companies sought drugs that had the potential of $1 billion or more in sales—the so-called blockbusters. For example, Lipitor, the drug that earned the highest revenue in 2009, accounted for $11.4 billion or 23% of Pfizer's $50 billion total revenues.[10]

The pharmaceutical industry had a significant amount of M&A activity in the previous decade. A number of companies, including Genzyme, turned to M&A to acquire promising drug compounds from companies that often did not have the resources to go through the FDA approval process and marketing (see **Exhibit 52.10** for recent major M&A deals in the biotech and pharmaceutical industry).

The M&A activity in the pharmaceutical industry had picked up in recent years in large part due to the "patent cliff" phenomenon. Under the Drug Price Competition and Patent Term Restoration Act of 1984, generic drug makers could file an application with the FDA to replicate a branded drug once its patent had expired. Additionally, the

---

[7]Michael Hay, Jesse Rosenthal, David Thomas, and John Craighead, "BIO/BioMedTracker Clinical Trial Success Rates Study," February 15, 2011.

[8]Booz & Co., "The Global Innovation 1000: Comparison of R&D Spending by Regions and Industries," 2013.

[9]Orphan drugs were granted additional tax credits as well as a seven-year exclusivity period, which began only after the drug was granted FDA approval.

[10]"Pfizer Reports Fourth-Quarter and Full-Year 2009 Results; Provides 2010 Financial Guidance and 2012 Financial Targets," Business Wire, February 3, 2010, http://www.businesswire.com/news/home/20100203005880/en/Pfizer-UK-Regulatory-Announcement-Pfizer-Reports-Fourth-Quarter#.VCmxsfldV8F (accessed Sept. 29, 2014).

Abbreviated New Drug Application allowed a generic drug to be approved in as few as six months, giving generic drug makers the ability to start producing a drug as soon as its patent protection expired. Without the burden of a lengthy R&D period, generic drug manufacturers could charge a much lower price than the original manufacturer, which enabled them to cannibalize as much as 90% of a pharmaceutical company's sales.[11] As a result, when a blockbuster drug approached its patent expiration, the company was said to be approaching a patent cliff. As of 2010, almost all the "Big Pharma" companies faced patent cliffs. For example, Pfizer was facing patent expiration for Lipitor in November 2011 (see **Exhibit 52.11** for top drugs facing patent expiration).

Sanofi-Aventis

Sanofi, based in Paris, France, traced its roots back to the 18th century, when Laboratoires Midy was founded in 1718 by a family of pharmacists. The modern Sanofi was founded in 1973 by Elf Aquitaine, a French oil company, which took control of the Labaz Group, a pharmaceutical company. In 1999, Sanofi merged with Synthélabo, a pharmaceutical company controlled by the French cosmetics group L'Oréal. In 2004, Sanofi-Synthélabo merged with Aventis, which was itself formed by the combination of Rhône-Poulenc and Hoechst in 1999, to create Sanofi.[12] By 2009, Sanofi had annual sales of more than EUR29 billion,[13] making it the fourth-largest pharmaceutical company in the world and the second-largest pharmaceutical company in Europe. The company had more than 105,000 employees and sales in more than 170 countries. Emerging-markets sales were expanding and accounted for more than 25% of sales.[14]

Sanofi mainly operated in two segments: pharmaceuticals and vaccines. The pharmaceuticals division contributed more than EUR25 billion of 2009 revenues. In pharmaceuticals, Sanofi was a major player in the diabetes market with the world's leading insulin product, Lantus. Other blockbusters included chemotherapy drug Taxotere, cardiovascular disease drug Plavix, antiplatelet agent Lovenox, sleep disorder medicine Ambien CR, multiple sclerosis drug Copaxone, and other internal medicines such as Allegra, an antihistamine. Sanofi was also a world leader in vaccines through its vaccine division, Sanofi Pasteur (EUR3 billion in sales in 2009). Lastly, Sanofi participated in a number of industry partnerships and joint ventures, such as an animal-health business with Merck that produced household names such as Frontline (which accounted for more than EUR2 billion in sales in 2009).[15]

Just like many other major pharmaceutical companies in the first two decades of the twenty-first century, Sanofi started to feel the effects of its looming patent cliffs. According to Deutsche Bank Securities Inc., as much as 45% of Sanofi's 2009 revenue

---

[11]Steve Christ, "Big Pharma's Worst Nightmare," *Wealth Daily*, July 30, 2011, http://www.wealthdaily.com/articles/weekend-big-pharmas-worst-nightmare/3176 (accessed Sept. 29, 2014).

[12]"Our History," Sanofi-Aventis website, http://en.sanofi.com/our_company/history/history.aspx (accessed Sept. 29, 2014).

[13]EUR = euros.

[14]Sanofi-Aventis SEC form 20-F, 2009.

[15]Sanofi-Aventis SEC form 20-F, 2009.

was at risk of patent expiration by 2015 (see **Exhibit 52.12**).[16] On July 23, 2010, the FDA decided to allow Momenta Pharmaceuticals and Sandoz to sell a generic version of Sanofi's Lovenox anticlotting medicine.[17] This development put additional pressure on Sanofi's new CEO, Chris Viehbacher, to offset the looming patent cliff. Viehbacher was previously a president of GlaxoSmithKline, and his appointment as CEO of Sanofi in December 2008 was a signal for change in a company long controlled by a small group of big French shareholders and homegrown management. Viehbacher, both a Canadian and German citizen, was seen as a sign that Sanofi's board of directors was serious about the lagging sales, poor drug pipeline, and expiring patents issue.

By early 2009, Viehbacher had indicated his intentions to review Sanofi's R&D efforts and pipeline and to seek diversification through M&A deals, actively talking to banks in preparation for a shopping spree.[18] By June 2009, Sanofi had cut 14 of its 65 internal-development programs, paving the way for acquisition of external drugs under development.[19] By the end of 2009, the company has spent $9 billion in acquisitions, most notably a $1.9 billion deal with Chattem, a maker of over-the-counter drugs and cosmetics that was based in Chattanooga, Tennessee.[20] When asked about his strategy, Viehbacher indicated a preference for drugs and treatments that did not rely solely on patents as barriers against competition. "Above all, what I'm looking for is businesses that are not dependent on patents," he told the Associated Press. "This is my fourth patent cliff in my career, and I'm looking to avoid a fifth."[21]

Sanofi Approaches Genzyme

Genzyme had appeared on Sanofi's radar screen as an ideal acquisition target in early 2010 for several reasons. First, the majority of Genzyme's products had patent lives that extended well beyond 2015 (**Exhibit 52.7**), providing relief to Sanofi's patent-cliff position. Biologics drugs were far more complex to produce than the chemical-based drugs produced by most of the large pharmaceutical companies. This complexity effectively extended the patent life, because the drugs were not only difficult to manufacture, but even more difficult to prove equivalent to the originals they copied. Because these drugs targeted specific patient and physician populations, Genzyme's existing relationships with these communities—and their brand recognition—provided additional protection against generic competitors.[22]

---

[16]Robyn Karnauskas, Navdeep Singh, and Colin Bristow, "DB-Biotech: What Fundamentals, Technicals, & Options Tell Us about Genzyme M&A," Deutsche Bank Securities Inc., August 16, 2010.

[17]"FDA Approves First Generic Enoxaparin Sodium Injection," FDA press release, July 23, 2010.

[18]Jeanne Whalen, "Sanofi Will Seek Growth via Small, Midsize Deals," *Wall Street Journal*, February 12, 2009; John Carroll, "Sanofi Prepared to Expand, Diversify with Buyouts," FierceBiotech, February 3, 2009; John Carroll, "Sanofi's Viehbacher to Review his R&D 'Children,'" FierceBiotech, February 12, 2009.

[19]John Carroll, "Viehbacher Readies an Overhaul of Sanofi R&D," FierceBiotech, June 24, 2009.

[20]Maureen Martino, "Viehbacher's $9 Billion Shopping Spree," FiercePharma, December 10, 2009.

[21]Tracy Staton, "Why Does Sanofi's CEO Consider 'Patent' a Dirty Word?," FiercePharma, July 30, 2010.

[22]Gina Chon, Anupreeta Das, and Dana Cimilluca, "Sanofi-Aventis Circles Genzyme for Potential Deal," *Wall Street Journal*, July 24, 2010.

Second, a Genzyme acquisition was in line with Sanofi's drive to diversify its business to avoid relying on a few specific disease areas and drugs. With a focus on rare genetic diseases, renal diseases, and MS, Genzyme's product portfolio was very different from Sanofi's, which was more focused on diabetes, vaccines, and oncology.

Third, Genzyme would bring a highly talented U.S. research team and access to Boston's world-leading life-science research universities. As Sanofi's global head of R&D put it, a Genzyme purchase would enable Sanofi to "inherit many years of investments in one transaction."[23]

Fourth, Genzyme's recent stock price provided favorable timing for Sanofi to "buy low." The manufacturing problem that first emerged in early 2009 appeared to still be a drag on Genzyme's stock price. In order to settle a proxy battle with Carl Icahn, Genzyme announced that it would repurchase $2 billion of stock, shed three noncore business units, as well as appoint two Icahn nominees onto Genzyme's board.[24] The settlement was generally viewed favorably; however, the stock was still fluctuating in the mid-$50 range as of June 2010 (**Exhibit 52.2**). After obtaining board seats, an active investor such as Icahn could facilitate the sale of the company, which is why Ichan's involvement in Genzyme was generally viewed as favorable for potential buyers such as Sanofi. But when a deal seemed about to take place and Sanofi put forth its offer of $69 per share in August 2010, Termeer and the rest of Genzyme's board rejected it as insufficient.

The Valuation of Genzyme

After the failed attempt to buy Genzyme from Termeer and the board in August 2010, Sanofi announced on October 5, 2010, that it would make a $69-per-share tender offer directly to Genzyme's shareholders.[25] Termeer remained very optimistic about the future of Genzyme and was not ready to relinquish his company's independence. Although the $69-per-share offer valued the company at $18.5 billion, Termeer continued to view it as low considering the higher stock prices Genzyme enjoyed in 2008. He also thought the company should be worth more in light of its recently launched shareholder-friendly initiatives, Cerezyme and Fabrazyme's return to normal production, and alemtuzumab, its promising new drug for MS.

Termeer was saving the morning to review the valuation of Genzyme. For the previous year, Genzyme had used Credit Suisse and Goldman Sachs as advisors to provide valuation data for a set of biotech companies that served as "market comparables" (**Exhibit 52.13**) as well as information about corporate and government interest rates (**Exhibit 52.14**). The comparables data included commonly used valuation multiples: price-to-earnings ratio (P/E), enterprise-value-to-EBITDA (EV/EBITDA),

[23]Chris V. Nicholson, "French Drug Maker to Buy Genzyme for $20.1 Billion," *New York Times*, February 17, 2011.

[24]Jonathan D. Rockoff and Joann S. Lublin, "Genzyme, Icahn Agree to End Proxy Fight," *Wall Street Journal*, June 10, 2010.

[25]Jessica Hall and James Regan, "Sanofi Makes $18.5 Billion Genzyme Offer Public," Reuters, August 29, 2010; Thomas Gryta, "Genzyme Rejects Sanofi's Overture," *Wall Street Journal*, August 31, 2010.

and enterprise-value-to-sales (EV/S). A recent Sanofi investor presentation argued that the $69-per-share offer was justified when compared to the valuation multiples in the biotech industry (**Exhibit 52.15**) and was also in line with stock price premiums paid in other large biotech transactions (**Exhibit 52.16**).

In addition to the valuation multiples and transaction premiums, Termeer wanted to construct a discounted cash flow analysis to value Genzyme. As a first step, Genzyme's investment bankers had presented the Genzyme finance team with two sets of operating profit (NOPAT) projections: a management scenario (**Exhibit 52.17**) and a market scenario (**Exhibit 52.18**). The market scenario reflected the average estimates of Wall Street analysts and was decidedly less optimistic than the projections from Genzyme management. Much of the difference between the two scenarios was in the pipeline revenues, the vast majority of which was due to alemtuzumab.[26] According to the investor presentation, Sanofi's $69-per-share offer was based on a valuation derived from estimates by Wall Street analysts (**Exhibit 52.19**).

To estimate Genzyme's fundamental value, Termeer and his finance team would need to complete a cash flow forecast and then conduct a discounted cash flow (DCF) analysis. The DCF model would also allow Termeer to show the board of directors the impact of specific line items, such as alemtuzumab revenues, upon the estimate of Genzyme's stock price. Armed with a solid understanding of the value drivers for the company, Termeer believed he and the board would be better positioned to respond to Sanofi's tender offer and potentially convince Sanofi to raise the offer to something closer to Genzyme's true value.

---

[26]Revenues for alemtuzumab were estimated as the expected revenue multiplied by the probability of the drug receiving FDA approval. Only 5% to 10% of drug candidates going into a Phase I clinical trial were able to successfully navigate the entire process, but drugs that reached a Phase III clinical trial, such as alemtuzumab, were assigned a 55% probability of success.

EXHIBIT 52.1 | Sanofi's Tender Offer Letter to Genzyme Shareholders

October 4, 2010
Mr. Henri Termeer
Chairman, President and Chief Executive Officer
Genzyme Corporation
500 Kendall Street
Cambridge, Massachusetts 02142

Dear Henri:

We are disappointed that you remain unwilling to have constructive discussions with us regarding our offer to acquire Genzyme Corporation. We continue to believe that our proposal is compelling for your shareholders and would provide them with immediate and substantial value that reflects the potential of Genzyme's business and pipeline.

Subsequent to making our offer public on August 29, 2010, we met with your largest shareholders owning collectively over 50% of Genzyme's outstanding shares. It was clear from our meetings that your shareholders are supportive of our initiative and, like us, are frustrated with your refusal to have meaningful discussions with us regarding our proposal. Your continued refusal to engage with us in a constructive manner is denying your shareholders an opportunity to receive a substantial premium, to realize immediate liquidity, and to protect against the risks associated with Genzyme's business and operations.

After several months of our repeated requests for a meeting with you, we finally met on September 20, 2010. Unfortunately, this meeting was not productive. In an effort to advance our discussions, I shared a very narrow information request focused on confirming your anticipated manufacturing recovery. Even though we and the market have analyzed and assessed the prospects for alemtuzumab, I proposed a meeting with your commercial team to understand their perspectives on the role alemtuzumab could play in the evolving multiple sclerosis market. You were unwilling to pursue either of these or any other path forward. You were also unwilling to provide us with your perspective on an appropriate valuation for Genzyme.

You have, therefore, left us no alternative but to commence a tender offer and take our offer directly to your shareholders. We strongly believe that our offer price of $69.00 per share in cash is compelling and represents substantial value for Genzyme's shareholders.

This offer represents a premium of 38% over Genzyme's unaffected share price of $49.86 on July 1, 2010, the day prior to the press speculation regarding Sanofi-Aventis' potential acquisition plans for a large US biotech company. It also represents a premium of almost 31% over the one-month historical average share price through July 22, 2010, the day prior to press speculation that Sanofi-Aventis had made an approach to acquire Genzyme.

We believe that a combination of our two businesses would be beneficial to our respective shareholders and employees, and the patients and physicians we serve. Sanofi-Aventis would put its full resources behind Genzyme to invest in developing new treatments, enhance penetration in existing markets and further expand into emerging markets. Sanofi-Aventis is well positioned to help Genzyme address its manufacturing problems. Genzyme would become the global center for excellence for Sanofi-Aventis in rare diseases and this unit would be managed as a stand-alone division under the Genzyme brand, with its own R&D, manufacturing and commercial infrastructure. Genzyme's management and employees would play a key role within Sanofi-Aventis, and the combination would further increase Sanofi-Aventis' presence in the greater Boston area.

It remains our strong preference to work together with you to reach a mutually agreeable transaction. However, given your unwillingness to engage in constructive discussions with us, we had no choice but to commence a tender offer. Given our commitment to this transaction, we will continue to consider all alternatives for consummating an acquisition of Genzyme. We believe it is in the best interests of both companies, and our respective shareholders and other constituencies, to move forward quickly to complete this transaction. We and our advisors are available to meet with you to discuss the terms of our offer and to conclude a transaction expeditiously.

Yours sincerely,

Christopher A. Viehbacher
Chief Executive Officer
Cc: Genzyme Board of Directors

EXHIBIT 52.2 | Genzyme (GENZ) Daily Closing Stock Price and Timeline of Events (October 2008–October 2010) and Market Indexes

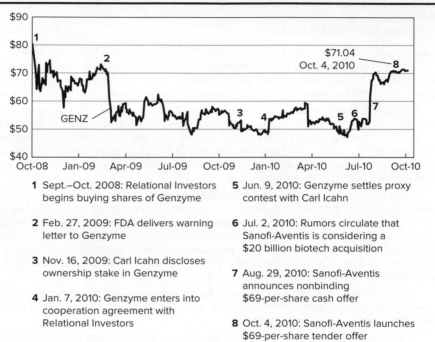

1 Sept.–Oct. 2008: Relational Investors begins buying shares of Genzyme

2 Feb. 27, 2009: FDA delivers warning letter to Genzyme

3 Nov. 16, 2009: Carl Icahn discloses ownership stake in Genzyme

4 Jan. 7, 2010: Genzyme enters into cooperation agreement with Relational Investors

5 Jun. 9, 2010: Genzyme settles proxy contest with Carl Icahn

6 Jul. 2, 2010: Rumors circulate that Sanofi-Aventis is considering a $20 billion biotech acquisition

7 Aug. 29, 2010: Sanofi-Aventis announces nonbinding $69-per-share cash offer

8 Oct. 4, 2010: Sanofi-Aventis launches $69-per-share tender offer

Data Sources: Capital IQ and case writers.

EXHIBIT 52.3 | 10-Year Stock Price Performance of Genzyme (GENZ) versus Sanofi-Aventis (SAN)

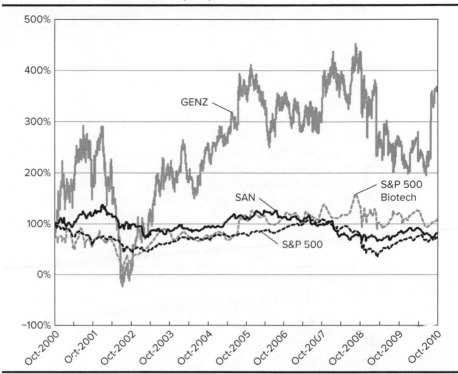

Note: Daily stock price performance is compared to the Standard & Poor's 500 Index (S&P 500) and the Standard & Poor's—Biotechnology Industry Group Index (S&P 500—Biotech). Base 100% = October 1, 2000.

Data Source: Capital IQ.

EXHIBIT 52.4 | Genzyme—Top Institutional Shareholders as of September 30, 2010

	Shares Held	%
BlackRock	15,206,690	6.0%
Icahn Capital	13,100,000	5.1%
ClearBridge Investments	11,321,909	4.4%
Relational Investors	10,606,248	4.2%
Vanguard	9,578,008	3.8%
State Street Global Advisors	9,527,545	3.7%
Invesco	6,322,453	2.5%
Sands Capital Management	6,306,517	2.5%
Fidelity Investments	5,649,165	2.2%
UBS Global Asset Management	5,061,493	2.0%
Wellington Management Company	4,951,537	1.9%
SAC Capital Advisors	4,889,476	1.9%
York Capital Management	4,629,908	1.8%
Total shares outstanding:	254,800,000	

Data Source: SEC form 13-F filing by each institution.

EXHIBIT 52.5 | Genzyme's M&A Activity, 1997–2009

Date	Value (in millions of dollars)	Company Acquired	Drug or Business Acquired	Segment
1997	112	PharmaGenics, Inc.	Created Genzyme molecular oncology	HO
2000	1,284	GelTex	Obtained RenaGel (formerly a joint venture)	CR
2000	875	Bio Matrix, Inc.	Became Genzyme Biosurgery division	BI
2001	17	Focal Inc.	Surgical biomaterials	BI
2003	596	SangStat Medical Corp.	Immune system treatment—Thymoglobulin	Other
2004	1,030	ILEX Oncology, Inc.	Cancer drugs—Campath and Clolar	HO
2005	659	Bone Care Int'l	Treatment of kidney disease—Hectorol	CR
2005	50	Verigen AG	Cartilage repair—MACI (launch in 2012)	BI
2005	12	Avigen	AV201—Parkinson's disease (launch in 2016)	GD
2006	589	AnorMED	Mozobil—stem cell transplant (approved 12/2008)	HO
2007	350	Bioenvision, Inc.	Evoltra (launch 2010–13)	HO
2007	53	Diagnostic Chemicals	Diagnostic division	Other
2008	1,900	Isis Pharmaceuticals	Mipomersen—cholesterol drug (launch in 2013)	Other
2009	350	Bayer Schering Pharma	Rights to Campath, Fludara, and Leukine	HO

Data Sources: LexisNexis, "Genzyme Corporation" Mergers and Acquisitions; Genzyme Corporation SEC 10-K filings, 2000–2007.

EXHIBIT 52.6 | Genzyme—Revenues by Segment

	2009 (in thousands of dollars)	% 2009 Total Revenues	2008 (in thousands of dollars)	% 2008 Total Revenues	% YoY Change
Genetic Diseases (GD): The core business of the company, focused on products to treat patients with genetic and other chronic debilitating diseases					
• **Cerezyme**: Enzyme replacement therapy for type 1 Gaucher's disease; launched in 1995	$ 793,024	18.9%	$1,238,977	29.5%	–36.0%
• **Fabrazyme**: Enzyme replacement therapy for patients with the inherited Fabry disease; launched in 2001	429,690	10.2%	494,260	11.8%	–13.1%
• **Myozyme**: Lysosomal glycogen-specific enzyme for use in patients with infantile-onset of Pompe disease; launched in 2006	324,545	7.7%	296,176	7.1%	9.6%
• **Aldurazyme**: For treatment of Mucopolysaccharidosis I (MPS I), a deficiency of a lysosomal enzyme; launched in 2003	155,065	3.7%	151,321	3.6%	2.5%
Other genetic diseases	72,195	1.7%	45,595	1.1%	58.3%
Total genetic diseases	1,774,519	43.5%	2,226,329	53.0%	–20.3%
Cardiometabolic and Renal (CR): Treatment of renal, endocrine, and cardiovascular diseases					
• **Renagel/Renvela**: Used by patients with chronic kidney disease on dialysis for the control of serum phosphorus	706,589	16.8%	677,729	16.1%	4.3%
• **Hectorol**: Treatment of secondary hyperparathyroidism in patients with stage 3 or 4 chronic kidney disease; acquired in 2005	130,757	3.1%	128,153	3.1%	2.0%
• **Thyrogen**: Treatment for thyroid cancer to allow patients to avoid traditional hypothyroidism treatment.	170,644	4.1%	148,448	3.5%	15.0%
Other cardiometabolic and renal	2,942	0.1%	1,595	0.0%	84.5%
Total cardiometabolic and renal	1,010,932	24.8%	955,925	22.8%	5.8%
Biosurgery (BI): Orthopedic products, via purchase of Bio Matrix in 2000					
• **Synvisc**: A local therapy to reduce osteoporosis knee pain, facilitating increased mobility	328,533	7.8%	263,094	6.3%	24.9%
• **Sepra**: A family of products used by to prevent adhesions after abdominal and pelvic open surgery, hysterectomy, etc.	148,538	3.5%	133,663	3.2%	11.1%
Other biosurgery	36,611	0.9%	48,931	1.2%	–25.2%
Total biosurgery	513,682	12.6%	445,688	10.6%	15.3%
Hematologic Oncology (HO): Cancer-treatment products	284,858	6.8%	101,217	2.4%	181.4%
Other product revenue (Other)	492,574	11.7%	467,748	11.1%	5.3%
Total product revenue	$4,076,665	100.0%	$4,196,907	100.0%	–2.9%

Data Sources: Genzyme Corporation SEC 10-K filings, 2008 and 2009.

EXHIBIT 52.7 | Genzyme's Drug Portfolio and Selected Late-Stage Pipeline Products as of 2010

Marketed Drugs				
Name	Main Indication	2009 Sales (in thousands of dollars)	Main Patent Expiration*	% of Total Sales
Cerezyme	Gaucher's disease	$793,024	2019	19.5%
Fabrazyme	Fabry disease	$429,690	2015	10.5%
Myozyme	Pompe disease	$324,545	2023	8.0%
Aldurazyme	MPS I	$155,065	2020	3.8%
Renagel/Renvela	High SP levels in CKD patients	$706,589	2014	17.3%
Hectorol	Hyperparathyroidism	$130,757	2016	3.2%
Thyrogen	Diagnostic in thyroid cancer	$170,644	2015	4.2%
Synvisc/Synvisc-One	Osteoarthritis pain	$328,533	2012	8.1%
Sepra	Healing after surgeries	$148,538	2013	3.6%

*Dates shown are for main patents (both United States and international).

Selected Pipeline Drugs Under Development			
Name	Main Indication	Clinical Trial Phase	Potential Approval**
Alemtuzumab/Campath	Multiple sclerosis	III	2011
Mipomersen	Hypercholesterolemia	III	2011
Ataluren	Cystic fibrosis	III	2011
Eliglustat	Gaucher's disease	III	2013
Clolar	Leukemia, MDS	Different stages	2010–2016
Mozobil	Tumor sensitization	I	2016

**Genzyme estimation.

Data Sources: Genzyme Corporation SEC 10-K filings, 2008 and 2009; Sanofi-Aventis tender offer, Genzyme shareholder presentation, SEC website, October 4, 2010, http://www.sec.gov/Archives/edgar/data/732485/000119312510223033/dex99a5c.htm (accessed Sept. 30, 2014).

EXHIBIT 52.8 | Genzyme Financials

Genzyme—Income Statement (in thousands of dollars)

	2007	2008	2009
Revenue			
Net product sales	$3,457,778	$4,196,907	$4,076,665
Net service sales	326,326	366,091	418,518
Research and development revenue	29,415	42,041	20,342
Total revenues	3,813,519	4,605,039	4,515,525
Operating Costs			
Cost of products and services sold	927,330	1,148,562	1,386,076
Selling and administrative expenses	1,187,184	1,338,190	1,428,596
Research and development	737,685	1,308,330	865,257
Amortization of goodwill	201,105	226,442	266,305
Contingent consideration expense	0	0	65,584
Purchase of in-process R&D	106,350	0	0
Charges for impaired assets	0	2,036	0
Total operating expenses	3,159,654	4,023,560	4,011,818
Operating Income (Loss)	653,865	581,479	503,707
Investment income	70,196	51,260	17,642
Interest expense	(12,147)	(4,418)	0
Equity method investments	20,465	(3,139)	(56)
Gain on acquisition of business	0	0	24,159
All other income (expenses)	3,295	356	(1,719)
Total other income (expenses)	81,809	44,059	40,026
Income before income taxes	735,674	625,538	543,733
Provision for income taxes	(255,481)	(204,457)	(121,433)
Net income (loss)	$ 480,193	$ 421,081	$ 422,300
Earnings per share			
Basic	$ 1.82	$ 1.57	$ 1.57
Diluted	$ 1.74	$ 1.50	$ 1.54

EXHIBIT 52.8 | *(continued)*

Genzyme—Balance Sheet (in thousands of dollars)

	2007	2008	2009
Assets			
Cash and equivalents*	$ 867,012	$ 572,106	$ 742,246
Short-term investments	80,445	57,507	163,630
Accounts receivable	904,101	1,036,940	899,731
Inventory	439,115	453,437	608,022
Other current assets	331,158	396,145	389,174
Total current assets	2,621,831	2,516,135	2,802,803
Property, plant, and equipment—net	1,968,402	2,306,567	2,809,349
Long-term investments	602,118	427,403	218,262
Goodwill	1,403,828	1,401,074	1,403,363
Other intangibles	1,555,652	1,654,698	2,313,262
Other long-term assets	162,544	365,399	513,685
Total assets	$8,314,375	$8,671,276	$10,060,724
Liabilities			
Accounts payable	$ 128,380	$ 127,869	$ 189,629
Accrued expenses payable	645,645	765,386	696,223
Current portion—long-term debt	696,625	7,566	169,531
Other short-term liabilities	13,277	13,462	24,747
Current liabilities	1,483,927	914,283	1,080,130
Long-term debt	113,748	124,341	116,434
Other liabilities	103,763	326,659	1,180,508
Total liabilities	1,701,438	1,365,283	2,377,072
Shareholders' equity			
Common stock and paid-in capital	5,387,814	5,783,460	5,691,398
Retained earnings	1,225,123	1,522,533	1,992,254
Total equity	6,612,937	7,305,993	7,683,652
Total liabilities and shareholders' equity	$8,314,375	$8,671,276	$10,060,724
Shares outstanding at December 31 (000)	266,008	270,704	268,841

*The cash position at the time of tender offer in October 2010 should be assumed to be higher by $921 million to reflect the sale of a genetics unit in September 2010.

EXHIBIT 52.8 | (continued)

Genzyme—Cash Flow Statement (in thousands of dollars)

	2006	2007	2008	2009
Cash from operations				
Net income	($ 16,797)	$480,193	$ 421,081	$ 422,300
Depreciation and amortization	331,389	338,196	374,664	456,364
Stock-based compensation	208,614	190,070	187,596	204,229
Change in operating assets	(73,311)	(117,862)	(90,615)	115,129
Purchase of in-process R&D	552,900	106,350	0	0
Charge for impaired assets	219,243	0	2,036	0
Deferred income tax benefit	(279,795)	(106,140)	(195,200)	(95,737)
Other operating cash flows	(53,674)	27,865	59,613	76,752
Cash from operations	888,569	918,672	759,175	1,179,037
Cash from investing				
Capital expenditure	(333,675)	(412,872)	(597,562)	(661,713)
Acquisitions, net of acquired cash	(568,953)	(342,456)	(16,561)	(51,336)
Net sale (purchase) of investments	13,168	205,614	188,127	(93,069)
Net sale (purchase) of equity securities	132,588	(1,282)	(80,062)	(4,366)
Other investing activities	(79,540)	(40,060)	(75,482)	−47078
Cash from investing	(836,412)	(591,056)	(581,540)	(671,424)
Cash from financing				
Net long-term debt issued/repaid	(4,501)	(5,909)	(693,961)	(7,492)
Issuance of common stock	158,305	285,762	318,753	100,521
Repurchase of common stock	0	(231,576)	(143,012)	(413,874)
Other financing activities	(5,751)	(1,051)	45,679	(15,771)
Cash from financing	148,053	47,226	(472,541)	(336,616)
Net change in cash and equivalents	$200,210	$374,842	($294,906)	$ 170,997

Data Source: Genzyme Corporation SEC 10-K filings, 2007–2009.

EXHIBIT 52.9 | Drug R&D and FDA Approval Process

Stage	Goal	Test In*	Time Needed*	Probability of Success*
Preclinical	Gather information on drug behavior in physiological setting	Animals	A few years	N/A
IND	Application submitted to the FDA for approval to conduct clinical trial		Several months	N/A
Phase I	Gather preliminary drug efficacy and safety, determine safe dosage, identify side effects	Healthy volunteers (between 20 and 80)	One to a few years	63%
Phase II	Evaluate drug efficacy against placebo or other treatments, observe drug safety, especially short-term side effects	A few dozen to a few hundred patients	One to a few years	33%
Phase III	Observe drug efficacy and safety in larger population, look for long-term safety and rare side effects	A few hundred to a few thousand patients	Two to several years	55%
NDA	Application submitted to the FDA for final market approval		Several months	80%

*May vary significantly in different diseases and scenarios.

Data Sources: "The FDA's Drug Review Process: Ensuring Drugs are Safe and Effective," FDA website, http://www.fda.gov/drugs/resourcesforyou/consumers/ucm143534.htm (accessed Sept. 30, 2014); Hay et al., "BIO/BioMedTracker Clinical Trial Success Rates Study," February 15, 2011.

EXHIBIT 52.10 | Selected Major M&A Deals in the Pharmaceutical Industry, 2007–2009

Date	Acquirer	Target	Value (in billions of dollars)
March 2007	Schering-Plough	Organon	$14.7
April 2007	AstraZeneca	MedImmune	$15.6
July 2008	Roche	Genentech	$46.8
October 2008	Eli Lilly	ImClone	$ 6.5
January 2009	Pfizer	Wyeth	$68.0
March 2009	Merck	Schering-Plough	$41.1

Data Source: Andreas Scherer, "M&A in Big Pharma: Holy Grail or Buying Time?," Contract Pharma, March 21, 2012, http://www.contractpharma.com/contents/view_expert-opinions/2012-03-21/ma-in-big-pharma/ (accessed Sept. 30, 2014).

EXHIBIT 52.11 | Selected Top-Brand Drugs with 2011–2015 Patent Expirations

Potential Expiration	Brand Name	Manufacturer	2008 U.S. Sales (in millions of dollars)
2011	Actos	Takeda	$2,569
2011	Zyprexa	Eli Lilly	$1,853
2011	Lipitor	Pfizer	$6,392
2011	Plavix	Sanofi-Aventis	$3,971
2011	Lovenox	Sanofi-Aventis	$1,107
2011	Levaquin	Ortho-McNeil-Janssen	$1,719
2012	Lexapro	Forest	$2,554
2012	Seroquel	AstraZeneca	$3,236
2012	Singulair	Merck	$3,204
2012	Diovan&HCT	Novartis	$2,404
2013	Aciphex	Eisai	$1,159
2013	Cymbalta	Eli Lilly	$2,294
2014	Nexium	AstraZeneca	$5,080
2014	Celebrex	Pfizer	$1,634
2015	Gleevec	Novartis	$ 902

Data Source: "Table 1: Selected Top Brand-Name Drugs with Patent Expirations from 2011 to 2020," USpharmacist.com, http://www.uspharmacist.com/CMSImagesContent/2012/6/USG1201-Patent_Table1.gif (accessed Sept. 30, 2014).

EXHIBIT 52.12 | Sanofi-Aventis's Drug Portfolio and Patent Cliff

Name	Main Indication	2009 Sales (in millions of euros)	Main Patent Expiration*	% of Total Sales
Lantus	Diabetes	3,080	2014	11.9%
Lovenox	Thrombosis	3,043	2011 in Europe,** no patent in United States	11.8%
Plavix	Atherothrombosis	2,623	2011 in United States, 2013 in Europe	10.2%
Taxotere	Cancers	2,177	2010	8.4%
Aprovel/CoAprovel	Hypertension	1,236	2011 in United States, 2012 in Europe	4.8%
Eloxatine	Colorectal cancer	957	Expired***	3.7%
Apidra	Diabetes	137	2018 in United States, 2019 in Europe	0.5%
Multaq	Atrial fibrillation	25	2011	0.1%
Stilnox/Ambien/Myslee	Sleep disorders	873	Expired	3.4%
Allegra	Allergic rhinitis	731	Expired	2.8%
Copaxone	Multiple sclerosis	467	2014 in United States, 2015 in Europe	1.8%
Tritace	Hypertension	429	Expired	1.7%
Amaryl	Diabetes	416	Expired	1.6%
Depakine	Epilepsy	329	Expired	1.3%
Xatral	Prostatic hypertrophy	296	Expired	1.1%
Actonel	Osteoporosis	264	2013 in United States, 2010 in Europe	1.0%
Nasacort	Allergic rhinitis	220	Expired	0.9%

*U.S./European patent shown; patent lives may vary in other parts of the world but in most cases are similar.

**European patent lives shown are for most of Europe; some European countries may have slightly different patent lives.

***Expired patents shown are for compound patents; formulation patents may provide further protection.

Data Source: Sanofi-Aventis SEC 20-F filing, 2009.

EXHIBIT 52.13 | Genzyme—Financial Data for Market Comparables as of Year-End 2009

	Genzyme (GENZ)	Amgen (AMGN)	Biogen (BIIB)	Celgene (CELG)	Gilead (GILD)	Life Tech (LIFE)
Revenues	$4,516	$14,642	$3,153	$2,567	$7,011	$3,280
EBIT	$504	$5,506	$1,295	$842	$3,529	$386
EBITDA	$770	$6,555	$2,013	$1,003	$3,742	$928
EBITDA margin (%)	17.1%	44.8%	63.8%	39.1%	53.4%	28.3%
Net income	$422	$4,605	$977	$777	$2,626	$145
Net income margin	9.3%	31.5%	31.0%	30.3%	37.5%	4.4%
Weighted avg. shares (in millions)	268	1,016	287	459	905	176
EPS (basic)	$1.57	$4.53	$3.40	$1.69	$2.90	$0.82
Stock price	$49.0	$56.6	$53.5	$27.8	$21.6	$52.2
Equity (market cap)	$13,159	$57,475	$15,371	$12,779	$19,584	$9,191
P/E (trailing)	31.2×	12.5×	15.7×	16.4×	7.5×	63.4×
Beta (value line)	0.70	0.65	0.75	0.80	0.65	0.80
Debt (interest bearing)	$124	$10,601	$1,100	$0	$1,161	$3,102
Equity	$7,684	$22,667	$6,262	$4,395	$6,505	$4,027
Debt/equity	1.6%	46.8%	17.6%	0.0%	17.8%	77.0%
Debt/market cap	0.9%	18.4%	7.2%	0.0%	5.9%	33.8%
Interest expense	($18)	$578	$0	$2	$28	$188
EBITDA/interest expense	NA	11.3	NA	501.5	133.6	4.9
Long-term debt rating (S&P)	A−	A+	BBB+	BBB+	A−	BBB
Enterprise value (EV)	$13,283	$68,076	$16,471	$12,779	$20,745	$12,293
EV/EBITDA	17.3×	10.4×	8.2×	12.7×	5.5×	13.2×
EV/sales	2.9×	4.6×	5.2×	5.0×	3.0×	3.7×

Data Sources: Company 10-K filings, Capital IQ, Bloomberg, Value Line, Standard & Poor's, GEO Investing.

EXHIBIT 52.14 | Market Interest Rates on October 5, 2010 (10-year maturity, yield to maturity)

Treasury Bond	2.48%
Corporate Bonds	
AAA	2.90%
AA	3.22%
A	3.76%
BBB	4.42%
BB	6.30%

Data Source: Bloomberg.

EXHIBIT 52.15 | Investor Presentation by Sanofi-Aventis—"Sanofi-Aventis Tender Offer to Acquire Genzyme" (October 4, 2010)

Our Offer Value Genzyme Significantly Higher than Peers despite Near-term Challenges and Recurrent Underperformance

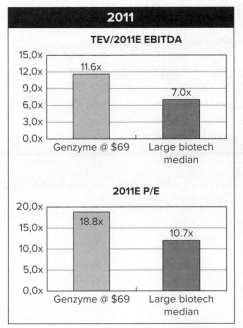

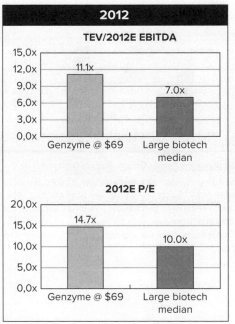

Source: "Sanofi-Aventis Tender Offer to Acquire Genzyme," SEC website, October 4, 2010, http://www.sec.gov/Archives/edgar/data/732485/000119312510223033/dex99a5c.htm (accessed Sept. 30, 2014).

EXHIBIT 52.16 | Investor Presentation by Sanofi-Aventis—"Sanofi-Aventis Tender Offer to Acquire Genzyme" (October 4, 2010)

Sanofi-aventis Offer Premiums are in Line with Large Biopharmaceutical Transactions

1-Day Premiums Paid

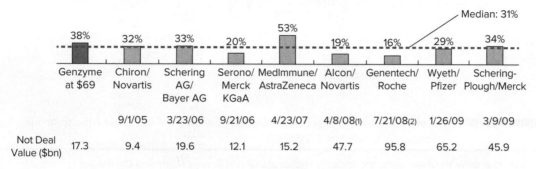

	Genzyme at $69	Chiron/ Novartis	Schering AG/ Bayer AG	Serono/ Merck KGaA	MedImmune/ AstraZeneca	Alcon/ Novartis	Genentech/ Roche	Wyeth/ Pfizer	Schering-Plough/Merck
	38%	32%	33%	20%	53%	19%	16%	29%	34%
		9/1/05	3/23/06	9/21/06	4/23/07	4/8/08(1)	7/21/08(2)	1/26/09	3/9/09
Not Deal Value ($bn)	17.3	9.4	19.6	12.1	15.2	47.7	95.8	65.2	45.9

Median: 31%

1-Month Premiums Paid

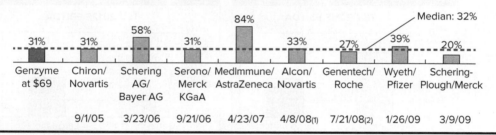

	Genzyme at $69	Chiron/ Novartis	Schering AG/ Bayer AG	Serono/ Merck KGaA	MedImmune/ AstraZeneca	Alcon/ Novartis	Genentech/ Roche	Wyeth/ Pfizer	Schering-Plough/Merck
	31%	31%	58%	31%	84%	33%	27%	39%	20%
		9/1/05	3/23/06	9/21/06	4/23/07	4/8/08(1)	7/21/08(2)	1/26/09	3/9/09

Median: 32%

Source: "Sanofi-Aventis Tender Offer to Acquire Genzyme."

Note: all permiums are relative to unaffected stock prices; Genzyme 1-day premium based on 7/1/10 and 1-month premium based on 1-month VWAP of $52.63 (as of 7/22/10): Genzyme net deal value adjusted for announced divestitures

(1) Date Novartis announced purchase of 25% state and call/put option; blended purchase price of the intital 25% for $10.4bn and remaining 75% at $180/share

(2) Date of intitial Roche offer, value grossed up 100% of Genentech (Roche owned ~55% at time of offer)

EXHIBIT 52.17 | Genzyme—Financial Forecasts (Management Scenario) in Millions of U.S. Dollars

	2009	2010	2011	2012	2013	2014	2015
			Projected				
Revenue Sources							
Personalized Genetic Health	$1,850.0	$1,757.5	$2,284.8	$2,513.2	$3,015.9	$3,468.3	$3,815.1
Renal and Endocrinology	$1,008.0	$1,058.4	$1,111.3	$1,166.9	$1,225.2	$980.2	$784.1
Biosurgery	$513.7	$590.8	$679.4	$781.3	$976.6	$1,171.9	$1,347.7
Hematology and Oncology	$509.8	$688.2	$929.1	$1,254.3	$1,630.6	$2,038.2	$2,445.9
Other	$29.1	$20.4	$21.4	$22.0	$22.7	$23.4	$24.1
Pipeline (probability adjusted)	$0.0	$0.0	$0.0	$25.0	$ 500.0	$1,100.0	$1,500.0
Revenues	$4,076.7	$4,115.3	$5,025.9	$5,762.7	$7,371.0	$8,782.0	$9,916.9
COGS	($1,386.1)	($1,316.9)	($1,532.9)	($1,671.2)	($2,027.0)	($2,283.3)	($2,578.4)
Gross Profit	$2,690.6	$2,798.4	$3,493.0	$4,091.5	$5,344.0	$6,498.6	$7,338.5
General & Administrative	($1,428.6)	($1,337.5)	($1,558.0)	($1,786.4)	($2,285.0)	($2,722.4)	($3,074.2)
R&D	($ 865.3)	($864.2)	($1,055.4)	($1,210.2)	($1,547.9)	($1,844.2)	($2,082.5)
Service and R&D Revenues	$438.9	$411.5	$502.6	$ 576.3	$737.1	$878.2	$991.7
EBITDA	$835.6	$1,008.2	$1,382.1	$1,671.2	$2,248.1	$2,810.2	$3,173.4
Depreciation & Amortization	($266.3)	($288.1)	($351.8)	($ 403.4)	($ 516.0)	($614.7)	($694.2)
Other Expenses	($65.6)	($205.8)	($50.3)	($57.6)	($73.7)	$0.0	$0.0
Operating Income (EBIT)	$503.7	$514.4	$980.1	$1,210.2	$1,658.5	$2,195.5	$2,479.2
Taxes	($121.4)	($180.0)	($343.0)	($ 423.6)	($ 580.5)	($768.4)	($867.7)
NOPAT (Net Op Profit After Tax)	$382.3	$334.4	$637.0	$786.6	$1,078.0	$1,427.1	$1,611.5

Sources: Analyst reports and case writer estimates.

EXHIBIT 52.18 | Genzyme—Financial Forecasts (Market Scenario) in Millions of U.S. Dollars

	2009	2010	2011	2012	2013	2014	2015
				Projected			
Revenue Sources							
Personalized Genetic Health	$1,850.0	$1,665.0	$2,164.5	$2,489.2	$2,787.9	$3,122.4	$3,497.1
Renal and Endocrinology	$1,008.0	$1,038.2	$1,069.4	$1,101.5	$1,134.5	$850.9	$595.6
Biosurgery	$513.7	$590.8	$679.4	$781.3	$898.5	$1,033.2	$1,157.2
Hematology and Oncology	$509.8	$688.2	$894.7	$1,118.4	$1,342.0	$1,543.4	$1,774.9
Other	$29.1	$20.4	$21.0	$21.6	$22.3	$22.9	$23.6
Pipeline (probability adjusted)	$0.0	$0.0	$0.0	$20.0	$70.0	$220.0	$300.0
Revenues	$4,076.7	$4,002.6	$4,828.9	$5,531.9	$6,255.2	$6,792.8	$7,348.4
COGS	($1,386.1)	($1,280.8)	($1,472.8)	($1,604.3)	($1,720.2)	($1,766.1)	($1,910.6)
Gross Profit	$2,690.6	$2,721.8	$3,356.1	$3,927.7	$4,535.0	$5,026.7	$5,437.8
General & Administrative	($1,428.6)	($1,300.8)	($1,497.0)	($1,631.9)	($1,845.3)	($2,003.9)	($2,167.8)
R&D	($865.3)	($840.5)	($1,014.1)	($1,161.7)	($1,313.6)	($1,426.5)	($1,543.2)
Service and R&D Revenues	$438.9	$400.3	$482.9	$553.2	$625.5	$679.3	$734.8
EBITDA	$835.6	$980.6	$1,328.0	$1,687.2	$2,001.7	$2,275.6	$2,461.7
Depreciation & Amortization	($266.3)	($280.2)	($338.0)	($387.2)	($437.9)	($475.5)	($514.4)
Other Expenses	($65.6)	($200.1)	($48.3)	($55.3)	($62.6)	$0.0	$0.0
Operating Income (EBIT)	$503.7	$500.3	$941.6	$1,244.7	$1,501.2	$1,800.1	$1,947.3
Taxes	($121.4)	($175.1)	($329.6)	($435.6)	($525.4)	($630.0)	($681.6)
NOPAT (Net Op Profit After Tax)	$382.3	$325.2	$612.1	$809.0	$975.8	$1,170.1	$1,265.8

Sources: Analyst reports and case writer estimates.

EXHIBIT 52.19 | Investor Presentation by Sanofi-Aventis—"Sanofi-Aventis Tender Offer to Acquire Genzyme" (October 4, 2010)

Our Offer Assumes Alemtuzumab Performs in Line with Analyst Expectations in Multiple Sclerosis

Peak Annual Sales Estimated ($m)

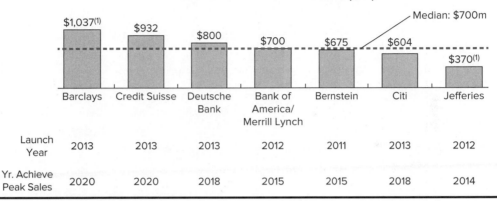

	Barclays	Credit Suisse	Deutsche Bank	Bank of America/ Merrill Lynch	Bernstein	Citi	Jefferies
	$1,037[1]	$932	$800	$700	$675	$604	$370[1]
Launch Year	2013	2013	2013	2012	2011	2013	2012
Yr. Achieve Peak Sales	2020	2020	2018	2015	2015	2018	2014

Median: $700m

Source: "Sanofi-Aventis Tender Offer to Acquire Genzyme."

■ *"According to our analysis, alemfuzumab can reach operating margins of only 28% by 2018. This is due to high payments to Bayers, relatively high COGS due to production at a third party, and building a global sales force that will be required in Multiple Sclerosis."* —September 17, 2009

■ *"Genzyme will pay Buyer a 20–35% royalty on sales in Multiple Sclerosis once the drug is approved in 2012"* —March 31, 2009

■ *"While Campath MS remains one of the more compelling disease modifying therapies for MS, we believe that unique autoimmune toxicities and pricing challenges remain to be addressed"* —June 14, 2010

■ *"We assume use in tysabri failures at a new patient add rate comparable to current Tysabri rate of 200/week"* —May 7, 2010

Delphi Corporation

We are clearly focused on Delphi's future. Emergence from the Chapter 11 process in the U.S. requires that we make difficult, yet necessary, decisions.

We are mindful of the impact the implementation of this plan will have on some of our stake-holders, including our employees and communities, yet ultimately, these actions will result in a stronger company with future global growth opportunities.

—Delphi Chairman and CEO Steve Miller[1]

January 2008 was proving to be a crucial time in the life of Delphi Corporation (Delphi). The company had been in Chapter 11 bankruptcy for more than two years; a vote was pending to approve the plan of reorganization (POR) filed in December 2007. A key objective of a Chapter 11 filing was to protect the company from its creditors while the courts orchestrated a reorganization plan to return the company to a competitive and profitable enterprise. Like most PORs, the Delphi plan called for a significant reduction of the company's leverage by exchanging the debt of the unsecured creditors with a mixture of new debt and new equity. The resulting reduction in interest expense would restore Delphi's profitability and make the restructured corporation a going concern.

Approval of the POR required a positive vote from all the classes of *impaired* creditors (i.e., Delphi's creditors who received less than the face value of their claims).[2] A claimant class was deemed to have accepted the plan if more than one-half of the claimants voted in favor of the plan and if their claims totaled at least two-thirds of the class's total claim. If the plan was rejected by any creditor class, then the judge would choose between several alternatives as the next step: liquidate the assets under Chapter 7 of the Bankruptcy Code; force the dissenting group to accept the POR via a *cramdown* or require management to construct a new plan for consideration by the claimants.

Chapter 7 liquidation was unusual in a large corporate bankruptcy because it rarely offered as much value to all the claimants relative to keeping the company intact as a

---

[1]"Delphi Outlines Transformation Plan; Outlines Strategic Path to 2007 Emergence from Chapter 11," PR Newswire, March 31, 2006.

[2]Shareholders were also classified as impaired because their claim was inferior to the debt holders.

going enterprise. Therefore, the judge would normally choose to cram down the existing POR or request the company to put together a new one. A cramdown was a process by which a dissenting class or classes were forced to accept the restructuring spelled out in the POR. Bankruptcy judges could resort to a cramdown if they thought the POR was "fair and equitable" and that a new POR was unlikely to offer significant improvement. Knowing that the judge had the option to conduct a cramdown also served the purpose of removing the incentive for a claimant class to continually reject the POR with the hope of getting a better offer.

Time was the enemy of impaired claimants because the bankruptcy process was expensive, and the sooner a company could exit Chapter 11, the sooner more value was available to spread among the claimants. To date, the legal, administrative, and financing costs associated with the Delphi bankruptcy had been estimated at more than $320 million. Just as important was the negative impact of the bankruptcy on Delphi's customer base, which would continue to erode while the company's status remained in limbo. Thus, all parties were feeling the pressure to follow management's appeal to accept the POR and get Delphi out of Chapter 11.

Delphi Corporation

After existing as a separate business unit within General Motors for eight years, Delphi was spun off in 1999 to pursue more strategic growth initiatives as an independent company. Leveraging on its technical and manufacturing experience, Delphi became one of the largest global suppliers of vehicle electronics, transportation components, integrated systems and modules, and other electronic technology. Although GM continued to be a key Delphi customer, Delphi developed relationships with every major global automotive OEM, including Ford Motor Company, DaimlerChrysler Corporation, Volkswagen Group, Hyundai, and Renault/Nissan Motor Company (**Exhibit 53.1**).

Delphi was profitable during the first two years after separation from GM, but then sales began to decline, and profits eroded (**Exhibits 53.2–53.4**). As Delphi struggled to be cost competitive, the company hired veteran turnaround specialist Steve Miller as its chairman and CEO. After discussions with GM and its major unions failed to result in a voluntary restructuring of its U.S. operations, however, Delphi filed voluntary petitions under Chapter 11 of the Bankruptcy Code in October 2005.

At the time, Delphi occupied spot 63 on the *Fortune* 500 list, and its petitions represented the ninth-largest bankruptcy filing in the history of the United States. Industry analysts viewed the filing as potentially the beginning for the much-needed restructuring of the U.S. auto industry, which was crumbling under the pressure of rising costs and increased competition from leaner competitors abroad. The key challenges facing Delphi ranged from claims against GM relating to legacy liabilities, burdensome restrictions in its U.S. labor agreements, and realignment of its global product portfolio and manufacturing footprints. The filing listed Delphi's consolidated assets and liabilities as $17.1 billion and $22.2 billion, respectively.

While in bankruptcy, Delphi continued to suffer losses and declining revenues. By year-end 2007, the company had losses in excess of $3 billion on sales of $22 billion. Delphi's bankruptcy was complicated by the company's global footprint and size: It maintained 290 sites, including manufacturing facilities, technical centers, customer centers, and sales offices in 34 countries. In addition to its global headquarters in Troy, Michigan, the company also had regional headquarters in Shanghai, Luxembourg, and São Paulo. Of Delphi's 169,500 employees, 141,100 were outside of the United States.

To emerge from bankruptcy, Delphi had identified five key areas in which to revamp its operations.

Labor agreements

In its court filing, Delphi had cited the cost of labor and liabilities associated with the labor unions as a major factor in its financial setback. Delphi reported that it paid its employees approximately $75 per hour in wages and benefits, more than three times the cost of the average U.S. auto supply worker. After a series of discussions between Delphi, GM, and the United Auto Workers union (UAW), Delphi proposed to eliminate 27,000 of 33,000 union jobs and change its hourly wage scale from $27 per hour to between $14 and $18.50 per hour.

Relationship with GM

Delphi wanted to redefine this relationship by having GM commit to supporting its legacy costs and clarify its business commitment to Delphi going forward. In addition, Delphi had certain supply contracts with GM that were unprofitable, which it wanted to renegotiate. GM had a strong incentive to agree to such changes because it depended on Delphi as its largest part supplier.

The POR specified that GM would receive $2.57 billion in cash, a second lien note, and junior preferred convertible stock. In addition, as agreed upon with Delphi during the spinoff, GM was liable to pay the healthcare and pension benefits for Delphi retirees in the event of a bankruptcy filing within eight years. According to analyst estimates, this guarantee could cost GM $6 billion at a time when it was struggling with declining U.S. market share and in the midst of its own restructuring.

Product portfolio

Delphi realigned its business operations to focus on the core technologies that the company thought gave it significant competitive and technological advantages. In this process, Delphi identified certain noncore product lines that would be sold or slowly discontinued (including approximately one-third of its global manufacturing sites) after consultation with its customers, unions, and other stakeholders.

Salaried work force

Delphi planned to reduce its global salaried work force by almost 8,500 employees to rationalize its SG&A costs and ensure that its cost structure was competitive and aligned with its product portfolio and manufacturing footprint. Delphi projected to realize savings of approximately $450 million per year from these initiatives. The company also developed executive and nonexecutive compensation programs to ensure retention of its key talent.

Pension costs

For the U.S. hourly and salaried employees, Delphi's pension and other postemployment benefit (OPEB) liabilities amounted to $12.5 billion as of December 31, 2007. The Internal Revenue Service (IRS) and Pension Benefit Guaranty Corporation (PBGC) had agreed to a funding plan that enabled Delphi to satisfy its pension funding obligations upon emergence from Chapter 11. The plan allowed Delphi to meet part of the obligations with cash contributions and transfer the rest to a pension plan sponsored by GM.

If the POR was rejected, Delphi would miss the PBGC's deadline to emerge from bankruptcy, in which case the PBGC had the right to initiate an involuntary plan termination. In addition, if the deadline was missed, the IRS could assess penalties on the missed pension-plan contributions of approximately $1.4 billion; however, if Delphi were forced to file for Chapter 7, the PBGC would have to assume responsibility for Delphi's unfunded pension liability, estimated as $5.9 billion.

Chapter 11 Reorganization

While under the protection of the court, a company enjoyed the benefit of the *automatic stay* provision. The automatic stay immediately arrested collection efforts by creditors, which, in turn, allowed management to focus on generating a POR. Before developing a POR, however, management needed to demonstrate to the bankruptcy judge that the firm had a higher value as a going concern rather than as liquidation. Once the judge ruled that reorganization was likely to provide more value, management developed the POR. After receiving the judge's approval, the POR was presented for a vote of approval by all holders of financial claims: debt holders, employees, and shareholders. If approved, the company was able to exit bankruptcy and implement its reorganization.

An important advantage of being in bankruptcy was being able to use DIP, or debtor-in-possession, financing. DIP financing was given top seniority status to make it an attractive opportunity for lenders who otherwise would avoid lending to a company in financial distress. By being granted the highest priority among the existing claimants, the risk to DIP lenders was radically reduced, encouraging the infusion of new money into the company. At the same time, the addition of DIP financing served to increase the risk of existing creditors who found themselves subordinated to a new debt claim. While in bankruptcy, Delphi had negotiated a $4.5 billion of DIP financing from a syndicate of lenders. The DIP Credit Facility consisted of a $1.75 billion first-priority revolving credit facility, a $250 million first-priority term loan, and a $2.5 billion second-priority term loan.

The primary challenge faced by a company in Chapter 11 was to restructure its balance sheet to have the right mix of debt and equity after emerging from bankruptcy. The purpose of the POR was to specify what each existing claimant would receive as payment for their claim. The payment could be either cash raised from the exit financing, or it could be new debt and equity securities issued in exchange for the existing securities. When the POR gave a claimant less than the face value of its claim, it was deemed to be impaired. For example, unsecured lenders were usually impaired in a bankruptcy and might receive shares of new equity valued at 60% of their original claim. It was the impaired claimants who were most likely to withhold their approval of the POR in an effort to improve their deal with a new POR.

The POR also specified how the cash settlement would be raised (i.e., the financing arrangement for getting the new debt and equity upon exit from bankruptcy). The climate for acquiring debt financing had become decidedly unfavorable following the credit crunch in August 2007. Despite the sluggish credit markets, however, Delphi had obtained exit financing commitments for a secured first-lien term facility of $3.7 billion and a senior secured second-lien term facility of $1.5 billion. The loan commitments were contingent upon the POR being approved by the end of January and upon the completion of the new equity issuance. The engagement letter mandated that the lenders syndicate financing on "commercially reasonable best efforts," which meant that they committed to supplying the $5.2 billion but that the interest rate would not be determined until the time of the deal. Due to the difficult lending environment, the judge had approved this as an acceptable risk for Delphi.

Finding equity investors had also proven difficult. During its two years in bankruptcy, Delphi had been forced to revise the equity commitment agreement of the POR twice. Recently, however, Delphi had received court approval for a group of investors to purchase $2.55 billion of new shares in the reorganized company.[3]

The POR

The financial restructuring of the POR proposed to use the proceeds from the exit financing to pay DIP lenders and other secured creditors in full with cash (**Exhibit 53.5**). The recoveries for the unsecured claims and equity holders consisted of various combinations of new debt, new equity, and warrants for the new equity. For example, the general unsecured and ERISA claims were to receive shares of the new common stock plus discount rights to buy new shares. The existing shareholders were to receive shares of the new stock plus rights to buy more shares plus warrants of various maturities and exercise prices to buy shares. The degree of recovery for the impaired classes depended upon the market value estimated for the new securities.

This made the valuation of the new shares critical for all the impaired classes. Delphi's investment banker had estimated a range of equity valuations based on assumptions about the future performance of Delphi (**Exhibits 53.6** and **53.7**). The valuation raised questions in the minds of some of the impaired stakeholders who were receiving equity and equity rights in lieu of full value for their claims (**Exhibit 53.8**). The POR used a midrange of $60/share as the Plan Value, which was used to determine the equity allocations for the various claimants.

At the time of the POR vote, existing common-stock holders had already lost most of their investment in Delphi (**Exhibit 53.9**). At a market price of only $0.14 per share

---

[3]The new equity group included private equity fund Appaloosa Management LP, Harbinger Capital Partners Master Fund I Ltd., Merrill Lynch, Pierce, Fenner & Smith Inc., UBS Securities LLC, Pardus Capital Management LP, and Goldman Sachs Group Inc.

and 562 million shares outstanding, the total market capitalization stood at $78.7 million. The POR proposed that the shareholders receive 461,552 new shares, which at the Plan Value of $60/share were worth $27.7 million. In addition, the shareholders would receive equity rights and warrants at various exercise prices to sweeten the deal.

The Bankruptcy Code[4] required that the POR satisfy the "best interest of creditors" test, which meant the company had to establish that the stakeholders would receive at least as much under the POR as in liquidation under Chapter 7 according to the *absolute priority* rule.[5] Delphi's POR demonstrated that the recoveries provided by the plan would be significantly better than those realized through liquidation (**Exhibit 53.10**). If at least one impaired creditor class voted in favor of POR, then the court could cram down the plan on all dissenting classes provided the plan was judged to be "fair and equitable" to all claimants.

Between filing for bankruptcy in 2005 and the end of 2007, Delphi had spent approximately $320 million on legal, accounting, and consulting fees; any delay in its emergence from bankruptcy would only increase these expenses. Most of the agreements negotiated with interested parties—such as General Motors, UAW, new investors, and tax authorities—had tight timelines for Delphi to get the plan approved by the court. If any timeline was not met, the party had the right to walk away from the deal, which would require additional time for more negotiations and almost certainly result in changes in the terms of settlement.

Delphi had set aside $87 million to pay cash bonuses to its top executives when it emerged from bankruptcy. This move drew criticism from the union workers, many of whom had accepted early retirement or buyout offers to help the company emerge from bankruptcy. Bankruptcy experts expected the court to pay special attention to this issue in its next hearing. This also triggered the debate about Delphi's expedited bankruptcy filing because corporate bankruptcy law, modified just nine days after the filing,[6] now placed restrictions on executive compensation to stop companies from giving retention and severance payment.

The POR required approval from all the claimant classes. The unimpaired classes would have no trouble accepting the plan, and in fact, were assumed by law to vote in favor of the plan. The impaired classes, however, might gamble that rejecting the plan would force Delphi to revise the POR to be more favorable toward them. Such renegotiations were always difficult because, for one class to improve, one or more of the other impaired classes had to lose something. Moreover, the negotiations were often time-consuming, which likely meant that all impaired classes would lose value due to the continued accumulation of costs and erosion of enterprise value while stuck in Chapter 11.

Absent the loss in value associated with remaining in bankruptcy, there were no compelling reasons for an impaired class to vote for acceptance. After all, if the judge ordered a cramdown, all classes would end up with the POR whether they voted for it

---

[4] See "A Managerial Primer on the U.S. Bankruptcy Code," UVA-QA-0633.

[5] The *absolute priority* rule required that creditors in a given class received value equal to the allowed amount of their claims before any claimant of lower priority could receive any distribution.

[6] Tom Krisher, "Bankruptcy Judge Approved Delphi Bankruptcy Exit Plan," *Associated Press*, June 7, 2006.

or not. Moreover, since a Chapter 7 liquidation would rarely deliver more value to all impaired classes, it was unlikely that a judge would opt for that course of action.

Exit Financing Risk

Steve Miller knew that if he got approval for the POR, he would need to move quickly to secure the exit financing as the final step in the process. The unimpaired creditors would be paid in full from the proceeds of the new debt and new equity, while the impaired classes would receive various combinations of new debt and equity. The catch was that no one knew for certain what the price of the new shares would be once Delphi actually emerged from Chapter 11. Furthermore, the credit markets were in turmoil, so even if the POR was accepted, there was a chance that the debt syndicate or the equity group could back out of the exit financing arrangement at the last minute. If the company was unable to raise the new funds, the judge would either have to demand a substantially amended POR or opt for liquidation via Chapter 7.

EXHIBIT 53.1 | Growth of Non-GM revenue (1999–2007)

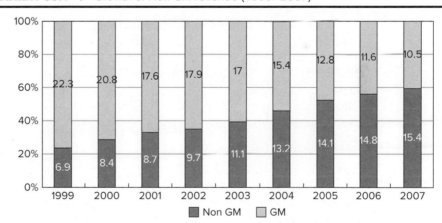

Data Source: Delphi annual reports, 1999–2007.

EXHIBIT 53.2 | Consolidated Statement of Operations, December 31, 2004–07 ($ in millions)

	2007	2006	2005	2004
Net sales				
General Motors and affiliates	8,301	11,636	12,860	15,417
Other customers	13,982	14,756	14,087	13,205
Total net sales	**22,283**	**26,392**	**26,947**	**28,622**
Operating expenses				
Cost of sales	21,066	25,416	25,701	25,989
U.S. employee special attrition charges	212	2,955	—	—
Selling, general and administrative	1,595	1,585	1,644	1,599
Depreciation and amortization	914	1,079	1,150	1,144
Impairment charges/others	441	215	623	372
Total operating expenses	**24,228**	**31,250**	**29,118**	**29,104**
Operating loss	(1,945)	(4,858)	(2,171)	(482)
Interest expense	(769)	(429)	(318)	(232)
Other adjustments	(116)	(41)	77	39
Income tax (expense) benefit	522	(136)	55	(4,143)
Loss from discontinuing operations	(757)	—	—	—
Net loss	**(3,065)**	**(5,464)**	**(2,357)**	**(4,818)**

Data Source: Delphi annual reports, 2004–2007.

EXHIBIT 53.3 | Consolidated Balance Sheet Statements, December 31, 2005–07
($ in millions)

	2007	2006	2005
Assets			
Cash and cash equivalents	1,036	1,667	2,221
Restricted cash	173	146	36
M receivables	1,257	2,078	1,920
Non-GM receivables	2,637	2,691	2,975
Total receivables	3,894	4,769	4,895
Inventory	1,808	2,175	1,874
Other current assets	1,308	458	528
Total current assets	8,219	9,215	9,554
Net property, plant, and equipment	3,863	4,695	5,108
Other assets	1,585	1,482	2,361
Total assets	**13,667**	**15,392**	**17,023**
Liabilities			
Notes payable plus current portion of long-term debt	749	3,089	3,117
Debtor-in-possession financing	2,746	250	—
Accounts payable	2,904	2,820	2,494
Other liabilities	2,693	2,211	1,192
Total current liabilities	9,092	8,370	6,803
Debtor-in-possession financing and long-term debt	59	49	273
Employee benefit plan obligations	443	550	310
Other liabilities	1,185	859	651
Total long-term liabilities	1,687	1,458	1,234
Liabilities subject to compromise	16,197	17,416	15,074
Total liabilities	26,976	27,244	23,111
Minority interest	163	203	157
Stockholders' equity (deficit)	(13,472)	(12,055)	(6,245)
Total liabilities and stockholders' deficit	**13,667**	**15,392**	**17,023**

Data Source: Delphi annual reports, 2005–2007.

EXHIBIT 53.4 | Consolidated Cash Flow Statements, December 31, 2004–07
($ in millions)

	2007	2006	2005	2004
Cash flows from operating activities				
Net loss	(3,065)	(5,464)	(2,357)	(4,818)
Adjustments				
Depreciation and amortization	914	1,079	1,150	1,144
Impairment charges	98	215	623	372
Pension and other postretirement benefit expenses	905	1,515	1,543	1,408
U.S. employee special attrition program charges	212	2,955	—	—
Changes in operating assets and liabilities	813	635	276	(157)
Other adjustments	(225)	(892)	(1,081)	3,576
Net cash provided by operating activities	**(348)**	**43**	**154**	**1,525**
Cash flows from investing activities				
Capital expenditures net of proceeds	(451)	(649)	(1,112)	(914)
Acquisition/divestitures	—	19	245	(61)
Proceeds from sale of non-U.S. trade bank notes	191	173	152	65
Others	(79)	(97)	(79)	92
Net cash used in investing activities	**(339)**	**(554)**	**(794)**	**(818)**
Cash flows from financing activities				
Repayment of debt securities	—	—	—	(500)
Net proceeds from term loan facility	(988)	—	971	—
Proceeds from revolving credit facility, net	(1,508)	2	1,484	—
Net proceeds from debtor-in-possession facility	2,441	—	218	—
Dividend payments	(50)	—	(64)	(157)
Other, net	47	(124)	(657)	(28)
Net cash (used in) provided by financing activities	**(58)**	**(122)**	**1,952**	**(685)**
Effect of exchange rate fluctuations	114	79	(41)	49
(Decrease) increase in cash and cash equivalents	**(631)**	**(554)**	**1,271**	**71**

Data Source: Delphi annual reports, 2004–2007.

EXHIBIT 53.5 | Summary of Recoveries for Different Stakeholders per the POR

Description	Amount due ($ in millions)	Impaired by Plan or Paid in Full	Recovery
DIP claims	3,427	Paid in full	100%
Administrative claims— expenses allowed under bankruptcy code	520	Paid in full	100%
Tax claims	50	Paid in full	100%
Secured claims	25	Paid in full	100%
General Motor's claim	2,573	Impaired by plan	(a) $1.073 billion in junior preferred securities
			(b) $1.5 billion in a combination of at least $750 million in cash and the balance in a second lien note
General unsecured and ERISA claims	4,424	Impaired by plan	(a) New common stock for 78% of claim value
			(b) Discount rights to buy equity at 36% discount to plan equity value for 22% of claim balance
Existing common stock of Delphi		Impaired by plan	(a) 462,000 shares of new stock[1]
			(b) Par value rights exercisable at the plane equity value
			(c) Seven-year warrants exercisable at a 21% premium to the plan equity value
			(d) Six-month warrants exercisable at a 9% premium to the plan equity value
			(e) Ten-year warrants exercisable at plan equity value

Data Source: Delphi court filings.

[1]At the time of reorganization there were approximately 562 million shares of Delphi stock that would be exchanged for shares of new stock.

EXHIBIT 53.6 | Projected Statement of Operations ($ in millions)

	2007	2008	2009	2010	2011
GM sales	10,546	5,996	5,465	5,479	5,736
Non-GM sales	15,423	13,712	14,821	16,484	17,923
Total sales	**25,969**	**19,708**	**20,286**	**21,963**	**23,659**
COGS	24,892	16,917	16,796	17,985	19,271
Selling, general and administrative	1,704	1,546	1,205	1,263	1,348
Securities litigation charge	332	0	0	0	0
Depreciation and amortization	1,859	1,698	1,218	1,221	1,235
Operating income (EBIT)	**(2,818)**	**(453)**	**1,067**	**1,494**	**1,805**
Reorganization items (income)/expense	(1,596)	21	0	0	0
Interest expense	347	572	561	518	452
Other income/(expense)	43	(78)	14	16	13
Pretax income	**(1,526)**	**(1,124)**	**520**	**992**	**1,366**
Income tax expense	144	143	238	329	367
Net income	**(1,670)**	**(1,267)**	**282**	**663**	**999**
Depreciation and amortization	1,859	1,698	1,218	1,221	1,235
Capital expenditures	(913)	(924)	(791)	(802)	(785)
Working capital adjustments	0	(328)	4	225	244

Data Source: Delphi court filings.

EXHIBIT 53.7 | Pro-Forma Balance Sheet ($ in millions)

	Pre-emergence	Debt/ Equity Discharge	Capital Transactions and Other	Fresh Start	Reorganized Balance Sheet
Cash and cash equivalents	1,000	(6,075)	6,664	—	1,589
GM receivables	1,481	—	—	—	1,481
Non-GM receivables	2,841	—	—	—	2,841
Total receivables	**4,322**	**—**	**—**	**—**	**4,322**
Inventory	1,926	—	—	100	2,026
Other current assets	498	—	—	248	746
Total current assets	**7,746**	**(6,075)**	**6,664**	**348**	**8,683**
Net property, plant and equipment	3,858	—	—	800	4,658
Other assets	1,070	—	167	4,460	5,697
Goodwill	428	—	—	4,327	4,755
Total assets	**13,102**	**(6,075)**	**6,831**	**9,935**	**23,793**
Current portion of long-term debt	4,177	(3,426)	37	—	788
Accounts payable	2,726	—	—	—	2,726
Pension	1,284	—	—	—	1,284
OPEB	152	—	—	—	152
Accrued liabilities	1,352	22	—	—	1,374
Total current liabilities	**9,691**	**(3,404)**	**37**	**—**	**6,324**
Debt	11	814	4,413	—	5,238
Pension	3,540	(2,118)	—	—	1,422
OPEB	9,297	(8,279)	—	—	1,018
Other liabilities	1,368	262	—	—	1,630
Total long-term liabilities	**14,216**	**(9,321)**	**4,413**	**—**	**9,308**
Liabilities subject to compromise	4,417	(4,417)	—	—	—
Total liabilities	**28,324**	**(17,142)**	**4,450**	**—**	**15,632**
Common stock and additional paid-in capital	2,782	4,191	1,624	(2,436)	6,161
Convertible preferred—plan investors	—	—	800		800
Preferred stock—GM	—	1,200	—	—	1,200
Retained earnings	(15,415)	5,676	(43)	9,782	—
Treasury stock	(96)	—	—	96	—
Accumulated comprehensive income	(2,602)	—	—	2,602	—
Other comprehensive income	109	—	—	(109)	—
Total stockholders' equity	**(15,222)**	**11,067**	**2,381**	**9,935**	**8,161**
Total liabilities and stockholders' equity	**13,102**	**(6,075)**	**6,831**	**9,935**	**23,793**

Data Source: Delphi court filings.

EXHIBIT 53.8 | Sensitivity of Recovery for General Unsecured Creditor Claims ($ in millions)

	Plan Value	Low End	Midpoint	High End
Total enterprise value	$13,900	$11,800	$13,300	$14,700
Less: pro-forma debt	6,025	6,025	6,025	6,025
Equity value	7,875	5,775	7,275	8,675
Shares outstanding	131.3	131.3	131.3	131.3
Implied share price	$ 60.0	$ 44.0	$ 55.4	$ 66.1
Recovery % of general unsecured claims	**100%**	**63%**	**89%**	**114%**

Source: Case writer estimates.

EXHIBIT 53.9 | Delphi Stock Price, 2004 through 2007 (in $ per share)

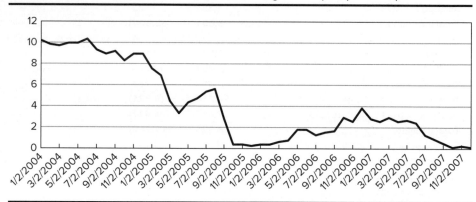

Data Source: Yahoo! Finance.

EXHIBIT 53.10 | Liquidation Analysis ($ in millions)

Assets	Low Estimate Net Book Value	Estimated Value	Realization	High Estimate Estimated Value	Realization
Cash and cash equivalents	117	117	100.0%	117	100.0%
Restricted cash	108	—	0.0%	—	0.0%
Accounts receivable	2,608	2,478	95.0%	2,608	100.0%
Interco receivables (pre-petition)	337	337	100.0%	337	100.0%
Interco receivables (post-petition)	283	283	100.0%	283	100.0%
Inventories	1,128	845	74.9%	939	83.3%
Prepaid exp and other current assets	544	181	33.3%	181	33.3%
Property, plant, and equipment	2,110	727	34.5%	1,145	54.3%
Investment in subsidiary	3,110	3,588	115.4%	5,094	163.8%
Other	234	715	305.2%	1,049	447.8%
Total assets / Proceeds	**10,579**	**9,271**	**87.6%**	**11,754**	**111.1%**
Trustee fees		85		110	
Winddown costs		1,597		1,042	
Professional fees		130		167	
Net proceeds available for distribution		**7,459**		**10,434**	

Recoveries	Estimated Allowed Claim	Estimated Payment	Payout %	Estimated Allowed Claim	Estimated Payment	Payout %
Less: Secured claims						
DIP facility, LCs, and other	4,200	4,200	100.0%	4,200	4,200	100.0%
Setoff rights and other	1,223	1,223	100.0%	221	221	100.0%
Total secured claims	**5,423**	**5,423**		**4,421**	**4,421**	
Remaining distributable value		2,036			6,014	
Less: admin and priority claims						
Reclamations	22	15	66.0%	22	22	100.0%
Trade accounts payable (post-petition)	1,166	769	66.0%	1,166	1,166	100.0%
Intercompany (post-petition)	301	198	66.0%	301	301	100.0%
Accrued liabilities, other admin and priority	1,628	1,054	64.7%	1,628	1,628	100.0%
Total admin and priority claims	**3,117**	**2,036**		**3,117**	**3,117**	
Remaining distributable value		—			2,897	
Less: General unsecured claims						
Funded debt	2,471	—		2,471	450	18.2%
Trade accounts payable	729	—		707	129	18.2%
Intercompany	90	—		90	16	18.2%
PBGC	5,900	—		5,900	1,074	18.2%
General motors benefit indemnity claim	7,203	—		6,100	1,111	18.2%
Other general unsecureds	661	—		644	117	18.2%
Total unsecured nonpriority claims	**17,055**	—		**15,912**	**2,897**	
Payout % for total unsecured claims		—			18.2%	
Distributable value available to equity		—			—	

Data Source: Delphi court filings.

Flinder Valves and Controls Inc.

In early May 2008, W. B. "Bill" Flinder, president of Flinder Valves and Controls Inc. (FVC), and Tom Eliot, chairman and chief executive officer of RSE International Corporation (RSE), were planning to negotiate a possible acquisition of FVC by RSE. Serious discussions for combining the two companies had started in March of that year, following casual conversations that dated back to late 2007. Those initial talks focused on the broad motives for each side to do a deal, and on the management issues, including compensation, in the new firm. What still remained was to negotiate a final term sheet on which the definitive agreement would be drafted and signed.

In the background, the past 12 months had been associated with mounting difficulty for the U.S. economy. The industries within which RSE and FVC operated were not immune from these effects. A recent analyst report summarized the market view for industrial manufacturing.

> Tighter borrowing standards and a severely weakened housing sector are weighing on the domestic economy, prompting consumers to cut back on spending and industrial manufacturers to reduce production. A similar situation now seems to be taking hold in western Europe.[1]

Both corporate leaders were concerned about the opportunities and risks of doing a deal in this increasingly challenging environment.

Flinder Valves and Controls Inc.

Flinder Valves and Controls, located in Southern California, manufactured specialty valves and heat exchangers. FVC maintained many standard items, but nearly 40% of its volume and 50% of its profits were derived from special applications for the defense and aerospace industries. Such products required extensive engineering experience of a kind only a few firms were capable of providing. FVC had a reputation for engineering excellence in the most complex phases of the business and, as a result, often did prime contract work on highly technical devices for the government.

---

[1] *Value Line Investment Survey,* April 25, 2008.

FVC was an outgrowth of a small company organized in 1980 for engineering and developmental work on an experimental heat-exchanger product. In 1987, as soon as the product was brought to the commercial stage, Flinder Valves and Controls Inc. was organized to acquire the properties, both owned and leased, of the engineering corporation. The president of the predecessor company, Bill Flinder, continued as the president of FVC. Eventually, the company acquired the patents it had licensed.

The raw materials used by the company were obtainable in ample supply from a number of competitive suppliers. Marketing arrangements presented no problems. Sales to machinery manufacturers were made directly by a staff of skilled sales engineers. The Auden Company, a large firm in a related field, was an important foreign distribution channel under a nonexclusive distributor arrangement. About 15% of FVC's sales came from Auden. Foreign sales through Auden and directly through FVC's own staff accounted for 30% of sales. Half the foreign sales originated in emerging economies, mainly Brazil, Korea, and Mexico. The other half originated in the United Kingdom, Italy, and Germany.

Although competitive erosion in the mid-2000s had temporarily interrupted FVC's sales growth, better economic conditions in the markets of developed countries, together with FVC's recent introduction of new products for the aerospace and defense industries, offered the company excellent prospects for improved performance. Sales in the first quarter of 2008 grew 23% over the corresponding period in 2007, at a time when many of FVC's competitors experienced limited growth prospects. **Exhibits 54.1** and **54.2** show the most recent financial statements for FVC.

FVC's plants, all of modern construction, were organized for efficient handling of small production orders. The main plant was served by switch tracks in a 15-car dock area of a leading railroad and also by a truck area for the company's own fleet of trucks. From 2005 to 2007, net additions to property totaled $7.6 million.

Bill Flinder, an outstanding researcher in his own right, had always stressed the research and development involved in improved products, with patent protection, although the company's leadership was believed to be based on its head start in the field and its practical experience.

FVC's success had brought numerous overtures from companies looking for diversification, plant capacity, management efficiency, financial resources, or an offset to cyclical business. For instance, when Flinder Valves was taken public in 1996, Auden Company, which later became a holder of 20% of FVC common stock, advanced a merger proposal. Rumors of possible antitrust action by the U.S. Department of Justice had circulated after the news of the proposed merger became public, and Auden withdrew from the discussions. FVC received various proposals from 1998 on, but none reached the stage of working out an agreement until the advances of RSE International Corporation.

FVC had come to RSE's attention with the FVC's disclosure of a U.S. government contract. FVC was to develop an advanced hydraulic-controls system, code-named "widening gyre," for use in numerous military applications. The technology was still in research and development, but was expected to have broad commercial value if the results were found to be economically successful.

RSE International Corporation

Tom Eliot had founded RSE International in 1970, grown it, taken it public, and firmly rooted it as a Russell 1000 company. In response to what he perceived to be the firm's growth challenges for the next decade, Eliot had persuaded RSE's board that the company should follow a policy of focused diversification, which would be achieved by an aggressive growth-by-acquisition program designed to create opportunities and entries into more dynamic markets than the ones RSE then served.

In 2008, RSE manufactured a broad range of products including advanced industrial components as well as chains, cables, nuts and bolts, castings and forgings, and other similar products. RSE then sold them (mostly indirectly) to various industrial users. One division produced parts for aerospace propulsion and control systems with a broad line of intermediate products. A second division produced a wide range of nautical navigation assemblies and allied products. The third division manufactured a line of components for missile and fire-control systems. These products were all well regarded by RSE's customers, and each was a significant factor in its respective market. **Exhibit 54.3** shows the RSE balance sheets for 2007; **Exhibit 54.4** presents the income statements from 2003 to 2007.

The company's raw material supply (sheets, plates, and coils) of various metals came from various producers. RSE International's plants were ample, modern, well-equipped with substantially newer machinery, and adequately served by railroad sidings. The firm was considered a low-cost producer that possessed unusual production knowledge. It was also known as a tough competitor.

Eliot and his management team had initiated several changes to help increase RSE's profit margins. Chief among them, in late 2006, had been the implementation of Project CORE, a business wide initiative to improve and unify the corporate wide information systems. This project had already identified numerous opportunities for improving profits and sales. As a result, RSE's latest sales and earnings forecasts projected a steady increase over the next five years. The current plan (excluding merger growth) called for sales to hit $3 billion within five years (**Exhibit 54.5**). Despite Eliot's confidence and optimism for the future of the company, he believed that the stock market still undervalued his firm's shares.

The Situation

During the early part of 2008, a series of group meetings had taken place between Tom Eliot and Bill Flinder and their respective advisers. It seemed clear to both parties that both FVC and RSE could profit from the merger. By early May, a broad outline of the merger seemed to be developing. Flinder Valves was to become a subsidiary of RSE International—the deal would be structured in such a way as to preserve FVC's identity. The two sides had explored some of the governance and compensation issues in the merger. Flinder would be retained along with his top management team and all other employees. No layoffs were contemplated. This reflected RSE's intention to invest in and grow the FVC operation. FVC's solid management team was one of the factors that had attracted RSE in the first place, and Eliot wanted to keep the same management in place after the merger. Flinder would receive a generous option-based incentive bonus that could result in a salary increase of between $50,000 and $200,000 per year. Because Flinder was 62 years old and nearing retirement, the compensation package was meant to retain him in the coming years as he trained a new chief executive.

The price of the deal was less clear. FVC's shares traded on the NASDAQ, whereas RSE's traded on the American Stock Exchange. The market capitalizations for FVC and RSE were approximately $100 million and $1.4 billion, respectively. Both companies had experienced recent rapid rises in share price due to strong performance despite the weak economic environment. **Exhibit 54.6** shows recent share prices for Flinder Valves and RSE.[2]

The financial advisors had collected a variety of relevant capital-market data. **Exhibit 54.7** provides valuation information on exchange-listed comparables for Flinder Valves and RSE. **Exhibit 54.8** presents information on recent related acquisitions. **Exhibit 54.9** presents historical money-market and stock-return data through May 2008. RSE's debt was currently rated Baa.

Flinder had shared FVC's current corporate-financial-statement forecast with Eliot but had emphasized that it did not include any benefits of the merger or the benefits of promising new technologies, such as the widening gyre (**Exhibit 54.10**). The reluctance to include the widening gyre project stemmed from the substantial uncertainty remaining regarding its potential economic benefits.

The companies had yet to settle on the form of consideration, either cash or RSE stock, that would best serve the parties to the deal. Eliot expected that RSE had the financial capacity to borrow the entire amount through its existing credit facilities. Roughly 70% of the Flinder Valves stock was held by its board of directors and their families, including the 20% owned by the Auden Company and 40% owned by Bill Flinder. The Auden Company did not object to the merger, but it had given notice that it would sell any RSE shares received in the deal. The Auden Company was about to undertake a new expansion of its own, and its executives were not disposed to keeping tag ends of minority interests in a company such as RSE. They saw no reason, however, for not maintaining their satisfactory business relationships with the Flinder Valves enterprise if it became a division of RSE International.

---

[2]RSE International's stock had a beta of 1.25; the beta for FVC was 1.00, based on the most recent year's trading prices. Both companies faced a marginal tax rate of approximately 40%.

EXHIBIT 54.1 | Consolidated Balance Sheet as of December 31, 2007 for Flinder Valves and Controls (dollars in thousands)

Assets

Cash	$1,884	
U.S. Treasury tax notes and other Treasury obligations	9,328	
Due from U.S. government	868	
Accounts receivable net	2,316	
Inventories, at lower of cost or market	6,888	
Other current assets	116	
Total current assets		$21,400
Investments		1,768
Land	92	
Buildings	6,240	
Equipment	18,904	
Less: allowance for depreciation	7,056	
Total plant, property, and equipment—gross	18,180	
Construction in process	88	
Total plant, property, and equipment—net*		18,268
Patents		156
Cash value of life insurance		376
Deferred assets		156
Total assets		42,124

Liabilities and Stockholders' Equity

Accounts payable	2,016	
Wages and salaries accrued	504	
Employees' pension cost accrued	208	
Tax accrued	72	
Dividends payable	560	
Provision for federal income tax	1,200	
Total current liabilities		4,560
Deferred federal income tax		800
Common stock at par (shares authorized and outstanding 2,440,000 shares)	1,220	
Capital surplus	7,180	
Earned surplus	28,364	
Total equity		36,764
Total liabilities and stockholders' equity		42,124

*Equivalent land in the area had a market value of $320,000, and the building had an estimated market worth of $16,800,000. Equipment had a replacement cost of approximately $24,000,000 but a market value of about $16,000,000 in an orderly liquidation.

EXHIBIT 54.2 | Summary of Consolidated Earnings and Dividends for Flinder Valves and Control
(dollars in thousands)

| | 2003 | 2004 | 2005 | 2006 | 2007 | (Unaudited) Three months ended 3/30 | |
						2007	2008
Sales	$36,312	$34,984	$35,252	$45,116	$49,364	$11,728	$14,162
Cost of goods sold	25,924	24,200	24,300	31,580	37,044	8,730	10,190
Gross profit	10,388	10,784	10,952	13,536	12,320	2,998	3,972
administrative	2,020	2,100	2,252	2,628	2,936	668	896
Other income—net	92	572	108	72	228	14	198
Income before taxes	8,460	9,256	8,808	10,980	9,612	2,344	3,274
Taxes	3,276	3,981	3,620	4,721	4,037	1,009	1,391
Net income	5,184	5,275	5,188	6,259	5,575	1,335	1,883
Cash dividends	1,680	2,008	2,016	2,304	2,304	576	753
Depreciation	784	924	1,088	1,280	1,508	364	394
Capital expenditures	1,486	1,826	2,011	2,213	2,433	580	640
Working capital needs	1,899	3,492	−1,200	4,289	4,757	1,130	1,365
Ratio analysis							
Sales	100.0	100.0	100.0	100.0	100.0	100.0	100.0
Cost of goods sold	71.4	69.2	68.9	70.0	75.0	74.4	72.0
Gross profit	28.6	30.8	31.1	30.0	25.0	25.6	28.0
administrative	5.6	6.0	6.4	5.8	5.9	5.7	6.3
Other income—net	0.3	1.6	0.3	0.2	0.5	0.1	1.4
Income before federal taxes	23.3	26.5	25.0	24.3	19.5	20.0	23.1
Net income	14.3	15.1	14.7	13.9	11.3	11.4	13.3

EXHIBIT 54.3 | Consolidated Balance Sheet for RSE International as of December 31, 2007 (dollar figures in thousands)

Assets		
Cash		$ 46,480
U.S. government securities, at cost		117,260
Trade accounts receivable		241,760
Inventories, at lower of cost or market		179,601
Prepaid taxes and insurance		2,120
Total current assets		587,221
Investment in wholly-owned Canadian subsidiary		158,080
Investment in supplier corporation		104,000
Cash value of life insurance		3,920
Miscellaneous assets		2,160
Property, plant, and equipment, at cost:		
Buildings, machinery, equipment	671,402	
Less: allowances for depreciation and amortization	260,001	
Property, plant, and equipment—net	411,402	
Land	22,082	
Property, plant, equipment, and land—net		433,484
Patents, at cost, less amortization		1,120
Total assets		$1,289,985

Liabilities and Stockholders' Equity		
Notes payable to bank		$ 5,795
Accounts payable and accrued expenses		90,512
Payrolls and other compensation		38,399
Taxes other than taxes on income		3,052
Provision for federal taxes on income refund, estimated		32,662
Current maturities of long-term debt		30,900
Total current liabilities		201,320
Note payable to bank[1]		119,100
Deferred federal income taxes		29,668
2% cumulative convertible preferred stock, $20 par,		27,783
1,389,160 shares outstanding[2]		
Common stock, $2 par; 96,000,000 shares authorized;		125,389
62,694,361 shares issued		
Capital surplus[3]		21,904
Retained earnings		764,821
Total equity		939,897
Total liabilities and stockholders' equity		$1,289,985

[1]$150,000,000 note, payable semiannually beginning June 30, 2008; $30,900,000 due within one year, shown in current liabilities. One covenant required the company not to pay cash dividends, except on preferred stock, or to make other distribution on its shares or acquire any stock, after December 31, 1999, in excess of net earnings after that date.

[2]Issued in January 2007; convertible at rate of 1.24 common share to one preferred share; redeemable beginning in 2012; sinking fund beginning in 2016.

[3]Resulting principally from the excess of par value of 827,800 shares of preferred stock over the pay value of common share issues in conversion in 2007.

EXHIBIT 54.4 | Summary of Consolidated Earnings and Dividends for RSE International (dollars in thousands)

	2003	2004	2005	2006	2007
Net sales	$1,623,963	$1,477,402	$1,498,645	$1,980,801	$2,187,208
Cost of products sold	1,271,563	1,180,444	1,140,469	1,642,084	1,793,511
Gross profit	352,400	296,958	358,176	338,717	393,697
Selling, general, and administrative	58,463	69,438	74,932	87,155	120,296
Earnings before federal income taxes	293,937	227,520	283,244	251,562	273,401
Tax expense	126,393	95,558	116,130	101,882	109,360
Net earnings	167,544	131,962	167,114	149,679	164,041
Depreciation	19,160	20,000	21,480	24,200	26,800
Cash dividends declared	85,754	77,052	53,116	77,340	92,238

EXHIBIT 54.5 | Forecast Financial Statements for RSE International for the Years Ended December 31, 2007–12 (dollars in thousands except per-share figures)

	Actual	Projected				
	2007	2008	2009	2010	2011	2012
Sales	$2,187,208	$2,329,373	$2,480,785	$2,642,037	$2,813,769	$2,996,658
Cost of goods sold	1,793,510	1,920,085	2,064,243	2,216,470	2,367,290	2,537,259
Gross profit	393,698	409,288	416,542	425,567	446,479	459,399
Selling, general, and admin.	120,296	129,786	139,481	151,027	161,315	169,826
Income before tax	273,402	279,502	277,061	274,540	285,164	289,573
Tax expense	109,361	111,801	110,824	109,816	114,066	115,829
Net income	164,041	167,701	166,237	164,724	171,098	173,744
Cash dividends	92,238	102,082	108,714	115,779	125,185	133,313
Depreciation	26,800	27,950	29,770	31,700	33,170	35,960
Net PPE	389,321	426,522	459,404	498,497	541,109	587,580
Net working capital	422,597	447,956	486,428	528,407	574,238	624,303
Earnings per share[1]	$2.62	$2.60	$2.58	$2.56	$2.66	$2.70
Divs. per share common stock[1]	$1.42	$1.58	$1.69	$1.80	$1.94	$2.07
Div. per share preferred stock[2]	$0.40					

[1]62,694,361 common shares in 2007. Thereafter, 64,416,919 shares reflecting conversion of the preferred stock.

[2]1,389,160 preferred shares in 2007. Conversion into 1,722,558 shares of common stock assumed in 2008.

EXHIBIT 54.6 | Market Prices of Flinder Valves and RSE International Corporation

	Flinder Valves and Controls			RSE International Corporation				
	Common Stock			Common Stock			Preferred Stock	
	High	Low	Close	High	Low	Close	High	Low
2003	$16.25	$8.75	$15.00	$12.31	$10.05	$11.88		
2004	24.75	14.00	22.63	14.36	11.77	13.16		
2005	25.00	20.00	22.25	12.81	9.27	11.13		
2006 Quarter Ended:								
March 31	24.38	20.75	21.50	14.13	12.83	13.95		
June 30	22.75	20.38	21.00	13.69	12.04	11.78		
September 30	22.75	20.38	21.50	12.83	10.48	11.26		
December 31	24.36	20.13	21.00	12.39	11.26	11.87		
2007 Quarter Ended:								
March 31	23.50	20.00	21.75	11.60	10.20	10.67	13.61	12.21
June 30	23.63	19.88	22.00	11.60	10.90	10.90	13.15	12.04
September 30	22.75	20.00	22.50	13.61	11.13	13.61	14.22	12.37
December 31	30.00	22.25	28.50	17.01	13.30	16.78	17.32	13.77
2008 Quarter Ended:								
March 31	32.13	26.00	31.50	20.73	15.08	20.69	17.32	13.98
May 1, 2008	$39.75	$38.90	$39.75	$22.58	$18.30	$21.98	$17.63	$15.35

EXHIBIT 54.7 | Market Information on Firms in the Industrial Machinery Sector

	Price/ Earnings Ratio	Beta	Dividend Yield	Expected Growth Rate to 2010	Debt/ Capital
Cascade Corp.					
Manufactures loading engagement devices	10.5	0.95	1.7%	5.1%	29%
Curtiss-Wright Corporation					
Manufactures highly engineered, advanced technologies that perform critical functions	17.2	1.0	0.7	12.3	36%
Flowserve Corp.					
Makes, designs, and markets fluid handling equipment (pumps, valves, and mechanical seals)	20.8	1.3	1.0	27.0	30%
Gardner Denver					
Manufacturers stationary air compressors, vacuum products, and blowers	10.9	1.3	Nil	NMF	19%
Idex Corp.					
Manufactures a wide range of pumps and machinery products	16.1	1.05	1.5	10.8	22%
Roper Inds.					
Manufacturers energy systems and controls, imaging equipment, and radio frequency products	19.7	1.2	0.5	10.8	29%
Tecumseh Products					
Manufactures compressors, condensers, and pumps	38.2	1.05	Nil	NMF	8%
Watts Industries					
Manufactures and sells and extensive line of valves for the plumbing and heating and water quality markets	15	1.3	1.5	8.4	32%

NMF = not meaningful figure.

Source: *Value Line Investment Survey,* April 25, 2008.

EXHIBIT 54.8 | Information on Selected Recent Mergers

Effective Date	Acquirer	Business	Target	Business
5/25/2006	Armor Holdings Inc	Law enforcement equip	Stewart & Stevenson	Turbine-driven products
6/26/2006	Bouygues SA	Construction	Alstom SA	Power generation equip
9/20/2006	Boeing Co	Aircraft	Aviall Inc	Vehicle parts
11/10/2006	Daikin Industries Ltd	Air conditioning sys	OYL Industries Bhd	Airconditioners
12/8/2006	Oshkosh Truck Corp	Heavy duty trucks	JLG Industries Inc	Excavators/telehandlers
4/11/2007	Rank Group Ltd	Investment holding co	SIG Holding AG	Packaging/plastics machinery
6/22/2007	Meggitt PLC	Aerospace/defense system	K&F Industries Holdings	Aircraft braking systems
7/31/2007	BAE Systems Inc	Electronic systems	Armor Holdings Inc	Law enforcement equip
12/3/2007	Carlyle Group LLC	Private equity firm	Sequa Corp	Aircraft engine component
12/20/2007	ITT Corp	Pumps/valves	EDO Corp	Electn system products
2/6/2008	London Acquisition BV	Investment holding co	Stork NV	Components
6/5/2008	Ingersoll-Rand Co Ltd	Industrial machinery/equip	Trane Inc	Airconditioners

Acquirer	Target	Transaction Size ($mm)	Target Net Sales Last 12 Months ($mm)	Equity Value/Target Net Income	Enterprise Value/Target Net Sales	Enterprise Value/Target Operating Income	Enterprise Value/Target Cash Flow	Premium 4 Weeks Prior to Announcement Date (%)
Armor Holdings Inc	Stewart & Stevenson	1,123	726	65.3	1.12	33.1	23.7	40.6
Bouygues SA	Alstom SA	2,467	17,679	nmf	1.48	77.9	22.5	–1.2
Boeing Co	Aviall Inc	2,057	1,371	28.9	1.53	18.7	14.9	27.2
Daikin Industries Ltd	OYL Industries Bhd	1,152	1,581	27.6	1.41	21.5	16.8	19.4
Oshkosh Truck Corp	JLG Industries Inc	3,252	2,289	20.5	1.30	11.9	10.7	52.3
Rank Group Ltd	SIG Holding AG	2,314	1,418	38.6	1.56	64.8	14.2	19.3
Meggitt PLC	K&F Industries Holdings	1,802	424	20.3	4.26	13.1	10.8	13.5
BAE Systems Inc	Armor Holdings Inc	4,328	2,805	30.5	1.71	17.1	14.3	29.3
Carlyle Group LLC	Sequa Corp	2,007	2,181	34.4	1.25	20.6	12.5	63.3
ITT Corp	EDO Corp	1,678	945	86.8	1.99	34.0	23.9	40.5
London Acquisition BV	Stork NV	2,347	2,153	17.1	0.02	na	na	35.2
Ingersoll-Rand Co Ltd	Trane Inc	9,751	8,328	21.2	1.39	14.9	11.6	na

na = not available.

Data Source: Thomson Financial's *SDC Platinum*.

EXHIBIT 54.9 | Capital Market Interest Rates and Stock Price Indexes
(averages per year except April 2008, which offers closing values for
April 25, 2008)

	2006	2007	April 2008
U.S. Treasury Yields			
3-month bills	4.70%	4.40%	1.28%
30-year bonds	5.00%	4.91%	4.52%
Corporate Bond Yields by			
Aaa	5.59%	5.56%	5.58%
Aa	5.80%	5.90%	5.96%
A	6.06%	6.09%	6.32%
Baa	6.48%	6.48%	6.98%
Stock Market			
S&P 500 Index	1,418	1,468	1,398
Price/earnings ratio	17.7×	18.3×	17.4×
Industrial Machinery Stocks			
Price/earnings ratio	13.9×	14.0×	
Dividend yield	1.4%	1.4%	
Historical return premium of equity over government debt (1926–2007)			
Geometric average	5.5%		
Arithmetic average	7.2%		

Data Source: *Value Line Investment Survey*, 25 April 2008; *Federal Reserve Bulletin*; Compustat.

EXHIBIT 54.10 | Forecast of Financial Statements for Flinder Valves and Controls for Years Ended
December 31, 2008–12 (dollars in thousands)

	Actual	Projected				
	2007	2008	2009	2010	2011	2012
Sales	$49,364	$59,600	$66,000	$73,200	$81,200	$90,000
Cost of goods sold	37,044	43,816	48,750	54,104	59,958	66,200
Gross profit	12,320	15,784	17,250	19,096	21,242	23,800
administrative	2,936	3,612	4,124	4,564	5,052	5,692
Other income, net	228	240	264	288	320	352
Income before taxes	9,612	12,412	13,390	14,820	16,510	18,460
Taxes	4,037	4,965	5,356	5,928	6,604	7,384
Net income	$ 5,575	$ 7,447	$ 8,034	$ 8,892	$ 9,906	$11,076
Depreciation	$ 1,508	$ 1,660	$ 1,828	$ 2,012	$ 2,212	$ 2,432
Net PPE	$18,268	$22,056	$24,424	$27,088	$30,049	$33,306
Net Working capital	$16,840	$20,331	$22,515	$24,971	$27,700	$30,702

Source: FVC Analysis.